Adolf Hitler

Volume II

Adolf Hitler

By JOHN TOLAND

Volume II

Doubleday & Company, Inc., Garden City, New York

Grateful acknowledgment is made for permission to quote portions from the following:

The Young Hitler I Knew by August Kubizek. Copyright © 1954 by Paul Popper and
Company. Reprinted by permission of the publisher, Houghton Mifflin Company,
Boston.

Hitler's Secret Conversations, 1941–1944, edited by H. R. Trevor-Roper, translated by
Norman Cameron and R. H. Stevens. Copyright © 1953 by Farrar, Straus and
Young, Inc. Reprinted with the permission of Farrar, Straus & Giroux, Inc., and of
George Weidenfeld & Nicolson Ltd., London.

The Testament of Adolf Hitler: The Hitler-Bormann Documents, February–April 1945,
edited by François Genoud and translated by R. H. Stevens. Copyright © 1959,
Libraire Arthème Fayard; English edition published by Cassell & Co., Ltd. Reprinted by permission of A. D. Peters & Co., Ltd.

Hitler's Interpreter by Paul Schmidt. Copyright © 1951 by Opera Mundi, Inc. Reprinted by permission of Opera Mundi, Inc.

Douze ans auprès d'Hitler: Confidences d'une secrétaire particulière d'Hitler, recorded
by Albert Zoller. Copyright © 1949 by Éditions René Julliard. Reprinted by permission of Éditions René Julliard.

Contents

Part 9 INTO THE ABYSS

List of Maps & Tables

Part 6

"TO THE VERY BRINK OF BOLDNESS"

Chapter Eighteen

CRYSTAL NIGHT
NOVEMBER 1938–MARCH 1939

1

The path of anti-Semitism in Hitler's Germany was tortuous. The first Jewish restrictions in 1933 were so inconclusive that it seemed as if the Führer were deliberately compromising his principles. Could this be an attempt to solve the Jewish question by rational means acceptable to those Germans who wanted Jews controlled but not persecuted? There followed a period of struggle between the racial radicals in the party and moderates in the government and civil service which came to a climax during the summer of 1935. At this time the latter took the offensive, objecting openly to the continuing mistreatment of Jews on the grounds that it was bad for business. The "unlawful" activity against Jews must end, Reich Bank President Schacht told a small, influential group including Interior Minister Frick, Finance Minister Schwerin von Krosigk, Justice Minister Gürtner and Education Minister Rust. Otherwise, he warned, he could not complete his task of economic rearmament. For example, the Jewish agent of Alliance Insurance in Egypt had been so harried that he resigned, leaving the market to the English. Many Jewish importers were canceling large orders and it was ridiculous to imagine that it was possible for a nation to succeed economically without Jewish business. Schacht had no objection to the public display of signs such as "Jews not wanted," since these could even be found in the United States, but he bitterly opposed those put up by Streicher proclaiming, "Whoever buys from a Jew is a traitor to the people." It was unanimously agreed by the group that "wild single actions" must cease so that the Jewish question could be solved legally.

The first steps in the direction of legalization were taken a few weeks later at Nuremberg by the Führer himself, when he proclaimed the Law for the Protection of German Blood and Honor, legalizing a number of repressive measures which were promptly justified by the official Catholic *Klervsblatt* as "indisputable safeguards for the qualitative make-up of the German people." Even Streicher seemed to be satisfied now that the matter was being solved "piece by piece" in the best German legal tradition. "We don't smash any windows and we don't smash Jews," he boasted. "Whoever engages in a single action of that kind is an enemy of the State, a provocateur, or even a Jew."

Were the Nuremberg laws an attempt by Hitler to solve the Jewish question by less harsh "acceptable" methods? Or was he merely biding his time before effecting his dream of extermination? In either case solution of the problem, for the time being at least, had been taken from the party and turned over to the law. This resulted in growing resentment among the more radical Nazi racists. Held in restraint during Hitler's ensuing expansion program, they finally broke out three years later, in 1938, with the destruction of synagogues in Munich, Nuremberg and Dortmund. A wave of Jew-baiting swept the nation. "The entire Kurfürstendamm," wrote Bella Fromm, a diplomatic correspondent from Berlin, "was plastered with scrawls and cartoons. 'Jew' was smeared all over the doors, windows, and walls in waterproof colors. It grew worse as we came to the part of town where poor little Jewish retail shops were to be found. The S.A. had created havoc. Everywhere were revolting and bloodthirsty pictures of Jews beheaded, hanged, tortured, and maimed, accompanied by obscene inscriptions. Windows were smashed, and loot from the miserable little shops was strewn over the pavement and floating in the gutter."

The tide of anti-Semitism was given impetus on November 7, 1938, when a young Jew, Herschel Grynszpan, shot a minor German Foreign Office official in Paris. Grynszpan, whose parents had been deported from Germany to Poland, had gone to the embassy to assassinate the ambassador only to be sidetracked by Counselor Ernst vom Rath. Himself an enemy of anti-Semitism, Rath was being investigated by the Gestapo but it was he who took the bullets intended for his superior.

"Being a Jew is not a crime," sobbed Grynszpan to the police. "I am not a dog. I have a right to live and the Jewish people have a right to exist on this earth. Wherever I have been I have been chased like an animal."

On the afternoon of November 9 Rath died. The news reached Hitler at the Munich town hall where he was attending a meeting of party leaders. He left the room with his escort, conferred briefly with Goebbels before boarding his special train. Goebbels returned to the meeting to announce that Rath's murder had inspired anti-Jewish riots in the districts of Kurhessen and Magdeburg-Anhalt. The Führer, he said, had decided that if the riots spread spontaneously throughout Germany they were not to be discouraged.

The party leaders took this to mean that they were to organize demonstrations while making it appear that they had nothing to do with them. But SA Chief Lutze either misunderstood Goebbels or refused to believe Hitler had given such a command. After assembling all Gruppenführer present, he ordered them not to participate in any actions against the Jews. While these SA officials were transmitting Lutze's instructions (which in some cases were ignored), the party leaders were telephoning conflicting orders to the provinces.

At first the SS did not participate in the ransacking of shops and burning of synagogues. Upon learning that Goebbels had ordered a pogrom, Himmler directed his men to prevent excessive looting, then dictated a file memorandum: "The order was given by the Propaganda Directorate, and I suspect that Goebbels, in his craving for power, which I noticed a long time ago, and also in his empty-headedness started this action just at the time when the foreign political situation is very grave." His castigation may have been only for the record. Hours earlier Himmler himself had violently attacked the Jews in a secret speech to his SS generals. The Jews, he said, were bent on destroying Germany and so had to be driven from the Reich "with unexampled ruthlessness." If Germany did not win this all-out battle against Jewry, "there won't be a single refuge for a true Teuton left, everybody will be starved and butchered."

If Himmler objected to the terrorism sweeping the country, his chief assistant did everything he could to capitalize on it. Soon after midnight Heydrich sent urgent teletypes to all headquarters and stations of the SD and police, enjoining them to co-operate with the party and SS leaders in "organizing the demonstrations." Finally, as many Jews, particularly rich ones, were to be arrested "as can be accommodated in existing prisons. For the time being, only healthy men, not too old, are to be arrested. Upon their arrest, the appropriate concentration camps should be contacted immediately in order to confine them in these camps as fast as possible."

It was a night of despair for the Jews in Germany, with the police standing by as witnesses of the destruction and beatings. One policeman was found by the deputy police chief of Berlin weeping in front of a looted shoe shop. It had been his duty to enforce order and yet, in violation of all his ideals, he had done nothing. By official count 814 shops, 171 homes were destroyed, and 191 synagogues put to the torch; 36 Jews were killed and another 36 seriously injured. But the figures, Heydrich himself admitted, "must have been exceeded considerably."

Otto Tolischus cabled the New York *Times* that he had just witnessed a wave of destruction unparalleled in Germany since the Thirty Years' War. "Beginning systematically in the early morning hours in almost every town and city in the country, the wrecking, looting and burning continued all day. Huge but mostly silent crowds looked on and the police confined themselves to regulating traffic and making wholesale arrests of Jews 'for their own protection.'"

The reaction from abroad was immediate and the acts of brutality were given an unforgettable name—inspired by the multitude of smashed windows—Crystal Night. On all sides Germany was assailed as a barbarous nation. Many Germans agreed and other party officials beside Himmler joined in the condemnation of Goebbels. Frau Funk, wife of the Minister of Economics, overheard her husband cursing him over the phone: "Are you crazy, Goebbels? To make such a mess of things! One has to be ashamed to be a German. We are losing our whole prestige abroad. I am trying, day and night, to conserve the national wealth, and you throw it willy-nilly out of the window. If this thing does not stop immediately, you can have the whole filthy mess."

Göring complained directly to the Führer that such events made it impossible for him to carry out his mission. "I was making every effort, in connection with the Four-Year Plan," he later testified, "to concentrate the entire economic field to the utmost. I had, in the course of speeches to the nation, been asking for every old toothpaste tube, every rusty nail, every bit of scrap material to be collected and utilized. It would not be tolerated that a man who was not responsible for these things should upset my difficult economic tasks by destroying so many things of economic value on the one hand and by causing so much disturbance in economic life on the other hand." Then Hitler, according to Göring's account, "made some apologies for Goebbels, but on the whole he agreed that such events were not to take place and must not be allowed to take place."

Hitler was already giving the impression that he knew nothing of Crystal Night and added his own complaints. "It is terrible," he told Frau Troost. "They have destroyed everything for me like elephants in a china shop . . . and much worse. I had the great hope that I was about to come to an understanding with France. And now that!" But Fritz Hesse, summoned to Munich from London for a special press conference, claimed he overheard otherwise from Hitler's own lips the very night Crystal Night was set into motion. At dinner the Führer was boasting how he had bluffed the English and French at Munich when an adjutant whispered something to Goebbels. He turned and muttered to Hitler. At first Hesse couldn't hear what was said, but when the others at the table lapsed into silence it became clear that the Propaganda Minister was explaining a mass attack which he and the SA were going to launch against the Jewish shops and synagogues in a few hours. There was no doubting the Führer's approval, recalled Hesse. "Hitler squealed with delight and slapped his thigh in his enthusiasm."*

The following day Hesse called on Ribbentrop, who was still irritated at not being invited to the previous day's press conference. First, he labeled the Munich Conference a piece of first-class stupidity. All it meant was that it postponed hostility for a year, when the English would be much stronger. "Believe me, it would have been much better if war had come now. We hold all the military trumps. Who knows what will happen in a year?" But the worst was that the Führer imagined he had called the English bluff. "For years I've tried to make it clear to him that he must be careful of the English because they are dangerous. But he won't believe it. . . . Instead he fools about and makes bombastic speeches. You heard him yourself yesterday! As for that little beast, Goebbels, have you heard what his gangs have done everywhere? These imbeciles have smashed up the Jewish shops—which have long been Aryan property anyhow. They've spoiled my game for me."†

Despite Hitler's protestations to moderates, the pogrom continued and by November 12 an estimated 20,000 Jews had been shipped to concentration camps. That day Göring, who had objected to the destruction of property on economic grounds, called a meeting of the Council of Ministers to determine who would have to pay for it. He began by announcing that this conference was of decisive importance and his next

---

* Johannes Popitz, the Prussian Minister of Finance, got a similar account from Göring. When Popitz remarked that those responsible for Crystal Night should be punished, the Reichsmarschall replied blandly: "My dear Popitz, do you wish to punish the Führer?"

† In reply to postwar claims that Goebbels had nothing to do with Crystal Night, his personal adviser, Leopold Gutterer, signed an affidavit to the effect that Goebbels admitted his involvement at a small party in 1942. "Influential circles of the National Socialist economic leadership," Goebbels reportedly said, "took the emphatic standpoint that one could not remove the Jews from the economic life of Germany to any greater extent than had been done to date. Therefore, we decided: 'Good, then we will mobilize the streets and in that way solve the problem within twenty-four hours.' "

words had a significance his listeners could not fathom at the time. "I have received a letter from Bormann sent me by order of the Führer, asking that the Jewish question be now, once and for all, treated in its entirety and settled in some way. Yesterday the Führer telephoned me to point out again that decisive measures must be undertaken in a coordinated manner." Inspired by this directive, the conferees agreed that the Jews themselves would have to pay for the damage in the form of a billion-mark fine.

"I certainly would not like to be a Jew in Germany!" remarked Göring and brought the four-hour meeting to a close with a grim forecast: "If in the near future the German Reich should come into conflict with foreign powers, it goes without saying that we in Germany should first come to a showdown with the Jews." Furthermore, the Führer was about to suggest to those foreign powers so concerned over the plight of German Jews that they be deported to the island of Madagascar. "He explained it to me November 9," concluded Göring. "He wants to say to the other countries: 'Why are you always talking about the Jews? Take them!'"

While this plan for the complete elimination of Jews from the Reich economy was getting under way, other Germans, including many party leaders, were privately expressing deep concern at the excesses of Crystal Night. The bureaucrats and party leaders, aware that such violent actions always get out of hand, protested that a pogrom was too costly and accomplished almost nothing in the battle against Jews. Others were repelled by the inhumanity of such actions but did little more than grumble cautiously. Gerhart Hauptmann, for instance, complained to a friend that Hitler had ruined Germany. "This scum will bring war to the whole world, this miserable brown comedian, this Nazi hangman is rushing us into a world of war, into destruction!" Then why didn't Hauptmann emigrate in protest like Mann and Zweig? "Because I'm a coward," replied the famous playwright, "do you understand? I'm a coward."

Those safe from reprisals were heaping abuse on Hitler. Almost every newspaper and radio commentator in the United States responded to Crystal Night with outrage. From Washington, Ambassador Dieckhoff wrote the Foreign Office that he hoped "the storm at present sweeping across the United States will subside again in the foreseeable future and we shall be able to work again." Until Crystal Night, he reported, most Americans ignored the anti-German propaganda but now even German-Americans were incensed. "What particularly strikes me is the fact that, with few exceptions, the respectable patriotic circles, which are thoroughly anti-Communist and, for the greater part, anti-Semitic in their outlook, also begin to turn away from us. The fact that the Jewish newspapers write still more excitedly than before is not surprising; but that men like Dewey, Hoover, Hearst, and many others who have hitherto maintained a cooperative reserve and have even, to some extent, expressd sympathy toward Germany, are now publicly adopting so violent and bitter an attitude against her is a serious matter. . . . In the general atmosphere of hate, the idea of boycotting German goods has received new fuel, and trade negotiations cannot be considered at the moment."

National outrage was climaxed by a rare denunciation from President Roosevelt. At a news conference on November 15 he read a prepared statement to the reporters. The news from Germany, he said, had deeply shocked American public opinion. "I myself could scarcely believe that such things could occur in twentieth century civilization. With a view to gaining a firsthand picture of the situation in Germany I have asked the Secretary of State to order our Ambassador in Berlin to return at once for report and consultation." But official condemnation did not extend beyond the verbal and the United States continued its trade relations with the Third Reich.

Perhaps the protests from abroad had some effect on him. A week after Crystal Night he supported the civil service, which sought to protect in the part-Jew "that part which is German," rather than the party which looked on the part-Jew as a carrier of the "Jewish influence." His support came in the form of the First Regulation to the Reich Citizenship Law which separated so-called non-Aryans into definite categories. A Jew was defined as anyone descended from at least three Jewish grandparents, or an individual with two Jewish grandparents who also belonged to the Jewish religious community or was married to a Jew.

Then came a curious category: the *Mischlinge* (half-breeds), those descended from only one Jewish grandparent, or those with two Jewish grandparents who neither practiced the Jewish religion nor were married to a Jew. In practice this split non-Aryans into two distinct groups with the Mischlinge no longer subject to repressive measures. With one bureaucratic stroke Hitler made it possible for a substantial portion of the hated enemy to escape his wrath. Was his resolve to exterminate Jews truly weakening or, again, was he merely waiting for a more suitable time to act decisively? Or was this a conscious or even unconscious attempt to save himself, since there was still the possibility that one of his own grandfathers was Jewish? The Mischlinge regulation also saved Jesus, who by Hitler's argument, being the son of God, had but two Jewish grandparents; neither did he practice the Jewish religion, nor was he married to a Jew.

2

From his youth Hitler had held cynical views of the democracies and their leaders' ability to speak one way while acting another. Consequently he was not as concerned about the vocal protests from the West throughout the latter part of 1938 as were many of his most faithful followers. Rudolf Hess, for one, was extremely downcast. On December 23 he spent two hours with the Bruckmanns, early supporters of the Führer, and told how he had implored Hitler in vain to stop the pogrom.

While Hitler must have been aware of the defection of these old adherents, he remained in such good spirits that he let himself be persuaded to wear tails for the New Year's Eve celebration at the Berghof. "My sister," Ilse Braun wrote in her diary, "had been at great pains to persuade him to dress with a minimum of good taste. 'Look at Mussolini,' she would say, 'he has a new uniform. And you, with those postman's caps.'" He kissed Ilse's hand, remarking that the Braun sisters were all beauties. "When he looked at me, beads of sweat formed between my breasts, and I did not have the courage to say *Danke schön*, though I had promised myself to make a great speech."

After accepting formal congratulations from the guests and his staff, the Führer participated in an ancient Teutonic ceremony. Molten lead was poured into a small basin of water and the shape it assumed supposedly determined the future. "Hitler did not seem satisfied with his results, for afterwards he sat down in an armchair, gazing dejectedly at the fire, and hardly spoke for the rest of the evening. Eva was extremely worried about him."

His dark mood was intensified a few days later by a revolt of bankers against his vast rearmament program. "The reckless expenditures of the Reich," read a memorandum composed by Hjalmar Schacht, president of the Reichsbank, and signed by every governor of the bank, "represents a most serious threat to the currency. The tremendous increase in such expenditures foils every attempt to draw up a regular budget; it is driving the finances of the country to the brink of ruin despite a great tightening of the tax screw, and by the same token it undermines the Reichsbank and the currency." The stability of the currency, warned Schacht, could not be stabilized in the face of such an inflationary expenditure policy and the "time has come now to call a halt."

Schacht knew that Hitler would be infuriated because the declaration in effect called for the end of military adventures. He told Schwerin von Krosigk what he had done, adding that he expected to be fired. (He had already lost his post as Minister of Economics to Walther Funk, whose powers were promptly annexed by Göring as chief of the Four-Year Plan.) The Finance Minister said that if Schacht went he would ask for his own dismissal, then composed a similar memorandum and sent it to the Führer.

Days passed but nothing happened. Finally at midnight of January 19, 1939, Schacht's phone rang. He was ordered to report to the Führer the following morning at nine. It was an unusual hour for an interview since Hitler rarely went to bed before three in the morning. According to Schacht, the Führer said, without preamble, "I have called you in order to hand you your dismissal as president of the Reichsbank." Schacht took the piece of paper extended to him. "You don't fit into the National Socialist picture," continued Hitler, then waited for some comment. Schacht remained silent until Hitler reprimanded him for condemning Crystal Night at a Christmas party of bank office boys. "If I had known that you approved of those happenings," Schacht finally said, "I might have kept silent."

This reply seemed to take Hitler's breath away. "In any case," he said indignantly, "I'm too much upset to talk to you any more now." Both men agreed that Schacht should take a long trip abroad and he left for India soon thereafter. Hitler was relieved to be rid of him. "When it is a question of a bit of sharp practice," Hitler later told his inner circle, "Schacht is a pearl beyond all price." But whenever he was called upon to show strength of character, he always failed.

Soon after Schacht's dismissal Captain Wiedemann was summoned to the winter garden. For the past months Hitler had been treating him with increasing coolness and Wiedemann guessed he too was going to be fired. Ever since Crystal Night the Führer had seemed to inhabit an imaginary world which had nothing in common with reality and whenever Wiedemann attempted to discuss any defect in the system Hitler ignored him.

"I have no use for people in high places and in my closest circle who do not agree with my politics," Hitler curtly told Wiedemann. "I hereby discharge you as my personal adjutant and appoint you consul general in San Francisco. You can accept or refuse this new position." Without hesitation Wiedemann accepted, adding that he hoped he wouldn't have to take a cut in salary. At this, Hitler's tone became milder. "I will always keep an open ear for your financial welfare." Thus, after four years' close association, the two war comrades parted without bitterness.

The exit of Schacht and Wiedemann signaled the return to grace of Josef Goebbels, who had fallen from favor due to his sexual adventures.

"Every woman inflames my very blood," he wrote in his twenties. "I pace back and forth like a wolf." Nor had marriage to Magda restrained him. At the same time he kept his numerous affairs under control, never compromising himself publicly. That is, until he fell in love with Czech actress Lida Baarova in the summer of the Olympics. Magda imagined it was one of his usual flirtations but finally lost her patience in 1938 and demanded a divorce. Hitler had shown remarkable tolerance to homosexuality but was distressed by the party leaders who abandoned mates who had helped in the rise to power. He demanded that Goebbels give up the actress. At first he refused, offering to resign from his ministry and become an ambassador to Japan or some such distant country. Finally he succumbed to pressure and renounced his great love. No sooner had Baarova returned to Czechoslovakia under "advice" from the police than Hitler summoned the entire Goebbels family to the Berghof. Pictures of the couple and three of their children at the entrance to the Kehlstein tea house were published as public proof that all was well with the household.

This stage reconciliation took place only a few weeks before Crystal Night and the anguish of losing Lida Baarova—along with a desire to rehabilitate himself with people like Himmler and Rosenberg who felt that the scandal had dealt "the severest kind of blow to the moral status of the party"—might have caused him to act so recklessly that November night.

The reinstatement of Goebbels coincided with Hitler's new approach to the Jewish question. On his most recent trip to her atelier in Munich, Frau Troost had urged Hitler to reinstate a Jewish composer, Arthur Piechler, to the school of music in Augsburg. Why shouldn't Jews be judged individually? she argued. The few she knew were not only experts in their field but valuable human beings.

"Those are your personal experiences," said Hitler after some thought. "If I'd had similar ones, then I never would have taken my path. But I had much different experiences—like those in Vienna." He must place the fate of the German people above all else. "The Jew lives and serves his own law but never that of the people or the nation where he has become a citizen. He does not belong to the German people and can therefore be among us only as a guest but not as it was during the period between 1918–1933 when he took all the top positions in art, culture, and the press, as well as in trade and the banks. It is my responsibility to see that our nation's future once more has a healthy and strong foundation based on national characteristics. I have made it my life work to build a safe existence and future for the German people and especially the German worker." This was all a prelude to refusing her request "on principle." Curiously, on his next visit to Munich he reversed himself and agreed to reinstate Professor Piechler.

Just as the false accusations of troop movements on the Czech borders early in 1938 had roused Hitler to premature action, so the storm of protests from abroad over Crystal Night may have hardened his resentment toward Jews and prompted him to look for new ways of dealing with them. An indication of this complete loss of objectivity came on January 21, 1939, when he told Czech Foreign Minister Chvalkovsky that no German guarantee would be given to a state which did not eliminate its Jews. "Our own kindness was nothing but weakness and we regret it," he said. "This vermin must be destroyed. The Jews are our sworn enemies and at the end of this year there will not be a Jew left in Germany." They were not going to get away with what they had done in November 1918. "The day of reckoning has come."

A few days later a Foreign Ministry circular on the Jewish question as a factor in foreign policy was dispatched to all diplomatic missions and consulates. "The ultimate aim of Germany's Jewish policy," it said, "is the emigration of all Jews living on German territories." Since the advent of National Socialism only slightly more than 100,000 Jews had legally or illegally left Germany to find homes in new host countries. Even this modest influx of Jews from Germany had already aroused the resistance of the native populations of America, France, Holland and Norway. Despite the moral denunciation of Germany, the Western nations were hermetically sealing their own boundaries against Hitler's Jews. This ground swell of anti-Semitism confirmed the validity of shipping out Jews en masse, and the goal of the new German policy, concluded the circular, "will be an international solution of the Jewish question in the future, not dictated by false sympathy for the 'Jewish religious minority which has been expelled,' but by the mature realization by all peoples of the danger which the Jews represent for the racial preservation of the nations."

On January 29 Hitler proclaimed his abrupt change in tactics even more explicitly. In a speech to the Reichstag on the sixth anniversary of the Nazi rise to power he declared war on world Jewry. Significantly, hours earlier he had ordered the navy to begin building a mighty submarine fleet to be completed within five years. England, America and France, he charged, were "continually being stirred up to hatred of Germany and the German people by Jewish and non-Jewish agitators," when all he wanted was peace and quiet. These lying attempts to bring about a war could not in the slightest influence Germany's manner of settling her Jewish problem, he said, and for the first time since his rise to power he publicly lifted the veil on his ultimate plan: "In the course of my life I have often been a prophet, and have usually been ridiculed for it. . . . I will once more be a prophet: If the international Jewish financiers in and outside Europe should succeed in plunging the nations once more into a world war, then the result will not be the Bolshevization of the earth, and thus the victory of Jewry, but the annihilation of the Jewish race in Europe!" He was crying out to the Jews the paranoiac warning: "Stop, before you force me to kill you!"

3

In the past year Hitler had destroyed one sovereign state, reduced and paralyzed another and, in the process, humbled the West. Nineteen thirty-nine promised even greater political conquests. On January 1 Mussolini finally made up his mind to accept the German offer of the past autumn and transform the Anti-Comintern Pact from a propaganda front to a full-fledged military alliance. "During this month," wrote Ciano in his diary, "he plans to prepare the acceptance of his views by public opinion, about which he doesn't give a damn." The reason: Mussolini feared war with the West was now inevitable.

In his New Year's message Hitler announced that the German government had but one wish: ". . . that in the coming year, too, we may succeed in contributing to the German pacification of the world." The next step in his "peaceful" program of pacification was the complete control of Czechoslovakia. For some time he had regretted the Munich Pact since it had become apparent he could have annexed the entire country without reprisals. Now he would have to find some acceptable excuse to march in and liquidate what was left.

In February he ordered Goebbels to launch a massive propaganda campaign against the Czech government: it was still terrorizing its ethnic German citizens, concentrating troops along the Sudeten borders, conspiring with the Soviets and grossly mistreating its Slovak population. The last accusation proved to be the most fruitful, for radical Slovak nationalists eagerly rose to the bait and began increasing their demands for complete independence. It was an explosive situation that needed but a single misstep from some inexperienced Czech in high places to set off another crisis —and give Hitler the excuse he needed.

In London the spirit of anti-appeasement was reinforced by a fallacious report from Erich Kordt of the German Foreign Office. He secretly informed a British official that Hitler was planning to bomb London in the near future. (It was a deliberate attempt by the anti-Hitler group in Germany to push England into a war with the Reich and was only the first of other false alarms to be planted by Kordt and other Foreign Office men in the plot.) Chamberlain took the bombing scare seriously enough to call a special cabinet meeting and, although no Nazi planes appeared, the temperature of suspicion was raised. Ambassador Henderson was brought from Berlin to report on possible Hitler military action and he did his utmost to convince Permanent Under Secretary of State for Foreign Affairs Cadogan that the Germans were not even "contemplating any immediate wild adventure and that their compass is pointing towards peace." The astute Cadogan was not so sanguine. He suggested that Hitler's intentions were "strictly dishonorable" yet he too was hesitant to believe reports that Hitler was about to engulf Czechoslovakia.

Henderson returned to his post in Berlin where he continued to send back optimistic assessments. Rumors of Nazi adventures in the Ukraine or in Holland were dying down, he reported. "Although it is suggested in some quarters that this calm may only be a prelude to another storm, I am not inclined to take that pessimistic view at present."

Yet the very next night even he was concerned by Hitler's actions at the annual banquet for the diplomatic corps. "The apparent friendliness which he had shown at the motor exhibition was notably absent at this dinner," Henderson wrote in his memoirs. "He kept his eyes fixed over my right shoulder and confined his remarks to general subjects, while stressing the point that it was not Britain's business to interfere with Germany in Central Europe." Although the Führer's attitude left Henderson "with a feeling of vague uneasiness," he did not bother to mention it in his next report to London.

Evidence of German intrigue was soon forthcoming. On March 6 British Ambassador Newton reported from Prague that relations between the Czechs and Slovaks "seem to be heading for a crisis." Matters had come to a head over a demand for financial assistance on the part of the Slovaks. What role, if any, "Germany is playing in the dispute is a matter for conjecture but it may be noted that the Slovak Minister of Commerce and Minister of Transport visited Berlin last week accompanied by experts."

For some reason this telegram was delayed forty-eight hours and by that time Henderson had recovered from his "vague uneasiness." On March 9 he wrote Halifax a long letter, expressing conviction that both Hitler and the German people longed for peace. "Hitler himself fought in the World War and his dislike of bloodshed, or anyway of dead Germans, is intense." Although Nazi extremists might be tempted to urge continued aggression, Hitler's inclination as a demagogue would be to please the majority rather than the fanatical minority. "That is one reason why, since I can find no justification for the theory that he is mad or even verging on madness, I am of the opinion that he is not thinking to-day in terms of war."

4

That evening the President of Czechoslovakia, Emil Hacha—who once admitted he understood very little about politics—finally committed the blunder Hitler was waiting for: he dismissed the Slovak government from office and ordered troops to prepare to move into the Slovakian district. The next day, Friday, Hacha declared martial law.

Hitler reacted with rapidity. He canceled his trip to Vienna to take part in the celebration of the Anschluss so that he could prepare for his next invasion. The slight but nagging fear that the Soviets might rush to Prague's aid was relieved almost immediately. Even as Hacha was resorting to martial law, Stalin told the Eighteenth Party Congress that they must be cautious and not allow the West to use the U.S.S.R. to pull its own chestnuts out of the fire. It was in line with Soviet policy to proclaim publicly that they were Czechoslovakia's only faithful ally while risking nothing. The excuse for inaction was that their pact with the Czechs required them to provide aid only *after* France had acted.

On Saturday, his favorite day for a coup, Hitler went into action, improvising with customary agility. First he instructed General Keitel to draft an ultimatum demanding that the Czechs submit to the military occupation of Moravia and Bohemia without resistance, then issued disruptive orders to agents in Czech and Slovak territory. At the same time Henderson was telephoning Halifax to proceed circumspectly. He doubted "whether Herr Hitler has yet taken any decision and I consider it therefore highly desirable that nothing should be said or published abroad during the weekend which will excite him to precipitate action."

Nothing was needed. That evening Hitler's two puppet leaders in Austria, accompanied by five German generals, drove across the Danube to break into a meeting of the new Slovak cabinet at their seat of government, Bratislava. The members were told to proclaim the independence of Slovakia but the new Prime Minister stalled for time by announcing that he would first have to discuss the situation with the Prague government. His predecessor, Josef Tiso—a Roman Catholic priest who was a Friar Tuck in the flesh—had been placed in a monastery under house arrest, but he now dramatically re-entered the scene. The corpulent Monsignor Tiso

("When I get worked up I eat half a pound of ham, and that soothes my nerves") escaped from his prison and demanded that a meeting of the new Slovak cabinet be held early Sunday morning, March 12.

At this secret convocation Tiso revealed that he had received an "invitation" to see Hitler in Berlin. He had accepted, he said, under threat of occupation by German and Hungarian troops. At exactly 7:40 P.M., March 13, Tiso was ushered into Hitler's office by Ribbentrop. The Führer, looking stern and implacable, was flanked by his two top military men, Brauchitsch and Keitel; orders had already been issued to the army and air force to stand by for a possible invasion of Czechoslovakia at six o'clock on the morning of the fifteenth.

"Czechoslovakia," said Hitler accusingly, "owes it only to Germany that she has not been mutilated further." Nor did the Czechs appreciate the great self-control exhibited by the Germans. He raised his voice, either in anger or a show of it, and asked what kind of a game they were playing. He assumed the Slovaks wanted independence and that was why he had prevented Hungary from seizing their territory. He wanted one question cleared up *"in a very short time."* He accented each of these words, then put the question directly to Tiso: did Slovakia want to lead an independent existence or not? "Tomorrow at midday," he said, "I shall begin military action against the Czechs, which will be carried out by General von Brauchitsch." He pointed to his commander-in-chief. "Germany does not intend to take Slovakia into her Lebensraum, and that is why you must either immediately proclaim the independence of Slovakia or I will disinterest myself in her fate. To make your choice I give you until tomorrow midday, when the Czechs will be crushed by the German steamroller."

Tiso hesitated briefly, then telephoned the Slovak cabinet in Bratislava and said in German that he was speaking from the Führer's office. He requested them to convene the Slovak parliament for the following morning. Once he was sure his stupefied listeners understood the message, Tiso rang off. He arrived in Bratislava in time to read to the assembled deputies a Slovak declaration of independence drafted by Ribbentrop. Opposition to the proclamation collapsed and a new Slovakia, independent in name only, was born.

That afternoon in London, Chamberlain stoutly parried angry questions in the House of Commons over the government's failure to stand up to Hitler. What about Britain's guarantee to Czechoslovakia? asked one critic. That guarantee, he retorted, referred only to unprovoked attack. "No such aggression," he said, "has taken place."

While Chamberlain was making excuses in Parliament, Hitler acted and, as usual, made it appear as if he were only reacting. His tool in the final step of the drama was President Hacha of Czechoslovakia. Harried and confused by the events of the past few days, Hacha now urgently requested an interview with the Führer—a case of the fly seeking an invitation to the spider's net.

After keeping Hacha in suspense for hours, Hitler finally agreed to see him. Already psychologically crushed, the President of Czechoslovakia, accompanied by his daughter and his Foreign Minister, boarded a train for Berlin. He could not fly because of a weak heart.

As he was leaving Prague a British newsman who had often seen Hitler at close quarters arrived. Sefton Delmer noticed that the habitués of cafés on Wenceslas Square were stolidly sipping their coffee unaware of what was going on. Suddenly, at dusk, troops of white-stockinged Sudeten Germans, six abreast, marched through the square, carrying Nazi banners and shouting: "Sieg Heil! Sieg Heil!" They were followed by Fascist collaborators waving the Czech tricolor. At first the crowds obeyed the demands to salute the Nazi banners. But once the factories closed and the workers flooded into the square there was a different spirit. They refused to make way for the marchers and fighting erupted. The police supported the demonstrators, who continued to march about shouting: "Ein Reich, ein Volk, ein Führer!" If Prague was symbolically German, the important Czech industrial town of Moravska Ostrava on the Polish border was already that in fact. Elite troops of Hitler's own bodyguard division occupied this area soon after dark to safeguard its modern steel mill from Polish seizure.

In Berlin Hitler and his guests were assembling in the drawing room of the chancellery to see a movie, *A Hopeless Case*. Next to the Führer sat General Keitel, on hand to issue, if necessary, executive orders to begin the invasion. At 10:40 P.M. the train from Prague pulled into Anhalt Station but it was not until an hour after midnight that Hacha was summoned by the Führer. He had waited that long, so he told Keitel, to give the old gentleman a chance to rest and recover from the tiring trip but the delay only increased Hacha's anxiety and by the time he and Foreign Minister Chvalkovsky passed by an SS guard of honor and entered Hitler's study his face was "flushed with agitation."

Hacha made a personal appeal by assuring the Führer that he had never mixed in politics. In a sad exhibition of abasement, he threw himself on Hitler's mercy. "He was convinced that the destiny of Czechoslovakia lay in the Führer's hands," read the official German minutes of the meeting, "and he believed it was in safekeeping in such hands."

Even this servility could not stem the vitriol stored up in Hitler. After repeating the alleged wrongs perpetrated by Masaryk and Beneš, he charged that "under the surface the Beneš spirit lived in the new Czechoslovakia." Frail little Hacha was a pitiable figure as he cringed under this attack. Abruptly Hitler—either from compassion or a need to change tactics—hastened to add that he did not mean to imply any distrust of Hacha, and he had "come to the conclusion that this journey by the President, despite his advanced years, might be of great benefit to this country because it was only a matter of hours now before Germany intervened."

Both Hacha and his Foreign Minister sat as if turned to stone until Hitler again gave them a glimmer of hope by insisting that he harbored no enmity against any nation and remained convinced of Hacha's loyalty. But this was extinguished by a declaration that the Beneš tendencies still flourished. The die had been cast on Sunday, said Hitler. The order for the invasion by the German troops and for the incorporation of Czechoslovakia into the German Reich had already been given.

The two Czechs sat stupefied. Hitler announced that his army would enter their country from all sides at 6 A.M. while the Luftwaffe occupied all Czech airfields.

Threat was again followed by promise. Hacha could serve Czechoslovakia by a simple decision. He would have to act quickly—or at six o'clock German troops and planes would go into action. "I would have irremediably lost face if I'd had to put this threat into execution," Hitler recalled several years later, "for at the hour mentioned fog was so thick over our airfields that none of our aircraft could have made its sortie."

He suggested that Hacha and his Foreign Minister withdraw to discuss privately what should be done, but to Hitler's relief Hacha said, "The position is quite clear." He admitted that resistance would be folly yet how could he possibly restrain the nation in less than four hours? Hitler replied that it had to be done somehow, then added hopefully that he saw dawning "the possibility of a long period of peace between the two peoples." If the decision was to resist, he concluded sharply, he saw "the annihilation of Czechoslovakia."

With these ominous words, Hitler ended the interview. As the two dejected Czechs were escorted to an adjoining room, Ribbentrop attempted to place a telephone call to Prague. The line was out of order and Schmidt was asked to try again. As the interpreter was dialing he heard Göring exclaim from the adjoining room that Hacha had fainted. A call went out for Dr. Morell, who had been kept on duty in case the ailing Czech President needed him. If anything happens to Hacha, thought Schmidt, the whole world will say tomorrow that he was murdered in the chancellery. Just then the line to Prague was opened. Schmidt went for Hacha and to his surprise found him recovered, thanks to Dr. Morell's vitamin injection. Hacha came to the phone and, after informing his cabinet what had happened, advised capitulation.

In the meantime Schmidt was making a fair copy of a brief official communiqué which had been composed beforehand. It stated that the President of Czechoslovakia confidently laid the fate of the Czech people and country in the hands of the Führer of the German Reich. It was, in reality, a document of surrender, and Hacha asked for another of Morell's injections. This revived him so much that he refused to sign it despite urgings of Ribbentrop and Göring. These two, according to the official French report, then proceeded to hound the two Czechs pitilessly. "They literally hunted Dr. Hacha and Mr. Chvalkovsky round the table on which the documents were lying, thrusting them continually before them, pushing pens into their hands, incessantly repeating that if they continued in their refusal, half of Prague would lie in ruins from bombing within two hours, and this would only be the beginning. Hundreds of bombers were waiting the order to take off, and they would receive that order at six in the morning if the signatures were not forthcoming."*

At last Hacha gave in and, face still flushed, signed the document at 3:55 A.M. with trembling hand. He turned to Dr. Morell and thanked him for his ministrations. The moment the pen dropped from Hacha's nerveless fingers the Führer rushed from the conference room to his office where his two middle-aged secretaries were waiting. His face was transfigured, recalled Christa Schröder, as he exclaimed, "Children, quickly, give me a kiss! Quickly!" Schröder and Wolf bussed him on both cheeks. "Hacha has just signed," he said in exultation. "It is the greatest triumph of my life! I shall go down in history as the great German!"

Late as it was, Hitler stayed up to savor the triumph. "I was sorry for the old gentleman," he confided to Hoffmann, and other intimates. "But sentimentality, in the circumstances, would have been out of place and might well have jeopardized success."

Dr. Morell interrupted to remark that but for him the communiqué might not have been signed. "Thank God," he said, "that I was on the spot and in time with my injections!"

"You go to hell with your damn injections!" exclaimed Hitler. "You made the old gentleman so lively that for a moment I feared he would re-

---

* Göring admitted at Nuremberg that he had told Hacha, "I should be sorry if I had to bomb beautiful Prague." But he hadn't intended doing it since "resistance could always be broken more easily without such bombing. But a point like that might, I thought, serve as an argument and accelerate the whole matter."

fuse to sign!" The celebration was briefly interrupted by Keitel, who reported that executive orders for the invasion of Czechoslovakia had been issued with the proviso not to open fire unless there were signs of resistance, and even then there would be attempts to negotiate before resorting to force of arms. He asked Hitler's permission to retire and was instructed to report back in a few hours so he could accompany the Führer to the special train which would take them to the Czech border.

5

At dawn on March 15 two disheveled men, "ashy-pale with fear," appeared at the American Legation in Prague to ask for asylum. They revealed they had been Czech spies in Germany and were known to the local Gestapo. "Their faces were twitching and their lips trembling when I sent them away," recalled George Kennan. A little later he had to follow instructions and turn two German fugitives from Hitler into the snow-swept street "where they were no more than hunted animals." Next came a Jewish acquaintance who had to be told he could stay only until he could calm his nerves. "He paced wretchedly up and down in the anteroom, through the long morning hours."

In London, Lord Halifax first learned of the invasion from his ambassador in Prague. Several hours later Henderson phoned from Berlin advising his chief to postpone the visit of the president of the Board of Trade to Germany. "It does not appear to me possible to prevent Germany from 'restoring order' but I would nevertheless deprecate visits at this juncture of any British Cabinet Minister."

Within the hour Henderson was on the phone again reading off the agreement signed by Hitler and Hacha, and at 11 A.M. he was dictating the text of a Hitler proclamation just issued to the German people: since Sunday, it read, "wild excesses" against Germans had taken place in many Czech villages, and from hour to hour the appeals from victims and persecuted had increased.

The shell-shocked Henderson at least realized that it was "the final shipwreck" of his mission to Berlin. "Do you wonder that I regard Berlin as a soul-scarifying job?" he hurriedly scrawled to Halifax in an informal letter. "Hitler has gone straight off the deep end again."

Hitler slept during most of the train trip from Berlin, not wakening until about noon on that memorable Ides of March. "I must be the first in Prague," he told his valet as he dressed. The closer they came to the frontier the more excited he became. At midafternoon his party disembarked near the frontier and transferred to a ten-vehicle motor convoy.

Hitler sat in the first car next to the driver, Kempka, as the column set off slowly in the blinding snowstorm. They passed through the open barriers of both customs stations and before long came upon German marching columns struggling in the drifts and ice. Kempka turned off the main road onto winding lanes and muddy byroads and it was dusk before they reached Prague. No one took notice of the convoy as it approached Hradschin Palace. The party was billeted in the castle and someone was sent into town to get cold Prague ham, rolls, butter, cheese, fruit and Pilsner beer. It was the first time Keitel ever saw Hitler drink beer.

The reaction to Germany's latest aggression was immediate and vehement. In response to public indignation, both the French and British governments gave military guarantees to Poland, Romania, Greece and Turkey and at the same time inaugurated political and military talks with the Soviets. Outrage extended to Hitler's own ally and that evening Ciano caustically wrote in his diary that the invasion of Czechoslovakia had destroyed the state established at Munich.

The Führer had already sent Prince Philip von Hesse to Rome with a letter of explanation. He hoped that Mussolini would understand and look at the latest move in the right light. Although Il Duce grumbled to Ciano, "The Italians will laugh at me; every time Hitler takes another state, he sends me a message," he decided that now, more than ever, it was essential to ally himself with a winner. "We cannot change our policy now," he said, "after all, we are not political whores." At the same time submission to his junior partner was humiliating; never before had Ciano seen his father-in-law in such distress.

Hitler was oblivious to criticism from home or abroad and his complacency seemed justified on March 16. As he surveyed his latest conquest from the walls of the castle of the Kings of Bohemia, the swastika flying from its battlements, he savored the pleasure of possessing an ancient city with so many historical memories to Teutons. In front of the City Hall twenty-seven leaders of the Protestant uprising against the Habsburgs had been beheaded in 1621; and in the Republikplatz Kaiser Wilhelm, Bismarck and Moltke had resided during the Prussian-Austrian War at the famous Hotel Zum blauen Stern. The magnificent structures of Prague, a number designed by German architects, owed much in his opinion to Teutonic culture. Only Germans built such bridges, towers and buildings!

An aide interrupted Hitler's revery to inform him that neither France nor Britain had mobilized. "I knew it," he said and made a prediction: "In fourteen days no one will talk about it any more." Of more interest to him was the report that pro-Nazi Czechs were already coursing through

Prague's streets marking Jewish shops in large colored letters: "JID" or "JUDE."

The factual dissolution of Czechoslovakia came later in the day when Monsignor Tiso sent a telegram to Berlin asserting Slovak independence and requesting German protection. Without delay Hitler's troops moved into Slovakia. The provinces of Ruthenia also asked to be absorbed into his orbit, but Hitler was more interested in appeasing the Hungarians, whose troops he allowed to swarm over the border and seize Ruthenian territory all the way to the Polish frontier. After a mere twenty years of independence all of Czechoslovakia was again in bondage.

Although they had stopped short of mobilization, the British were infuriated. "I can well understand Herr Hitler's taste for bloodless victories," Halifax warned the German ambassador, "but one of these days he will find himself up against something that will not be bloodless."

For some time he as well as the outspoken Cadogan had objected to aspects of Chamberlain's appeasement policy yet had supported him out of loyalty. But the moment had come to take a stand. The Foreign Secretary went to Chamberlain and made it clear that the nation, the party and the House of Commons demanded that Hitler's aggressions be condemned publicly and positively.

Chamberlain heeded this advice. On the eighteenth Ambassador Henderson was temporarily recalled from Berlin and that night, the eve of his seventieth birthday, the Prime Minister made a speech at Birmingham which changed the course of British foreign policy. He warned that it would be a great mistake to suppose that Great Britain, despite its detestation of war, "has so lost its fibre that it will not take part to the uttermost of its power in resisting such a challenge if it were made." It was hardly an inspiring call to arms but, coming from this symbol of conciliation, it aroused the audience to enthusiasm, for it did mean the virtual end of appeasement.

It also revealed that Hitler had made his first serious miscalculation. Czechoslovakia was his by threat of force but in time it would inevitably have fallen peaceably into his orbit; and by breaking an international agreement, freely entered into by his own government, he had completely reversed official and public opinion in both France and England. No longer would Chamberlain and his followers take Hitler at his word. He had broken the rules of the game—and not for a good enough cause.

How, then, had the Führer come to make such an obvious blunder? First, he had not expected his move to provoke such a violent reaction. Hadn't the West accepted the same excuses for restoring law and order in Austria? Hadn't they been satisfied with just as specious arguments at

Munich? He had been convinced he must seize the territory Germany needed to guarantee the future of the Teutonic race while he still had his physical vigor and Germany's military strength was still superior to that of its enemies.

When he marched into Czechoslovakia he was not certain where he would strike next or against whom, only that he must have Bohemia and Moravia before launching (or threatening to launch) any further military action. And so in Hitler's eyes he had committed no blunder, only sustained a public relations setback. What concerned him was the next step.

Chapter Nineteen

THE FOX AND THE BEAR
JANUARY–AUGUST 24, 1939

1

On the day Hitler announced the protectorate of Bohemia and Moravia from Hradschin Castle, the British Foreign Office was warned by the Romanian ambassador that secret sources indicated Hitler would take over Romania and Hungary within the next few months. Those hastily reconstructing foreign policy in London were led further astray by an alarming note from their own ambassador in Paris. It was filled with errors since Sir Eric Phipps typed it himself for the sake of secrecy. "Hitler's personal wish," he wrote, "backed by Goering, Himmler, Ribbentrop, Goebbels and Reichenau, is to make war on Great Britain before June or July." The information had probably been planted by the German anti-Hitler faction in their continuing effort to start a shooting conflict. The Führer, in fact, had no desire to fight England, and the proposed domination of both Romania and Hungary was still only in the economic sphere. His sights were set on a solution of Germany's festering differences with Poland, which had been created after the World War by the Allies primarily to contain German aggression. Not only had the Reich lost most of the provinces of West Prussia and Posen but a corridor was cut to the Baltic along the Vistula River to give landlocked Poland an outlet to the sea. Danzig, at the end of this corridor, was made a free city so it could serve Poland as a seaport. Nothing aroused patriotic Germans more than this so-called Polish Corridor which isolated their province of East Prussia from the rest of the Fatherland. And the focal point of resentment lay in Danzig, which was populated almost exclusively by Germans.

Surprisingly, the most nationalistic of Germans devoted little space to the Polish question in *Mein Kampf* and his early speeches. It was not that Hitler entertained friendly feelings for the Poles—a non-Aryan inferior people according to his standards—but that he was obsessed by the Soviet Union, the only country large enough to meet Germany's needs for living space. From the beginning of his regime Hitler had minimized the Polish question and in 1934 signed a ten-year non-aggression pact with Warsaw. Publicly he made a show of German-Polish friendship and at Munich, it will be remembered, graciously invited the Poles to join in the dismemberment of Czechoslovakia. This they did with relish, not realizing that the guests at such banquets usually pay the bill in the end. It was presented a month after Munich when Ambassador Josef Lipski was invited to have lunch with Ribbentrop at the Grand Hotel in Berchtesgaden. At last the time had come, said Ribbentrop, to settle their differences. He proposed—and his manner was friendly—that Poland return Danzig and allow Germany to construct its own corridor linking East Prussia with the rest of the Reich. In return Germany would let Poland use Danzig as a free port, guarantee her existing borders and extend their pact. Ribbentrop further suggested that the two countries co-operate on the emigration of Jews from Poland and establish "a joint policy towards Russia on the basis of the Anti-Comintern Pact."

Since many influential Poles shared Hitler's fear of Red Russia and hatred of Jews, the prospects of a peaceful settlement seemed hopeful. But the Polish Foreign Minister, Colonel Josef Beck, kept avoiding Hitler's invitations to Germany while doing his best to strengthen links with Russia. Late in 1938 a joint statement of Russo-Polish friendship was issued and trade talks were initiated.

This double game could not be played indefinitely with a man such as Hitler and at last Beck was forced to accept his hospitality. Early in January 1939 he came to the Berghof. If he feared being browbeaten like Schuschnigg, Tiso and Hacha, he was pleasantly surprised. There were no threats, only inducements as Hitler hinted of possible liquidation of Czechoslovakia with further benefits to Poland. This approach failed. As diplomatically as possible Beck refused even to consider the return of Danzig.

Several weeks later Ribbentrop journeyed to Warsaw so he could repeat the German offer. He was treated to a round of dancing, theater and hunting along with an endless supply of caviar and green vodka but at the conference table he got nothing but more Polish charm. It was rumored at the Wilhelmstrasse that Hitler, offended at Beck's continued refusal to accept what he considered a most generous offer, shouted that the only way to deal with the Poles was by threat. This tactic, used so successfully against Austria and Czechoslovakia, was implemented that March. Ribbentrop warned Warsaw that Polish outrages against the German minority were becoming intolerable. This pronouncement was followed by a press campaign with Göring's newspaper, *Die Zeitung*, charging that German women and children were being molested in Polish streets while German houses and shops were smeared with tar. Far from intimidated, Beck summoned the German ambassador on Tuesday and made his own threat: any attempt to change the status quo of Danzig would be regarded as an act of aggression against Poland.

"You want to negotiate at the point of a bayonet!" exclaimed the German ambassador.

"That is your own method," said Beck.

This and other indications of Polish pluck were rewarded by a startling offer of military assistance from London in case of Nazi aggression. Beck accepted "without hesitation" and on the last day of March Chamberlain, "looking gaunt and ill," walked into the House of Commons and dropped wearily into his chair. A few minutes later he rose and began reading a statement slowly and quietly, head lowered as if he could barely make out the words. "In the event of any action, which clearly threatens Polish independence," he said, "and which the Polish Government accordingly considers it vital to resist with their national forces, His Majesty's Government would feel themselves bound at once to lend the Polish Government all support in their power." The Poles, he added, had been assured to this effect, and the French had authorized him to announce that they joined Britain in these assurances. As he sat down there was spontaneous cheering, the first genuine display of approval since his return from Munich. The unconditional offer was the first material proof that Chamberlain had indeed abandoned appeasement. At last England was united and committed.

The following day, April 1, the Führer responded to this unanimity with a satirical speech. What right, he asked, had the English to interfere with Germany's right to live? "If today a British statesman demands that every problem in the realm of vital German rights must first be discussed in England, then I could demand just as well that every British problem must first be discussed with us. Certainly, this Englishman might give me the answer that Palestine is no affair of the Germans. We do not want to have anything to do with Palestine. However, just as we Germans have no business in Palestine, so England has no business in Germany's living space." And if England maintained that the Germans had no right to do this or that, what right had the English to shoot down Arabs in Palestine who were only standing up for their homeland?

He turned from sarcasm to threat. "The German Reich," he said, "is in no sense prepared to tolerate intimidation permanently, or even a policy of encirclement." This was relatively mild and it must have taken will power to control his feelings so well. Privately he seethed, and, upon receiving confirmation of the British guarantee to the Poles that afternoon from Admiral Canaris, he flared up. Features distorted by rage, he stormed about the room, hammering his fists on the marble table and spewing curses. "I'll cook them a stew they'll choke on!" Could he have been thinking of a pact with Stalin?

Perhaps Hitler's remarkable poise during the speech that evening came from the conviction that he was speaking from strength. Madrid had fallen to Franco, and the Civil War in Spain had just officially ended. In addition, England's attention was being diverted that very day by "fresh rumors of Italian pressure" on Albania, a diversion that fitted neatly into Hitler's plan. He summoned Keitel and told him the Polish problem imperatively demanded a solution. What a tragedy it was, he said, that sly old Marshal Pilsudski, with whom he had signed the non-aggression pact, had died so prematurely. But the same might happen to himself at any time. "That was why he would have to try as soon as possible to resolve this intolerable position for Germany's future whereby East Prussia was geographically cut off from the rest of the Reich; he could not postpone this job until later, or bequeath it to his successor." He was sure, he added, that Britain would turn her back on Poland once she saw Germany's determination.

And so, as a result of his failure to realize that Britain had jettisoned appeasement in fact as well as in words, Hitler issued a war directive on April 3 marked "Most Secret" and delivered by hand to senior commanders only. "Since the situation on Germany's eastern frontier has become intolerable, and all political possibilities of peaceful settlement have been exhausted," it began, "I have decided upon a solution by force." The attack on Poland, Operation White, would begin on the first of September.

The responsibility for opening hostilities on the western front would be left to England and France. If these nations attacked Germany in retaliation, the Wehrmacht was to conserve its strength in this quarter as much as possible. "The right to order offensive operations is reserved absolutely in me." So was decision regarding any air attack on London.

This indicated that he did not take seriously the Anglo-French pledge to support Poland. The Allies might, at worst, declare war but it would only be to save face and if the Germans restrained themselves from responding offensively a deal could be worked out. On such miscalculations are the fates of nations decided. This directive was countersigned by Keitel who, together with all the commanders he consulted, opposed any conflict with Poland. All agreed that Germany was not yet ready for war.

Hitler's charge that political possibilities of a peaceful settlement with Poland had been exhausted was not without foundation. Not only was Colonel Beck avoiding discussions with Hitler but he had just arrived in Dover to consummate the pact with the British. He was welcomed warmly by officials and public alike. Beck enjoyed the lavish entertainment, particularly an intimate lunch with the King and Queen, but being aloof, secretive and suspicious, he embarked on the formal talks in a less receptive mood. He objected strenuously when Chamberlain, having swallowed his own suspicions of Russia, suggested that they both join the Soviets in an anti-Hitler front. Fearing a Russian attack far more than one from the Nazis, Beck refused to do anything to precipitate a war with Hitler. On this point he would not budge and the temporary mutual assistance pact with the British which he signed April 6 excluded any Soviet participation.

Most nations operate their foreign policy on the pragmatic proposition that at least two irons in the fire are better than one. The Soviet Union, no exception, was negotiating simultaneously with England and Germany. This urgent need for allies stemmed in part from the dangerous weakening of the Red Army brought about two years earlier by Stalin's bloody purge (inspired, incidentally, by Hitler's elimination of the Röhm circle) of Marshal Tukhachevsky and other top military leaders.* Although it was not generally known, Germany had been secretly strengthening the Red Army for almost two decades. Both Germany and the Soviet Union had been excluded from the negotiations leading to the Versailles Treaty and, since outcast nations are often drawn together by

---

* Afterward Heydrich boasted that this emasculation of the Red Army was his work. Upon receiving information that the Tukhachevsky clique was plotting to eliminate Stalin, Heydrich fed it back to Stalin, through President Beneš, along with forged supportive papers. Before long a Soviet representative was in Berlin negotiating with Heydrich for the incriminating papers. He was paid three million rubles in bills that must have been marked; whenever a German agent tried to spend one in Russia he was arrested. Marked money was not the only piece of Russian trickery. It was Stalin himself who had leaked the original material to the unsuspecting Heydrich; Tukhachevsky had become too powerful and was a threat to Stalin's dictatorship.

shared grievances, they covertly began an extensive military collaboration. Its chief architect was the commander of the tiny postwar German army, General Hans von Seeckt. Late in 1920 he created an administrative organization within the Defense Ministry with offices in Berlin and Moscow. Before long the Junkers Corporation was granted concessions for the manufacture of airplane motors in a suburb of Moscow while Bersol, a joint stock company, began manufacturing poison gases in Samara Province. More significantly, German technical experts were helping the Russians establish three ammunition plants while a staff of sixty German military and civilian instructors trained a squadron of the Red Air Force composed solely of Germans. Similarly, German tank officers were being trained by German experts at a so-called "heavy vehicle experimental and test station" near Kazan.

This mutually profitable secret arrangement developed, it will be recalled, into a political rapprochement which was formalized on Easter Sunday, 1922, by the Treaty of Rapallo. It was an effective alliance against the Versailles powers, giving assurance to the Soviets that Germany would not join in any international consortium to exploit their economy while freeing the Germans from threat of complete encirclement. But the rise of Hitler marked a turning point in Soviet-German relations which, by 1938, were practically at an end. The tide again changed dramatically when the Munich Pact was signed by France and England without consulting the Soviets.

Ignored by the West, the Soviet Union once more looked to Germany. Early in 1939 it accepted a Hitler overture to discuss a new trade treaty by inviting one of Ribbentrop's aides to Moscow; and a few days later Stalin gave credence to a sensational story in the London *News Chronicle* that he was signing a non-aggression pact with the Nazis. In a speech to the eighteenth congress of the Communist Party he declared that the Soviet Union was not going to be drawn by the West into any war with Germany. "We are in favor of peace and consolidation of our business relations with all countries." German newspapers seized upon the *all* as a further overture to the Reich, and Soviet newspapers responded by congratulating them for their discernment.

Within a month Peter Kleist, Ribbentrop's expert for Poland and the Baltic states, was instructed to improve his personal relations with the people at the Soviet Embassy in Berlin. Kleist wondered if this was a prelude to another dramatic change in foreign policy and it was with mixed feelings, a few days later, that he accompanied a German specialist in East European economic affairs to the Soviet Embassy in its stately quarters on Unter den Linden. They had been invited to tea by Georgi Astakhov, the mild, ascetic-looking Soviet chargé d'affaires. It was obviously an unusual occasion; no other Russian was present. After chatting about French Impressionism, Astakhov suggested they get down to business. It was absurd, he said, for Germany and the Soviet Union to fight each other over ideological subtleties. Why not establish a common policy? Kleist remarked that ideological subtleties had become important realities but Astakhov waved this aside with a movement of his hand. Stalin and Hitler, he said, were men who created those realities and never let themselves be dominated by them.

Kleist left the embassy in a thoughtful mood. Obviously Astakhov was passing along a signal from the Kremlin to Ribbentrop. But to Kleist's surprise Ribbentrop, who had ordered him to make the initial overture, now told him to avoid further contact with Astakhov. "I do not think the Führer would wish that conversation to be continued."

Stalin took the next step. On April 17 Soviet Ambassador Alexei Merekalov called on Ribbentrop's chief subordinate, Baron von Weizsäcker. It was the Russian's first visit in ten months and the excuse for coming was a matter ordinarily handled at a lower echelon. Toward the end of their conversation Merekalov asked what Weizsäcker thought of Russian-German relations. His reply was: Germany always desired mutually satisfactory commercial relations with Russia. Ambassador Merekalov's answer was an unmistakable signal for rapprochement: there existed for Russia no reason why she should not live with Germany on a normal footing. "And from normal, the relations might become better and better."

In the meantime the Soviets continued to woo the other side. But Chamberlain did not want to be rushed into closer diplomatic relations with Russia. He could not believe that she had the same aims and objects as Britain had, let alone any sympathy with democracy. The Prime Minister was convinced that a Russian alliance would divide Balkan resistance to Germany. And so, while playing "hard to get" with the Soviets, he buttressed the guarantee of assistance to Poland by offering another to Romania.

On April 19 Romania's Foreign Minister, Grégoire Gafencu, called at the Reich chancellery and received a firsthand impression of Hitler's reaction to this proposed guarantee. At first mention of England, he sprang from his chair and paced the room. Why, he shouted, couldn't the English see that he only wished to reach an agreement with them? If England wanted war she could have it! "And it will be a war of unimaginable destructiveness," he warned. "How can the English picture a modern war when they can't even put two fully equipped divisions in the field?"

The next day, April 20, was Hitler's fiftieth birthday and perhaps his recent show of anger was an indication of impatience. Time was fleeting and he believed he had only a few more years of good health to accomplish his mission. The 1939 birthday was celebrated as usual by a major military parade. This magnificent spectacle—with all three branches of the Wehrmacht as well as the *Waffen* (armed) SS represented—was designed as a warning to enemies. At Hitler's express request the latest medium artillery, heavy tank guns, anti-aircraft guns and air force searchlight units were displayed. Overhead roared a menacing cloud of fighter and bomber squadrons. The attending foreign diplomats were suitably impressed by this greatest military display in German history, nor did they miss the significance of the guest of honor at Hitler's side, President Hacha of Czechoslovakia.

Although numerous Germans were appalled by the demonstration, the majority felt a surge of pride to see such armed might. The fiftieth birthday was also an excuse to subject the public to another flood of propaganda in praise of Hitler.

For a multitude of worshipers he was Germany's savior: "The Führer is the only man in our century who has possessed the strength to take into his hand the thunderbolt of God and fashion it anew for mankind." For others he was more than Messiah—God himself: "My children look upon the Führer as He who gives orders for everything, arranges everything. To them the Führer is the Creator of the world."

School children were taught to give homage in song:

> *Adolf Hitler is our savior, our hero,*
> *He is the noblest being in the whole wide world.*
> *For Hitler we live,*
> *For Hitler we die.*
> *Our Hitler is our Lord,*
> *Who rules a brave new world.*

Hitler himself even forbade the use of the term Third Reich and complained to his inner circle of the growth of this cult worship, which in some instances went to ludicrous lengths. During a recent study course arranged by the party, a lady lecturer had told in all seriousness of her experience with a talking dog. When asked "Who is Adolf Hitler?" the dog replied, "Mein Führer." The lecturer was interrupted by an indignant Nazi who shouted that it was abominable taste to relate such a ridiculous story. The lecturer, on the verge of tears, replied, "This clever animal knows that Adolf Hitler has caused laws to be passed against vivisection and the Jews' ritual slaughter of animals, and out of gratitude this small canine brain recognized Adolf Hitler as his Führer."

If the Church looked upon Hitler as neither the Messiah nor God, it nevertheless honored him on his fiftieth anniversary. Special votive masses were celebrated in every German church "to implore God's blessing upon Führer and people," and the Bishop of Mainz called upon Catholics in his diocese to pray specifically for "the Führer and Chancellor, the inspirer, enlarger and protector of the Reich." The Pope did not fail to send his congratulations.

These honors did nothing to temper the anger Hitler had revealed to the Romanian ambassador nor was his resentment solely directed at England. Hitler was outraged by the recent appearance in the United States of an unauthorized condensed version of *Mein Kampf* which included passages omitted from the authorized American edition as well as editorial comments by Alan Cranston calling attention to Hitler's distortions. Printed in tabloid form and priced at ten cents, half a million copies were sold in ten days. On the cover was printed: "Not one cent of royalty to Adolf Hitler."* This affront was followed by another from President Roosevelt in the form of a joint message to Hitler and Mussolini (who had just invaded Albania) appealing for assurances against further aggressions. "You have repeatedly asserted that you and the German people have no desire for war," Roosevelt told Hitler. "If this is true there need be no war."

Ruffled, Hitler delivered his answer on April 28. Never before had a speech such a large audience, for it was broadcast not only throughout Germany and parts of Europe but carried by the major networks in the United States, an incredible contrast to the days in Vienna when Hitler would lecture to whoever would listen—if only the trees. Then his auditors often ignored or ridiculed him. Now the world trembled.

The immense audience inspired him. William Shirer, for one, never had heard the Führer speak so eloquently. He opened with a brilliant defense of his foreign policy that turned into a denunciation of Britain's new foreign policy which, he charged, thereby removed the basis for their naval treaty of 1935. This unexpected abrogation of a treaty he himself had so

---

* The Führer's agents promptly sued on the grounds that his copyright had been violated. The court decided in favor of Hitler, ordering the publishers to cease and desist from printing and distributing any more copies of the Cranston version. "It was a beautiful example of democracy in action," said Cranston, now United States senator from California, in 1974. He admitted that legally Hitler was right and he was wrong. "But those 500,000 copies we sold helped awaken a great many Americans to how wrong Hitler was in those monstrous policies of his that were soon to plunge us into World War."

eagerly sought was followed by an equally devastating attack on Poland
and cancellation of the Polish-German non-aggression pact since it had
been "unilaterally infringed" by the Poles. Having torn up two treaties,
Hitler proceeded to welcome new negotiations so long as they were on
equal terms. "No one," he said, "would be happier than I at the prospect."

It was a remarkable display of mental gymnastics soon surpassed by
an assault on Roosevelt which—for the German audience, at least—was a
masterpiece of irony and sarcasm. This was the Hitler of the early years,
the beer-hall entertainer and debater. He took up the President's message
point by point, demolishing each one like a schoolmaster. His heavy sarcasm fell upon delighted ears in the Reichstag and with each riposte the
laughter and applause grew louder. The presiding officer, Göring, led the
uproar, his sides shaking.* When the Führer at last came to the President's request for assurance that Germany would launch no more aggression, his answer was a sardonic counterattack that brought still heartier
laughs—yet failed to respond to the question: Was he going to invade
Poland?

The speech was designed more to satisfy Hitler's people than to persuade his enemies. What he needed was time to bring the Polish question
to a favorable conclusion and, feeling that his address had accomplished
its purpose, he went into virtual seclusion at his semi-official vacation residence, the Berghof. He refused to make a single attempt to approach Poland during the ensuing hot summer but to Russia he was readily available.
The tentative offer of friendship so slyly advanced to Kleist over teacups
was developing into true romance. Shortly after the explosive Reichstag
speech a seemingly innocuous item appeared on a back page of Soviet
newspapers: Maxim Litvinov had been succeeded by V. M. Molotov. It
was sensational news and nowhere was it more appreciated than in the
German Embassy. That evening the German chargé telegraphed the Wilhelmstrasse that the Foreign Commissariat was giving no explanations but
the dismissal appeared to be the result of differences of opinion between
Stalin and Litvinov, whose wife, Ivy, was English. He himself symbolized
collective security against the Axis, and his exit meant that Stalin was
abandoning this line. The replacement of the Jewish Litvinov by a gentile
further indicated that Stalin, already distrustful of Britain's tentative overtures, was opening the door wider to his fellow anti-Semite in Berlin. The
embarrassing fact that Molotov had a Jewish wife was kept from Hitler,
not only by the Russians but by his own diplomats.

* When Göring was shown a movie of this speech at the Nuremberg Trials he again
laughed uncontrollably.

The news of Litvinov's replacement by Molotov struck the Führer "like a cannon ball." Beyond their common violent hatred and fear of Jews, he had long grudgingly admired Stalin's ruthless methods. Even so Hitler was not yet convinced that collaboration with the Soviets was wise. On May 10 he summoned an expert on Russian affairs to Berchtesgaden to determine whether Stalin was prepared for a genuine understanding with Germany. Gustav Hilger, economic attaché at the German Embassy in Moscow, with two decades' experience in Russia, was somewhat taken aback by such a query. He was "tempted to give Hitler a résumé of German-Soviet relations since 1933, and to remind him how often the Soviet government, during the first years of his rule, had expressed the desire of maintaining the old friendly relationship" but restrained himself, merely reminding Hitler of Stalin's declaration to the party congress exactly two months ago that there was no reason for war with Germany. To Hilger's surprise neither Hitler nor Ribbentrop could remember the substance of Stalin's remarks.

Hitler listened to Hilger's lengthy thesis that the Soviet Union was no military threat since she needed peace to build up her economy, but remarked as soon as Hilger left that he was "a bit of a Russian himself now" and might have succumbed to Soviet propaganda. "But if he is right then I must not fall in with Stalin's peace overtures. I must interrupt the internal consolidation of that giant as quickly as possible." He ordered Ribbentrop to mark time with the Soviets.

On his part, Stalin ordered Astakhov to resume trade talks with the Germans. On May 20 Molotov inserted himself into the negotiations by inviting Ambassador von der Schulenburg to the Kremlin. The usually dour Molotov was a genial host but beneath the veneer of amiability lay a flintlike obduracy and once serious discussion got under way he complained that Hitler's apparent reluctance to conclude a new economic agreement gave the Soviets the impression that the Germans were not in earnest and were only playing at negotiating for political reasons.

For the present, at least, the Führer was more concerned with strengthening his ties with Mussolini. Upset as he was by Il Duce's surprise invasion of Albania (Hitler had wanted a diversion, not the real thing), he had been negotiating ever since then for a more binding Axis treaty. This was signed with considerable ceremony in Berlin on May 22. Dubbed the Pact of Steel, it bound Italy's destiny inextricably to Germany's. To Hitler the agreement was a diplomatic triumph, pledging as it did each party to support the other in case of war "with all its military forces on land, on sea, and in the air." Incredibly Mussolini had been so anxious to please Hitler that he had not had his cabinet or his political and legal experts check the text, which did not even include a clause specifying that it was in effect only in case of attack by an enemy. Il Duce had carelessly placed the fate of Italy in his partner's hands.

It was almost as if Hitler had received a license to risk war and the next day a confident Führer gathered the senior Wehrmacht officers in his study at the chancellery. The solution of Germany's economic problems, he explained, had somehow become inextricably tied to her differences with Poland. "Danzig is not the subject of the dispute at all. It is a question of expanding our Lebensraum in the East and of securing our food supplies, of the settlement of the Baltic problems."

Therefore Poland (which would always side with Germany's enemies despite treaties of friendship) must be destroyed. "We cannot expect a repetition of the Czech affair," he warned. "There will be war. Our task is to isolate Poland." He reserved to himself the right to give the final order to attack since battle with Poland would be successful only if the West stayed on the sidelines. "If this is impossible, then it will be better to attack in the West and settle Poland at the same time."

The contradiction puzzled his listeners and, while most were staggered by Hitler's words, faithful Keitel convinced himself that the Führer was only trying to show his commanders that their misgivings were unfounded and that war would not really break out. This despite Hitler's next words: a bald prediction of a "life and death" war against England and France. "The idea that we can get off cheaply is dangerous; there is no such possibility. We must burn our boats, and it is no longer a question of justice or injustice, but of life or death for eighty million human beings." The basic aim was to force England to her knees. "We shall not be forced into a war," he said, "but we shall not be able to avoid one."

This was not the irrational ranting of a man possessed by the will to conquer but an admission that Germany could not continue as a great nation without war. Only the limitless resources of the East could save the Reich; and the alternative, accommodation with the West, entailed unacceptable risks. If he exposed to the world that he had been bluffing and shirked the test of war, German prestige and power would deflate like a leaky balloon.

With the possible exception of Keitel and Raeder, the other listeners filed out of the winter garden in shock. As for the Führer, he set out for his refuge on the Obersalzberg in high spirits, stopping off at Augsburg to see a local production of *Lohengrin*. Even as he relaxed at the Berghof, Hitler kept exploring the possibilities of a deal in the East. Although he had ordered Schulenburg to "sit tight" he began fretting about the English negotiations in Moscow. What if they concluded a treaty with the

Bolsheviks before he did? If so, what would Stalin do if Germany invaded Poland? He had to know and on May 26 Ribbentrop dictated instructions for Schulenburg to inform Molotov that Germany's former policy of hostility to the Comintern was to be abandoned if Hitler could be assured that the Soviets had, in fact, renounced their aggressive struggle against Germany as indicated by Stalin's recent speech. If so, then the time had come "to envisage the tranquilization and normalization of German-Russian foreign political relations."

Hitler was willing to postpone the dream of Lebensraum. He instructed Schulenburg to convince Molotov that the Germans had no intention at all of expanding into the Ukraine. The Russians also should not fear the recent Pact of Steel, which was aimed exclusively at the Anglo-French combination. Schulenburg was further enjoined to assure Molotov that, should Hitler find it necessary to use military force against Poland, the Soviet Union would not suffer. Furthermore, a pact with Germany was far more practical than one with perfidious Albion, which only wanted someone else to do her dirty work—as usual. The offer was tempting, for behind the diplomatic language was an obvious invitation to divide up Poland. And the argument that England and France could not, or would not, come to Poland's aid in time was one to appeal to a pragmatist like Stalin.

This offer was made so spontaneously that the Wilhelmstrasse was thrown into a mild panic. First Ribbentrop hastily informed the Japanese ambassador of Hitler's proposal, then urged him to wire Tokyo for concurrence. While General Oshima's critics at home looked upon him as Hitler's toady, he could, if the occasion demanded, be extremely intransigent. He refused even to send such a telegram, arguing that any Axis accord with the Soviet Union (whose troops and tanks were battling the Japanese on the Manchurian-Outer Mongolian border in a bitter if undeclared war) would destroy all chances of bringing Japan into the three-power pact with Germany and Italy that Hitler desired and the Japanese had kept side-stepping.

Disconcerted, Ribbentrop telephoned Ambassador Attolico for his opinion—not, he said, as ambassador but as expert on Russian affairs. Attolico agreed with Oshima that any Axis approach to the Kremlin would only make it easier for the Russians to "sell more dearly its own goods" in Paris and London. The harried Ribbentrop must have discussed the matter by phone with Hitler in Berchtesgaden and received new instructions. That evening another telegram went to Moscow canceling the offer to the Russians. Ambassador von der Schulenburg should make no move without further orders.

Concluding that he had approached the Russians on too high a level, Hitler ordered Weizsäcker to sound out Astakhov. He did so on the last day of May and the tone and content of their talk was so reassuring that the Führer authorized a message to Schulenburg later that same day instructing him to "undertake definite negotiations with the Soviet Union." On the heels of this message came another suggesting that economic talks with the Russians also be resumed. But Stalin's suspicions exceeded Hitler's and when nothing substantive had been achieved by the end of June the latter reluctantly ordered suspension of negotiations. The honeymoon that each side seemed so eager to consummate was off.

2

Stalin's Western suitors were no nearer to a treaty than Hitler. In London Lord Halifax was reaching the end of his patience with the Kremlin's reluctance to get down to business. Saying no to everything, he complained to Ambassador Maisky, was not his idea of negotiation since it had "a striking resemblance to Nazi methods of dealing with international questions." The Soviet answer was a tart article in *Pravda* on June 29 with this headline: BRITISH AND FRENCH GOVERNMENTS DO NOT WANT A TREATY ON THE BASIS OF EQUALITY FOR THE USSR. What actually lay behind Soviet hesitation was a lively suspicion that the British aimed to get Russia embroiled in a war with Hitler while reducing their own military contribution to a minimum. The Japanese ambassador in London, equally skeptical, reported to Tokyo his impression that the English were playing their usual double game: using the Soviet treaty negotiations as a threat against Hitler while utilizing a German-oriented peace plan against Stalin.

In the meantime Hitler remained at the Berghof much of the summer, removing himself from the diplomatic scene and making no important announcements. Perhaps this silence was born of his own uncertainty, perhaps it was in line with his conviction that most problems solved themselves if left alone. In any case, he could have done nothing more calculated to confuse his opponents. It was a season for passivity. He listened patiently to a written warning from Mussolini delivered in person by one of his generals. War was inevitable, said Il Duce, but added that their two countries needed peace. "It is from 1943 onwards that a war effort will have the greatest prospects of victory." Hitler did not deign to argue as the general read on of Mussolini's reluctance to anticipate a European war. The Führer's own intent was to localize the war by isolating Poland and he needed no advice from an Italian about how to do it.

To his adjutants he appeared markedly relaxed. He left his mountain fastness in mid-July for a brief stay in Munich where he attended a special performance of *Tannhäuser* at the State Opera House. This production boasted a new feature added for the personal benefit of the artist-bohemian Hitler: two nude girls, one posing as Europa astride a bull and the other depicting Leda with her swan.

A week later he was at Bayreuth enjoying the year's Wagner festival which, besides *The Ring*, included stirring performances of *Tristan* and *Parsifal*. He had invited his old school friend Kubizek to attend every performance but did not see him until August 3, the day after the final performance of *Götterdämmerung*. That afternoon an SS officer escorted Kubizek to Haus Wahnfried. Hitler grasped his old friend's right hand in both of his, and Kubizek could hardly speak.

Kubizek hesitatingly brought out a large bundle of postcards with the Führer's picture and wondered if they could be autographed for friends back in Austria. Hitler put on his reading glasses—he was careful to remove them for photographers—and obligingly began signing cards as Kubizek methodically blotted each signature. Afterward Hitler led him into the garden to Wagner's tomb. "I am happy," he said, "that we have met once more on this spot which always was the most venerable spot for us both."

This episode was one of the rare evidences of Hitler's private life, which had become overshadowed by his responsibilities as Führer. He had little time for Eva Braun, and it was not until the beginning of 1939 that she was moved into quarters in the chancellery. She slept in Hindenburg's former bedroom, whose main decoration was a large picture of Bismarck, and there were standing orders from the Führer never to open the window curtains. This bleak room, along with an adjoining boudoir, led directly to Hitler's library, but she was required to enter his suite through the servants' entrance.

Although they lived as husband and wife, the two went through an elaborate charade to persuade the staff that they were merely good friends. In the morning she would address him as "Mein Führer," and this form of address became such a habit that she used it, so she confessed to her best friend, even in private. The circle privy to their secret was beginning to widen, however, because of at least one ridiculous slip in security. Just before his dismissal, Captain Wiedemann went to the Führer's room one morning to deliver an emergency message and to his surprise saw outside the door Eva's petite Viennese shoes next to Hitler's boots—left to be shined as if it were a hotel. "I could not help recalling La Fontaine's fable," he wrote in his memoirs, "and I burst out laughing as I went downstairs."

When important guests arrived at either the chancellery or at Berchtesgaden, where Eva's pleasant apartment adjoined the Führer's, she was confined to quarters and this was hard to endure. She longed to meet Admiral Horthy, President Hoover, King Carol of Romania, the Aga Khan and other notables and yet was forced to stay in her room like a child. She was particularly disturbed, she confided to friends, when Hitler refused her pleas to meet the Duchess of Windsor since the two women, she thought, had so much in common. She did console herself with the thrill of knowing that the great of the world were coming from all over the world to honor her lover. This knowledge made her "Back Street" existence endurable. Moreover, anything was better than the earlier days of loneliness and doubt which had led to two attempted suicides.

On the political front Ribbentrop authorized resumption of talks with Astakhov on the day Hitler was enjoying *Tristan* at Bayreuth. Although the results delighted the Foreign Minister, Peter Kleist warned him not to let Stalin see that Germany was in a hurry and, above all, not to negotiate any special offers merely to conclude a pact. They should wait and probably within six months reach an agreement that would satisfy both parties. Ribbentrop laughed. They could sign a pact within a fortnight! He ignored Kleist's advice to be patient and, in his eagerness to complete a treaty that would checkmate England, instructed Schulenburg to meet Molotov again and propose serious political talks. At this meeting on August 3, the German ambassador got the impression, so he reported, that the Soviets were determined to sign with England and France "if they fulfill all Soviet wishes." This was certainly the impression Molotov hoped to make. Both he and Stalin had noted the eagerness in the Wilhelmstrasse and were tempting the Germans while leading on the British.

By this time Hitler had become even more impatient than Ribbentrop. His campaign deadline against Poland was less than a month off and he needed assurance from Stalin that the Red Army would not intervene. At this point he either forced the issue or was blessed by luck. The day after Schulenburg's inconclusive talk with Molotov a crisis in Poland arose. Danzig Nazis informed the Polish customs officials that they could no longer carry out their normal duties. Poland responded with an irate demand to withdraw the order, whereupon the president of the Senate of the Free City of Danzig indignantly denied that any such order had been issued and charged that Poland was only looking for a pretext to threaten Danzig.

If it was indeed a case of the tail wagging the dog, the latter quickly took command on August 9. Berlin warned Warsaw that any repetition of the ultimatum to Danzig "would lead to greater tension in the relationship between Germany and Poland." The tempest in the teapot grew into a serious crisis with Poland's retort that she would consider any possible German intervention an aggression.

The controlled German press was already in full cry. POLAND! LOOK OUT! warned one headline. WARSAW THREATENS BOMBARDMENT OF DANZIG—UNBELIEVABLE AGITATION OF POLISH MEGALOMANIA! blared another. While Goebbels shouted, the Foreign Office waged its campaign in a lower key with Julius Schnurre, Ribbentrop's economic expert, assuring Astakhov that German interests in Poland were really quite limited. "They do not at all need to collide with Soviet interests of any kind," he said, "but we must know those interests."

From his mountain retreat Hitler became personally involved by sending his private plane to Danzig for Carl Burckhardt, the League of Nations' high commissioner for the Free City. Burckhardt arrived at the Obersalzberg on August 11 and was driven up to the tea house on the Kehlstein.

Hitler was occupied by a different matter. "Perhaps something enormously important will happen soon," he remarked to Speer as they rode up in the elevator to the main room. Almost as though speaking to himself, he mentioned something about sending Göring on a mission. "But if need be I would even go myself. I am staking everything on this card." He was referring to a treaty with Stalin but by the time Burckhardt walked in he had worked himself into an excess of rage over Poland. "If the slightest thing happens without warning," he exclaimed, "I will pounce on the Poles like lightning with all the power of mechanized forces which they don't even dream of!" He shouted at the top of his voice, "Do you understand me?"

"Very well, Monsieur Chancellor, I quite realize that means a general war."

A look of pain and fury came over Hitler's face. "Very well," he said, "if I am forced into this conflict, I prefer to do it today rather than tomorrow. I will not conduct it like Wilhelm II, who always had scruples of conscience before waging total warfare. I will fight relentlessly to the bitter end."

He calmed down as if he had let off sufficient steam and quietly assured his guest that he had no desire to fight Britain and France. "I have no romantic aspiration," he said pleasantly, "no appetite for domination. Above all I seek nothing in the West. Neither today nor tomorrow." But he had to have a free hand in the East. "I must obtain a sufficient quantity of wheat for my country." He also needed a colony outside of Europe for timber. That was as far as his ambitions extended. "Once and for all," he said somberly, "it is necessary that you realize that I am ready to negotiate and discuss all these matters."

He reaffirmed that, given freedom in the East, he would happily conclude a pact with the British and guarantee all their possessions. This promise was obviously meant to be transmitted to London, as was the threat that followed. "Everything that I have in mind is directed against Russia; if the West is too stupid and blind to understand this then I will be forced to come to terms with the Russians, to crush the West and then after its defeat, turn with all my forces against the Soviet Union. I need the Ukraine so they can't starve us out as in the last war."

3

What Burckhardt did not know was that the British had recently made a secret offer to Hitler through one of Chamberlain's top advisers. In a private conversation at his house in West Kensington, Sir Horace Wilson assured Fritz Hesse, Ribbentrop's undercover representative, that the Prime Minister would be prepared to offer the Führer a defensive alliance for twenty-five years that could include economic advantages for the Reich and the return of German colonies by stages "in due course." In return Hitler must promise to take no more aggressive action in Europe.

Hesse was not sure he had heard right and asked Sir Horace to explain again in detail. He did. "If I were Hitler," said the astounded Hesse, "I would accept your proposition. But whether he will do so, no one can tell." Hesse transmitted the offer to the Foreign Office and before long was on a special plane bound for the Reich with a typewritten sheet provided by Wilson summarizing the proposals. While impressed, Ribbentrop wondered how he could convince Hitler that they should be taken seriously. Did Hesse really think the British would go to war on Hitler's side in case the Soviets attacked Germany? Would they break off their conversations in Moscow before negotiating with Germany? Hesse believed they would.

When Hitler first heard the proposals, so an eyewitness informed Hesse, he was transported with joy. "It's the greatest news I've had for a long time!" he exclaimed and began romancing like a child. The dream of his life, an alliance with mighty England, was coming true! But almost immediately he had misgivings and accused Wilson of laying a trap to save the Poles from a well-deserved thrashing. "What does Hitler want?" Hesse asked his informant—Walther Hewel, Ribbentrop's liaison man at the chancellery. The answer was: the Führer had his heart set on forcing the Poles to capitulate.

That week Ribbentrop asked Hesse if he was "completely convinced" that England would go to war over Danzig. All of his sources, he answered, indicated that Chamberlain could not act otherwise. Any invasion of Polish territory would result in war. "The Führer doesn't believe this at all!" exclaimed Ribbentrop. "Some donkeys told him that the English would only bluff and a German counterbluff would drive them to their knees." Puzzled by the contradiction between Ribbentrop's personal convictions and his public posture, Hesse asked if he really thought the English were bluffing. The Foreign Minister asserted that he *had* warned the Führer that the English were not soft and degenerate and would fight if they believed the balance of power in Europe depended on it or their empire was seriously threatened.

Two days later Ribbentrop told Hesse that he had transmitted all of the latter's arguments to Hitler. But he remained convinced that if the English were really ready to plunge into war over such a trivial matter as Danzig, then war with England was absolutely inevitable.

Ribbentrop promised to speak again to Hitler and marveled at the "surprisingly calm way" the Führer considered Hesse's alternatives. Still, Hitler was consumed by fear that it was merely a maneuver to trick him. What guarantee was there that the English would keep their word? "The Führer," Ribbentrop reported, "would only consider solid guarantees." This hardened attitude was reflected in Ribbentrop's own diplomatic posture upon meeting Mussolini's son-in-law on August 11 in Salzburg. Ciano had come with emphatic instructions from Mussolini to insist upon postponement of any invasion of Poland. The matter must be solved by conference.

Ribbentrop, as well as his Führer, had resented Il Duce's sending an emissary instead of coming himself. Besides both despised Ciano for the drinking bouts and sexual escapades he reportedly indulged in whenever he visited the Reich. Ribbentrop dutifully mouthed his master's thoughts at the meeting with Ciano. Perhaps the Foreign Minister had even come to share them. At any rate, he acted like a carbon copy of Hitler as he peremptorily brushed aside all of Ciano's eloquent pleas for a peaceful solution. Finally Ciano asked what Ribbentrop wanted: the Corridor or Danzig? "Not that any more," was the answer. "We want war."

The coolness between Ciano and Ribbentrop spread to their secretaries and scarcely a word was exchanged during lunch. At one point Ciano, pale and shaken, whispered to a compatriot, "We are almost at blows."

Surprisingly Ciano, who had allowed himself to be bullied by Ribbentrop, stood up to the Führer the following day at the Berghof. During lunch Ciano poked fun at the floral decorations, which interpreter Dollmann guessed had been arranged by Eva Braun; and once serious discussions began, he countered Hitler's arguments with energy and wit. He warned that a war with Poland could not be confined to that country since this time the West would surely declare war. In the most explicit terms, Ciano pointed out that Italy was not prepared for a general war, in fact, didn't have sufficient matériel to remain in combat for more than a few months. All affability, Hitler suggested they postpone further talk until morning and drive up to his retreat on Kehlstein mountain while there was still good light. Ciano complied with obvious lack of enthusiasm and, as Hitler drew him to a window and expatiated on the scenic grandeur that lay outside, shivered uncomfortably. He then proceeded to drink cup after cup of hot tea, which he disliked. The trip to the mountaintop left Ciano disconsolate and that evening he telephoned his father-in-law: "The position is serious."

By morning Ciano was a beaten man. At the second talk with Hitler he said not a word of Italy's inability to take part in the war. His brilliant debating power had suddenly deserted him, and to Schmidt's amazement, "he folded up like a jackknife." Gone was the cool decisiveness and statesmanship of yesterday as he listened apathetically to the Führer's assurance that England and France would never go to war on Poland's account. "You have been proved right so often before when we others held the opposite view," said Ciano, "that I think it very possible that this time, too, you see things more clearly than we do."

A few hours later a dispirited Ciano was airbound for home. "I return to Rome," he wrote in his diary, "completely disgusted with the Germans, with their leader, and their way of doing things. Now they have dragged us into an adventure which we have not wanted and which might compromise the regime and the country as a whole."

Soon after Ciano's departure Hesse was ordered to meet Ribbentrop at a hotel in Salzburg. After staring silently at a writing table for ten minutes the Foreign Minister finally looked up somberly at Hesse. "I have just come from the Führer," he said. "He is, unfortunately, not in a position to discuss Chamberlain's offer." He was referring to Wilson's proposals. "He has quite different intentions. Chamberlain's offer will not be discarded. We shall return to it when the time has come." He instructed Hesse to fly back to London at once and keep his ears open. "The Führer means to play a very dangerous game. I do not know whether it will suc-

ceed or not. In any case, we don't want a war with England. Give us a signal in good time if the danger becomes acute."

The supreme confidence exuded by Hitler to Ciano was largely play-
acting. He was deeply concerned at Stalin's reluctance to come to an
agreement. This anxiety was aggravated by a report that a British-French
delegation had recently arrived in Moscow and was about to conclude successful negotiations with the Soviets. In truth, the Russians were in no
mood to negotiate, concerned as they were that the Allies were toying
with them. First the Anglo-French delegation had taken six days to arrive
by slow cargo-passenger ship and train when they could have made it in a
single day. Next the British senior officer had come without proper credentials, and when the talks finally got under way it seemed that the British
were not at all serious: a Soviet offer to provide 136 divisions for a common defense against the Nazis was matched by a British proposal to provide one mechanized and five infantry divisions.

Not knowing all this, the Führer ordered Ribbentrop to put more
pressure on the Kremlin, and a conference between Molotov and Schulenburg was hastily arranged. On the evening of August 15 the Foreign
Commissar listened attentively to everything the German ambassador had
to say but could give no quick answer. First, he said, an understanding
must be reached on several points. Would the Germans, for example, be
willing to influence Japan to take a different attitude toward the Soviets?
Would the Germans conclude a pact of non-aggression? If so, under what
conditions?

Hitler was too impatient for deliberations. He ordered Ribbentrop to
reach an understanding at once with Molotov; and thereby let his adver-
sary set the pace of events. Stalin took immediate advantage. Through
Molotov he replied that before any political pacts could be signed their
economic agreements must be concluded. Ribbentrop responded with a
further plea to Schulenburg for haste, pointing out that the first stage of
the economic agreements had just been completed. His instructions became almost hysterical. The next conversation with Molotov, he said,
should be conducted "by pressing emphatically . . . for a rapid realization
of my trip and by opposing appropriately any possible new Russian objections. In this connection you must keep in mind the decisive fact that an
early outbreak of open German-Polish conflict is probable and that we
therefore have the greatest interest in my having my visit to Moscow take
place immediately."

Stalin realized that every hour of delay was painful to Hitler (perhaps
his agents had learned of Hitler's September 1 deadline) and so ordered
Molotov to procrastinate as usual at his next meeting with Schulenburg on

August 19. The Foreign Commissar consequently argued tediously over every point despite his guest's repeated and emphatic pleas for action. But half an hour after Schulenburg departed the Soviets surprisingly reversed their tactics. Molotov invited the German back to the Kremlin. He arrived late that afternoon and it was immediately apparent that Molotov had good news. After apologizing for inconveniencing Schulenburg, the Foreign Commissar said he had just been authorized to hand over a draft of a non-aggression pact and to receive Herr von Ribbentrop in Moscow. He did not explain, naturally, that the Anglo-French-Soviet military talks in Moscow had reached such an impasse that Stalin had lost all patience with the West. Perhaps he had intended to join with Hitler all along and only used the Anglo-French talks as a maneuver to get better conditions from Hitler.

Even so the Russians proceeded deliberately. Molotov told Schulenburg he could not receive Ribbentrop until a week *after* the signing of their economic agreement. If that took place today, the date would be August 26, if tomorrow, the twenty-seventh. Hitler must have read Schulenburg's report with mixed feelings—delight at the probability of concluding the treaty and exasperation at Stalin's insistence on first signing their economic agreement. It was little better than blackmail but Hitler felt there was no alternative. The trade agreement was rushed through and signed in Berlin two hours after midnight. It granted the Soviet Union a merchandise credit of 200 million Reichsmarks, at the reasonable interest of five per cent, to be used to finance Soviet orders of machine tools and industrial installations. Armaments "in the broader sense," such as optical supplies and armor plate, were to be supplied in proportionately smaller amounts. The credit would be liquidated by Soviet raw materials.

Outmaneuvered by Stalin, just as he had outmaneuvered the Austrians and Czechs, Hitler could not possibly wait the week that Molotov proposed. He composed a personal message to Stalin which was dispatched from Berlin at 4:35 P.M., August 20. In it Hitler sincerely welcomed the signing of the new German-Soviet commercial agreement as a first step in the reordering of German-Soviet relations. He also accepted the Soviet draft of the non-aggression pact although there were a few questions connected with it which should be clarified as soon as possible. Then he got down to the crux of the matter: speed in concluding this pact, he said, was of the utmost importance since tension between Germany and Poland was becoming intolerable. A crisis might arise "any day."

Two hours after Schulenburg delivered the message to the Kremlin, he was summoned back for a personal reply from Stalin himself: "I thank you for the letter," it began. He hoped the pact would mark a decided turn in their political relations. "The people of our countries need peaceful relations with each other." He agreed to see Ribbentrop on August 23.

Throughout the twentieth Hitler had been silently pacing up and down the great hall in the Berghof waiting anxiously for news from Moscow; the expression on his face kept anyone from disturbing him. In expectation he had already sent the pocket battleship *Graf Spee* to a waiting position in the Atlantic; twenty-one U-boats were in offensive positions around the British Isles.

At dinner (according to Speer) Hitler was handed a telegram. After reading it, his face flushed a deep red and he stared vacantly out the window. All at once he slammed both fists on the table, making the glasses rattle. "I have them!" he exclaimed in a voice choked with emotion. "I have them!" He slumped back and, since no one dared to ask any questions, the meal resumed in silence.

After coffee a euphoric Hitler told his guests that Germany was concluding a non-aggression pact with Russia. "Here, read this," he said. "A telegram from Stalin." Hoffmann recalled that the Führer was so delighted he slapped his knee, something the photographer had never seen him do before. There was great ado as Kannenberg, the major-domo, brought out champagne. Glasses were clinked and the entourage drank a toast to the great diplomatic coup. Presently Hitler led everyone to the little movie theater in the basement to see a film of Stalin reviewing a massive Red Army parade. How lucky, remarked the Führer, that such military might was now neutralized.

Hoffmann worried about repercussions among the faithful National Socialists who had been fighting the Reds for decades. "The party will be just as astounded as the rest of the world," Hitler purportedly replied, "but my party members know and trust me; they know I will never depart from my basic principles, and they will realize that the ultimate aim of this last gamble is to remove the Eastern danger and thus to facilitate, under my leadership, of course, a swifter unification of Europe."

On the face of it, Stalin and Hitler *were* most unlikely allies. What could they possibly have in common? In fact, there were a number of similarities. One admired Peter the Great while the other saw himself as the heir of Frederick the Great. Both were advocates of ruthless force and operated under ideologies that were not essentially different. Communists and Nazis alike were self-righteous and dogmatic; both were totalitarian and both believed that the end justified the means, sanctifying injustice, as it were, in the name of the state and progress.

Hitler had long admired Stalin, regarding him as "one of the extraor-

dinary figures in world history," and once shocked a group of intimates by
asserting that he and the Soviet leader had much in common since both
had risen from the lower classes, and when one listener protested compari-
son with a former bank robber, he replied, "If Stalin did commit a bank
robbery, it was not to fill his own pockets but to help his party and movement. You cannot consider that bank robbery."

Nor did the Führer look upon Stalin as a true Communist. "In actual
fact, he identifies himself with the Russia of the Czars, and he has merely
resurrected the tradition of Pan-Slavism. [Perhaps Hitler was unconsciously speaking of himself and Germany.] For him Bolshevism is only a
means, a disguise designed to trick the Germanic and Latin peoples."

Both Stalin and Hitler felt sure they could use each other. Both dictators were wrong but in that hectic summer of 1939 there was not a
major nation in the world which was not operating under some miscon-
ception. Europe was a cauldron of distrusts, deceit and double-dealing.
Even as Ribbentrop prepared to leave for Moscow, Stalin had not completely abandoned the hope of an Anglo-French-Soviet military alliance
against Hitler. And while the English were doing their halfhearted best to
consummate this agreement, they were secretly inviting Göring to England. On all sides nation was dealing behind the back of nation, each
mouthing platitudes of sincerity or uttering threats.

4

The apparent winner was Hitler. He wakened on the morning of August 22 full of confidence. After Ribbentrop had left the Berghof with
final instructions for his mission to Moscow, the Führer summoned his
senior commanders and their chiefs of staff for a special meeting in the
spacious reception hall. It was a lecture, not a conference, with Hitler sitting behind a large desk doing all the talking. "I have called you together
to give you a picture of the political situation, in order that you may have
insight into the various elements on which I have based my decision to
act, and in order to strengthen your confidence." The conflict with
Poland, he said, was bound to come sooner or later and there were a number of reasons why it was best to act promptly. "First of all two personal
factors: my own personality and that of Mussolini. Essentially all depends
on me, on my existence, because of my political talents. Probably no one
will ever again have the confidence of the German people as I have. There
will probably never again be a man with more authority than I have. My
life is, therefore, a factor of great value. But I can be eliminated at any
time by a criminal or an idiot." The second personal factor was Il Duce. If

something happened to him, Italy's loyalty to their alliance would be questionable.

On the other hand there was no outstanding personality in either England or France. "Our enemies have men who are below average. No personalities. No master, no men of action . . ." Furthermore, the political situation was favorable, with rivalry in the Mediterranean and tension in the Orient. All these fortunate circumstances would no longer prevail in two or three years. "No one knows how long I shall live. Therefore conflict is better now."

Then he became specific. Relations with Poland, he said, had become unbearable. "We are facing the alternative to strike or to be destroyed with certainty sooner or later." What could the West do? Either attack from the Maginot Line or blockade the Reich. The first was improbable and the second would be ineffective since now the Soviets would supply Germany with grain, cattle, coal, lead and zinc. "I am only afraid that in the last minute some *Schweinehund* will produce a plan of mediation!"

The commanders, led by Göring, clapped enthusiastically.* "Mein Führer," said the Reichsmarschall "the Wehrmacht will do its duty!" Despite their applause, Göring and the other military commanders were unanimously against war since all were convinced that Germany was not yet properly prepared to wage one. There was only a six weeks' supply of ammunition, as well as alarming shortages of steel, oil and other important materials.

Hitler was as aware of all this as his generals but envisaged a different type of warfare: the *Blitzkrieg*, a sudden all-out attack of such force and intensity that victory would be assured quickly. The concept was strategic as well as tactical. The dehumanizing years of trench combat in the Great War, not to mention the deprivations of those on the home front, were still searing memories to Hitler. He had vowed that the misery of a long conflict would never again be visited on Germany. That is why he geared the Wehrmacht to armament in breadth rather than in depth. He had purposely organized Germany's economy for a relatively high production of ready armaments but not to wage long-range war with mass-productive powers. His goal was to produce armaments quickly, not to increase Germany's armament-producing plant or to retool her armament-producing machinery.

A series of Blitzkrieg attacks—sustained by short, intensive bursts of production—would permit Hitler to act as if Germany were stronger than

---

* According to one colorful account which stretches all credulity, Göring jumped on the table and danced around triumphantly like a savage, which would indeed have been a sight to behold.

she actually was by avoiding the massive production for conventional war that would have meant economic ruin. His was a poor man's philosophy that could only succeed with audacity. Already he had achieved a series of cheap victories by risking a conflict that his more affluent enemies were eager to avoid at almost any cost.

Blitzkrieg not only appealed to his gambling instinct but was perfectly suited to his position of dictator. A democracy could hardly have sustained the necessary bursts of economic effort, the concentration on turning out tanks, for instance, followed by an abrupt concentration on civilian items. What would have brought down a democracy did not apply to the National Socialist state with the peculiar weaknesses and strengths of its economy.

By choosing Blitzkrieg, Hitler confounded some of his own generals, whose theories were still rooted in the past. They did not realize, as he did, that Germany was far readier for combat than England and France. It was a gamble but he figured he could achieve victory over Poland so rapidly that he would never even have to cross swords with England or France. The odds were that they would then see the futility of retaliation. Somehow he had to neutralize the West—whether by threat or force of arms—so that by 1943 he could achieve his true aim, conquest of Russia. With eyes open, Adolf Hitler was prepared to meet his destiny.

On the morning of August 22 not one of the military men listening to Hitler's blueprint for invasion uttered a word of criticism, nor was there any protest from the field commanders, who were brought in after lunch for their inspirational message. The Führer exhorted them to have no mercy. "Might is right," he said and announced that the invasion would likely begin at dawn on Saturday, August 26.

Early that evening Ribbentrop and his party took off for Moscow in two Condors. There was a general feeling of extreme tension. "Nobody," recalled Peter Kleist, "could guarantee that the Soviets would not spring on us an Anglo-French agreement, all neatly tied up, when we arrived in Moscow." Nor could anyone predict whether Ribbentrop would be forced into the "long, soul-destroying negotiations" habitually conducted by the Russians.

The news of Ribbentrop's trip took Japanese Ambassador Oshima by complete surprise and that midnight he made a special trip to Weizsäcker's home in Berlin to express his displeasure. Ordinarily a man of poise, Oshima's face was rigid and gray. How, he asked, could such a turnabout be explained to Tokyo?

Early the next afternoon, August 23, Henderson handed over Chamberlain's letter to the Führer. It declared categorically that Britain was determined to fulfill its promises to Poland. At the same time Chamberlain made another plea for peace. Why couldn't there be a truce so that Germany and Poland could discuss their problems directly? "At this moment," he concluded, "I confess I can see no other way to avoid a catastrophe that will involve Europe in war."

Hitler replied excitably in violent language; and Henderson expressed the hope that a solution might be found if their two nations co-operated. Hitler curtly retorted that this should have been done before. This brought a protest that the British government had given guarantees and must honor them. "Then honor them," snapped the Führer. "If you have given a blank check you must also meet it."

Henderson stoutly defended the British position but insisted on doing it in German, a language whose subtleties he had not yet mastered. Hitler brushed aside his arguments and began to threaten. The slightest attempt by Poland to make any further move against the Germans or Danzig, he said, would mean immediate intervention. Furthermore, mobilization in the West would be answered by German mobilization.

"Is that a threat?" asked Henderson.

"No, a protective measure!" In vain Henderson tried to assure Hitler that Chamberlain had always championed Germany. "I too believed that until this spring," said Hitler almost sadly. Thereupon Henderson blurted out that he personally had never believed in an Anglo-French-Russian pact. He preferred that Germany rather than England should have a treaty with Russia. Hitler's answer was ominous. "Make no mistake," he said, "it will be a long treaty." Henderson was not content to let this subject alone. He argued that the Führer knew as well as he did that the Russians always made difficulties. In any case he was convinced that Chamberlain had not changed in his attitude to Germany.

"I must judge by deeds in this matter," said Hitler and resumed recriminations. This brought a threat from Henderson that any direct action by Germany would mean war, which in turn touched off another display of almost hysterical violence. In such a war, exclaimed Hitler, Germany had nothing to lose and Great Britain much. He had no desire for war but would not shrink from it and his people were much more behind him than last September. He abruptly ended the conversation by stating that a written reply to Chamberlain would be handed over to Henderson in the afternoon.

Weizsäcker, a silent witness to this uneven duel, was as convinced as Henderson of Hitler's genuine agitation. But no sooner had the door closed behind the Englishman than the Führer slapped himself on the thigh (it was becoming a habit) and laughed. "Chamberlain won't survive that conversation," he said triumphantly. "His cabinet will fall this evening."

While waiting for the Führer's written answer, Henderson returned to Salzburg where he telephoned his subordinates in Berlin instructing them to inform London that Hitler was "entirely uncompromising and unsatisfactory but I cannot say anything further until I have received his written reply." A little later came a summons to return to the Berghof. This time Hitler, according to Henderson's report, had recovered his calm and "never raised his voice once." But he was no less obdurate, charging that "England was determined to destroy and exterminate Germany."

Henderson protested that war between their two countries would only benefit the lesser races of the world. To this Hitler replied that it was England who was fighting for the lesser races whereas he was only fighting for Germany and this time the Germans would battle to the last man. It would have been different in 1914 if he had been Chancellor then! "At the next instance of Polish provocation," he continued, "I shall act." He repeated his threat of the morning but this time without histrionics. "The questions of Danzig and the Corridor will be settled one way or another. Please take note of this. Believe me, last year—on October 2—I would have marched either way. I give you my word of honor on that!"

That afternoon the two German Condors landed at Moscow airport where Ribbentrop was pleased to see the swastika flying side by side with the hammer and sickle. After the Foreign Minister reviewed an honor guard of the Soviet air force, he was driven to his quarters, the former Austrian Embassy. (Was this Tartar irony?) Count von der Schulenburg informed him that he was expected in the Kremlin at 6 P.M. but couldn't say whether it would be Molotov or Stalin who would negotiate with him. "Odd Moscow customs," thought Ribbentrop to himself.

After Schulenburg and Hilger had made their reports, both advised Ribbentrop to allow himself plenty of time and not give the impression of being in a hurry. Interrupting with an impatient movement of the hand, he enjoined the ambassador to inform the Russians that he had to be back in Berlin within twenty-four hours. So saying, he hastily had a snack before heading for the Kremlin.

At 6 P.M. Ribbentrop was facing Stalin. He was affable, good-natured. Molotov was impassive. Ribbentrop spoke first, expressing his nation's desire to establish German-Soviet relations on a new footing. He understood from Stalin's March speech that he felt the same. Stalin turned to

Molotov. Did he want to speak first? The Foreign Commissar dutifully replied that it was Stalin's prerogative to reply.

He did in a manner which Ribbentrop had never encountered before. "For years," said Stalin concisely, "we have poured pails of manure at one another. That should not stop us from coming to an understanding. This was the drift of my speech in March, the meaning of which you have understood perfectly." With a notebook opened in front of him for reference, he continued without pause to practical matters: the spheres of influence in the countries between Germany and the U.S.S.R. were defined, with Finland, most of the Baltic States and Bessarabia in the Russian orbit; in the event of war between Germany and Poland they would meet at a definite "line of demarcation."

It was obvious that Stalin had come to the room to do business, not dally, and by the end of three hours he and Ribbentrop had agreed upon everything except two Baltic ports which Stalin insisted on having in his sphere. Ribbentrop said he would have to check with the Führer first and the talks were adjourned so he could do so.

Hitler was as eager to do business as Stalin. Within an hour a phone call from the Wilhelmstrasse brought this laconic reply: "Answer is yes. Agreed." In the meantime Ribbentrop sat down to another quick meal at his quarters, bubbling over with enthusiasm for Stalin and Molotov.

The Foreign Minister was in high spirits as he drove back to the Kremlin with the favorable answer from Hitler, this time with a larger retinue, which included two photographers. Secret police rushed out of the darkness as the German cars slowly moved into the mysterious inner city and proceeded past the largest cannon of its time, so huge that no one had ever dared fire it, past little wooden houses and cathedrals. Finally the procession reached a modern administration building where Stalin was waiting. In short order, final agreement on the non-aggression pact was reached. It was a concise, clear contract. Each party was to desist from any aggressive action against the other and lend no support to any power attacking the other. The treaty was to last for ten years and continue for another five unless renounced by either party a year prior to its expiration.

It was a conventional agreement, but not so its secret protocol, which carved up Eastern Europe. Equally extraordinary was Stalin's willingness to be photographed at the signing of the documents. He entered into the spirit and stage-managed the best-known picture of the signing. He beckoned to Ribbentrop's SS adjutant, Richard Schulze, to join the group but this young man couldn't imagine Stalin meant him. Finally Stalin took the extremely tall Schulze by the arm and placed him next to Ribbentrop. Perhaps Stalin wanted to add youthful appeal to the picture; perhaps he knew that Schulze's younger brother was Hitler's SS ordnance officer.

Toast followed toast but the most noteworthy was one from Stalin that was never revealed to the Russian people: "I know how much the German nation loves its Führer," he said. "I should therefore like to drink to his health." One of the most important treaties in world history had been completed and signed without argument in a few hours, proof that both Hitler and Stalin wanted the agreement, that both knew exactly what they would give to get what they wanted, and that both wished the deed done swiftly.

To Hitler the pact was *his* triumph, not Stalin's. He had apparently forgotten his own prediction in *Mein Kampf* that any German-Russian alliance would inevitably bring a war which would cause "the end of Germany." He had since changed his mind, so he confided to Bormann several years later, and hoped an entente with the Soviets would be "honestly sincere if not unreservedly friendly." He imagined after so many years of power that Stalin, the realist, would have shed the nebulous Marxist ideology, retaining it only as a poison for external use. The brutal manner in which he treated the Jewish intelligentsia encouraged such a belief. "In a spirit of implacable realism on both sides we could have created a situation in which a durable entente would have been possible. . . . An entente, in short, watched over by an eagle eye and with a finger on the trigger!"

Upon learning the treaty was signed, Hitler jumped up from the dinner table, exclaiming, "We've won!" Although he had waived the opportunity to seize all of Poland, the argument had neutralized Russia. Now he was free to proceed against Poland. Without the Soviet Union on their side, neither England nor France would do more than mouth threats. In addition he was assured of getting from the East all those raw materials he might be deprived of by a possible British blockade.

He was paying Stalin to do exactly what he would undoubtedly have done without a pact. The economy of the Soviet Union as well as its military efficiency was still in such disarray after the purges that Stalin could not even think of fighting the Reich. In fact he had never seriously sought a protective alliance against Hitler. What he and his associates in the Kremlin desired above all was neutrality; the pact with Germany not only gave this but fulfilled their aim of provoking war among the capitalist powers. To Stalin, Nazi Germany was just another capitalist enemy.

At about 3 A.M., August 24, Hitler led his entourage onto the Berghof terrace. The sky on the north and northwestern horizon blazed with the colors of the rainbow. Across the valley, a startling red glow from these

Northern Lights was cast on the Unterberg, a mountain of legend. "The last act of *Götterdämmerung*," recalled Speer, "could not have been more effectively staged. The same red light bathed our faces and our hands."

Hitler abruptly turned to his Luftwaffe adjutant, Below. "Looks like a great deal of blood," he said. "This time we won't bring it off without violence."

Chapter Twenty

"A CALAMITY WITHOUT
PARALLEL IN HISTORY"
AUGUST 24–SEPTEMBER 3, 1939

1

The world awakened Thursday morning, August 24, to headlines proclaiming a treaty that was a traumatic shock not only to ordinary citizens but to diplomats. "I anticipate an ultimatum to Poland," Henderson reported from Berlin. "Whether eleventh hour attempt of Polish Government to re-establish contact will avail, I much doubt. But I regard it as *last* hope, if any, of peace: if there is a last hope."

The Polish people were extremely upset by the German-Soviet pact despite attempts by their newspapers to belittle it as a sign of German weakness. The government itself expressed supreme confidence that British and French assistance would turn the tide in case of war with Hitler. French Communists seemed to be torn between loyalty to their own country and Mother Russia. Confusion was even greater among their American colleagues. At first the *Daily Worker* ignored the treaty as if waiting for instructions from Moscow. Finally Earl Browder, the party leader, announced that it had weakened Hitler. With nary a qualm most extreme left-wing "progressives" obediently accepted a new party line: the agreement with Hitler had been consummated so that Russia could prepare herself for the eventual battle against Fascism. President Roosevelt's response was to send another of his moral telegrams to Hitler urging him "to refrain from any positive act of hostility for a reasonable and stipulated period" but, like its predecessor, it was filed and forgotten.

In Moscow Stalin was congratulating himself. Convinced that the British would compromise in the face of political reality, he imagined that the spheres of influence he had been granted would fall to him bloodlessly, by negotiation. Hitler's other allies were not so sanguine. The Italians, while admitting that Hitler had "struck a master blow," were uneasy and the Japanese feared that the alliance would encourage Stalin to increase pressure on Manchuria. Prime Minister Hiranuma, whose cabinet had already held more than seventy meetings in a futile effort to reach agreement on a concordat with Germany and Italy, was so embarrassed and dismayed that he announced, "The cabinet herewith resigns because of complicated and inscrutable situations recently arising in Europe."

The German public was generally pleased and relieved: the threat of encirclement, a war on two fronts, had miraculously evaporated thanks to the Führer. Those who found the pact the hardest to swallow were his staunchest followers but most of them quickly convinced themselves that the Chief knew exactly what he was doing.

Hitler flew up to Berlin to greet the returning hero, Ribbentrop, and he spent the evening in the chancellery listening to his Foreign Minister rhapsodize over the masters of the Kremlin, who made him feel "as if he were among old party comrades." Further, a picture of Czar Nicholas in the Winter Palace had convinced Ribbentrop that they could do business with Russia since it indicated that the Communists themselves revered a Czar who worked for the people. While Hitler took all this in with some interest, he was much more enthralled by the pictures Hoffmann had taken. Hitler, it seemed, had requested a close-up of the Soviet leader to see if his earlobes were "ingrown and Jewish, or separate and Aryan." One profile view in particular was most reassuring. His new brother-in-arms, according to the earlobe test, was no Jew.

But Hitler shook his head disapprovingly at the photographs of the final ceremonies. Every one showed Stalin with a cigarette. "The signing of the pact is a solemn act which one does not approach with a cigarette dangling from one's lips," he said and instructed the photographer to paint out the cigarettes before releasing the pictures to the press.

The Führer also interrogated at length the ordnance officer who had accompanied Ribbentrop. He reported that Stalin, before inviting his guests to sit down at the celebration dinner, had carefully inspected the table to see that everything was in order. This reminded Fräulein Schröder of the Führer himself and the secretary imprudently remarked on the similarity. Hitler did not appreciate the analogy. "*My* servants and *my* house," he said with some irritation, "are always perfect!"

The following day, Friday, August 25, was a crucial and crowded one. It began with a letter to Mussolini, explaining with some embarrassment what had taken place in Moscow. After giving assurances that the treaty only strengthened the Axis, Hitler trusted that Il Duce would understand why he had been forced to take such a drastic step. Hitler's next act was to ask Schmidt to translate the key passages of the speech Chamberlain had made in Commons the previous day. He listened intently to the Prime Minister's admission that the Moscow Pact had come as "a surprise of a very unpleasant character," but that the Germans were laboring under a "dangerous illusion" if they believed that the British and French would no longer fulfill their obligations to Poland.

"These words," recalled Schmidt, "made Hitler pensive, but he said nothing." Perhaps this confirmed a nagging uncertainty. The assault on Poland was scheduled to start early next morning but he was in such doubt that just before noon he instructed the high command to postpone the issuance of the executive order to attack for one hour—until three that afternoon. Then he summoned the British ambassador to the chancellery. Henderson arrived at 1:30 P.M. to find the Führer in a conciliatory mood. He was now prepared "to make a move toward England which should be as decisive as the move towards Russia which had led to the recent agreement." His conscience, Hitler said, compelled him to make this final effort to secure good relations. But this was his last attempt.

To Henderson he appeared to be calm and normal. But he did lose his temper as soon as he began enumerating the charges against the Poles, such as firing on civilian aircraft. These conditions, he shouted, "must cease!" The Danzig problem and the Corridor must be solved without further delay. The only result of Chamberlain's last speech could be "a bloody and unpredictable war between Germany and England." But this time Germany would not have to fight on two fronts. "Russia and Germany will never again take up arms against each other."

When Henderson kept repeating stolidly that England could not go back on her word to Poland, Hitler's threatening posture reverted to one of reasonableness. Once the Polish question was solved, he was prepared and determined to approach Britain again with a large comprehensive offer: he would, for instance, accept the British Empire and pledge himself personally to its continued existence. But if the British rejected his proposal, he concluded ominously, "there will be war." And this was his last offer.

Half an hour later, at exactly 3:02 P.M., he confirmed the order to attack Poland at dawn. On the surface his gamble appeared to have been motivated by mere opportunism. Admittedly a cunning virtuoso of day-to-day politics, his foreign policy did have a basic thrust: a step-by-step play to gain domination over continental Europe that was closely allied to his radical anti-Semitic program. In Rome his ambassador, accompanied by Ciano, was just entering the Palazzo Venezia with the text of the unusual letter written earlier in the day. At three-twenty Ambassador Hans Georg von Mackensen handed over the document to Il Duce. The pact had mightily impressed Mussolini, who, like all politicians, appreciated a brilliant coup. Yet he was realistic enough to face the fact that his own army, which had performed so feebly in Albania, was not endowed with sufficient morale, training or skill to wage a genuine war. He did not say so to Mackensen, only mouthed protestations of agreeability: he was in complete accord with the Moscow Pact while remaining an "unswerving anti-Communist," and stood behind the Führer come what may (this he emphasized expressly), "unconditionally and with all his resources."

No sooner had Mackensen left the room than Il Duce either changed his mind or had it changed for him. According to Ciano, it was he who convinced Mussolini to compose an answer to Hitler, admitting frankly that Italy was not ready for war and could only participate if Germany immediately delivered sufficient "military supplies and raw materials to resist the attack which the French and English would predominantly direct against us."

At the same time the Italian ambassador in Berlin was explaining to the Führer that Il Duce's answer was on its way. While Hitler was waiting for the next visitor, French Ambassador Coulondre, an aide brought in a news report from England which Schmidt glimpsed over his employer's shoulder. England and Poland had just concluded a pact of mutual assistance in London. Visibly concerned, the Führer brooded in silence. For months the signing of this agreement had been delayed for one reason or another. That it should take place on this of all days, a few hours after he had made his "last" offer to England, was no coincidence. This guarantee of military aid (even though it could never be implemented) might give the Poles such a false sense of security that they would refuse to negotiate with Germany.

At 5:30 P.M. Coulondre was finally escorted into the office. After exhibiting rage over Polish provocations, Hitler expressed regret over a possible war between Germany and France. "I had the impression at times," recalled Schmidt, "that he was mechanically repeating what he said to Henderson, and that his thoughts were elsewhere. It was obvious that he was in a hurry to bring the interview to an end." He half rose to his feet in a gesture of dismissal but the elegant Coulondre would not be put off without a retort. He spoke with forcible words that Schmidt would never forget: "In a situation as critical as this, Herr Reichskanzler, misunderstandings are the most dangerous things of all. Therefore, to make the matter quite clear, I give you my word of honor as a French officer that the French army will fight by the side of Poland if that country should be attacked." Then he assured Hitler that his government was prepared to do everything for the maintenance of peace right up to the last.

"Why then," exclaimed Hitler angrily, "did you give Poland a blank check to act as she pleased?" Before the Frenchman could reply, the Führer leaped to his feet for another tirade against the Poles. "It is painful for me to have to go to war against France; but the decision does not depend on me." With a wave of the hand he dismissed the ambassador.

A minute later, at 6 P.M., Attolico entered. He bore with him the text of Mussolini's letter, which had been dictated over the phone by Ciano. The announcement that Italy was not prepared for war, on the heels of the British-Polish pact and Coulondre's crystal-clear declaration of France's intentions, hit the Führer like "a bombshell." To him it was the completely unexpected defection "of an ally." But he controlled himself, dismissing Il Duce's envoy with the curt comment that he would send an immediate reply. As Attolico went out the door Schmidt heard Hitler mutter, "The Italians are behaving just as they did in 1914."

The waiting room was a pit of rumor and counterrumor as scraps of information were passed around. War seemed inevitable. Weizsäcker, for instance, saw only a two per cent possibility of preventing a world war in which Italy would leave Germany in the lurch. Inside his office Hitler was telling General Keitel: "Stop everything at once. Get Brauchitsch immediately. I need time for negotiations."

Keitel rushed out into the anteroom. "The order to advance must be delayed again," he excitedly told his aide. The news spread that the threat of war had been averted at the last minute. The Führer was returning to negotiation! There was general relief except from Hitler's chief adjutant, Rudolf Schmundt, who was glum. "Don't celebrate too soon," he told Warlimont. "This is only a postponement." Major Engel shared Schmundt's deep concern. Never before had the army adjutant seen the Chancellor in such "total confusion." The Führer was even arguing bitterly with Hewel, whose opinion he usually respected. Hitler bet that if war started with Poland the English would surely not join in. "Mein

Führer," asserted Hewel, "do not underestimate the British. When they see there is no other alternative, they stubbornly go their own way." Hitler was too angry to argue and turned away.

Göring was also convinced that the English were not merely mouthing words of warning and was surreptitiously negotiating for peace. A man of action, he had already initiated discussions with England without consulting Ribbentrop, whom he distrusted. It was not as daring as it appeared, for he intended keeping his Führer informed of any developments. His desire for peace was hardly altruistic. Being a freebooter with the touch of the gangster, his prime aim in life was to enjoy the fruits of the plunder he was amassing thanks to his privileged position. War could bring an end to his sybaritic existence. On the other hand, Hitler was driven by principle, warped though it was, and could not be bribed. He might compromise but only if it brought him closer to his long-range goal. Realizing all this, Göring carried on his devious policy of peace with caution. As unofficial go-between in this intrigue he selected a wealthy Swedish businessman named Birger Dahlerus. He had a German wife as well as interests in the Reich and so shared Göring's desire to prevent war between Germany and England. Furthermore, he was in a position to do something about it, for he had influential English friends who were willing to work clandestinely on the project.

Earlier that month Dahlerus had arranged a secret meeting between Göring and seven Englishmen in a house conveniently close to the Danish border. Here it was that the Reichsmarschall first expounded his views and hopes for peace to the foreign businessmen. Little was done except talk until the historic military conference at the Berghof two weeks later. This spurred Göring to telephone Dahlerus in Stockholm and urge him to come as soon as possible. The situation, he guardedly revealed, had worsened and the chances of a peaceful solution were rapidly diminishing. Göring persuaded Dahlerus to fly at once to England with an unofficial message to the Chamberlain government, urging that negotiations between Germany and England take place as soon as possible.

And so on that eventful morning of August 25 Dahlerus had flown to London by ordinary passenger plane but it was not until early evening that he was ushered into the office of Lord Halifax. The Foreign Secretary was in an optimistic mood and—since Hitler, it will be recalled, had just called off the invasion—it did not appear that the services of a neutral would be of further use. Dahlerus was not so optimistic and telephoned Göring for his opinion. The Reichsmarschall's reply was alarming. He feared that "war might break out at any moment."

Dahlerus repeated these words to Halifax the next morning and offered to deliver to Göring—the only German in his opinion who could prevent war—a personal message from Halifax confirming England's genuine desire to reach a peaceful settlement. Lord Halifax excused himself so he could discuss the matter with Chamberlain. In half an hour he returned with the Prime Minister's approval. The letter was written and Dahlerus was rushed to Croydon airdrome.

In Berlin Ambassador Attolico was on his way to the chancellery with another message from Mussolini. It contained an imposing list of the material Italy would need if she participated in a war: six million tons of coal; seven million tons of petroleum, two million tons of steel and a million tons of lumber. Since Attolico was opposed to war, he deliberately made Mussolini's terms impossible to fulfill. To Ribbentrop's icy query as to when this vast amount of material was to be delivered, Attolico answered, "Why, at once, before hostilities begin."

It was an unreasonable demand. Surprising, considering the strain he must have been under, was Hitler's calm reply, which was relayed to Mussolini by telephone at 3:08 P.M. He could meet Italy's requirements in most areas, he said, but regretted it was impossible to deliver before the outbreak of war for technical reasons. "In these circumstances, Duce, I understand your position, and would only ask you to try to achieve the pinning down of Anglo-French forces by active propaganda and suitable military demonstrations such as you have already proposed to me." In the light of his pact with Stalin, he concluded, he did not "shrink from solving the Eastern question even at the risk of complications in the West."

It was no idle threat. The Wehrmacht was now prepared to attack on September 1 and was only waiting for the Führer's final confirmation. An oppressive heat lay over Berlin that Saturday afternoon. Despite the headlines in the papers—IN CORRIDOR MANY GERMAN FARMHOUSES IN FLAMES! POLISH SOLDIERS PUSH TO EDGE OF GERMAN BORDER!—many Berliners were enjoying themselves at the surrounding lakes. The less fortunate were more concerned by the temperature than by politics.

At 6:42 P.M. Attolico got another call from Rome. It was Ciano with another urgent message for the Führer. In it Mussolini apologetically explained that Attolico had misunderstood the delivery date. He didn't expect the raw materials for a year. He regretted not being more helpful at such a crucial time and then, unexpectedly, made a plea for peace. A satisfactory political solution, he said, was still possible. When Hitler read these words he concluded that his ally was abandoning him. Somehow he controlled his feelings and sent off another conciliatory reply. "I respect the reasons and motives which led you to take this decision," he said and tried to infuse his partner with his own optimism.

Disappointed and exhausted, the Führer retired earlier than usual, only to be awakened soon after midnight. Göring had to see him at once on urgent business: the Swedish go-between he had mentioned the other day was back with an interesting letter from Lord Halifax. It was about 12:30 A.M. August 27, when Dahlerus was ushered into the Führer's study. Hitler waited solemnly, staring fixedly at the neutral who was striving for peace. Göring stood beside him, looking pleased with himself. After a brief friendly greeting, Hitler launched into a lecture on Germany's desire to reach an understanding with the English, which degenerated into an excited diatribe. After describing his latest proposals to Henderson, he exclaimed, "This is my last magnanimous offer to England." His face stiffened and his gesticulations became "very peculiar" as he boasted of the Reich's superior armed might.

Dahlerus pointed out that England and France also had greatly improved their armed forces and were in good position to blockade Germany. Without answering, Hitler paced up and down, then suddenly stopped in his tracks, stared and began talking again (Dahlerus recalled), this time as if in a trance. "If there should be a war, then I will build U-boats, build U-boats, build U-boats, build U-boats, U-boats, U-boats." It was like a stuck record. His voice became more and more indistinct. Abruptly he was orating as if to a huge audience, but still repeating himself. "I will build airplanes, build airplanes, airplanes and I will destroy my enemies!" In consternation, Dahlerus turned to see how Göring was reacting. But the Reichsmarschall appeared not at all perturbed. Dahlerus was horrified: so this was the man whose actions could influence the entire world!

"War doesn't frighten me," continued Hitler, "encirclement of Germany is an impossibility, my people admire and follow me faithfully." He would spur them to superhuman efforts. His eyes went glassy. "If there should be no butter, I shall be the first to stop eating butter, eating butter." There was a pause. "If the enemy can hold out for several years," he finally said, "I, with my power over the German people, can hold out one year longer. Thereby I know that I am superior to all the others." All at once he asked why it was that the English continually refused to come to an agreement with him.

Dahlerus hesitated to answer honestly but finally said that the trouble was founded on England's lack of confidence in Hitler. At this the Führer struck his breast. "Idiots!" he exclaimed. "Have I ever told a lie in my life?" He continued to pace, again stopped. Dahlerus, he said, had heard his side. He must return to England at once and tell it to the Chamberlain government. "I do not think Henderson understood me, and I really want to bring about an understanding."

Dahlerus protested that he was a private citizen and could go only if the British government requested it. First he must have a clear definition of the vital points on which agreement could be reached. For example, what exactly was Hitler's proposed corridor to Danzig? Hitler smiled. "Well," he said, turning to Göring, "Henderson never asked about *that*." The Reichsmarschall tore a page out of an atlas and began outlining with a red pencil the territory Germany wanted.

This led to a clarifying discussion of the main points in Hitler's offer to Henderson: Germany wanted a treaty with Britain that would eliminate all disputes of a political or economic nature; England was to help Germany get Danzig and the Corridor; in return Germany would guarantee Poland's boundaries and let her have a corridor to Gdynia; the German minority in Poland would be protected; and, finally, Germany would give military aid whenever the British Empire came under attack.

Dahlerus ingenuously took Göring at face value and was inclined to think the best of Hitler. Moreover, he had no training in diplomacy. In his favor were a sincere desire for peace, courage and admirable persistence. As soon as he returned to his hotel he put in a long-distance call to an English friend. Before long he had assurance that the British government would welcome him as a messenger. At eight that peaceful Sunday morning he boarded a German plane at Tempelhof. As it headed at low level for London he wondered if he was merely a pawn in a game of intrigue. He was fairly sure that Göring was honestly working for a peaceful settlement. But was Hitler?

Hitler treated that Sabbath as a weekday. Having canceled the imminent celebration in Nuremberg which bore the inappropriate title "Party Day of Peace," he introduced a wartime measure of food and clothes rationing. Then the armed forces were placed on a semi-emergency basis with all naval, army and air attachés ordered to remain in Berlin until further notice.

Under the pall of this martial atmosphere Peter Kleist of Ribbentrop's office was secretly approached by two important Polish diplomats with a mediation proposal. They hinted that Foreign Minister Beck was being forced to act belligerently toward Germany only to satisfy a rabid group of Polish patriots. What Beck needed was time to calm things down. Kleist dutifully reported this to Ribbentrop and was soon explaining the details to Hitler himself. He listened with barely concealed impatience and then announced peremptorily that if Beck could not even assert himself in Poland there was no help for him. Furthermore, Kleist was to cease making any more semi-official contacts with the Poles. He gave this order with some acrimony, adding that Herr von Ribbentrop should have issued such an order long ago. As Kleist walked thoughtfully out of the chancellery he was certain that the decision had at last been reached—and it was war!

That sultry Sunday Hitler also took time to answer a plea for peace from Premier Daladier, doing so as one veteran to another. "As an old front-line soldier," he wrote, "I know, as you do, the horrors of war." There was no longer any need for dispute since the return of the Saar had ended all further German claims on France. The mischief-maker was England, which had unleased "a savage press campaign against Germany" instead of persuading the Poles to be reasonable. He begged Daladier, a patriotic Frenchman, to put himself in Hitler's place. What if some French city—say Marseilles—were prevented from professing allegiance to France as a result of defeat in battle? What if Frenchmen living in that area were persecuted, beaten, bestially murdered? "I cannot in any circumstances imagine, Monsieur Daladier, that Germany would fight against you on these grounds." Hitler agreed with everything Daladier had written in his letter and again called on their common experiences as front-line soldiers to understand that it was impossible for a nation of honor to renounce nearly two million of its people and see them ill-treated on its own frontiers. Danzig and the Corridor must, in all honor, return to Germany.

A little after noon a German plane landed at Croydon. Birger Dahlerus stepped out. The place seemed dead since civilian air traffic between England and the Continent had come to a standstill. He was driven to the Foreign Office past air raid wardens patrolling streets where shopwindows were pasted over with strips of paper, then taken through back alleys to 10 Downing Street. Chamberlain, Halifax and Cadogan were waiting. They were grave but "perfectly calm." As Dahlerus told about the long meeting with Hitler he sensed an air of skepticism. His report differed from that of Henderson on several points and Chamberlain asked if he was absolutely certain he'd understood what Hitler said. Dahlerus, whose command of German was superior to Henderson's, replied that any misinterpretation was out of the question.

Throughout this conversation Chamberlain's remarks were colored by distrust of Hitler; he asked what impression the Führer had made on Dahlerus. The answer ("I shouldn't like to have him as a partner in my business") brought the only smile of the day from the Prime Minister. Since the British doubted his interpretation of Hitler's demands, Dahlerus suggested that they allow him to return to Berlin with their reactions.

Chamberlain hesitated. Ambassador Henderson, presently in London, was scheduled to fly back to Berlin that day with their answer to Hitler's proposals. Dahlerus suggested that the ambassador wait a day. Then he could let the British know exactly how Hitler felt *before* they made an official reply based only on Henderson's assessment.

He suggested phoning Göring so he could ask point-blank if the German government would agree to Henderson waiting a full day. "Do you intend to phone from the Foreign Office?" asked Chamberlain. Dahlerus did and Chamberlain agreed. In a few minutes the go-between was in Cadogan's room hearing Göring say that he could not possibly give an immediate answer without conferring with the Führer. Half an hour later Dahlerus again phoned. This time Göring announced that Hitler accepted the plan "on the condition that it was genuine." Cadogan insisted that Dahlerus fly back to Berlin secretly, so the plane which had brought him to England was transferred from Croydon to a smaller field, Heston.

It was 11 P.M. by the time Dahlerus arrived at Göring's Berlin residence. After assuring the Reichsmarschall of his personal conviction that both the English government and her people truly wanted peace and were acting in good faith, Dahlerus outlined the British response to the Hitler proposals. Göring rubbed his nose. The British reply, he said, was hardly satisfactory and the whole situation was highly precarious. He would have to confer with Hitler alone. Dahlerus nervously paced the floor of his hotel room as he waited for the answer. Finally at 1:30 A.M. Göring telephoned. Hitler, he said in a robust voice, *did* respect England's views and welcomed her desire to reach a peaceful agreement. He also respected England's decision to honor her guarantee of Poland's boundaries as well as her insistence on an international guarantee in this matter of five great powers. Dahlerus was particularly relieved by his last concession since it surely meant that Hitler had shelved any other plans he might have had for Poland.

2

Often amateur diplomats merely confuse matters, but this time Dahlerus had succeeded in breaking a log jam. By 9 P.M. when Henderson's plane landed at the Berlin airport matters had progressed substantially. The ambassador had returned to his post armed with an official version of the offer Dahlerus had delivered unofficially. It also contained a clause stating that Beck had just agreed to enter at once into direct discussions with Germany.

The streets of the capital were pitch-dark from the blackout and the few people abroad reminded Henderson of apparitions. The exertions of the past months had left the ambassador exhausted. He had recently undergone an operation for cancer only to discover his was a terminal case. But he kept his condition private and never complained about the pressure of work. No sooner had Henderson begun a hurried meal at the embassy than word came from the chancellery: Hitler wanted to see him without delay. Fortified by half a bottle of champagne, Henderson drove out of the embassy driveway. A considerable crowd was waiting at the gate in absolute silence but, as far as he could see, with no hostility.

As Hitler read the German translation of the British note he registered no emotion even though it ended with the mixed expression of promise and threat that had become the Führer's own trademark: a just settlement of the questions between Germany and Poland could open the way to world peace; failure to reach it would bring Germany and Great Britain "into conflict and might well plunge the whole world into war. Such an outcome would be a calamity without parallel in history."

Hitler passed the note to Ribbentrop without comment, amazing Schmidt with such a calm reaction. Henderson's next move was even more surprising. He took the offensive for the first time in memory and did more talking than Hitler. Ordinarily this would have caused an eruption but Hitler sat calmly, occasionally staring out at the dark garden where his famed predecessor, Bismarck, had so often strolled.

In the meantime Henderson was proclaiming that England's word was her bond and she "had never and would never break it." In the old days Germany's word also had the same value and he quoted Field Marshal von Blücher's exhortation to his troops when hurrying to support Wellington at Waterloo: "Forward, my children, forward; I have given my word to my brother Wellington, and you cannot wish me to break it." Things were quite a bit different a hundred and twenty-five years ago, commented Hitler but with no asperity, and then insisted that while *he* was quite ready to settle his differences with Poland on a reasonable basis the Poles were continuing their violence against Germans. Such acts seemed to be a matter of indifference to the British.

Henderson—perhaps it was the champagne—somehow took this as a personal insult, heatedly replying that he had done everything in his power to prevent war and bloodshed. Herr Hitler, he said, must choose between friendship with England and excessive demands on Poland. The choice between war and peace was his. Still retaining his calm, Hitler replied that this was not a correct picture of the situation. His alternatives were either to defend the rights of the German people or to abandon them at the cost of an agreement with England. And there could be no choice: his duty was to defend the rights of all Germans.

At the end of this extraordinary colloquy Hitler again expressed a desire for agreement with England. It left Henderson with some optimism. He was also cheered by Schmidt's parting remark: "You were quite marvelous."

But there was pessimism at the chancellery. The Führer, Engel wrote in his diary, "is exceptionally irritated, bitter and sharp," and he made it clear to his adjutants that he would not take advice from the military on the question of peace or war. "He simply could not understand a German soldier who feared war. Frederick the Great would turn in his grave if he saw today's generals." All he wanted was liquidation of the unjust conditions of the Poles, not war with the Western Allies. "If they were stupid enough to take part that was their fault and they would have to be destroyed."

The air of depression and anxiety in the winter garden heightened as Hitler composed an answer to the British, and this turned to alarm when the noon papers reported in glaring headlines that at least six German nationals had been murdered in Poland. Whether this report was true or not, Hitler himself believed it and was incensed. And so by the time Henderson reappeared early that evening there was a feeling in the waiting rooms and corridors of the chancellery that little less than a miracle could prevent war. The ambassador was still hoping for the best and, as on the day before, wore a red carnation, his private signal to insiders that he still had hope. Once Henderson entered Hitler's study and was handed a copy of the German reply, however, he sensed an attitude more uncompromising than last night. With the Führer and Ribbentrop eying him closely, he began reading the German note. It started reasonably. Germany readily consented to the proposed mediation by the British; Hitler was pleased to receive a Polish emissary in Berlin with full powers to negotiate. But the next words were completely unacceptable: the German government calculated that "this delegate will arrive on Wednesday, 30 August, 1939."

"It sounds like an ultimatum," protested Henderson. "The Poles are given barely twenty-four hours to make their plans." Supported by Ribbentrop, the Führer heatedly denied the charge. "The time is short," he explained, "because there is the danger that fresh provocation may result in the outbreak of fighting."

Henderson was not impressed. He still could not accept such a time limit. It was the Diktat of Bad Godesberg all over again. Hitler argued that he was being pressed by his General Staff. "My soldiers," he said, "are asking me 'yes' or 'no.'" The Wehrmacht was ready to strike and its commanders were complaining that a week had been lost already. Another week might bring them into the rainy season.

But the ambassador would not budge and Hitler at last lost his temper. He angrily made a countercharge: neither Henderson nor his government cared a row of pins how many Germans were being slaughtered in Poland. Henderson shouted back that he would not listen to such language from Hitler or anybody else. It seemed the ambassador had also lost his temper, but he explained in his report that this was a trick; the time had come to play Herr Hitler at his own game. Glaring into his opponent's eyes, at the top of his voice he bellowed that if Hitler wanted war he could have it! England was every bit as resolute as Germany and would in fact "hold out a little bit longer than Germany could!"

The Führer took this new departure in British diplomacy with relative grace and, once the clamor subsided, asserted his constant desire to win Britain's friendship, his respect for the Empire, and his liking for Englishmen in general. But genuine as Hitler's expression of admiration for the English appeared to be, it was still apparent to Henderson that their two countries had reached an impasse. As he was leaving the chancellery he was "filled with the gloomiest of forebodings." In the farewell to his German escort, Henderson glumly expressed the fear that he would never again wear a red carnation in Germany.

Later that evening Göring summoned Dahlerus to his residence and revealed a secret: Hitler was working on a *grosszügiges Angebot* (magnanimous offer) to Poland. It was going to be presented the next morning and would include a lasting and just solution of the Corridor by a plebiscite. Once more Göring tore a page out of an atlas and hastily sketched with a green pencil the territory that would be settled by plebiscite; then he outlined in red the area Hitler regarded as pure Polish.

Göring urged Dahlerus to fly immediately to London so he could once more stress Germany's determination to negotiate and "hint confidentially" that Hitler was going to present the Poles with an offer so generous they would be bound to accept.

The next morning was one of reaffirmation for Chamberlain. The most pressing matter on his agenda was Hitler's invitation to the Poles. The Prime Minister's Foreign Secretary was convinced that it was "of course unreasonable to expect that we can produce a Polish representative in Berlin today" nor should the Germans expect it; and his ambassador in Warsaw telephoned that he saw little chance of inducing the Poles to send Beck or any other representative to Berlin immediately. "They would certainly sooner fight and perish rather than submit to such humiliation especially after the examples of Czechoslovakia, Lithuania and Austria."

Chamberlain himself was now so determined to resist Hitler that he never even asked the Poles if they would submit and by the time Dahlerus was back at 10 Downing Street negotiation seemed impossible. Chamberlain, Wilson and Cadogan listened to the Swede, but their reaction to Hitler's "magnanimous offer" was that it was all talk and only a trick to gain time. Why not phone Göring and find out if the offer had actually been typed up? suggested Dahlerus. In a few minutes he was talking to the Reichsmarschall, who assured him that the note to Poland was not only finished but its terms were more generous than he had predicted.

Encouraged, Dahlerus did his utmost to allay British distrust, going over the terms of the offer with the help of the map Göring had marked up. While the terms seemed reasonable, the British were still disturbed by Hitler's insistence that a Polish delegate present himself in Berlin on the thirtieth, that very day. Beyond the time limit, Chamberlain and his colleagues opposed the place, Berlin. Look what had happened to Tiso and Hacha!

Dahlerus phoned Göring again, this time with the suggestion that the negotiations with Poland take place out of Berlin, preferably in a neutral territory. "Nonsense," was the annoyed reply, "the negotiations must take place in Berlin where Hitler had his headquarters, and anyhow I can see no reason why the Poles should find it difficult to send emissaries to Berlin." Despite the rebuff, as well as their own continuing distrust, the British decided to at least keep the door to peace open. Dahlerus was urged to fly back to Berlin and reassure Hitler that England remained willing to negotiate. Further, as evidence of good faith, Halifax telegraphed Warsaw cautioning the Poles not to fire on troublemakers from their German minority and to stop inflammatory radio propaganda.

The Polish response was to order a general mobilization. Hitler was indignant, for his Foreign Office had spent the day drafting an offer to Poland so generous that his objective interpreter, Schmidt, could scarcely believe his eyes. Besides suggesting a plebiscite in the Corridor under an international commission, it gave the Poles an international road and railway through territory which would become German. "It was a real League of Nations proposal," recalled Schmidt. "I felt I was back in Geneva." Despite his wrath at the Polish mobilization, Hitler instructed Brauchitsch and Keitel to postpone the invasion of Poland another twenty-four hours. This, he said, was the final postponement. Unless his demands were accepted by Warsaw the attack was to begin at 4:30 A.M. September 1. By nightfall there was still no word from Warsaw and the news from London was inconclusive: the British were considering Hitler's latest note "with all urgency" and would send a reply later in the day. In the meantime they advised Colonel Beck to negotiate with the Germans "without delay." It was an ironic request after their own long delay. Perhaps the British irresolution was aroused, if not occasioned, by secret revelations earlier in the day from a German civilian in close contact with the Wehrmacht. Ewald von Kleist-Schmenzin revealed to the British military attaché a number of German military secrets along with an assurance that Hitler had recently suffered a nervous breakdown and the General Staff planned to take advantage of this to stage a military coup.

It was 10 P.M. Berlin time before Henderson finally got permission to present the reply to the Germans. He phoned Ribbentrop proposing they meet at midnight. This happened to be the deadline for the Polish representative to arrive in Berlin and Ribbentrop thought it was deliberate. It was done in all innocence—more time was needed to decipher the London message—but it set an unwholesome atmosphere of suspicion for the interview. After Henderson suggested the Germans follow normal procedure by transmitting their proposals through the Polish Embassy in Berlin, Ribbentrop leaped to his feet. "That's out of the question after what has happened!" he shouted, the last vestige of self-control gone. "We demand that a negotiator empowered by his government with full authority should come here to Berlin."

Henderson's face grew red. London had warned him to keep calm this time and his hands trembled as he read the official answer to Hitler's last memorandum. Ribbentrop fumed as if listening under duress. Undoubtedly he knew its contents since most telephone calls at the British Embassy, particularly the overseas line to London, were being monitored by a German intelligence agency known as the Research Office. The note itself, while conciliatory in tone, offered little more than the previous phone messages of the day.

"That's an unheard-of suggestion!" Ribbentrop angrily interrupted at the suggestion that no aggressive military action take place during the negotiations. Crossing his arms belligerently, he glared at Henderson. "Have you anything more to say?" Perhaps he was paying the ambassador back for yesterday's shouting match with the Führer. The Englishman responded to this rudeness by remarking that His Majesty's Government had information the Germans were committing acts of sabotage in Poland.

This time Ribbentrop was truly enraged. "That's a damned lie of the Polish government!" he shouted. "I can only tell you, Herr Henderson, that the position is damned serious."

Henderson half rose in his seat and shouted in return, "You have just said 'damned!'" He wagged an admonitory finger like an outraged schoolmaster. "That's no word for a statesman to use in so grave a situation."

Ribbentrop looked as if a glass of cold water had been thrown in his face. For a split second he was the picture of shock and indignation. To be reprimanded by an arrogant Englishman! He jumped to his feet. "What did you say?" Henderson was also on his feet and the two men glared at each other like fighting cocks. "According to diplomatic convention," recalled Schmidt, "I too should have risen; but to be frank I did not quite know how an interpreter should behave when speakers passed from words to deeds—and I really feared they might do so now." He kept his seat, pretending to be writing in his notebook. When he heard heavy breathing above, he feared the German Foreign Minister was about to throw His Majesty's ambassador bodily through the doorway. Over the years as interpreter he had rather enjoyed grotesque situations but this one was extremely painful. He heard more heavy breathing to right and left but finally Ribbentrop and then Henderson sat down. Cautiously the interpreter raised his head. All clear. The storm was over.

The conversation continued in relative calm for a few minutes. Then Ribbentrop took a paper out of his pocket. It was Hitler's offer to Poland which had so surprised Schmidt. Ribbentrop began reading the sixteen points in German. Henderson had difficulty in understanding them, he later complained, because Ribbentrop "garbled through" the document at top speed and he asked for the text so he could transmit it to his government. It was such normal diplomatic procedure that Schmidt wondered why the ambassador bothered asking at all and he could scarcely believe what he heard next. "No," said Ribbentrop quietly, with an uneasy smile, "I cannot hand you those proposals." He couldn't explain that the Führer had expressly forbidden him to let the document out of his hand.

Henderson, also unable to believe his ears, repeated his request. Once more Ribbentrop refused, this time emotionally slapping the document on the table. "It is out of date, anyhow," he said, "As the Polish envoy has not appeared."

Watching in agitation, Schmidt suddenly realized that Hitler was playing a game: he feared that if the British passed on the proposals to the Poles they might accept them. It was a mortal sin for an interpreter to make a comment but he did stare fixedly and "invitingly" at Henderson, silently willing him to ask for an English translation. Ribbentrop could hardly refuse such a request and Schmidt was determined to translate with such deliberation that the ambassador could copy every word in longhand. But Henderson did not understand the signal and all the interpreter could do was make a thick red mark in his notebook, a personal notation meaning that the die was cast for war.

Thus ended the stormy interview which, according to Ribbentrop, was conducted "with discourtesy" by Henderson and "with coolness" by himself. Despite the late hour, the Foreign Minister reported immediately to Hitler at the chancellery and suggested that Henderson be given the German proposals in writing. The Führer refused.

3

Early the next morning Henderson telephoned the secretary of the Polish Embassy, warning him that he had information "from an unquestionably accurate source that there would be war if Poland did not undertake to do something within two or three hours."

Every word was taken down by Hitler's wire tappers. So was Henderson's message to London fifteen minutes later, repeating the same information with the comment that while it might be a bluff there was an equal possibility it was not. Although the Germans were still not privy to all the British ciphers, Henderson's indiscreet use of the telephone was making their task easier. (The security in the British Embassy in Rome, incidentally, was even slacker. Lord Perth's safe was regularly burgled each week by a professional thief in the employ of Italian intelligence authorities. Besides copying confidential material that revealed all British diplomatic codes and ciphers, the thief one night appropriated Lady Perth's tiara for himself. But even this loss brought no improvement in the embassy security measures. Fortunately for England, Mussolini was not yet turning over foreign codes and ciphers to his ally.)

The last day of August was a frantic one for men of good will. Dahlerus got permission from Henderson to telephone London and a little after noon was telling Sir Horace Wilson that Hitler's proposals were "extremely liberal." According to Göring, he said, the Führer had put forward such terms with the sole intention of showing the British how anxious he was to secure a friendly settlement with the English. As Dahlerus was speaking, Wilson heard a German voice repeating the words. Realizing the phone was tapped, he instructed Dahlerus to give his information to Henderson, but the amateur diplomat did not get the hint. Nor did he stop when Wilson warned that he should not "get ahead of the clock." Finally Wilson told Dahlerus in plain language to shut up and, when he did not, slammed down the receiver.

While the professional and amateur diplomats were grasping for a peaceful solution, the program for war proceeded relentlessly. That noon

Hitler issued the second order for invasion, driven to this extremity (according to A. I. Berndt, his liaison man with DNB) by a gross lie. Berndt thought the reported number of German nationals killed by Poles too small and simply added a nought. At first Hitler refused to believe such a large figure but, when Berndt replied that it may have been somewhat exaggerated but something monstrous must have happened to give rise to such stories, Hitler shouted, "They'll pay for this! Now no one will stop me from teaching these fellows a lesson they'll never forget! I will not have my Germans butchered like cattle!" At this point the Führer went to the phone and, in Berndt's presence, ordered Keitel to issue "Directive No. 1 for the Conduct of the War."

Already prepared, its opening words were tailored to fit the moment: "Since the situation on Germany's eastern frontier has become intolerable and all political possibilities of peaceful settlement have been exhausted, I have decided upon a *solution by force.*" The attack on Poland was definitely set for the following day, Friday, the first of September, and no action would be taken in the West. The directive was hand-carried to all senior commanders, who transmitted, with the greatest possible secrecy, special orders to field commanders. At 4 P.M. the executive order to begin the invasion was confirmed; troops and equipment began moving up to forward positions near the frontier. Simultaneously special orders were transmitted to a secret German unit on the Polish border by the chief of the SS Security Service. Reinhard Heydrich had concocted a diabolical scheme—Operation Himmler—to give Hitler a perfect excuse for launching his attack. SD detachments disguised as Polish soldiers and guerrillas would create incidents along the border the night before the invasion. In exactly four hours they were to attack a forestry station, destroy a German customs building and, most important, briefly occupy the German radio station at Gleiwitz. After shouting anti-German slogans into the microphone the "Poles" would retreat, leaving behind a number of dead bodies as proof that a fight had taken place. The bodies presented no problem. Heydrich had already selected the victims—they were called "canned goods"—from concentration camps.

In Berlin Ambassador Lipski, after a five-and-a-half-hour delay, was finally escorted into Ribbentrop's office at 6:30 P.M. Fatigued and nervous, Lipski read a brief communication stating that his government was "favorably considering" British proposals for direct negotiations between Germany and Poland and would make "a formal reply on the subject within the next few hours." He added pointedly that he had been trying to make this declaration since 1 P.M.

Have you come as an emissary empowered to negotiate? asked Ribbentrop coolly, to which Lipski replied that he merely had instructions "for the time being" to transmit the message he had just read. Ribbentrop protested that he had expected Lipski to come as a fully empowered delegate. "Have you authority to negotiate with us now on the German proposals?" he persisted. Lipski did not. "Well, then there is no point to our continuing the conversation."

So ended one of the briefest interviews in Schmidt's experience. Lipski never asked to see Hitler's sixteen-point proposal and even if Ribbentrop had volunteered it he was not authorized to receive it. He was following his orders "not to enter into any concrete negotiations." The Poles were apparently so confident they could whip the Germans (with help from their allies) that they were not interested in discussing Hitler's offer. Nor were England and France extending themselves to persuade the Poles to negotiate. When Lipski arrived back at his embassy he attempted to phone Warsaw. The line was dead. The Germans had cut communications. There was no more they needed to know.

At the chancellery Adolf Hitler was conversing with Italian Ambassador Attolico, who had arrived at 7 P.M. Once again Attolico urged peace. Would Hitler agree to Il Duce acting as last-minute mediator? "We must first await the course of events," said the Führer. These now marched on schedule. At exactly 8 P.M. Heydrich's fake "Polish" attack on the radio station at Gleiwitz took place. An hour later all German stations canceled regular programs so that an official statement could be read. The sixteen-point offer was repeated word for word and even unfriendly foreign correspondents were impressed by its reasonableness.

The Poles never for a moment considered accepting the German proposal. Instead of sending a hurried request to resume negotiations that might possibly have thrown Hitler's plot off balance, they retaliated aggressively with their own broadcast at 11 P.M. It charged that the German broadcast clearly exposed Hitler's aims. "Words can no longer veil the aggressive plans of the new Huns. Germany is aiming at the domination of Europe and is canceling the rights of nations with as yet unprecedented cynicism. This impudent proposal shows clearly how necessary were the military orders [mobilization] given by the Polish government."

Ribbentrop went to the chancellery to see how the Führer reacted to the Polish broadcast. Nothing else can be done, said Hitler. Things are now in motion. He was noticeably composed. After weeks of worry and doubt, the course for the future was at last set. He went to bed assured that England and France would not take action. Perhaps the greatest assurance that night to Hitler (he had recently told his military that the treaty with Stalin had been "a pact with Satan to drive out the devil")

was a brief message from Moscow that the Supreme Soviet had finally
ratified the treaty with Germany after a "brilliant" speech by Molotov.

To Hitler the invasion of Poland was not war, only a coup to seize
what was rightfully Germany's. It was a localized action which both England and France, after making face-saving gestures, would surely accept as
a fait accompli. Time and again his adjutants had heard him say at the
dinner table, "The English will leave the Poles in the lurch as they did the
Czechs."

Although intercepts from his own Research Office clearly indicated it
was probable that both England and France would intervene in the event
of a German-Polish war, Hitler could not bring himself to believe this
since (according to his personal adjutant, Schaub) it "disturbed the formation of his intuition." He preferred to put more credence in a personal
conviction that neither Britain nor France would act. "England is
bluffing," he recently had told his court photographer, then added with a
rare impish grin, "And so am I!"

Göring was in his private train when word came that Hitler had made
the final decision for war. Beside himself with anger, he got Ribbentrop
on the phone. "Now you've got your damned war! It's all your doing!" he
shouted and slammed down the receiver. It was ironic. Perhaps no one
had warned the Führer more often than Ribbentrop that England would
surely fight if pushed to the limit.

4

At four forty-five Friday morning, September 1, the German cruiser
Schleswig-Holstein, in Danzig harbor on a courtesy visit, began shelling
the little peninsula where Poland maintained a military depot and eighty-
eight soldiers. Simultaneously artillery fire crashed along the Polish-German border, followed by a massive surge eastward of German infantry and
tanks. There was no formal declaration of war but within the hour Hitler
broadcast a proclamation to his troops. He had no other choice, he said,
"than to meet force with force."

In Rome Il Duce was outwardly calm. A few hours earlier, spurred by
his own fear and a deluge of cautionary advice, he had come to a wise but
embarrassing decision: Italy would remain neutral. He personally telephoned Attolico and urged him to beg the Führer to send him a telegram releasing him from the obligation of their alliance. Hitler quickly
composed an answer that hid his anger. "I am convinced that we can carry
out the task imposed upon us with the military forces of Germany," he
said and thanked Mussolini for everything he could do in the future "for

the common cause of Fascism and National Socialism." He signed the note at 9:40 A.M., then headed for the Kroll Opera House to address the Reichstag. The onlookers were surprised to see Hitler step briskly onto the stage in a tailored field-gray uniform. It looked like military dress but was merely the party uniform in a new color. The audience listened intently as —in a low, raucous voice—he hammered out his case against Poland, point by point, all the time working himself into a state of indignation. He also regretted that the Western powers thought their interests were involved. "I have repeatedly offered England our friendship, and if necessary closest co-operation. Love, however, is not a one-sided affair, but must be responded to by the other side." Eva Braun, in the audience, turned to her sister and whispered, "This means war, Ilse, and he'll leave—what will become of me?"

Perhaps because of its extemporaneous nature, the speech was not one of the Führer's best efforts and Helmut Sündermann, along with others in the Dietrich office, was frantically correcting the grammar and removing the redundancies so a presentable version could be submitted to the press. Hitler went on to promise that he would never wage war against women and children and then announced that Polish soldiers had fired the first shots in German territory and Wehrmacht troops were only returning the fire. "Who fights with poison," he threatened, "will be fought with poison. Who disregards the rules of human warfare can only expect us to take the same steps. I will carry on this fight, no matter against whom, until the safety of the Reich and its rights are secured! . . . From this moment, my whole life shall belong more than ever to my people. I now want to be nothing but the first soldier of the German Reich. Therefore, I have once again put on that uniform which was always so sacred to and dear to me. I shall not take it off until after the victory—or I shall not live to see the end!"

The audience cheered and in the fanatical excitement it went unnoticed that Eva Braun had covered her face and was weeping. "If something happens to him," she finally told her sister, "I will die too." Hitler was announcing that if anything *should* happen to him Göring would be his successor. If the Reichsmarschall fell Hess would take over. It was a unilateral decision, perhaps made on the spur of the moment, and indicated that there was really no longer a German government. The Führer was Germany.

In startling contrast to the wild cheers of "Sieg Heil" in the opera house, the streets outside were almost deathly quiet. The few people abroad were serious as if oppressed with concern for the future. There were no signs of the jubilation as on that August day, twenty-five years before, when the Kaiser announced his war. Today there was no eager young Adolf Hitler in the streets, eyes alight with exultation. In 1914 the majority of Europeans had found relief in war. "We must never forget," wrote D. H. Lawrence of the war which he had vigorously opposed, "that mankind lives by a two-fold motive: the motive of peace and increase, and the motive of contest and martial triumph. As soon as the appetite for martial adventure and triumph in conflict is satisfied, the appetite for peace and increase manifests itself and *vice versa*. It seems a law of life." Between the armistice and today there had been little peace or increase. This generation had no immediate past of dull daily life, no desire for adventure or escape. Aware that the last war had settled nothing, these Germans knew from experience that war was long, tragic and inglorious, that it might radically alter their lives for the worse.

As Eva Braun dejectedly left the opera house with Dr. Brandt, he tried to cheer her up. "Don't worry, Fräulein Braun," he said. "The Führer told me that there will be peace again in three weeks' time." She managed to force a smile.

Henderson telegraphed London that immediately after the speech Hitler had returned to the chancellery and told his generals that "his policy had broken down and that guns alone could now speak. Herr Hitler broke down and left the room without completing the speech." It could have been true. Early that afternoon Göring summoned Dahlerus to the chancellery. Hitler wished to see him. The Führer thanked Dahlerus for all his efforts, then blamed England that they had been in vain. There was now no longer any hope of an agreement. A moment later he interrupted a Göring irrelevancy to say he was determined to crush Polish resistance and annihilate Poland as a nation. If England still wanted to talk, however, he was willing to meet her halfway. Abruptly he began to shout and gesticulate. Göring averted his head in embarrassment. "If England wants to fight for a year, I shall fight two years. . . ." Hitler cut himself short but after a moment's pause bellowed even louder, as his arms milled about wildly. "If England wants to fight for three years, I shall fight for three years!" He clenched his fist and shouted: "And if it is necessary, I will fight ten years!" From a crouch he smashed his fist down so low it almost touched the floor.

When Hitler emerged into the anteroom a little later, however, he appeared to be in a state of "joyful excitement." He exclaimed to Ribbentrop and two of his adjutants that the progress of his troops was beyond his wildest hopes; the entire campaign would be over before the West had time to draw up notes of protest. At this point Otto Abetz, a French expert, offered his unsought opinion that France would declare war. Turning to Ribbentrop, Hitler raised his hands in mock terror. "Please spare me the verdicts of your experts," he said and heaped sarcasm on German diplomats who received the highest salaries, possessed the most modern means of communication, yet always came up with the wrong answer. They had predicted war over conscription, the Rhineland, the annexation of Austria, the Sudeten crisis and the occupation of Prague. His military attachés were just as bad. "Either their wits have been so dulled by their fatiguing breakfast duty that they are unable to get a better over-all picture of the situation in their countries than I can get from Berlin, or my policy does not suit them and they falsify the true position in their reports in order to put obstacles in my path. You must understand, Ribbentrop, that I have at last decided to do without the opinions of people who have misinformed me on a dozen occasions, or even lied to me, and I shall rely on my own judgment, which has in all these cases given me better counsel than the competent experts."

In London, Polish Ambassador Edward Raczynski had already taken it upon himself to call on Lord Halifax at 10 Downing Street and say, on his own responsibility, that his government considered the invasion a case of aggression under Article 1 of the Anglo-Polish Treaty of Mutual Assistance.

"I have very little doubt about it," said Halifax. As the two men emerged into the hall, ministers were already arriving for an emergency cabinet meeting. Sir John Simon, the Chancellor of the Exchequer, grasped Raczynski's hand. "We can shake hands now," he said. "We are all in the same boat. . . . Britain is not in the habit of deserting her friends." Minutes later Chamberlain was suggesting to his cabinet that Hitler be given a final warning: unless hostilities ceased, England would fulfill her obligations to Poland. The message, he warned, should be worded cautiously, not as an ultimatum. Otherwise the Germans might immediately attack British ships.

The world was shocked by the sudden attack even though it was expected. There was no condemnation from the Vatican, which had been secretly exerting pressure on the Polish government, through Cardinal Hlond, to negotiate with Hitler. President Roosevelt's first action was a plea that both belligerents promise not to bomb civilians or "unfortified cities." It was a vow that Hitler had already publicly made and Roosevelt's statement only annoyed him. His irritation escalated to indignation when his chargé in Washington reported that the deputy of the press chief in the U. S. State Department had told the DNB representative: "We only pity you people, your government already stands convicted; they are condemned from one end of the earth to the other; for this bloodbath, if it now comes to war between Britain, France and Germany, will have been absolutely unnecessary. The whole manner of conducting negotiations was as stupid as it could possibly be." Hitler blamed American hostility on the Jewish-controlled press and the Jews around President "Rosenfeld." He retaliated by prohibiting all German Jews, as enemies of the state, from henceforth going outdoors after 8 P.M. in the winter and 9 P.M. in the summer. Before long all Jewish radios would be confiscated.

Late that afternoon the British message to Germany was finally dispatched to Henderson, who was instructed to take it at once, in the company of his French colleague, to Ribbentrop. He should explain that it was a warning, not an ultimatum—but for his own information (and incidentally that of Hitler's wire tappers) that if the German reply was unsatisfactory the next stage would be either an ultimatum with a time limit or an immediate declaration of war.

Henderson and Coulondre arrived at the Wilhelmstrasse just before 9:30 P.M. But Ribbentrop refused to meet them together. First he saw the British ambassador, receiving him with pointed courtesy. Ribbentrop remarked that it was Poland which had provoked Germany and began arguing, though not raucously. This time they did not stand nose to nose but conducted themselves correctly. No sooner had Henderson left than Coulondre entered with an almost identical note from France. Ribbentrop repeated that it was Poland's fault, not Germany's, but promised to pass on the message to Hitler.

In London Chamberlain was telling the Commons about the note sent to Hitler. England's only quarrel with the German people, he said, was that they allowed themselves to be governed by a Nazi government. "As long as that government exists and pursues the methods it has so persistently followed during the last two years, there will be no peace in Europe. We shall merely pass from one crisis to another, and see one country after another attacked by methods which have now become familiar to us in their sickening technique. We are resolved that these methods must come to an end." There were cheers from all benches.

5

Despite indications that Hitler would resent further attempts at mediation from Rome, Mussolini decided to make a final effort and the next morning suggested a big-power conference to settle the dispute. But the Führer was not enthusiastic while both France and England were reluctant. "There is only one chance," Fritz Hesse in London phoned Hewel of the Wilhelmstrasse, "namely that we immediately move out of Poland

and offer reparation payment for damages. If Hitler does that there is probably one chance in a million of avoiding the catastrophe." Within two hours Hewel called back. A deep voice broke in, Ribbentrop's. "You know who is speaking," he said but asked not to be mentioned by name. "Please go immediately to your confidant—you know who I mean [he was referring to Sir Horace Wilson]—and tell him this: the Führer is prepared to move out of Poland and to offer reparation damages provided that we receive Danzig and a road through the Corridor, if England will act as mediator in the German-Polish conflict. You are empowered by the Führer to submit this proposal to the British cabinet and initiate negotiations immediately."

Hesse was flabbergasted. Had a specter of things to come finally dawned on the Führer at the last moment? Or was it just a charade to see how far the British would compromise with the sword of war dangling overhead? Hesse asked Ribbentrop to repeat the offer. He did, adding, "So there will be no misunderstanding, point out again that you are acting on the express instructions of Hitler and that this is no private action of mine."

Hesse phoned 10 Downing Street. He was informed that Wilson would not be available for some time. A few minutes later, at exactly 7:44 p.m., Chamberlain walked into the House of Commons to make his statement. "We waited there exactly like a court awaiting the verdict of the jury," recalled Harold Nicolson. But from the beginning the Prime Minister's speech was a letdown. "His voice betrayed some emotion as if he were sickening for a cold. He is a strange man. We expected one of his dramatic speeches. But none came." After assuring his listeners that His Majesty's Government was bound to take action unless Hitler withdrew his forces from Poland, Chamberlain astounded them by asserting an agreement to do so would return matters to pre-invasion status—"that is to say, the way would be open to discussions between the German and Polish governments of the matters at issue between them, on the understanding that the settlement arrived at was one that safeguarded the vital interests of Poland and was secured by an international guarantee."

In other words, Chamberlain still hesitated. (Later, according to Ambassador Kennedy, he said that the "Americans and the world Jews had forced him into the war.") There were indignant cries of "Speak for England, Arthur!" as acting Labour leader Arthur Greenwood sprang to his feet. "I wonder," he said, "how long we are prepared to vacillate at a time when Britain and all that Britain stands for, and human civilization, are in peril."

A mutiny of the MPs was in the air, many demanding that an ultimatum to Hitler be issued at once without the French. But Chamberlain insisted on acting in concert. At 9:50 P.M. he phoned Daladier and proposed a compromise. Daladier hedged: his cabinet insisted on giving Hitler until noon tomorrow to withdraw from Poland. Almost at the moment they hung up, Hesse arrived at 10 Downing Street to see Wilson. Sir Horace was "visibly impressed" by Hitler's new proposal to quit Poland but was reluctant to present it to the cabinet. The situation, he said, had changed drastically since their last meeting: Roosevelt had secretly promised to help Chamberlain if he declared war and Russia certainly would not fight on Germany's side.

Hesse persisted. "I see in this offer," he said, "the last and only chance to avoid war and also a sign that Hitler recognizes he has made a mistake. Otherwise I would not have this proposal in my hands."

Sir Horace could not believe that Hitler had changed his mind. Would he make a public apology for his acts of violence? If so, there might still be a chance. Such a suggestion, said Hesse, was a psychological error. In Hitler's eyes at least, the responsibility for the present crisis was not solely his. This brought an unusually loud rejoinder from Wilson. Hitler and Hitler alone was responsible for the situation!

"If this proposal fails merely because Hitler won't apologize," said Hesse in desperation, "then the world will believe that Chamberlain wanted the war, inasmuch as he had the chance of avoiding it."

Wilson thought this over. "All right," he said, "repeat your suggestion again; perhaps I can transmit it to the cabinet." After Hesse did so, Sir Horace paced up and down, hands behind his back. There was a knock at the door. A servant handed Wilson a slip of paper. After reading it twice he held it over the flame of a candle, paced anew. Finally he turned to Hesse. "I cannot forward your suggestion to the cabinet," he said. The note undoubtedly was that Chamberlain had just decided to act even if it had to be without France. At 11:30 P.M. the cabinet met once more in emergency session. Chamberlain said he wanted to make a statement to the British people the following noon. "I therefore suggest," he said, "that Sir Nevile Henderson should be instructed to see Herr von Ribbentrop at 9 A.M. tomorrow, and to say that unless a reply is received by 12 noon a state of war will exist between England and Germany as from that hour." It was possible, he added, that this decision might spur the French to act earlier but he doubted it.

Simon protested that the noon ultimatum would not give Chamberlain time to make his statement to the people; it should be 11 A.M. There was general agreement and the meeting ended. Then came a loud clap of thunder and through the window could be seen a flash of lightning.

The Führer, according to his valet, spent that evening at the chancellery quietly discussing the Polish campaign. But upon reading Hesse's report of the futile meeting with Wilson—it arrived two hours after midnight—he purportedly lost his temper and began blaming Ribbentrop for Italy's refusal to take part in the war. Nor was the harried Foreign Minister's day yet over. At about 4 A.M. the British Embassy telephoned to say that Henderson wished to give Ribbentrop an important communication at 9 A.M. It was obviously a disagreeable message and might even contain an ultimatum. Ribbentrop didn't feel like facing this. He turned to Schmidt, who happened to be on hand, and told him to receive Henderson in his place.

6

Sunday, September 3, dawned clear and balmy. It was a lovely day and ordinarily Berliners would be streaming out to the nearby woods and lakes to enjoy the holiday. Today they were depressed and confused to find themselves at the threshold of a major war.

Of all mornings, this was the one that Schmidt, in bed only a few hours, overslept. Rushing by taxi to the Foreign Office, he saw Henderson enter the building and himself raced into a side entrance. He was standing, somewhat breathless, in Ribbentrop's office as the hour of nine struck and Henderson was announced. The ambassador shook hands but declined Schmidt's invitation to sit down. "I regret that on the instructions of my government," he said with deep emotion, "I have to hand you an ultimatum for the German government." He read out the statement, which called for war unless Germany gave assurances that all troops would be withdrawn from Poland by eleven o'clock, British Summer Time.

Henderson extended the document. "I am sincerely sorry," he said, "that I must hand such a document to you in particular as you have always been most anxious to help." While Henderson would not be remembered for astuteness, retaining as he did a naïve conception of the Führer to the end, he had succeeded in outshouting him and staring down Ribbentrop on successive evenings, feats worthy of some applause.

In a few minutes Schmidt was at the chancellery. He made his way with some difficulty through the crowd gathered outside of the Führer's office. To anxious questions on his mission, he said cryptically, "Classroom dismissed." Hitler was at his desk; Ribbentrop stood by the window. Both turned expectantly as Schmidt entered. He slowly translated the British ultimatum. At last Hitler turned to Ribbentrop and abruptly said, "What now?"

"I assume," said Ribbentrop quietly, "that the French will hand in a similar ultimatum within the hour."

Schmidt was engulfed in the anteroom by eager questions but once he revealed that England was declaring war in two hours there was complete silence. Finally Göring said, "If we lose this war, then God have mercy on us!" Everywhere Schmidt saw grave faces. Even the usually ebullient Goebbels stood in a corner, downcast and self-absorbed.

One man refused to give up hope. Dahlerus located Göring at his private train. Why didn't the Reichsmarschall fly to London and negotiate with the British? Göring was persuaded to telephone Hitler. Surprisingly, he reported, the Führer liked the idea, but first wanted British concurrence. Dahlerus telephoned the counselor at the British Embassy, who replied that the Germans must first answer the ultimatum. Undeterred, Dahlerus phoned the Foreign Office in London. He got the same answer. Still he persisted. He somehow persuaded Göring to ring up Hitler again and suggest sending a conciliatory official reply to the British. Dahlerus waited outside the train, nervously pacing up and down, while Göring talked with the Führer. Finally Göring stepped out of the train, seating himself at a large collapsible table in a stand of beech trees. He muttered that a plane was standing by to take him to England. But Dahlerus concluded from the "disappointed" look on his face that he had been refused by the Führer; but the Swede was not perspicacious (at Nuremberg he dolefully admitted that he had been misled in general by both Hitler and Göring) and could have been taken in by Göring's play-acting. The extent of Dahlerus' naïveté was revealed in his own recorded reaction to the moment: "My blood boiled as I saw the hopelessness of this powerful man. And I could not understand why, knowing what he did, he did not jump into his car, drive to the chancellery and tell them what he really thought —always supposing he really meant all the things he had been telling me for the past two months." So ended the stout, if amateurish, efforts of Dahlerus to prevent war.

At 11:15 A.M. Ambassador Henderson received a message to call upon Ribbentrop. Within fifteen minutes he was handed Germany's reply to the ultimatum—a flat refusal. Henderson looked up from the statement and remarked that it "would be left to history to judge where the blame really lay." Ribbentrop replied that "nobody had striven harder for peace and good relations with England than Herr Hitler had done," and wished Henderson well personally.

At noon loudspeakers in the streets of Berlin blared out the news of war with England to shocked listeners.

London, where it was 11 A.M., was hot and summery and Chamberlain was steeling himself for his broadcast to the people. Fifteen minutes later he announced that England was at war. The British government, he said, had done everything possible to establish peace and had a clear conscience. "Now may God bless you all and may He defend the right."

Even as he was speaking, Coulondre handed over to Ribbentrop France's ultimatum—and was told that France would therefore be the aggressor. But it was England that bore the brunt of Hitler's resentment. He who so readily perceived British weakness had completely failed to judge British strength. His localized war was turning into a general conflagration because of this miscalculation. It was an impasse born of his first crucial mistake: the decision to seize all of Czechoslovakia. If he had not done so and had waited for that country to fall in his lap, it is doubtful that the English would have reacted so positively to his demands on Poland. What Hitler had refused to accept—even though he may have guessed as much —was that an Englishman will go so far but not one inch farther. Despite information to the contrary by Hesse and intelligence reports, Hitler had been misled by his own distorted picture of British character. It was with unprecedented embarrassment, therefore, that he informed Admiral Raeder of the Western ultimatum.

There was little doubt that the occupants of the Kremlin were surprised by the British declaration. "The news of war," reported the Moscow correspondent of the London *Daily Telegraph*, "astonished the Russians. They expected a compromise." Curiously the Soviets showed so little inclination to join the attack on Poland that Ribbentrop invited them to do so in a telegram dispatched early that evening to Ambassador von der Schulenburg. "In our estimation," explained Ribbentrop, "this would be not only a relief for us, but also be in the sense of the Moscow agreements, and in the Soviet interest as well."

Hitler was already preparing to leave the chancellery with his entourage to board a special train bound for the fighting front. Nine minutes before it left Berlin, the Führer sent off a message to the ally who had failed to support him in his greatest crisis. Unlike the telegram to Moscow, this one to Mussolini was sent in the clear and was replete with dramatic phrases. He was aware, said Hitler, that this was "a struggle of life and death" but he had chosen to wage war with "deliberation," and his faith remained as "firm as a rock." As the Führer's train pulled out of the station at exactly 9 P.M. he did not show the confidence of this letter.

One secretary, Gerda Daranowsky, noticed he was very quiet, pale and thoughtful; never before had she seen him like that. And another, Christa Schröder, overheard him say to Hess: "Now, all my work crumbles. I wrote my book for nothing."

But to his valet he seemed the epitome of assurance; there was, he said, nothing to worry about in the West; Britain and France would "break their teeth" on the Westwall. As the train headed east Hitler called Linge to the dining salon and ordered an even more spartan diet from that day on. "You will see to it," he said, "that I have only what the ordinary people of Germany can have. It is my duty to set an example."

Part 7

BY FORCE OF ARMS

Candid shot of Hitler on the veranda of the Berghof in 1938. WÜNSCHE

Hitler standing in limousine outside the Rheinhotel Dreesen in Bad Godesberg, where he was to meet with British Prime Minister Neville Chamberlain. September 1938. IMPERIAL WAR MUSEUM

Hitler, Chamberlain and Ribbentrop talk peace in Munich one week later. BUNDESARCHIV

Left, General von Fritsch, shortly before his death in Poland. IMPERIAL WAR MUSEUM. Right, General Halder, wearing rimless glasses, and Field Marshal von Brauchitsch pose over map. July 3, 1939. IMPERIAL WAR MUSEUM

Left, two months after invading Poland in 1939 Hitler narrowly escapes death at Hofbräuhaus in Munich. A bomb hidden in a column behind Hitler exploded a few minutes after he unexpectedly ended his speech and rushed to the railroad station. That afternoon Frau Troost had warned him of possible assassination and he decided to take earlier train. The ordnance officer in charge of scheduling, Max Wünsche, stares intently at his chief from the front row. BIBLIO. FÜR ZEIT. Right, Polish Jews humiliated by Nazis. IMPERIAL WAR MUSEUM

Rare pictures of Hitler planning invasion of the West in early 1940 in the old Reich Chancellery. Left, Göring and Captain von Puttkamer, the Führer's naval adjutant, watch Hitler explain how to skirt the Maginot Line. Almost all his commanders opposed the unorthodox plan—which worked. PUTTKAMER. Right, Keitel, Jodl, Hitler, Schmundt (chief adjutant) and Puttkamer. PUTTKAMER

Hitler's military inner circle, May 1940. Front row, l. to r., Brückner (personal adjutant), Otto Dietrich (press chief), Keitel, Hitler, Jodl, Bormann, Below (Hitler's Luftwaffe adjutant), Hoffmann the photographer. Middle row, Bodenschatz (Göring's chief of staff), Schmundt, Wolf, Dr. Morell (Hitler's chief physician), Hansgeorg Schulze (Hitler's ordnance officer, killed in battle and replaced by his brother Richard). Back row, Engel (Hitler's army adjutant), Dr. Brandt (Hitler's surgeon), Puttkamer, Lorenz (DNB), Walther Hewel (Foreign Office), unknown, Schaub (Hitler's personal adjutant), Wünsche. BIBLIO. FÜR ZEIT.

The jig that never was. Hitler's elation at news that France had surrendered was briefly filmed by Walter Frentz at Brûly-de-Pesche, not, as generally believed, in Compiègne. The following frames (and there were no others, Frentz revealed to the author) were cleverly "looped" (repeated) by a Canadian film expert, making it appear that Hitler was executing a dance. The same technique was later used in cat food commercials. TRANSIT FILM, MUNICH

Hitler tells a joke. Extreme right, Below.
FRENTZ

"Never again trench warfare," he assures entourage. PUTTKAMER

Bormann, Himmler, Keitel, Hitler and Puttkamer. PUTTKAMER

Fun on the auto tour. Arno Breker, the sculptor, threatened with a dagger by his wife if he ever should be disloyal. Left, Gerda Daranowsky Christian, Hitler's secretary and former employee of Elizabeth Arden. FRENTZ

Hitler in Paris with Speer and Breker. U. S. ARMY

Hitler in Paris, l. to r., Architect Giesler, Breker, Keitel, Hitler, Bodenschatz, Engel, Bormann, Schaub and Speer. FRENTZ

Two faces of Adolf Hitler. PUTTKAMER

Generalissimo Franco leans forward from train car to speak with Hitler and the German interpreter. October 1940. Part Jewish, Franco refused Hitler's offer to join the Axis. U. S. ARMY

Hitler talks peace with Soviet Foreign Minister Molotov, November 1940. The man in the center is Stalin's interpreter. After this meeting Hitler decides definitely to invade Russia. IMPERIAL WAR MUSEUM

Hitler and Papen on the Berghof veranda. FRENTZ

Hitler celebrates Christmas 1940 with young Luftwaffe officers. FRENTZ

The same day. Engel is promoted to major. Puttkamer affixes the new insignia. FRENTZ

Bormann at wheel with Frau Hess. Hess in jump seat; in back Professor Haushofer, the geopolitician, and Hildegard Fath, Hess's secretary. FATH

Hess with his wife on a skiing holiday in the mid-thirties. He usually kept a stiff upper lip—to cover his buck teeth. FATH

Athlete Hess takes off. FATH

Just before his flight to England in May 1941, Hess and his son. The girl is Bormann's daughter. FATH

Chapter Twenty-one

VICTORY IN THE WEST
SEPTEMBER 3, 1939–JUNE 25, 1940

1

The invasion of Poland proceeded rapidly. Polish cavalrymen, carrying long lances, were no match for German tanks. In a concentrated land and air attack, the defenders were overwhelmed. Harried from the air by fighter planes, bombers and screeching Stukas, the Polish ground forces were quickly dispersed by a million and a half men supported by heavy self-propelled guns and tanks. It was this incredible mass of Panzers in particular which wreaked havoc. They burst through defenses and ravaged the rear. The Blitzkrieg was almost as terrifying to foreign observers as the victims, for it presaged a frightening turning point in the art of warfare. By morning of September 5 the Polish air force was destroyed, the battle for the Corridor ended. Two days later most of Poland's thirty-five divisions were either routed or surrounded.

Hitler closely followed the action in his special train, designating it as Führer Headquarters even though Jodl's operations staff remained in Berlin. Once he had donned a uniform his way of life changed drastically. Assuming the old role of front-line soldier, he imposed on Führer Headquarters an austere simplicity. His new motto was: "Front-line troops must be assured that their leader shares their privations." Every morning, after dictating orders of the day to Fräulein Schröder, he set out for the battlefield with pistol and oxhide whip. He rode in an open vehicle, weather permitting, so the troops would recognize him while his valet and adjutant tossed out packs of cigarettes. To the wonder of his entourage, he began devoting himself tirelessly to the most minute details of operations. He spent hours, for example, personally inspecting kitchens and mess halls, tyrannically imposing the enlisted man's diet on officers. This aspect of the new regimen soon ended but in all matters of the battlefield he continued to have unflagging interest—that is, with one significant exception. When Schmundt asked him to speak to the first trainload of wounded he could not do so. The sight of their suffering, he confessed, would be intolerable.

As the one-sided campaign drew to a close an unexpected visitor appeared at Führer Headquarters. Fritz Hesse had come to report that the German official delegation in London had been given a friendly farewell not only by their high-ranking British friends but by the population. A crowd outside the embassy had shouted, "See you at Christmas!" Hesse had also come to Poland out of personal concern; he understood he was in disfavor because of his persistence in seeking peace. But Hewel, who presently enjoyed Hitler's complete confidence, assured him that the Führer had sincerely sought negotiations with the British. What provoked him into invading Poland were the reports of atrocities inflicted on German nationals. Hesse could not believe that the order to invade had come in a moment of rage. "Yes, this was without a doubt the cause," insisted Hewel. "And he soon regretted that he had given way to his temper." That was why he had permitted Hesse to negotiate with Sir Horace Wilson after the invasion. "Yes, Hitler would have just liked to say, 'Everybody about face, march, march!'"

"My God," exclaimed Hesse bitterly, "couldn't anyone make it clear to him that although a dictator can order, 'About face, march, march!' it is impossible in a parliamentary nation to cancel a decision for war made after long and thoughtful preparation? How can he imagine such a thing? I always warned that there was a war party in England and that the collapse of Chamberlain's foreign policy would certainly bring victory to this war party. Didn't anyone read this report?"

After a silence the disconcerted Hewel admitted that the Führer had a rather strange concept of the workings of a democracy. "He snorted at me when I tried to explain to him your report on the statements Chamberlain made in the House of Commons. He simply did not want to believe it. Don't be afraid though. In the meantime he has realized your report was correct. But for heaven's sake don't make use of this. Nothing irritates the Führer more than people who were right when he was wrong."

What concerned Hitler more than England—for there was no action at all on the western front—was the reluctance of the Soviet Union to join in the attack on Poland. Apparently Stalin wanted to wait until the last possible moment so as to minimize Red Army losses. It was not until 2 A.M., September 17, that the German ambassador in Moscow was personally informed by Stalin that the Red Army would cross the Polish frontier in several hours. At 4 A.M. local time the Red Army crossed the long eastern frontier of Poland. At one point men of the Polish Frontier Corps saw a horde of horse-drawn carts filled with soldiers coming through the morning mist. "Don't shoot," shouted the Red Army men, "we've come to help you against the Germans." The defenders were so confused—white flags were attached to the leading Russian vehicles—that the Soviets passed through in many places without receiving a shot. It was the end of eastern Poland.

Ribbentrop was not awakened until 8 A.M. and when he learned that Schmidt had let him sleep three hours he shouted angrily, "The German and Russian armies are rushing toward each other—there may be clashes —and all because you were too slack to waken me!" The interpreter tried to calm him by reminding him that a demarcation line had been set up. But the Foreign Minister, his face lathered, continued to rage as he brandished a razor: "You have meddled with the course of world history! You have not enough experience for that!" What really infuriated Ribbentrop, who was up front with a skeleton staff, was that the delay allowed Goebbels and not his own office to issue the news to foreign journalists in Berlin.

The only contest now was between the victors. Before the first day of Russian participation ended the two allies were wrangling over the text of the joint communiqué which would attempt to justify the conquest of Poland. Stalin objected to the German draft ("it presented the facts all too frankly"), then wrote out in his own hand a new version. No sooner had Hitler bowed to this revision than Stalin presented another far more important one: an out-and-out partition of the spoils which would deprive the Poles of even the semblance of independence. On the face of it the Russian proposal was advantageous to Germany but Hitler's suspicion was such that it was four days before Ribbentrop was empowered to endorse it.

The Foreign Minister arrived in the Russian capital at 5:50 P.M., September 27, to negotiate the new treaty. It seemed to have been timed auspiciously since Warsaw had just capitulated to German arms. That was, until Ribbentrop received a warning from Berlin of imminent Soviet attacks on Estonia and Latvia. It was, therefore, with apprehension that Ribbentrop set out for the Kremlin later that evening. He already was sure that Stalin was going to make him a tempting offer but feared the price might be too high. At 10 P.M. the conference began. As expected, Stalin formally offered all Polish territory east of the Vistula, which included most of Poland's populated areas. In return, all he wanted was the third Baltic state, Lithuania.

After the three-hour meeting ended, Ribbentrop sent off a message by telephone to the Führer. Stalin's proposal, he reported, had one very attractive feature, namely that, with control of the bulk of their population, "the Polish national problem might be dealt with as Germany saw fit."

Shrewd Stalin knew his Hitler. Beyond a need for continuing good relations with the Soviets, the Führer could not resist the opportunity of controlling this breeding ground of Jews. He authorized Ribbentrop to sign the treaty and presented Stalin with the last of the Baltic States. It was a heavy price to pay for keeping his rear in the East free while he dealt with the West. On the surface it looked like another instance of opportunism, sacrificing the future for the present. But Hitler was so convinced of the weakness of the Red Army that he must have felt he could easily take back by force what he had given away on paper. During the next day's final negotiations the Soviets insisted that Ribbentrop telephone the Führer for definite approval of all angles of the treaty. Hitler affirmed the agreement although Ribbentrop sensed that it was with some misgivings. "I want to establish quite firm and close relations," he said and when Ribbentrop reported these words Stalin replied laconically, "Hitler knows his business."

Stalin beamed upon Molotov and Ribbentrop as they signed the pact at 5 A.M. on the twenty-ninth, but Ribbentrop's remark that Russians and Germans must never again fight brought an embarrassing silence. Finally Stalin replied, "This ought to be the case." The coolness of the tone and the unusual phrasing impelled Ribbentrop to ask the interpreter for confirmation. A second Stalin remark was equally vague: when Ribbentrop wondered whether the Soviets were willing to go beyond the friendship agreement and conclude an alliance for the coming battles with the West, the answer was: "I shall never allow Germany to become weak." The words were uttered so spontaneously that Ribbentrop concluded they must have expressed Stalin's conviction.

He returned to Berlin still puzzling over the two remarks. Hitler was even more concerned, interpreting Stalin's words to mean that the chasm between their philosophies was too wide for bridging and that a dispute was bound to arise. Only then did the Führer explain that he had made the Lithuanian concession to prove to Stalin "his intention of settling questions with his Eastern neighbor for good and of establishing real confidence from the start." Taking these words at face value as he had those of Stalin, Ribbentrop remained convinced that Hitler really sought a permanent understanding with the Soviets.

While Stalin was digesting the three Baltic States and eastern Poland, Hitler was transforming the rest of that nation into a massive killing ground. He had already ordered Jews from the Reich massed in specific Polish cities having good rail connections. Object: "final solution, which will take some time," as Heydrich explained to SS commanders on September 21. He was talking of the extermination of the Jews, already an open secret among many high-ranking party officials.

These grisly preparations were augmented by a "house cleaning" of Polish intelligentsia, clergy and nobility by five murder squads known as *Einsatzgruppen* (Special Groups). Hitler's hatred of Poles was of relatively recent origin. He was convinced that during the past few years numerous atrocities had been inflicted on the German minority in Poland. "Tens of thousands were carried off, mistreated, and murdered in the most gruesome manner," he told a partisan crowd in Danzig on September 19. "Sadistic beasts vented their perverted instincts—and this democratic, religious world looked on without even a whimper." But, he added, "Almighty God has now blessed our weapons." Now he was getting his revenge. By mid-autumn 3500 intelligentsia (whom Hitler considered "carriers of Polish nationalism") were liquidated. "It is only in this manner," he explained, "that we can acquire the vital territory which we need. After all, who today remembers the extermination of the Armenians!" This terror was accompanied by the ruthless expulsion of 1,200,000 ordinary Poles from their ancestral homes so that Germans from the Baltic and outlying portions of Poland could be properly housed. In the ensuing bitter months more Poles lost their lives in the resettlement from exposure to zero weather than those on the execution list.

2

Even as the SS carried out Hitler's radical program in the East, he turned his attention to the West.* With the better part of Poland his, he

---

* Since the SS comprised a number of sections, each with different duties and characteristics, each should be judged separately. See Glossary, page 1016. The Waffen (armed) SS, for instance, was purely a military aggregation of elitists, and its members' allegiance was to the Reich and Hitler, not Himmler. They fought better than

sought to end the war with France and England, one way or the other.
First he launched a peace offensive in press and radio. "Hitler will again
reach an understanding with the English," Hewel assured Fritz Hesse,
"and wants to make it as easy as possible for them." The Führer, he said,
was also prepared to let Hesse resume his sub rosa negotiations with Sir
Horace Wilson so long as Germany was guaranteed an absolutely free
hand in the East. Hitler could not agree, for instance, to refrain from attacking Russia. Hesse was puzzled and if it had not been anyone as close to
Hitler as Hewel he would have dismissed such a fantastic idea. Why then,
he asked, did the Führer make a pact with Stalin if he intended to attack
the Soviet Union?

Hewel explained that Hitler had made the deal for one reason: to
keep the English neutral. Since it had failed to do so, he was already
thinking of breaking it. Stalin's greed for territory had exasperated the
Führer, who had given up the Baltic "only with a bleeding heart." Hesse
protested that this completely contradicted Ribbentrop's assessment.

"In Hitler's eyes," was Hewel's surprising reply, "Ribbentrop plays no
role at all." Hitler looked upon him merely as a sort of secretary. That was
why the Führer had been playing the English game through unofficial
channels like Hesse, Göring and Dahlerus. Later that September he encouraged the last to make another trip to London. "The British can
have peace if they want it," said Hitler, "but they will have to hurry." But
while he talked peace to Dahlerus he was privately determined to make
war. Within hours he was telling the commanders of the army, navy and
air force of his decision to launch an early attack in the West "since the
Franco-British army is not yet prepared." He set the date: November 12.
Colonel Warlimont noticed that everyone, including Göring, was "clearly
entirely taken aback." The Führer occasionally glanced at a small piece of
paper as he gave the background of his decision and outlined the broad
directives for operations. He did not, for example, intend to use the
Schlieffen plan of 1914 but would attack through Belgium and Luxembourg in approximately a west-northwest direction so as to gain the Chan-

---

army troops, being better motivated and more democratically organized. There was
little differentiation between officers and enlisted men. In the Wehrmacht the men
were forbidden to keep their footlockers open so as to prevent stealing; but the Waffen
SS considered themselves "a band of brothers" and it was forbidden to lock them. Any
stealing was punished by the men themselves; and a thief was cashiered on their
recommendation. Many myths about the Waffen SS still persist. Its notorious tattoo,
for example, had no sinister symbolism. It was merely a man's blood type in case he
was wounded and needed a battlefield transfusion. Himmler, whom the "band of
brothers" regarded as an outsider, was not tattooed.

nel ports. No one spoke a word in protest and as soon as Hitler finished speaking he tossed his notes into the fire.

Dahlerus, granted free transit by both sides, was back in London on September 28. He talked to Cadogan that morning for more than two hours but the latter predictably was not at all impressed. "He really hadn't much to say," Cadogan wrote in his diary. "He's like a wasp at a picnic— one can't beat him off. He's brought very little from Berlin." Dahlerus was no more successful with Chamberlain and Halifax, but Hitler was not daunted. On October 6 he made a public appeal for peace at the Kroll Opera House. "Why should this war in the West be fought? For restoration of Poland? Poland of the Versailles Treaty will never rise again." The establishment of the Polish state, he said, was a problem to be solved by Russia and Germany—not the West. What other reason was there for war? Admittedly there were numerous problems of great importance which had to be solved sooner or later. Was it not more "sensible" to do so at the conference table before millions of men were uselessly killed and billions of riches destroyed?

Courtship was followed by dire prediction. "Destiny will decide who is right. One thing only is certain. In the course of world history there have never been two victors, but very often only vanquished." He prayed that God might show the Third Reich and all other nations the correct course. "If, however, the opinions of Messrs. Churchill and followers should prevail, this statement will have been my last. Then we shall fight. . . . There will never be another November 1918 in German history!"

Almost certainly Hitler had no intention of accepting a permanent peace with two great powers capable of threatening the Reich's security. A temporary one, however, might enable him to divide France from England and so vanquish them separately. That was why he could speak so sincerely. Throughout Germany there was a feeling of widespread relief over the Führer's plea for peace and even premature celebrations of joy, only slightly dampened by Daladier's quick answer the following day. France, he declared, would never lay down arms until assured of a "real peace and general security." But as the days passed without word from London hope grew in Berlin. The Führer, however, was preparing for the worst. On October 9 he issued Directive No. 6 for the Conduct of War, which outlined an invasion through Luxembourg, Belgium and Holland.

The next morning at eleven, seven of his military commanders reported to the chancellery. Before presenting the new directive Hitler read out a memorandum of his own composition which indicated that he was a student of military and political history. Germany and the West, he said, had been enemies since the dissolution of the First German Reich in 1648 and this struggle "would have to be fought out one way or the other." But he had no objection "to ending the war immediately," so long as the gains in Poland were accepted. His listeners were not asked for comment nor did they volunteer any. They were called upon only to endorse the German war aim: "the destruction of the power and ability of the Western powers ever again to be able to oppose the state consolidation and further development of the German people in Europe."

He acknowledged the objections to haste in launching the attack. But time was on the enemy's side. Because of the Russian treaty and the great victory in Poland, Germany was at last in position—for the first time in many years—to make war on a single front. With the East secured, the Wehrmacht could throw all its forces against England and France. It was a situation that could terminate abruptly. "By no treaty or pact can a lasting neutrality of Soviet Russia be insured with certainty." The greatest safeguard against any Soviet attack lay "in a prompt demonstration of German strength."

Furthermore, hope of Italian support depended primarily on how long Mussolini remained alive. The situation in Rome could change in a flash. So could the neutrality of Belgium, Holland and the United States. Time was working against Germany in many ways. At present she enjoyed military superiority but England and France were closing the gap since their war industries could call upon the resources of most of the world. A long war presented great dangers. The Reich had limited supplies of food and raw materials, and the fount of war production, the Ruhr, was dangerously vulnerable to air attack and long-range artillery.

He proceeded to purely military matters. They must avoid the trench warfare of 1914–18. The attack, he said, would depend on the new tank and air tactics developed in Poland. Panzers would lead the breakthrough. He urged his commanders to improvise, improvise; and illustrated how they could "prevent fronts from becoming stable by massed drives through identified weakly held positions."

It was a brilliant display but almost every one of his commanders remained convinced that the Wehrmacht was not yet prepared or suitably supplied for war with the West. Yet there was not a single objection, not even after the Führer's announcement that the start of the attack could not begin "too early. It is to take place in all circumstances (if at all possible) this autumn."*

---

* About this same time he also issued an order legalizing euthanasia for those patients deemed "incurable." Perhaps he was thinking of his mother's suffering from cancer but more likely it was an opportunity to get rid of the mentally ill, the elderly non-productive and those groups he regarded as racially harmful.

In London, Chamberlain was still pondering an answer to Hitler's latest peace offer. As he walked into the cabinet meeting on the day the Führer's invasion directive was issued, he was perturbed by the first enthusiastic American reaction to Hitler's "very attractive series of proposals." He was clear in his own mind that the Hitler speech offered no real advance toward a reasonable peace and he told the cabinet that their reply should be "stiff." The ministers agreed but it was decided to hold up the answer two days.

On the morning of October 11 it was rumored in Berlin that the Chamberlain government had fallen and an armistice was imminent. The old women in the capital's vegetable markets, reported an assistant correspondent on the New York *Herald Tribune,* threw cabbages in the air and wrecked their own stands in sheer joy. A holiday spirit spread through the city until Berlin radio denied the report.

The following afternoon, after a week's delay, Chamberlain finally answered Hitler. He announced in Commons that the German proposals were hereby rejected as "vague and uncertain." If Hitler wanted peace, "acts, not words alone must be forthcoming"; he must supply "convincing proof" that he truly sought peace. Applause from the House was moderate.

In Berlin a circular from the Press Department of the Foreign Ministry was immediately telegraphed, in the clear, to all foreign stations. It denounced the Prime Minister's reply as an outrageous affront. To Hitler the rejection was disappointing but not unexpected. He summoned Göring and the two men responsible for Luftwaffe production—Field Marshal Erhard Milch and Colonel General Ernst Udet. "My attempts to make peace with the West have failed," he said. "The war continues. Now we can and must manufacture the bombs."

3

As word spread of Hitler's decision to attack the West, various resistance groups inside Germany concocted plans for coups d'état and assassinations. Some wanted to execute the Führer; others simply to kidnap him and set up either a military junta or a democratic regime. Lists of ministers were drawn up; peace feelers were extended to the United States and other neutrals. The most serious group of conspirators came from the OKW itself and its leading spirit was an impetuous cavalry officer, Colonel Hans Oster. As chief assistant to Admiral Canaris in the *Abwehr,* the Intelligence Service, this impatient, often imprudent man could not have been in a more strategic position. Moreover, he had connections with every faction in the Wehrmacht, private individuals like Schacht, the Foreign Ministry, and even the SS.

Oster found a valuable recruit in a Munich lawyer, Josef Müller, who had detested Hitler for years. Müller—a devout Catholic—made a clandestine trip to Rome early that October with the connivance of Oster, his object to discover if the British were prepared to make peace with an anti-Nazi regime. He met Pius XII and found him willing to act as intermediary. The Pope's secretary sounded out the British minister and was informed that Great Britain was not averse to making a "soft peace" with an anti-Hitler Germany.

Müller was empowered to take this information orally back to Germany but begged for something in writing that would prove to the Abwehr and military commanders that this peace proposal was authorized by the Holy Father himself. Surprisingly, the Vatican agreed and a letter was written by the Pope's private secretary outlining the main bases for peace with England.

The Oster group was cheered. Of all their attempts to make contact with the West, this was the most promising. Perhaps the Pope's promise of participation would at last induce Brauchitsch to take an active part in the conspiracy. But the army commander-in-chief was not impressed. He was convinced that the German people were "all for Hitler." General Halder proved to be almost as timid, but under pressure from Oster and others he finally agreed to help carry out a Putsch. All at once it appeared as if the leading officers were willing to take action. The conspirators were even assured that Brauchitsch himself was prepared to join them if Hitler refused to call off the invasion.

A showdown between army chief and Führer was set for Sunday, November 5—the day the troops were scheduled to move to attack positions on the western front. Brauchitsch appeared as scheduled at the chancellery. After presenting a memorandum, he elaborated on the main arguments against the invasion. It would be impossible, he said, to mount such a massive offensive in the autumn or spring rains. "It rains on the enemy too," replied Hitler curtly. In desperation, Brauchitsch argued that the Polish campaign indicated that the fighting spirit of the German infantryman was far below that of the World War. There were even signs of insubordination similar to those in 1918.

Hitler had been listening politely, if coolly. This remark enraged him. "In what units have there been any cases of lack of discipline?" he demanded. "What happened? Where?" Brauchitsch had deliberately exaggerated "to deter Hitler" and he shrank before such fury. "What action has been taken by the army commander?" demanded the Führer. "How many death sentences have been carried out?"

He turned his vitriol on the army. It had never been loyal or had confidence in his genius and had consistently sabotaged rearmament by deliberate slowdown methods. The army, in fact, was afraid to fight! Suddenly Hitler spun around and marched out of the room. Brauchitsch was still in a state of shock when he staggered into army headquarters at Zossen, eighteen miles away, and stammered out an incoherent account of what had taken place. Almost simultaneously a telephone call from the chancellery reaffirmed November 12 as the date for invasion. An exact hour was set—7:15 A.M. General Halder requested written confirmation and got it immediately by messenger.

The army conspirators now had the necessary documentary evidence to overthrow Hitler. But there was no call for revolt, no signal for assassination. Instead they furtively burned all incriminating papers. Colonel Oster alone did not panic; through Count Albrecht von Bernstorff, whose father had been ambassador to Washington during the Great War, he warned the Belgian and Netherlands legations to expect an attack at dawn on November 12.

Sunday's storm in the chancellery was followed by anticlimax. The Luftwaffe needed five consecutive days of good weather to destroy the French air force and the meteorological report on Tuesday the seventh was so unpromising that Hitler postponed A-Day.

Although Hitler knew nothing of the military plot, Göring had warned him against Brauchitsch and Halder: "My Führer, get rid of these birds of ill omen." A more definite admonition came from the Swiss astrologer, Karl Ernst Krafft, hired by Himmler's secret intelligence service as an astral adviser. He had recently submitted a paper indicating that Hitler would be in danger of assassination between November 7 and 10; but the document was hastily filed since astrological speculation concerning the Führer was *verboten*.

When Hitler came to Munich on the morning of November 8 to attend the annual reunion of the Old Fighters, Frau Troost, the architect, also sounded a note of warning. She asked why he was so lax about security measures, coming as he did to her studio with only one or two bodyguards. He replied that a man must have faith in Providence, then slapped his trouser pocket. "See, I always carry a pistol but even that would be useless. If my end is decided, only this will protect me." He put hand over heart. "One must listen to an inner voice and believe in one's fate. And I believe very deeply that destiny has selected me for the German nation.

So long as I am needed by the people, so long as I am responsible for the life of the Reich, I shall live." He pictured himself as another Christ. "And when I am no longer needed, after my mission is accomplished, then I shall be called away."

Even though the talk switched to architecture, Frau Troost noticed Hitler's uneasiness. "I must change the schedule today," he suddenly said and muttered something about checking with Schaub. But he did nothing, being so occupied with other matters. He visited Unity Mitford, who had shot herself in the temple and was recuperating in a Munich clinic.* By this time she had regained consciousness and when she asked to go home Hitler promised to send her by special train to Switzerland as soon as she was strong enough to travel.

He spent much of the afternoon on a speech he had just decided to make that evening at the Bürgerbräukeller. It would be another attack on England, designed primarily for German ears. The main room of the vast beer hall was already gaily decorated with banners and flags and by late afternoon the microphones were in place and tested. At dusk a small, pale man with a high forehead and clear bright eyes entered carrying a box. He was a skilled artisan named Georg Elser and he had recently been discharged from Dachau concentration camp where he had been held as a Communist sympathizer. His goal was peace and he had come here to kill Hitler. In the box was a timing device connected to sticks of dynamite. As waiters and party officials made the final preparations for the meeting Elser inconspicuously walked up to the gallery and hid behind the pillar rising from the back of the festooned speakers' platform. Several days earlier he had cut the wooden paneling of the pillar with a special saw— he was a cabinetmaker as well as a mechanic—fixed several hinges and replaced the piece of wood as a little door.

At last the lights of the hall were extinguished, the doors closed. Elser waited another half hour, then placed the bomb in the pillar and set it to detonate at about 11:20 P.M. The Führer would start speaking at 10 P.M. and the explosion would come midway in the speech.†

---

* "If it comes to war," Unity Mitford told her sister Diana at the Bayreuth Festival, "I shall kill myself." She did not care to live, she said, if the two countries she loved took up arms against each other. After the radio blared out the news of England's declaration of war she walked into the English Gardens, and tried to kill herself with a small pistol. She was taken to a clinic in the Nussbaumstrasse where, at Hitler's orders, she was treated by a distinguished surgeon, Professor Magnus. He decided it was too dangerous to extract the bullet still lodged in her temple. News of the suicide attempt was suppressed: Unity's parents were informed discreetly through the German minister in Berne.

† There had already been a number of attempts to assassinate Hitler. One he knew nothing about was plotted by a disillusioned SS guard who, about 1929, planted a

At his apartment on the Prinzregentenplatz, Hitler summoned his young ordnance officer, Max Wünsche. Would it be possible, he asked, to leave Munich earlier than planned? Wünsche assured him it would be no problem; there were always two trains at the Führer's disposal as a security precaution. The young man immediately made arrangements to use the early one.

The Führer was greeted at the Bürgerbräukeller with such wild acclaim that he did not begin speaking until ten minutes past ten. His audience reveled in the insults and jibes he heaped upon the English. It took little, in fact, to draw applause and there were so many interruptions that Wünsche, seated in the front row, feared the Führer would miss the early train.

At 11:07 P.M. Hitler unexpectedly brought his tirade to a hurried conclusion. A few yards away, inside the pillar, Elser's clock was ticking. In thirteen minutes the bomb was supposed to explode. Ordinarily Hitler spent considerable time after a speech chatting with the comrades of the Putsch but tonight, without shaking hands, he rushed out of the building accompanied by Hess and several adjutants and into the car waiting outside. Kempka headed directly for the railroad station. Before they arrived —exactly eight minutes after Hitler left the Bürgerbräukeller—Wünsche heard a distant explosion. He wondered what it was. If Hitler heard the noise he did not think it worth mentioning.

In the hubbub that followed the explosion—the shrieking of sirens from police cars and ambulances—a rumor started that the war was over. It might have been if Hitler had been standing on the platform. He surely would have died. The bomb killed seven and wounded sixty-three, including Eva Braun's father, who had gained admission thanks to a special low-numbered membership card, though he was actually party member No. 5,021,670. His daughter, accompanied by her best friend, Herta Schneider, arrived at the station just as the Führer's train was leaving. Aboard they found an air of carefree gaiety. No one knew of the explosion and almost everyone was drinking. The lone teetotaler, Hitler, was animated but it was Goebbels who enlivened the conversation with his caustic wit.

At Nuremberg the propaganda chief left the train to send several messages and gather the latest news. When he returned to the Führer's

---

bomb under the podium just before a speech in the Sportpalast. During the speech the malcontented SS man had a sudden urge to go to the toilet; by chance someone locked him in the men's room and he was unable to set off the bomb. "It was the joke of the century," recalled a friend of the would-be assassin. "The history of the world might have been changed if he hadn't had to go to the bathroom."

compartment he told of the bomb in a trembling voice. Hitler thought it
was a joke until he noticed Goebbels' pale face. His own became a grim
mask. Finally in a voice hoarse with emotion he exclaimed, "Now I am
completely content! The fact that I left the Bürgerbräukeller earlier than
usual is a corroboration of Providence's intention to let me reach my goal."

First he demanded information on the wounded and charged Schaub
with the task of doing everything possible for them, then he began to
hypothesize out loud on possible conspirators. He concluded that the
bombing must have been planned by two known British intelligence
agents. Captain S. Payne Best and Major R. Stevens were privately negotiating with one of Heydrich's secret agents who was posing as an OKW
captain in the anti-Nazi conspiracy. Acting immediately on Hitler's conjecture, Himmler detrained and telephoned an order to kidnap the two
Britons in Holland.

The following afternoon Stevens and Best were trapped in Venlo and
brought across the border to Germany for questioning. Hours later the
real bomber was arrested at the Swiss border and returned to Munich.
Under glaring arc lights in an interrogation room at Gestapo headquarters
Elser admitted he had planted the bomb. No, he had no accomplices. He
had done it to end the war. He described in detail how he had cut the
panel and come back to set the clock.

Upon reading the Gestapo report Hitler angrily scrawled on it:
"What idiot conducted this interrogation?" It was ridiculous, he thought,
to imagine that Elser was a lone wolf. Wasn't it obvious that this was a
wide conspiracy involving his worst enemies: the English, the Jews, the
Freemasons and Otto Strasser?

Himmler personally tried to beat the truth out of the prisoner. According to one witness, he cursed wildly as he drove his boots hard into
the body of the handcuffed Elser. Despite the kicks and a beating "with a
whip or some similar instrument," the little cabinetmaker stubbornly
held to his testimony. Even under hypnosis, Elser repeated his story. This
convinced Heydrich that Elser had no accomplice, but the Führer bitterly
reproached Himmler for failing to find the real criminals.*

* Perhaps that is why Himmler saw to it that Elser was not brought to public trial and
executed. Instead he was installed as a privileged prisoner in a concentration camp;
Elser alone could confirm that the SD had, in fact, found the one and only criminal.
Later Elser smuggled a letter to Captain Best, a fellow prisoner. In it he swore that he
had been summoned to the office of the commandant of Dachau in October 1939
where two men—presumably Heydrich agents—persuaded him to plant a bomb in the
Bürgerbräukeller. It was to explode as soon as Hitler left the building and kill a group of
traitors who were plotting against the Führer. Elser agreed and was released from the
concentration camp to install the bomb. At Berlin Gestapo headquarters he was told by

The official version of the plot was bizarre: Elser was a Communist "deviationist" who had been persuaded by the National Socialist "deviationist," Otto Strasser, to become the tool of the British Secret Service. To this main plot propagandists added subplots. One pamphlet claimed that the English agents not only set off the bomb in Munich but were responsible for the political murders and mysterious deaths of such notable figures as Lord Kitchener, Archduke Franz Ferdinand and King Alexander of Yugoslavia.

Besides inciting hatred for England, the attempted assassination was exploited to bolster the Führer's popularity. Messages of congratulation on his narrow escape arrived from Germans on every level of society. The Catholic press throughout the Reich piously declared that it was the miraculous working of Providence which had protected the Führer. Cardinal Faulhaber sent a telegram and instructed that a Te Deum be sung in the cathedral of Munich, "to thank Divine Providence in the name of the archdiocese for the Führer's fortunate escape." The Pope, who had yet to explicitly condemn Germany's liquidation of Poland, sent his special personal congratulations. But Hitler doubted his sincerity. "He would much rather have seen the plot succeed," he told a group at dinner and, when Frank protested that Pius XII had always been a good friend of Germany, added "That's possible but he's no friend of mine."

Hitler gave thanks to his own inner voice as well as to Providence for quitting the beer hall ahead of time. He told Hoffmann: "I had the most extraordinary feeling and I don't myself know how or why—but I felt compelled to leave the cellar just as quickly as I could." Foreign observers, however, had other theories. "Most of us think it smells of another Reichstag fire," wrote Shirer in his diary.

4

Twelve days after the bombing Hitler issued War Directive No. 8. The land invasion would be conducted as planned but he forbade bombardment of centers of population in Holland, Belgium and Luxembourg "without compelling military necessity." This was more pragmatic than humanitarian and revealed Hitler's ultimate goal. His real intent in attacking the West was to secure his rear for the assault on Russia, not to con-

---

the same two agents that he was going to be used as a prosecution witness at a trial of the English agents. He would testify that Otto Strasser had introduced him to Best and Stevens, who paid him to plant the bomb. But Best and Stevens were never tried and survived five years in various concentration camps.

quer territory in Europe or destroy England, which might later be in-veigled into condoning his drive to the East.

A few days later he called a special conference, this time inviting not only his commanders-in-chief but those who would lead the attack. The meeting took place in the chancellery at noon, November 23, and began on a low key. "The purpose of this conference," he explained, "is to give you an idea of the world of my thoughts, which governs me in the face of future events, and to tell you my decisions." Next he revealed what all his listeners should have already known: that the military with its proud tradition had degenerated into a subservient weapon of a one-man dictatorship. "I have doubted for a long time whether I should strike in the East and then in the West," he said. "Basically I did not organize the armed forces in order *not* to strike. The decision to strike was always in me. Sooner or later I wanted to solve the problem."

It was an open declaration of mastery but there was not a murmur of dissent. It would have defied understanding, so Göring testified later, if any of those present *had* protested. "The Supreme Commander had decided and therefore there was nothing left for a soldier to discuss; and that applies to a field marshal as well as to the ordinary soldier."

Hitler went on to say, "in all modesty," that he was irreplaceable. "The fate of the Reich depends only on me. I shall deal accordingly." He admitted that his entire plan was a gamble, yet somehow made his admission aggressive. "I have to choose between victory or destruction," he said. "I choose victory." It was a historical choice, to be compared with the momentous decision of Frederick the Great before the First Silesian War. "I have decided to live my life so that I can stand unashamed if I have to die." Remarkably, he ended with a grim prophecy of his own fate. "I shall stand or fall in this struggle. I shall never survive the defeat of my people." These were truthful words. For Hitler there was only black or white; only complete victory or Götterdämmerung.

That afternoon Hitler read Brauchitsch and Halder a personal lecture on the defeatism of the army high command. Stricken, the former offered his resignation. But Hitler refused to accept it, reminding him that a general had to fulfill his duty and obligation "just like every other soldier." It had been a harrowing day for the military, one described with eloquent brevity in Halder's diary: "A day of crisis!" Both he and Brauchitsch had been so thoroughly cowed by Hitler's threat to annihilate everyone who stood in his way that they made frantic efforts to disassociate themselves from the Resistance.

Exactly one week later it was Stalin's turn to startle the world. On November 30 he invaded Finland, which had repelled a Communist rebellion in 1918 with the help of German troops. It was an embarrassment for Hitler, not only because of the extremely friendly relations between Germans and Finns but also because it weakened the already tenuous bonds with Mussolini. The Italians, from the first opponents of the Russo-German pact, were as indignant over the unprovoked Soviet invasion of Finland as the West. The official organ of the papacy, *Osservatore Romano*, which had followed the Pope's lead in failing to condemn Fascist or Nazi incursions, now joined him in excoriating the Soviet attack as a calculated act of aggression. So much pressure was exerted on Mussolini from church and civilian sources that, "for the first time," wrote Ciano, "he desired German defeat." In fact, on December 26 he authorized his son-in-law to inform the representatives of Belgium and Holland that they were about to be invaded by Hitler.*

For a week Mussolini was in a turmoil, vacillating between fear that his ally might succeed and hope that he would. On New Year's Eve he considered entering the war on Hitler's side but when signs multiplied that Germany was on the point of invading the West he sat down and in the role of big brother wrote his junior partner a letter of advice. Never had Il Duce spoken out so boldly and his own frankness concerned him so that it was not until January 5, 1940, that he finally gave Ciano permission to send it off. He urged Hitler to refrain from invading the West. Both sides would lose such a war. "Now that you have secured your eastern frontiers and created the Greater Reich of ninety million inhabitants, is it worth while to risk all—including the regime—and sacrifice the flower of German generations in order to hasten the fall of a fruit which must of necessity fall and be harvested by us, who represent the new forces of Europe? The big democracies carry within themselves the seeds of their decadence."

He then criticized the treaty with Russia in a manner that he must have known would provoke the Führer. "I feel that you cannot abandon the anti-Semitic and anti-Bolshevist banner which you have been flying for twenty years and for which so many of your comrades have died; you cannot renounce your gospel, in which the German people have blindly believed." Four months ago the Soviet Union was world enemy number one; how could she now be friend number one? "The day when we shall have demolished Bolshevism we shall have kept faith with our two Revolutions."

Attolico delivered this unique letter by hand on the afternoon of January 8. The Führer, understandably, was in no mood to answer and put it

---

* The Belgian ambassador in Rome rashly transmitted this warning to Brussels by telegram. The message was intercepted and deciphered by the Germans.

aside. This was the high point of Mussolini's effort to free himself from domination by his ally but, having asserted himself, he experienced an almost immediate predictable reaction and began slipping back into his servile role.

5

Neither Hitler nor Mussolini knew that the British were seriously considering declaring war on the U.S.S.R. over the Finnish invasion, thanks in large part to the pressure exerted by church groups and the Cliveden Set, which argued that the real enemy was Red Russia, not Germany. After all, Hitler's demands on Poland were reasonable and only his manner was obnoxious. In the meantime the shooting war against Hitler had diminished to one in name only. On a train trip skirting the French frontier, the crew told William Shirer that not a shot had been fired on this front since the war began. Then he saw for himself that both sides seemed to be observing an unofficial armistice. "For that matter one blast from a French '75' could have liquidated our train. The Germans were hauling up guns and supplies on the railroad line, but the French did not disturb them. Queer kind of war." So queer, in fact, that when a former First Lord of the Admiralty suggested that the RAF bomb the timber areas of southwestern Germany, the British Air Minister, Sir Kingsley Wood, replied: "Oh, you can't do that. That's private property. You'll be asking me to bomb the Ruhr next."

Hitler's main offensive weapon in these unsettled days was Goebbels, brought back to full favor by the outbreak of war. The force of his propaganda campaign was directed against the French; his purpose was to divide them from the British. Goebbels visited the Westwall in the bitter rain and snow so he could determine first hand what the poilu a few hundred yards away in the Maginot Line was experiencing. He concluded that the average French soldier was so weary, miserable and bored that he would be a ready victim of his concerns and prejudices. "Goebbels knew," recalled his secretary, Werner Naumann, "that the average little French soldier only wanted a good bed, a woman, a warm room, his garden and peace of mind." He worried about the Jews, the English and, above all, this ridiculous war. The Propaganda Minister, therefore, instructed German soldiers to shout friendly greetings across no man's land and engage the French in brotherly conversation. Propaganda teams blasted information and news over loudspeakers, aimed at proving that France and Germany were really not enemies. At night sentimental French songs were broadcast to the Maginot Line and before signing off the announcer would say something like: "Good night, dear enemy, we don't like this war any more than you do. Who is responsible? Not you or I and so why shoot each other? Another day has ended and we will all have a good night's sleep." The final touch would be a recorded lullaby. In the daytime the French troops were showered with leaflets showing a shivering poilu at the front in one picture and his wife in bed with an English soldier in another.

The French civilians were approached differently. They were bombarded with broadcasts over secret transmitters illustrating the corruption of their government, the profiteering of Jews and the terrifying might of Hitler's army and air force. One particularly effective leaflet was a German version of the prophecies of Nostradamus which foretold the conquest of France by the Third Reich.

At home Goebbels ordered Germans to harden themselves for the coming battle. Their very existence was at stake since the enemy was "determined to annihilate Germany for good." In mid-December he forbade newspapers to print a word about peace. "In line with this point of view any sentimental note in connection with Christmas must be avoided in the press and on the radio." Only one day would be celebrated, December 24. To unite front and homeland, the theme of 1939's radio Christmas program would be: "Soldiers' Christmas—People's Christmas."

The British soldiers in France were not at all concerned by Goebbels' propaganda. The war, in fact, had turned into a contest of lame jokes. British civilians were as bored as their troops and referred to it as the *Sitzkrieg* or Phony War. More and more members of Parliament dozed as Chamberlain read off his weekly reports.

Hitler was waiting for a stretch of five clear days to turn a joke into grim battle. His own air chief was in a quandary. Göring had to give the impression of being eager while privately praying for a continuation of the bad weather since he feared his Luftwaffe was not yet ready for combat. He attended the daily weather conferences, pestering Chief Meteorologist Diesing for additional information. Hitler also pressed Diesing for longer-range forecasts but he stubbornly refused. "Mein Führer," he replied, "I will gladly be bold and predict weather for three days; but not foolhardy—not five days!"

In desperation Göring hired a rainmaker, Herr Schwefler, for 100,000 marks. It is not clear whether the field marshal ordered him to bring five clear days or to continue the bad weather but it would not have made any difference since Schwefler's only equipment turned out to be a defunct commercial radio set. On the other hand, Milch was hoping for good weather since he agreed with Hitler that time was on the side of the enemy. Despite its deficiencies, the Luftwaffe still enjoyed air superiority, an advantage that was steadily decreasing with the flow of planes to both England and France from the United States.

On January 10, 1940, the impatient Führer fixed another specific date for invasion: a week later at exactly fifteen minutes before sunrise. Fate intervened before the day was over. A light Luftwaffe plane strayed across the frontier, crash-landing in Belgium. Of all of the German planes in the sky that day, this was the most important. It carried an unauthorized passenger, Major Helmut Reinberger, who had a briefcase filled with the operation plans for the airborne attack on Belgium. While Reinberger was burning the papers he was seized by Belgian soldiers; but he reported optimistically to Luftwaffe headquarters through the German Embassy in Brussels that he had succeeded in burning the plans to "insignificant fragments, the size of the palm of his hand." Göring, in a state of consternation, experimented by burning a similar packet of papers. The results were so inconclusive that his wife suggested using clairvoyants, not unusual advice to a man who utilized a rainmaker. The team of clairvoyants unanimously agreed that not a scrap of the documents remained.

Their report may have relieved Göring but not Hitler. He canceled the invasion order on the assumption that the plans had been revealed to the enemy. He, not the clairvoyants, was correct. Enough fragments had remained for the Belgians to learn of the invasion. This information was passed on to London where it was received with considerable suspicion. Halifax, for instance, told the cabinet, "I doubt very much whether the documents are genuine." The General Staff agreed; obviously the papers had been planted. They were engrossed in their own offensive, the landing of an expeditionary force in Norway. The very concept of such a *coup de main* appealed to Churchill, the new First Lord of the Admiralty; and, despite his sad experience in a similar venture in the Great War, he pressed the issue until the cabinet was won over.

Hitler was also preparing to seize Norway. He had not even considered such action—after all, these were Nordic peoples who could be counted on to remain neutral as they had in 1914—until his ally, Stalin, upset calculations by invading Finland. This, Hitler feared, might give the Allies an excuse to move into Norway, thus outflanking Germany from the north. He authorized a study of a possible invasion but it was given low priority. Then, late in February, alarming reports of an imminent British landing in Scandinavia turned the Führer into an ardent advocate—out of concern that a British foothold in Norway would close off the Baltic and bottle up all his submarines. Equally foreboding was the economic threat. More than half of Germany's iron ore came from Norway and Sweden; an end to this supply would cripple her war production. On March 1, 1940, therefore, Hitler issued a directive for the simultaneous occupation of Denmark and Norway. It was to have "the character of a *peaceful* occupation, designed to protect by force of arms the neutrality of the northern countries," but resistance would be "broken by all means available."

Hitler became so concerned by the time element that within two days he decided to launch his attack—the "most daring and most important undertaking in the history of warfare"—before invading the West. It would begin on March 15.

In the meantime he had been attempting to shore up deteriorating relations with his two allies. Those with Russia, in particular, had entered a disturbing phase. Negotiations for a trade agreement had started soon after the conquest of Poland. A visit of a thirty-seven-man German economic delegation to Moscow was followed by an even larger Soviet mission to Berlin, which brought a list of industrial and military orders totaling more than one and a half billion Reichsmarks. The Germans were dismayed since most of the orders were for machinery and armaments essential to their own war production. The result was a bitter and lengthy wrangle finally brought to a head by Stalin himself. He querulously declared that if Germany did not give way "the treaty would not be concluded."

Hitler could not permit this, and early in February Ribbentrop was instructed to send a personal letter to Stalin urging him to re-examine the German position. Apparently Stalin, whose hardheaded negotiations had already wrung concessions from the Germans, realized he had pushed his ally to the limit. (Two months earlier his archenemy, Trotsky, had observed: "Before the hour of Hitler's defeat strikes, many, very many in Europe will be wiped out. Stalin does not want to be among them and so he is wary of detaching himself from Hitler too early.") In one of his lightning changes, Stalin called for an end of bickering. He agreed to accept German deliveries over a period of twenty-seven months while promising delivery of raw materials over a period of eighteen months. With all difficulties removed, the trade pact was signed three days later. The German delegation was delighted. "The agreement," reported the chairman, "means a wide-open door to the East for us."

Hitler was pleased as well as relieved. He had become even more fascinated by his counterpart in the Kremlin. Stalin was the only world leader he wanted to know intimately and he interrogated envoys from Russia at length for the most trivial details about his ally. Often, recalled Christa Schröder, he would interrupt to exclaim enthusiastically, "That Stalin is a brute, but really you must admit he's an extraordinary fellow." It was almost as if he were talking about himself.

The solution of this Russian problem was accompanied by the termination of another when the Finns were forced to accept harsh Soviet peace terms that March to end their brief, bloody war. Greatly relieved at being freed from the embarrassment of having to give moral support to such an unpopular cause, Hitler turned to more productive arenas. One of these was Italy. He had just made a step in this direction by finally answering Mussolini's letter of unwelcome advice. Hitler vindicated all his actions in minute detail, taking time out to rhapsodize about Italy, using as many italicized words as a schoolgirl writing of her latest crush.

Naturally a letter delayed so long could only be delivered by a prestigious messenger. And so the following day, March 9, Foreign Minister von Ribbentrop left Berlin with a large retinue: advisers, secretaries, barbers, a doctor, a gymnastics teacher and a masseur. At their first meeting Il Duce gave a guarded answer to Ribbentrop's question: Would Italy participate in the war? He intended, he said, "to intervene in the conflict and to fight a war parallel to that of Germany." *But* he must be free to choose the date. Ribbentrop attempted in vain to tie Mussolini down more definitely but he would merely agree to see Hitler. The following Monday, March 18, the two dictators met at the Brenner Pass in a snowstorm. The session was cordial with Hitler dominating the conversation. But he spoke quietly and made few gestures. He had come, he said, "simply to explain the situation" so Il Duce could make his own decision.

To Schmidt's surprise, Mussolini used his few minutes of talk to reassert emphatically his intention of coming into a war. It was merely a matter of choosing the best moment, he said. The two men departed in an aura of eternal trust and friendship. But Hitler instructed Schmidt not to submit a copy of the interview to the Italians. "One never knows who may read this document on the Italian side, and what Allied diplomats may be told." For his part, Il Duce seemed to belie his recent vow to join the war. On the return trip to Rome he pointed out the train window to the thick fall of snowflakes with the remark that he would need snow as far south as Etna to turn Italians into a race of warriors. Although irritated that the Führer had done almost all the talking, he was now convinced his ally was not preparing to launch any land offensive.

6

Recently the Schirachs had come upon the Führer in the chancellery library reading a book with the help of glasses.* He hurriedly put them

---

* Hitler's secretaries used a special large-print typewriter so he could read in public without glasses.

away (Hoffmann was forbidden to take pictures when he wore them) and rubbed his eyes. "You see," he confessed, "I need glasses. I am getting old and that is why I prefer to wage war at fifty rather than sixty." He ruffled the pages of his book, a picture album containing photographs of London. "How gratifying not to find any baroque buildings," he murmured, then snapped the book shut. "I must not look at this sort of thing any more."

He was determined that Germany should be first in Norway and on April 2 ordered the invasion to begin at 5:15 A.M. a week later. The anti-Hitler conspirators were just as determined to hamstring the invasion. To do so they needed Halder. He had recently promised to help but was wavering and, to bring him to action, he was shown Müller's memorandum summarizing the Pope's participation in secret peace negotiations with the English. The chief of the army General Staff was impressed but reduced to tears. His conscience, he sobbed, would not permit him to act.

The failure of this plot failed to discourage the redoubtable Colonel Oster. He decided to stop Hitler by personal action and early in April secretly informed the Dutch military attaché that Norway was about to be invaded. But the information was forwarded to a member of the Norwegian Legation in Berlin who did not think it worth relaying to Oslo. The British also failed to believe similar reports that Hitler was doing what they themselves planned to do a day or so later. Remarkably, an aura of overconfidence had enveloped 10 Downing Street.

On Sunday morning, April 7, five German naval groups put to sea destined for six Norwegian cities. At three of these ports—Narvik, Trondheim and Stavanger—waited German merchant ships with combat troops hidden in their holds. British ships were laying mines in Norwegian waters below Narvik in preparation for their own invasion and HMS *Glowworm* sighted two German destroyers. It was assumed in London that these ships were part of a limited force intent on capturing Narvik. Not until Monday morning did the cabinet learn that enemy warships were also approaching at least three other Norwegian ports. The ministers were aghast but it was too late to thwart Hitler.

Early Tuesday morning the Germans struck. By 8 A.M. Narvik was seized by two battalions of special mountain troops under the command of Brigadier General Eduard Dietl, an intimate of the Führer since the Beer Hall Putsch. Before noon four other important ports fell but the raiders were delayed long enough by defenders in the ancient fortress of Oskarberg to allow the royal family, the government and members of Parliament to escape from Oslo by special train while twenty-three trucks

were carting off the gold of the Bank of Norway and the secret papers of
the Foreign Office.

In Denmark the Germans met little resistance, their plan working as
it had been laid out on paper. For some reason the Danish navy never
opened fire and the land troops only managed to inflict twenty casualties
on the invaders. It was all over by midmorning. The King capitulated, ordering all resistance to cease. He assured the chief of staff of the German
task force that he would do everything possible to keep peace and order in
the country. Then he turned complimentary. "You Germans," he said,
"have done the incredible again! One must admit that it is magnificent
work!"

By the end of the day it appeared as if Hitler had scored a complete
triumph in Norway as well—until the British navy unexpectedly appeared.
On Wednesday morning five destroyers broke into Narvik harbor to sink
two destroyers and all but one cargo ship. Three days later the *Warspite*
returned with a flotilla of destroyers and sank the rest of the German vessels.

This news so agitated Hitler that he told Brauchitsch it didn't look as
though they could possibly hold Narvik. By April 17 his vexation was apparent. He railed at everyone in sight. While Brauchitsch, Keitel and
Halder held their tongues, Chief of Operations Jodl brusquely announced
that there was but one thing to do: "Concentrate, hold on and do not
give up." To the consternation of the onlookers, he and Hitler began arguing as if they were equals. Finally, in a temper, the chief of operations
stormed out of the room, slamming the door. Hitler said not a word.
Tight-lipped, he left by another door but that night he signed an order to
Dietl: "Hold on as long as possible." The nineteenth brought a new crisis.
From his hide-out on the rugged northern coast of Norway, King Haakon
VII, the sole monarch of the century elected to the throne by popular
vote, steadfastly refused to name a government headed by Vidkun Quis-
ling, the leader of a Norwegian Fascist party and a disciple of Rosenberg.

By this time the British had finally landed two brigades of 13,000
men near Narvik and Trondheim. As their attack gained momentum more
British arrived, and by the end of the week the Germans were in desperate
straits. But Milch came to the rescue by taking personal command of the
Luftwaffe attack. He sent two huge seaplanes loaded with mountain
troops to Narvik; then supervised dive-bombing strikes that weakened the
British and Norwegian resistance in central Norway. By April 28 the British ordered evacuation of the bulk of their troops. The following day King
Haakon and members of his government were transferred by British

cruiser to Tromsö, a city far above the Arctic Circle, where a provisional capital was established.

Most of Norway was now under German control except for Narvik where Dietl's 6000 men still gallantly held off 20,000 Allied troops. On the last day of April Jodl informed Hitler that communications had finally been established overland between Oslo and Trondheim. At lunch Hitler, "beside himself with joy," admitted his error and thanked Jodl for his contributions to the victory. The Führer also showed his gratitude to Dietl and Milch with promotions. He was unstinting in his praise of the latter, remarking at one conference how Milch had taken over the Luftwaffe in Norway when it appeared that all was lost. "And why?" he asked rhetorically, conveniently forgetting his own argument with Jodl. "Because there was a man like me, who just did not know the word 'impossible.'"

With the northern flank secure, Hitler again devoted his energy to the invasion of the West. He had never liked the original plan of attack, an unimaginative version of that used in the World War: an attack through northern France and Belgium to the Channel ports. Its objective was not only to smash the French army but, by occupying the Channel coast, to cut the British off from their ally while establishing submarine and air bases for attacks on the British Isles.

"This is just the old Schlieffen plan," he objected to Keitel and Jodl, "with a strong right flank along the Atlantic coast; you won't get away with an operation like that twice running." Even if it succeeded, it violated his principle of Blitzkrieg warfare and he had vowed never to allow this generation to suffer what *he* had in Flanders. He envisioned a daring thrust farther south through the Ardennes with a sudden armored breakthrough at Sedan and a sweep to the Channel. The main force would then swing to the north, in a reversal of the Schlieffen plan, for a drive into the rear of the retreating Anglo-French army. Night after night his adjutants would see him poring over a specially constructed relief map to make sure that the Sedan was, after all, the correct place to penetrate.

Independently, perhaps the most brilliant strategist of the Wehrmacht, Colonel General Fritz Erich von Manstein, had devised a similar offensive. He presented it to Brauchitsch, who rejected it on the grounds that it was too risky. But the Führer heard talk of Manstein's "risky" proposal and asked him for the details. To Manstein's surprise, Hitler was delighted with what he heard. It not only reinforced his own convictions but contained a number of improvements to his own plan. The supreme command liked Hitler's revised version no more than they had Manstein's. To a man they opposed it but the Führer overrode all objections, deriding opponents as "Schlieffen worshipers," embalmed in a "petrified" strategy. "They should have read more Karl May!"

The Hitler-Manstein offensive was formally adopted in late February and by the time the battle for Norway was ended there were 136 German divisions ready for action along the western front. They waited only for a stretch of good weather. On May Day Hitler set the invasion for the fifth but forty-eight hours later, after another unfavorable meteorological report, he postponed X-Day until the seventh—and then the eighth. Göring was pleading for still more time when alarming news arrived from Holland: cancellation of furloughs, evacuations and road blocks. Agitated, Hitler agreed to another postponement until Friday, May 10, but added, "not a day longer!" The sustained effort at the front to keep two million men at the point of attack, he said, was becoming increasingly difficult.

By now he was determined to strike without waiting for the five-day favorable weather prerequisite which had already cost three months. He was gambling on the tool that had proved so valuable in the past—his "intuition," that is, a suspension of logic born of impatience. On Thursday morning a corps commander near Aachen reported heavy fog in his area. This was followed by a prediction that the fog would lift and the tenth would be a good day. Hitler ordered his special train prepared for departure from a small station outside of Berlin and went through elaborate measures to keep his own inner circle in the dark as to its destination and purpose. Outwardly calm during the tedious train trip, he was gnawed with worry that evening as the deadline for confirmation of the attack order approached. The train stopped near Hannover for a final weather report. This time Chief Meteorologist Diesing (who later got a gold watch as a reward) predicted good weather for the tenth. Hitler confirmed the order to attack at dawn, then retired earlier than usual. But he could not get to sleep. Despite the report he kept worrying about the weather.

A greater peril to success came from his own intelligence service. Of the few Hitler had entrusted with the final details of the invasion, one was Admiral Canaris and whatever he knew was passed on to his impetuous deputy, Colonel Oster. Earlier that evening Oster had reported to his old friend the Dutch military attaché, over the dinner table, that Hitler had issued the final attack order. After the meal Oster stopped off at OKW headquarters in the Bendlerstrasse and got information that there would be no last-minute postponement. "The swine has gone to the western front," he told the Dutch attaché, who first informed a Belgian colleague, then phoned The Hague in code: "Tomorrow, at dawn. Hold tight!"

At 4:25 A.M. on the tenth the Führer's train reached its destination, Euskirchen, a town near the Holland-Belgian borders. Under a canopy of stars, the party was driven to the Führer's new headquarters, *Felsennest* (Rocky Nest). Dawn was breaking as they settled into the bunker installation which had been blasted out of a wooded mountaintop. Checking his watch, Hitler got an unwelcome surprise ("I was filled with rage"). Dawn had come fifteen minutes earlier than he had been told it would.

Twenty-five miles to the west his troops were charging across the Belgian, Holland and Luxembourg borders. The air was darkened with his Luftwaffe. Twenty-five hundred aircraft had been gathered for the attack, far outnumbering those the Allies could send up. Wave after wave of German planes swept westward to devastate more than seventy enemy airfields. Airborne troops captured key points in Holland while glider forces swooped down prepared to capture Belgian fortresses by surprise. The Führer was patricularly interested in the attack on Fort Eben Emael. He had personally briefed the commanders and non-coms involved in this glider operation, using a scale model for the purpose, and he awaited reports "feverishly." By noon of the eleventh, this supposedly impregnable fortress, along with a bridge over the Meuse, was in German hands. On hearing this Hitler literally hugged himself with joy. Later came even more meaningful information: the enemy were striking back! "When the news came that the enemy was advancing along the whole front," Hitler recalled, "I could have wept for joy; they'd fallen into the trap! It had been a clever piece of work to attack Liège. We had to make them believe we were remaining faithful to the old Schlieffen plan."

7

On May 10 England and France were caught by surprise, their General Staffs not heeding the warnings from Brussels and The Hague or their own intelligence experts.* Pale and somber, Chamberlain wanted to stay on as Prime Minister but he was persuaded to step down. King George VI accepted his resignation regretfully and suggested that Halifax succeed him. But it was obvious that Winston Churchill alone had the confidence of the nation and at 6 P.M. His Majesty summmoned him to the palace.

---

* In 1938 MI-6, the British secret intelligence service, had bought the secret of a German cipher machine (called "Enigma") from a Polish mathematician for £10,000, a British passport and a resident's permit in France for himself and his wife. He had memorized diagrams of the main parts of the machine and created a replica in an apartment on the Left Bank in Paris. A working model of Enigma was successfully completed and installed in Bletchley Park, a Victorian mansion forty miles north of London. By the time England declared war in 1939 the machine, code-named Ultra, was operational; and its first major contribution was to warn the British General Staff of Hitler's plan to invade the West.

Churchill had once paid a grudging compliment to the Führer in a letter to the *Times*: "I have always said that I hoped if Great Britain were beaten in a war we should find a Hitler who would lead us back to our rightful place among nations." These words had not mollified the Führer, who continued to look upon Churchill as his worst enemy, the tool of those English Jews who had scotched an Anglo-German alliance. It was a profound hatred contrasting strangely with his admiration for Stalin, and Churchill's elevation to Prime Minister was galling news.

As Hitler's troops and tanks advanced into Holland and Belgium, Goebbels prepared his staff for the next step in the propaganda war. "The minister," read the secret staff meeting of May 11, "formulates the principle for the immediate future that anything in enemy reports that is not correct or even anything that could be dangerous to us must immediately be denied. There is no need at all to examine whether the report is factually correct or not—the decisive point is merely whether the enemy's assertions could in any way be damaging to us." More important, the French and English must be told again and again that it was they who had declared war. "It was *their* war which was now bursting upon them. On no account must we allow ourselves to be maneuvered once more into the role of aggressor."

The drive into western Belgium gained the most impressive victories. This, of course, was part of Hitler's plan to divert attention from the main attack through the hills of the Ardennes. By May 13 these troops had crossed the Meuse at several points to approach Sedan where Hitler hoped to break through the weak link in the Maginot Line.

Despite the steady advance in the north, Hitler was disturbed by the stubborn defense put up by the outnumbered Dutch troops and, on the morning of the fourteenth, issued a directive to break this resistance "speedily." Detachments of the Luftwaffe were sent from the Belgian area "to facilitate the rapid conquest of Fortress Holland." Within hours the Luftwaffe dropped ninety-eight tons of high explosives on Rotterdam. The intent was to eliminate Dutch resistance at the bridges over the Nieuwe Maas but the bombs slammed into the center of the city, killing 814 civilians. The facts were grossly misrepresented by the democratic press, which listed the death toll as between 25,000 and 30,000. Nor did Western newspapers reveal that the tacit agreement between the two sides to limit bombing to military targets had been first violated by the British. Three days earlier, over strenuous French objections, thirty-five Royal Air Force bombers had attacked an industrial city in the Rhineland, killing four civilians, including an Englishwoman. "This raid on the night of 11th May, although in itself trivial, was an epoch-making event," commented F. J. P.

Veale, an English jurist, "since it was the first deliberate breach of the fundamental rule of civilized warfare that hostilities must only be waged against the enemy combatant forces." Despite Hitler's frightful retaliation in Holland, he resisted proposals to bomb London itself. He was not willing to go that far—as yet. The tragedy of Rotterdam ended Dutch resistance, the commander-in-chief of the Dutch forces ordering his men to lay down arms a few hours later. That same day German tanks burst through the French Ninth and Second Armies at Sedan. Supported by screaming Stuka dive bombers, three long columns of Panzers rattled and rumbled toward the English Channel.

Churchill was wakened the next morning by a telephone call from Paris. "We have been defeated!" exclaimed Premier Reynaud. "We are beaten!" Churchill could not believe it, nor could his generals, who had misread the armored conquest of Poland as a simple maneuver against an inept, primitive defense.

The terror that seized France was aggravated by Goebbels. "The task of the secret transmitter, from now on," he told his staff on May 17, "is to use every means to create a mood of panic in France. . . . It must further utter an urgent warning against the dangers of a 'Fifth Column' which undoubtedly includes all German refugees. It should point out that, in the present situation, even the Jews from Germany are nothing but German agents." That morning Hitler motored forward to Bastogne in the heart of the Ardennes. "All the world hearkens!" he declared triumphantly. He had come to the headquarters of Army Group A, commanded by General Gerd von Rundstedt, to discuss progress of the main drive to the Channel and was in such an expansive mood that he stayed for lunch and later walked among the men exuding success.

Back in the homeland, it was the rare German who did not share his exultation. Most of those who had once feared Hitler was traveling too fast and too dangerously had become true believers in his infallibility. Four industrialists, including Alfried Krupp, grew so excited as they listened to the radio reports of the drive through Holland that they began poking their fingers at a map of northeastern Europe jabbering: "This one here is yours; that one there is ours; we shall have that man arrested; he has two factories. . . ." One industrialist left the hubbub to phone a subordinate to get Wehrmacht permission for two of the group to visit Holland at once.

By the morning of May 19 several armored divisions were within fifty miles of the Channel and one, the 2nd, rolled into Abbeville at the mouth of the Somme the following evening. The trap was sprung and inside the giant net were the Belgians, the entire British Expeditionary Force and three French armies. Hitler was so surprised when Brauchitsch telephoned him of the capture of Abbeville that his voice choked with emotion. He praised everyone. Jodl wrote in his diary that the Führer went into raptures. "Talks in words of appreciation of the German Army and its leadership. Busies himself with the peace treaty which shall express this theme: return of territory robbed over the last 400 years from the German people, and of other values."

Things were turning out exactly as he had dreamed. Within three days the tanks of Army Group A had wheeled north, closing on the Channel ports of Calais and Dunkirk, whose capture would cut off the British from a sea retreat to England. Göring slammed his big hand on a table when he heard the report. "This is a special job for the Luftwaffe!" he exclaimed. "I must speak to the Führer at once. Get a line through by phone!" In moments he was assuring Hitler unconditionally that the Luftwaffe by itself could annihilate the trapped remnants of the enemy. All he asked was withdrawal of German tanks and ground troops so that they wouldn't be hit by friendly bombs. Having resumed his feud with both the Wehrmacht and army high commands, Hitler might have seen this as an opportunity to strengthen his hold on the military. He gave Göring consent to finish off the enemy from the air.

Overhearing this, Jodl sarcastically remarked to an adjutant, "There goes Göring shooting off his big mouth again!" then dutifully began making the necessary arrangements over the phone with Göring's chief of staff. "We have done it!" Göring exulted to Milch on his return to air force headquarters. "The Luftwaffe is to wipe out the British on the beaches. I have managed to talk the Führer round to halting the army." Milch did not share his enthusiasm and objected that their bombs would sink too deeply into the sand before exploding. Besides, the Luftwaffe was not strong enough for such an operation. "Leave it to me, it's not your business," said Göring and returned to his boasting. "The army always wants to act like gentlemen. They round up the British as prisoners with as little harm to them as possible. But the Führer wants to teach them a lesson they won't easily forget."

The following morning, May 24, Hitler visited Rundstedt and his staff at Group A's forward headquarters. In high spirits, the Führer predicted that the war would be over in six weeks. Then the way would be free for an agreement with the English. All he wanted from them was their acknowledgment of Germany's position on the Continent. When they got down to tactics, General von Rundstedt did not oppose the use of planes to reduce the entrapped enemy at Dunkirk. He proposed that tanks be halted at the canal below the besieged city. Hitler agreed with his observation that this armor should be saved for operations against the French. At 12:45 P.M. the halt order was issued to the Fourth Army in the Führer's name.

That evening four Panzer divisions were stopped at the Aa Canal. The tank crews were astounded. No fire was coming from the opposite shore. Beyond they could make out the peaceful spires of Dunkirk. Had Operations gone crazy? The division commanders were even more amazed. They knew they could take Dunkirk with little trouble since the British were still heavily engaged near Lille. Why weren't they allowed to seize the last escape port to England?

Army Chief of Staff Halder was contemptuous. "Our left wing, consisting of armor and motorized forces," he wrote in his diary, "will thus be stopped in its tracks on the direct order of the Führer! Finishing off the encircled army is to be left to the Luftwaffe!" Halder was convinced, with some reason, that Göring was merely looking for personal glory and had won over the Führer by arguing that if the army generals got the victory Hitler's own prestige at home would be damaged beyond repair.

The ground commanders reiterated their request to move into Dunkirk with tanks and infantry, but Hitler would not listen. It was only on May 26, after reports of heavy shipping in the Channel (was it possible the British were preparing to evacuate their forces?), that he grudgingly authorized an advance on Dunkirk from the west. But that same day Göring assured him that the Luftwaffe had destroyed Dunkirk harbor. "Only fish bait will reach the other side. I hope the Tommies are good swimmers."

As the English and Allied troops fell back into the cul-de-sac, a crazy-quilt fleet of almost 900 vessels began leaving dozens of English ports. There were warships and sailboats, launches and strange-looking Dutch craft—manned by career officers, fishermen, tugboat operators, expert amateur seamen and Sunday sailors who had never before ventured beyond the three-mile limit. This was Operation Dynamo, a mission to evacuate 45,000 men in two days. But this modest estimate had not taken into consideration Hitler's low opinion of democracy in action. He was completely surprised by a sporting operation carried out gallantly and effectively by a pickup group of amateurs and professionals. By the thirtieth of May, 126,606 men were back in England—and more were coming every hour.

Hitler's commanders were no more perceptive. That day Halder wrote in his diary that the encircled enemy was disintegrating. Admittedly some were fleeing across the Channel "on anything that floats," but he described this disparagingly as another *Le Débâcle*, a reference to Zola's novel about the French rout in the Franco-Prussian War. By midday, however, the German high command finally realized the extent of the evacuation and massive bombing attacks were mounted. But fog came to the rescue of the British. Not only was Dunkirk itself enshrouded but all the Luftwaffe fields were blanketed by low clouds which grounded their three thousand bombers.

In the meantime the Stukas of the Eighth Air Corps were doing surprisingly little damage to the flotilla of small vessels; and those bombs dropped on the beaches dug so deeply before exploding that casualties were low. Equally surprising was the performance of a new British fighter plane, the Spitfire, which ravaged Göring's fighter squadrons; and once the weather cleared enough for bombers to get into the air, they too were picked off by the deadly little Spitfires.

Oddly, the continuing evacuation did not seem to perturb Hitler. It was almost as though it was no concern of his. While Brauchitsch and Halder frantically looked for ways to stop the steady flow to England, the Führer responded haltingly, almost lackadaisically. It was the commanders who waved their arms at conferences these days, not he. In striking contrast to the Narvik crisis, he pounded no tables, made no threats, called for no frantic measure to stop the exodus to England. He let his subordinates carry the burden of decision.

The thin perimeter of the Dunkirk defense line held until June 4 but by then 338,226 British and Allied troops had been ferried to England to fight another day. Now speculation arose on both sides of the Channel regarding Hitler's strange behavior. Why had he given Göring the license to bomb the encircled army "to teach them a lesson," then apparently assisted in their escape by not acting forcefully? His own words only confused matters. He told his naval adjutant that he had expected the BEF would fight to the last man as they had done in *his* war, and hoped to contain them until they ran out of ammunition, thus gaining for himself a mass of prisoners for use in peace negotiations. Yet when this strategy failed—if it had been his strategy—and almost no British were captured, he showed no signs of rage or even petulance.

A variation on this theme was his remark to Linge as they surveyed the pock-marked beaches of Dunkirk, strewn with books, photographs, shoes, rifles, bicycles and other possessions: "It is always good to let a broken army return home to show the civilian population what a beating they have had." He also told Bormann that he had purposely spared the English. "Churchill," he complained, "was quite unable to appreciate the sporting spirit of which I had given proof by refraining from creating an irreparable breach between the British and ourselves."

The military men, including all the adjutants, smiled at those who believed the Führer had been motivated by political or humanitarian considerations. "That Hitler purposely let the British escape, belongs to the realm of fables," commented Puttkamer. Others equally close to Hitler were sure he had been moved to pity by his affection for the English. "The blood of every single Englishman is too valuable to be shed," he told Frau Troost. "Our two people belong together, racially and traditionally—this is and always has been my aim even if our generals can't grasp it." Competent foreign observers gave some credence to this theory. François-Poncet, for instance, was convinced that Hitler never really wanted to war with the English—only to neutralize them.

He had given witness to this recently by sending Unity Mitford home via Zurich in a special train. He deeply regretted her fate, he told Engel. "She lost her nerve, just when, for the first time, I could really have used her." It was a hostile England to which she returned; her brother-in-law, Sir Oswald Mosley, together with other leaders of the British Union of Fascists, were jailed without trial three days after Hitler invaded Belgium to prevent his propaganda for peace. Mosley had already admonished his Blackshirts to remain steadfast and loyal to their native land. His attitude was: "I will fight to the last day to keep England and Germany friends and prevent war, but the moment war is declared I will fight for my country." Lady Diana Mosley soon followed her husband into prison on the order of her relative, the Prime Minister, while she was still nursing her eleven-week-old son. The authorities gave her permission to take the baby into Holloway prison, but not his ninteen-month-old brother. One child to a mother was the rule, and she decided to take neither so that they would not be separated. It was fortunate since her cell, its floor swimming in water, had no bed, only a thin mattress. When Mosley became gravely ill three years later, he and his wife were finally released. Public uproar ensued which was derided by George Bernard Shaw. "I think this Mosley panic shameful," he told a girl reporter. "What sort of people are they who can be frightened out of their wits by a single man? Even if Mosley were in rude health, it was high time to release him with apologies for having let him frighten us into scrapping the Habeas Corpus Act. . . . We are still afraid to let Mosley defend himself and we have produced the ridiculous situation in which we may buy Hitler's *Mein Kampf* in any bookshop in Britain, but may not buy ten lines written by Mosley. The whole affair has become too silly for words. Good evening."

Unity Mitford arrived home, the bullet still in her head. Sad and depressed, she was unable to feed herself. She died eight years later when the bullet moved on its own.

8

Hitler left Felsennest on the eve of the fall of Dunkirk with instructions to preserve the entire area as a "national monument." Every room in the complex was to be kept intact, every name-plate to remain on its door. Führer Headquarters was moved to the small Belgian village of Brûly-de-Pesche, near the border of France. By the time Hitler arrived the place was deserted, every inhabitant evacuated. A special garden had been laid out along with gravel paths but the cement of the Führer bunker was still wet. He gave this peaceful scene a warlike name, *Wolfsschlucht* (Wolf's Gorge), after his own nickname of early party days.

By this time King Leopold had not only surrendered Belgium but refused to go into exile. "I have decided to stay," he told his Prime Minister. "The cause of the Allies is lost." This seemed certain on June 5 when 143 German divisions turned on the remnants of the French army—65 divisions. The defenders had few tanks and almost no air cover and the Wehrmacht swept forward on a 400-mile front. In Paris Reynaud made a desperate impossible plea to Roosevelt for "clouds of planes," then packed his bags.

It was an auspicious moment to enter the war on Hitler's side and Mussolini expressed his desire to join the lists. But his ally urged him to wait until the Luftwaffe wiped out the French air force. Il Duce could only restrain himself until June 10 before declaring war, and the supremely confident tone of his explanatory letter to Hitler brought this burst of sarcasm: "I have quite often in the past wondered about his naïveté," the Führer told his military staff. "The whole letter is proof that in the future I must be much more careful with the Italians in political matters. Evidently Mussolini thinks of this as a walk in *Passo romano*." The Italians would get a rude surprise. "First they were too cowardly to take part, now they are in a hurry so that they can share in the spoils."

At dawn thirty-two Italian divisions attacked six French divisions in the south, but with such a lack of drive that any advance had to be measured in feet. By this time both ends of the French line in the north had crumbled and on the morning of the fourteenth German troops began entering Paris. It was one of the few times in the history of modern warfare that the commander of an operation reached the objective before his troops. General von Bock, chief of Army Group B, had flown ahead in his liaison plane, arriving at the Arc de Triomphe just in time to take the salute of the first combat troops. It was a parade, not a battle, and Bock took time off to visit the tomb of Napoleon before having lunch at the Ritz and doing a little shopping.

At Wolf's Gorge, Göring was trying to persuade Hitler to avenge the British bombing of residential areas in Germany. As they conversed in the village square, Colonel Warlimont overheard Göring announce that he could not tolerate these British atrocities any longer and wanted to "give them back ten bombs for every one of theirs." But Hitler could not be swayed. He said, so Warlimont recalled, "he thought it quite possible that the British government was so shaken by Dunkirk that it had temporarily lost its head, alternatively that the reason for the attacks on the civilian population was that the British bombers had inaccuarate bomb sights and were flown by untrained crews. In any case he thought we should wait before taking countermeasures."

The Führer was in a negotiating mood. Capitalizing on the excitement of the fall of Paris, he made a statement to the West by means of a unique interview with Karl von Wiegand of the Hearst press. He asserted that he had had no intention of attacking "the beautiful French capital" so long as it remained an open city, then vehemently denied it had been his aim or intention to destroy the British Empire. And all he asked from the United States was a regional Monroe Doctrine: America for Americans, Europe for Europeans.

While German troops continued to advance, the Italians in the south seemed to be marching in place. Fortunately for Il Duce, events in the north soon precluded the necessity for any action at all in the south. By evening of the sixteenth Germans were pouring through the haphazard French defenses almost at will. Late the next morning, as Hitler was discussing the situation with his military advisers at Wolf's Gorge, word came that the French wanted an armistice. Throwing dignity to the winds, he slapped his thigh and jerked up a knee in a spontaneous spasm of ecstasy.* "He was literally shaken by frantic exuberance," recalled Fräulein Schröder. The staff gaped in wonder but Keitel rose to the moment. "Mein Führer," he said ponderously, "you are the greatest *Feldherr* [field commander] of all time!"

Although the British were stricken by the French capitulation, Churchill revived their courage with talk of England's "finest hour." And

* The Western newsreel version turned this brief moment into an extended scene. According to Laurence Stallings, the film was doctored by John Grierson, the documentary producer then serving as propagandist in the Canadian army. By "looping" the frames (a technique subsequently used in TV cat food commercials), Grierson transformed Hitler's gesture into a ludicrous series of gay pirouettes. Hitler's official cameraman, Walter Frentz, filmed the scene; he asserts that there were only eight frames, and provided them to the author.

from the British Broadcasting Corporation came another voice of resistance, this beamed to France. "The flame of French resistance cannot go out," proclaimed General Charles de Gaulle from Studio B-2. "It will not go out." France, he said, had lost only a battle. "She has not lost the war." Neither man noted that it was June 18, the hundred and twenty-fifth anniversary of the Battle of Waterloo, a contest ultimately decided by Blücher's German troops.

At noon Hitler met with Mussolini in the Führerbau, scene of the latter's personal trimph at the historic Munich Conference of 1938. This time the Italian dictator was noticeably subdued. His own declaration of war had been a military fraud, a diplomatic gamble. Hitler had achieved victory without help and would, of course, have the last word today. Both Ciano and Mussolini were startled to find Hitler in a peace-loving, magnanimous mood. Hitler made "many reservations on the desirability of demolishing the British Empire, which he considers, even today, to be an important factor in world equilibrium," then, in the face of Mussolini's objections, stoutly supported Ribbentrop's proposal of lenient peace terms to the French. "Hitler is now the gambler who has made a big scoop and would like to get up from the table, risking nothing more," Ciano wrote in his diary. "Today he speaks with a reserve and perspicacity which, after such a victory, are really astonishing. I cannot be accused of excessive tenderness toward him, but today I truly admire him."

The two dictators took time off to autograph souvenir postcards of their meeting. On one such card Mussolini scratched in his bold, upright hand: "Men make history!" Underneath, in his much softer script, Hitler wrote: "History makes men." Mussolini left for Rome in dejection. "In truth," wrote Ciano that evening, "the Duce fears that the hour of peace is growing near and sees fading once again that unattainable dream of his life: glory on the field of battle."

Two days later, on the first day of summer, Hitler motored to the same woods near Compiègne where the Kaiser's representative had surrendered. It was a vindictive as well as historic choice. There stood the famous wooden railroad dining car used on that occasion, hoisted from its museum through a torn-out wall to the original site. At exactly 3:15 P.M. the Führer motorcade arrived. Hitler walked toward the car with springy step, face grave, manner solemn. He stopped at a granite block which read:

HERE ON THE ELEVENTH OF NOVEMBER 1918 SUCCUMBED
THE CRIMINAL PRIDE OF THE GERMAN EMPIRE—VANQUISHED
BY THE FREE PEOPLE WHICH IT TRIED TO ENSLAVE

William Shirer was watching through binoculars to catch Hitler's expression. "I have seen that face many times at the great moments of his life. But today! It is afire with scorn, anger, hate, revenge, triumph." He was muttering, so recalled Linge, something that sounded like "We will destroy everything that can remind the world of that shameful day in 1918."

A long plain table had been set up in the old railroad car with half a dozen chairs on each side for the two delegations. At the head stood Schmidt where he would be able to hear both groups. After the Führer seated himself next to his interpreter, Göring, Raeder, Brauchitsch, Ribbentrop and Hess took their places. Several minutes later General Charles Huntziger led in the French delegation—an admiral, an air force general, and a former ambassador, their faces still showing the shock of learning at the last moment where the negotiations would take place.

Hitler and his associates rose. Not a word was spoken. Both delegations bowed and sat down. First Keitel read out the preamble to the armistice conditions, which had been composed by Hitler. The French and the Germans stared at each other, thought Schmidt, like wax figures as Keitel spoke the Führer's words: Germany did not intend that the conditions should cast any aspersion on so courageous an enemy. "The aim of the German demands is to prevent a resumption of hostilities, to give Germany security for the further conduct of the war against England which she has no choice but to continue, and also to create the conditions for a new peace which will repair the injustice inflicted by force on the German Reich." It seemed as though Hitler addressed England rather than France, offering them an honorable peace too if they chose. This became more evident in the stipulations which included German renouncement of any intent to challenge Britain's sea power. He solemnly swore he would not take over the French war fleet for his own use in the war or, indeed, use any French naval equipment (for a possible crossing of the Channel). Hitler had included this promise against advice from his own navy to make good the heavy losses in the Norway campaign with French ships; a proposal he curtly rejected out of both fear and hope. He feared seizure of the French fleet would harden English determination to fight since it would challenge their supremacy of the seas; he hoped his appeasement would lead to peace with a tacit gentlemen's agreement that Britannia should continue to rule the waves while Germania turned east for Lebensraum.

Once Schmidt finished reading the French text, Hitler got to his feet. So did the others. After more polite bows, the Führer left with most of his followers. Keitel and Schmidt stayed behind and were joined directly by

Jodl and several other German officers. After the French had re-examined
the terms, they insisted upon transmitting them to their government at
Bordeaux. "Absolutely impossible!" said Keitel. "You must sign at once."

But the French stubbornly demanded the same courtesy extended to
the German delegation in 1918 and in a few minutes Huntziger was talking to General Weygand, the French commander-in-chief. "I am telephoning from the coach"—he paused—"from the coach you know." He
reported that the conditions were hard but not dishonorable. Even so,
Huntziger felt they were "merciless," far worse than the conditions
France had forced on Germany in the previous war, and the negotiations
continued without resolution until dusk. They resumed the following
morning, June 22, dragging on into late afternoon. By 6 P.M. Keitel lost all
patience and sent Schmidt to the French with an ultimatum: "If we cannot reach an agreement within an hour, the negotiations will be broken
off, and the delegation will be conducted back to the French lines."

There was no alternative. At 6:50 P.M., after more telephone conversations with Bordeaux, General Huntziger signed the armistice treaty.
After the ceremony Keitel asked him to stay a moment. When they were
alone the two generals looked at each other silently and Schmidt noticed
both had tears in their eyes. Controlling his emotion, Keitel congratulated
the Frenchman for having represented his country's interests with such
dignity, then held out his hand. Huntziger shook it.

All these events were being radioed back to Germany as they occurred
and as soon as the proud but downcast Huntziger stepped down from the
old dining car, there was a brisk recorded rendition of "Then we strike,
then we strike, then we strike at England!" that must have stirred German
hearts. It was the Goebbels touch. He had music for all occasions; but his
choice this time was provoking to his Führer, who had been trying to give
the opposite impression in the treaty.

Back at Wolf's Gorge Hitler was planning a sightseeing tour of Paris.
He had summoned a sculptor and his two favorite architects—Speer and
Giesler—to go along as guides. "Paris has always fascinated me," he told
Arno Breker, whose heroic-classical works were also admired by Stalin.
Hitler admitted that it had long been one of his most ardent wishes to
visit the City of Light. It was a metropolis of art and that was why he
insisted on seeing it first with his artists. He was sure they would find inspiration for the rebuilding of important German cities. "I am interested
in actually seeing the buildings with which I am theoretically familiar."

It was pitch-dark when the party—which included Keitel and
Bormann and several adjutants—arrived at a meadow outside Brûly-de-
Pesche and climbed into a plane piloted by Baur, but by the time they

reached Le Bourget the sun was up. June 23 was going to be a bright, hot day. Hitler climbed into the first open car of a motor column, seating himself as usual beside the driver. Behind him sat the rest of the party. As they headed for the first stop, the Opéra, the streets of the city were deserted except for an occasional gendarme who would dutifully greet the Führer with a smart salute. Breker had spent his most decisive years in Paris and was shocked to see the almost complete absence of life.

Hitler's features slowly relaxed as he took in the architectural wonders of the Opéra, which he had admired since his early days in Vienna. He was as familiar with the building as with his own chancellery and his eyes shone with excitement. "This is the most beautiful theater in the world!" he called out to his entourage. He inspected the boxes and noted that one room was missing. The white-haired attendant who had been accompanying them with stiff pride announced coolly that it had been eliminated years ago. "There, you see how well I know my way about!" said Hitler with the pride of a schoolboy.

After a stop at the Eiffel Tower they visited Napoleon's tomb. Here Hitler placed cap over heart, bowed and gazed for some time down into the deep round crypt. He was very moved. Finally he turned to Giesler and said quietly, "You will build my tomb."* He lapsed into pensive silence, then instructed Bormann to transfer the bones of young Napoleon from Vienna to his father's side.

The three-hour tour ended on the heights of Montmartre, the mecca of art students. Perhaps it reminded Hitler of his own student days. Lost in thought for some moments, he finally turned to Giesler, Breker and Speer. "Now your work begins," he said. The rebuilding of cities and monuments was entrusted to them. "Bormann," he said, "help me with this. Take care of my artists." Hitler again surveyed the city which stretched below. "I thank Fate to have seen this city whose magic atmosphere has always fascinated me," he said. That was why he had ordered his troops to by-pass Paris and to avoid combat in its vicinity. "So that picture below us would be preserved for the future." But the few Parisians who saw him that morning were reduced to panic. As his cavalcade came upon a group of boisterous market women the fattest pointed in terror at Hitler. Her shriek of "It's him! It's him!" spread pandemonium.

The next day Hitler instructed Speer to draw up a decree in his name to resume full-scale work on the Berlin buildings. "Wasn't Paris beautiful?" he said. "But Berlin must be made more beautiful." Hitler also took

---

* Later he gave Giesler explicit instructions. His tomb was to be extremely simple and it would be placed in Munich. "Here I was truly born," he said. "Here I started my movement and here is my heart."

Breker aside and began rhapsodizing on what they had seen the previous morning. "I love Paris—it has been a place of artistic importance since the nineteenth century—just as you do. And like you, I would have studied here if Fate had not pushed me into politics since my ambitions before the World War were in the field of art."

The armistice was scheduled to go into effect an hour and thirty-five minutes past midnight and there was an atmosphere of jollity as they sat down to a late dinner at a table lit by candles. The sky darkened, thunder rumbled in the distance. Just before midnight an aide reported enemy planes approaching. The lights were extinguished and they sat in pitch-darkness, faces periodically lit up by flashes of lightning.

Champagne glasses were passed around. There was an unearthly silence as watches were checked. At 1:35 A.M. came the startling brassy cry of a bugle. Someone whispered to Breker that it was the traditional signal for "Weapons at rest." Someone else, overcome by emotion, blew his nose. Keitel stood and in the darkness made a short speech. He raised his glass and called for three "Hocks" to the Führer, their Supreme Commander.

Everyone rose and clinked glasses while Hitler sat somewhat uneasily —he didn't like such displays but was bowing to the tradition of the Wehrmacht. He brought glass to mouth as a courtesy but did not drink, then slumped, head bowed, a man alone in this jubilant company. At last he said almost inaudibly, "It was a great responsibility," and left the room.

Chapter Twenty-two

"EV'N VICTORS BY
VICTORY ARE UNDONE"
(DRYDEN)
JUNE–OCTOBER 28, 1940

1

That summer Hitler made it evident he was more interested in negotiating than in fighting. In France his weapons were persuasion and the projection of himself as the magnanimous victor who offered the French a share in the fruits of a united and prosperous Fascist Europe, a hegemony designed not only for moral regeneration but as a bulwark against Godless Bolshevism. One of the first acts in this campaign was a demand that his troops act like liberators, not conquerors. "I do not wish my soldiers to behave in France the way the French behaved in the Rhineland after the first war!" He told Hoffmann that anyone found looting would be shot on the spot. "I want to come to a real understanding with France."

Consequently troops who entered Paris did not swagger around the city demanding homage and free food. They conscientiously paid for every purchase and enjoyed the late June sun outside the cafés of the Champs-Élysées side by side with Frenchmen. It was an embarrassed, often silent and indifferent companionship but fear was leaving Parisians who had expected their women to be raped and their shops and banks to be sacked. By now it was common knowledge that the Wehrmacht was actually assisting those refugees trekking back to the capital, and there was some acceptance of the placard plastered all over the city showing a child in the arms of a friendly German with the admonition: "Frenchmen! Trust the German soldier!"

Hitler would have been proud of his troops. They were neat, quiet and ingratiating; courteous to women but not too gallant, and respectful to their mates. They stood bareheaded at the tomb of the Unknown Soldier, armed only with cameras. They acted more like a horde of tourists brought in at special holiday rates than the fearsome creatures who had just humiliated the French armies. It was astute public relations, part of a program designed to turn France into a working and productive vassal.

Hitler himself was playing the tourist with a special group including his adjutants and his World War sergeant, Max Amann. For two days this lighthearted group was guided by the Führer around the old battlefields of the conflict that had helped lead to this one. It was a sentimental journey with Hitler enjoying every moment. He pointed out the fields of Flanders that had formerly been a hellish morass, the old trenches that had been kept as memorials and attractions for sightseers. Instead of surveying the scenes in quiet solemnity, the Führer talked interminably, explaining the minutest detail of what had happened here and over there. As he drove through Lille, which he had memorialized in water color, a woman looking out of the window recognized him. "The Devil!" she gasped. Amused at first, he vowed he would erase that image from the minds of the conquered.

The sentimental junket ended on June 26 and he turned his mind to the unpleasant task ahead: subjugation of the English. It was a chore not to be relished, he reiterated to his adjutants. War with England was a war of brothers and the destruction of their empire would, in truth, be cause for German distress. That was why, he confided to Hewel, he was reluctant to invade England. "I do not want to conquer her," he said, "I want to come to terms with her, I want to force her to accept my friendship and to drive out the whole Jewish rabble that is agitating against me."

Hitler still had no definite plan for the invasion of the British Isles. Victory in the West, in fact, had come so quickly that there was not a single landing craft or barge ready for launching across the Channel. He seemed to be waiting instead for England to sue for peace. But such expectations were rudely jolted on July 3 by the surprise Royal Navy bombardment of the French fleet lying at anchor in the Algerian port of Mers-el-Kebir. Within thirteen minutes the battleship *Bretagne* was sunk with the loss of 977 men, and three other vessels, including the *Dunkerque*, were badly damaged with heavy losses in life. The rest of the fleet escaped. The victors paid a heavy price for their fear that Hitler might possibly use these warships in her invasion of England. With British evacuation from Dunkirk still a bitter memory to most Frenchmen, this attack, particularly after Admiral Darlan's sincere vows to deny Hitler their ships, roused deep animosity throughout France. "Perfidious Albion" became a café phrase.

The shelling also confirmed the convictions of those who felt that collaboration with Hitler was France's only salvation. Recently the country itself had been physically divided by the armistice terms into two zones: Occupied France in the north and Vichy France in the south under a regime headed by Marshal Pétain. The bombardment made more difficult his task of preventing Deputy Premier Laval from leading France into an ever closer collaboration with Hitler while simplifying for Jean Giraudoux and other Fascist intellectuals the effort to seek new converts. Alfred Fabre-Luce in his quasi diary wrote: "In one day England killed more French sailors than Germany did during the whole war." The British blunder at Mers-el-Kebir, he predicted, was hastening Hitler's One Europe. It also wakened the Führer from his complacent dream of a quick settlement with England while emphasizing his own inability to either control the French fleet or checkmate the Royal Navy. He who was practically landbound was stunned by the shocking mobility of sea power. The explosive naval action reinforced his earlier fear that even if the British fleet did not thwart an invasion of England it would enable her rulers to set up headquarters in Canada or Australia and rule the seas from there.

He hovered in an agony of indecision between negotiation and force. "I must not give up," he told Puttkamer. "The English will eventually see it my way." But when Brauchitsch and Halder flew to the Berghof on July 13 he readily approved their plan to invade England, yet moments later protested that he had no desire to fight his English brothers. He had no desire to dismantle the Empire; bloodshed would only draw the jackals eager to share in the spoils. Why was England still so unwilling to make peace? he asked and answered, so Halder wrote in his diary, "that England still has some hopes of action on the part of Russia."

Three days after, he issued a specific invasion directive designed to eliminate the English homeland as a base for the prosecution of the war against Germany and, if necessary, to occupy it completely. The operation was given an imaginative code name: Sea Lion. No sooner had Hitler approved it than he decided to make a peace proposal of his own. "The Führer is going to make a very magnanimous peace offer to England,"

Ribbentrop told Schmidt. "When Lloyd George hears of it, he will probably want to fall on our necks." When it came on July 19, it began with a
derisive attack on Churchill, continued with a threat that any battle between their two countries would surely end in the annihilation of England, and concluded with a vague proposal: "I can see no reason why this
war should continue."

The first English reply to Hitler's bleak offer came from someone who
knew him well. Sefton Delmer, now working for BBC, was on the air
within the hour. "Herr Hitler," he said in his most deferential German,
"you have on occasion in the past consulted me as to the mood of the
British public. So permit me to render Your Excellency this little service
once again tonight. Let me tell you what we here in Britain think of this
appeal of yours to what you are pleased to call our reason and common
sense. *Herr Führer* and *Reichskanzler*, we hurl it right back to you, right
in your evil-smelling teeth." Shirer heard this at the Berlin studio while
waiting to make his own broadcast to America and observed its effect on
the officials there. "Can you make it out?" one shouted to Shirer. "Can you
understand those British fools? To turn down peace now? They're crazy."

President Roosevelt too was unimpressed by Hitler's offer. Later that
evening, in a radio address from the White House accepting the nomina-
tion for the presidency, he declared there was only one way to deal with a
totalitarian country—by resistance, not appeasement. Never, reported Ambassador Dieckhoff to Berlin, had Roosevelt's "complicity" in the outbreak and prolongation of this war come out so clearly as in this speech.
"England is to be prevented from changing her course, English resistance
is to be strengthened and the war is to be continued."*

Still no official rejection came from London and when Hitler summoned his commanders to Berlin for a conference on Sunday, July 21, he
seemed more puzzled than bellicose. "England's situation is hopeless," he
said. "The war has been won by us. A reversal of the prospects of success
is impossible." He speculated on the chances of a new cabinet under
Lloyd George before lapsing into grim conjecture.

Suddenly the musing ended. He called for "a speedy ending of the
war" and suggested that Sea Lion was the most effective way to do so. But

---

* A few days later a press adviser of the Washington Embassy submitted the following
memorandum to the German Foreign Minister after a talk with Fulton Lewis, Jr., political commentator for the Mutual Broadcasting Company: "L. who travels a good
deal, and in connection with the Republican and Democratic conventions met Americans from all classes and parts of the country, stated that people did not want any war,
but were rather helpless before Roosevelt's cunning tactics, especially now when by a
cornucopia of enormous orders in all the states he had reduced the Congress to a
rubber stamp without a will of its own."

his assurance—or show of it—almost immediately began to dissipate. He warned that invasion across the Channel commanded by the enemy was no one-way trip as in Norway. There could be no element of surprise. How could they solve the problem of logistic supply? He went on and on, pointing out grave problems that Admiral Raeder (who was taking diligent notes) silently seconded. Complete air superiority was essential and first-wave landings must be completed by mid-September before worsening weather prevented the Luftwaffe from full participation. He turned to Raeder. When could the navy give him a clear picture on technical preparations? When would they complete emplacement of coastal artillery? To what extent could they protect the bridging of the Channel?

The discomfited admiral was thinking of other problems: they would have to transport most of the troops in river and canal barges which were still to be hauled from the Reich. And how could this enfeebled fleet of combat vessels hold off the Royal Navy? After the Norway losses there were only forty-eight U-boats, one heavy cruiser, four destroyers and three torpedo boats fit for action. With some embarrassment Raeder replied that he hoped to have an answer on technical details in a few days but how could he commence practical preparations until air superiority was a fact? Brauchitsch responded to his pessimism with a positive expression of faith. He liked Sea Lion. Göring's deputy said the Luftwaffe was only waiting for the word to start a massive air offensive; without comment, Hitler instructed Raeder to submit his report as soon as possible. "If preparations cannot be completed with certainty by the beginning of September, it is necessary to consider other plans." The burden of Sea Lion was on the navy.

When they were alone, Hitler told Brauchitsch, "Stalin is flirting with England to keep England at war and tie us down, to gain time for taking what he wants and what cannot be taken if peace breaks out." While admitting that there were at present no signs of Soviet activity against the Reich, he conceded that the Russians posed a problem that had to be dealt with. "We must begin thinking about them."

An Englishman gifted with foresight had recently perceived that Hitler's true goal was Lebensraum at the expense of the Soviet Union. "When one compares his utterances of a year or so ago with those made fifteen years earlier," wrote George Orwell in a review of the English edition of *Mein Kampf*, "a thing that strikes one is the rigidity of his mind, the way in which his world view *doesn't* develop. It is the fixed vision of a monomaniac and not likely to be much affected by the temporary maneuvers of power politics. Probably, in Hitler's mind, the Russo-German Pact represents no more than an alteration of time-table. The plan laid down in

Mein Kampf was to smash Russia first, with the implied intention of smashing England afterwards. Now, as it has turned out, England has got to be dealt with first, because Russia was the more easily bribed of the two but Russia's turn will come when England is out of the picture—that, no doubt, is how Hitler sees it."

Although Hitler had achieved an astounding military victory in the West it had not brought him the political stability he needed to begin his holy war against Russia. His blows against England had merely made this stubborn nation more stubborn and his attempts to placate the Vichy French into joining his crusade were being thwarted by a reluctant compliance that stopped short of active assistance.

These failures notwithstanding, he was still confident he could prevent the conflict from becoming a world war, still so sure England was on the verge of surrender that he ordered an immediate intensification of the propaganda war against England. One of Goebbels' first acts was to broadcast over the secret transmitter system those Nostradamus prophecies which had already come to pass and ending with the one foretelling the destruction of London in 1940. Modern interpretations of Nostradamus were supplied by Krafft, the astrologer who had predicted the beer-hall bombing.

During this season of misgivings Hitler took time off for another reunion with his old friend Kubizek, to whom he had sent tickets to the 1940 Wagner festival. During the first interval of *Götterdämmerung* on July 23 the two met in the drawing room. After greeting Kubizek warmly Hitler complained that the war had checked his rebuilding program. "I still have so infinitely much to do. Who else is there to do it? And here I have to stand by and watch the war robbing me of my best years. . . . We are growing older, Kubizek. Not many more years—and it will be too late to do what remains to be done."

Today's personal encounter with Kubizek was a rare intrusion in Hitler's growing public responsibilities. Paradoxically, his relationship with Eva Braun had become more conjugal. Rather than separating them, the war brought them closer together since he could now spend much more time at the Berghof. Gone were the elaborate attempts to convince everyone that they were merely friends; the staff and servants treated her with the greatest respect, among themselves referring to her as *Chefin*, wife of the Chief. She addressed Hitler openly with the familiar *Du* and he replied in kind, sometimes calling her "Tschapperl," a Viennese diminutive meaning little thing. In front of close friends he would even occasionally stroke her hand or give some other sign of overt affection. According to intimates, their sexual relations were normal, keeping in mind that Hitler was almost fifty and completely absorbed in work. At last the accepted mistress of the Berghof, Eva had gained in self-assurance and elegance. Difficult though her life might be, the conviction that she no longer had rivals was solace enough for her.

That summer Hitler decided that the time had come for Lebensraum and to destroy Bolshevism. He instructed the military to make preparations in this direction and on July 29, 1940, Jodl journeyed to the Bad Reichenhall railroad station to discuss the matter with Colonel Warlimont, chief of OKW's planning section, in his special train. Warlimont and his three senior officers thought the unusual visit might mean promotion or some award. To their mystification, Jodl checked to see that all doors and windows of the dining car were closed and then abruptly announced in a quiet, dry voice that Hitler had decided to rid the world "once and for all" of the danger of Bolshevism. A surprise attack was to be launched on the Soviet Union as soon as possible—May 1941. "The effect of Jodl's words was electric," recalled Warlimont, who at the time grasped his chair because he could not believe his own ears. "That's impossible!" burst out a colonel named Lossberg. How could Hitler fight Russia before England was defeated! Jodl gave a curious answer: "The Führer is afraid that the mood of the people after a victory over England would hardly permit him to embark on a new war against Russia."

A chorus of protests erupted. This was the two-front war which had defeated Germany in the First World War. And why this sudden change after the Moscow Pact? Hadn't Stalin kept his promise to deliver raw materials and food punctually and fully? Jodl tersely answered every objection: a collision with Bolshevism was inevitable; it was better to attack now at the peak of German armed strength. The answers did not convince Warlimont but Jodl, who had presented similar protests to Hitler, cut short the debate. "Gentlemen," he said, "it is not a question for discussion but a decision of the Führer!" He ordered Warlimont to prepare planning papers under the code name Build-up East.

On the last day of July the Führer summoned his commanders to the Berghof for a conference that purported to concern Sea Lion but would lead in the opposite direction. Admiral Raeder spoke first. Preparations were in full swing: matériel had been brought up according to plan and the conversion of barges would be finished by the end of August. On the other hand, the merchant shipping situation was unfavorable due to losses sustained in Norway and from mines; and while minesweeping had com-

menced it was hampered by Allied air superiority. Therefore, he concluded, it would be better to postpone the invasion until the following
May.

Hitler protested. Waiting that long, he said, would enable England
to improve her army and stockpile considerable supplies from America—
and perhaps even Russia. "How can we bridge the gap until May?" he
asked and set the operation for September 15. No sooner had he made
this categorical decision than he diluted it. That is, he added, if a concentrated weeklong bombing attack on southern England could damage the
RAF, the Royal Navy and key harbors. "Otherwise it is postponed until
May 1941."

If this was a decision it was the kind of halfhearted one that pleased
Raeder. It gave him top priority to prepare Sea Lion while shifting the
burden of responsibility onto the Luftwaffe. More important, it gave Hitler
the option of turning the war from West to East, and once the two navy
men, Raeder and Puttkamer, left the room, he began belittling Sea Lion's
chances. "Our little navy," he sighed, "only fifteen per cent of that of the
enemy!" Moreover, the Channel was far more formidable than it appeared
on a map as any voyager on that treacherous body of water in foul weather
could testify.

It was almost as though he had dismissed the invasion of England.
"Russia needs only to hint to England that she does not wish to see Germany too strong and the English, like a drowning man, will regain hope
that things will be entirely different in six to eight months. But if Russia is
smashed, England's last hope is extinguished. Then Germany will be the
master of Europe and the Balkans." This time his musings came to a resolute conclusion. "Decision," he said curtly. "In view of these considerations Russia must be liquidated. Spring '41." Gone was the hesitation
of the past few conferences. Again he was the old Führer, the man of destiny. "The sooner we smash Russia the better. The operation only makes
sense if we smash the state to its core in one blow. Mere conquest of land
areas will not suffice." The offensive, he said, must be carried out as a single, unbroken operation. He would not make Napoleon's mistake and be
whipped by the Russian winter. We will wait, he said, until May. "Five
months' time," he said with satisfaction, "to prepare."

He was carried away by his vision. "Object," he said with animation,
"annihilation of Russia's vital energy." The war lord personified, he rapidly outlined an attack of some 120 divisions: first a drive to Kiev; second,
one through the Baltic toward Moscow; finally, a convergence from north
and south followed by a special operation against the Baku oil area. The
dream was materializing into a reality.

2

Within twenty-four hours the man of decision was again vacillating. He issued two directives, one calling for quick conquest of Britain and the other expressing doubt of its execution. The first began in confidence: "In order to establish the conditions necessary for the final subjugation of England, I intend to intensify the air and naval war against the English homeland." The Luftwaffe was to overpower the RAF as quickly as possible, then stand by in force for Operation Sea Lion. "I reserve for myself," he pointed out, "the decision on terror attacks as a means of reprisal."

The second order, signed by Keitel in the name of the Führer, directed preparations for Sea Lion to be completed by mid-September, then stated: "Eight to fourteen days after the launching of the air offensive against Britain, scheduled to begin about August 5, the Führer will decide whether the invasion will take place this year or not; his decision will depend largely on the outcome of the air offensive."

Even as Keitel sent out this directive he sensed Hitler's ambivalence. "Although the Führer appeared to be throwing himself into all the preparations with great enthusiasm and demanded the adoption of every conceivable improvisation to speed the preparations, I could not help gaining the impression that when it came to the question of actually *executing* the operation, he was in the grip of doubts and inhibitions: he was wide awake to the enormous risk he would be running and to the responsibility he was being called upon to shoulder." Keitel also had the feeling that above all Hitler was "reluctant to countenance the inevitable loss of his last chance of settling the war with Britain by diplomatic means, something which I am convinced he was at that time hoping to achieve." It never occurred to Keitel that this might have been more than an exercise in vacillation; that Hitler might possibly be using the showy preparations for Sea Lion to mask his attack on Russia.

Nor did it occur to Hitler that the substance of his two directives on that August 1 had been decoded by Ultra. The messages assured Churchill that he truly possessed the German code and his faith was confirmed beyond doubt when Ultra shortly decoded a signal from Göring designating August 13 as the beginning of Operation Eagle, the all-out air assault on England.

The offensive began on schedule, but because of worsening weather only the Third Air Force took part. There were almost five hundred bombing sorties but, thanks primarily to radar and secondarily to the Ultra warning, damage was slight and German losses were serious: 45

Luftwaffe aircraft against 13 RAF fighters. The next day was equally disappointing to Göring. On the fifteenth he launched all three of his air fleets. This time Ultra disclosed exactly what forces Göring would use and approximately where each would strike and with this knowledge the RAF was able to assemble its few fighter squadrons at the right place and altitude, parceling them so economically that each German wave met fierce resistance. In the greatest air battle to date, the RAF shot down 75 planes while losing 34. Operation Eagle was turning sour: on the seventeenth the score was 70 to 27. That was the day the slow Stuka dive bomber, which had wreaked such havoc in France, was taken out of the campaign by Göring. It was simply no match for the Spitfires.

Bad weather began on the nineteenth and kept the Luftwaffe grounded four days. During the respite Göring summoned his commanders. The daylight attacks on aircraft factories and other such targets, he said, would have to be replaced by night raids. Göring also took the opportunity to bitterly reproach the single- and double-engine fighter pilots for their performances. "Neither type of fighter is allowed to break off its escort mission because of weather," he ordered. Any pilot who did so would be court-martialed.

When the weather lifted on August 23 the Luftwaffe came over the Channel that night en masse. One flight of a dozen bombers strayed off course and, instead of hitting aircraft factories and oil tanks outside of London, dropped their loads directly on the city. Nine civilians were killed and the RAF, assuming it had been done on purpose, retaliated the next night by bombing Berlin. Little damage was suffered but the Berliners were stunned. "They did not think it could happen," Shirer wrote in his diary. "When this war began Göring assured them it couldn't. . . . They believed him. Their disillusionment today therefore is all the greater. You have to see their faces to measure it."

The RAF returned to Berlin three nights later, this time killing ten civilians and wounding twenty-nine others. Hitler was outraged since the German attack on London had been due to a navigational error, yet still refused to let the Luftwaffe bomb the English capital. Berlin was hit twice more. Aroused to action, he finally threatened dire retaliation on the afternoon of September 4, in an unscheduled speech at the Sportpalast. His audience of women social workers and nurses cheered at his promise to surpass Churchill's bombings. "When the British air force drops two or three or four thousand kilograms of bombs," he said, "then we will in one night drop 150-, 230-, or 400,000 kilograms." The din in the auditorium forced him to pause. "When they declare that they will increase the attacks on our cities, then we will raze their cities to the ground. We will stop the handiwork of these air pirates, so help us God! The hour will come when one of us will break, and it will not be National Socialist Germany!"

The answer was a frenzied: "Never, never!"

3

Two days later Admiral Raeder reported to Hitler at the chancellery. The two discussed Sea Lion cautiously as if neither had much faith in it, the admiral concluding his comments with a question that should have drawn a hot retort: "What," he asked, "are the Führer's political and military directives in the event that Operation Sea Lion does not take place?"

But Hitler was not at all ruffled and it was with some satisfaction that Raeder reported to his colleagues, "Decision of the Führer to land in England is by no means yet firm since the Führer has the conviction that the submission of England will be achieved even without landing. Landing is, however, now as before, regarded by the Führer as the means by which, according to every prospect, an immediate crushing end can be made of the war. Yet the Führer has no thought of executing the landing if the *risk* of the operation is too high." It was obvious that Hitler could not tolerate a miscarriage of Sea Lion since that would decisively redound to the prestige of Great Britain. He wanted a triumphant blitz finale to the end of the war—but one without risks. What particularly disturbed him was Puttkamer's eyewitness report of a recent exercise near Boulogne in which landing barges drawn by tugs were thrown into complete disorder by the tide. In Puttkamer's opinion, a similar landing operation on the English coast would be equally catastrophic.

The success of invasion or capitulation depended on the air assault and Hitler sanctioned mass raids on London the day after his desultory meeting with Raeder. Wave after wave of planes took off for England. Late that afternoon the first group of 320 bombers, heavily protected by fighters, passed over the head of Göring, who was watching from the cliffs of Cape Blanc Nez. The tightly massed planes swarmed over the Channel, then flew up the Thames to blast Woolwich Arsenal, power stations and docks. As soon as Göring got the report that the last target was "a sea of flames," he hurried to a microphone and began broadcasting that London was being destroyed. His planes, he boasted, were striking "right into the enemy's heart." The devastating attack continued until dawn and was resumed the following dusk. Eight hundred and forty-two Londoners died in those two days of terror. Making good his threat to "raze their cities to the ground," Hitler authorized another massive raid for September 15. This would be the grand finale, designed not only to punish London but to destroy the RAF.

Again Ultra warned Churchill and, four days before the raid, he broadcast an exhortation to the nation. "There is no doubt that Herr Hitler is using up his fighter force at a very high rate, and that if he goes on for many more weeks he will wear down and ruin the vital part of his air force." At the same time he warned that "no one should blind himself to the fact that a heavy full-scale invasion of this island is being prepared with all the usual German thoroughness and method, and that it may be launched now—upon England, upon Scotland, or upon Ireland, or upon all three." It could come in the next few days. "Therefore, we must regard the next week or so as a very important period in our history. It ranks with the days when the Spanish Armada was approaching the Channel, and Drake was finishing his game of bowls; or when Nelson stood between us and Napoleon's Grand Army at Boulogne." His words lifted spirits in the fortress island, inspiring civilians to feel that they too were involved in the battle.

Although Hitler was putting on a public show of confidence, he revealed considerable concern at a Führer conference on September 14. After praising the Luftwaffe for the "terrific" effect of Operation Eagle, he admitted that the prerequisites for Sea Lion were "not yet on hand." Bad weather had prevented the Luftwaffe from gaining complete air command. But he still refused to call off the invasion. The air attacks were having a devastating effect on English nerves and mass hysteria would break out in ten or twelve days.

Göring's deputy seized on this to advance his scheme of bombing civilians into submission. Raeder, who seemed enthusiastic about everything but a sea invasion, gave his hearty approval but Hitler insisted that the Luftwaffe confine itself to vital military targets. "Bombing with the object of causing mass panic must be the last resort."

All the talk subsided and what had apparently been a decision to launch Sea Lion was only an agreement to make one on September 17. In the meantime the Battle of Britain intensified, with increasingly heavy German losses. On the fifteenth, for instance, 60 planes were destroyed while the British were losing 26. Consequently Hitler was forced at last to face reality on Tuesday, the seventeenth. He admitted to himself that bombing would probably never bring the English to their knees, then curtly announced his decision: due to inability to achieve air superiority, Operation Sea Lion was hereby postponed until further notice. Postponement meant cancellation; from that moment on the invasion of England existed only on paper. Ultra and a small band of British pilots, typifying the united spirit of the people, had dealt Adolf Hitler his first military defeat. "This blessed plot, this earth, this realm, this England," was saved.

"We have conquered France at the cost of 30,000 men," the Führer told Puttkamer once the decision was made. "During one night of crossing the Channel we could lose many times that—and success is not certain." He seemed happy, thought his naval adjutant, now that Sea Lion was shelved.

That same day Ultra learned that Hitler had authorized the dismantling of air-loading equipment at all Dutch airfields. Churchill summoned the chiefs of staff in the evening. "It was," F. W. Winterbotham recalled, "as if someone cut all the strings of the violins in the middle of a dreary concerto. There were controlled smiles on the faces of these men." Then the chief of the air staff said what everyone privately hoped: in his opinion Hitler had abandoned Sea Lion, at least for the year. "There was a very broad smile on Churchill's face now as he lit up his massive cigar and suggested that we should all take a little fresh air."

4

Hitler still hoped to bring England to the negotiating table, if not by air or sea assault, by the capture of the most strategic mass of rock in the world, Gibraltar. Its seizure would not only keep the Royal Navy out of the Mediterranean and thus insure German take-over of North Africa and the Mideast but drastically lengthen the Empire's life lines to the Far East. How could the British continue a war on such a basis? reasoned Hitler. Particularly since he was willing to give them an honorable peace and let them be a silent partner in the crusade against Bolshevism.

It so happened that Franco's Minister of the Interior, Ramon Serrano Suñer, was then in Berlin to discuss Spain's entry into the war in general and a possible attack on Gibraltar in particular. On the way to the chancellery on that eventful morning he was in an apprehensive mood. Yesterday's conference with Ribbentrop had left him both disturbed and irritated, for he feared Ribbentrop's arrogant behavior was merely a reflection of his master's irritation with the Franco regime.

The Spaniard was pleasantly surprised to be received by Hitler with serene politeness and it was with some confidence that he explained he had been sent as personal agent of Franco as well as a representative of the Spanish government. He was married to the former Zita Polo, sister of the Generalissimo's wife. He had come, he said, to clarify the conditions under which Spain would join Germany in the war. That would be "whenever Spain's supply of foodstuffs and war material was secure."

The Führer seemed more interested in politics than war. Europe, he said, must be united into a continental political system by establishing her own Monroe Doctrine, with Africa under her protection. His allusions to Spain's entry into the war, however, were "indirect and vague." Only when his guest stressed the need for artillery in the Gibraltar area did Hitler become specific—and then about the superiority of bombs over shells. Rattling off figures, he explained that a long-barreled cannon needed repairs after firing about 200 rounds, each containing 75 kilograms of explosives, while a Stuka squadron of 36 machines could indefinitely drop 120 bombs of 1000 kilograms at a time. How long, argued Hitler, could the enemy resist these dive bombers? At the mere sight of them, the Royal Navy would flee from Gibraltar. Therefore there was no need for artillery. Besides, he added, the Germans could not possibly supply 38-centimeter guns for the Gibraltar operation. This virtuoso verbal performance, which left his listener speechless with wonder, was followed by an assurance that Germany would do everything in her power to help Spain.

Serrano Suñer left the chancellery so relieved that his host had not once used a threatening or even pressing tone that he advised Franco to accept Hitler's suggestion that the two leaders meet at the Spanish frontier in the near future for a more definite discussion. Equally impressed by Serrano Suñer, Hitler decided to approach his brother-in-law more forthrightly. "Spain's entry into the war on the side of the Axis Powers," he wrote Franco the next morning, "must begin with the expulsion of the English fleet from Gibraltar and immediately thereafter the seizure of the fortified rock." Once Spain came over to the Axis side, he promised with the persuasiveness of a salesman, Germany would supply not only military but economic aid to the greatest extent possible. In other words, quick victory was to be followed by quick profits.

In his reply on September 22 Franco seemed to agree with almost everything Hitler proposed but a meeting between Serrano Suñer and Ribbentrop two days later foretold difficulties. The Spaniard objected politely but firmly to German claims for several strategic islands off Africa. Even the interpreter thought Serrano Suñer was being quite "niggardly" about these bases after a wholesale offer by Ribbentrop of territory in Africa. "This," Schmidt observed, "brought the first chill to the warm friendship between Franco and Hitler."

If Ribbentrop was frustrated at the difficulties of negotiating with Franco's relative, he had cause for celebration later in the month when his brain child, the Tripartite Pact with Japan and Italy, was signed in Berlin. In it Japan agreed to recognize the leadership of Germany and Italy in the establishment of a new order in Europe as long as they recog-

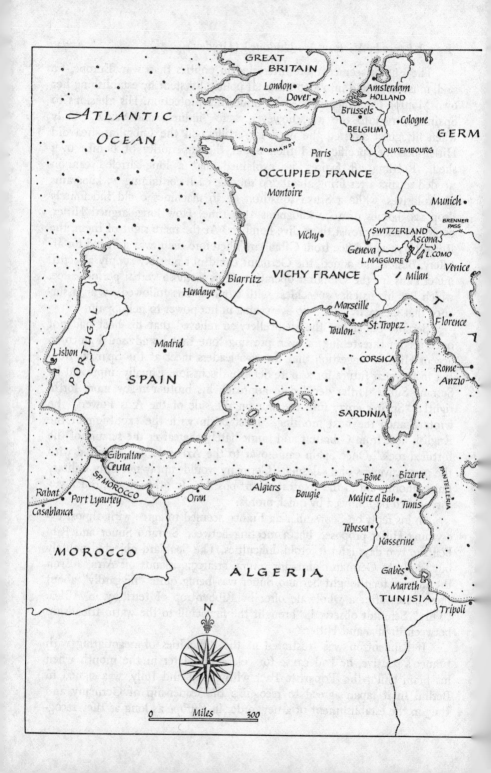

nized her new order in Asia. The signatories also promised "to assist one
another with all political, economic and military means when one of the
three Contracting Parties is attacked by a power at present not involved in
the European War or in the Sino-Japanese Conflict."

To the British and Americans this was further evidence that Japan
was no better than Nazi Germany and Fascist Italy, and that the three
"gangster" nations had joined forces to conquer the world. The Soviets
were disturbed but Ribbentrop assured Molotov that the treaty was
directed exclusively against the warmonger elements in America. Why not
make it a quadripartite pact? he urged, and then wrote a long letter to
Stalin saying that it was "the historical mission of the four powers—the
Soviet Union, Japan, Italy, and Germany—to adopt a long-range policy
and to direct the future development of their peoples into the right channels by delimitation of their interests for the ages."

5

Hitler devoted October to diplomacy. On the fourth he met Mussolini at the Brenner Pass. "The war is won! The rest is only a question of
time," he said. While admitting that the Luftwaffe had not yet achieved
air supremacy, he claimed that British planes were being knocked out of
the air at a ratio of three to one. For some reason, however, England
continued to hold out even though her military situation was hopeless.
Her people were under inhuman strain. Why does she keep on? he complained and answered his own question: hope of American and Russian
aid.

That, he said, was an illusion. The Tripartite Pact was already having
a "dampening effect" on the cowardly American leaders and forty German
divisions on the eastern front discouraged any Russian intervention.
Therefore the time was ripe to strike a new blow at the very roots of the
British Empire: to seize Gibraltar. This digressed into a diatribe against the
Spaniards, who demanded 400,000 tons of grain and considerable gasoline
as their price for entry into the war. And, complained Hitler, when he had
brought up the matter of eventual repayment, Franco had the gall to reply
that this "was a matter of confusing idealism with materialism." Almost
beside himself with resentment, Hitler exclaimed that he had been practically represented "as if I were a little Jew who was haggling about the
most sacred possessions of mankind!"

After the two dictators parted in a spirit of warmth and trust, the
Führer made for Berchtesgaden "to think over quietly the new political
scheme." He paced the rooms of the Berghof and took long walks by him-

self on the slopes of the Obersalzberg. He spoke out some thoughts over the dinner table, some at conferences. The result of these monologues was a decision to sound out the French during his trip to see Franco. Then, and only then, would he speak to the Russians.

His special train (it bore the curious name *Amerika*) left Germany on the twenty-second, arriving that evening at Montoire in west central France. Here Laval, Deputy Premier of Vichy France, came aboard for a brief conference. It dealt primarily with arrangements for a meeting with Marshal Pétain in two days. At this time the Führer planned to extend his program reducing France to complete vassalage. He hoped to do it with the willing help of the victims but was ready to use force and ruthless reprisals if necessary. Beyond subjecting France, as he had other con-quered nations, to what Göring blandly called plunder economy (which included the outright theft of everything of value from raw materials and slave labor to national art treasures), he hoped to gain Vichy France as an active ally against England. From Laval's attitude, Hitler was assured that this could be done and he was in a confident mood as the train con-tinued its journey through the night for the crucial meeting with Franco.

They were to meet next day at a little French border town more suit-able for a holiday than a conference of world importance. Hendaye lay just below Biarritz in the resort area of southwest France, with beaches and palm trees worthy of a travel poster. The rendezvous was at the edge of town where the French narrow-gauge and Spanish wide-gauge rails met. The Führer train arrived in good time for the two o'clock meeting but there was no Spanish train on the adjoining platform. It was a sparkling, clear October day, so pleasant that the punctual Germans were not an-noyed. After all, what could you expect from those lazy Spaniards with their interminable siestas?

Hitler was convinced that once he met Franco face to face he would bring him around just as he had Chamberlain, Laval and the others. Where would the Generalissimo be without the help of Germany? It was not, as devout Spaniards believed, the intervention of the Mother of God which had won the Civil War but the bombs German squadrons had "rained from the heavens that decided the issue."

While they waited, Hitler and Ribbentrop chatted on the platform. "We cannot at the moment," Schmidt overheard the Führer say, "give the Spaniards any written promises about transfers of territory from the French colonial possessions. If they get hold of anything in writing on this ticklish question with these talkative Latins, the French are sure to hear something about it sooner or later." Tomorrow he wanted to induce Pétain to start active hostilities against England and so could not give away French territory today. "Quite apart from that," he continued, "if such an agreement with the Spaniards became known, the French colonial empire would probably go over bodily to De Gaulle."

At last, an hour late, the Spanish train appeared on the International Bridge over the Bidassoa River. The tardiness had been deliberate, not due to any siesta. "This is the most important meeting of my life," Franco told one of his officers. "I'll have to use every trick I can—and this is one of them. If I make Hitler wait, he will be at a psychological disadvantage from the start." The *Caudillo* (Leader) was short and plump with dark, piercing eyes. In a nation of distinguished-looking men, he appeared to be a nonentity, a Sancho Panza, who had risen to power by luck and perseverance. His success was hard-won. Coming from Galicia, a province noted for its sober pragmatists, he brought to his high rank a grim sense of reality and shrewdness.

Although a peasant at heart, Franco was not even a man of the people. He also was too close to the Church and the monarchists and, while giving lip service to the Falangists (a Fascist-type party), it was obvious he was not one of them. The true Falangists, such as his brother-in-law, who had recently been promoted to Foreign Minister, were much more pro-German. Despite his recent unhappy experiences in Berlin, Serrano Suñer remained convinced that Germany was invincible and that Spain should go over to the winning side. Franco was skeptical. "I tell you that the English will never give in," he told his generals. "They'll fight and go on fighting: and if they are driven out of Britain, they'll carry on the fight from Canada: they'll get the Americans to come in with them. Germany has not won the war." At the same time he did not want to exhaust Hitler's patience and subject Spain to the fate of Czechoslovakia and the succeeding line of small countries which had stood in his way.

As his train drew alongside of Hitler's, Franco knew the fate of his country rested on his ability to keep it out of the European conflict. The Civil War had left Spain's economy in a shambles and with the failure of last year's harvest his people faced starvation. But would Hitler let him remain neutral? If he gave the Führer a flat refusal, what could stop a German invasion? The solution was to give the impression of joining the Axis, yet find some slight point that needed further clarification. His Galician heritage was his armor as he stepped onto the platform and started toward Hitler to the accompanying blast of military music.

Franco began with a set speech laden with compliments and vocal promises. Spain had always been "spiritually united with the German people without any reservation and in complete loyalty," and, in fact, "at every moment felt herself united with the Axis." Historically there were only forces of unity between their two nations and, in the present war, "Spain would gladly fight at Germany's side." The difficulties of doing so, he added, were well known to the Führer: in particular the food shortage and the difficulties anti-Axis elements were making for his poor country in America and Europe. "Therefore, Spain must mark time and often look kindly toward things of which she thoroughly disapproves." He said this with a tone of regret but quickly noted that despite all these problems Spain—mindful of her spiritual alliance with the Axis—was assuming "the same attitude toward the war as had Italy in the past autumn." This artful dodge was followed by a promise from Hitler. In return for Spanish co-operation in the war, he said, Germany would let Franco have Gibraltar—it would be seized on the tenth of January—as well as some colonial territories in Africa.

Franco sat huddled silently in his chair, face expressionless. Finally he began to talk, slowly and deliberately, offering up excuses while insisting on more concessions. His country, he said, needed several hundred thousand tons of wheat immediately. Fixing Hitler with "a slyly watchful expression," he asked if Germany was prepared to deliver it. And what about the large number of heavy guns Spain needed to defend the coast from attacks by the Royal Navy, not to mention anti-aircraft guns? He shifted in seemingly haphazard manner from one subject to another, from recompense for the certain loss of the Canary Islands to the impossibility of accepting Gibraltar as a present from foreign soldiers. That fortress must be taken by Spaniards! Abruptly he pragmatically assessed Hitler's chances of clearing the British out of Africa: to the edge of the desert, perhaps, but no farther. "As an old African campaigner I am quite clear about that." Similarly, he cast doubt on the Führer's ability to conquer Britain itself. At best England might fall but Churchill's government would flee to Canada and continue the war with America's aid.

Franco spoke in a monotonous singsong that reminded Schmidt of a muezzin calling the faithful to prayer. It only frustrated Hitler, who finally shot to his feet and blurted out that it was futile to continue. He immediately sat down again, as if regretting his display of nerves, and once more tried to persuade Franco to sign a treaty. Of course! said Franco. What would be more logical? As long as Germany supplied the food and armaments, of course; and as long as Spain was given the option to decide the right moment for war. Having come full circle, the meeting was adjourned.

As a disgruntled Hitler departed for his private compartment, the two Foreign Ministers walked down the platform to Ribbentrop's train for further discussions. After some sparring, Ribbentrop revealed that the Führer

had come to Hendaye "to ascertain whether the Spanish claims and the
French hopes were compatible with one another." Surely the Caudillo
would understand Hitler's dilemma and sign a secret protocol to which
Italy would later add her signature. Whereupon Ribbentrop handed over
a Spanish translation of the proposal. It stated that Spain would receive
territories from French colonial possessions "to the extent that France can
be indemnified from British colonial possessions."

With a show of surprise, Serrano Suñer exclaimed that evidently a
new course was to be followed in the African question and Germany's attitude toward France apparently had changed! This made Spain's compensation for entering the war very vague. And Franco, he concluded with a
little smile, would have "to define more exactly the rewards of victory" to
his people. Ribbentrop was no match for such verbal gymnastics and
fought to restrain his anger as the Spaniard made a dramatic but elegantly
formal exit.

That evening the Germans entertained the Spaniards at a state dinner in the dining car of the Führer's train. Franco was warm and friendly,
his brother-in-law charming. Perhaps their ingratiating manner throughout
the meal encouraged Hitler to draw Franco aside as the guests were rising
to depart. For almost two hours the two men talked in private with the
Führer becoming increasingly agitated at his inability to manipulate the
imperturbable Caudillo, who stood firm on every important point. He
believed, for instance, that the eastern gate of the Mediterranean, the
Suez Canal, should be closed before the western gate, Gibraltar; nor was
he moved by Hitler's protests. Even when his firmness drove Hitler from
insistence to an outburst of temper, Franco remained impassive, insisting
that if Spain did not get the ten million quintals of wheat, history (he was
referring to the rising against Napoleon) might repeat itself. The Führer
left the banquet car in a fume. "Franco is a little major!" he told
Puttkamer. To Linge he reduced him in rank: "In Germany, that man
would never rise higher than sergeant!" Another heard him bring down
the Caudillo to corporal, his own World War grade. He was even more
annoyed at the cunning tactics of his Foreign Minister. "Suñer has Franco
in his pocket," he told Keitel and threatened to break off the talks with
the Spaniards there and then.

In the meantime Ribbentrop was in his train trying to work out an
agreement with Suñer, but he had become as frustrated as the Führer with
the Spaniard's polite but insistent objections. Losing all patience, he
dismissed Serrano Suñer and his aides as if they were schoolboys, instructing them to bring in the completed text by eight in the morning.

Serrano Suñer failed to appear in person on the twenty-fourth, en trusting the text instead to his subordinate, a former ambassador to Berlin who spoke German with a Viennese accent. Ribbentrop was so infuriated at the substitution that his rude shouts could be heard outside the train. "Unsatisfactory!" exclaimed Ribbentrop in his role as schoolmaster after reading Serrano Suñer's draft, which described the French Zone of Morocco as a territory later to belong to Spain. He demanded that the Spaniards submit a new draft, then drove off with Schmidt to the nearest airport so they could reach Montoire in time for the Hitler-Pétain meeting. Spluttering with rage all the way, the Foreign Minister cursed Suñer as a "Jesuit" and Franco as an "ungrateful coward." Secretly the interpreter was delighted by the tactics of the Spaniards. For the first time Hitler had been outwitted before he could play his own tricks.

He had already arrived in Montoire and was waiting in his train to meet Marshal Pétain, who had recently elevated himself from Premier to Head of State, a new title disassociating him from the old republican regime. It would have made the Führer even unhappier with Franco to know that he had already warned Pétain not to assume the burden of leading France out of chaos. "Make your age your excuse," he had said. "Let those who lost the war sign the peace. . . . You are the hero of Verdun. Don't let your name be mingled with the others who have been defeated." "I know, General," Pétain had replied, "but my country calls me, and I am hers. . . . It may be the last service I can do for her."

The aged marshal, smartly uniformed, was greeted at the entrance of the railway station by Keitel. Pétain returned his salute and walked erectly past the German honor guard, eyes front, with Ribbentrop and Laval at his heels. They silently filed through the station to the Führer's train. As Pétain emerged from the ticket hall, Hitler came forward, hand outstretched. The marshal allowed himself to be led into the private coach but sat very straight facing Hitler, listening to Schmidt translate—he was talking rather loudly for the old man's benefit—"with calm indolence." He seemed confident rather than servile. Laval, next to him, was a vivid contrast. He was dying for a cigarette and knew smoking was anathema to both Hitler and Pétain. Laval's searching eyes darted alternately from Hitler to Ribbentrop as the former pointed out that he was aware the marshal did not belong among those who had favored declaring war on Germany. "If this were not the case," he said, "this talk could not have taken place."

After listing French sins in a moderate tone, the Führer repeated what he had said to Franco: "We have already won the war. England is beaten and will sooner or later have to admit it." And, he added meaningfully, it was obvious someone would have to pay for the lost war. "That will be either France or England. If England bears the cost, then France can take the place in Europe which is due her, and can fully retain her position as a colonial power." To do this, of course, France would have to protect her colonial empire from attack as well as reconquer the central African colonies, which had gone over to De Gaulle. At this point he indirectly suggested that France join the war against Britain by asking Pétain what France would do if the English continued to attack her battleships as she had at Mers-el-Kebir and a few weeks later at Dakar.

While admitting that both of these attacks affronted most Frenchmen, Pétain replied that his country was in no position to wage another war. He countered with a request for a final peace treaty "so that France may be clear about her fate, and the two million French prisoners of war may return to their families as soon as possible." Hitler glided over this problem and the two Frenchmen, in turn, made no response to another hint that France should enter the war. The two sides were at cross-purposes and although Pétain expressed his personal admiration for the Führer and seemed to agree with many of his opinions, he expressed himself so curtly that Schmidt took it as an overt rebuff. "The great stake for which Hitler had played," recalled the interpreter, "had been lost as a result of the prudent reticence shown by Pétain and Laval." In his opinion France was not shamed by the actions of their two representatives at Montoire.

It was with honor, Pétain told his countrymen a few days later over the radio, that he accepted collaboration with Germany. He did so to maintain French unity. It would also lighten the weight of France's sufferings and better the lot of her prisoners. "This collaboration," he warned, "must be sincere. It must exclude all idea of aggression. It must carry with it a patient and confident effort." France had numerous obligations to the victor. Hadn't Hitler let France keep her sovereignty? "So far," continued Pétain, "I have spoken to you as a father. Today I am addressing you as a leader. Follow me. Trust in eternal France."

The mood aboard the Führer train was glum. Hitler had failed to get what he wanted at both Hendaye and Montoire. The third disappointment came before *Amerika* crossed the border of France with delivery of a letter from Mussolini dated six days earlier. In it he venomously attacked the French. In their hearts, he wrote, they hated the Axis and, despite the sweet words coming from Vichy, "one cannot think of their collaboration." Anxious lest Il Duce's vengeful attitude toward France endanger his own plan to draw Vichy into the anti-democratic crusade, Hitler instructed Ribbentrop to move up his meeting with Mussolini in Florence to October 28. Ribbentrop's telephone call to Ciano a few minutes later caused a minor panic in Rome. "This rush of the Führer to Italy so soon after his conference with Pétain," Ciano wrote in his diary, "is not at all pleasing to me. I hope he will not offer us a cup of hemlock because of our claims against France. This will be a bitter pill for the Italian people, even more so than the Versailles delusion."

Rather than return to Berlin as planned, Hitler ordered his train to Munich so he could rest and prepare for the hastily updated trip to Italy. On October 27, just before heading south late that afternoon, word came from the German military attaché in Rome that it was now "practically certain" that Mussolini would attack Greece early the next morning. According to Schmidt, the Führer "was beside himself" at this news and that evening at supper Ribbentrop reflected his master's ire. "The Italians will never get anywhere against the Greeks in the autumn rains and winter snows," he said. "Besides the consequences of war in the Balkans are quite unpredictable. The Führer intends at all costs to hold up this crazy scheme of the Duce's, so we are to go to Italy at once, to talk to Mussolini personally."

Ribbentrop could not have meant this seriously. He himself had set the meeting two days earlier. Further, he was aware that the Führer had just refused to sign a message to Rome, composed by his own staff, which criticized any such attack in straight language. "Ribbentrop," recalled Weizsäcker, who had written the message, "approved this, but Hitler said he did not want to cross Mussolini. Hitler's silence meant indirectly giving Italy the sign to go ahead with her decisive and dangerous step to the Balkans."

The next morning at 10 A.M., as *Amerika* was passing through Bologna, Hitler learned that the Italians had just marched into Greece. His first outburst of swearing and cursing, recalled Engel, was directed not at Mussolini but at the German liaison staffs and attachés who had "spoiled many a recipe for him." Only then did Hitler begin berating the Italians for their duplicity. "This is the revenge for Norway and France!" he exclaimed, then complained that "every second Italian is either a traitor or a spy." His emotions released, he turned to a more sober analysis of the situation. Il Duce, he guessed, had gone into Greece to counter Germany's growing economic influence in the Balkans. "I am greatly disturbed," he said. The Italian invasion, he feared, would have "grave consequences and give the British a welcome opportunity to set up an air base in the Balkans."

An hour later his train pulled into the gaily decorated station of Florence. An exuberant Duce rushed forward to embrace his ally. "Führer," he exclaimed, "we are on the march!" Hitler controlled himself. The damage had been done and it would be useless to complain. His greeting was aloof, a far cry from the usual warm reception he gave Mussolini, but even this coolness was momentary. In moments both dictators, being politicians, were put in good spirits by the ecstatic cries of "Führer, Heil Führer! Duce! Duce!" from the crowd outside the Palazzo Pitti where the talks would take place. Several times the two dictators had to appear at the balcony to appease the crowd. "It was a greeting such as the Romans gave their Caesars," Hitler later told his valet. "But they did not deceive me. They are trying to soften me now because of the way they have messed up my plans."

During the talk Hitler controlled himself well to Schmidt's surprise, with not "the slightest sign of his mental gnashing of teeth." Mussolini was in exceptional good humor. Any guilt he may have felt for doing what Hitler had only given reluctant consent to had been dispelled by his own resentment over Hitler's recent dispatch of troops to Romania days after they both had promised at the Brenner Pass to preserve peace in the Balkans. "Hitler always faces me with a fait accompli," he had complained to Ciano. "This time I am going to pay him back in his own coin. He will find out from the papers that I have occupied Greece. In this way the equilibrium will be re-established."

Apparently he had succeeded, for the Führer never uttered a syllable of complaint about Greece. Instead he devoted most of his time to the problem that had brought him to Florence. He told Mussolini of the meeting with Pétain and Laval in which he had been much impressed by the dignity of the former—and had not been at all deceived by the servility of the latter. He described his talks with Franco as an ordeal and rather than go through another he would "prefer to have three or four teeth out." The Caudillo, he complained, had been "very vague" about entering the war; he must have become leader of Spain by an accident.

The long meeting ended in brotherliness with Hitler repeating the promise made at the Brenner Pass that he would "on no account conclude peace with France if the claims of Italy were not completely satisfied." On his part, Mussolini observed that their two countries were, as always, completely in accord. Once aboard *Amerika,* however, Hitler began fulminating against Il Duce's new "adventure," the outcome of which could only be military catastrophe. Why on earth, he exclaimed, didn't Mussolini attack Malta or Crete? That would still make some sense in the context of their war with England in the Mediterranean. Particularly with the Italian troops in such straits in North Africa that they had just requested a German armored division!

The return trip through the snow-covered Alps was a morose one for the Führer. In little more than six months he had conquered more land than even the most optimistic German could have imagined. Norway, Denmark, Luxembourg, Belgium, Holland and France were his. He had outstripped Alexander and Napoleon. Yet nothing, it seems, fails like success; this incredible string of victories had been followed by frustration at Hendaye, Montoire and Florence. The mediocre leader of a second-rate country and the chief of a defeated nation were avoiding being led into the crusade against England and his own dependable ally was stupidly endangering the Axis position in the Mediterranean out of need for personal glory on the battlefield. As if that were not enough, the air campaign designed to bring England to the green table was now an admitted failure—at a frightful cost in planes.

Unable to hide his annoyance during the tedious voyage back to the Fatherland, he railed at "deceiving" collaborators and ungrateful, unreliable friends. What other conqueror had ever been faced with such a superfluity of frustrations! Much of his display must have been theater. Hitler could not have been as disturbed by Pétain's lack of commitment as he pretended and he surely knew he could have prevented the incursion into Greece if he had been willing to put pressure on Mussolini. But his bitterness at Franco's refusal to commit himself was sincere. The Caudillo must be forced into compliance, for he was the key to Gibraltar and seizure of this fortress could checkmate the English—and clear the way for the crusade in the East.

Chapter Twenty-three

"THE WORLD WILL HOLD
ITS BREATH"
NOVEMBER 12, 1940–JUNE 22, 1941

1

Although Hitler had given only reluctant support to the Tripartite Pact with Japan and Italy, he was persuaded by its father, Ribbentrop, to invite the Soviets to make it a four-power agreement. And so, on November 12, 1940, Foreign Commissar Molotov arrived in Berlin to talk of coalition. The meeting began without Hitler at Ribbentrop's new office in the former presidential palace and the host did his utmost to make the Soviet delegation feel at home, bestowing smiles on all sides. "Only at long intervals," recalled Schmidt, "did Molotov reciprocate, when a frosty smile glided over his intelligent, chess player's face." He listened impassively to Ribbentrop voice loud assurance that the Tripartite Pact was not aimed against the Soviet Union. In fact, Ribbentrop observed, Japan had already turned her face to the south and would be occupied for centuries in consolidating her territorial gains in Southeast Asia. "For her Lebensraum Germany, too, will seek expansion in a southerly direction, that is in central Africa, in the territories of the former German colonies." Everyone, he said reassuringly, was going south, as if talking of the latest fad. He suggested in his heavy-handed manner that the Soviets also head south and named the Persian Gulf and other areas in which Germany was disinterested. It was an obvious reference to India but Molotov just peered without expression through his old-fashioned pince-nez.

Disconcerted, Ribbentrop suggested that the Soviet Union join the Tripartite Pact. But Molotov, whose unerring logic in the presentation of arguments reminded Schmidt of his mathematics teacher, was saving his ammunition for Hitler. That afternoon Molotov listened impassively to the Führer, but when Hitler finally stopped talking complained politely that his statements had been of too general a nature. He wanted details; and began posing a succession of embarrassing questions: "Does the German-Soviet agreement of 1939 still apply to Finland? What does the New Order in Europe and Asia amount to, and what part is the U.S.S.R. to play in it? What is the position with regard to Bulgaria, Romania and Turkey; and how do matters stand with regard to the safeguarding of Russian interests in the Balkans and on the Black Sea?"

No foreigner had ever before dared to express himself quite so boldly and Schmidt wondered if Hitler would rush irately out the door as he had two years earlier when Sir Horace Wilson handed him Chamberlain's letter. But he meekly supplied reassuring answers. The Tripartite Pact, he said, would only regulate conditions in Europe; there would be no settlement without Russian collaboration—not only in Europe but in the Far East.

Molotov was skeptical. "If we are to be treated as equal partners and not mere dummies," he said, "we could, in principle, join the Tripartite Pact. But first the aim and object of the pact must be closely defined, and I must be more precisely informed about the boundaries of the Greater Asia area." Obviously disconcerted at being put on the defensive, Hitler abruptly ended the interrogation with the announcement that they would have to break off their discussion. "Otherwise we shall be caught by the air-raid warning."

He sent the Russians an invitation for luncheon on the thirteenth even though he disliked eating with foreigners. But the rare concession to cordiality did not moderate his guest's persistence. Molotov opened the second conference with continuing aggression. He brought up Finland, which Hitler was secretly planning to use as a military ally in case of war with Russia. The mere mention of Finland turned the Führer from genial luncheon host to testy litigant. "We have no political interest there," he protested.

Molotov was not convinced. "If good relations are maintained between Russia and Germany," he said with studied calm, "the Finnish question can be settled without war. But in that case there must be no

German troops in Finland and no demonstrations against the Soviet government there." Hitler controlled himself, answering in a quiet but emphatic tone that the only German troops in Finland were in transit to northern Norway.

Molotov's suspicions were not allayed and Hitler became so ruffled he began to repeat himself. "We must have peace with Finland, because of their nickel and timber." But the next sentence, perhaps unwittingly, exposed his ultimate plan. "A conflict in the Baltic would put a severe strain on Russo-German relations—with unpredictable consequences." If Molotov did not see that this was a threat, he ignored it, thereby making a grave diplomatic error. "It's not a question of the Baltic but of Finland," he replied sharply.

"No war with Finland!" said Hitler obstinately.

"Then you are departing from our agreement of last year," said Molotov with equal obstinence.

This was a far grimmer, if less spectacular, contest than the debate with the British and Ribbentrop saw his cherished policy of Russian-German entente in grave danger. He intervened conciliatingly and Hitler took the cue to sound the Ribbentrop theme of Southward Ho! "After the conquest of England," he said, "the British Empire will be apportioned as a gigantic world-wide estate in bankruptcy of forty million square kilometers." Like the promoter of a new real estate development, Hitler painted a tempting picture. "In this bankrupt estate Russia will get access to the ice-free and really open seas. Thus far, a minority of 45 million Englishmen have ruled 600 million inhabitants of the British Empire. I am about to crush this minority." Germany, he said, wanted no diversion from her struggle against the heart of the Empire, the British Isles. This was why he opposed any Baltic war.

But this excursion did not mollify Molotov, who resumed his complaints. "You have given a guarantee to Romania which displeases us," he said with characteristic brusqueness. This referred to Germany's recent guarantee of Romania's new frontiers from foreign attacks. "Is this guarantee also valid against us?"

In diplomacy it is considered a blunder to pin down an opponent. "It applies to anyone who attacks Romania," Hitler said flatly and a few moments later abruptly adjourned the meeting, using the same excuse as yesterday—possible English air raid.

Hitler did not attend the banquet at the Russian Embassy that evening, an occasion marred by the appearance of British planes just as Molotov was proposing a friendly toast. Ribbentrop escorted the host to his own air shelter in the Wilhelmstrasse and while there took the opportunity to show Molotov a draft of the four-power treaty he so devoutly sought. It called for Germany, Russia, Japan and Italy to respect each other's natural spheres of influence and settle any dispute "in an amicable way." It defined the Soviet's "territorial aspirations" as south "in the direction of the Indian Ocean."

Molotov was not impressed. Russia, he said, was more interested in Europe and the Dardanelles than the Indian Ocean. "Consequently," he said, "paper agreements will not suffice for the Soviet Union; she would have to insist on effective guarantees of her security." He made an exhaustive list of other Soviet interests: Swedish neutrality, access to the Baltic Sea; and the fate of Romania, Hungary, Bulgaria, Yugoslavia and Greece.

Ribbentrop was so taken aback that, according to the minutes of that meeting, he could "only repeat again and again that the decisive question was whether the Soviet Union was prepared and in a position to co-operate with us in the liquidation of the British Empire." Molotov replied with sarcasm: if Germany was waging a life-and-death struggle against England as Hitler had remarked that afternoon, he could only assume this meant that Germany was fighting "for life" and England "for death." And when Ribbentrop persisted that England was beaten but didn't know it, the Russian replied, "If that is so, why are we sitting in this air-raid shelter? And whose bombs are those that are falling so close that their explosions are heard even here?"

Molotov won the argument but lost the case. When Hitler read the report of the air-shelter discussion he was galled. Convinced that the Russians were not serious about a four-power pact, he gave up the last scant hope of entente and resolved to do what he had vowed to do since 1928. At last he irrevocably decided to attack Russia, confiding later to Bormann that Molotov's visit had convinced him "that sooner or later Stalin would abandon us and go over to the enemy." He could not submit to Soviet blackmail regarding Finland, Romania, Bulgaria and Turkey. "The Third Reich, defender and protector of Europe, could not have sacrificed these friendly countries on the altar of Communism. Such behavior would have been dishonorable, and we should have been punished for it. From the moral as well as from the strategic point of view it would have been a miserable gambit. War with Russia had become inevitable, whatever we did; and to postpone it only meant that we should later have to fight under conditions far less favorable. I therefore decided, as soon as Molotov departed, that I would settle accounts with Russia as soon as fair weather permitted." One encouragement was the miserable performance of the Red Army against little Finland. He had also come to regard himself as a man of destiny, superior to any other human being, whose genius and will power would conquer any enemy. Mesmerized by his political and military victories, he explained to one Nazi commander that he was the first and only mortal who had emerged into a "superhuman state." His nature was "more godlike than human," and therefore as the first of the new race of supermen he was "bound by none of the conventions of human morality" and stood "above the law."

2

Hitler kept his decision to himself, however, leaving his commanders under the impression that England was still the primary target. On the day of Molotov's arrival in Berlin he had issued a directive aimed at bringing England to her knees without having to risk an invasion across the Channel. This plan called for a combination of blows to finish what the Italians had so ineptly started in Egypt and Greece. These attacks—combined with seizure of Gibraltar, the Canaries, Azores, Madeira and parts of Morocco—would assuredly cut off England from the Empire and force her to capitulate.

It was a chancy if clever plan since it involved co-operation with a dubious collaborator, an unstable ally and a reluctant neutral. No one was more aware of the difficulties of such a complex campaign than the Führer, but despite recent frustrations he was confident of bringing Pétain, Mussolini and Franco to heel. He began with the last. "I have decided to attack Gibraltar," he told the Caudillo's envoy, Serrano Suñer, on November 18. "All that is required is the signal to begin, and a beginning must be made."

But Franco's brother-in-law was as impossible to pin down as ever. He repeated Spain's dire need for grain and renewed her territorial demands. Hitler refused the latter outright, pointing out how well paid Spain would be if she joined the victorious side. Serrano Suñer observed that Spain, as Napoleon had found to his dismay, had always been ready to resist *any* invasion of its territory. This was succeeded by a final observation which somehow managed to combine another threat with the promise of compliance: Spain would have to use the remaining period of neutrality to buy wheat from the West. It was a tantalizing performance that left Hitler irritated and frustrated, and he later told intimates that Serrano Suñer was "the most evil spirit . . . the (gravedigger) of modern Spain!"

Convinced that Franco would eventually join the war, the Führer held the final briefing on the seizure of Gibraltar, Operation Felix, early in December. He told his commanders that he would undoubtedly get Franco's formal consent in the near future and then sent a personal friend of Franco's to bring him to terms. His choice, Canaris, was disastrous. The admiral, working against Hitler since 1938, formally presented Hitler's arguments, then informally advised Franco to stay out of a war that the Axis was bound to lose.*

When Canaris reported that Franco would enter the war only "when England was about ready to collapse," Hitler lost his patience; on December 10 he instructed his commanders to abandon Felix as a lost cause. But a few weeks later he made another appeal to Franco. In a long plaintive letter he promised to deliver grain immediately if the Caudillo would only approve an early assault on Gibraltar. He made a pledge never to forsake Franco that was followed by a final plea: "I believe, Caudillo, that we three men, the Duce, you and I, are linked to one another by the most implacable force of history, and that we should therefore, in this historic conflict, obey the supreme commandment to realize that in grave times such as these nations can be saved by stout hearts rather than by seemingly prudent caution."

Once more Franco appeared to agree with everything Hitler said, yet did nothing. It was by will power alone that he stalled Felix and saved Gibraltar for England, and by so doing he kept the Mediterranean open to the West while confining Adolf Hitler to the continent of Europe. If the Mediterranean had been closed, it is most likely that all of North Africa and the Middle East would have fallen to the Reich. The entire Arab world would have enthusiastically joined the Axis with all its resources—because of their hatred of the Jews. Apart from Spain's desperate economic situation and his fear of aligning himself with an eventual loser, there was a compelling personal motive for Franco's decision to thwart Hitler. He was part Jewish.†

3

Stalin waited almost two weeks before informing the Germans that the Soviets would join Hitler's proposed four-power pact on several condi-

---

* After the war the Marquis de Valdeglesias, in the presence of Franco, asked General Vigon (a close friend of Canaris) if it was true that the admiral had worked against Spanish interests. Franco lunged from his chair. "No, no," he exclaimed, "Canaris was an excellent friend of Spain!" "Perhaps," observed the marquis, "he was a closer friend of Spain than his own country." At this point, recalled Valdeglesias, "the Caudillo's extreme excitement confirmed my impression that this was true."

† This was known by the British ambassador to Spain, Sir Samuel Hoare, and others in the diplomatic community but it is extremely doubtful that Hitler—who had recently complained that Franco treated him like a little haggling Jew—had been informed of this by his own diplomats, who had also hidden from him the fact that Molotov's wife was Jewish.

tions, such as withdrawal of troops from Finland. The demands were not excessive but, to the surprise of the Foreign Office, Hitler did not deign to haggle—or even bother to send Moscow a reply.

His mind was set on force of arms and late in the month his field commanders began a series of war games involving the attack on Russia. A day after their conclusion, on December 5, the chiefs of staff of the three army groups involved met with Hitler, Brauchitsch and Halder. While approving Halder's basic plan of attack, the Führer was averse to imitating Napoleon with a main drive on Moscow. Seizure of the capital, he said, "was not so very important." Brauchitsch protested that Moscow was of supreme importance not only as the focal point of the Soviet communications network but as an armament center. This brought forth a heated retort. "Only completely ossified brains, absorbed in the ideas of past centuries," said Hitler, "could see any worth-while objective in taking the capital." *His* interest lay in Leningrad and Stalingrad, the Bolshevik breeding grounds. With these two nests destroyed, Bolshevism would be dead. And that was the primary aim of their attack.

Brauchitsch's protest that this was the aim of a politician led to a lecture proving that politics and military strategy were interdependent. "Hegemony over Europe," said Hitler, "will be decided in battle against *Russia.*" The defeat of the Soviet Union, for example, would help bring his secondary enemy, England, to terms. Five days later Hitler began preparing his own people for the coming crusade with a ringing speech in Berlin on the inequitable distribution of the riches of the earth. It was not fair, he said, for Germans to live 360 persons per square mile while other countries were sparsely populated. "We must solve these problems," he concluded, "and, therefore, we will solve them."

At the same time Goebbels was preparing Germany for hard times ahead. The prolonged Yuletide atmosphere, he told his associates, must be confined exclusively to two days. "Even then the feast of Christmas itself should be fitted into the framework of present-day happenings. A sloppy Christmas tree atmosphere lasting several weeks is out of tune with the militant mood of the German people." There would also be a raising of Germany's moral tone—outside of the big cities. "No strip dancers are to perform in rural areas, in small towns, or in front of soldiers." Comedians were also forbidden in the future to make political jibes or "lewd erotic jokes."

The revised plan of attack was presented to Hitler on December 17. He altered it to delay the drive on Moscow until the Baltic States were cleared and Leningrad captured, then changed the name of the operation from Otto to a more meaningful title: Barbarossa (Red Beard) after

Frederick I, the Holy Roman Emperor who had marched east in 1190 with his legions to take the Holy Land. The bulk of the Red Army standing on its western frontier, he directed, would be "destroyed by daring operations led by deeply penetrating armored spearheads." Those forces still capable of giving battle would be prevented from withdrawing into the depths of the U.S.S.R. "The final objective of the operation is to erect a barrier against Asiatic Russia on the general line Volga–Archangel. The last surviving area of Russia in the Urals can then, if necessary, be eliminated by the air force."

Halder suspected that Hitler was only bluffing and asked Engel if this was a genuine plan. The adjutant believed that Hitler himself did not yet know. But the die indeed was cast, the crusade set in motion. Hitler had no patience with those who, counseling moderation in triumph, wanted Germany to cease its aggression and enjoy the fruits of conquest. Most of Europe, they argued, was Hitler's and if he bided his time England too would recognize the reality of his hegemony. But to Adolf Hitler such a passive policy was unacceptable. The aim of National Socialism was the destruction of Bolshevism. How could he turn his back on his mission in life?

"I had always maintained that we ought at all costs to avoid waging war on two fronts," he later told Bormann, "and you may rest assured that I pondered long and anxiously over Napoleon, and his experiences in Russia. Why, then, you may ask, this war against Russia, and why at the time that I selected?" There was no hope of ending the war by invasion of England and hostilities would have gone on interminably with the Americans playing an increasingly active role. The one and only chance of vanquishing the Soviet Union was to take the initiative. Why attack in 1941? Because time was working in Russia's favor and against the Germans. Only when he held the territories of Russia would time be on *Germany's* side.

4

On the surface relations between the two unnatural allies prospered. Within days after setting Barbarossa into action—on January 10, 1941— Hitler authorized promulgation of two agreements with the Soviets: an economic treaty specifying reciprocal deliveries of commodities; and a secret protocol in which Germany renounced its previous claim to a strip of Lithuanian territory for 7,500,000 gold dollars.

Behind the façade of amity, however, dissension increased between the trade delegations. The flow of raw materials from the Soviet Union was steady and on schedule, while German deliveries were painfully slow and erratic. Whenever, for instance, machine tools were ready for shipment to Russia some inspector from the Air or War Ministry would appear to praise the workmanship, then hijack the tools in the name of national defense. This organized slowdown extended to warships. Hitler himself ordered work stopped on a heavy cruiser promised to Stalin so more submarines could be produced. The Germans did offer to tow the hull to Leningrad and arm it with 380-mm. Krupp guns but they wrangled so insistently over price that the ship was still in Wilhelmshaven.

Stalin became involved in the argument over German deliveries but he always restrained his own negotiators. He was determined to maintain good relations with his obstreperous ally for as long as possible. While he was striving for peace—at least until the Red Army was brought up to fighting strength—Hitler continued to prepare his people for war and the New Order. He did so in an ominously oblique manner in his annual January 30 address at the Sportpalast. After a rousing introductory speech by Goebbels, he strode rigidly to the platform, raising an arm diffidently in the party salute, amidst wild cheers. He stood silent for a moment and then began speaking. "His voice," recalled Shirer's replacement at CBS, "was first a slow, low rumble." Then, with sudden vehemence, his arms began sweeping in wide gestures.

He could have been thinking of Barbarossa and the racial cleansing that would follow when he said, "I am convinced that 1941 will be the crucial year of the great New Order in Europe," but the enemy he attacked was Britain, leader of the "pluto-democracies," which, he charged, were under the control of an international Jewish clique and supported by dissident émigrés. These words provided cover for his attack on the Soviet Union while preparing his own people for the final assault on Jewry and, upon hearing Halder's report four days later that German troop strength would be equal to Russia's and far superior in quality, Hitler exclaimed, "When Barbarossa commences the world will hold its breath and make no comment!" His vision of conquest, in fact, soared beyond the limits of his own continent; on February 17 he ordered preparation of a drive to the heart of Britain's empire, India. This would be accompanied by seizure of the Near East in a pincer movement: on the left from Russia across Iran and on the right from North Africa toward the Suez Canal. While these grandiose plans were primarily designed to force Britain onto the side of Germany, they indicated the extent of Hitler's vaulting aspirations. Russia was as good as won and his restless mind was already seeking new worlds to conquer, new enemies, America and Roosevelt in particular, to bring to heel.

For a dreamer Hitler could, quite often, be practical. No sooner had he envisaged vast fields of conquest than he began devoting himself to a relatively modest one. The defeat of Italian troops in Albania and Greece had, in his own words, indirectly "struck a blow at the belief of our invincibility, that was held by friend and foe alike." Greece, therefore, had to be occupied and order re-established throughout the area before Barbarossa could safely be launched. This was not his sole motivation. Hitler also looked upon Italian failure in the Balkans as a golden opportunity to gain more territory and economic assets.

The occupation of Greece, no simple matter, was particularly complicated by geography. Four countries lay between Hitler and his target—Hungary, Romania, Bulgaria and Yugoslavia. The first two, virtual German satellites, had been invested by his troops for some months; and the third, under considerable pressure, had joined the Tripartite Pact on the first of March. While this gave German troops a clear road to Greece, strategic Yugoslavia remained a military as well as political concern. Its leaders wanted neither German nor Russian intervention in the Balkans and, after veiled threats and vague promises failed to bring them into the Axis, Hitler invited Prince Paul, the Yugoslav Regent, to the Berghof so that he could exert his personal influence.

Tempted as he was by Hitler's promise to guarantee Yugoslavia territorial integrity, Prince Paul protested that the decision was most difficult for personal reasons: his wife's Greek ancestry, her personal sympathies for England and his own antagonism toward Mussolini. The Prince left without giving an answer but three days later—an interminable wait for Hitler —he replied that he was willing to sign the Tripartite Pact, provided Yugoslavia was not required to lend any military assistance or allow passage of German troops through its territory. This was unsatisfactory but Hitler, controlling his feelings, sent back word that Germany accepted these conditions. This conciliatory offer unexpectedly brought a rebuff. The Yugoslavs could do nothing that might involve them in a war, "possibly with America or even Russia."

By mid-March it was evident that the Yugoslav government would not yield and the strain on the Führer was visible as he spoke on the sixteenth at the Memorial Day ceremony in the Berlin War Museum. "His face was drawn and haggard," recalled Louis Lochner, "his skin was ashy gray, his eyes devoid of their usual luster. Care and worry was stamped on him. But that was not the most striking thing. What amazed me was the matter of fact, uninterested, detached way in which he rattled off his usual platitudes appropriate to such an occasion." He read the brief speech as though it bored him, making no attempt to rouse the millions listening to him over the radio.

The next day the situation in Yugoslavia changed with dramatic suddenness. The Crown Council agreed to sign the Tripartite Pact. This brought a public outcry of indignation and, after three ministers resigned in protest, high-ranking air force officers led a revolt. By dawn of March 27 the rebels had overthrown the government and the youthful heir to the throne, Peter, was King.

In Berlin that morning, Hitler was congratulating himself on the happy conclusion of the Yugoslav problem; he had just received a message that the local population had been "universally most impressed" by Yugoslavia's acceptance of the new pact and that the government was "entirely master of the situation." Five minutes before noon, as he was preparing himself for an important conference with Japanese Foreign Minister Matsuoka, a telegram arrived from Belgrade. When Hitler read that the former members of the Yugoslav government were reportedly under arrest, he first thought it was a joke. Then he was seized with indignation. To be robbed of victory at the last moment was insupportable. This time his rage was genuine. He felt he'd been "personally insulted." He shouted an order for military commanders to report at once to the chancellery, sent an emergency call for Ribbentrop, who was talking with Matsuoka at the Wilhelmstrasse, then burst into the conference room where Jodl and Keitel were waiting for the daily briefing. Brandishing the telegram, Hitler exclaimed that he was now going to smash Yugoslavia once and for all!

Like a lover spurned moments after being accepted, the more he talked the angrier and more excited he became. He vowed he would issue orders for immediate, simultaneous attacks from north and east. Keitel protested that such an ambitious operation was impossible. The Barbarossa deadline could not be postponed since troop movements were already proceeding according to their planned maximum railway-capacity program. Furthermore, List's army in Bulgaria was too weak to pit against Yugoslavia and only a fool would rely on help from the Hungarians.

"That is the very reason why I have called in Brauchitsch and Halder," said Hitler. They would have to find some solution. "Now I intend to make a clean sweep of the Balkans—it is time people got to know me better."

By ones and twos, Brauchitsch, Halder, Göring, Ribbentrop and their adjutants joined the meeting. All listened in awe as Hitler declared in a harsh and vengeful tone that he was determined "to smash Yugoslavia militarily and as a state." To Ribbentrop's protest that they should first confront the Yugoslavs with an ultimatum, Hitler replied acidly, "Is that how you size up the situation? The Yugoslavs would swear black is white. Of course, they say they have no warlike intentions, and when we march into Greece they will stab us in the back." The attack, he exclaimed, must start as soon as possible! "Politically it is especially important that the blow against Yugoslavia be carried out with merciless harshness and that the military destruction be done in Blitzkrieg style." That would frighten the Turks as well as Greece. Göring's main task was to eliminate the Yugoslav air force ground installations before destroying the capital "in attacks by waves."

Hitler disposed of the hastily summoned Hungarian and Bulgarian ministers with dispatch. In a fifteen-minute meeting with the former his comment on the revolt in Belgrade was reduced to a quotation: "Whom the gods would destroy they first make mad." This was followed by a promise: if Hungary helped on this crisis, she would win back the long-coveted Banat area. It was a unique opportunity for Hungary to obtain revisions she might otherwise not get for years. "You can believe me that I am not pretending, for I am not saying more than I can be answerable for."

The next interview took but five minutes. Hitler told the Bulgarian minister that he was relieved by the events in Yugoslavia. "The everlasting uncertainty down there is over," he said and used Macedonia as the bait for continued Bulgarian co-operation with the Axis. The dispensing of largesse—of other people's property—was abruptly followed by rage. "The storm," he exclaimed, "will burst over Yugoslavia with a rapidity that will dumfound those gentlemen!"

With orders for attack issued and two hesitant allies bribed into line, Hitler at last found time that afternoon to see the Japanese envoy. Hitler hoped that America could be kept out of the war and suggested that the best way might be for Japan to seize Singapore. This should be done quickly since another such golden opportunity would not soon occur. And Japan, he added, need have no fear that Russia could counter with an attack in Manchuria in view of the strength of the German army.

Matsuoka, a graduate of the University of Oregon, answered slowly and deliberately in English. He was convinced, he said, that the German proposal was the right one, then added: "But I can give no firm promise on behalf of Japan at the moment." He hastily assured the visibly disappointed Hitler that he himself was for action. In truth, he was so eager for it that the Japanese army had sent Colonel Yatsugi Nagai along on this trip to see that he made no harsh promises about Singapore. Consequently Matsuoka was forced to respond evasively to every mention of the British stronghold. Even when Hermann Göring, after accepting a scroll of Mount Fuji, jokingly promised to come and see the real thing "if Japan takes Singapore," the envoy nodded toward the edgy Colonel Nagai and said, "You'll have to ask him."

Matsuoka was not at all reticent about a treaty he hoped to make with Stalin in the near future and was surprised to hear Ribbentrop, who had given him the idea of a grand four-power treaty, say, "How can you conclude such a pact at this time? Just remember, the U.S.S.R. never gives anything for nothing." Nagai took this to be a warning, but Matsuoka's enthusiasm could not be damped even when Ambassador Oshima told him in confidence that there was a strong likelihood that Germany and Russia would soon be at war.

The meeting with Matsuoka was not the end of Hitler's day. He signed Directive No. 25 calling for simultaneous attacks on Yugoslavia and Greece before sitting down at midnight to tell Mussolini about Yugoslavia. "Now I do not regard this situation as disastrous, to be sure," he wrote, "but nevertheless as one which is so difficult that we, for our part, must avoid making any mistakes if we do not want ultimately to imperil our entire position." He had, therefore, taken all necessary measures to meet any developing crisis with the necessary military means. "I now urgently request you, Duce, not to carry out any further operations in Albania for the next few days." After this polite reminder not to endanger the situation with another hopeless adventure, he called for "*absolute secrecy*," underlining these words for emphasis.

The letter with all its punctilious courtesy emphasized the new relationship between the two men. After the misadventures in Greece and Africa, Mussolini was no longer the "senior partner." In the Führer's eyes, he was branded with the unforgivable defect of failure. The list of Hitler's grievances was formidable, if debatable: the abortive Grecian campaign had not only encouraged the British to launch a successful offensive in Libya, and discouraged Franco from supporting the Gibraltar operation, but forced Germany to deal with the dissident Yugoslavs at a most inappropriate time. Barbarossa would have to be postponed for at least a month.

5

Although Hitler blamed the delay of Barbarossa on the Yugoslav campaign, the general shortage of equipment for the Wehrmacht—his responsibility—could have been a more determining factor. In any event, he did not regard the postponement as a calamity despite a gnawing dread: "I was haunted by the obsession that the Russians might take the offensive." He did not seem perturbed when he summoned his field commanders to the chancellery to announce a definite date of attack and, more important, deliver a doctrinal lecture on the coming "struggle of two opposing ideologies." By 11 A.M. March 30 the senior commanders for Barbarossa, along with their leading staff officers, were gathered in the small cabinet chamber where a speaker's lectern had been set up. More than two hundred were seated in long rows according to rank and seniority by the time Hitler entered from the rear. With a shuffling of chairs the assemblage smartly rose, then sat down once Hitler stepped to the rostrum. His mood was grave as he spoke of the military and political situation. The United States could not reach the peak of production and military power for four years. Consequently this was the time to clean up Europe. War with Russia was inevitable, he said, and merely to sit back and wait would be disastrous. The attack would begin on June 22.

It could not be postponed, he said, since no successor would ever again exercise sufficient authority to accept responsibility for unleashing it. He and he alone could stop the Bolshevik steamroller before all Europe succumbed to it. He called for the destruction of the Bolshevik state and the annihilation of the Red Army, adding an assurance that victory would be quick and overwhelming. The only problem, he added ominously, was how to deal with the conquered Russians, how to treat prisoners of war and non-combatants.

The military sat stiff in their chairs, wondering if they would be called upon to take part in this program. As military professionals most of them had been repelled by Hitler's ruthless measures, after the conquest of Poland, against Polish Jews, intelligentsia, clergy and nobility. Their fears were quickened by Hitler's next loud threat: "The war against Russia will be such that it cannot be fought in a knightly fashion! This struggle is one of ideologies and racial differences and will have to be conducted with unprecedented, merciless and unrelenting harshness." There was no utterance of protest, any more than there had been in Poland, not even an involuntary gesture of protest.

That morning Hitler had put his military leaders to the final humiliating test with his demand that they compromise their honor as warriors. Now they, like so many in Germany who shared his fear and hatred of Jews and Slavs, were reluctant partners in his crusade. Today Lebensraum, which they considered just recompense for the Russian territories won in battle but lost at Versailles, had been relegated to the background and Hitler's real grounds for invasion lay exposed: annihilation of Bolshevism —that is, annihilation of the Jews.

In the meantime preparations for the Yugoslav-Greek invasions were brought to a conclusion. In Belgrade there were daily patriotic demonstrations, some instigated by local Communists carrying out Soviet Balkan policy. Russia, in fact, was so eager to bolster the Yugoslavs against German incursion that she signed a pact with the new government on April 5. This did not daunt Hitler. The following dawn German troops crossed the Yugoslav border in overwhelming force. Bombers began systematically destroying Belgrade in an operation to which Hitler had given a significant code name, Punishment. The Soviet leaders, their signature hardly dry on the treaty with Yugoslavia, reacted with striking indifference, relegating the attack on Yugoslavia and Greece to the back pages of *Pravda*. Mere passing mention was made of the devastating air raids on Belgrade which were continuing around the clock.

Hitler warned Goebbels that the entire campaign would take at least two months and this information was passed on to the people. It was based on a gross overestimation of enemy strength. Within a single week German and Hungarian troops marched into a shattered Belgrade which was little more than rubble. In the process of Punishment, 17,000 civilians had died. On the seventeenth the remnants of the Yugoslav army surrendered. Ten days later the Grecian campaign was virtually concluded when German tanks rumbled into Athens. Twenty-nine German divisions had been transported into the battle zones over primitive roads and rail systems at an extravagant cost of energy, fuel and time. Of this huge force, only ten divisions saw action for more than six days. A sledge hammer had been used to kill mosquitoes. It was this shocking failure of German intelligence which was more responsible for the delay of Barbarossa than Mussolini.

Hitler's dismay at the cost of the Balkan invasion was more than mitigated by a startling development in North Africa. With only three divisions at his disposal, General Erwin Rommel burst across Cyrenaica to within a few miles of Egypt. This triumph, which surprised Hitler as much as the enemy, compromised Britain's hold on the entire eastern Mediterranean. It also damaged British prestige and persuaded Stalin to maintain good relations with the Germans despite provocations. Besides shutting his eyes to their aggressions in the Balkans, the Soviet leader persistently ignored the growing rumors that Hitler was planning to invade his own country. Warnings had already come from numerous sources, including the U. S. State Department. Foreign diplomats in Moscow talked openly of an imminent clash. "Thus, the [Jewish] wife of the American Ambassador Steinhardt," reported a German diplomat to Berlin, "remarked that she would like to be out of Moscow before the troops entered it."

For months the Soviet intelligence service itself had been predicting the attack. But Stalin did not trust his own informants and his paranoia increased with the volume of reports. Convinced that Hitler would not be stupid enough to attack Russia without first neutralizing England, he imagined these were rumors manufactured by the capitalist West, which hoped to come between him and Hitler. He wrote in red ink on one alarming report from a Czech agent: "This information is a British provocation. Find out where it comes from and punish the culprit."

Marshal Yeremenko confirmed Stalin's irrational suspicions in his memoirs: "That was why he failed to authorize all urgent or decisive defense measures along the frontier, for fear that this would serve the Hitlerites as a pretext to believe the rumors since his own hope was for the capitalists and Nazis to destroy each other. In any event, he wanted to avoid provoking Hitler into an attack before the Red Army was fully armed."

He was equally anxious to placate Japan. He treated Foreign Minister Matsuoka, fresh from Berlin, as an honored guest, making a public show of his delight when a neutrality pact was signed. At the celebration party in the Kremlin—it came on the day Belgrade fell—Stalin personally brought plates of food to the Japanese envoys, embraced them, kissed them and danced around. The treaty was a coup for his diplomacy, convincing proof that he could disregard rumors of a German attack on Russia. Certainly Hitler would never have permitted Japan to conclude this agreement if he had any such notion.

Stalin was in such a good humor that he followed the Japanese delegation to the station platform for a final tipsy good-by. He kissed General Nagai, then, encompassing the diminutive Matsuoka in a bear hug, gave him several affectionate smacks. "There is nothing to fear in Europe," he said, "now that there is a Japan-Soviet neutrality pact!"

A few minutes later, as the Japanese train moved off, he threw an arm around German Ambassador von der Schulenburg. "We must remain friends," he said, "and you must now do everything to that end!" He turned to a colonel, checked to make sure he too was a German, and roared out: "We shall remain friends with you—*in any event!*" He was probably referring to the numerous flights of German planes over Russian territory. In the past two weeks alone there had been fifty such incursions. Two days after embracing Schulenburg, however, Stalin was spurred to action by the emergency landing of a German plane almost a hundred miles inside the Soviet Union; aboard were found a camera, unexposed rolls of film and a torn topographical map of the districts of the U.S.S.R. The Soviets lodged a formal complaint with Berlin, adding that eighty other violations of Soviet air space had occurred since the end of March. Still it was a mild protest and Stalin persisted in ignoring a new flood of warnings, the latest from British Ambassador Cripps, who predicted Hitler would attack on June 22.*

While everyone in the German Foreign Office suspected an attack on Russia might be imminent, it was not until now that Hitler told Ribbentrop of Barbarossa. The unhappy Foreign Minister "wanted to try one more diplomatic approach to Moscow but Hitler refused to allow any further démarche." He forbade Ribbentrop to discuss the matter with anyone, and then assured Ambassador von der Schulenburg in Moscow: "I do not intend a war against Russia." Two days later Hitler again confirmed the attack date, the one Cripps had mentioned, June 22.

There was no doubt that Germany was entering this contest with the most powerful armed force in the world. Yet she had no valid ally. Japan was on the other side of the world; Italy was a liability; Spain was intransigent; and Vichy France was unreliable. Hitler's alliances had been diminished by victory. His easy conquests had made all his friends—including little ones like Yugoslavia, Hungary and Romania—uneasy. His only strength was the Wehrmacht and reliance on force was fatal for any conqueror. Wars are won by politics, not by arms. Napoleon had learned this hard lesson from the British, who had a tradition of losing battles and winning wars. They had lost the battle against Hitler on the Continent but had already won the battle for their dominions and the battle for American aid.

Hitler's only chance for victory in the East was an alliance with those millions in the Soviet Union who hated Stalin but, unless he followed the advice of the Rosenberg group to treat them liberally, he would not only lose his last chance for a genuine Grand Alliance but turn potential allies into relentless enemies.

---

* For some time members of the Ultra team had been attempting to relay vital information to the Soviets without revealing the source. "For this purpose," recalled Hugh Trevor-Roper, "we had a special liaison officer in Moscow. But such was the Russian distrust that he was never able to make contact with his Russian opposite number. I remember he once told me that the nearest he had got to him was when the Russian, a general, waved to him in the opera."

"We were luckier with the Russians in London," said Asher Lee, "and gave them the guts but not the teeth of Ultra." Lee dealt with a mixed bag: an officer in the NKVD, an air attaché, a test pilot and a member of the Supreme Soviet with the rank of colonel. But they too were suspicious and, according to Lee, "virtually ignored Ultra material, at any rate for the pre-Stalingrad period."

6

Although Hitler's military leaders had first been appalled by the thought of invading Russia, they now almost universally shared his conviction that victory would come quickly. The consensus was that the campaign would be successfully completed within three months and Field Marshal von Brauchitsch had just drastically reduced this estimate. After "up to four weeks" of major battle, he predicted, the war would degenerate into a mopping-up operation against "minor resistance." The hardheaded Jodl concurred and curtly silenced Warlimont who questioned the categorical statement that "the Russian colossus will be proved to be a pig's bladder; prick it and it will burst."

The Führer, according to General Guderian, "had succeeded in infecting his immediate military entourage with his own baseless optimism. The OKW and OKH were so serenely confident of victory before winter set in that winter clothing had only been prepared for every fifth man in the army." There were, of course, a few dissidents in high places. From the beginning Ribbentrop and Admiral Raeder openly opposed Barbarossa. Keitel, too, had serious reservations but he had learned to keep any objections to himself. There was also opposition within Hitler's inner circle. Rudolf Hess—second in line after Göring to succeed the Führer—heartily approved the theory of Lebensraum but opposed attacking Russia so long as the war with England continued. The Bolsheviks alone, he confided to Schwerin von Krosigk, were profiting by this unfortunate conflict. Determined to resolve the question of how to neutralize Britain, he had met with Professor Karl Haushofer, the geopolitician, in the Grunewald Forest the previous summer. Until two in the morning they discussed the best means of negotiating a peace. Haushofer suggested a secret rendezvous with some prominent Englishman in a neutral city. From this modest beginning sprang an adventure that would intrigue the world.

Excited by the prospect of a secret mission, Hess took the plan to Hitler, hoping perhaps that this would restore his own waning influence. Despite Hess's lofty rank, Hitler had not taken him seriously for over a year. "I hope he never becomes my successor," he reportedly told Hanfstaengl. "I wouldn't know whom to be more sorry for, Hess or the party." But his affection for *"mein Hesserl,"* his second Kubizek, had not diminished and he gave the Deputy Führer grudging approval to make inquiries through Albrecht Haushofer, the professor's elder son, who worked in the Foreign Office.

Young Haushofer, a member of the Resistance for several years, diffidently suggested to Hess that the best possibility would be a meeting with his own closest English friend, the Duke of Hamilton, since he had ready access to Churchill and the King. Hess left the meeting with enthusiasm but Albrecht wrote his father that "the whole thing is a fool's errand." At the same time he decided to do what he could, as a patriotic German, to make peace with England. He wrote the Duke of Hamilton proposing a meeting with Hess in Lisbon. He signed the message "A" and sent it, via Hess's brother, to a Mrs. V. Roberts in Lisbon. She transmitted it to England but the letter was intercepted by the British censor. He turned it over to the Secret Service, which eventually instructed RAF intelligence to take appropriate action. So much time had passed by then that Hess decided to act on his own without the knowledge of the Haushofers or Hitler. His plan was to embark on the mission himself, doing so in a dramatic manner that would strike the English as a sporting gesture. He would fly over the estate of the Duke of Hamilton, land by parachute and secretly conduct negotiations under a false name. He was an expert flier, a flight officer in the First World War, the winner in 1934 of the hazardous air race around the Zugspitze, Germany's highest peak, near Garmisch. A solo flight over enemy lines to a remote area of Scotland would surely appeal to young Hamilton, the first to fly over Mount Everest. "I was confronted by a very hard decision," Hess later told interrogators. "I do not think I could have arrived at my final choice unless I had continually kept before my eyes the vision of an endless line of children's coffins with weeping mothers behind them, both English and German; and another line of coffins of mothers with mourning children." Hess was convinced that only by such an original stratagem could the Führer's dream of a coalition between Germany and England be effectuated. If he failed, it would not involve Hitler; if he succeeded, he would give the Führer credit for the scheme. Admittedly the chances were slim that he would even reach Scotland alive—perhaps ten to one. But the prize was worth the hazard.

Hess was sure that Hitler would welcome a novel peace venture but would never allow him to risk his life in the attempt. Hadn't he already refused to let Hess fly at the front? Therefore secrecy was essential. It was the decision of a naïve, not too bright acolyte who, according to Adjutant Wiedemann, was the Führer's "most devoted and dedicated subordinate." A painfully shy man whose greatest ambition was to further his master's career, Hess hid behind tightly stern lips, heavy jowls, fanatic eyes and a fearsome pair of eyebrows. But this was no Teutonic Oliver Cromwell. Once he smiled the severity vanished.

It was this Parsifal who conjured up the dream of flight to the enemy, this man of culture without judgment, this completely devoted servant who convinced himself that he was carrying out the *true* will of his master. If it was a woolly scheme, it was organized and prepared with exquisite efficiency. He persuaded Willy Messerschmidt, the aeronautical engineer, to let him borrow an ME-110 two-man plane for practice flights, then criticized its limited range. It should, he said, have two auxiliary tanks of 700 liters fitted on each wing. After reluctantly making this change, Messerschmidt was talked into adding special radio equipment. Then came training under the excuse of recreation, and after twenty flights Hess felt he had mastered the modified plane. In the meantime, contrary to wartime regulations, he had acquired a new leather flying suit, persuaded Baur (Hitler's personal pilot) to get him a secret map of forbidden air zones, and installed a new radio in his home on the outskirts of Munich.

It was quite possible, he later wrote his wife from prison, "that I became not quite normal. The flight and its purpose had taken hold of me with the force of a fixed idea. Anything else, I seemed to see and hear only partly . . ." He lived and moved in those early days of May in a world of instruments, piston pressures, detachable petrol containers, auxiliary air pumps, cooling temperatures and radio bearings.

His secretary, Hildegard Fath, noticed that Hess often did not listen to what she was saying. His wife was equally aware of his preoccupation. What surprised her even more was the unusual amount of time he spent with their four-year-old son, who bore Hitler's secret name, Wolf. Surprising too, in view of Hess's reluctance to pose for pictures, was his own recent suggestion that photographs of father and son be taken.

Hess rose early on the morning of May 10, a Saturday, and, upon learning that the weather forecast was good, he made arrangements for the flight. Never had he been more gallant to his wife. After tea he kissed her hand and then stood gravely at the door of the nursery "with an air of one deep in thought and almost hesitating." She asked him when he was returning and, told it would be Monday at the latest, she bluntly said, "I cannot believe it. You will not come back as soon as that!" She guessed he was bound for a meeting with someone like Pétain but he feared that she had guessed the truth. He "turned hot and cold in turns" and, before she could say anything more, he dashed into the nursery to take a last look at their slumbering son.

At 6 P.M., after giving his adjutant a letter for Hitler, Hess took off from the Augsburg airport and headed for the North Sea. Abruptly, contrary to the weather report, the cloud cover vanished and for a moment he thought of turning back. But he kept going and found England covered by a veil of mist. Seeking shelter, he dived down with full throttle, at first unaware that a Spitfire was on his tail. Outdistancing the pursuer, he hedgehopped over the dark countryside at more than 450 miles an hour, narrowly skimming trees and houses. Baur had always claimed Hess was the type of pilot who liked to fly through open hangar doors and it was in this barnstormer's spirit that he aimed at the mountain looming ahead. It was his guidepost and he literally climbed up the steep slope and slid down the other side, always keeping within a few yards of the ground. Just before 11 P.M. he turned east and picked out a railway and small lake which he remembered were just south of the duke's residence. He climbed to 6000 feet, a safe height from which to parachute, and switched off the motor. He opened the hatch—then suddenly realized he had overlooked one step in his elaborate training: "I had never asked how to jump; I thought it was too simple!" As the ME-110 plummeted, he recalled a friend mentioning that a plane should be on its back. After a half roll, he found himself upside down, held inside by centrifugal force. He began to see stars; just before passing out, he thought: "Soon the crash must come!" Regaining consciousness, he saw the speed gauge indicate zero. He flung himself out of the plane, pulled at the parachute ring. Fortunately, while unconscious, he had automatically brought the plane out of its semi-looping curve to finish almost perpendicular on its tail. And so, to his amazement, he found himself safely in mid-air.

He hit the ground, stumbled forward and blacked out a second time. He was found by a farmer, marched off to the Home Guard and brought to a barracks in Glasgow. Insisting that he was one Oberleutnant Alfred Horn, he asked to see the Duke of Hamilton.

It was not until Sunday morning that his letter was delivered to Hitler at the Berghof. While Engel was making his daily report, Martin Bormann's brother Albert broke in to announce that Hess's adjutant wanted to see the Führer on a very urgent matter. Albert was driven out with an angry "Can't you see I'm in the middle of a military report and do not wish to be disturbed!" A minute later Albert, face ashen, sidled in again. But this time he would not be put off. Insisting the matter was important and possibly dangerous, he extended the letter from Hess. Hitler put on his glasses and began to read indifferently but as soon as he saw the words "My Führer, when you receive this letter I shall be in England" he dropped into a chair and shouted so loudly he could be heard downstairs: "Oh, my God, my God! He has flown to England!" He hastily read of the technical difficulties of the flight and that Hess's goal was to further the

Führer's own aim of alliance with England but he had kept the flight secret since he knew the Führer would have forbidden it.

> And if, my Führer, this project—which I admit has but very little chance of success—ends in failure and the fates decide against me, this can have no detrimental results either for you or for Germany; it will always be possible for you to deny all responsibility. Simply say I am crazy.

Chalk white, the Führer ordered Engel to get the Reichsmarschall on the phone. As soon as he was located near Nuremberg, Hitler shouted, "Göring, come here immediately!" He yelled at Albert Bormann to fetch his brother and Ribbentrop, placed Hess's hapless adjutant under arrest, and began pacing the room angrily. When Martin Bormann arrived out of breath, Hitler demanded to know if Hess could possibly reach England in an ME-110. The question was answered by the famous ace of the Great War, Luftwaffe General Udet. Never, he said, not with its limited range. And the Führer muttered, "I hope he falls into the sea!"

As the day wore on, Hitler's anger developed into a rage. Private guests, confined to the upper floor, wondered in fear what had happened, while Hitler agitatedly stalked his study trying to work out a believable explanation for the public. Would the Japanese and Italians suspect that Germany was after a separate peace? Would his own soldiers fight less hard? Worst of all, had Hess revealed the plans for Barbarossa? After many drafts a communiqué was finally drawn up explaining that Hess had commandeered a plane against orders and disappeared. It was assumed he had crashed. A letter left behind "unfortunately showed traces of a mental disturbance which justifies the fear that Hess was a victim of hallucinations."

Fräulein Fath heard a broadcast of this announcement while dining. Its tone was so unfriendly that she thought: "Is this the thanks for his lifetime devotion?" She phoned Hess's brother, Alfred, and they mulled over the possibilities. Frau Hess was watching a movie with chauffeurs, servants and adjutants when she was called out by the most junior adjutant. Distraught, he begged her to put on her things. It was such a senseless request that swift dread crossed her mind. But upon learning that it was only a radio broadcast presuming that her husband was dead, she angrily replied: "Nonsense!" She doubted that anything tragic had occurred and put in a priority call to the Berghof, intending to speak to the Führer. But she got Bormann, who said he had absolutely no information. Knowing her husband's assistant as she did, she did not believe him. She phoned Alfred Hess in Berlin. He too could not believe Rudolf was dead.

No announcement had yet come from England even though Hess,

admitting his true identify to the Duke of Hamilton, told about his mission of peace and how he and Albrecht Haushofer had tried to arrange a meeting in Lisbon. Hamilton rushed off to see Churchill, who said, "Well, Hess or no Hess, I am going to see the Marx brothers." Only after the film ended did the Prime Minister interrogate Hamilton thoroughly.

A few hours following the German announcement that Hess was missing, the British finally revealed that he had arrived in England. No details were released. German newspapers were already putting out a reprint of the radio broadcast but the news from London made it necessary to concoct a fuller official version. This one, published on Tuesday the thirteenth, acknowledged the landing of the Deputy Führer in Britain before enlarging on his mental state:

> As is well known in party circles, Hess had undergone severe physical suffering for some years. Recently he had sought relief to an increasing extent in various methods practiced by mesmerists and astrologers, etc. An attempt is also being made to determine to what extent these persons are responsible for bringing about the condition of mental distraction which led him to take this step. . . .

Such an admission caused confusion in Germany that extended to the highest levels. Goebbels told his staff, "Our job is for the moment to keep a stiff upper lip, not to react, not to explain anything, not to enter into polemics. The affair will be fully cleared up in the course of the afternoon and I shall issue detailed instructions from the Obersalzberg this afternoon." He tried to assure his people that the Hess flight, admittedly embarrassing at the moment, would be seen in the future as a mere dramatic episode. "However, there are no grounds for letting our wings droop in any way or for thinking that we shall never live this down."

From this meeting Goebbels flew to Berchtesgaden to attend an emergency convocation of Gauleiters and Reichsleiters. After Bormann had read aloud the Hess letter, the Führer appeared. Hans Frank had not seen him for some time and was shocked at his "disturbed appearance." At first he spoke about Hess "very softly, hesitatingly and with a deep sense of melancholy," but soon his tone changed to one of anger. The flight, he said, was sheer insanity. "Hess is first of all a deserter and if I ever catch him, he will pay for this as any ordinary traitor. Furthermore, it seems to me that this step was strongly influenced by astrological cliques which Hess kept around him. It is time, therefore, to put an end to all these stargazers.* Because of this insanity our position is made much more

---

* There were wholesale arrests of astrologers and occultists suspected of knowing Hess. Performances involving demonstrations of an occult, spiritualist, clairvoyant, telepathic or astrological nature were outlawed.

difficult though not shaken, particularly my belief that the victory in this Jewish war against National Socialism belongs to our unblemished flag." His listeners had already heard stories of Hess's pet lion, as well as his interest in homeopathic medicine and astrology, and were prepared to believe he was mentally disturbed. Yet they wondered, as ordinary citizens did, why then had Hitler retained him in high office?

It was significant that the Führer mentioned not a word to his party leaders about the coming invasion of Russia and his fear that Hess might have revealed it to the English. He need not have worried. Under the interrogation of Hamilton and Sir Ivone Kirkpatrick, Hess insisted there was "no foundation for the rumors now being spread that Hitler is contemplating an early attack on Russia." What he wanted to talk about was peace with England. He had come without Hitler's permission, he said, to "convince responsible persons that since England could not win the war, the wisest course was to make peace now."

As soon as Albrecht Haushofer learned of the flight he hurried to his father's study. "And with such fools we make politics!" he exclaimed. The English would never deal with such a man under such ridiculous circumstances! His father sadly agreed it was a "terrible sacrifice all in vain." Young Haushofer was ordered to Obersalzberg, placed under guard and given pen and paper to write a report for the Führer, who refused to see him. Entitled "English Connections and the Possibility of Utilizing Them," it revealed as much of the truth as possible without implicating friends in the Resistance. Albrecht told of his friendship with the Duke of Hamilton and of the letter he had written at Hess's behest, adding that he himself would be indispensable in case of future negotiations with the English because of his many connections. This report persuaded Hitler not to act hastily. He ordered Haushofer transported to the Gestapo prison in Berlin on the Prince Albrecht Strasse for further interrogation. His father was spared but drew Hitler's special rage. "The Jewish-tainted professor has Hess on his conscience!" he said and reproached himself for not taking steps earlier "to tear apart that whole Munich breed and silence them."

Others connected with Hess were arrested—his brother Alfred, adjutants, orderlies, secretaries and chauffeurs. Ilse Hess was not imprisoned but Martin Bormann did his utmost to humiliate her. He also put as much distance as possible between himself and his former chief. He changed the praenomina of his two children, Rudolf and Ilse, named after the Hesses, and appointed more appropriate godparents. Selected as Hess's successor, he eliminated everything that reminded him of his former employer. All photographs of Hess, books and official literature bearing his picture were destroyed. He even attempted to confiscate the Hess home but this was too much even for Hitler. He refused to sign the eviction notice.

The guests at the Berghof were released from the top floor but no one dared speak of the flight to England, not after someone innocently asked why Hess's adjutant was not at the table and Bormann replied that he was in prison—"and he will not come out again." "Typically," commented Engel in his diary, "the only one who walks around this beehive expectantly is Bormann; we all agree that he considers this *his* hour."

In England the government had decided not to make public the interrogations of Hess; it would be best to keep the Nazis guessing. Hess was transported secretly to the Tower of London during the night of May 16 to become the world's most famous prisoner of war. A few days later A. P. Herbert summarized in verse the Englishman's view of Hess:

> *He is insane. He is a Dove of Peace.*
> *He is Messiah. He is Hitler's niece.*
> *He is the one clean honest man they've got.*
> *He is the worst assassin of the lot.*
> *He has a mission to preserve mankind.*
> *He's non-alcoholic. He was a "blind."*
> *He has been dotty since the age of ten,*
> *But all the time was top of Hitler's men. . . .*

Stalin was far more perturbed by the Hess flight than Mussolini who, according to his son-in-law, was "glad of it because this will have the effect of bringing down German stock, even with the Italians." Those in the Kremlin, particularly in light of the invasion rumors, suspected the British were really intriguing with Hitler. New regulations were imposed. Travel outside of Moscow by foreigners was forbidden except in rare cases.

Irate as he was, Hitler confided to several intimates that he respected Hess for his willingness to sacrifice himself on such a dangerous mission. On reflection he realized that his deputy had made the hazardous flight for him. Hitler did not believe that Hess was mad, only foolish not to have seen what a disastrous political mistake he was making.

This more sober judgment was corroborated some months later when Hitler consoled Frau Bruckmann on the death of her husband: "We all have our graves and grow more and more lonely, but we have to overcome and go on living, my dear gracious lady! I, too, am now deprived of the only two human beings among all those around me to whom I have been truly and inwardly attached: Dr. Todt [builder of the Westwall and Autobahn] is dead and Hess has flown away from me!"

"That is what you say now and to me," reportedly replied Frau Bruckmann, who had a reputation for frankness, "but what does your official press say? Year after year we all go to Bayreuth and are deeply moved, but who understands the real meaning? When our unhappy age at last produces a man who, like the Valkyrie, fulfills the deeper meaning of Wotan's command—seeks to carry out *your* most sacred wish with heroism and self-sacrifice—then he is described as insane!" She expected the Führer would retort sharply but he remained quiet and thoughtful. "Is it not enough, what I have said to you—and to you alone—about my real feeling?" he finally said. "Is that not enough for you?"

As for Hess, it was enough that he had done his utmost. He was glad, he wrote his wife from the Tower of London, that he had been impelled to fly to England, an urge which he described as "the obstinate dragon" that would not let him go. "True, I achieved nothing. I was not able to stop the madness of the war and could not prevent what I saw coming. I could not save the people but it makes me happy to think that I tried to do it."*

7

The day after learning about Hess, Hitler issued two repressive decrees. One declared that Russian civilians taking arms against the Wehrmacht in the coming invasion should be considered outlaws and shot without trial. The other empowered Himmler to carry out "special tasks which result from the struggle which has to be carried out between two opposing political systems." He was to act independently of the Wehrmacht "under his own responsibility." There would be no interference from any source and "the highest personalities of the government and party" were to be forbidden entrance into the occupied Russian areas which would be "cleansed" of Jews and other troublemakers by special SS units of assassins known as *Einsatzgruppen* (Special Action Groups).

Both directives troubled Alfred Rosenberg, who had recently been appointed Commissioner for the Central Control of Questions Connected with the East European Region. A Balt himself, he believed the Soviet people should be treated as anti-Stalinists rather than as enemies of the

---

* As a reward Hess—described by Wiedemann as "the straightest character" among the Nazi leaders—has already served more than thirty years of solitary confinement. He remains the last Allied prisoner at Spandau prison. In all those years he has been separated from visitors by a wide table. Never has he been allowed to embrace or kiss a loved one.

Reich. He assured Hitler that they would welcome the Germans as liberators from Bolshevik-Stalinist tyranny and could be trusted with a certain
amount of self-rule. Each state would have to be treated differently. The
Ukraine, for instance, would be "an independent state in alliance with
Germany" but Caucasia must be ruled by a German "plenipotentiary."

Convinced that a heavy-handed policy in the East would destroy the
spirit of Lebensraum, Rosenberg submitted a memorandum to Hitler objecting to the two directives. How could one possibly build a civil administration in the occupied areas without using the Soviet civil commissars
and officials now administering them? He recommended that "only senior
and very senior officials" should be "liquidated." Hitler gave no definite
answer. Characteristically, he was content to take no active part in the
power struggle between Himmler and Rosenberg that would surely begin
once the Wehrmacht advanced into the Soviet Union. Bormann, the rising star in the National Socialist hierarchy, would be a decisive factor in
this contest. He had already joined forces with Himmler.

In the meantime, final preparations for Barbarossa continued. Admiral Raeder informed Hitler on May 22 that he would cease delivering important materials to Russia. Comparatively few shipments had, in fact,
been sent to the Soviet Union, while many had come from the East. In
addition to almost 1,500,000 tons of grain, the Soviets had delivered
100,000 tons of cotton, 2,000,000 tons of petroleum products, 1,500,000
tons of timber, 140,000 tons of manganese and 25,000 tons of chromium.
Despite suspicions over the Hess flight, Stalin was still so eager to appease
Hitler that he authorized further shipments by express trains from the Far
East of other important raw materials, such as copper.

On the same day a meeting with Molotov reinforced Ambassador
von der Schulenburg's earlier conjecture that the recent consolidation of
power by Stalin merely meant that the foreign policy of the Soviet Union
was completely in his hands. In hopes of staving off Barbarossa, Schulenburg reported that the Soviet attitude toward Germany had improved
markedly in the past few weeks. But Hitler was not to be dissuaded by his
diplomats any more than he was by his naval chief. On May 30, three days
after German paratroopers wrested the strategic island of Crete from the
British, Admiral Raeder attempted to turn Hitler's attention from the
East by urging him to mount a substantial offensive against Egypt and
Suez. Now, he urged, was the time to strike. With reinforcements General
Rommel could score a decisive victory. "This stroke," he said, "would be
more deadly to the British Empire than the capture of London!"

Hitler was beyond such advice. Barbarossa was in motion and nothing
short of catastrophe could postpone it. His greatest concern was security.

Haunted by the mishap in Belgium a year earlier, he still had not informed Mussolini of the invasion. When he met his senior ally at the Brenner Pass on June 2, he talked at length of his determination to force British capitulation (this time by U-boats), of Hess, and of the situation in the Balkans. Not a word did he utter about Barbarossa, not only for the sake of secrecy but because Il Duce had already cautioned him in explicit terms not to attack Russia, which had become "a running sore" to Germany.

The roads and rail lines leading east were dense with traffic as the final phase of preparations for Barbarossa began. On June 6 Hitler summoned Japanese Ambassador Oshima to Berchtesgaden and revealed that large numbers of troops were being sent east because of Soviet border violations. "Under such circumstances," he concluded with a confidence that impressed his listener, "war might be unavoidable between us." To Oshima this was tantamount to a declaration of war and he immediately warned Tokyo that an invasion of Russia was imminent.

It was a significant day for the Führer. He legalized his threat to wage ruthless ideological warfare by instructing Field Marshal von Brauchitsch to issue a directive to liquidate captured Soviet commissars as bearers of an ideology diametrically opposed to National Socialism. His commander-in-chief objected violently until Hitler curtly said, "I cannot demand that my generals should understand my orders, but I do demand that they follow them." The terms of this directive could not be misinterpreted. "These commissars are the originators of barbarous, Asiatic methods of warfare, and they must therefore be treated with all possible severity and dispatch. . . . Whether captured during battle or while offering resistance, they must be shot at once." This ideologically motivated order was to be executed by the Wehrmacht together with Himmler's Einsatzgruppen and its issuance by OKW was more than another victory for Hitler over the military. It bound them to his political program and made them unwilling accomplices, along with the SS, in his grand plan of the future.

To achieve this goal he must first conquer the Red Army and to do this he needed the help of those states bordering the Soviet Union that could be trusted—and that, sharing his own fear and hatred of Bolshevism, had accounts of their own to settle with Stalin. The Finns, forced to accept harsh terms to end their brief, bloody war with Russia, needed little urging to join the crusade; and on June 8 the first elements of a German infantry division landed in Finland. Two days later Field Marshal Mannerheim ordered a partial mobilization. Hitler also trusted Romania and on June 11 he intimated to General Ion Antonescu that he had decided to attack Russia. He was by no means asking Antonescu for assistance in such a war, he said, and "merely expected of Romania that in her own interest she do everything to facilitate a successful conclusion of this conflict." Stirred by visions of spoils and military glory, the Romanian dictator hastily declared that he wanted to be in on the fight from the first day.

8

On June 14 Soviet secret agent Sorge dispatched a definite warning from Tokyo: "War begins June 22." But Stalin still chose not to credit this or similar alarums. He had reassured himself, despite qualms, that the war could not possibly start until 1942 and that very day ordered publication of a Tass communiqué ridiculing the numerous rumors of war: "All this is nothing but clumsy propaganda by forces hostile to the U.S.S.R. and Germany and interested in an extension of the war." This statement was so reassuring that there was an easing of tension in the forward positions of the Red Army.

In Berlin selected combat officers were arriving at the chancellery for a special briefing and luncheon. By now each one had digested his own orders and become reconciled (if grudgingly) to the inhumane methods Hitler had imposed on the enemy. At 2 P.M. there was a break for lunch and this, unlike so many other meals at the chancellery, was mellow and relaxed. Nor was the atmosphere of camaraderie dispelled when Hitler ascended to the podium and began a persuasive lecture on the need to launch Barbarossa. The collapse of Russia, he said, would lead to England's surrender.

A final signal went out on June 17 confirming 3 A.M., Sunday, June 22, as zero hour. That day a German sergeant, who had struck an officer and feared execution, crossed into Soviet lines to surrender. He revealed that the German attack would begin before dawn on the twenty-second. Front-line officers who learned of the report were disturbed but their commanding general's reaction was: "No use beating an alarm."

As zero hour approached, Hitler appeared calm and confident. On Friday the twentieth he sent for Frank—formerly his personal lawyer and now governor general of German-occupied Poland. "We are facing a war with the Soviet Union," he said and, when the other reacted with consternation, added, "Calm yourself." He promised that the German attack units would soon pass through Frank's area and then waved off his attempt to make another objection. "I understand your problem very well. But I must insist that you come to an understanding with Himmler." He was referring to their conflicting concepts of treating the occupied areas. "I

Hitler with Keitel and Engel aboard the special Führer train. FRENTZ

Hitler reads latest radio dispatch. FRENTZ

Hitler and his dog Blondi inspect Flak crew. To his right, Albert Bormann (brother of Martin), valet Linge and Richard Schulze (Hitler's ordnance officer). FRENTZ

Engel, Puttkamer and Jodl outside train. PUTTKAMER

Göring's favorite trains, in his basement at Karinhall. FRENTZ

Left, on February 15, 1942, after the military reverses in Russia of November–December 1941, Hitler exhorts recent SS officer graduates to stem the Red tide and save civilization. Behind: Schaub and Schulze. The latter, recently made the Führer's personal adjutant, was so moved he wanted to join the fight. The young lieutenants, Schulze recalled, jumped onto their seats and cheered in a spontaneous demonstration. SCHULZE

Below, a few days later Hitler loses his Minister of Armaments, the famed engineer Fritz Todt, in a mysterious plane crash on the eastern front. Todt was replaced by architect Speer. PUTTKAMER

Mussolini flies over the Russian lines in 1942. Moments after this unusual picture was taken, he insisted on taking the controls from pilot Baur. Hitler consented, to his regret. Il Duce maneuvered the plane with boyish élan. PUTTKAMER

Mussolini's son-in-law, Count Ciano, visits Hitler at Wolf's Lair, his headquarters in Poland. Behind: Schmundt, Ribbentrop and Schulze. BIBLIO. FÜR ZEIT.

Hitler and Speer at Wolf's Lair. Behind is Otto Günsche, Hitler's SS adjutant. GÜNSCHE

In July 1942 Hitler moves east to Werewolf, the new headquarters in the Ukraine, so he can personally direct the attack on Stalingrad. Birthday celebration that August for Bormann's secretary Fräulein Wahlmann. L. to r., Schaub, Hewel, Fräulein Wahlmann, Bormann, Engel, Fräulein Fugger (another Bormann secretary) and Heinrich Heim, instructed by Bormann to note down surreptitiously Hitler's table conversations. PUTTKAMER

A month later the inner circle celebrates Below's birthday. L. to r., Schulze, Johanna Wolf (Hitler's secretary), Below, Christa Schröder (Hitler's secretary), Dr. Brandt, Hewel, Albert Bormann, Schaub, Puttkamer, Engel. PUTTKAMER

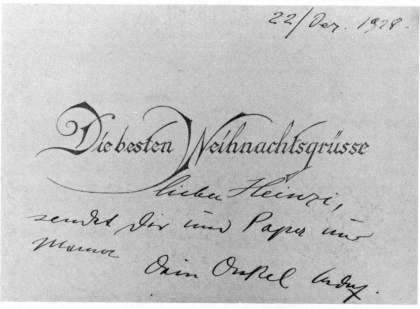

22/Dez. 1938.

Die besten Weihnachtsgrüsse

Christmas card from Uncle Adolf to his favorite nephew, son of Alois Hitler, Jr., Heinz Hitler, who was later captured at Stalingrad. HANS HITLER

can tolerate no more differences; you two must come to an under-standing." That evening Hitler's proclamation to the troops was secretly distributed and, under cover of darkness, assault units began moving forward. By dawn of the twenty-first more than three million men were in attack position.

In London Cripps, home for consultations, was sounding another warning that Hitler was about to invade Russia. "Well," he told Soviet Ambassador Maisky, "we have reliable information that this attack will take place tomorrow, 22 June, or at the very latest 29 June. . . . You know that Hitler always attacks on Sundays." Maisky sent an urgent cipher message to Moscow. At last Stalin sanctioned an alert for the armed forces. He also instructed his ambassador in Berlin to present a verbal note to Ribbentrop vigorously objecting to the 180 German overflights since April, which "assumed a systematic and intentional character."

There was tension at the Bendlerstrasse as the clock neared 1:30 P.M., the final moment the attack could be called off. No word came from the chancellery. Barbarossa was on! At the chancellery Hitler was trying to explain to Mussolini why he was launching Barbarossa: "Duce!" he wrote. "I am writing this letter to you at a moment when months of anxious deliberations and continuous nerve-racking waiting are ending in the hardest decision of my life." The concentration of Soviet forces at the Reich border, he said, was tremendous, and time was on the side of the enemy. "I have therefore, after constantly racking my brains, finally reached the decision to cut the noose before it can be drawn tight."

He made no criticism of Italy's disastrous ventures in Greece and Africa nor hinted at other grievances. He maintained a tone of respect, approaching supplication, throughout and ended the letter almost as if he were in the confessional: "The partnership with the Soviet Union, in spite of the complete sincerity of the efforts to bring about a final conciliation, was nevertheless often very irksome to me, for in some way or other it seemed to me to be a break with my whole origin, my concepts, and my former obligations. I am happy now to be relieved of these mental agonies."

In Moscow Molotov had just summoned Ambassador von der Schulenburg. The Foreign Commissar wanted to add weight to the *note verbale* which his ambassador in Berlin had not yet been able to deliver to Ribbentrop. "There are a number of indications," he told Schulenburg, "that the German government is dissatisfied with the Soviet government. Rumors are even current that a war is impending between Germany and the Soviet Union." It was an embarrassing situation and all Schulenburg could do was promise to transmit the question to Berlin. He returned to his office as ignorant as Molotov that an attack was coming in a few hours.

One of the eastern front commanders was reading out Hitler's exhortation to the troops. "Weighed down for many months by grave anxieties, compelled to keep silent, I can at last speak openly to you, my soldiers." He told of the Russian build-up on the German frontier, of the numerous border violations. That was why they had been brought up to the "greatest front in world history" along with allies from Finland and Romania. "German soldiers! You are about to join battle, a hard and crucial battle. The destiny of Europe, and future of the German Reich, the existence of our nation now lie in your hands alone."

All along the tortuous 930-mile front, from the Baltic to the Black Sea, three million men listened and believed. With fear and expectation they huddled in their positions. It was the shortest night of the year, the summer solstice, but it seemed endless to those waiting in the pale light for the command to attack. Just before midnight the Moscow–Berlin express rumbled over the frontier bridge into German territory. It was followed by a long freight train filled with grain, the last delivery Stalin would make to his ally, Adolf Hitler.

In Berlin that evening there was an air of expectation. The international journalists were gathered at the Foreign Press Club in the Fasenstrasse, hoping to get some information from a group of Foreign Office officials, but as midnight approached with no official announcement the newsmen began to leave for home. At the chancellery there was such unusual activity that even those like Hitler's press chief, Dietrich, who knew nothing of Barbarossa, felt sure "that some tremendous action against Russia was in progress." Hitler was the personification of confidence. "In three months at the latest," he told one adjutant, "there will be a collapse on the part of the Russians such as the world has never before seen." But this was only a sham. He could not close his eyes that night any more than he could on the eve of the invasion of the West.

At 3 A.M., June 22—exactly a year after the surrender of France at Compiègne—German infantrymen moved forward. Fifteen minutes later flame and smoke burst out all along the eastern front. The pale night sky was turned to day by the flash of guns. Barbarossa, long a dream, was reality. But its creator was already nagged by concern. The five-week delay caused by the Yugoslav venture loomed more ominously. Being of historic bent, perhaps Hitler recalled that on that same day in June a hundred and twenty-nine years before Napoleon had crossed the Niemen River on his way to Moscow.

Fifteen minutes before zero hour Ambassador von Bismarck delivered Hitler's long letter to Ciano, who immediately telephoned Il Duce.

Mussolini was incensed as much by the ungodly hour as by having been kept uninformed. "Not even I disturb my servants at night," he grumbled to his son-in-law, "but the Germans make me jump out of bed at any hour without the least consideration."

In Moscow Schulenburg was en route to the Kremlin with an accusation that the Soviet Union was about to "fall on Germany's back." Consequently the Führer had ordered the Wehrmacht "to oppose this threat with all the means at its disposal." Molotov listened silently to a solemn reading of the statement, then said bitterly, "It is war. Your aircraft have just bombarded some ten open villages. Do you believe that we deserved that?"

At the Wilhelmstrasse Ribbentrop finally sent word that he would see the Russian ambassador at 4 A.M. Never before had Schmidt seen his chief so excited. Pacing up and down the room like a caged animal, Ribbentrop kept repeating, "The Führer is absolutely right to attack Russia now." It seemed, thought Schmidt, as if he were trying to reassure himself. "The Russians would certainly themselves attack us, if we did not do so now."

At exactly 4 A.M. Soviet Ambassador Dekanozov entered, right hand innocently extended. Ribbentrop interrupted his attempt to relay the Soviet grievances. "That is not the question now," he said and announced that the Soviet government's hostility had compelled the Reich to take military countermeasures. "I regret that I can say nothing further," he said, "especially as I myself have come to the conclusion that, in spite of serious endeavors, I have not succeeded in establishing reasonable relations between our two countries."

Quickly regaining his composure, Dekanozov expressed his own regret at the course of events, laying the entire blame on the non-co-operative attitude of the Germans. He rose, bowed perfunctorily, and left the room without offering Ribbentrop another handshake.

Correspondents all over Berlin were being wakened for a 6 A.M. press conference at the Foreign Office. Several heard the news en route to the Wilhelmstrasse from outdoor loudspeakers as a message from the Führer was broadcast: "People of Germany! National Socialists! The hour has come. Oppressed by grave cares, doomed to months of silence, I can at last speak frankly." He told of the machinations of Russia and England to crush the Axis with the aid of American supplies. "I therefore decided today to lay the fate and future of the German Reich in the hands of our soldiers. May God help us above all in this fight!"

Chapter Twenty-four

"A DOOR INTO
A DARK, UNSEEN ROOM"
JUNE 22–DECEMBER 19, 1941

1

By early morning of June 22 single-sheet extra editions of Berlin newspapers were on the streets. Although confused by the abrupt attack on an ally, the public felt a sense of relief since few had been able to understand why a treaty had been made with the Reds in the first place. Hitler set Goebbels the task of explanation and that morning the propaganda chief began laying down the guidelines to his subordinates: "Now that the Führer has unmasked the treachery of the Bolshevik rulers, National Socialism, and hence the German people, are reverting to the principles which impelled them—the struggle against plutocracy and Bolshevism." The Führer, he added, had assured him the Russian campaign would end within four months. "But I tell you it will take only eight weeks."

That afternoon he was repeating his prophecy to guests at a party. Turning to film star Olga Tschechowa, the niece of Chekhov, he said, "We have a Russian expert here. Will we be in Moscow by Christmas?" Irritated by both his manner and the question, her answer was terse: "You know Russia, the endless land. Even Napoleon had to retreat." For once Goebbels was at a loss for words and could only say, "So." But within ten minutes his adjutant was telling the actress, "I imagine, madame, you are ready to leave. The car is outside."

The Soviet Union was in disarray. Within hours the Red Air Force had admittedly lost 1200 aircraft, and infantry resistance was unco-ordinated. Refusing to believe in the gravity of first reports, Stalin ordered the Red Army to keep out of German territory and the Red Air Force to restrict raids to within ninety miles of the frontier. He was so convinced that the Nazi invasion was a mistake and he could halt the war by diplomatic means that he kept open radio communications with the Wilhelmstrasse while requesting Japan to mediate any political and economic differences between Germany and the Soviet Union.

His ambassador in England was under no such illusion. Maisky called upon Foreign Secretary Eden and asked directly whether the British government was going to reduce its war effort somewhat and perhaps now listen to Hitler's "peace offensive." Eden firmly replied in the negative, and that evening Churchill (who had recently remarked: "If Hitler invaded Hell, I would make at least a favourable reference to the Devil in the House of Commons") made it official in a stirring broadcast to the nation. "We are resolved to destroy Hitler and every vestige of the Nazi regime. From this nothing will turn us—nothing. We will never parley, we will never negotiate with Hitler or any of his gang." He pledged to give the utmost help to the Russians. "We shall appeal to all our friends and allies in every part of the world to take the same course and pursue it, as we shall faithfully and steadfastly to the end."

George Kennan, assigned to the American Embassy in Berlin, had reservations which he passed on in a personal note to a friend in the State Department: "It seems to me that to welcome Russia as an associate in the defense of democracy would invite misunderstanding of our own position and would lend to the German war effort a gratuitous and sorely needed aura of morality. In following such a course I do not see how we could help but identify ourselves with the Russian destruction of the Baltic states, with the attack against Finnish independence, with the partitioning of Poland and Rumania, with the crushing of religion throughout Eastern Europe, and with the domestic policy of a regime which is widely feared and detested throughout this part of the world and the methods of which are far from democratic." At the same time this should not prohibit "the extension of material aid whenever called for by our own self-interest. It would, however, preclude anything which might identify us politically or ideologically with the Russian war effort."

Roosevelt was equally aware of Stalin's dictatorial policies, his secretiveness and greed for territory. But he feared Hitler far more and promptly approved a State Department declaration that giving assistance to Communism would benefit American security. He told reporters: "Of course we are going to give all the aid we possibly can to Russia"—but failed to add when or how this could be done.

The Pope's attitude was not at all vague. While taking no definite stand on the German invasion, he made it clear that he backed the Nazi fight against Bolshevism, describing it as "high-minded gallantry in defense of the foundations of Christian culture." A number of German bishops, predictably, openly supported the attack. One called it "a European crusade," a mission similar to that of the Teutonic Knights. He exhorted all Catholics to fight for "a victory that will allow Europe to breathe freely again and will promise all nations a new future."

Within twenty-four hours German public interest began to slacken. After the first rush for the newspapers, which contained only general reports from the front, the citizens returned to their normal life as if it were only another of Hitler's exploits. At 12:30 P.M. on June 23 he and his entourage left the capital in the Führer train: destination *Wolfsschanze* (Wolf's Lair), the new headquarters in a forest several miles from Rastenburg, East Prussia. Confidence in a quick victory ran high among the staff as they settled into the wooden huts and concrete bunkers but the Führer had mixed feelings. "We have only to kick in the door and the whole rotten structure will come crashing down," he told Jodl, yet shortly remarked to an aide, "At the beginning of each campaign one pushes a door into a dark, unseen room. One can never know what is hiding inside."

The early victories seemed to justify the highest hopes. Within two days hordes of prisoners were taken and bridges seized intact. There seemed to be no organized enemy resistance as German tanks burst through Soviet lines and roamed at will. For a week no details were given to the German public, then on Sunday, the twenty-ninth, ten special communiqués, personally prepared by Hitler, were announced over the radio at hourly intervals. Goebbels had objected to this abrupt flood of information but Hitler thought it a brilliant idea. As the day wore on, however, he received complaints that a spectacle was being made of the war, and when Otto Dietrich reported that Sunday radio listeners were extremely annoyed at having to keep to their apartments on such a fine day he retorted that he knew the mentality and emotion of the masses better than Dietrich "and all the other intellectuals put together."

There were such piercing advances, such mass surrenders—almost half a million to date—that Halder wrote in his diary on July 3, "It is no exaggeration to say that the campaign against Russia has been won in fourteen days." The Führer also told his entourage that "to all intents and purposes the Russians have lost the war." How fortunate it was, he exulted, "that we smashed the Russian armor and air force right at the beginning!" Never, he said, could the Russians replace them. Many Western military experts shared this estimate and talk in the Pentagon was that the Red Army would fold up in a month or so.

2

Following in the wake of the advancing troops were four SS Einsatzgruppen of 3000 men each, whose mission was to insure the security of the operational zone; that is, prevent resistance by civilians. These were police of a very special nature, given an additional task by their chief, Reinhard Heydrich. They were to round up and liquidate not only Bolshevik leaders but all Jews, as well as gypsies, "Asiatic inferiors" and "useless eaters," such as the deranged and incurably sick.

To supervise this mass killing, Heydrich and Himmler had been inspired to select officers who, for the most part, were professional men. They included a Protestant pastor, a physician, a professional opera singer and numerous lawyers. The majority were intellectuals in their early thirties and it might be supposed such men were unsuited for this work. On the contrary, they brought to the brutal task their considerable skills and training and became, despite qualms, efficient executioners.

The majority of the victims were Jews. They had no idea of Hitler's "racial cleansing" program since few German anti-Semitic atrocities were reported in the Soviet press. Consequently, many Jews welcomed the Germans as liberators and were easily trapped by the Special Units. "Contrary to the opinion of the National Socialists that the Jews were a highly organized group," testified Obergruppenführer von dem Bach-Zelewski, the senior SS and police commander for Central Russia, the appalling fact was that they were taken completely by surprise. It gave the lie to the old anti-Semitic myth that the Jews were conspiring to dominate the world and were thus highly organized. "Never before has a people gone as unsuspectingly to its disaster. Nothing was prepared. Absolutely nothing."

The exterminations proceeded with cool calculation. It was a tidy, businesslike operation; and the reports were couched in the arid language of bureaucracy as if the executioners were dealing with cabbages, not human beings. The methodical work of the killing units was rarely marred by resistance. "Strange is the calmness with which the delinquents allow themselves to be shot," reported one commander, "and that goes for non-Jews as well as Jews. Their fear of death appears to have been blunted by a kind of indifference which has been created in the course of twenty years of Soviet rule."

Heydrich's most awkward problem was coping with the psychological effects of the exterminators. Some enlisted men had nervous breakdowns or took to drinking, and a number of the officers suffered from serious stomach and intestinal ailments. Others took to their task with excess enthusiasm and sadistically beat the prisoners in violation of Himmler's orders to exterminate as humanely as possible.

He himself was witness to the demoralizing effect of daily murder. On a visit to Minsk that summer he asked the commander of Einsatzgruppe B to shoot a hundred prisoners so he could observe the actual liquidation. As the firing squad raised rifles, he noticed one young man was blond and blue-eyed, the hallmark of the true Teuton, and did not belong in this group. Himmler asked if he was a Jew. He was. Both parents? Yes. Did he have any antecedents who were not Jewish? No. Himmler stamped his foot. "Then I cannot help you."

The squad fired but Himmler, who had come to see, stared into the ground. He shuffled nervously. Then came a second volley. Again he promptly averted his eyes. Glancing up, he saw that two women still writhed. "Don't torture those women!" he shouted. "Get on with it, shoot quickly!" This was the opportunity Bach-Zelewski was hoping for. He asked Himmler to note how deeply shaken the firing squad was. "They are finished for the rest of their lives!" the SS man said. "What kind of followers are we creating by these things? Either neurotics or brutes!"

Himmler impulsively ordered everyone to gather around so he could make a speech. Theirs was a disgusting task, he said, but as good Germans they should not enjoy doing it. Their conscience, however, should be in no way affected because they were soldiers who had to carry out every order without question. He alone, before God and the Führer, bore the terrible responsibility for what had to be done. Surely they had noticed that this bloody work was as odious to him and moved him to the depths of his soul. But he too was obeying the highest law by doing his duty.

Rumors of these atrocities distressed Rosenberg, ordered by Hitler to draw up a blueprint for occupation of the conquered Eastern territories. He had envisaged a far different program with a degree of self-rule. Since the Führer had earlier agreed to establish "weak socialist states" in the conquered lands of Russia, Rosenberg optimistically assumed that Hitler approved his own plan in principle and that it would be accepted at a special conference on the subject to be held at the Wolfsschanze on July 16. "It is essential," said Hitler (according to Bormann's notes of the meeting), "that we do not proclaim our views before the whole world. There is no need for that but the main thing is that we ourselves know what we want." If this did not reveal to Rosenberg that Hitler had changed his mind about establishing "weak socialist states," what followed surely did. "This need not prevent our taking all necessary measures—shooting, resettlement, etc.—and we shall take them. . . . In principle we must now face the task of cutting up the giant cake according to our needs in order to be able: first, to dominate it; second, to administer it; third, to exploit it. The Russians have now given an order for partisan warfare behind our front. This guerrilla activity again has some advantage for us; it enables us to exterminate everyone who opposes us."

Although Rosenberg left the meeting with the title of Reich Minister of the East, it was a hollow one, for he realized his own dream of the East now had little chance to materialize. What a tragedy, he thought, that Hitler still maintained the false conception of Slavs, born during his youthful days in Vienna out of inflammatory pamphlets which described the Slavs as lazy primitives, a hopelessly second-class race. Equally disastrous was Hitler's complete misunderstanding of the structure of the Soviet Union. The Ukrainians and other tribes under the yoke of the Great Russians were potential allies of the Third Reich and could be a bulwark of defense against Bolshevism if treated properly and given a measure of self-rule. But the Führer had been persuaded by Bormann and Göring that they were enemies to be controlled by the whip. The struggle to turn Hitler from this path seemed hopeless but Rosenberg resolved to keep trying. It was a diluted resolve, for no one knew better than he that, once the Führer looked into his eyes, he would, as usual, be too frightened to speak out.

3

O what can ail thee, Knight at arms,
Alone and palely loitering?—Keats

During these early summer days of 1941 Hitler became sick. To begin with there were recurrent stomach pains which may have been of hysterical nature. His system was already undermined by an overdose of drugs— 120 to 150 anti-gas pills a week as well as ten injections of Ultraseptyl, a strong sulfonamide. Then he was struck down by dysentery—a common malady in the swampy surroundings of the Wolfsschanze. A victim of diarrhea, nausea and aching limbs, he would shiver one moment, sweat the next. A more serious threat to his health came to light during a hot argument with Ribbentrop late in July. The Foreign Minister, opposed to Barbarossa from the beginning, lost his temper and began to shout his disapproval. Hitler paled at the extraordinary attack. He tried to defend himself but halted in mid-sentence, clutched his heart and sank into a chair. There was a frightening moment of silence. "I thought I was going to have a heart attack," Hitler finally said. "You must never again oppose me in this manner!"

Dr. Morell was so perturbed he sent an electrocardiogram of the Führer's heart to Professor Dr. Karl Weber, director of the Heart Institute at Bad Nauheim and a leading authority on heart disease. He had no idea that the patient was Hitler, only that he was "a very busy diplomat." His diagnosis was: a rapidly progressive coronary sclerosis, a virtually incurable heart disease. Morell probably did not pass this information on to Hitler; at least once announcing in his presence that the Führer's heart was in good shape. Morell did add a number of other medicines to his patient's growing list of prescriptions: a heart tonic, Cardiazol (a quite harmless solution for circulatory weakness, fainting and exhaustion) and Sympathol 3, one per cent as efficacious as adrenalin.

Hitler's illness came at the height of a bitter conflict with his commanders on the conduct of the campaign in the East. He had already ordered the direct attack on Moscow halted; he stripped Army Group Center of its most powerful armored units, one being sent north to facilitate the capture of Leningrad, the other south to bolster the drive into the Ukraine. Both these areas, in Hitler's opinion, superseded Moscow in importance; the first because it was a key industrial center (and was named after Lenin), and the second because of its economic importance. Not only was the Ukraine vital for its industry and grain but the Crimea itself was a potential Soviet aircraft carrier for the bombing of the Ploesti oilfields in Romania. Further, once the Crimea was occupied, the Wehrmacht would have easy access to the Caucasus.

Hitler's sick spell gave Brauchitsch and Halder the chance to sabotage the Führer's strategy. Quietly they began trying to put their own plan into operation, with Halder exerting his personal influence on Jodl to gain his support. It was not until Hitler was on the road to recovery in mid-August that he fully realized what had been going on behind his back: neither his own strategy nor that of Halder had been put into effect but a compromise of both. To clarify the situation, Hitler composed an order on August 21 that could not possibly be misunderstood: "The most important objective to be reached by winter is not Moscow, but the Crimea." The attack on Moscow could not begin until Leningrad had been isolated and the Russian Fifth Army in the south destroyed. This order was followed a few hours later by a lengthy memorandum, dictated in anger and read with indignation. Little better than a stern lecture on how to wage a campaign, it charged that unnamed commanders were driven by "selfish desires" and "despotic dispositions," then characterized the army high command as a gathering of minds "fossilized in out-of-date theories."

"A black day for the army!" Engel wrote in his diary. "Unbearable!" scrawled Halder in his. "Unheard of! The limit!" He spent hours on the twenty-second with Brauchitsch complaining about the Führer's "inadmissible" interference with army affairs, ending with the suggestion that the two of them resign. But the dispirited, ailing marshal refused on the grounds that "it wouldn't be practical and would change nothing." He even did his utmost to quell rebellion in his own staff by assuring them that the Führer had personally promised that, once victory was certain in the Ukraine, all available forces would be thrown into the attack on Moscow. The rebellion—if it could be dignified as such—died out in a diminishing chorus of grumbles.

4

This minor crisis was soon overshadowed by the highly publicized visit of Mussolini to the front. He was coming to persuade Hitler to enlarge the Italian Expeditionary Force on the Russian front and so share some of the glory of crushing Communism. But as his special train approached Wolfsschanze Il Duce was in poor condition to match wits with his ally; he was still pale and grieving over the recent loss of his son Bruno in an air crash.

Hitler met Mussolini at the little railroad station near the Wolfsschanze and for the rest of the day scarcely gave him a chance to open his mouth. The Führer talked incessantly of the forthcoming victory in the East, the stupidity of France and the evil machinations of the Jewish clique that surrounded Roosevelt. When his guest finally managed to make his offer of more troops Hitler changed the subject. His almost incessant monologue continued for the next few days until Mussolini became so tired of hearing of German glory and exploits that he began a long discourse on the triumphs of ancient Rome in general and Trajan, who had fought in the region they were inspecting, in particular.

Later in the day, at Uman in the Ukraine, they inspected an Italian division and as Bersaglieri with waving feathers in their steel helmets roared past on motorcycles shouting "Duce!" Mussolini's face glowed. But Hitler soon regained the limelight once they entered the still smoking ruins of Uman and he was cheered by *his* soldiers. After lunch he left Mussolini behind and walked informally among his troops. Il Duce felt insulted but got his revenge on the return flight. He went forward to talk with Baur, Hitler's pilot, who was delighted at his enthusiasm and particularly Mussolini's request to take over the controls. Caught off guard, Hitler gave his consent but immediately regretted it, constantly fidgeting while his erstwhile idol maneuvered the craft with boyish élan.

It was only a passing triumph. On the long rail trip back home Mussolini was dejected. He had not only failed to get approval for a large Italian contingent but had gained the uneasy feeling that the war in the East would be a lengthy and bloody one. His depression changed to rage upon learning that Ribbentrop was not going to publish the agreed joint communiqué of the visit; the Foreign Minister's name, it seemed, had been mentioned *after* Keitel's.

This time Hitler bowed to Mussolini and asked Ribbentrop to get into line. His honor avenged, Il Duce's spirit rose. He summoned Dino Alfieri, his ambassador to Berlin, and gave him directives for a report on their visit to the front. "Don't forget to mention," he said, "that for a considerable part of the way I piloted the Führer's four-engined plane myself."

At the Wolfsschanze Hitler changed his mind and decided it was now time to launch the attack on Moscow. During tea in the casino with his secretaries and aides, he stared fixedly at a large map on the wall. "In several weeks we will be in Moscow," he said in a deep, rough voice. "There is no doubt of it. I will raze that damned city and I will construct in its place an artificial lake with central lighting. The name of Moscow will disappear forever." And so on the afternoon of September 5 he told Halder, "Get started on the central front within eight to ten days." His mood at supper that night was light, almost frolicsome. His comments were noted down by Werner Koeppen, Rosenberg's liaison man at Führer Headquarters. Since early July that year, at Rosenberg's behest, he had been circumspectly recording the Führer's table conversations. Koeppen assumed Hitler knew what he was doing and would furtively jot down notes on his paper napkin, then immediately after the meal write out only those parts of the conversation he could distinctly remember. An original and one copy of his records were forwarded to Berlin by courier.

Unbeknown to Koeppen, there was a second Boswell at the main table. Shortly after their arrival at Wolfsschanze, Bormann had suggested almost offhandedly to Heinrich Heim, his adjutant, that he surreptitiously note down what the Chief said. So Hitler wouldn't know he was being put on record, Bormann instructed his adjutant to rely on his memory. But Heim wanted more accurate results and on his own initiative he began making copious notes on index cards which he hid on his lap. Bormann

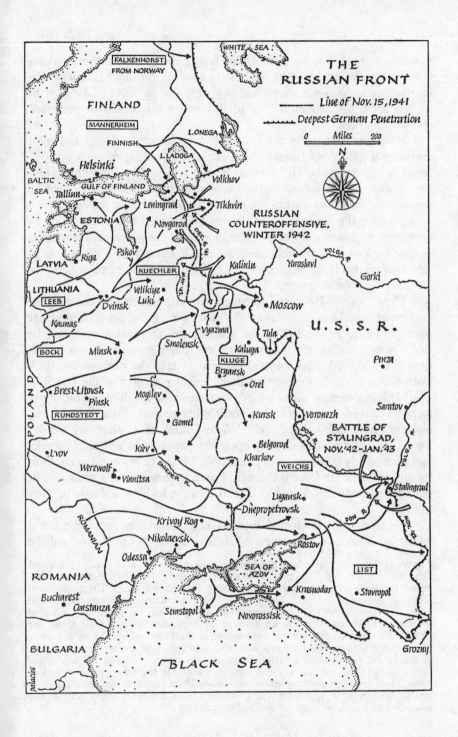

was taken aback but he gave Heim tacit approval to continue taking notes.* "So the matter went on," Heim recalled, "without Bormann giving me any instructions, expressing any wishes or anything else except to silently show his happiness that in this way much would be preserved and not forgotten."

Heim was constantly faced with two problems: to select the most meaningful reflections (sometimes what he was writing down was superseded in importance by Hitler's next words) and to keep the Führer from seeing what he was doing. At the noon meal and the evening supper he was able to mask his activities but during the late night tea sessions, which took place in the bunker, he had to rely on memory alone, except for an occasional scribbled word or two. Heimchen, as the gentle soul was affectionately called, was so unobtrusive (as was Koeppen) that Hitler continued to speak freely, spontaneously on a limitless variety of subjects in an oral stream of consciousness.

The records of Heim and Koeppen gave rare insight into the momentous events unfolding each day on the eastern front. On September 17, for instance, Hitler expounded on the spirit of decision, which consisted, he said, "in not hesitating when an inner conviction commands you to act. Last year I needed great spiritual strength to take the decision to attack Bolshevism. I had to foresee that Stalin might pass over to the attack in 1941. It was therefore necessary to get started without delay, in order not to be forestalled—and that wasn't possible before June. Even to make war, one must have luck on one's side. When I think of it, what luck we did have!" The tremendous military operation presently in progress, he said, had been widely criticized as impracticable. "I had to throw all my authority into the scales to force it through. I note in passing that a great part of our successes have originated in 'mistakes' we've had the audacity to commit."

He assured his fascinated listeners that the hegemony of the world would be decided by the seizure of Russian space. "Thus Europe will be

* Some of these notes were later published in various editions in England, France and Germany, the last under the title *Hitler's Tischgespräche*, by Henry Picker, who deputized for Heim as court reporter from March through July 1942. Heim was never consulted by any of the publishers or given the opportunity of commenting on the notes and correcting misconceptions on their history. While the published portion of his notes sounds quite accurate, he misses many important passages. Only about one sixth of his original notes, for instance, appear in the Picker edition. Heim is positive that Hitler never knew his table talk was being recorded. After the war he was assured of this by Hitler's personal adjutant, Schaub. Heim presently lives in Munich within blocks of Koeppen but was unaware until recently that the other was also making notes. Their two accounts complement each other. Heim purposely omitted all military matters for security; Koeppen did not. The latter's notes, moreover, are valuable as corroboration of Heim's far more detailed and personalized minutes.

an impregnable fortress, safe from all threat of blockade. All this opens up economic vistas which, one might think, will incline the most liberal of the Western democrats toward the New Order. The essential thing, for the moment, is to conquer. After that everything will be simply a question of organization." The Slavs, he said, were born slaves who felt the need of a master and Germany's role in Russia would be analogous to that of England in India. "Like the English, we shall rule this empire with a handful of men."

He talked at length of his plans to make the Ukraine the granary for all Europe and to keep its conquered people happy with scarves and glass beads, then ended in a confession: while everyone else was dreaming of a world peace conference, he preferred to wage war for another ten years rather than be cheated of the spoils of victory.

The capture of Kiev, three days later, caused elation at Wolfsschanze. It meant, predicted Hitler, the early conquest of the entire Ukraine and justified his insistence on giving priority to the southern offensive. At dinner on September 21 Hitler glowed with satisfaction as he told of the capture of 145,000 prisoners in the valley near Kiev. This battle of encirclement, he claimed, was the most confused in the entire history of warfare. The Soviet Union was on the verge of collapse.

At the noon meal on September 25 he revealed his fear of the subhuman farther east: Europe would be endangered until these Asians had been driven back behind the Urals. "They are brutes, and neither Bolshevism nor Czarism makes any difference—they are brutes in a state of nature." Late that evening he extolled the virtues of battle by comparing a soldier's first battle to a woman's first sexual encounter, as if he regarded each as an act of aggression. "In a few days a youth becomes a man. If I weren't myself hardened by this experience, I would have been incapable of undertaking this Cyclopean task which the building of an empire means for a single man." It was with feelings of pure idealism that he had set out for the front in 1914. "Then I saw men falling around me in thousands. Thus I learned that life is a struggle and has no other object but the preservation of the species."

The table talk was almost exclusively of the battle in the East, since there was little action on the only other active war front, North Africa. The British effort to throw back Rommel had failed miserably; and by the beginning of autumn there was a standoff in the desert with neither side prepared to mount another offensive. Hitler's energy and the might of the Wehrmacht were being concentrated for an all-out assault on Moscow but Field Marshal von Bock warned that it was too late in the season. Why not spend the winter in fortified positions? Hitler replied with an allegory of sorts: "Before I became Chancellor, I used to think the General Staff was like a mastiff which had to be held tight by the collar to keep it from attacking anyone in sight." But it had turned out to be anything but ferocious. It had opposed rearmament, the occupation of the Rhineland, the invasion of Austria and Czechoslovakia, and even the war in Poland. "It is I who have always had to goad on this mastiff."

He insisted upon attacking the capital in force and the operation, code-named Typhoon, was launched on the last day of September by Bock. His mission was to destroy the central Soviet forces with a fearsome aggregation of sixty-nine divisions before advancing on the capital; his basic strategy was a drive aimed at Moscow with a double tank envelopment, the pincers meeting eighty miles behind the Red Army.

The Soviet high command, unable to conceive of a major offensive started so late in the year, was caught so completely by surprise that Guderian's 2nd Panzer Group raced fifty miles in the first twenty-four hours through the Red Army ranks. German infantrymen rushed into the vacuum to mop up disintegrating pockets of resistance.

By October 2 Hitler was confident enough of victory to set off for Berlin in his special train. He had not spoken to the people for months and the next afternoon he strode into the Sportpalast purportedly to make an appeal in support of the Wartime Winter Assistance Program. But he had come to issue a major proclamation. "On the morning of June 22," he said, his words booming over loudspeakers throughout the Reich, "the greatest battle in the history of the world began." Everything had gone according to plan, he said, and then announced that the enemy was "already beaten and would never rise again!" The audience broke into wild acclaim.

He began listing the statistics of victory: 2,500,000 prisoners, 22,000 destroyed or captured artillery pieces, 18,000 destroyed or captured tanks, more than 14,500 destroyed planes. The figures rolled on: German soldiers had advanced up to 1000 kilometers ("This is as the crow flies!"), over 25,000 kilometers of Russian railway were again in operation with most of this already converted to the German narrow gauge. For a man who had just professed that Russia was beaten and would never rise again, he entertained deep concerns. The war in the East, he admitted, was one of ideologies, therefore all the best elements in Germany must now be welded into one indissoluble community. "Only when the entire German people becomes a single community of sacrifice can we hope and expect that Providence will stand by us in the future. Almighty God never helped a lazy man. Nor does He help a coward."

It was a remarkable speech, one boasting of victory while calling for further sacrifice to ward off destruction. By evening the people's thoughts were diverted solely to triumph with the news that Orel had been seized so rapidly by Guderian's tankers that passengers in streetcars waved, assuming they were Russians; and vital factory equipment destined for evacuation to the Urals was seized intact.

The following day Hitler was back at Wolfsschanze and Koeppen noted that at supper he was in a particularly good mood. The noonday meal on October 6 was devoted to Czechoslovakia where there was considerable underground activity. His solution: deport all Jews "far to the East." This reminded him that, since Jews were the source through which all enemy information is spread, they should also think of deporting Jews from Berlin and Vienna to the same destination.

During the day Bryansk was taken as Guderian completed the encirclement of three entire Soviet armies. At supper Hitler was in a light-hearted mood and there was no talk of politics. Instead he made a lame joke: Major Engel had just been bitten by a dog and that explained the epidemic of madness ravaging Führer Headquarters. Victory continued and within two days reports from the front indicated that the Red Army could "essentially be considered defeated." With conquest of Moscow in sight, Hitler ordered that not a single German soldier should enter the capital. "The city," he said, "will be destroyed and completely wiped from the earth."

As Hitler emerged from the military conference on October 9 he called out to Otto Dietrich that the public could now be informed of the latest operations. Half an hour later, as he paced his study in the bunker with vigorous strides, Hitler dictated word for word the victory statement Dietrich was to submit to the press. Dietrich did so the next day in Berlin, then raised his fist high in the air. "And on that, gentlemen," he shouted, "I stake my whole journalistic reputation!" "Axis and Balkan correspondents applauded and cheered," recalled Howard K. Smith of the New York *Times*, "then stood and raised their arms in salute to Dietrich."

That morning German newspapers told of a great victory: two Soviet army groups had been encircled. The public reaction was electric. Faces previously wan and drawn were now beaming. In beer-restaurants, people stood and saluted when the radio played "Horst Wessel" and "Deutschland über Alles." Rumors spread throughout the capital that Moscow had fallen.

Significantly, on that same day Field Marshal von Reichenau, the first general to espouse National Socialism, issued an order to the Sixth Army for sterner treatment of partisans. This was no ordinary war, he said, but a struggle to the death between German culture and the Jewish-Bolshevist system. "Therefore, the soldier must have full understanding of the necessity for harsh but just measures of atonement against Jewish subhumanity." Similar orders came from Rundstedt, Manstein and other senior commanders.

Hitler's declaration that the Soviets were defeated and total victory assured was not merely propaganda to raise morale at home. He believed what he said. But he had not quite convinced his pragmatic propaganda chief. Josef Goebbels started the briefing to his subordinates on the fourteenth with the optimism of a Dietrich: "Militarily this war has already been decided. All that remains to be done is of predominantly political character both at home and abroad." Then he contradicted himself by warning that the German people must reconcile themselves to continued fighting in the East for another ten years. Therefore it was the task of the German press to help strengthen the people's "staying power" and when that was done "the rest will follow of its own accord, so that, within a very short space of time, no one will notice that no peace has been concluded at all."

If Hitler had similar reservations they were dispelled upon learning that the Soviet diplomatic corps had fled Moscow on October 15 for Kuibyshev, six hundred miles to the east. Panic was truly sweeping the city and at the Kremlin Stalin reputedly had lost his nerve. A report that two German tanks had reached a suburb caused stampedes at railway stations. High-ranking party officials and secret police joined the pell-mell flight in cars, causing the first traffic jam in Soviet history. Pedestrians stormed the stalled cars, robbing and blackmailing the occupants, particularly those thought to be Jews.

Other bands of deserters and workers were plundering stores since no police were on hand to stop them. One rumor circulated that Lenin's body had been removed from Red Square for safekeeping, another that Stalin himself had taken to his heels. A grim minority was building barricades and preparing to die rather than let a single Nazi pass, but most Moscovites were demoralized, awaiting the Germans with a strange mixture of expectancy and apathy. Many of them bought German-Russian dictionaries so they could greet the conquerors in their own language.

In Berlin there was talk in the halls of the Wilhelmstrasse that Stalin had made an offer of peace through King Boris of Bulgaria. Fritz Hesse asked Ribbentrop whether it was true and was told in strict secrecy that Hitler had rejected the offer "clearly because he was convinced he could stand the immediate test and emerge victorious in the end." Most of Hitler's commanders shared his confidence. Jodl, for instance, had no doubt that the Soviets had used up their last reserves. At supper on the seventeenth Hitler's talk was mostly of the bright future. As far as he was concerned Lebensraum was a fact.

Two days after Hitler's euphoric monologue, the man he admired and derided had regained his aplomb. Reappearing in the Kremlin, Stalin asked the chairman of the Moscow Soviet, "Should we defend Moscow?" and without waiting for an answer proclaimed a state of siege. Breaches of law and order were to be dealt with promptly; all spies, diversionists and agents provocateurs were to be shot without trial. With firm direction from the top, morale throughout the city began to lift.

Before Moscow, the Soviet troops stiffened and the German spearheads which had driven to within forty miles of the capital were slowed. Then came a break in the weather. The fall rains began and while the powerful German Mark IVs became mired in the muddy roads, the more maneuverable Soviet T-34 tanks rolled free. Hitler's victories of the past two years had come through the superior mobility and firepower brought about by massed Panzer attacks closely supported by tactical air forces. But the seas of mud below foundered the armor and the low visibility above grounded the Luftwaffe, which had already gained air supremacy. With mobility went firepower—and Blitzkrieg, upon which Hitler based his hopes.

To say that Typhoon was stemmed by the mud and freezing rain and the Red Army was only partially true. The principal reason for failure, so asserted most of his commanders, was Hitler's refusal to launch it a month earlier. If he had followed their advice Moscow would have been a mass of rubble and the Soviet government and its forces defeated. But Captain von Puttkamer, for one, was convinced that it was the fault of Brauchitsch and Halder for sabotaging the Führer's basic plan during his illness.

In late October the sleet turned into snow and the mud froze. Conditions for the troops were almost unbearable. There were few advances along the entire line and these were modest ones. By the end of the month the situation was so desperate that Giesler, the architect, was ordered to stop work on the reconstruction of German cities. All workers, engineers, building materials and machinery were to be transported at once to the East to construct highways, repair railroad tracks and construct stations and locomotive sheds.

At meals Hitler appeared as confident as ever. On the eve of his departure for the annual celebration of the Munich Putsch he enlivened supper with jokes and reminiscences. In Moscow his admired enemy was making a speech at the annual Eve-of-Revolution Day meeting in the huge hall of the Mayakovsky subway station. It was an odd mixture of dejection and confidence. First Stalin admitted that the building of socialism had been greatly impeded by the war and that casualties on the battlefield already were almost 1,700,000. But the Nazi claim that the Soviet regime was collapsing had no basis in fact. "Instead," he said, "the Soviet rear is today more solid than ever. It is probable that any other country, having lost as much territory as we have, would have collapsed." Admittedly Russia faced a tremendous task since the Germans were fighting with numerous allies—Finns, Romanians, Italians and Hungarians—while not a single English or American soldier was yet in position to help the Soviet Union.

He made an impassioned appeal to Russian national pride in the name of Plekhanov and Lenin, Belinsky and Chernyshevsky, Pushkin and Tolstoy, Gorki and Chekhov, Glinka and Tschaikovsky, Sechenov and Pavlov, Suvorov and Kutuzov. "The German invaders want a war of extermination against the peoples of the Soviet Union. Very well then! If they want a war of extermination, they shall have it."

Stalin was back in command and the next morning, November 7, he spoke with equal force to troops gathered in Red Square. In the distance guns boomed and overhead came the snarl of patrolling Soviet fighter planes as he compared their position with that of twenty-three years ago. How could anyone doubt that they could and must defeat the German invaders? Again he shrewdly used names of the past—the conquerors of the Teutonic Knights, the Tartars, the Poles and Napoleon—as a rallying cry. "May you be inspired by the heroic figures of our great ancestors, Alexander Nevsky, Dimitri Donskoi, Minin and Pozharsky, Alexander Suvorov, Michael Kutuzov!"

Hitler arrived in Munich the following afternoon. He made an impassioned appeal to a convocation of Reichsleiters and Gauleiters and later delivered a speech at the Löwenbräukeller which included a warning to President Roosevelt that if an American ship shot at a German vessel "it will do so at its own risk." His threatening words did not have Stalin's forceful ring. In fact, he was depressed by the stalemate on the eastern front and the next day reminded his staff what had befallen Napoleon's army in Russia. "The recognition that neither force is capable of annihilating the other," he predicted, "will lead to a compromise peace."

But Marshal von Bock argued against such pessimism. He urged that their offensive be continued. So did Brauchitsch and Halder. On November 12 the latter was the picture of optimism as he announced that in his opinion the Russians were on the verge of collapse. Hitler was impressed and three days later the push for Moscow resumed.

At first the weather was good but soon ice, mud and snow began taking control of the battlefield. When General Oshima appeared at

Wolfsschanze on one of his periodic visits Hitler explained winter had come much earlier than his weather man had predicted. Then, in the strictest confidence, he admitted that it was doubtful if they could take Moscow that year. Gone was the season of good humor. There were no jokes at mealtime and the request for seats at his table diminished.

The cold intensified, provoking bitter denunciation of Hitler's earlier edict prohibiting the preparation of winter clothing. On November 21 Guderian phoned Halder to say that his troops had reached the end of their endurance. He was going to visit Bock and request that the orders he had just received be changed since he could "see no way of carrying them out." But the marshal, under direct pressure from the Führer, would not listen to Guderian's pleas and ordered the attack on Moscow resumed. After short, spasmodic advances the drive once more faltered. Taking over personal direction from an advanced command post, Bock called for another assault on November 24 despite a brewing storm. The attack was halted by snow, ice and fanatic Soviet resistance.

Frustration in the center was compounded five days later by a crisis in the south. Field Marshal von Rundstedt was forced to evacuate Rostov, the gate to the Caucasus, captured only a week previously. Angered by this thirty-mile retreat, Hitler telegraphed Rundstedt to remain where he was. The marshal immediately wired back:

IT IS MADNESS TO ATTEMPT TO HOLD. FIRST THE TROOPS CANNOT DO IT AND SECOND IF THEY DO NOT RETREAT THEY WILL BE DESTROYED. I REPEAT THAT THIS ORDER MUST BE RESCINDED OR THAT YOU FIND SOMEONE ELSE.

The message was drafted by a subordinate, except for the last sentence, which Rundstedt added in his own hand. It was these final words that infuriated Hitler and, without consulting the commander-in-chief of the army, he replied that same night:

I AM ACCEDING TO YOUR REQUEST. PLEASE GIVE UP YOUR COMMAND.

After replacing Rundstedt with Field Marshal von Reichenau, one of the few who dared speak openly to him, the Führer flew to Mariupol for firsthand information. He sought out an old comrade, Sepp Dietrich, commander of the SS Leibstandarte, but to his chagrin learned that the officers of this elite division agreed with Rundstedt that they would have been wiped out if they had not fallen back.

After giving Reichenau orders to do what he had fired his predecessor for doing, Hitler summoned Rundstedt. He was packing to go home and thought the Führer might make some sort of apology. But their personal discussion turned into a threat; Hitler said that in the future he would not tolerate any more applications to resign. "I myself, for instance, am not in a position to go to my superior, God Almighty, and say to Him, 'I am not going on with it, because I don't want to take the responsibility.'"

Announcement of the fall of Rostov caused gloom in Berlin in both the Propaganda Ministry and the Foreign Office. But this defeat soon paled before a looming disaster on the central front. The all-out offensive against Moscow was foundering. Although an infantry reconnaissance reached the edge of Moscow early in December and sighted the Kremlin's spires, it was dispersed by several Red Army tanks and an emergency force of factory workers. Field Marshal von Bock, suffering from severe stomach cramps, admitted to Brauchitsch on the phone that the entire attack had no depth and the troops were physically exhausted. On December 3 Bock phoned Halder. This call was even more pessimistic and when Bock suggested going over to the defensive the chief of the General Staff tried to inspirit him with the kind of admonition that comes from those far from the front line; he said that "the best defense was to stick to the attack."

The following day Guderian reported that the thermometer was down to 31 degrees below zero. It took fires under the tank engines to get them started and the cold made telescopic sights useless. Worse, there were still no winter overcoats and long woolen stockings and the men suffered intensely. On the fifth it was five degrees colder. Guderian not only broke off his attack but began to withdraw his foremost units into defensive positions.

That same night the new Soviet commander of the central front, General Georgi Zhukov, launched a massive counteroffensive—one hundred divisions—on a two-hundred-mile front. This combined infantry-tank-air assault caught the Germans off guard and Hitler had not only lost Moscow but seemed destined to suffer Napoleon's fate in the winter snows of Russia. Despair and consternation swept the German Supreme Command, Commander-in-Chief of the Army von Brauchitsch, sick and discouraged, wanted to resign.

Hitler himself was confused. In the Great War the Russian infantrymen had fought poorly; now they were tigers. Why? Despondent, he admitted on December 6 to Jodl that "victory could no longer be achieved."

5

For the past two years Hitler had been sedulously avoiding confrontation with the United States. Convinced that the entire nation was in the clutches of the "Jewish clique," which not only dominated Washington but controlled the press, radio and cinema, he exercised the utmost restraint in the face of Roosevelt's increasing aid to Britain. Although he despised Americans as fighters, he did acknowledge their industrial strength and was set upon keeping them neutral—until he was prepared to deal with them properly.

Despite the steady flow of war matériel to the British Isles, Hitler was so eager to avoid incidents that he had forbidden attacks on United States naval or merchant ships. "Weapons," he ordered, "are to be used only if *U.S. ships fire the first shot.*" But Roosevelt's quick reaction to Barbarossa threatened to end Hitler's patience. On the day after the attack the President authorized Acting Secretary of State Sumner Welles to release a statement that Hitler must be stopped even if it meant giving aid to another totalitarian country. Although Roosevelt was vague as to how this was to be done, he soon made it clear, first by releasing some forty million dollars in frozen Soviet assets, and then by announcing that the provisions of the Neutrality Act did not apply to the Soviet Union, thus leaving the port of Vladivostok open to American shipping.

Two weeks later, July 7, German claims that Roosevelt was intervening in the European war were reinforced; it was revealed that American forces had arrived in Iceland to eventually replace British forces then occupying that strategic island. The German chargé d'affaires in Washington, Hans Thomsen, cabled the Wilhelmstrasse that this was a further attempt on FDR's part to provoke Hitler into attacking America through some naval incident so she could declare war on Germany.

Disturbed by these reports, Hitler made a proposition to Ambassador Oshima in mid-July that was a reversal of his former determination to limit Japan to the task of holding off England and keeping America neutral. "The United States and England will always be our enemies," he said. "This realization must be the basis of our foreign policy." It was a sacred conviction reached after lengthy deliberations. "America and England will always turn against whomever, in their eyes, is isolated. Today there are only two states whose interests cannot conflict with one another, and these are Germany and Japan." Wasn't it obvious that America under Roosevelt, bent on a new imperialism, was exerting pressure alternately on the European and Asiatic Lebensraum? "Therefore," he concluded, "I am of the opinion that we must jointly destroy them." As bait, he suggested Japan help "liquidate the assets" of the defeated Soviet Union and occupy its Far Eastern territories.

The proposition was received in Tokyo with polite reserve. The Japanese had already decided not to attack Russia from the east but instead move south to Indochina. They did so and its peaceful seizure brought a quick response from Roosevelt on the night of July 26. Taking the advice of those like Harold Ickes, who had long been urging him to act forcefully against all aggressors, the President ordered Japanese assets in America frozen, an act which deprived Japan of her major source of oil. To the New York *Times* it was "the most drastic blow short of war." To Japan's leaders it was the last step in the encirclement of the Empire by the ABCD (American, British, Chinese, Dutch) powers, denying Nippon her rightful place as leader of Asia, a challenge to her existence. In any case, it was a giant step toward war in the Far East and, to some observers, Roosevelt's backdoor entrance to war against Hitler.

A month later the President went further when he met Churchill at sea off Newfoundland and signed the Atlantic Charter, a joint declaration of British and American war aims. Its terms not only left no doubt that Roosevelt was Hitler's implacable enemy but, ironically, disillusioned the Führer's enemies inside Germany, for no difference was made between a Nazi and an anti-Nazi. Those in the Resistance regarded the charter as Roosevelt's unofficial declaration of war against all Germans. They particularly resented Point 8, which stipulated that Germans must be disarmed after the war; a demand which, Hassell wrote in his journal, "destroys every reasonable chance for peace."

Roosevelt's determination to smash Hitler was opposed to the sentiments of millions of Americans. In addition to the right-wing America Firsters of Charles Lindbergh and the German-American Bund, there was the traditional isolationist Midwest which, though sympathetic to Britain and China, wanted no part of a shooting war. Other Americans hated Communism so intensely that they resented any aid going to the Soviet Union. Roosevelt was undeterred by violent press and radio attacks. "From now on," he announced in a radio broadcast on September 11, "if German or Italian vessels of war enter these waters [i.e., Iceland and similar areas under United States protection] they do so at their peril." Although this was a ready excuse for Hitler to remove the last restrictions on U-boat warfare, he could not be provoked into a misstep. He ordered Admiral Raeder "to avoid any incidents in the war on merchant shipping before the middle of October." By then, he explained, the Russian campaign would be as good as over.

Hitler's hope of avoiding a major incident vanished on the last day of October when the United States destroyer *Reuben James*, escorting a convoy six hundred miles west of Iceland, was torpedoed. It sank with 101 Americans aboard. Roosevelt withheld comment but his Secretary of the Navy told an audience of marines that the French liner *Normandie* would be expropriated, loaded with 400 airplanes and sent to Murmansk. The San Francisco *Chronicle* demanded that the Neutrality Act be repealed immediately and the Cleveland *Plain Dealer* called for immediate "action." But isolationist Senator Nye urged restraint: "You can't walk into a barroom brawl and hope to stay out of the fight!" and another senator, who was not isolationist, advised, "Let us keep cool."

The storm of anti-German sentiment couldn't have come at a more propitious time for Roosevelt. A week later the Office of Lend-Lease Administration was directed to do everything in its power to supply military and economic aid to the Soviet Union. One billion dollars was immediately allocated to that end.

The following day, November 8, Hitler made his belligerent speech at Munich, which was, in fact, an excuse for the sinking of the *Reuben James.* "President Roosevelt has ordered his ships to shoot the moment they sight German ships!" he shouted. "I have ordered German ships not to shoot when they sight American vessels but to defend themselves as soon as attacked. I will have any German officer court-martialed who fails to defend himself." Despite the show of anger this merely indicated that the Führer still wanted to avoid war. Say what he would, he feared Franklin Roosevelt and the industrial power of America.

He revealed as much in spite of himself in an interview early that autumn at Wolfsschanze. "I will outlast your President Roosevelt," he explained to Pierre Huss of INS. "I can afford to wait and take my time to win this war in my own way." They were outdoors and Hitler, wearing his long greatcoat of rubberized field gray, stood with hands folded behind his back staring vacantly, lost in thought. Suddenly he said, "I am Führer of a Reich that will last for a thousand years to come." He slapped a glove into his left palm. "No power can shake the German Reich now. Divine Providence has willed it that I carry the fulfillment of a Germanic task." Although he talked of his own destiny, he was obsessed by resentment of Churchill and Roosevelt, whom he disparaged as minor characters on the world stage. "They are sitting over there in their plutocratic little world, surrounded and enslaved by everything proved obsolete in the last decade. The money bags and Jews run the show behind the scenes; a parliamentary circus tramples on what is left in rights and privileges of their people. I have my people behind me and they have faith in me, their Führer." As the two men continued their walk, followed by a small group of guards and subordinates, Hitler resumed his complaint about "the madmen" who had driven him to war. "I had plans and work for my people for fifty years to come, and didn't need a war to stay in office like the

Daladiers and Chamberlains. And, for that matter, Herr Roosevelt of America."

Huss noted his brow pucker into a slight frown at the mention of the President. "It struck me suddenly, with unmistakable clarity," recalled Huss, "that I had stumbled on a secret locked within the Führer's breast, a secret he would never let out and which he may never admit having." Hitler by instinct *feared* Franklin D. Roosevelt. "Ja, Herr Roosevelt—and his Jews!" exclaimed Hitler. "He wants to run the world and rob us all of a place in the sun. He says he wants to save England but he means he wants to be ruler and heir of the British Empire."

Hitler's hardening attitude toward America was reflected by Ribbentrop. On the evening of November 28 he summoned General Oshima and urged Japan to declare war against both the United States and Britain. Oshima was surprised. "Is Your Excellency indicating that a state of actual war is to be established between Germany and the United States?" Ribbentrop had not meant to go that far. "Roosevelt is a fanatic," he explained, "so it is impossible to tell what he would do." He promised that if Japan should fight the United States, Germany would join her ally. "There is absolutely no possibility of Germany's entering into a separate peace with the United States under such circumstances. The Führer is determined on this point."

This information was a great relief to the Japanese high command. A carrier task force was already en route to Pearl Harbor. On the last day of November Oshima was ordered to inform Hitler and Ribbentrop immediately that the English and Americans were planning to move military forces into East Asia and this must be countered:

. . . SAY VERY SECRETLY TO THEM THAT THERE IS EXTREME DANGER THAT WAR MAY SUDDENLY BREAK OUT BETWEEN JAPAN AND THE ANGLO-SAXON NATIONS THROUGH SOME CLASH OF ARMS AND ADD THAT THE TIME OF THE BREAKING OUT OF THAT WAR MAY COME QUICKER THAN ANYONE DREAMS.

These instructions were quickly followed by orders to obtain specific pledges from the Germans, yet when Oshima approached Ribbentrop late on the evening of December 1 the Foreign Minister was surprisingly evasive. He excused himself on the grounds that he would first have to consult with the Führer, who was still at the Wolfsschanze. Both men knew that Hitler had little time to devote to the drama brewing on the other side of the world and so Oshima was not surprised that he did not receive a draft treaty until 3 A.M. on the fifth. In it Germany promised to join Japan in any war against the United States and not to conclude a separate peace.

The first to learn of Pearl Harbor at the Wolfsschanze was Otto Dietrich. Late in the afternoon of December 7 he hurried to Hitler's bunker with word that he was bearing an extremely important message. Hitler had just received depressing reports from the Russian front and feared Dietrich was bringing more bad news, but as his press chief hastily read the message his look of surprise was unmistakable. He brightened. Extremely excited, he asked, "Is this report correct?"

Dietrich said that he had received a telephone confirmation from his office. Hitler snatched the paper and, without putting on coat or hat, strode to the military bunker. Keitel and Jodl were amazed to see him, telegram in hand, a "stunned" look on his face. It seemed to Keitel as if the war between Japan and America had suddenly relieved Hitler of "a nightmare burden." With Hewel, the Führer could barely conceal the elation in his voice. "We cannot lose the war!" he exclaimed. "Now we have a partner who has not been defeated in three thousand years."

6

The desperate reports streaming in from the Russian front on Pearl Harbor day forced Hitler to draft a new directive which he issued twenty-four hours later. "The severe winter weather," it began, "which has come surprisingly early in the East, and the consequent difficulties in bringing up supplies, compel us to abandon immediately all major offensive operations and to go over to the defensive." He set down the general principles for defense while turning over to Halder the task of issuing subsequent instructions. Then he set off for Berlin to take personal charge of the crisis raised by Pearl Harbor. By this time his initial relief at the Japanese attack had been replaced by concern. In one stroke, Pearl Harbor had freed Stalin from worry over attack from the east; he could now transfer almost all his strength in Asia against Germany. "This war against America is a tragedy," Hitler later admitted to Bormann. "It is illogical and devoid of any foundation of reality. It is one of those queer twists of history that just as I was assuming power in Germany, Roosevelt, the elect of the Jews, was taking command in the United States. Without the Jews and without this lackey of theirs, things could have been quite different. From every point of view Germany and the United States should have been able, if not to understand each other and sympathize with each other, then at least to support each other without undue strain on either of them."

One of Hitler's first visitors in Berlin on the morning of the ninth was Ribbentrop with the unwelcome information that General Oshima was requesting an immediate declaration of war against America. But the Foreign Minister didn't think Germany was obligated to do so since, according to the Tripartite Pact, she was bound to assist her ally only in case of a direct attack upon Japan.

Hitler could not accept this loophole. "If we don't stand on the side of Japan, the pact is politically dead," he said. "But that is not the main reason. The chief reason is that the United States already is shooting at our ships. They have been a forceful factor in this war and through their actions have already created a situation of war."

His decision to declare war on America was not lightly taken, nor was its motivation simple. Beyond upholding the spirit of the Tripartite Pact there were far weightier arguments: the assistance received from Japan would considerably offset the disadvantages caused by America's entry into the war; from a propaganda point of view the acquisition of a new, powerful ally would have a tremendously heartening effect after the recent setbacks in Russia. Further, an outright declaration of war was in line with his ideological world view. Why not make 1941 the year in which he declared total war upon the two major enemies of human survival—international Marxism (Russia) and international finance capitalism (America), both the creatures of international Jewry?

His Foreign Office regarded the decision as a colossal mistake. In addition to the obvious reasons it neatly solved another of Roosevelt's domestic problems. The President would not have to declare war on Germany and risk opposition from a substantial segment of the citizenry. American national unity, so unexpectedly won by the surprise attack at Pearl Harbor, would remain intact.

On December 11 Hitler convoked the Reichstag. "We will always strike first!" he said. Roosevelt was as "mad" as Woodrow Wilson. "First he incites war, then falsifies the causes, then odiously wraps himself in a cloak of Christian hypocrisy and slowly but surely leads mankind to war, not without calling God to witness the honesty of his attack." After equating international Jewry with Bolshevik Russia and Roosevelt's regime, Hitler made his declaration of hostilities. "I have therefore arranged for passports to be handed to the American chargé d'affaires today and the following . . ." His words were drowned in a bedlam of cheers, and it was some time before he could announce that Germany was "at war with the United States, as from today." The chief of operations of OKW listened to this speech with more concern than enthusiasm and as soon as Jodl left the Kroll Opera House he telephoned his deputy, General Warlimont, in

Wolfsschanze. "You have heard that the Führer has just declared war on America?"

Warlimont had just been discussing the matter with staff officers and said they couldn't be more surprised. "The staff," said Jodl, "must now examine where the United States is most likely to employ the bulk of her forces initially, the Far East or Europe. We cannot take further decisions until that has been clarified."

"Agreed; this examination is obviously necessary, but so far we have never even considered a war against the United States and so have no data on which to base this examination; we can hardly undertake this job just like that."

"See what you can do," said Jodl. "When I get back tomorrow we will talk about this in more detail."

Anxiety over America was soon overridden by new reverses in the East. The German retreat on the central front threatened to degenerate into panic flight. The area west of Moscow and the Tula area was a snow-covered graveyard of abandoned guns, trucks and tanks. German despondency was accompanied by rising Russian confidence. On December 13 the Soviets publicly announced the failure of Hitler's attempt to surround Moscow and two days later the Politburo ordered the principal organs of government to return to the capital.

The exhausted Brauchitsch wanted to continue the withdrawal but Hitler overruled him and sent out a general order that spread despair among the military hierarchy: "Stand fast, not one step back!" Marshal von Bock, commander of the central front, already suffering from a stomach ailment, reported himself physically unfit for duty. He was replaced by Kluge. The next day, the nineteenth, Brauchitsch—just recovering from a heart attack—summoned up nerve enough to face Hitler. For two hours they argued in private. Brauchitsch left the Führer, ashen and shaken. "I am going home," he told Keitel. "He has sacked me. I can't go on any longer."

"What is going to happen now, then?" asked Keitel.

"I don't know; ask him yourself."

A few hours later Keitel was summoned. The Führer read out a brief Order of the Day he had composed. He was assuming personal command of the army, inextricably binding the fate of Germany with his own. The news was to be kept secret for the moment but he felt Halder should be informed at once. Hitler did so, minimizing the difficulties of the post. "This little affair of operational command is something anybody can do," he said. "The commander-in-chief's job is to train the army in the National Socialist idea and I know of no general who could do that as I want it done. For that reason I have taken over command of the army myself."

Previously he had been de facto commander of the army, keeping himself in the background and allowing the military to take blame for all setbacks. Now he was the official commander-in-chief and would have to accept praise or blame for whatever happened.

Part 8

THE FOURTH HORSEMAN

And I looked, and behold a pale horse: and his name that sat on him was Death, and Hell followed with him. And power was given unto them over the fourth part of the earth, to kill with sword, and with hunger, and with death, and with the beasts of the earth.

REVELATION 6:8

"AND HELL FOLLOWED
WITH HIM"
1941–1943

1

Two days after the invasion of the Soviet Union the man responsible
for the deportation of Jews, Reinhard Heydrich, complained in writing
that this was no answer to the Jewish problem. Deporting these misfits to
the French island of Madagascar, for instance, would have to be dropped
in favor of a more practical solution. It was fitting, therefore, that on the
last day of July Heydrich received a cryptic order (signed by Göring upon
instructions from the Führer) instructing him "to make all necessary preparations regarding organizations and financial matters to bring about a
complete solution of the Jewish question in the German sphere of
influence in Europe."*

Behind the innocuous bureaucratic language lay sweeping authority
for the SS to organize the extermination of European Jewry. As a preliminary step, Himmler—still shaken by his experience in Minsk—asked the

---

* Three weeks earlier Hitler had hinted to Hewel what he intended to do. "I feel like a
Robert Koch in politics," he said during a long, late night discussion in the hot bunker.
"He found the bacillus and with it showed medical science a new way. I discovered the
Jew as a bacillus and the ferment of all social decomposition . . . and one thing I have
proven is that a state can live without Jews; that economy, art, culture, etc., can exist
even better without Jews, which is the worst blow I could give the Jews."

chief physician of the SS what was the best method of mass extermination. The answer was: gas chambers. The next step was to summon Rudolf Höss, the commandant of the largest concentration camp in Poland, and give him secret oral instructions. "He told me," testified Höss, "something to the effect—I do not remember the exact words—that the Führer had given the order for a final solution of the Jewish question. We, the SS, must carry out that order. If it is not carried out now the Jews will later on destroy the German people." Himmler said he had chosen Höss's camp since Auschwitz, strategically located near the border of Germany, afforded space for measures requiring isolation. Höss was warned that this operation was to be treated as a secret Reich matter. He was forbidden to discuss the matter with his immediate superior. And so Höss returned to Poland and, behind the back of the inspector of concentration camps, quietly began to expand his grounds with intent to turn them into the greatest killing center in man's history. He did not even tell his wife what he was doing.

Hitler's concept of concentration camps as well as the practicality of genocide owed much, so he claimed, to his studies of English and United States history. He admired the camps for Boer prisoners in South Africa and for the Indians in the wild West; and often praised to his inner circle the efficiency of America's extermination—by starvation and uneven combat—of the red savages who could not be tamed by captivity.

Until now he had scrupulously integrated his own general policy with that of Germany, since both led in the same general direction. The resurgence of German honor and military might, the seizure of lost Germanic territories, and even Lebensraum in the East were approved heartily by most of his countrymen. But at last had come the crossroads where Hitler must take his personal detour and solve, once and for all, the Jewish question. While many Germans were willing to join this racist crusade, the great majority merely wanted a continuation of the limited Jewish persecution which had already received the tacit approval of millions of Westerners.

It was Hitler's intent to start eliminating the Jews secretly before leaking out the truth a little at a time to his own people. Eventually the time would be ripe for revelations that would tie all Germans to his own fate; his destiny would become Germany's. Complicity in his crusade to cleanse Europe of Jewry would make it a national mission and rouse the people to greater efforts and sacrifices. It would also burn all bridges behind the hesitant and weak-hearted.

Until now all this was kept secret from Hitler's innermost circle—the secretaries, adjutants, servants and personal staff. But in the autumn of

1941 the Führer began making overt remarks during his table conversations, perhaps as an experiment in revelation. In mid-October, after lecturing on the necessity of bringing decency into civil life, he said, "But the first thing, above all, is to get rid of the Jews. Without that, it will be useless to clean the Augean stables." Two days later he was more explicit. "From the rostrum of the Reichstag, I prophesied to Jewry that, in the event of war's proving inevitable, the Jew would disappear from Europe. That race of criminals has on its conscience the two million dead of the First World War, and now already hundreds and thousands more. Let nobody tell me that all the same we can't park them in the marshy parts of Russia! Who's worrying about our troops? It's not a bad idea, by the way, that public rumor attributes to us a plan to exterminate the Jews. Terror is a salutary thing." He predicted that the attempt to create a Jewish state would be a failure. "I have numerous accounts to settle, about which I cannot think today. But that doesn't mean I forget them. I write them down. The time will come to bring out the big book! Even with regard to the Jews, I've found myself remaining inactive. There's no sense in adding uselessly to the difficulties of the moment. One acts shrewdly when one bides one's time."

One reason Hitler had delayed implementing the Final Solution was hope that his implied threat to exterminate the Jews would keep Roosevelt out of the war. But Pearl Harbor ended this faint expectation and Hitler's hope turned into bitterness, with extermination becoming a form of international reprisal.

The decision taken, the Führer made it known to those entrusted with the Final Solution that the killings should be done as humanely as possible. This was in line with his conviction that he was observing God's injunction to cleanse the world of vermin. Still a member in good standing of the Church of Rome despite detestation of its hierarchy ("I am now as before a Catholic and will always remain so"), he carried within him its teaching that the Jew was the killer of God. The extermination, therefore, could be done without a twinge of conscience since he was merely acting as the avenging hand of God—so long as it was done impersonally, without cruelty. Himmler was pleased to murder with mercy. He ordered technical experts to devise gas chambers which would eliminate masses of Jews efficiently and "humanely," then crowded the victims into boxcars and sent them east to stay in ghettos until the killing centers in Poland were completed.

The time had come to establish the bureaucracy of liquidation and the man in charge, Heydrich, sent out invitations to a number of state secretaries and chiefs of the SS main offices for a "Final Solution" Conference, to take place on December 10, 1941. The recipients of his invitation, aware only that Jews were being deported to the East, had little idea of the meaning of "final solution" and awaited the conference with expectation and keen interest.

Their curiosity was whetted by a six-week postponement. Frank, head of the *Generalgouvernement* (German-occupied Poland), became so impatient that he sent Philipp Bouhler, his deputy, to Heydrich for more details, then convened a conference of his own at Cracow in mid-December. "I want to say to you quite openly," said Hitler's former lawyer, "that we shall have to finish the Jews, one way or another." He told about the important conference soon to take place in Berlin which Bouhler would attend for the Generalgouvernement. "Certainly the major migration is about to start. But what is to happen to the Jews? Do you think they will actually be settled in Eastern villages? We were told in Berlin, 'Why all this fuss? We can't use them in the *Ostland* either; let the dead bury their dead!'" He urged his listeners to arm themselves against all feelings of sympathy. "We have to annihilate the Jews wherever we find them and wherever it is at all possible." It was a gigantic task and could not be carried out by legal methods. Judges and courts could not take the heavy responsibility for such an extreme policy. He estimated—and it was a gross overestimate—that there were 3,500,000 Jews in the Generalgouvernement alone. "We can't shoot these 3,500,000 Jews, we can't poison them, but we can take steps which, one way or another, will lead to an annihilation success, and I am referring to the measures under discussion in the Reich. The Generalgouvernement will have to become just as free of Jews as the Reich itself. Where and how this is going to happen is the task for the agencies which we will have to create and establish here, and I am going to tell you how they will work when the time comes."

When Bouhler arrived in Berlin on January 20, 1942, for the Heydrich conference he was far better prepared than most of the conferees to understand the generalities uttered. At about 11 A.M. fifteen men gathered in a room at the Reich Security Main Office at number 56–58 Grossen Wannsee. There were representatives from Rosenberg's East Ministry, Göring's Four-Year Plan agency, the Interior Ministry, the Justice Ministry, the Foreign Office and the party chancellery. Once they had seated themselves informally at tables, Chairman Heydrich began to speak. He had been given, he said, "the responsibility for working out the final solution of the Jewish problem regardless of geographical boundaries." This euphemism was followed by a veiled and puzzling remark which involved Hitler himself. "Instead of emigration," he said, "there is now a further possible solution to which the Führer has already signified his consent—namely deportation to the East."

At this point Heydrich exhibited a chart indicating which Jewish communities were to be evacuated, and gave a hint as to their fate. Those fit to work would be formed into labor gangs but even those who survived the rigors would not be allowed to go free and so "form a new germ cell from which the Jewish race would again arise. History teaches us that." Georg Leibbrandt, of Rosenberg's office, was at a loss. Martin Luther of the Foreign Office was also confused. He protested that mass Jewish evacuations would create grave difficulties in such countries as Denmark and Norway. Why not confine the deportations to the Balkans and western Europe? The conferees left Berlin with a variety of impressions. Bouhler knew exactly what Heydrich was talking about but Luther assured Fritz Hesse that there were no plans at all to kill the Jews. Leibbrandt and his superior, Alfred Meyer, gave a similar report to Rosenberg. Not a word, they agreed, had been said of extermination.

Thirty copies of the conference record were distributed to the ministries and SS main offices and the term "Final Solution" became known throughout the Reich bureaucracy yet the true meaning of what Heydrich had said was fathomed only by those privy to the killing operations, and many of this select group, curiously, were convinced that Adolf Hitler himself was not totally aware that mass murder was being plotted. SS Lieutenant Colonel Adolf Eichmann, in charge of the Gestapo's Jewish Evacuation Office, for one knew this was a myth. After the Wannsee conference he sat "cozily around a fireplace" with Gestapo Chief Müller and Heydrich, drinking and singing songs. "After a while we climbed onto the chairs and drank a toast; then onto the table and traipsed round and round—on the chairs and on the table again." Eichmann joined in this celebration with no qualms. "At that moment," he later testified, "I sensed a kind of Pontius Pilate feeling, for I was free of all guilt. . . . Who was I to judge? Who was I to have my own thoughts in this matter?" He, Müller and Heydrich were only carrying out the laws of the land as prescribed by the Führer himself.

A few days later Hitler confirmed in spite of himself, that he was indeed the architect of the Final Solution. "One must act radically," he said at lunch on January 23, in the presence of Himmler. "When one pulls out a tooth, one does it with a single tug, and the pain quickly goes away. The Jew must clear out of Europe. It's the Jew who prevents everything. When I think about it, I realize that I'm extraordinarily humane. At the time of the rules of the Popes the Jews were mistreated in Rome. Until 1830, eight Jews mounted on donkeys were led once a year through the streets of Rome. For my part, I restrict myself to telling them they must go away. If they break their pipes on the journey, I can't do anything about it. But if they refuse to go voluntarily I see no other solution but extermination." Never before had he talked so openly to his inner circle and he was so absorbed by the subject that on the twenty-seventh he again demanded the disappearance of all Jews from Europe.

His obsession with Jews was publicly expressed a few days later in a speech at the Sportpalast on the ninth anniversary of National Socialism's rise to power. "I do not even want to speak of the Jews," he said, and proceeded to do so at length. "They are simply our old enemies, their plans have suffered shipwreck through us, and they rightly hate us, just as we hate them. We realize that this war can only end either in the wiping out of the Germanic nations, or by the disappearance of Jewry from Europe." He reminded the audience, which included some forty high-ranking military officers, of his 1939 prophecy that the Jews would be destroyed. "For the first time, it will not be the others who will bleed to death, but for the first time the genuine ancient Jewish law, 'an eye for an eye, a tooth for a tooth,' is being applied. The more this struggle spreads, the more anti-Semitism will spread—and world Jewry may rely on this. It will find nourishment in every prision camp, it will find nourishment in every family which is being enlightened as to why it is being called upon to make such sacrifices, and the hour will come when the worst enemy in the world will have finished his part for at least a thousand years to come."

To those presently engaged in designing gas chambers, to those constructing the killing centers in Poland, and particularly to those who were being prepared to administer the mechanics of the final solution, this statement was a clarion call for genocide. But to foreign observers, such as Arvid Fredborg, Hitler's words and appearance that afternoon seemed to foreshadow a German disaster. "His face," wrote the Swedish journalist, "now seemed ravaged and his manner uncertain."

2

To the Führer the extermination of Jews and Slavs was as important as Lebensraum. He had turned the invasion into ideological warfare and his military decisions, therefore, could only be understood in this context. What appeared irrational to his generals was no sudden mental lapse but the fruit of decisions made in 1928. Ironically, never had he shown more military acumen than after the shocking defeats at the gates of Moscow. Surrounded by demoralized military leaders pleading for general retreat, Hitler did not lose his nerve. He refused to grant any requests to withdraw. He was not swayed by the most successful tank commander, Guderian, who argued that taking up positional warfare in such unsuitable terrain would lead to the useless sacrifice of the best part of the army. He accused Guderian of being too deeply impressed by the suffering of the soldiers. "You feel too much pity for them. You should stand back more. Believe me, things appear clearer when examined at longer range."

Enforcing his order ruthlessly, Hitler managed to rally the army and stem the Russian advance. The cost was great but a number of his generals, including Jodl, were forced to agree that he had personally saved his troops from the fate of Napoleon's army. "I intervened ruthlessly," he told Milch and Speer, and explained that his top commanders were willing to retreat all the way to the German border to save their troops. "I could only tell these gentlemen, 'Mein Herren, return personally to Germany as soon as possible but leave the army to my leadership.'"

All was well on the other war fronts. In France the Resistance, still hopelessly splintered, was of little concern; and in the Mediterranean, U-boats, Italian "human torpedoes" and mines had recently sunk or crippled a carrier, three battleships and two cruisers, thus eliminating Great Britain's Eastern battle fleet as a fighting force. Moreover, Rommel was almost ready to launch another major offensive in North Africa and Germany's Japanese allies were continuing their unbroken series of victories in the Pacific. At the same time Hitler knew the crisis in the East was by no means over and so ordered a general mobilization of the industry and economy of the Reich. The present effort, he said, was insufficient and the Blitzkrieg strategy must be abandoned. Although he couched this call for a long war in hopeful terms, he privately retained the nagging fear, so recently confided to Jodl, that victory could no longer be achieved.

Such dark doubts were never revealed in his table conversations. He continued to chat about the evils of smoking, the joys of motoring, dogs, the origin of Tristan and Isolde, the beauty of Frau Hanfstaengl and Jews. Of the grim struggle at the front he spoke little and then with optimism. At the height of the winter crisis, for instance, he declared that no cause was hopeless provided the leadership stood firm. "As long as there is one stouthearted man to hold up the banner, nothing has been lost. Faith moves mountains. In this respect, I am ice cold: if the German people are not prepared to give everything for the sake of their self-preservation, very well! Then let them disappear!"

Such imperturbable performances at mealtime were belied by his appearance. "He is not the man he was," Hewel told a friend. "He has grown gloomy and obdurate. He will shrink from no sacrifice and show no mercy or forgiveness. You would not recognize him if you saw him." His morale received a crushing blow on February 8 when Fritz Todt, builder of the Westwall and the Autobahn system, died in a plane crash. At the breakfast table there was speculation on who would take over Todt's position as Minister of Armaments and Munitions, one of the most crucial posts in the Reich. Everyone agreed that Todt was irreplaceable; and Albert Speer, who had spent most of the night talking to Hitler about the Berlin and Nuremberg building projects, was thunderstruck when the Führer appointed him next morning. The architect's protest that he knew nothing about such matters was cut short. "I have confidence in you. I know you will manage it. Besides I have no one else."

At the funeral of Todt in the Mosaic Hall of the Reich chancellery, Hitler was so shaken that during his eulogy he could hardly continue and, once the ceremony ended, he took refuge in his apartment. Somehow he managed to recover his composure enough in the next few days to address 10,000 newly appointed Wehrmacht and Waffen SS lieutenants at the Sportpalast. Grim-faced, he told of the disaster in Russia, sparing no details. You young officers, he said, are going East to save Germany and Western civilization from the Reds. It was such a stirring speech that many in the audience wept. Standing at his side, Richard Schulze, recently promoted to personal adjutant, was so moved he wanted to join in the fight. "I felt ashamed to stay home at such a time." The new lieutenants had been ordered not to applaud but when Hitler started down the aisle they could not restrain themselves. They cheered wildly, many jumping onto their chairs.

This spontaneous outburst was a tonic to Hitler but by the time he returned to the Wolfsschanze he was again depressed. He looked exhausted and sallow. The blanket of snow covering the area deepened his despondency. "I've always detested snow," he confided to his shadow. "Bormann, you know I've always hated it. Now I know why. It was a presentiment."

Hitler despaired upon reading the report of casualties in Russia up to February 20: 199,448 dead, 708,351 wounded, 44,342 missing, 112,627 cases of frostbite. Yet he soon rebounded. Confidence abruptly regained, he began to talk at the dinner table of the terrible winter as an ordeal successfully, miraculously endured. He announced to the company with a sigh of relief that Sunday would be the first of March. "Boys, you can't imagine what that means to me—how much the last three months have worn out my strength, tested my nervous resistance." He revealed that during the first two weeks of December alone a thousand tanks had been lost and two thousand locomotives put out of operation. But the worst of winter was at last over. "Now that January and February are past, our enemies can give up the hope of our suffering the fate of Napoleon. . . . Now we're about to switch over to squaring the account. What a relief!" His high spirits were no longer spurious and he began to boast. "I've noticed, on the occasion of such events, that when everybody loses his nerve, I'm the only one who keeps calm. It was the same thing at the time of the struggle for power."

In the meantime preparations for the Final Solution were maturing and Himmler's Einsatzgruppen had begun another deadly sweep. While this second roundup of Jews, commissars and partisans was carried out in a co-ordinated manner in the military areas, progress in civilian territories proceeded less smoothly. Even so the death toll was massive and Rosenberg's staff begged him once more to urge Hitler to treat the peoples of the occupied areas as allies, not enemies. Rosenberg's aides warmly supported his relatively liberal concept of setting up separate states with varying degrees of self-government, but his turn toward liberalism had not been accompanied by a strengthening of character and he still trembled at the thought of antagonizing his Führer. A stronger man might have proved as ineffective; to approach the Führer it was necessary to go through Bormann, who had solidly aligned himself with Himmler and Heydrich. Rosenberg's liaison man at Wolfsschanze, Koeppen, was finding it increasingly difficult to convey to Hitler the true story of what was going on in the East. Before the Hess flight, he had simply passed on memoranda directly to Hitler but now Bormann insisted on acting as go-between with the excuse that the Führer was too busy with military matters. And so, concluded Koeppen, Hitler only saw the problem of the occupied East through the eyes of his right-hand man. "Therein lay the fateful development which, in my opinion, cost us victory in the East."

While it was true that Hitler had little time for internal matters, it was more likely that Bormann always followed his personal instructions; and there was no doubt that Hitler always took time to oversee the Final Solution. In this matter he neither needed nor took advice. He made this clear in his message on the anniversary of the promulgation of the party program in late February. "My prophecy," he said, "shall be fulfilled that this war will not destroy Aryan humanity but it will exterminate the Jew. Whatever the battle may bring in its course or however long it may last, that will be its final course." The elimination of Jewry overrode victory itself.

Despite such open hints, few had yet been initiated into the secret. Goebbels himself still did not realize the enormity of the measures being prepared. One of his employees, Hans Fritzsche, did learn about the Einsatzgruppen killings from a letter sent by an SS man in the Ukraine. The writer complained that he had suffered a nervous breakdown after receiving an order to kill Jews and Ukrainian intelligentsia. He could not protest through official channels and asked for help. Fritzsche immediately went to Heydrich and asked point-blank, "Is the SS there for the purpose of committing mass murders?" Heydrich indignantly denied the charge, promising to start an investigation at once. He reported back the next day that the culprit was Gauleiter Koch, who had acted without the Führer's knowledge, then vowed that the killings would cease. "Believe me, Herr Fritzsche," said Heydrich, "anyone who has the reputation of being cruel does not have to be cruel; he can act humanely."

Only that March did Goebbels himself learn the exact meaning of Final Solution. Then Hitler told him flatly that Europe must be cleansed of all Jews, "if necessary by applying the most brutal methods." The Führer was so explicit that Goebbels could now write in his diary:

> . . . A judgment is being visited upon the Jews that, while barbaric, is fully deserved. . . . One must not be sentimental in these matters. If we did not fight the Jew, they would destroy us. It's a life-and-death struggle between the Aryan race and the Jewish bacillus. No other government and no other regime would have the strength for such a global solution of this question.

By spring six killing centers had been set up in Poland. There were four in Frank's Generalgouvernement: Treblinka, Sobibor, Belzec and Lublin; two in the incorporated territories: Kulmhof and Auschwitz. The first four gassed the Jews by engine-exhaust fumes but Rudolf Höss, commandant of the huge complex near Auschwitz, thought this too "inefficient" and introduced to his camp a more lethal gas, hydrogen cyanide, marketed commercially under the name of Zyklon B.

Spring revitalized the Führer. His health improved, his spirits rose. The Soviet winter counteroffensive had ground to a complete halt and a lull set in all along the front. This gave him more time to think of future policies and on April 24 he telephoned Goebbels that he wanted to deliver a major speech before the Reichstag. The following Sunday at 3 P.M. he denounced Bolshevism as "the dictatorship of Jews" and labeled the Jew "a parasitic germ" who had to be dealt with ruthlessly. But the thrust of his speech was a vocal reaffirmation of renewed faith in eventual triumph. At the same time he made no effort to conceal how close the army had come to disaster. He exaggerated the situation to make his personal role more effective. "Deputies," he exclaimed dramatically, "a world struggle was decided during the winter." He compared himself with Napoleon. "We have mastered destiny which broke another man a hundred and thirty years ago." To prevent a similar crisis he went on to demand passage of a law granting him plenary powers. Its terms were sweeping. Every German was henceforth obliged to follow his personal orders—or suffer dire punishment. He was now officially above the law with the power of life and death. He had, in essence, appointed himself God's deputy and could do the Lord's work: wipe out the vermin and create a race of supermen.

The members of the Reichstag, stirred to the roots by his manner and words, unanimously approved the measure "enthusiastically and noisily." To foreign observers there seemed little reason for such a law. Hitler already had grasped more de facto power than Stalin or Mussolini, more, in fact, than either Caesar or Napoleon had enjoyed. He had done so, he claimed, to end war profiteering and the black market, and to prune the overgrown staffs of bureaucracy for additional manpower in the battle of production. He ignored the fact that the bleeding of the German economy had been caused not only by the conservatism in the civil service and the judiciary, but by corruption within the party itself. The plundering by such men as Göring, along with the widespread venality and inefficiency on every level of National Socialism, had been draining the strength of the Reich for almost a decade.

Three days later the Führer met Mussolini at the baroque Klessheim Castle near Salzburg. The Italians, unlike the enrapt audience at the Sportpalast, had been depressed by Hitler's oratory and they entered the first conference with some foreboding. The Führer talked interminably but said little of interest, glossing over the misfortunes of the eastern front ("The German army this winter wrote the finest pages of its history"). He declared that America was a big bluff, and again favorably compared himself to Napoleon. He also expounded on India, Japan and practically every country in Europe, with categorical pronouncements in each case. On the second day, after lunch, although everything had been said, Hitler continued talking uninterrupted for another hour and forty minutes, as Mussolini kept checking his wrist watch. Hitler's own commanders were bored. "General Jodl," recalled Ciano, "after an epic struggle, finally went to sleep on the divan."

3

Within the SD it was no secret that Himmler distrusted Heydrich, who had monumental files on everyone in the party, including the Führer, and was despised in return. (One day Heydrich showed a subordinate, Günter Syrup, a picture of Himmler. Covering the upper part of his face, he said, "The top half is the teacher but the lower half is a sadist.") But Hitler had great plans for Heydrich. He was even considering him as a successor now that Göring had fallen from favor after the disappointing performance of his Luftwaffe, and made him Acting Protector of Moravia and Bohemia in addition to his other high offices. After initiating a wave of terror in Czechoslovakia that quickly crushed the resistance movement, Heydrich adopted the guise of benefactor, particularly to workers and peasants. He raised the fat ration for industrial laborers, improved the social security system and requisitioned luxury hotels for the working class. "He plays cat and mouse with the Czechs," observed his fellow intellectual, Goebbels, "and they swallow everything he places before them. He has carried out a number of extremely popular measures, particularly the almost complete conquest of the black market."

The Reich Protector's achievements in Czechoslovakia roused the Czech government-in-exile to action. Since it appeared that the population might passively accept domination by the Third Reich under such a benevolent despot, they decided to assassinate Heydrich. Two non-coms, Jan Kubis and Josef Gabcik, trained at a school for sabotage in Scotland, were parachuted into the protectorate from a British plane.

On the morning of May 27 the assassins, accompanied by two compatriots, hid at a curve on the road between Heydrich's country villa and Hradschin Castle in Prague. As the Protector's green open Mercedes was approaching, Gabcik jumped to the road and pressed the trigger of his Sten. Nothing happened. He cocked the gun. Again it jammed. Behind him, Kubis lobbed a grenade at the car, which was slowing to a halt. Heydrich shouted, "Step on it, man!" but the driver, a last-minute substitute, kept slamming on the brakes. The grenade exploded, wrecking the rear of the car. Apparently unwounded, Heydrich leaped to the road, revolver in hand, shooting and yelling as if he were "the central figure in a scene out of any Western." Kubis escaped on a bicycle; Gabcik, still unhurt, stood momentarily immobilized when his weapon jammed, then escaped. Suddenly Heydrich dropped his revolver, grasped his right hip and staggered. Fragments of leather and steel springs from the Mercedes' upholstery had penetrated his ribs and stomach. He was taken to a nearby hospital but his wound did not seem serious and he refused to be attended by any but a German doctor. One was finally found who announced that an operation was necessary since grenade fragments were lodged in the membrane between the ribs and lungs as well as the spleen.

Himmler, at temporary headquarters near Wolfsschanze, wept upon learning that his right-hand man was dying, but some SS men were convinced these were crocodile tears since he resented Heydrich's rise to favor with Hitler. As Heydrich lay dying in Prague he whispered a warning to his subordinate Syrup to beware of Himmler.

Later, while surveying the death mask of Heydrich, Himmler remarked to Walter Schellenberg, chief of the SS Foreign Intelligence Service, "Yes, as the Führer said at the funeral, he was indeed a man with an iron heart. And at the height of his power fate purposefully took him away." His voice was somber but Schellenberg could never forget "the nod of Buddha-like approval that accompanied these words, while the small cold eyes behind the pince-nez were suddenly lit with sparkle like the eyes of a basilisk."

The two assassins, along with five other members of the Czech Resistance, were finally trapped in a Budapest church by the SS and executed. But this was only the beginning of the reprisal. A reign of terror which made Heydrich's actions seem benevolent descended on Bohemia and Moravia. More than 1300 Czechs were executed out of hand, including all the male inhabitants of Lidice on the fake charge that these villagers had harbored the assassins. Lidice itself was burned, the ruins dynamited and the ground leveled. The eradication of this obscure village not only aroused the disgust and indignation of the Western world but rekindled the spirit of resistance within Czechoslovakia.*

It was the Jews who suffered most by the assassination. On the day Heydrich died 152 were executed in Berlin. Three thousand others were removed from the concentration camp of Theresienstadt and shipped to Poland where the killing centers were already receiving a steady flow of victims.

Perhaps the most diabolical innovation of the Final Solution was the establishment of Jewish Councils to administer their own deportation and destruction. This organization, comprising those leaders of the community who believed that co-operation with the Germans was the best policy, discouraged resistance. "I will not be afraid to sacrifice 50,000 of our community," reasoned a typical leader, Moses Merin, "in order to save the other 50,000."

By early summer the mass exterminations began under the authority

---

* "This was our general idea when we flew in a party to murder Heydrich in Czechoslovakia," admitted British Labour M.P. R. T. Paget, after the war. "The main Czech Resistance movement was the direct result of the consequent SS reprisals."

of a written order from Himmler. Eichmann showed this authorization to one of his assistants, Dieter Wisliceny, with the explanation that Final Solution meant the biological extermination of the Jewish race. "May God forbid," exclaimed the appalled Wisliceny, "that our enemies should ever do anything similar to the German people!"

"Don't be sentimental," said Eichmann. "This is a Führer order." This was corroborated by Himmler in a letter to the chief of the SS Main Office at the end of July: "The occupied Eastern territories will be cleared of Jews. The implementation of this very hard order has been placed on my shoulders by the Führer. No one can release me from this responsibility in any case. So I forbid all interference."

What Kurt Gerstein learned, as head of the Technical Disinfection Service of the Waffen SS, had already driven him to despair. "He was so appalled by the satanic practices of the Nazis," recalled a friend, "that their eventual victory did not seem to him impossible." During a tour that summer of the four extermination camps in the Generalgouvernement, Gerstein saw with his own eyes what he had read about. At the first camp he and two companions—Eichmann's deputy and a professor of hygiene named Pfannenstiel—were informed that Hitler and Himmler had just ordered "all action speeded up." At Belzec, two days later, Gerstein saw these words translated into reality.

"There are not ten people alive," he was told by the man in charge, Kriminalkommissar Christian Wirth, "who have seen or will see as much as you." Gerstein witnessed the entire procedure from the arrival of 6000 Jews in boxcars, 1450 of whom were already dead. As the survivors were driven out of the cars with whips, they were ordered over a loudspeaker to remove all clothing, artificial limbs, and spectacles and turn in all valuables and money. Women and young girls were to have their hair cut off. "That's to make something special for U-boat crews," explained an SS man, "nice slippers."

Revolted, Gerstein watched the march to the death chambers. Men, women, children—all stark naked—filed past in ghastly parade as a burly SS man promised in a loud, priestlike voice that nothing terrible was going to happen to them. "All you have to do is breathe in deeply. That strengthens the lungs. Inhaling is a means of preventing infectious diseases. It's a good method of disinfection." To those who timorously asked what their fate would be, the SS man gave more reassurance: the men would build roads and houses; the women would do housework or help in the kitchen. But the odor from the death chambers was telltale and those at the head of the column had to be shoved by those behind. Most were silent, but one woman, eyes flashing, cursed her murderers. She was spurred on by whiplashes from Wirth, a former chief of criminal police in Stuttgart. Some prayed, others asked, "Who will give us water to wash the dead?" Gerstein prayed with them.

By now the chambers were jammed with humanity. But the driver of the diesel truck, whose exhaust gases would exterminate the Jews, could not start the engine. Incensed at the delay, Wirth began lashing at the driver with his whip. Two hours and forty-nine minutes later the engine started. After another interminable twenty-five minutes Gerstein peered into one chamber. Most of the occupants were already dead. At the end of thirty-two minutes all were lifeless. They were standing erect, recalled Gerstein, "like pillars of basalt, since there had not been an inch of space for them to fall in or even lean. Families could still be seen holding hands, even in death." The horror continued as one group of workers began tearing open the mouths of the dead with iron hooks, while others searched anuses and genital organs for jewelry. Wirth was in his element. "See for yourself," he said, pointing to a large can filled with teeth. "Just look at the amount of gold there is! And we have collected as much only yesterday and the day before. You can't imagine what we find every day—dollars, diamonds, gold! You'll see!"

Gerstein forced himself to watch the final process. The bodies were flung into trenches, each some hundred yards long, conveniently located near the gas chambers. He was told that the bodies would swell from gas after a few days, raising the mound as much as six to ten feet. Once the swelling subsided, the bodies would be piled on railway ties covered with diesel oil and burned to cinders.

The following day the Gerstein party was driven to Treblinka near Warsaw where they saw almost identical installations but on a larger scale: "eight gas chambers and veritable mountains of clothing and underwear, 115 to 130 feet high." In honor of their visit, a banquet was held for employees. "When one sees the bodies of these Jews," Professor Pfannenstiel told them, "one understands the greatness of the work you are doing!" After dinner the guests were offered butter, meat and alcohol as going-away presents. Gerstein lied that he was adequately supplied from his own farm and so Pfannenstiel took the former's share as well as his own.

Upon arrival in Warsaw, Gerstein set off immediately for Berlin, resolved to tell those who would listen of the ghastly sights he had witnessed. A modern Ancient Mariner, he began spreading the truth to incredulous colleagues. As a rock thrown into a pond creates ever widening ripples, so did the tale of Kurt Gerstein.

4

The coming of spring 1942 saw almost no change in Germany's military situation. The eastern front remained stagnant and Rommel was still not quite ready for his new desert offensive. There was little of cheer to report except continuing Japanese victories and Hitler's enthusiasm over these was dampened by his ally's polite but stubborn refusal to conduct the war as he saw it. Ribbentrop persistently pressed the Japanese, through Ambassador Oshima, to turn their major attack toward India, but to no avail. Nor was Hitler any more successful when he invited Oshima to Wolfsschanze and repeated the request. The Wehrmacht, he said, was about to invade the Caucasus and once that oil region was seized the road to Persia would be open. Then the Germans and Japanese could catch all the British Far East forces in a giant pincers movement. It was tempting but the Japanese declined the opportunity. They were already contemplating negotiations with the West. Prime Minister Tojo had been summoned to the palace and instructed by the Emperor "not to miss any opportunity to terminate the war." Tojo summoned the German ambassador, General Eugen Ott, and suggested that their two nations secretly approach the Allies; he would fly to Berlin as a personal representative of the Emperor if Hitler would send a long-range bomber. The Führer's reply was polite but lukewarm; he could not take the risk of Tojo crashing in a German plane.

Determined to defeat Russia even without the aid of Japan, Hitler proceeded as planned with his contemplated drive into the Caucasus. He stressed the importance of the area in words that alarmed his field commanders. If they didn't seize the oilfields at Maikop and Grozny, he said, "I shall have to liquidate the war."

The ambitious operation, code-named Blau, was slowed for weeks by heavy spring rains and it was not launched by Marshal von Bock until June 28. Six Hungarian and seventeen German divisions drove toward Kursk. Forty-eight hours later the powerful Sixth Army, consisting of eighteen divisions, struck just to the south. The Russians made the mistake of committing their tanks piecemeal and within forty-eight hours the two German forces met, encircling large number of prisoners. Just ahead lay the Don and the strategic city of Voronezh, but Bock was reluctant to press the attack. He finally took the city on July 6 but by this time Hitler was so disgusted with his dilatory tactics that he relieved him permanently.

As Bock headed west into retirement, complaining of mistreatment, Hitler moved his headquarters deep into the Ukraine, occupying a camp in the woods a few miles northeast of Vinnitsa. Christened Werewolf by himself, it was an uncamouflaged collection of wooden huts located in a dreary area. There were no hills, no trees, simply an endless expanse of nothingness. Under the cloudless July sky, the heat was stifling and this in turn markedly affected Hitler, contributing to the arguments and explosions which would reach unprecedented heights in the weeks to come.

Perhaps the heat also contributed to a crucial mistake. Hitler quixotically decided to mount a major attack on Stalingrad, an industrial city on the Volga, while continuing the drive to the Caucasus. Halder, for one, complained openly that it was impossible to take both Stalingrad and the Caucasus simultaneously and urged that they concentrate on the former alone. But Hitler remained convinced that the Russians were "finished."

There was deep concern within the Soviet high command itself. Stalin replaced the commander of the Stalingrad front and ordered the city to be readied for a siege. As at Moscow and Leningrad, thousands of workers began constructing three lines of defense works around the city. Home guard and worker battalions were sent west to back up retreating Red Army forces.

The arguments at Werewolf intensified. After one stormy session Hitler told his personal adjutant, "If I listen to Halder much longer, I'll become a pacifist!" Debate became outright rancor on July 30 at the daily Führer conference when Jodl solemnly stated that the fate of the Caucasus would be decided at Stalingrad, and that the Fourth Panzer Army, earlier diverted to the former, must be returned to the latter. Hitler exploded—and then agreed to do so. If this tank army had never been shifted to the south, Stalingrad would probably already have been in German hands, but by now the Soviets had gathered enough strength in front of the Volga to slow if not stem the new assault. On such apparently minor decisions do great issues often depend. With Stalingrad invested by midsummer, the entire Soviet defense system might have been irrevocably split by winter. It was another revealing example of Hitler's dangerous dispersion of forces. First had come his insistence on striking simultaneously at both Leningrad and the Ukraine, before belatedly pressing on to Moscow. All this was accompanied by a further diffusion of energy through waging political and ideological warfare while pursuing his personal goal of exterminating Jews. Similarly in the present dilemma— Stalingrad or the Caucasus?—he was insisting on taking both, at the risk of taking neither. The ancient Greeks would have called it hubris, the overweening pride that eventually overtakes all conquerors.

If Hitler had qualms over the jeopardy in which his overleaping ambition had placed the Wehrmacht, they were not apparent. A week later he was blandly assuring an Italian visitor that Stalingrad and the Caucasus would both be taken. His optimism seemed to be well founded. The over-all military situation was auspicious. Rommel had won an unexpected victory in North Africa by taking Tobruk, the linchpin to the British defenses, and then pushing on to El Alamein, only sixty-five miles from Alexandria. This triumph was followed by announcement of an even greater one at Midway. Hitler had believed the Japanese, whose communiqués had been much more accurate than those of the Americans. But this time it turned out to be his ally who grossly exaggerated; Nippon had not only lost four carriers and the cream of her naval aviators but the tide of battle in the Pacific had swung. The extent of defeat was confirmed by the news that the Americans had just landed in force on Guadalcanal, a strategic island deep inside Japan's defense perimeter.

It was a colossal setback and so unexpected that it was no wonder the arguments at Werewolf grew even more intense. A violent one erupted on August 24 following Halder's request that a unit presently under heavy Soviet attack be permitted to withdraw to a shorter line. Hitler shouted that his army chief of staff always came with the same proposal—withdrawal! "I expect my commanders to be as tough as the fighting troops."

Ordinarily Halder could restrain his resentment but today he retorted that brave Germans were falling in thousands simply because their commanders were not allowed to make reasonable decisions. Hitler recoiled. He stared fixedly, then said hoarsely, "Colonel General Halder, how dare you use language like that in front of me! Do you think you can teach me what the man at the front is thinking? What do you know about what goes on at the front? Where were you in the First World War? And you try to pretend to me that I don't understand what it's like at the front. I won't stand that! It's outrageous." The other military men sidled out of the conference room, heads bowed. It was obvious that Halder's days at Führer Headquarters were numbered.

By late August fighting began in the northern outskirts of Stalingrad. Already set afire by heavy bombings, the city was temporarily cut off when the Red Army communication networks broke down. But apparent victory did not mellow Hitler. He felt he had been lied to by commanders in the field and deceived by those at his own headquarters. His suspicion of both groups was growing pathological and he rarely listened to advice, never to criticism. Oppressed by the summer torpor, he began making hasty decisions in the grip of anger and recrimination. He was particularly incensed with Bock's replacement, Marshal List, and when he left the conference of August 31 Hitler began to insult and revile him. List's days too were numbered.

5

Hitler's conviction that he was surrounded by traitors was confirmed by the discovery late in August of a spy ring, the *Rote Kapelle* (Red Orchestra), which was comprised of prominent Germans. This group had succeeded in informing Moscow about the attack on Maikop, the fuel situation in Germany, the location of chemical warfare materials in the Reich, and Hitler's insistence on taking Stalingrad. After wholesale arrests, forty-six members of the ring, including Mildred Harnack, an American citizen, were executed. But secret information continued to flow to Moscow from another German spy, Rudolf Rössler, a publisher of leftist Catholic books in Lucerne. Rössler, whose code name was Lucy, had informants inside Germany, including General Fritz Thiele, the number two man in the OKW signal organizations; and his reports consequently were far more important than those of the Rote Kapelle; he could provide the Red Army with the German daily order of battle.

Hitler suspected there was a spy at Führer Headquarters since all his moves seemed to be anticipated. Suspicion bred irritability and his military leaders took the brunt of it. The argument on September 7 was the most tempestuous of all. That morning Hitler sent Jodl, one of the few staff officers still in his good graces, to the Caucasus to find out why List was making such slow progress in the mountain passes leading out to the Black Sea. After a long interview with List and the commander of the Mountain Corps, Jodl concluded that the situation was hopeless. He flew back to Vinnitsa and reported that List was adhering strictly to the instructions he had received.

The Führer jumped to his feet. "That's a lie!" he shouted and accused Jodl of having colluded with List. He was only supposed to transmit orders. Never had Jodl seen such an outburst of rage from a human being. Stung, he struck back. If Hitler had wanted a mere messenger, he said, why hadn't he sent a young lieutenant? Infuriated that Jodl had "wounded" him in the presence of others, Hitler stalked out of the room, casting glares at everyone. More convinced than ever that he was the victim of lies, Hitler shut himself up in his bunker.

The briefing conferences now took place in his hut. He pointedly refused to shake hands with any staff officer. The atmosphere of the meetings was glacial, with stenographers recording every word of the Führer's instructions. He was determined that never again would his orders be disputed. It was also the end of the camaraderie at mealtimes that he cherished. From now on the Führer ate alone in his room, attended only by Blondi, the Alsatian bitch which Bormann had recently given him to take his mind off escalating problems.*

The military community at Vinnitsa waited in anxious silence. No one felt secure. On September 9 Hitler summarily removed List and took personal command of Army Group A. Then came rumors that Halder, Jodl and Keitel were soon to be released. Although the latter had never been on intimate terms with General Warlimont, he now sought out his advice. Was it possible, he forced himself to ask, to keep his position and retain his self-respect? "Only you can answer that," replied Warlimont in embarrassment. He recalled how petrified Keitel had become the time Hitler angrily threw a file on the table. As it tumbled to the floor the chief of staff, forgetting his exalted position, had stood petrified as if he were a junior officer. It was a typical case, thought Warlimont, "of a man given a position for which he was unqualified." Poor Keitel had overreached himself; it was tragic since he had never wanted the job.

At conferences Hitler continued to display dogged confidence. When General von Weichs of Army Group B and General Friedrich Paulus, the field commander whose task it was to take Stalingrad, warned of the extremely long and lightly held Don front on the northern flank, the Führer made light of their concern. He assured them that the Russians were at the end of their resources and the resistance at Stalingrad was "a purely local affair." Since the Russians were no longer capable of launching a major counteroffensive, there was no real danger on the Don flank. The vital thing, he said, was "to concentrate every available man and capture as quickly as possible the whole of Stalingrad itself and the banks of the Volga." That was why he proposed to reinforce Paulus' Sixth Army with three more divisions.

This time there were some grounds for Hitler's optimism. Disorder was rampant among Soviet troops in the Stalingrad area. Numerous units between the Don and the Volga had already disintegrated as officers and troops deserted or fled to the rear. Columns of refugees, taking cattle and farm equipment with them, cluttered all roads to the east. One recently assigned commander found that his armor had vanished without orders and that leading artillery, anti-tank and engineer commanders, some hold-

---

* Heim never took another note of table conversation but Koeppen, upon Hitler's return to the communal table several months later, made notes until the following January. Thereafter a few inconsequential table conversations were recorded by Bormann or a reporter named Müller.

ing the rank of general, had decamped. By September 14 disaster seemed imminent. Luftwaffe planes were already mining the Volga behind Stalingrad as German infantrymen ranged through the center of the city, seizing the main railroad station and driving as far as the waterfront. Abruptly the Soviet defense stiffened. Reinforcements, ferried across the river, began challenging the Germans. On the fifteenth the main railroad station changed hands several times and Paulus felt obliged to narrow his attack. The fighting became listless and this had a marked effect on Hitler, so Warlimont noted upon his return to the briefing sessions after an absence of two weeks. As the Führer fixed him with a long, malevolent stare, Warlimont thought: "The man's confidence has gone with realization that the Soviets cannot be beaten"; that was why he could no longer abide those generals who had witnessed "his faults, his errors, his illusions and his daydreams."

"He trusts none of the generals," wrote Engel in his diary; ". . . he would promote a major to a general and make him chief of staff, if he only knew such a man. Nothing seems to suit him and he curses himself for having gone to war with such poor generals." Hitler decided to rid himself of Halder, who had annoyed him above all others as a prophet of doom, but whom he tolerated for his competence. The end came on September 24. "You and I have been suffering from nerves," said Hitler. "Half of my exhaustion is due to you. It is not worth while going on. We need National Socialist ardor now, not professional ability. I cannot expect this of an officer of the old school such as you." Tears welled in Halder's eyes, a sign of weakness to Hitler, further grounds for dismissal. Halder said not a word in his own behalf. He rose when Hitler finished his tirade. "I am leaving," he said simply, and walked out of the room with dignity. He was convinced that Hitler was dominated by feminine characteristics. "The intuition which mastered him instead of pure logic," he later wrote, "was only one of the many proofs of this fact."

As a replacement, Hitler wanted the antithesis of Halder, and chose Kurt Zeitzler. A newly appointed major general, he had none of the advantages of seniority and authority enjoyed by Halder and it seemed doubtful he could have much influence with OKW and the army group commanders. But Zeitzler's relative youth and inexperience made him all the more attractive to the Führer. He promoted Zeitzler two grades to colonel general.

In appearance he did not fit the role. An extremely short, heavy man, he seemed to be constructed of three balls. But in his first meeting with Hitler in the presence of some twenty officers Zeitzler did not fawn. He listened stolidly as the Führer excoriated the General Staff for doubts and fears. Once the scorching attack, aimed at almost everyone in the room, ended, Zeitzler said, "Mein Führer, if you have any further objections to the General Staff, please tell them to me under four eyes but not in the presence of so many other officers. Otherwise, you must seek a new chief of the General Staff." He saluted and marched out of the room. The other officers waited for the expected explosion but Hitler was impressed. "Eh," he said with a little grin, "he will be back, *ja?*"

Those expecting a new spirit of defiance at Führer Headquarters were quickly disillusioned. In his inaugural address to the officers of OKH, Zeitzler said, "I require the following from every staff officer: he must believe in the Führer and in his method of command. He must on every occasion radiate this confidence to his subordinate and those around him. I have no use for anybody on the General Staff who cannot meet these requirements."

Reassured that he had at last found the right army chief of staff, Hitler set out for Berlin to make another speech. It came on the last day of September at the Sportpalast rally for Winter Relief. Eagerly awaited by a hand-picked audience which had no idea what their Führer would say, it was a short, uninspired speech delivered without the usual sparkle. It struck many foreign listeners as pure bombast of no import, but they missed the implications of the anti-Semitic remarks that accompanied Hitler's pledge to take Stalingrad. Perhaps it was because his words about the Jews had been so oft repeated. For the third time that year he reiterated his prediction that if the Jews instigated "an international war to exterminate the Aryan peoples it would not be the Aryan peoples that would be annihilated but Jewry itself." The motivation for this repetition was obscure except to those privy to the secret of the Final Solution. Each mention was a public acknowledgment of his program of extermination; each gave reassurance and authority to the elite charged with the task of mass murder. Noteworthy too was his repetition of the false date of the original prophecy. It was made on January 30, 1939, not, as he kept saying, on the first of September. This could not have been a slip of the tongue since Hitler repeated it three times. By changing the date to that of the attack on Poland, the beginning of the Second World War, he linked his racial program to the war. He was preparing the people for the hard truth they must eventually face: the extermination of the Jews was an integral part of the war from the very first day of combat.

He was also announcing, if obscurely, that his twin program—the Final Solution and Lebensraum—was progressing as planned. His listeners left the auditorium with a generally uneasy impression. They themselves had contributed the only lift to the meeting, the unison rendition of "The

Song of the Eastern Campaign," whose melody even foreign correspondents found extremely moving:

> *We have been standing guard for Germany,*
> *Keeping the eternal watch.*
> *Now at last the sun is rising in the East,*
> *Calling millions into battle.*

Their spirit was not shared by a number of officials, shocked by the repressive measures in the East. The most forceful rebukes came from Rosenberg's Ministry for the East Territories, and these despite its chief's reluctance to do battle with the formidable combine of Himmler, Bormann and Erich Koch, the Reich commissar for the Ukraine. The last, a former railroad conductor, had delusions of grandeur and rode around in a horse-drawn carriage like a little emperor. Cowed by the ruthless measures of this trio, Rosenberg had recently made them a peace offering: he fired Georg Leibbrandt, symbol of his own more liberal principles for governing occupied areas. But remaining subordinates continued to increase pressure on Rosenberg to by-pass Bormann and go directly to the Führer; they kept submitting new suggestions and reports. The most damning indictment of the Bormann-Himmler-Koch policy was a thirteen-page memorandum from Otto Bräutigam, who had spent seven years in the Soviet Union. The Germans, he said, had been greeted as liberators but the occupied peoples soon discovered that the slogan "Liberation from Bolshevism" was merely a blind for enslavement. Instead of gaining allies against Stalinism, the Germans were creating bitter enemies. "Our policy," charged Bräutigam, "has forced both Bolsheviks and Russian nationalists into a common front against us. The Russian fights today with exceptional bravery and self-sacrifice for nothing more or less than recognition of his human dignity." There was only one solution, concluded Bräutigam: "The Russian people must be told something concrete about their future." If Hitler ever read this memorandum, he never followed its advice. He was determined to win or lose on his own terms.

6

November proved to be a month of disaster for Germany with the enemy scoring victories in both East and West. Since conquest of Egypt was low among Hitler's priorities, he had made defeat in North Africa inevitable by failing to send Rommel sufficient supplies and reinforcements. With the pyramids practically in sight, the Desert Fox was forced into defensive warfare. When his southern section (held by Italians) was pierced by British General Montgomery, Rommel radioed for permission to retreat. On the evening of November 2 the Führer sent his reply: Do not fall back "one inch." The troops must "triumph or die."

Just before receiving this message Rommel radioed that he had been forced to withdraw; in fact a retreat had been under way for five hours. This information reached OKW at 3 A.M. and since the Operations Staff duty officer knew nothing of Hitler's original message, he did not think it important enough to pass on to the Führer.

Hitler, of course, was angry that he had not been awakened. He summoned Warlimont but as the deputy operations chief started down the path toward his office Keitel shouted from a distance in a highly unmilitary manner, "You, Warlimont, come here! Hitler doesn't want to ever see you again!" He was informed that he was relieved of his post.

Rommel's retreat, an augury of total defeat in the desert, was closely followed on November 7 by a disturbing report: a huge armada of Allied ships had entered the Mediterranean and was approaching the north coast of Africa. Although these ships had been sighted outside Gibraltar for several days Hitler and OKW had assumed they were bound for Sardinia or Sicily. The main reason for German surprise, explained Jodl, "probably was that we did not expect such a political false play after the upright, one can properly say, noble treatment which France had received [from Germany] since the collapse in the Forest of Compiègne. For this landing was only possible in agreement with the French and not against the will of France."

Hitler neither bothered to make excuses nor reflected the alarm of his military commanders. He cut short the midday briefing conference and, accompanied by most of the high-ranking population of Wolfsschanze, boarded his special train. Their destination was Munich; the occasion, the nineteenth anniversary of the Putsch. While the Führer slept, the first American and British troops landed on the beaches of Morocco and Algeria. Early reports indicated the French were repelling the landings and Hitler chided his advisers for their initial panic. To their dismay he ordered reinforcements sent to Crete at the other end of the Mediterranean. Outwardly, at least, he was more concerned about the address he was to make to old comrades at the Löwenbräukeller at 6 P.M. It was a fighting speech. Defending himself against the charge that his insistence on taking the city, which "happens to bear the name of Stalin," was as costly to the German army as Verdun, he warned that he was no Wilhelm II, a weakling who had surrendered the Reich's vast Eastern conquests because of a few traitors' sudden desire for an accommodation with the West. "All our enemies may rest assured that while the Germany of that time laid down its arms at a quarter of twelve, I on principle have never finished before five minutes past twelve."

By evening the reports from Africa were too grim for Hitler to ignore. He ordered Ribbentrop to summon Mussolini for an immediate conference. Roused from bed for the second time within twenty-four hours, Ciano was persuaded to waken Mussolini. But Il Duce refused to make the trip to Bavaria. Already ill, he did not relish facing the Führer under the shadow of defeat. By the time his substitute, Ciano, arrived in Munich, Hitler had accepted the significance of the Africa landings. It was clear to him that "the God of war had now turned from Germany and gone over to the other camp." At the same time he reacted violently to Ribbentrop's suggestion that Stalin be approached through Madame Kollontai, the Soviet ambassador in Stockholm. A proposal that most of the conquered territories in the East be given up, "if need be," brought the Führer to his feet. "All I want to discuss," he said with a violence that terrorized Ribbentrop, "is Africa—nothing else!"

He also rejected another Japanese attempt to secure a peace with Russia, as well as a formal request for the Germans to go over to the defensive in the East and shift the bulk of their forces to the West. "I understand Japanese reasoning," Hitler told Ambassador Oshima. It was a good idea but impossible to execute. In such cold country it was extremely difficult to dig defensive positions. But this was merely rhetoric, designed to make refusal palatable to an ally. Any accommodation with Stalin was impossible for a man whose program stood or fell on victory over Bolshevism. And if he could not have victory in the East, Hitler was condemned by his mission to hold back the Red Army until he could rid Europe of Jews.

There were increasing rumors in Berlin that Hitler had gone mad. At one large gathering the wife of Reichsminister Funk reportedly told the wife of Reichsminister Frick, "The Führer is leading us headlong into disaster." "Yes," replied Frau Frick, "the man is insane." This opinion was echoed by Dr. Ferdinand Sauerbruch, the noted surgeon. He told friends that during a recent visit to the Führer he had heard an old and broken Hitler muttering such disjointed phrases as, "I must go to India," or "For one German who is killed ten of the enemy must die."

7

Hitler faced another defeat at Stalingrad. For weeks the Sixth Army of Paulus had made little progress. Advances were measured in yards and the cost of each yard was exorbitant. Both Paulus and Lieutenant Colonel

Reinhard Gehlen, chief of intelligence in the East, warned of dangerous enemy concentrations to the north. "While it is not possible to make any over-all assessments of the enemy situation with the picture as uncertain as it is at present," reported Gehlen on November 12, "we must expect an early attack on the Romanian Third Army, with the interruption of our railroad to Stalingrad as its objective so as to endanger all German forces further to the east and to compel our forces in Stalingrad to withdraw."

Hitler was at the Berghof and did not read this ominous report. But he too was concerned about the Romanians and specifically asked if something was brewing in their area. The answer was no, repeatedly no, recalled Puttkamer, who attended every military conference that week. Since bad news notoriously travels slowly, the Führer was not informed of the gravity of the situation. There was still some doubt as to the strength of the Soviet build-up and the high command, stung by a recent Hitler criticism that it "repeatedly overestimated the enemy," was reluctant to repeat their timorous miscalculations in Poland and France.

At dawn November 19 forty Soviet divisions attacked the Romanians. The defenders fought ably and with gallantry but were crushed by overwhelming numbers. The Army Group B commander reacted quickly. First he ordered Paulus to cease attacking Stalingrad and prepare units to meet the threat to his left flank; then once it became obvious that the Romanians would collapse, he suggested immediate withdrawal of the Sixth Army.

Hitler peremptorily vetoed this. Convinced by earlier reports that the Soviets had been bled to the point of death and this counteroffensive was only a last gasp, he ordered the men at Stalingrad to stand firm. Help was on the way. The reassuring words did not reflect the state of disarray within Hitler's headquarters itself. Major Engel recorded in his diary that there was complete confusion. "Führer himself completely unsure what is to be done." During these trying hours he incessantly paced the great hall of the Berghof, inveighing against his commanders for repeating the same old mistakes.

The tanks he had sent so reluctantly into the battle had already been thrown back and by November 21 the Romanians, half of whose tanks had been disabled by mice which had gnawed through wires, were cut off. "Absolute dismay," hastily scrawled one Romanian officer in his diary. "What sins have we or our forebears committed? Why must we suffer so?" Only that day did Paulus and his chief of staff, Major General Arthur Schmidt, realize their own peril. The appearance of Soviet tanks a few miles from their battle headquarters confirmed that vital links in Sixth Army lines of communication had been captured. After hastily transferring his own headquarters, Paulus asked permission to withdraw. His superior approved the proposal and passed it on to OKW. At the evening's conference in the Berghof, Jodl proposed a general evacuation of the Sixth Army but again the Führer said no. "No matter what happens we must hold the area around Stalingrad."

The next morning, the twenty-second, the two arms of a tremendous Soviet pincer movement met, encircling the entire Sixth Army. More than 200,000 of Germany's finest troops along with 100 tanks, 1800 big guns and more than 10,000 vehicles were caught in a giant *Kessel* (cauldron). At a Sixth Army conference that morning someone suggested they break out to the southwest. "We can't," said Chief of Staff Schmidt, "because we haven't got the necessary fuel. And if we tried we should end up with a catastrophe like that of Napoleon." Sixth Army, he added, would have to go into a "hedgehog" defense. By afternoon the situation had worsened so much that Schmidt began to question his own argument. At this point Paulus received fresh orders: Stand fast and await further orders. "Well," said Paulus, turning to his chief of staff, "now we'll have time to think over what we ought to do. This we'll do separately. Meet me, please, in an hour's time and we'll compare the conclusions we have reached." They were identical: break out to the southwest.

Hitler, now en route back to Wolfsschanze, could not contemplate retreat. That evening he sent a personal message to Paulus. "Sixth Army must know," he said, "that I am doing everything to help and to relieve it. I shall issue my orders in good time." Paulus accepted the decision but one of his corps commanders began a withdrawal on his own initiative in order to force Paulus into ordering a general retreat. Paulus had authority to remove or arrest him but did neither, since the situation was so critical. Ironically, once Hitler learned a retreat was under way, he put the blame on the innocent Paulus and rewarded the guilty man, in whom he had great faith, by giving him an independent command.

His suspicion of Paulus was one reason Hitler ignored a personal plea from the Sixth Army commander, late on the night of November 23, to break out of the trap. Instead he chose to accept Göring's assurance that the Luftwaffe could keep the encircled Sixth Army supplied by air despite the Reichsmarschall's poor performance record, and he dispatched a radio signal next morning ordering Paulus to hold "at all costs" since supplies were coming by air. In a display of wishful thinking, Hitler eagerly seized upon Göring's rash promise and declared Stalingrad a fortress, thus sealing the fate of the almost 250,000 German and allied troops.

Having lost faith in Paulus' superior, Hitler turned over most of that commander's responsibility to Field Marshal von Manstein, whose ingenious invasion plan of the West had coincided so closely with his own. Manstein was to command a new force, Army Group Don, his task to halt the Soviet advance westward so as to take all pressure off the defenders of Stalingrad. Manstein sent a reassuring message to Paulus that noon: "We will do all we can to get you out of this mess." Paulus' present task, he added, was to "maintain the Volga and north front according to the Führer's order and prepare strong forces to break out to the rear." Taking this to mean that Sixth Army was to stand firm while Manstein opened up a corridor, Paulus and Schmidt abandoned their own plan to break out without Hitler's permission.

Twenty-two of the planes flying supplies to Stalingrad were shot down before the end of the day. On the twenty-fifth another nine were destroyed, and a mere seventy-five tons of food and armaments reached Paulus. Back at Wolfsschanze Army Chief of Staff Zeitzler braved Hitler's wrath on the twenty-sixth by suggesting that Paulus be given "freedom of action"; that is, to attempt to break out or, that failing, have tacit permission to capitulate. Hitler rejected this proposal out of hand, agreeing only to a relief action on the part of Manstein. To all protests the Führer referred to Göring's repeated hollow assurances of sufficient air supply. "We are horrified by so much optimism," noted Engel in his diary, "which even Luftwaffe General Staff officers do not share."

That day Paulus sent a handwritten letter to Manstein, thanking him for the recent promise to help Sixth Army. He told of his request to Hitler asking for freedom of action if it should become necessary. "I wanted to have this authority," he explained, "in order to guard against issuing the only possible order in that situation too late. I have no means of proving that I should only issue such an order in an extreme emergency and I can merely ask you to accept my word for this."

Paulus got his answer from the Führer at five minutes before midnight. In a personal message to the men of Sixth Army, Hitler ordered them to stand fast with the assurance that he would do all in his power to send them relief.

The relief operation, Winter Storm, was relatively stingy, consisting of a single thrust by two armored divisions. Scheduled to begin in early December, there were so many delays in assembling this minimal force that it was not mounted until the morning of December 12. As 230 tanks rolled northeast toward Stalingrad, some sixty miles distant, there was very little resistance. In some places there were no Russians at all and the Germans were puzzled. Even so only twelve miles were made; the frozen ground began to melt under the sun's rays and slopes were turned into slippery traps.

At the noon conference Hitler's first question was, "Has there been some disaster?" and, when told that the sole enemy attacks were at the sector held by Italian troops, began grumbling. "I've had more sleepless nights over this business in the south than anything else. One doesn't know what's going on."

For six days the men of Sixth Army anxiously waited for sight of friendly tanks but all they could see were streams of Russians plodding west to stem Winter Storm. Manstein was equally depressed and requested permission on the eighteenth for Paulus to break out so that most of his men could be saved. Zeitzler "very urgently" approved the measure, but Hitler remained adamant since the Italian Eighth Army had collapsed that day, opening a huge hole north of the relief force.

The following afternoon Manstein once more radioed Hitler for permission to break out Sixth Army. At first Hitler refused but he showed signs of relenting under Zeitzler's continued urgings. His indecision encouraged some staff officers to hope against hope that Paulus, on his own responsibility, would attempt the breakout. Paulus would have done so if he could. He was prepared to disobey the Führer's original order, but by now had less than a hundred tanks with fuel enough, at best, for twenty miles. Moreover, there was hardly enough ammunition for defense, let alone an offensive. He and Schmidt rested their hopes on the columns driving to their relief.

But the tanks coming to their aid would get no farther east. On December 23 Manstein was forced to call off the relief attack since one Panzer division of this force had to be diverted to plug up the hole left by the fleeing Italians. At 5:40 P.M. he got in touch with Paulus by teleprinter and asked, "if worst came to worst," could he break out? Did this mean, asked Paulus, that he was now authorized to initiate the move? "Once it is launched," he said, "there'll be no turning back."

"I can't give you full authority today," replied Manstein. "But I hope to get a decision tomorrow."

At his headquarters Hitler remained reluctant to make it and, on Christmas Eve, Manstein had only gloomy words and holiday wishes for the Sixth Army. That evening Manstein radioed Wolfsschanze that the stamina of the troops at Stalingrad had diminished considerably and would continue to do so at an increasing rate. "It might be possible to provide for the men a little longer but then they would be quite incapable of fighting their way out. The end of the month is, in my opinion, the last possible date." Even as Manstein signed the message he knew that Hitler would not listen. The Sixth Army was already doomed. Much as Paulus wanted to break out, he knew it would now be suicidal. He agreed with Manstein that it was the end. But should he explain the situation to his men? Troops without hope would not fight.

Goebbels tried to give it to them in his New Year message. In an address directed specifically to front-line troops he promised that 1943 would bring the Reich closer to its "final victory," its "ultimate victory." He spoke far more frankly to his staff. Propaganda for the coming months, he said, must avoid producing a basically defensive attitude among the people. "Since the beginning of the war our propaganda has taken the following mistaken line of development. First year of the war: We have won. Second year: We will win. Third year: We must win. Fourth year: We cannot be defeated." Such a development, he said, was disastrous. "Instead, the German public must be made to realize that we are also *able* to win because the prerequisites exist as soon as work and effort in the country are fully placed at the service of the war." It was a grim picture and foreshadowed a Führer decree, a fortnight later, ordering the total mobilization of the homeland for the war effort.

8

Just before the New Year Hitler sent his personal pilot, Baur, to the Stalingrad pocket with instructions to bring back General Hans Hube, commander of the 14th Panzer Corps. At Führer Headquarters the puzzled Hube, who had lost a hand in the First World War, was asked to give an accurate report of Sixth Army's position. Hube's fearless and blunt revelation of the desperate plight of his comrades impressed Hitler, who listened in silence. "Much of this is new to me," he said and promised to send the SS Panzer Corps, presently in France, to the relief of Stalingrad. In the meantime the airlift would be increased at all costs. With deep emotion the Führer vowed that he would turn the setback at Stalingrad into victory just as he had done after last winter's crisis.

Hube flew back to the battle with orders to instill new hope in his comrades. He arrived on the eighth, the day enemy planes dropped leaflets containing a Soviet ultimatum to capitulate or die. Heartened by Hube's news, Paulus told his corps commanders that there could be no question of surrender.

Two days later the main Soviet assault began and Sixth Army's western front was slowly pushed back. Food and ammunition supplies rapidly dwindled; the daily ration of most big guns was a single round and each man got a slice of bread and a little horse meat. The amount of supplies coming into the pocket remained far below that promised by Göring and by now Hitler was disillusioned to the point of biting sarcasm, referring to him as "this fellow Göring, this fat, well-fed pig!" Perhaps the greatest insult was selecting a subordinate to reorganize the airlift and save Sixth Army. The Führer had already twice praised Field Marshal Milch as one who did not know the word "impossible." In mid-January he was brought to Wolfsschanze and instructed by Hitler to get three hundred tons of supplies daily into the cauldron. To do so he was given special powers, including authority to issue orders to any military command. Milch's energetic reforms raised the daily level of supply from sixty to eighty tons and there was a glimmer of hope inside the pocket. But it soon became obvious that even Milch could do little better and finally he himself realized his mission was impossible.

By January 20 the pocket, already reduced to half its size, showed unmistakable signs of disintegration, particularly in those areas where the fighting was fiercest. Moved by the suffering he saw with his own eyes, Paulus felt duty-bound to appeal once more to higher authority. That day he summoned Schmidt and two staff members for their opinion. Only one of the three, an operations officer, favored continuing the fight and Paulus dispatched identical messages to Manstein and Führer Headquarters requesting permission, once operations were no longer possible, "to avoid complete annihilation."

Both Manstein and Zeitzler urged Hitler to reply favorably but he continued to demand that Sixth Army "fight to the last man." In a last desperate measure to bring him around, a major named Zitzewitz was flown out of Stalingrad to make a firsthand report of the hopeless situation. Hitler gripped both Zitzewitz's hands when he was presented on January 22. "You have come from a deplorable situation," he said, then talked of another relief drive through enemy lines by a battalion of new Panther tanks.

Zitzewitz was flabbergasted. How could a battalion succeed where an entire Panzer army had failed? During a pause in Hitler's dissertation the major read off figures from a slip of paper he had prepared. He spoke movingly of the trapped men's hunger and frostbite, the dwindling supplies, the feeling that they had been written off. "My Führer," he concluded, "permit me to state that the troops at Stalingrad can no longer be ordered to fight to their last round because they are no longer physically capable of fighting and because they no longer have a last round."

Hitler turned to him in surprise, and, Zitzewitz felt, stared straight through him. "Man recovers very quickly," Hitler said. He dismissed the major and ordered this message sent to Paulus: "Surrender out of the question. Troops will resist to the end."

Hitler himself had gnawing doubts but two days later his spirits were lifted by a startling announcement that Roosevelt had just called for the unconditional surrender of the Axis at the conclusion of an Allied conference in Casablanca. (For some time the Germans believed Casablanca was the code name for the White House and that the conference had taken place in Washington.) By making any political settlement of the world conflict quite impossible, the President had handed Hitler an invaluable piece of propaganda to incite his people to resistance to the end. It was a ray of hope, for Hitler himself had been forced at last to accept the hopeless situation at Stalingrad. He had reportedly ordered Chief Adjutant Schmundt to fly to Stalingrad and give Paulus a pistol to use on himself—at the last moment.

Isolated groups of Germans were already surrendering in considerable numbers but Paulus himself stood firm. He told two divisional commanders who brought up the subject of capitulation that the general situation did not permit such action. They must obey the Führer's injunction to hold out to the last possible moment. His own decision weighed heavily on his conscience since he knew the torments his men were suffering. Until recently their fighting spirit had been remarkable. With faith in their leaders, they had taken it for granted that relief was coming. Today, the tenth anniversary of the National Socialist take-over, an air of hopelessness pervaded the air. There was no place to put the newly wounded since every cellar in Stalingrad was crowded almost to suffocation. The supply of drugs, medicines and bandages was fast disappearing. It was no longer possible to bury the dead in the frozen ground.

Forcing himself to rise to the occasion of the day, Paulus radioed Hitler:

ON THE ANNIVERSARY OF YOUR ASSUMPTION OF POWER, THE SIXTH ARMY SENDS GREETINGS TO THE FÜHRER. THE SWASTIKA STILL FLUTTERS OVER STALINGRAD. MAY OUR STRUGGLE STAND AS AN EXAMPLE TO GENERATIONS AS YET UNBORN, NEVER TO SURRENDER, HOWEVER DESPERATE THE ODDS. THEN GERMANY WILL BE VICTORIOUS.

In another personal message, Paulus informed the Führer that his nephew, Leo Raubal, was wounded. Should he be evacuated by air? The reply was negative: as a soldier he must remain with his comrades. Thus the brother of Hitler's true love, Geli, was consigned to almost certain death.*

In a final letter Paulus wrote his wife, a Romanian of noble birth, "I stand and fight—these are my orders!" On the evening of January 30 he armed himself with a rifle for his last battle. Then came word from Wolfsschanze that the Führer had promoted him to the rank of field marshal. It was an honor that every officer dreamed of, yet at this moment it seemed of little consequence. The promotion was followed, after midnight, by a message from Zeitzler, which was its price tag: "The Führer asks me to point out that each day the fortress of Stalingrad can continue to hold out is of importance."

Just before dawn of the thirty-first, Chief of Staff Schmidt peered out a window and in the glare of innumerable fires saw an incredible sight. In the market place a large group of German and Russian soldiers were standing together, smoking cigarettes, talking animatedly. Schmidt told Paulus that the end had come. Further local resistance was senseless unless they were willing to fire at their own troops. Paulus agreed that surrender was the only alternative. Within the hour the two men were in a Soviet car bound for the headquarters of General M. S. Shumilov's Sixty-fourth Army.

When Shumilov suggested they go to lunch Paulus said he could not eat a bite until the Russians promised to provide food and medicine for his men. "We are human," said Shumilov sympathetically. "Of course we will do all this." They stepped outside. It was bitter cold but the sun shone brilliantly. Shumilov spread his arms. "Ah, a wonderful spring day!" At lunch Shumilov proposed a toast to victory for the Red Army. After some hestitation Paulus held up his glass. "I drink to the victory of German arms!" Affronted, Shumilov put down his own glass, then said good-naturedly, "Forget it. Prosit!"

Early the following morning, February 1, Moscow announced the surrender of Paulus and Schmidt. At the midday conference Zeitzler could not believe this was true but Hitler had no doubts. "They have surrendered there formally and absolutely," he insisted. "Otherwise they would have

* Hitler had two other relatives on this front: Hans Hitler, whose father was the Führer's first cousin; and Heinz Hitler, son of his half brother, Alois, Jr. Hans escaped to Germany; both Leo and Heinz were captured. According to Stalin's daughter, the Germans proposed exchanging one of their prisoners (it could have been either Leo or Heinz) for her brother Yasha. But Stalin told her, "I won't do it. War is war." Reportedly young Stalin was shot by the Germans. Heinz Hitler died in captivity but Geli's brother returned home in 1955, reconciled to the fact that his uncle had done nothing to save him and more than ever convinced that Hitler was "absolutely innocent" of his sister's death.

closed ranks, formed a hedgehog, and shot themselves with their last bullets." Zeitzler continued to express doubt that Paulus had capitulated. Perhaps he was lying somewhere badly wounded. "No, it is true," said Hitler. "They'll be brought straight to Moscow and put into the hands of the GPU and they'll blurt out orders for the northern pocket to surrender too." He rambled on, commending those military men who, unlike Paulus, ended their problems with a shot in the head. "How easy it is to do that! A revolver—makes it easy. What cowardice to be afraid of that. Ha! Better be buried alive! And in a situation like this where he knows well enough that his death would set the example for behavior in the pocket next door. If he sets an example like this, one can hardly expect people to go on fighting."

He continued to berate Paulus. "What hurts me the most personally is that I promoted him to field marshal. I wanted to give him this final satisfaction. That's the last field marshal I shall appoint in this war. You mustn't count your chickens before they're hatched. I don't understand it at all. When a man sees so many men die—I must really say: how easy it is for our . . ." His words became incoherent. ". . . he can't have thought of that. It's ridiculous, a thing like this. So many men have to die and then a man like this besmirches the heroism of so many others. He could have got out of his vale of tears and into eternity and been immortalized by the nation, but he'd rather go to Moscow. What kind of a choice is that? It just doesn't make any sense!"

The next day the northern pocket surrendered. The Soviets claimed the capture of 91,000 prisoners including 24 generals and 2500 officers. Thanks in large part to Hitler's own brutal treatment of Soviet prisoners, these men were treated inhumanely. Reportedly more than 400,000 German, Italian and Romanian prisoners of war died between February and April 1942. Starvation was the chief cause of death and cannibalism became a common practice. The strong alone survived and these lived on excrement from which undigested corn and mullet was picked and washed. Only a few thousand of those captured at Stalingrad would ever return to Germany. One was Paulus, who pleased the Soviets by publicly condemning Hitler and Nazism.

After visiting the wreckage of Stalingrad, General Charles de Gaulle remarked to a correspondent, "Ah, Stalingrad, a remarkable people, a very great people." The correspondent assumed he was talking of the Russians. "*Mais non*, I'm not speaking of the Russians but of the Germans. To have come so far!"

Chapter Twenty-six

THE FAMILY CIRCLE
1943

1

After the traumatic scene with Jodl, Hitler retreated to his bunker at Werewolf. Here he ate and slept in solitude, his sole companion Blondi, the Alsatian bitch. As the Battle of Stalingrad approached its climax the Führer returned to Wolfsschanze and slowly emerged from solitary confinement. Occasionally he would invite an adjutant or visitor from Berlin to share his meager repast. As the group enlarged to include the secretaries and other select members of the family circle, the meals were transferred back to the communal dining hall. The military leaders were still excluded and he still refused to shake hands with them at briefings. For their part, they felt constrained in his presence, most considering him a tyrant and more than a little mad.

Even in the depth of his depression the Führer had treated his adjutants with polite consideration and his interest in the younger ones, like Richard Schulze, a former Ribbentrop aide, was avuncular. This was the side of Hitler that the Halders never knew. They did not see the man who could be gracious to servants and at ease with chauffeurs and secretaries. Isolation from the military drove him even closer to this family circle and so his new secretary, Gertraud Humps, had a special opportunity to get to know her Führer. She was brought to the Wolfsschanze early that winter to replace the attractive and ebullient Gerda Daranowsky. "Dara" had left a job with Elizabeth Arden to work for Hitler and now was marrying his Luftwaffe liaison officer.

Traudl Humps, the granddaughter of a general, was twenty-two, naïve and impressionable. She was so nervous the first time she took dictation that Hitler soothed her as if she were a child. "You don't have to get excited," he said, "I myself will make far more mistakes during the dictation than you will." She was summoned again on January 3, 1943. This time Hitler asked if she would like the job of permanent private secretary. It was an exciting and flattering offer and, without hesitation, she accepted it. She soon became accustomed to this new, strange world. With no full office routine or fixed duty time, she had leisure to spend much of the day wandering in the snow-covered forest. She particularly enjoyed watching her new employer play with Blondi in the morning. The big dog would jump through hoops, leap over a six-foot wooden wall, climb up a ladder, then beg at the top. Whenever Hitler noticed Traudl, he would come over, shake hands and ask how she was doing.

This affable Hitler was not in evidence at the military briefings. After the fall of Stalingrad his irascibility was such that attendance at situation conferences was kept to a minimum. Guderian, who hadn't seen the Führer since the failure to take Moscow, noticed that, while he hadn't aged greatly, he "easily lost his temper and raged, and was then unpredictable in what he said and decided."

At mealtimes he managed to control his temper with the family circle but his conversation deteriorated in quality. "After Stalingrad," recalled Fräulein Schröder "Hitler would not listen to music any more, and every evening we had to listen to his monologues instead. But his table talk was by now as overplayed as his gramophone records. It was always the same: his early days in Vienna, the *Kampfzeit*, the history of man, the microcosm and the macrocosm. On every subject we all knew in advance what he would say. In the course of time these monologues bored us. But world affairs and events at the front were never mentioned: everything to do with the war was taboo."

In Berlin, Goebbels proclaimed a three-day mourning in honor of Stalingrad's dead. During that period all places of entertainment, including theaters and cinemas, were closed. He also began preparing the nation for hard times ahead. Everywhere—on trains, walls, shopwindows and billboards—was splattered the slogan: "The Wheels Must Turn Only for Victory." On February 15 he issued a decree addressed to Reichsleiters,

Gauleiters and all army headquarters demanding complete mobilization for victory.

That same day in a speech at Düsseldorf, entitled, "Do You Want Total War?" he all but announced Hitler's Final Solution. Two thousand years of Western civilization, he said, were in danger from a Russian victory, one forged by international Jewry. There were cries from the audience of "Hang them!" and Goebbels promised that Germany *would* retaliate "with the total and radical extermination and elimination of Jewry!" This brought wild shouts and manic laughter.

The gravity of the military situation was underlined, next day, in a letter from Bormann to his wife, whom he addressed as his dearest Mummy-Girl. "Should the war take a turn for the worse, either now or at some later stage, it would be better for you to move to the West, because you simply must do everything in your power to keep your—our—children out of any danger. In due course they will have to carry on the work of the future."

On the eighteenth Goebbels again presented his theme of total war in a speech at the Sportpalast to a select audience of trusted party members. It was a staged affair in every detail. The crowd arrived in civilian clothes rather than uniforms for the visual effect. The songs they sang, their shouts of approval, their spoken choruses were admirably orchestrated. On the podium Goebbels was more actor than orator and what he said was not as important as how he said it. In a rhetorical tour de force, he raised his listeners to such frenzy that when he shouted, "Do you want total war? Do you want total war? Do you want it, if necessary, to be even more total and radical than can even be imagined today?" the response was a mighty chorus of Ja's. And when he asked: "Do you accept the fact that anyone who detracts from the war effort will lose his head?" there was thundering approval. "What an hour of idiocy!" he later cynically remarked to his entourage. "If I had told these people to jump from the fourth floor of the Columbus House they would have done it."

So dedicated was Goebbels to the concept of total war that he took it upon himself to organize the highest ranks of the party into an ad hoc committee of action. Early in March he drove up to Göring's home on the Obersalzberg to enlist his help. Matters, he said, would have to be taken out of the Führer's hands; Hitler had aged fifteen years since the war and it was tragic that he had become such a recluse and led such an unhealthy life. It was essential therefore that they make up for the present lack of leadership in domestic and foreign policy. "One must not bother the Führer with everything." He impressed upon Göring that war must be waged politically and that the political leadership of the Reich must be transferred to the Ministerial Council for the Defense of the Reich. Its membership should be bolstered by ruthless men, dedicated to victory at all costs.

Goebbels reassured Göring that they would be acting in Hitler's behalf. "We have no other ambition than that of supporting each other and of forming a solid phalanx around the Führer. The Führer sometimes wavers in his decisions if the same matter is brought to him from different sides. Nor does he always react to people as he should. That's where he needs help."

Göring promised to do his best to bring Himmler into their group and Goebbels revealed that he had already won over such important officials as Funk, Ley and Speer, all men of unparalleled fidelity to the Führer. "The cause is greater than any of us; that goes without saying. The men who helped the Führer win the revolution will now have to help him win the war. They were not bureaucrats then, they must not be bureaucrats today."

Göring never considered approaching Director of Air Armament Field Marshal Milch. Besides lacking qualification as a National Socialist, he made no secret of his opposition to the Reichsmarschall. A few days after the conspiratorial Göring-Goebbels conversation Milch took the opportunity, while dining alone with Hitler, to advise replacement of Göring, whom he suspected of reverting to narcotics. He also had the nerve to tell the latest Göring-Goebbels joke. When those two went to heaven, St. Peter ordered the first to run to a distant cloud and back as punishment for lying so often. St. Peter then looked around for Goebbels. "Where is the little one with the clubfoot?" he asked. "Oh," explained an angel, "he returned to earth for his motorcycle."

After supper Milch said that he had a long list of recommendations and hoped the Führer would not be offended by his frankness. First he urged Hitler to abandon the offensive designed to retake Kursk and go over to the defense. The Wehrmacht was weak, supplies were scanty and lines must be shortened. "You cannot persuade me," said Hitler mildly and made a dot on his pad. The next response was just as radical: Hitler should cancel his daily staff discussions and appoint a new chief of the General Staff—Manstein, for instance. "Give him control of all fronts, not only one area. All under your command. You remain supreme commander while he acts as your assistant." Hitler said nothing but made another pencil mark that Milch took for nervousness. For another hour the field marshal listed equally provoking suggestions. Finally he came to the last and most unpalatable one. "Mein Führer," he said, "Stalingrad has been the gravest crisis for both Reich and Wehrmacht. You simply must act decisively to bring Germany out of this war. I assure you many agree with me. There is still time. You must act at once. Do so without ceremony but, above all, act now!"

It was past midnight. Milch was sweating from exertion and apprehension. He apologized for annoying the Führer with twenty contradictions. Hitler glanced at the dots on his pad. "You have contradicted me twenty-four times, not twenty," he said. He did not seem at all angry or even upset. "I thank you for telling me this. No one else has given me such a clear picture."

2

Correspondent Louis Lochner had already made several attempts to inform Roosevelt of the resistance movement inside the Reich. In hopes of convincing Roosevelt that not all Germans were Nazis, Lochner was prepared to give him the radio code of two separate groups opposed to Hitler so that Roosevelt could inform them directly what political administration in Germany would be acceptable to the Allies. After failing to reach the President through his appointments secretary, Lochner wrote a personal note revealing the existence of these codes and emphasizing that they could be handed over to Roosevelt alone. There was no reply but several days later Lochner was informed that his insistence was viewed by official sources as "most embarrassing." Would he please desist? What Lochner did not know was that the President's refusal to see him was official American policy in line with unconditional surrender, designed not only to withhold encouragement to German resisters but to avoid any important contact. Recognition of the existence of any anti-Hitler movement within Germany was forbidden.

The Resistance was discouraged but continued to plot the overthrow of Hitler. It was agreed that seizure of power alone was not sufficient. The Führer himself must first be assassinated and General Oster and his group selected General Henning von Tresckow, Field Marshal von Kluge's chief of staff, as executioner. He decided to lure Hitler up front, then plant a bomb in his plane that would explode on the return flight. On the evening of March 13, 1943, one of Tresckow's junior officers, Fabian von Schlabrendorff, arrived at the airport with a parcel supposedly containing two bottles of brandy. It was a bomb made from British plastic explosives. Using a key, Schlabrendorff pressed down hard on the fuse, triggering the bomb. Moments later he delivered the parcel to a colonel in Hitler's party who had promised to deliver it to a friend at Wolfsschanze.

The Führer boarded the plane and it took off. The bomb was expected to explode above Minsk but two hours passed without news of any accident. Then came word that the plane had landed safely in Rastenburg. The conspirators were confounded. Now they had to retrieve the erratic bomb before it exploded or was discovered. Schlabrendorff did so and discovered that its firing pin had been released but the detonator was a dud.

A few days later the conspirators tried again. Near midnight, March 20, in a room at a Berlin hotel, the Eden, Schlabrendorff turned over plastic explosives to Colonel Rudolf Christoph Freiherr von Gerstdorff, Kluge's chief of intelligence. His mission was suicidal. He was to approach the Führer at tomorrow's celebration of Heroes' Memorial Day at the Zeughaus in Berlin and blow himself and Hitler to bits.

The next day Gerstdorff appeared at the Zeughaus, a bomb in each overcoat pocket. At 1 P.M. Hitler arrived, and after listening to a passage from Bruckner by the Berlin Symphony he gave a short speech in the inner court. As he headed for the exhibition hall where captured Russian trophies were on display, Gerstdorff reached into his left pocket and broke the acid capsule of the British fuse, which needed at least ten minutes to detonate. Hitler was accompanied by Himmler, Keitel, Göring and a dozen others but the would-be assassin had no difficulty getting to his left side.

Schmundt had assured Gerstdorff that the Führer would spend half an hour at the exhibit but he showed little interest and, to Gerstdorff's consternation, was out of the building in five minutes. There was no possibility of following and Gerstdorff knew he had only another five minutes to dispose of the fuse without being observed. He elbowed his way to the corridor. Finally he found a men's room. Fortunately it was empty. He hastily removed the fuse from his pocket and—seconds before it was due to explode—flushed it down the toilet and left the building with the bombs.

Although the Gestapo had no suspicion of these two attempts against the Führer's life, they suspected that traitors infested the Abwehr. Fifteen days later they arrested Hans von Dohnanyi at Abwehr headquarters. Oster managed to destroy most of the papers incriminating himself but before long he too was placed under arrest. The conspirators had lost not only an able leader but their best means of communicating with each other and any friends in the West.

3

Early that April Hitler and his entourage boarded the train for Berchtesgaden, which would be a welcome respite from the gloomy surroundings at the Wolfsschanze. It was a clear, mild winter night and as they left the snow-covered forest of Rastenburg, Traudl Humps was a bit saddened to leave, yet exhilarated by the promise of new experiences. There was every comfort on the train including a special car equipped with showers and bathtubs; the food was excellent and the seats could be converted into comfortable beds. As the train rolled quietly toward its destination the next morning, she thought of other trains in the Reich, without light or heat, their passengers uncomfortable and hungry. Her thoughts were interrupted by an invitation to join the Führer for lunch. The following morning she breakfasted in less exalted company. The gossip among the servants and secretaries was about Eva Braun, who was to board the train at Munich. To them she was "the lady at the Berghof," and as such was silently accepted by all guests. That is, except by the wives of Ribbentrop, Göring and Goebbels. The first ignored her regally; the other two snubbed her openly, despite Hitler's request that she be treated with respect.

Traudl was given a tour of the Berghof by one of the older secretaries. They started on the second floor where the Führer lived. The walls of the hallway were decorated with paintings by the old masters, beautiful pieces of sculpture and exotic vases. Everything, thought Traudl, was wonderful but strange and impersonal. There was deadly silence since the Führer still slept. In front of one door were two black Scotch terriers—Eva's dogs, Stasi and Negus. Next came Hitler's bedroom. The two rooms, it seemed, were connected by a large bathroom and it was apparent they lived discreetly as man and wife. Traudl was taken downstairs to the large living room which was separated from the famous picture-window room by a heavy velvet curtain. The furnishings were luxurious but despite the beautiful Gobelins and thick carpets she got the impression of coldness. The accommodations were far superior to those at Wolfsschanze but here she felt ill at ease. While she was treated as a guest, she was not there of her own free will but as an employee.

The daily schedule at the Berghof was something of a strain even though it never varied. Hitler's noon briefing rarely ended before midafternoon and it was usually 4 P.M. before the last officer left and the Führer entered the living room where his hungry guests were gathered. As if by signal, Eva would then make her appearance, accompanied by her two scampering dogs. Hitler would kiss her hand, before greeting each guest with a handshake. The transformation of man of state burdened by the tragedies of battle to jovial host eager to please guests and helpmate was unexpected and somewhat ludicrous. His private life in fact was not much different from that of a very successful businessman.

The men addressed Eva with a slight bow and a polite "Gnädiges Fräulein"; the women called her Fräulein Braun. Several seemed very intimate, particularly Herta Schneider, a school friend. The women began an animated discussion on children, fashion and personal experiences. Finally Hitler interrupted, ridiculing Eva's dogs as "hand-sweepers." She blithely retorted that Hitler's dog, Blondi, was a calf.

The banal pleasantries, enlivened by not so much as an aperitif, were ended when Hitler escorted one of the ladies to the table. They were followed by Bormann and Eva, who heartily disliked him, primarily for his flagrant philandering.* "Anything in skirts is his target," remarked one adjutant, "except, of course, Eva herself."

The guests enjoyed sauerbraten but Hitler kept to the vegetarian meals cooked under the supervision of Dr. Werner Zabel in his Berchtesgaden clinic and warmed over at the Berghof kitchen. Nothing would induce Eva to so much as tastè Hitler's thick gruel, oatmeal soup or baked potato liberally soaked in raw linseed oil. The Führer teased her about her own meager diet. "When I first met you," he said, "you were pleasingly plump and now you are quite thin." Women underwent these sacrifices, he added sardonically, "only to make their girl friends envious."

The conversation was gay and superficial until Hitler abruptly began propagandizing for vegetarianism by describing in detail the horrors of a slaughterhouse he had recently visited in the Ukraine. The guests blanched as he described work girls in rubber boots, standing in fresh blood up to their ankles. One, Otto Dietrich, laid down knife and fork with the comment that he was no longer hungry.

After lunch Hitler set out on the daily twenty-minute walk to his tea house. It was a round stone building located below the Berghof, reminding some of the guests of a silo or power plant. Tea was served in a large round room whose six large windows provided a wide vista. From one end there was a magnificent view of the Ach River roaring down the mountainside between houses that looked like matchboxes. Beyond lay the baroque towers of Salzburg.

---

* Somehow he managed to convince his wife, whom he kept almost permanently pregnant, that his infidelities were for the greater good of National Socialism In one remarkable letter she suggested he bring his latest mistress, M., to their Berchtesgaden home and then expressed the hope that Bormann see to it that "one year M. has a child, and the next year I, so that you always have a wife who is mobile."

Hitler drank apple-peel tea while Eva talked of plays and movies. His only comment was that he could not watch a film while the people were making so many sacrifices. "Besides, I must save my eyes for studying maps and reading front-line reports." The conversation that day palled on Hitler. He closed his eyes and shortly was asleep. His guests continued to chat but in lowered voices, and when the Führer wakened he joined in as if he had just closed his eyes momentarily to think.

At 7 P.M. a parade of vehicles arrived at the Berghof, and the business of government resumed. Two hours later Hitler left the conference and led the way to the dining room where he ate mashed potatoes and a to-mato salad while his guests dined on cold meat. He charmed everyone with tales of his youth, until he noticed the lipstick on Eva's napkin. Did she know what it consisted of? Eva protested that she only used French lipstick made of the finest materials. With a pitying smile Hitler said, "If you women knew that lipstick, particularly from Paris, is manufactured from the grease of waste water, you certainly wouldn't color your lips any more." Everyone laughed. He had won another argument—if no adherents.

An adjutant quietly informed Hitler that everyone had arrived for the evening military conference. Not wanting his guests, particularly the women, to come in contact with the military, he told them to remain seated. "It won't take too long," he said and left, head lowered but with a strong step. The secretaries went to an office to type air raid reports, while Eva and most of the guests descended to the basement to see a movie. Before it concluded a telephone rang: a servant reported that the conference was over and the Führer expected everyone in the main hall. Eva hurried to her room to refresh her make-up; her sister Gretl smoked a last ciga-rette, then chewed peppermint candy to camouflage her breath; and the rest dutifully repaired to the great hall. It was almost midnight by the time Hitler came down the stairs and seated himself at the fireplace next to Eva and her two little terriers. Since they did not get along with Blondi, the latter was excluded except on the rare occasions when Hitler asked Eva to banish her two darlings so his dog could have a moment in the limelight.

Liquor was served but Hitler took tea and apple cake. The group sat silently around the fire in the semidarkness waiting for him to begin the general conversation. Finally he raised his voice for another lecture on the evils of tobacco. His dentist declared that smoking disinfected the mouth. In moderation, it was not at all dangerous. Hitler dissented. "I wouldn't offer a cigar or cigarette to anyone I admired or loved since I would be doing them a bad service. It is universally agreed that non-smokers live

even though the idea seemed a little odd. He stared at her for some time before slowly getting to his feet. She too rose. It was apparent he was trying to control himself but suddenly he burst out angrily: "You are a sentimentalist! What business of yours is it? The Jewesses are none of your business!" As he continued to shout, she ran up the stairs to her room. An adjutant reached her before she could close the door. "Why did you have to do this?" he asked. "You have made him very angry. Please leave at once!"

On the eve of his fifty-fourth birthday, Hitler celebrated by inviting Blondi to the tea session and putting her through her paces. She begged; she played schoolgirl. She even gave a concert and the more her master praised the more intensely she sang. Just before midnight the large doors opened dramatically and orderlies entered with trays of glasses. All were filled with champagne except Hitler's, which contained a sweet white wine. At the last stroke of twelve glasses were touched. Some of the guests voiced simple congratulations and others made little speeches.

On April 20 Hitler came downstairs earlier than usual so he could look over his presents. At lunch Traudl's escort was Himmler. She disliked him, not because he gave the impression of brutality but because of his attempt to charm her. He kissed her hand, talked in a soft voice and perpetually presented a genial, obliging countenance. Even his eyes smiled endlessly. Goebbels impressed her. "He was not good-looking at all," she remembered, "but now I could understand why the girls at the chancellery used to run to the window to see the propaganda chief leave his ministry while they scarcely took notice of the Führer." She noticed that most of the ladies at the Berghof flirted with him as much for his wit as his charm.

Shortly after the birthday celebration Hitler learned that Traudl had become engaged to Hans Junge, one of his valets. "I really have such bad luck with my people," he remarked at lunch with an exaggerated sigh. "First Christian married Dara and took my best secretary; then I found a satisfactory replacement and now Traudl Humps is going to leave me—and take with her my best servant." He suggested that they get married at once since Junge was scheduled to leave for the eastern front. Traudl wanted to postpone such a decisive step after so short an acquaintance. "But you love each other!" was Hitler's surprising reply. "Therefore it is best to get married right away. If you're married, you know, then I can protect you any time someone tries to molest you. I couldn't do that if you were only engaged. And you can still work for me after you're married." Traudl had to keep from laughing and was tempted to ask why *he* didn't marry Eva Braun if love was that important.

4

On May 7 Hitler made a sad pilgrimage to the capital to attend the funeral of another old comrade. Viktor Lutze, the successor to Röhm, had died in an auto accident. At least that was the official story; some survivors of the Röhm Putsch suspected foul play. After the funeral Reichleiters and Gauleiters attended a luncheon at the chancellery. This was followed by a detailed survey of the general situation which began with the Führer's statement that in 1939 Germany—a revolutionary state —had faced only bourgeois states. It was easy, he explained, to knock out such nations since they were quite inferior in upbringing and attitude. A country with an ideology always had the edge over a bourgeois state since it rested upon a firm spiritual foundation. This superiority, however, had ended with Barbarossa. There the Germans had met an opponent which also sponsored an ideology, if a wrong one. He praised Stalin for purging the Red Army of defeatists and installing political commissars with the fighting forces. Stalin enjoyed the further advantage of having rid himself of "high society" by other liquidations so that Bolshevism could devote all its energy to fighting the enemy.

Another reason for failure in the East was the poor performance of Germany's allies, particularly the Hungarians. Lasting resistance to the Soviets, he concluded, could be offered in Europe only by the Germans since victory in battle was linked with ideology. Consequently the anti-Semitism which formerly animated party members must once more become the focal point of their spiritual struggle. It should also be a rallying cry for the troops; if they did not stand firm as a wall, the hordes of the East would sweep into Europe. A constant, untiring effort must therefore focus on taking the necessary measures for the security of European culture. "If it be true today that the Bolshevism of the East is mainly under Jewish leadership and that the Jews are also the dominant influence in the Western plutocracies, then our anti-Semitic propaganda must begin at this point." That was why there was practically no possibility of any compromise with the Soviets. "They must be knocked out, exactly as we formerly had to knock out our own Communists to attain power. At that time we never thought of a compromise either."

Despite the vigorous tenor of his talk, it was apparent that Hitler's health was failing. Dr. Morell doubled the hormone injections as well as adding still another drug, Prostakrin, but there was little improvement. Another electrocardiogram indicated a worsening of his heart condition. Fearing that the diet regime of Dr. Zabel was aggravating matters, Morell recommended that the Führer hire a special cook. They settled on a woman from Vienna, a Frau von Exner, who would surely know how to please an Austrian palate. Neither was aware there was Jewish blood in her mother's family.

On May 12 Hitler returned to Wolfsschanze satisfied that his leadership had ended the withdrawals after the fall of Stalingrad. His complacency ended the next day upon learning that two German-Italian armies in Tunisia, some 300,000 men, had been bagged by the Allies. It was another Stalingrad. A week later there was worse news. Mussolini's regime was close to collapse. Italians in high places were using phrases such as "you never know what's going to happen" and "when the war is over." On the streets German soldiers were openly cursed as enemies.

In mid-June Hitler's youngest secretary married his valet Junge. After a short honeymoon the groom went to the eastern front while Traudl returned to her duties at Wolfsschanze. "You've become very pale and thin," was Hitler's first observation. Kindly meant, it caused Traudl embarrassment when Linge, Schaub and Bormann broke into knowing leers. No longer was she the naïve girl who first came to Führer Headquarters. The daily routine of the loftiest circle in the Reich was causing a curious depression. She tried to express some of this in her diary, then spoke to others, particularly the sympathetic Hewel, of her misgivings. She discovered that most of the others shared the vague sense of dissatisfaction and gloom. They too suffered from "cabin fever" but nobody could give a concrete reason for their common uneasiness.

That June Hitler persuaded Dara Christian to return. She arrived with many suitcases and soon filled the bunker and barracks with her effervescence. Her songs, jokes and gaiety raised everyone's spirits. By this time Traudl had lost her bashfulness and one day asked Hitler point-blank why he was so eager to get everyone else married when he hadn't done so himself. The reply was that he did not want to be a father. "I think the children of a genius have a hard time in this world. One expects such a child to be a replica of his famous father and don't forgive him for being average." Until now he had seemed quite modest and she was disturbed by the complacent announcement that he was a genius.

Despite the reverses in North Africa, Hitler was still considering the all-out attack on Kursk so vigorously opposed by Milch. Armored expert Guderian came to Berlin and added his objections: first on the grounds that the new Panther tank had a limited supply of spare parts; and second —in answer to the Führer's argument that the attack was necessary for political reasons—that few people even knew where Kursk (on the southern wing of the central front) was. Hitler confessed that the mere thought of this offensive churned his stomach, but in the ensuing days he was persuaded by both Zeitzler and Kluge to launch it while there was still time. The operation was entitled Citadel and, on the first of July, Hitler addressed his senior commanders. Germany, he said, must either tenaciously hold on to all conquered territory or fall. The German soldier had to realize he must stand and fight to the end. He admitted Citadel was a gamble yet felt sure it would succeed. Hadn't he been right, against all military advice, about Austria, Czechoslovakia, Poland and the Soviet Union? His inclusion of the last country struck a chill in the audience.

Manstein's attack force in the north consisted of eighteen divisions but less than 1000 tanks and 150 assault guns were fit for combat. In the south General Model had fifteen divisions and only 900 tanks. The assault began at an unusual hour, 3 P.M. on the fourth of July. It was hot and sultry. Thunder rumbled threateningly in the distance. At first it seemed as if the Soviets had been caught by surprise, for Red Army artillery did not respond until long after dark. But visions of a quick victory vanished once heavy rains began to fall. By dawn roads and trails were veritable quagmires. Later that morning a cloudburst transformed streams into roaring cascades, and it took sappers twelve hours to bridge them for tanks.

By July 9 the leading German tanks were still fifty-five miles from Kursk. The disappointment was followed next day by news that an Anglo-American force had landed on Sicily and were meeting a spiritless defense. This came as no surprise to Hitler and on July 13 he stopped the offensive he had so reluctantly supported so he could send reinforcements, including the SS Panzer Corps, to western Europe. Manstein argued that failure to continue the Kursk operation would endanger a long salient stretching all the way to the Black Sea. A gambler, Hitler accepted the loss of Kursk in return for more probable success in another quarter. But Citadel turned out to be more than a lost campaign. Thereafter the initiative in the East would belong to the Soviets.

5

Turning his back on the East, Hitler journeyed to northern Italy for another meeting with Il Duce, their thirteenth, on July 19. The conference, held at the imposing Villa Gaggia near Feltre, began promptly at 11 A.M. with the two men facing each other from large armchairs. Circling them was an elite group of military and diplomatic dignitaries. There were a few moments of embarrassed silence as both Mussolini and Hitler waited for the other to begin. It was a strange prelude, more like the stiff meeting of two families arranging a dowry. At last the Führer began speaking quietly of the general military and political situation. Il Duce sat cross-legged, hands clasped on knees, on the edge of a chair that was too large and too deep, listening with impassive patience. Then he began to fidget and he nervously passed a hand over the lower part of his face as Hitler abruptly assailed the Italians for their defeatism.

Occasionally Mussolini would press a spot behind his back that apparently pained him; occasionally he would heave a deep sigh as if resigned but wearied by a monologue which grew increasingly strident. Struggling to hide his distress, he mopped his brow with a handkerchief. Hitler showed no mercy, and even after an adjutant whispered something into his ear at five minutes to one, he did not pause in his reiterated assurance to the wilting Duce that the crisis could be overridden if Italy emulated Germany's fanatic determination to fight. Every German, he said, was imbued with the will to conquer. Lads of fifteen were manning AA batteries. "If anyone tells me that our task can be left for another generation, I reply that this is not the case. No one can say that the future generation will be a generation of giants. Germany took thirty years to recover; Rome never rose again. This is the voice of history."

At exactly 1 P.M. the adjutant again whispered to Hitler and the others imagined it must indeed be an urgent message. This time, after a look of annoyance, he ended his sermon. The meeting was over, he announced, and luncheon was served. The other Italians were distressed at Mussolini's silence during the harangue. Not once had he protested or even attempted to explain that within a month most Italian soldiers would no longer have the means or the will to offer effective resistance.

Five days later Il Duce was forced to listen to another diatribe, this from his own Fascist Grand Council, which was convening for the first time since 1939. After a long exhausting debate on his conduct of the war, a resolution was proposed demanding restoration of a constitutional monarchy with the King in command of the armed forces. The vote was taken and the motion passed 19 to 8. The next day, July 25, a sultry Sunday, Mussolini called on Victor Emmanuel III. He tried to control himself, but the notes in his hand rattled. The King stopped his arguments; it was useless to go on; Italy was defeated and the soldiers would no longer fight for Fascism. He requested Mussolini's resignation, then revealed he had already appointed Marshal Pietro Badoglio as head of government. "I am sorry, I am sorry," he was heard to say through the door. "But the solution could not have been otherwise." The little King accompanied Il Duce to the front door where he shook his hand warmly. As

Mussolini stepped out of the villa he was approached by a Carabinieri officer who said His Majesty had charged him with the protection of Il Duce's person. Mussolini, protesting that it was not necessary, was led into an ambulance. He was under arrest.

At nine-thirty that night Hitler shocked his military advisers by announcing, "The Duce has resigned." The government had been taken over by Badoglio, their bitterest enemy. He quelled the rising panic and when Jodl suggested they do nothing until receiving a complete report from Rome Hitler curtly replied: "Certainly, but we have to plan ahead. Undoubtedly, in their treachery, they will proclaim that they will remain loyal to us; but this is treachery. Of course, they won't remain loyal. . . . Anyway what's-his-name [Badoglio] said straightaway that the war would be continued but that doesn't mean a thing. They have to say that. But we can play the same game; we'll get ready to grab the whole mess, all that rabble. I'll send a man down tomorrow with orders to the commandant of the 3rd Panzer Grenadier Division to take a special detachment into Rome and arrest the whole government, the King—all that scum but most of all the Crown Prince—to grab all that riffraff, particularly Badoglio and the entire gang. And then you watch them creep and crawl and in two or three days there'll be another coup."

At a midnight conference Hitler issued more instructions. The 2nd Parachute Division was to prepare a jump in the capital area. "Rome must be occupied. Nobody is to leave Rome and then the 3rd Panzer Grenadier Division moves in." Someone wanted to know if the exits to the Vatican should be occupied. "That doesn't matter," said Hitler, "I'll go right into the Vatican. Do you think I worry about the Vatican? We'll take that right off. All the diplomatic corps will be hiding in there. I don't give a damn; if the entire crew's in there, we'll get the whole lot of swine out. Afterward, we can say we're sorry. We can easily do that. We've got a war on."

In the presence of his secretaries he managed to gain control of himself. "Mussolini is much weaker than I thought," he muttered, as if talking to himself. "I personally protected his rear and he has given way. Well, we never could depend on our Italian allies and I believe we'll be better off without such an irresponsible nation."

He sent for the two men he felt he could depend on most in a crisis —Goebbels and Göring. (Of the latter, he told his military leaders, "At such a time one can't have a better adviser than the Reichsmarschall. In time of crisis the Reichsmarschall is brutal and ice cold. I've always noticed that when it comes to the breaking point he is a man of iron without scruples." The three met at ten in the morning and half an hour later were joined by Ribbentrop, who was recovering from an attack of pneumonia. With quiet "self-assurance" Hitler expressed a suspicion that Mussolini had not resigned voluntarily. He had been arrested. That meant Fascism was in mortal danger and they must seize any possibility of averting its collapse. He told of his plan to drop a parachute division around Rome and arrest the King and his family along with Badoglio and his henchmen.

The catastrophe in Italy was almost immediately followed by the carpet bombing of Hamburg. By the morning of August 3 the city was a blazing mass of ruins. More than 6000 acres of homes, factories and office buildings were gutted. Seventy thousand people were dead. Hitler was enraged, convinced as he was that such terror raids were a product of the Jews; he accused the leading British air commanders, including Portal and Harris, of being Jews or part Jewish. Psychologically Hamburg's destruction was as devastating as Stalingrad, not only to ordinary citizens but to Hitler's paladins. Goebbels was in a "blue funk" after inspecting the ruins of Hamburg, according to the diary of his own press officer, and for the first time posed the question: "What if we lose?" to his subordinates. He armed himself with a pistol.

The chief of the Luftwaffe, so recently characterized as "ice cold," was even more crushed by the bombings. "We were met with a shattering picture," recalled Adolf Galland, one of those hastily summoned to his office. "Göring had completely broken down. His head buried in his arm on the table, he moaned some indistinguishable words. We stood there for some time in embarrassment. At last Göring pulled himself together and said we were witnessing his deepest moments of despair. The Führer had lost faith in him."

6

Negotiation with the enemy had become a common, if covert, topic at the Foreign Office ever since receipt of another peace feeler from Stalin soon after the Battle of Stalingrad. Admiral Canaris (who himself had tried in vain to deal secretly with Roosevelt, through former Governor of Pennsylvania George Earle) was so convinced this was a serious offer that he persuaded Ribbentrop to present it to the Führer. He did so in the form of a memorandum which Hitler angrily tore up with a threat to execute anyone attempting to mediate on his own. There would be no negotiations, he said, until the Wehrmacht regained the initiative. He forbade Ribbentrop even to mention the matter again, and when his Foreign

Minister timidly proposed they reduce the program of conquest in Europe so as to make it more acceptable to the Allies, Hitler was incensed. "Believe me, we shall win," he said. "The blow that has fallen is a sign telling me to grow harder and harder and risk all we have. If we do, we shall win in the end."

In the strictest confidence, Ribbentrop revealed all this to Fritz Hesse. For safety's sake, their conversation took place on a walk through a wood near Wolfsschanze in a March snow flurry. "All we can hope for now," he said, "is that at least one of our opponents will grow sensible. Surely the English must realize that it would be madness to deliver us into the hands of the Russians." Tears came to his eyes but he pulled himself together. He pledged Hesse to secrecy.

A few days later they went for another walk in the snow. "There must be some way," said Ribbentrop, "of persuading the British and Americans of the insanity of the war they are waging against us." Didn't they understand that the defeat of Germany would only help Stalin and upset the balance of power in Europe? Wasn't it possible to make them see that their own position throughout the world would be compromised? The Soviet military potential was already superior to that of the Western Allies. "Can't we somehow make the British and Americans see that the victory of the Soviets is the opposite of what they want?" Having spent years in England, Hesse did not think this was possible. The two Allies were not unduly worried about a Russian victory. Unlike the Germans, neither had experienced the firsthand terrors of Bolshevism.

One of Ribbentrop's men, Peter Kleist, was already resuming his personal efforts to seek peace with Russia despite Hitler's definite injunction to cease further contact with Madame Kollontai, the Soviet ambassador to Sweden. His middleman was Edgar Clauss, a nondescript businessman who came from East Europe, spoke Russian and German with equal ineptitude and lived in Sweden with a Swedish wife of Russian extraction. Clauss had met Stalin and Trotsky before the Revolution and had connections with the Soviet Embassy in Stockholm; local Germans regarded him as "either a braggart or a spy." After two long talks with members of the embassy, Clauss reported to Kleist on June 18, 1943, that the Soviets were determined "not to fight for a day or even a minute—'ni odnu minitu'— longer than necessary on behalf of British and American interests." They felt that Hitler, blinded by ideology, had allowed himself to be pushed into the war by the intrigues of the capitalist powers. While confident that the Red Army could stand off the Wehrmacht, they feared it would be in an extremely weakened position after victory when it would have to "confront the cold steel" of the Western Powers. The Soviets distrusted the Americans and British since they had not yet come forward with any definite statements about war aims and territorial boundaries; nor had they promised anything definite on the so-called Second Front in Europe. The Anglo-American landing in Africa seemed more like an attempt to protect their own flank from the Soviet Union than an attack on the Axis. Stalin therefore could not attach any real value to the promises of Roosevelt and Churchill, said Clauss. On the other hand, the vast Soviet areas held by Hitler were a negotiable object, and a concrete deal could be concluded immediately.

Stalin wanted only two things: a guarantee that peace would be preserved and economic aid. It was a tempting proposal since it seemed clear that Clauss had received his information directly from the Soviets but there was always the chance that Kleist himself might be the victim of a Soviet trick. For hours that night he wandered the streets of Stockholm, debating with himself. Finally he decided that if there was the slightest possibility of ending the war and saving Europe from a Soviet invasion he had no choice. The next morning he flew to Berlin intending to "confess" his forbidden conversation but as he stepped out of the plane at Tempelhof he was arrested on the charge that he had been conniving with "the Jew Clauss."

Kleist was interrogated by Heydrich's successor, Ernst Kaltenbrunner, a burly man six foot seven with a lantern jaw, a saber cut across one cadaverous cheek and dangling, simian arms. He was impressed by Kleist's straightforward account. It rang true, he said. Kaltenbrunner also believed his denial that Clauss was a Jew and so only placed Kleist under house arrest. A fortnight later this was canceled and he turned to the less dangerous operation of resettling Estonian Swedes. To his surprise, the question of peace was soon raised again, this time by Ribbentrop. The defeat at Kursk that summer had convinced him that German defeat was now irreversible and he should brave the Führer's wrath. He summoned Kleist to Wolfsschanze on August 16 and said, "I have asked you here because I want to hear that absurd story again of what went on up north. I mean your meeting with the Jew in Stockholm—before it's finally filed and put away." For the next few hours the two men thoroughly analyzed every detail about the possible motives of the Kremlin.

Ignoring Hitler's order never to bring up negotiations again, Ribbentrop told him about the conversation with Kleist. The Führer did not explode but repeated that there could never be any question of negotiating with Moscow; the war was to be fought relentlessly until victory. At the same time he would allow Kleist to keep in touch with Clauss and if the Kremlin had any kind of offer it was to be transmitted at once to Berlin.

Kleist did not see Clauss again for almost three weeks. At their meeting in early September the go-between (who may very well have been misleading both the Russians and Germans about the extent of his intimacy with each of them) showed his displeasure. He was sick, he said, of playing at politics with people who didn't know what they wanted. A Soviet contact, it seemed, had stayed in Stockholm for nine days waiting in vain for Kleist. Not even a refusal had come from Berlin! Kleist managed to pacify Clauss, then persuaded him to pay his respects to Madame Kollontai and resume the contact.

Clauss returned with bad news. The Soviets, bolstered by continuing success in battle, would not negotiate unless the Germans gave a sign they were serious: for example, dismissing Rosenberg and Ribbentrop. Kleist could barely restrain a grin; that was going to be a delightful point to put into his report to the Foreign Minister; but he respectfully pointed out that Hitler had no intention of negotiating. Clauss was not at all surprised. He sighed. The Germans didn't understand anything about negotiating. To do so one needed patience and knowledge of one's partner. The Führer failed on both counts.

Surprisingly, four days later Kleist found Clauss extraordinarily excited. His source at the Soviet Embassy had just informed him that Moscow was about to take another dramatic step! Vice-Commissar for Foreign Affairs Dekanozov, former ambassador in Berlin, would arrive in a week or so with authorization to speak directly to Kleist. There were conditions: Kleist must return to Stockholm *before* Dekanozov's arrival; and the Germans must release a previously agreed-upon sign—the resignation of Ribbentrop and Rosenberg—which would confirm that Kleist was authorized to take part in the talks. "What do you say now?" asked Clauss, his face flushed with eagerness and impatience. "We have managed to refloat the wreck! Now all Hitler has to do is to get on board and set sail, and he'll be out of his dilemma. Will he do it?"

On September 10 Kleist reported all this to Ribbentrop. Predictably, the Foreign Minister was hurt and angry that, after all he had done to bring about Soviet-German rapport, his own resignation was a prerequisite for negotiations! He was also dubious that a man of Dekanozov's standing would be used in this kind of game. The next moment his press officer interrupted with an announcement from Radio Moscow: Dekanozov was about to leave for Sofia to become ambassador. That, exclaimed Ribbentrop, proved his point. On the contrary, said Kleist, who knew more about Soviet tactics, this was confirmation from the Kremlin that Dekanozov *was* involved and would appear on neutral soil for talks. He suggested they reply with an announcement that Schulenburg had just been appointed

Germany's ambassador to Sofia. Ribbentrop shook his head vigorously. The Führer would never send Schulenburg to Sofia! Kleist patiently explained that Stalin hadn't really intended to send Dekanozov there either. "Both announcements would merely act as a sign understood only by the 'augurs' and by nobody else in the world."

Ribbentrop saw the light and, with renewed enthusiasm, left immediately for the Wolfsschanze. He returned late at night somewhat sheepishly with inhibiting instructions from Hitler: Kleist was to tell Clauss privately that he was unable to get back to Sweden for the time being. "Try to hold on to the thread," said Ribbentrop. "The Führer is interested to find out how far the Russians will go." The next day Kleist was recalled for another interview, this one completely discouraging. The Führer had decided to avoid *any* direct contact with the Soviets however fleeting. Kleist left the room utterly dejected. They had come so close—to no avail.

7

Hitler's categorical refusal to negotiate with Stalin came at a curious time. Forty-eight hours earlier, on September 8, shortly after Allied troops breached the narrow channel between Sicily and the toe of Italy, it had been announced that the new Italian regime under Marshal Badoglio had signed an armistice with the West. Hitler was badly shaken even though he himself had predicted Badoglio would betray Germany. But he hadn't thought it possible (so he told the hastily summoned Goebbels) that this treachery would be committed so dishonorably.

Hitler's concern over the fate of 54,000 German troops in Sardinia and Corsica was succeeded by fear that the Allies might take the opportunity to launch their second front; the recent heavy English bombings were certainly suspicious. He was similarly haunted by another critical situation on the eastern front: the Wehrmacht, under heavy Soviet pressure, was withdrawing to the Dnieper.

At this point Goebbels wondered whether anything might be done with Stalin. "Not for a moment," said Hitler. It would be easier to make a deal with the English. At a given moment they would come to their senses. Goebbels disagreed. Stalin was more approachable, being a practical politician. Churchill was a romantic adventurer with whom one could not even talk sensibly. "Sooner or later," predicted Goebbels, "we shall have to face the question of inclining toward one enemy side or the other. Germany has never yet had luck with a two-front war; it won't be able to stand this one in the long run either." Concessions would have to be made, he said, pointing out how they had not come to power in 1933 by making unqualified demands. "We did present absolute demands on August 13, 1932, but failed because of them." The first thing to do was admit that Italy was lost, and he urged Hitler to address the nation on this subject without delay. The people were entitled to frankness, as well as a word of encouragement and solace from the Führer.

With reluctance Hitler agreed and on the night of September 10, from his bunker at Wolf's Lair, delivered a twenty-page speech which was taped in Berlin and broadcast to the nation. "My right to believe unconditionally in success," he said, "is founded not only on my own life but also on the destiny of our people." Neither time nor force of arms would ever bring the German people down.

Those who joined Hitler at tea after the speech were revivified by his own display of good spirits. "I must admit," wrote Goebbels' press officer in his diary, "that for a while I was completely captivated. What secret strength comes from this man who can, with a look and a handshake, totally confuse a sober, realistic man such as myself!" Even so, the rather stilted words he broadcast must have sounded hollow to civilians undergoing devastating air raids and to troops on the eastern front who were falling back with frightening losses.

Hitler, too, realized that words alone could not bolster his people's morale and decided to act drastically, dramatically. He would rescue Mussolini, now held prisoner in a hotel near the top of Gran Sasso, the loftiest peak in the Apennines range of mountains a hundred miles from Rome. An attack up the steep, rocky slope would not only cost many casualties but give guards time to kill Mussolini. Parachuting into such terrain was about as risky and so it was decided to use gliders. To carry off this piece of derring-do, Hitler chose a fellow Austrian. SS Captain Otto Skorzeny, a Viennese who stood six foot four, was, apart from his size, an imposing figure. He bore deep scars on his face from the fourteen duels he had fought as a student and carried himself with the air of a fourteenth-century condottiere. Skorzeny was not only a bold man of action but a canny one who believed commando operations should be carried out with a minimum force and as few casualties to both sides as possible. At 1 P.M. on Sunday, September 12, he and 107 men boarded gliders which, once airborne, began jerking erratically on their tow lines. The plan was to land on what appeared in photographs to be flat grassy meadow near Il Duce's hotel.

Mussolini, who had been threatening to commit suicide, was sitting by an open window with arms folded when a glider suddenly loomed and a parachute, acting as a brake, blossomed behind just before it crashed with a shattering noise a hundred yards away. Four or five men in khaki piled out and began assembling a machine gun. Mussolini had no idea who they were, only that they were not English. An alarm rang and Carabinieri guards and police excitedly rushed from their barracks, as other gliders began landing. One skidded to rest less than twenty yards from the hotel. It was Skorzeny's. Looking up, he saw Il Duce staring out at him. "Away from the window!" he shouted and lunged into the lobby.

Skorzeny and his band literally bowled over the detachment of soldiers trying to stop them; then he bolted up a staircase, three steps at a time, to the next floor and flung open a door. Mussolini stood in the middle of the room. "Duce," he said, "the Führer has sent me. You are free!" Mussolini embraced him. "I knew my friend Adolf Hitler would not abandon me," he said and profusely thanked his rescuer. Skorzeny was surprised at Il Duce's appearance. He looked sick and unkempt in ill-fitting civilian clothes. He was unshaven; his usually smooth head was covered with short, stubbly hair.

By 3 P.M. they were in a small Fieseler-Storch which had managed to land safely on the sloping meadow. While happy to be free, Mussolini was apprehensive. Being a pilot, he knew how risky the take-off from this unlikely strip would be. As the plane gathered speed it bumped erratically over rocks toward a yawning gully. The Storch finally lifted but its left wheel almost immediately struck the ground. The little plane bounced into space, then plunged straight into the gully. Skorzeny closed his eyes and held his breath, awaiting the inevitable crash. Somehow the pilot managed to pull the plane out of its dive and, to the shouts and waves of Germans and Italians on the meadow, guided it safely down into the valley.*

Nobody uttered a word. Only now, in "most unsoldierly fashion," did Skorzeny lay a reassuring hand on Il Duce's shoulder. Within the hour they landed in Rome, transferred to a trimotor Heinkel and were bound for Vienna. They arrived late at night and were driven to the Hotel Imperial. When Skorzeny brought Il Duce a pair of pajamas he rejected them. "I never wear anything at night," he said, "and I would advise you to do the same, Captain Skorzeny." He grinned roguishly. "Especially if you sleep with a woman."

As midnight struck Skorzeny's telephone rang. It was Hitler, who until he received word of the rescue had been "like a caged lion, pacing to and fro, listening for every ring of the telephone." His voice was husky

---

* Skorzeny's men escaped by cable car with their only casualties, ten men injured in a glider crash.

with emotion. "You have performed a military feat which will become part of history," he said. "You have given me back my friend Mussolini."

After a stopover in Munich, where Mussolini was reunited with his family, he and Skorzeny set off for East Prussia early on the morning of September 14. The Führer was waiting at the Wolfsschanze airstrip. He warmly embraced his ally and for some time the two stood hand in hand. Finally Hitler turned to Skorzeny, who had discreetly waited before disembarking, and thanked him effusively. This one daring feat had forever endeared him to Hitler. It had also captured the imagination and admiration of foes as well as friends. More important, the spirits of Germans were uplifted not only by the rescue of Mussolini but by the manner in which it was done.

The Führer expected Mussolini to wreak vengeance on Badoglio and the regime in power. But Il Duce's only ambition was retirement to the Romagna. Privately he knew that his political life was over. His only future was as Hitler's pawn and the latter reacted with sarcasm and resentment. "What is this sort of Fascism which melts like snow before the sun!" he said. "For years I have explained to my generals that Fascism was the soundest alliance for the German people. I have never concealed my distrust of the Italian monarchy; at your insistence, however, I did nothing to obstruct the work which you carried out to the advantage of your King. But I must confess to you that we Germans have never understood your attitude in this respect." These words of intimidation were followed by a promise—even more ominous—to treat Italy well despite Badoglio's treachery *if* Il Duce would assume his role in a new republic. "The war must be won and once it is won Italy will be restored to her rights. The fundamental condition is that Fascism be reborn and that the traitors be brought to justice." Otherwise Hitler would be forced to treat Italy as an enemy. The country would be occupied and governed by Germans.

Mussolini wilted. If Hitler did not have his way the Italian people would undoubtedly suffer. Renouncing his plans to retire, he issued an official communiqué announcing that he had today assumed the supreme direction of Fascism in Italy. This was accompanied by four orders of the day which reinstated those authorities dismissed by Badoglio, reconstituted the Fascist militia, instructed the party to support the Wehrmacht and investigate the conduct of members relative to the July 25 coup d'état. By sheer force of will, Hitler had turned things around in Italy. But he no longer had any illusions about his partner. "I admit that I was deceived," he told his family circle. "It has turned out that Mussolini is only a little man."

During his guest's brief stay Hitler remarked that he wanted to settle with Russia. It was only said to impress Mussolini but Ribbentrop, who happened to be present, took it seriously and promptly asked for instructions. Hitler put him off but, once they were alone, again forbade Ribbentrop to make any overtures. He must have noticed his Foreign Minister's dejection, for he later took the trouble to call at his quarters. "You know, Ribbentrop," he said, "if I settled with Russia today I would only come to grips with her again tomorrow—I just can't help it."

Ever the wishful thinker, Ribbentrop still felt Hitler might relent. Late in the evening of September 22 he telephoned Kleist and asked if he could fly to Stockholm the next day. Kleist was astonished. It would be pointless to take such a trip, he said, without definite instructions. Ribbentrop admitted he had none to give but ordered Kleist to go anyway as soon as possible!

The following day it was Goebbels, taking advantage of a seat near Hitler at dinner, who urged him to seek some sort of peace. With either England or Russia. But Hitler said that negotiating with Churchill would be useless since he was "guided by hatred and not by reason," and Stalin could not possibly accede to German demands in the East.

And so, against this background, Kleist set off again for Sweden, this time with a feeling ranging between annoyance and despair. It seemed obvious that Hitler was only flirting with peace. In Stockholm Kleist was informed by a depressed Clauss that the recent German refusal to accept terms for the talks had made him persona non grata at the Soviet Embassy. Germany, he said, had lost her last chance in the East. He was right. Ten days earlier Stalin had rejected another peace bid by the Japanese and promptly reported it to Washington. Then, following months of excuses, he agreed to a conference with Churchill and Roosevelt at Teheran. It took place late that November and bound the Grand Alliance, so it seemed, inextricably together.

"AND WITH THE BEASTS
OF THE EARTH"
APRIL 1943–APRIL 1944

1

To most Germans, Hitler's treatment of the Jews was a matter of minor importance. They had been indifferent to the lot of Jewish neighbors forced to wear the Star of David—after all, didn't they deserve it? And even after the same neighbors began to disappear it was assumed they had been deported. It was only wise to discount unspeakable rumors in a land where listening to a foreign broadcast was punishable by death.

Not many knew about the killing centers. These were all in Poland and each was surrounded by a barren stretch several miles wide posted with notices that trespassers would be shot on sight. To ensure secrecy, the process from deportation to murder was not only executed speedily but done so under a smoke screen of euphemism: the over-all operation was referred to as "special treatment"; collectively the centers were described as the "East"; individual installations were called labor, concentration, transit or PW camps; and gas chambers and crematorium units were "bathhouses" and "corpse cellars."

Rumors of atrocities were answered by lies. When an important Nazi official, Hans Lammers, brought Himmler several reports that Jews were being executed in large numbers, the Reichsführer was vehement in denial. He explained that the so-called Final Solution order, received from the Führer through Heydrich, merely entailed evacuation of Jews from the homeland. During these movements there had unfortunately been some deaths from sickness and attacks by enemy aircraft—and a number of Jews, he admitted, had to be killed during revolts as examples. Himmler assured Lammers that the majority of Jews were being "accommodated" in camps in the East and brought out photo albums to show how they were working for the war effort as shoemakers, tailors and such. "This is the order of the Führer," emphasized Himmler. "If you believe you have to take action, then tell the Führer and tell me the names of the people who made these reports to you." Lammers refused to divulge any information and sought more information from Hitler himself. He gave almost identical information. "I shall later on decide where these Jews will be taken," he said, then added reassuringly—"and in the meantime they are being cared for there."

While some of those closest to Hitler truly did not know what was going on in the East, many others, victims of self-deception, guessed if they did not know the terrifying facts. "Don't let anyone tell you he had no idea," Hans Frank later wrote, including himself in the accusation. "Everyone sensed that there was something horribly wrong with this system, even if we didn't know all the details. We didn't *want* to know! It was too comfortable to live on the system, to support our families in royal style, and to believe that it was all right."

This was the man who had recently told his subordinates that they were all accomplices in the elimination of the Jews which, disagreeable as it might be, "was necessary in the interests of Europe." In his role as head of the Generalgouvernement in Poland, Frank knew the order had come directly from the Führer. But the average German still was convinced that Hitler had no part in any brutality. "People are now clinging to the hope that the Führer doesn't know about such things, can't know, otherwise he would take some steps," wrote an ardent Nazi woman to a friend in reference to the Euthanasia Program, the overture to the Final Solution. "Anyway, they think he can't know how this is being done or on what scale. I feel, however, that this can't go on much longer without even this hope being lost."

Those in Hitler's family circle could not imagine Uncle Adi authorizing the murder of Jews. It was unthinkable. Hadn't both Schmundt and Engel successfully persuaded the Führer to let a number of part Jewish Wehrmacht officers keep their commissions? The villain had to be either Bormann or Himmler, acting behind his back. But these two were only

Hitler's faithful agents. He alone conceived the Final Solution and he alone could have ordered its execution. Without him there would have been no Final Solution, and he was confident he could get away with it if it were presented to the world as a fait accompli. There would be threats of retribution but the memories of men are short. Who today recalled the bitter condemnation of Turks for massacring a million Armenians during the Great War?

In a secret conversation on June 19, 1943, the Führer instructed Himmler to proceed with the deportation of Jews to the East "regardless of any unrest it might cause during the next three or four months." It must be carried out, he added, "in an all-embracing way." While these words would certainly not have convinced the family circle that Hitler was a mass murderer, those he uttered some time later to Bormann would have. "For us," he said after proudly admitting that he had purged the German world of the Jewish poison, "this has been an essential process of disinfection, which we have prosecuted to its ultimate limit and without which we should ourselves have been asphyxiated and destroyed." Hadn't he always been absolutely fair in his dealings with the Jews? "On the eve of the war, I gave them one final warning. I told them that, if they precipitated another war, they would not be spared and that I would exterminate the vermin throughout Europe, and this time once and for all. To this warning they retorted with a declaration of war and affirmed that wherever in the world there was a Jew, there, too, was an implacable enemy of National Socialist Germany. Well, we have lanced the Jewish abscess; and the world of the future will be eternally grateful to us."

One particularly horrifying aspect of Hitler's Final Solution had recently come to an apocalyptical ending. Of the 380,000 Jews crowded into the Warsaw ghetto, all but 70,000 had been deported to the killing centers in an operation devoid of resistance. By this time, however, those left behind had come to the realization that deportation meant death. With this in mind, Jewish political parties within the ghetto finally resolved their differences and banded together to resist further shipments with force. They did so to Himmler's amazement and he thereupon ordered the total dissolution of the Warsaw ghetto. At three in the morning of April 9, 1943, more than 2000 Waffen SS infantrymen—accompanied by tanks, flame throwers and dynamite squads—invaded the ghetto, expecting an easy conquest, only to be met by determined fire from 1500 fighters armed with weapons smuggled into the ghetto over a long period several light machine guns, hand grenades, a hundred or so rifles and carbines, several hundred pistols and revolvers, and Molotov cocktails. Himmler had expected the action to take three days but by nightfall his forces had to withdraw. The one-sided battle continued day after day to the bewilderment of the SS commander, General Jürgen Stroop, who could not understand why "this trash and subhumanity" refused to abandon a hopeless cause. He reported that, although his men had initially captured "considerable numbers of Jews, who are cowards by nature," it was becoming more and more difficult. "Over and over again new battle groups consisting of twenty to thirty Jewish men, accompanied by a corresponding number of women, kindled new resistance." The women, he noted, had the disconcerting habit of suddenly hurling grenades they had hidden in their bloomers.

On the fifth day of frustration Himmler ordered the ghetto combed out "with the greatest severity and relentless tenacity." Stroop decided to do this by setting fire to the entire Jewish area, block by block. The Jews, he reported, remained in the burning buildings until the last possible moment before jumping from the upper stories to the street. "With their bones broken, they still tried to crawl across the street into buildings which had not yet been set on fire. . . . Despite the danger of being burned alive the Jews and bandits often preferred to return into the flames rather than risk being caught by us."

The defenders fought two, three weeks with reckless heroism, taking refuge, as a last resort, in the sewers. Finally, on May 15, firing from the few remaining Jewish nests of resistance became sporadic and the following day General Stroop blew up the Tlomacki Synagogue, in the "Aryan" section of Warsaw, to celebrate the end of the battle. For exactly four weeks the little Jewish army had held off superior, well-armed forces until almost the last man was killed or wounded. Of the 56,065 who were rounded up, 7000 were shot out of hand; 22,000 were sent to Treblinka and Lublin; the remainder to labor camps. The German losses were 16 dead and 85 wounded. Of far more significance was the blow dealt to Hitler's concept of Jewish cowardice.

2

Early that June Pius XII secretly addressed the Sacred College of Cardinals on the extermination of the Jews. "Every word We address to the competent authority on this subject, and all Our public utterances," he said in explanation of his reluctance to express more open condemnation, "have to be carefully weighed and measured by Us in the interests of the victims themselves, lest, contrary to Our intentions, We make their situation worse and harder to bear." He did not add that another reason for proceeding cautiously was that he regarded Bolshevism as a far greater danger than Nazism.

The position of the Holy See was deplorable but it was an offense of omission rather than commission. The Church, under the Pope's guidance, had already saved the lives of more Jews than all other churches, religious institutions and rescue organizations combined, and was presently hiding thousands of Jews in monasteries, convents and Vatican City itself. The record of the Allies was far more shameful. The British and Americans, despite lofty pronouncements, had not only avoided taking any meaningful action but gave sanctuary to few persecuted Jews. The Moscow Declaration of that year—signed by Roosevelt, Churchill and Stalin— methodically listed Hitler's victims as Polish, Italian, French, Dutch, Belgian, Norwegian, Soviet and Cretan. The curious omission of Jews (a policy emulated by the U. S. Office of War Information) was protested vehemently but uselessly by the World Jewish Congress. By the simple expedient of converting the Jews of Poland into Poles, and so on, the Final Solution was lost in the Big Three's general classification of Nazi terrorism.

Contrasting with their reluctance to face the issue of systematic Jewish extermination was the forthrightness and courage of the Danes, who defied German occupation by transporting to Sweden almost every one of their 6500 Jews; of the Finns, allies of Hitler, who saved all but four of their 4000 Jews; and of the Japanese, another ally, who provided refuge in Manchuria for some 5000 wandering European Jews in recognition of financial aid given by the Jewish firm of Kuhn, Loeb & Company during the Russo-Japanese War of 1904–5.

But the man who did most to hinder the atrocities in the East was a thirty-four-year-old German lawyer who worked for Himmler. Konrad Morgen, son of a railroad conductor, had become imbued with the ethics of law from his student days and even as an assistant SS judge was outspoken in his disapproval of illegality whoever committed it. His judgments, based strictly on the evidence, so exasperated his superiors that Morgen was posted to a front-line SS division as punishment. Because of his outstanding reputation he was transferred in 1943 to the SD's Financial Crimes Office with the understanding that he was not to deal with political cases. Early that summer he was given a routine investigative mission to clear up a long-standing corruption case at Buchenwald concentration camp. The commandant, Karl Koch, had been suspected of hiring out camp laborers to civilian employers, racketeering in food supplies and, in general, running the camp for his own personal profit. The initial investigation had failed to bring conviction when a parade of witnesses categorically supported Koch's plea of innocence.

Morgen journeyed in July to Weimar where he installed himself in Hitler's favorite local hostelry, the Elephant Hotel, and quietly began his research. To his surprise he found the concentration camp, located on a hill above Weimar, a prospect pleasing to the eye. The installations were clean and freshly painted; the grounds covered with grass and flowers. The prisoners appeared to be healthy, sun-tanned, normally fed. They enjoyed regular mail service and a large camp library which boasted books in foreign languages. There were variety shows, movies, sporting contests and even a brothel. As Morgen began to dig deeper he learned that the corruption at Buchenwald had started with the influx of Jews after Crystal Night. Unfortunately, the closer he got to the truth about Koch, the further he was from proof. Too often for coincidence he found that prisoners said to have information of corruption were now dead. From their files he discovered that the dates of death were years apart and in each case a different cause was given. Suspecting murder, he ordered an investigation but his own special agent could not find a single clue and refused to continue his search.

An ordinary man would have abandoned the investigation, but Morgen was so convinced that crime had been committed that he turned detective himself. He went to local banks where he briefly displayed official-looking papers and pretended that he had been authorized by Himmler to examine Koch's accounts. His persistence was rewarded. At one bank he found undeniable evidence that Koch had embezzled 100,000 marks. Finally proof of murder came when Morgen burrowed deep into the prison records to discover that witnesses were taken to a secret cell and eliminated.

Armed with a bulging briefcase of records and affidavits, Morgen set out for Berlin. His superior, the chief of criminal police, blanched at the evidence. He had not expected Morgen to take his assignment so seriously and hurriedly passed him on to Kaltenbrunner. Heydrich's successor was equally aghast—or pretended to be—and said, "That's not my business. Take it to your own boss in Munich." Morgen dutifully took the evidence to the head of the SS Legal Department, who was just as unwilling to take any responsibility. "You'll have to tell all that to Himmler," he said. Morgen proceeded to the Reichsführer's field headquarters where he was refused an interview. With the help of a sympathetic member of Himmler's personal staff, Morgen proceeded to draft a cautiously worded telegram outlining the case. The problem was to get it delivered personally. Somehow it was slipped through the bureaucratic barrier and came to

Himmler's attention. To the amazement of almost everyone, he gave Morgen complete authority to proceed against Koch, his wife and anyone else connected with the sordid case. Some thought it was because of Himmler's mistrust of Oswald Pohl, the administrator of all concentration camps; others believed that he did not realize the case was a potential Pandora's box; but those who knew Himmler most intimately felt it was another instance of his peculiar sense of honor.

3

"Cruelty has a human heart."

WILLIAM BLAKE

There was no more paradoxical figure in the higher reaches of National Socialism than Heinrich Himmler. He impressed many by his charm and politeness, his modesty at meetings, his reasonableness. Diplomats described him as a man of sober judgment and the resistance movement regarded him as the sole leading Nazi who could be utilized in ending Hitler's rule. To General Hossbach he was the Führer's evil spirit, cold and calculating, the "most unscrupulous figure in the Third Reich." To Max Amann he was "a kind of Robespierre or witch-burning Jesuit." What made him sinister to Carl Burckhardt, the former League of Nations High Commissioner of Danzig, was "his capacity to concentrate upon little things, his pettifogging conscientiousness and his inhuman methodology; he had a touch of the robot." To his young daughter Gudrun he was a loving father. "Whatever is said about my *Papi*," she recently said, "what has been written or shall be written in the future about him—he was my father, the best father I could have and I loved him and still love him."

Most of his subordinates regarded Himmler as a warm, thoughtful employer with a deep sense of democracy. He played skat with secretaries and soccer with aides and adjutants. Once he invited a dozen young charwomen to his birthday dinner and ordered his reluctant officers to choose them as table companions, then himself led off the head charwoman.

The key to this enigmatic character did not lie in his youth. He came from a well-to-do Bavarian middle-class family and was named after his father's most famous pupil, Prince Heinrich von Wittelsbach. Young Himmler was neither more nor less anti-Semitic than the average young Bavarian of his class and the remarks about Jews in his diary were those of a bigot trying to be fair rather than of a racist. He had rigid convictions concerning sex and these were not unusual for his day. In short, he seemed to be the predictable product of Bavarian education and training—a promising young bureaucrat, meticulous and regulated.

By 1922, at age twenty-two, Himmler was a typical young nationalist with anti-Semitic leanings and a romantic vision of military life. That year he wrote a poem on the flyleaf of his diary, which revealed his dream of dying for a cause:

> *Although they may pierce you,*
> *Fight, resist, stand by.*
> *You yourself may perish*
> *But keep the banner high.*

It was not strange that a young man of such bent should be attracted by the theories of National Socialism and its charismatic leader; a bureaucrat by training and loyal by nature, he was a perfect Nazi career man. As he rose in the party he became the victim of a battle raging within himself. He was a Bavarian, yet fervently admired Prussian kings like Frederick the Great and constantly praised Prussian austerity and hardness. Himself dark, of average size and somewhat oriental features, he believed fanatically that the ideal German was Nordic and, like his master, preferred to surround himself with tall, blond, blue-eyed subordinates.* He admired physical perfection as well as athletic skill, yet was constantly suffering from stomach cramps. He presented a ridiculous figure on skis or in the water and once collapsed trying to win a lowly bronze medal in the mile run.

With more personal power than anyone in the Reich except Hitler, he remained unpretentious and conscientious. Born and bred a Catholic,

---

* Himmler was determined to breed out, within a hundred years, the dark German types (like himself and Hitler) by mating them exclusively with blonde women. To promote this racial policy he established *Lebensborn* (Spring of Life), an SS maternity organization whose main function was to adopt racially suitable children for childless SS families and to assist racially sound unwed mothers and their children. Thousands of children in the occupied territories were kidnaped and raised in special SS installations. "All good blood in the world," Himmler told his SS generals, "all Germanic blood which is not on the side of the Reich can one day be our destruction. Therefore . . . every German of the best blood whom we can bring to Germany and make into a self-aware German is a fighter for us, and one less on the other side. I really have the intention of fetching German blood from all over the world; to rob and steal where I can." Lurid postwar accounts describe Lebensborn as "stud farms" where SS men and suitable young women were mated to breed a master race. While Himmler's program did nothing to discourage illegitimacy, there is no evidence that he sponsored illicit sexual liaisons, nor is there proof that the kidnaping of children was done on a large scale. The fact that there were only 700 employees in all the Lebensborn homes casts doubts on such claims. Certainly Himmler envisaged a huge operation but Lebensborn never realized anywhere near its full potential because of the overriding needs of the resettlement and extermination operations.

he now relentlessly attacked the Church and yet, according to a close associate, conscientiously rebuilt his SS on Jesuit principles by assiduously copying "the service statutes and spiritual exercises presented by Ignatius Loyola."

Dreaded by millions, he trembled before the Führer who, he confessed to a subordinate, made him feel like a schoolboy who hadn't done his homework. Like his Führer, Himmler was indifferent to things material and, unlike Göring and others, never profited from his position. He lived in frugal simplicity, eating moderately, drinking sparingly and restricting himself to two cigars a day. He maintained one household on the Tegernsee for his wife and daughter, another near the Königsec for his personal secretary, Hedwig Potthast, who bore him a son and a daughter. And as a man of responsibility, he provided for each family in a style which left him very little for his personal use.

Some of his tenets were so eccentric that even his faithful followers found them difficult to accept: glacial cosmogony, magnetism, homeopathy, mesmerism, natural eugenics, clairvoyance, faith healing and sorcery. He sponsored experiments in obtaining gasoline by having water run over coal and in producing gold out of base metals.

While his power had all come from Hitler, the Führer wanted nothing to do with him personally. "I need such policemen," he told Schaub, who had been entreated by Himmler to get him an invitation to the Berghof, "but I don't like them." Hitler went so far as to order his personal adjutant, Schulze, an SS captain, not to keep his nominal chief informed about the daily military discussions.

At the same time, he put the Reichsführer in full charge of the operation closest to his heart, the Final Solution. In some respects it was an appropriate appointment. From the beginning Himmler had been under Hitler's spell and he remained totally Hitler's man, his disciple and subject. Furthermore, Himmler was the epitome of National Socialism, for it was as a diligent professional party worker that Himmler had overcome his own problems of identity. He was the Führer's faithful right hand who, despite squeamishness in the face of blood or beatings, had become a mass killer by remote control, an efficient businessman murderer.

He had done so while retaining his sentimentality. "I've often bagged a deer," he confided to his personal physician, "but I must tell you I've had a bad conscience each time I've looked into its dead eyes." Recently, at some personal risk, he had connived with Field Marshal Milch to save the lives of 14,000 Jewish skilled laborers in Holland. He had also released from Ravensbrück concentration camp the mother of a Luftwaffe colonel who refused to renounce her belief as a Jehovah's Witness.* He did so under Milch's threat never to speak to him again; he so wanted to be considered a "good fellow."

If approached diplomatically he found it difficult to resist a reasonable plea for mercy. In one case he freed a deserter; in another, forgave an official for writing a biting critique of SS treatment of the Poles. But his sense of honor forbade him to show mercy to his own flesh and blood. When a nephew, an SS officer, was brought up on charges of homosexuality he immediately signed the order sending him to a punishment camp. During imprisonment, the young man committed other homosexual acts and the uncle ordered his execution. Rolf Wehser, an SS judge, urged leniency but Himmler refused. "I do not want anyone to say that I was more lenient because it was my own nephew." It was Hitler himself who had to revoke the judgment of death.

Under Himmler's supervision the work of the killing centers reached the peak of efficiency by the fall of 1943. At Auschwitz those selected for death marched to the gas chambers, unaware of their fate, past an inmate symphony orchestra conducted by the Jewish violinist Alma Rose. At Treblinka, however, the Jews almost always knew they were about to die and would cry and laugh from shock. Annoyed guards lashed away at them; babies, who hindered attendants while shaving their mothers' hair, would be smashed against a wall. If there was any resistance, guards and Kapos (trusties) would use whips to drive the naked victims into trucks bound for the gas chamber.

The thought of refusing the order to murder never entered the heads of the executioners. "I could only say Jawohl," Höss, the commandant of Auschwitz, later confessed. "It didn't occur to me at all that I would be held responsible. You see, in Germany it was understood that if something went wrong, then the man who gave the orders was responsible." Nor did these executioners ever question whether the Jews deserved their fate. "Don't you see, we SS men were not supposed to think about these things; it never even occurred to us. . . . We were all so trained to obey orders, without even thinking, that the thought of disobeying an order would simply never have occurred to anybody, and somebody else would have done it just as well if I hadn't." Besides, those who participated in the exterminations had been trained so rigorously "that one would shoot his own brother if ordered to. Orders were everything."†

---

* These were among the most indomitable of Hitler's victims and most of those imprisoned refused a standing offer of freedom if they would but renounce their faith.
† The experiments made by Stanley Milgram in the United States as described in his book, Obedience to Authority, indicate that blind obedience is not limited to Germans.

Some of the executioners thoroughly enjoyed their work but these were sadistic at the peril of punishment from their chief. Years earlier Himmler had forbidden independent action against the Jews by any member of his organization. "The SS commander must be hard but not hardened," he instructed one Sturmbannführer. "If, during your work, you come across cases in which some commander exceeds his duty or shows signs that his restraint is becoming blurred, intervene at once." Recently he had passed down a similar judgment to the SS Legal Department in regard to unauthorized shootings of Jews. "If the motive is selfish, sadistic or sexual, judicial punishment should be imposed for murder or manslaughter as the case may be." That was undoubtedly why he had authorized Morgen to bring the commandant of Buchenwald to trial.

Training his men to become hard but not hardened was a difficult task for Himmler and he attempted to do so by transforming the SS into an order of knights with the motto: "Loyalty is my honor." He imbued the SS, therefore, not only with a sense of racial superiority but with the hard virtues of loyalty, comradeship, duty, truth, diligence, honesty and knighthood. His SS, as the elite of the party, was the elite of the German Volk, and therefore the elite of the entire world. By establishing castles of the order to indoctrinate SS members in his ideals, he hoped to breed a New Man, "far finer and more valuable than the world had yet seen." He also lectured his men on good manners and good breeding. "Whether it is a dinner you are giving or the organization of a march, wherever there are guests, I insist that you attend to the slightest details, for I want the SS to set an example of propriety everywhere, and show the utmost courtesy and consideration to all fellow Germans." His SS men were to be models of neatness. "I do not want to see a single white vest with the slightest spot of dirt." Furthermore they must drink like gentlemen "or you will be sent a pistol and asked to put an end to it."

They were to be gentlemen, in fact, no matter how atrocious their mission. And with this in mind, Himmler summoned his SS generals to Posen on October 4, 1943. His primary purpose was to enlarge the circle of those privy to the extermination of the Jews. The recent revelations by Morgen, combined with persistent rumors of terrors in the concentration camps, were causing apprehension and some revulsion among the most loyal adherents of the Führer. Now that the truth was leaking out, he had decided to involve the party and the military in his Final Solution. By

---

During the Milgram experiments only thirty-five per cent of those tested refused an order to inflict pain on fellow human beings. The majority simply obeyed the voice of authority. These tests made in 1960 were corroborated by Vietnam and, to an extent, by Watergate.

making them, in effect, co-conspirators, he would force them to fight on to the end. The war was probably lost, but this would give him time to fulfill his main ambition. If worse came to worst he would take millions of Jews to death with him.

The speech to the SS officers was only the first in a series of information lectures by Himmler that were to include many civilian leaders and Wehrmacht officers. In a sense, the first was the most important of the scheduled speeches since he must convince the SS that the execution of this distasteful deed was not at variance with the highest principles of their order. He said he wanted to talk to them quite frankly, on a very grave matter. "Among ourselves it should be mentioned once, quite openly, but we will never speak of it publicly." His reluctance to proceed was obvious but finally he said, "I mean the evacuation of the Jews, the extermination of the Jewish race. It's one of those things it is easy to talk about—'The Jewish race is being exterminated,' says one party member, 'that's quite clear, it's in our program—elimination of the Jews, and we're doing it, exterminating them.' "

These plain words, after years of rhetoric and sloganeering, were shocking despite the unwelcome suspicions raised by Morgen and Kurt Gerstein. More so was Himmler's condemnation of those who had been profiting by the Final Solution. "A number of SS men—there are not very many of them—have fallen short, and they will die without mercy. We had the moral right, we had the duty of our people, to destroy this race which wanted to destroy us. But we have not the right to enrich ourselves with so much as a fur, a watch, a mark, or a cigarette or anything else. Because we have exterminated a bacterium we do not want to be eventually infected by the bacterium or die of it. I will not allow so much as a sepsis to appear here or gain a hold. Wherever it may form, we must cauterize it. In the final analysis, however, we can say that we have fulfilled this most difficult duty for the love of our people. And our spirit, our soul, our character have not suffered injury from it."

Two days later Himmler spoke in the same vein to a group of Gauleiters and Reichsleiters. "The sentence 'The Jews must be exterminated,' with its few words, gentlemen, can be uttered easily. But what that sentence demands of the man who must execute it is the hardest and toughest thing in existence." It was apparent to his listeners that they were about to hear what they had been closing their ears to for months. "I ask you really only to hear and never to talk about what I tell you in this circle. When the question arose, 'What should be done with the women and children?' I decided here also to adopt a clear solution. I did not deem myself justified in exterminating the men, that is to say, to kill them or let them be killed, while allowing their children to grow up to avenge themselves on our sons and grandchildren. The hard decision had to be taken— *this people must disappear from the face of the earth."*

This was, he said, the most onerous assignment the SS ever had. "It was carried out—I think I can say—without our men and our leaders suffering the slightest damage to spirit or soul." They had remained knights despite mass extermination. A leaden silence fell over the hall. "He spoke," recalled Baldur von Schirach, "with such icy coldness of the extermination of men, women and children, as a businessman speaks of his balance sheet. There was nothing emotional in his speech, nothing that suggested an inner involvement."

After enlarging on the difficulties of this awesome task, Himmler brought the subject to a close. "You now know what is what and you must keep it to yourself. Perhaps at a much later time we shall consider whether something about it can be told to the German people. But it is probably better to bear the responsibility on behalf of our people (a responsibility for the deed as well as for the idea) and take the secret with us into our graves." He was like Brutus, forcing his colleagues to dip their hands in Caesar's blood. The Final Solution was no longer the burden only of Hitler and Himmler but theirs, a burden they must carry in silence.

Bormann closed the meeting with an invitation to lunch in the adjoining hall. During the meal Schirach and the other Gauleiters and Reichsleiters wordlessly avoided each other's eyes. Most guessed that Himmler had only revealed the truth so as to make them accomplices and that evening they drank so much that a good number had to be helped into the train that was taking them to the Wolfsschanze. Albert Speer, who had addressed the same audience just before Himmler, was so disgusted by the drunken spectacle that the next day he urged Hitler to read his party leaders a lecture on temperance.*

4

The Jews were not the only victims of Hitler's New Order. Millions of others, particularly in occupied Russia, had been shot, gassed and

* Speer claims to this day that he knew nothing of the Final Solution. Some scholars have accused him of attending Himmler's speech since during it the Reichsführer specifically addressed him. Speer insists he left for Rastenburg immediately after his own speech. Field Marshal Milch confirmed this. Granted that Speer was not present, it is difficult to believe he did not know of the extermination camps. From the text of Himmler's speech it is clear that he *thought* he was talking directly to Speer—and assuming that he was one of the high-ranking conspirators.

beaten to death. During a recent visit to Wolfsschanze Peter Kleist had voiced opposition to this policy to the Führer himself in a long detailed memorandum. "You've given me a very unpleasant picture of conditions in occupied Russia," said Hitler after reading it. "Isn't this idea of improving conditions by giving in to the ambitious demands of any nationalist politician that comes along nothing but an illusion? These nationalists will just think we are weak, and their ambition will spur them on to make more and more demands." Kleist spoke out boldly, explaining that he did not mean they should give in to demands, rather create conditions that would make the peoples of the East choose Germany instead of the Soviet Union. As he continued, Hitler listened thoughtfully, eyes on the floor. This gave Kleist the rare opportunity of observing his face at leisure. "I had always been struck by the way in which his expression was split up into many different units. It seemed to be composed of single elements that did not combine to form any real unity."

Finally Hitler interrupted. He was not at all angry but completely cool, calm and thoughtful as if talking to himself. "I cannot turn back now," he said, gazing into space. "Any change in my attitude would certainly be misunderstood as giving in, the military situation being what it is, and would bring a landslide." He did promise to consider a more liberal course once he had gained the military initiative, but Kleist felt this was only rhetoric. How could you change such a mind?

Abruptly Hitler looked up at Kleist. Gone was the calm, contemplative mood. "It's an illusion," he exclaimed with some violence. "You have a right to think only of the moment and of the situation weighing upon us at the present time, but that is also where you fall short. I have a duty to think of tomorrow, and the day after tomorrow. I cannot forget the future for the sake of a few momentary successes." In a hundred years Germany would be a nation of 120,000,000. "For that population I need empty space. I cannot grant the Eastern peoples any sovereign rights of independence and replace Soviet Russia with a new national Russia which is, for that very reason, much more firmly knit together. Policy is made not with illusions but with facts. Space is the deciding question for me in the East!"

And so his policy of oppression continued, accompanied by the ruthless starvation of Soviet prisoners of war. Alfred Rosenberg himself bore witness to this inhumanity in a scorching letter to Keitel that must have been prepared and thrust upon the Minister for the Occupied Eastern Territories by more forceful subordinates. It charged that of the 3,600,000 Soviet prisoners of war only a few hundred thousand were in good health.

The great majority had been starved or shot out of hand in a series of atrocities that ignored "potential understanding."

Countless other Soviet prisoners, along with non-Jewish inmates of concentration camps, were dying in a series of medical experiments: some after lying naked in snow or icy water; some during high-altitude tests; some as guinea pigs for mustard gas and poison bullets. Polish women at the Ravensbrück camp were inflicted with gas gangrene wounds; gypsies at Dachau and Buchenwald satisfied the curiosity of a group of doctors who wanted to know how long human beings could live on salt water.

The administration of occupied territories throughout Europe had also resulted in manifold executions as reprisals for acts of sabotage and rebellion. These were legalized by an order issued by the Führer on Pearl Harbor Day, once he realized all hope of taking Moscow was gone and eventual victory was dubious. Bearing the odd but apt title, "Night and Fog Decree," it ordered that all persons endangering German security, except those to be executed immediately, were to "vanish" without leaving a trace. Their families were to be told nothing of their fate.

By the fall of 1943 Hitler's New Order in Western Europe, which purported to be an amalgamation of states for the common good, was exposed for what it was: a plunder economy. Faced with millions reluctant to become mere vassals, Hitler turned from persuasion to sheer force. Acts of work stoppage and sabotage were answered by enforced labor and the execution of hostages. In Holland and France the death toll was more than 20,000. Legalized pillage had become the order of the day with boxcars of loot (including food, clothing and art treasures) converging on the homeland from Norway, Holland, Belgium, Luxembourg, France and Denmark. This did not include enormous occupation assessments. France alone was paying seven billion marks a year for membership in the New Order.

Hitler revealed the truth to the entire party leadership at a meeting in Berlin. "All that rubbish of small states still existing in Europe must be liquidated as fast as possible. The aim of our struggle must be to create a unified Europe: the Germans alone can really organize Europe."

A unified Europe, of course, meant one completely dominated by Germany; one kept orderly by the Gestapo and collaboration police. Yet with all its oppressions and brutal reprisals, Hitler's New Order had not aroused the spirit of rebellion among the masses. Most of the occupied peoples still co-operated with Nazi authorities so that they could lead comparatively normal lives, convinced that general strikes, attacks on German overseers or attempts to disrupt the administration and economy of their nation would inevitably lead to massive reprisals at worst or a lowering of their own standard of living at best. It was easier and more prudent to make common cause with an occupation that probably would last indefinitely. It was this will to survive that reduced resistance activities to a minimum. Few, indeed, belonged to the underground and too often, as in France, there was bloody, debilitating rivalry between Communist and non-Communist partisan units. The only substantial resistance movement was in Yugoslavia and this too was blunted by the internecine quarrel between Tito, a Communist, who strove to unite all anti-Hitler elements, and Mihailovic, the Serbian nationalist.

Although Hitler's ultimate aim to transform most of Europe into a Germanic empire was now in the open, the extent of his ambitions was not. Even many of his enemies surmised he would restrict himself to Europe; they would have been confounded to read his secret handwritten notes on the subject.*

> England for the good of the world must remain unchanged in its present form.
> Consequently, after final victory, we must effect a reconciliation.
> Only the King must go—in his place the Duke of Windsor. With him we will make a permanent treaty of friendship instead of a peace treaty.

Scandinavia and the Iberian Peninsula, he continued, would be joined under the New Order, thus materializing that United Europe envisaged by Charles the Great, Prince Eugene and Napoleon.

> The most important point of final victory will be the exclusion of the United States from world politics for all time and the destruction of their Jewish community.
> For this purpose Dr. Goebbels will have dictatorial authority as Governor to accomplish the total re-education of the racially mixed and inferior population. Göring will also help in this respect, above all by mobilizing all those with German blood, at least fifty per cent of the inhabitants, so they can be educated militarily and regenerated nationalistically.

5

While Hitler envisaged grandiose plans of conquest that encompassed five continents, his armies in the East were being steadily driven back toward the homeland. Inspired by success in repelling Operation Citadel, the Soviet high command had gone over to the attack with confidence and daring. In the last six months of 1943 the Red Army had

* These documents are presently in the Müllern-Schönhausen Collection.

advanced in some places as much as two hundred and fifty miles, throwing the Germans in the south and center back across the Dnieper River.

This only spurred Hitler to accelerate the Final Solution and early in 1944 he allowed the secret to be revealed to a large non-party, non-SS group. On January 26, 1944, Himmler made his third address, this to some 260 high-ranking army and navy officers in a theater at Posen. In his cool, antiseptic manner he told how Hitler had given him the mission of extermination. "I can assure you that the Jewish question has been solved. Six million have been killed." A wave of applause swept the auditorium. One Wehrmacht officer near Colonel von Gerstdorff (who had tried in vain to bomb Hitler and himself to bits) stood up on a chair in his enthusiasm. From the rear of the hall an aghast general checked to see how many of his colleagues were *not* applauding. He could count but five.

Himmler continued this campaign of enlightenment in the next weeks. He admitted to a group of navy leaders that he had ordered women and children killed. "I would be a weakling, a criminal to our descendants if I allowed hate-filled sons to grow to manhood in this battle of humans against subhumans . . . but we must recognize more and more that we are engaged in a primitive, original, natural racial battle." He told much the same story to another group of generals at Sonthofen. "The Jewish question in Germany and in general throughout the occupied territories is solved," he said. And when he added that it had been done "without compromise," there was applause. In all, Himmler made some fifteen speeches on the Final Solution, covering a wide range of audiences but, significantly, never one of Foreign Office personnel.

The last days of 1943 were oppressive ones for Hitler. Not only did his troops face new setbacks at Leningrad and throughout the Ukraine, but his extermination program was threatened when SS Judge Morgen finally uncovered the network of corruption at Buchenwald. An accomplice of Camp Commandant Koch's, named Köhler, lost his nerve and agreed to testify. He was jailed as a material witness but within days was found dead in his cell. In the light of such damning evidence, Koch wilted under Morgen's relentless interrogation. He confessed that, besides enriching himself at the expense of the inmates, he had executed a number of them to cover up his secret.

The successful prosecution of Koch by no means satisfied Morgen's sense of justice. He pursued the trail of corruption to Poland. In Lublin Morgen was warmly greeted by the camp's commandant, Kriminalkommissar Wirth, who had acted as Gerstein's guide in Belzec. He revealed with pride that it was he who had not only built the four extermination camps in the Lublin area but organized the system of extermination. Each establishment, he said, had been built up like a Potemkin village. As trains pulled into a dummy railroad station, the occupants imagined they were entering a city or town. With relish, Wirth described how he or one of his representatives would greet the newcomers with a set speech: "Jews, you were brought here to be resettled but before we organize the future Jewish state, you must of course learn how to work. You must learn a new trade." After these calming words the victims would innocently start off on their march to death.

Wirth's description of the entire process seemed "completely fantastic" to Morgen but not after he toured the buildings which housed the loot. From the massive piles—including one incredible heap of watches—he realized that "something frightful was going on here." Never had he seen so much money at one time, particularly foreign currency. There were coins from all over the world. He gaped in wonder at the gold-smelting furnace and its prodigious stack of gold bars.

Morgen inspected all four camps built by Wirth—Maidanek, Treblinka, Sobibor and Belzec. In each one he saw evidence of execution —the gas chambers, the ovens, the mass graves. Here was crime on a ghastly scale, yet he was helpless to act since the order had come directly from the Führer's chancellery. Morgen's only recourse was to prosecute the "arbitrary killings" of prisoners; these could be brought before the SS judicial system. He set out to get evidence and persevered, despite continued hindrances, until he found sufficient proof to bring charges of murder against the two top officials at Maidanek.

The guiding spirit of all four camps, the helpful Christian Wirth, continued to talk freely to Morgen. One day he remarked casually that a man named Höss ran another large extermination complex near Auschwitz. This sounded like fertile ground for Morgen, but his authority was limited and he had to find some good reason to go so far afield. He soon found his excuse: an unsolved case of gold smuggling involving several men on Höss's staff. And so by early 1944 the doughty Morgen was investigating the death camps near Auschwitz. He had no trouble locating numerous sheds loaded with loot, gas chambers and crematories. But investigations of "illegal" killings and corruption were blocked every time one of his men got too close to the truth and Morgen decided to return to Germany so he could attend to a more important matter—the mass official killing themselves. Morgen decided to approach Himmler personally and make it clear that the extermination system was leading Germany "straight into the abyss." To reach the Reichsführer he again had to go through channels. First on the list was his immediate superior, the chief of the criminal police. Nebe listened in shocked silence ("I could see his hair stand on end when I made my report") and when he found tongue he told Morgen to report the matter immediately to Kaltenbrunner. He too was appalled and promised to take his protest to both Himmler and Hitler. Next came Chief Justice of the SS Court Breithaupt. He was so incensed that he promised to arrange a meeting between Himmler and Morgen. But this time the machinery of bureaucracy prevented Morgen from getting beyond the Reichsführer's anteroom. This convinced Morgen that he would have to take a more practical route to justice: "that is, by removing from this system of destruction the leaders and important elements through the means offered by the system itself. I could not do this with regard to the killings ordered by the head of the state, but I could do it for killings outside of this order, or against this order, or for other serious charges."

He returned to his task with spirit, determined to institute proceedings against as many leaders as possible in hopes of undermining the entire system of mass murder. He expanded the scope of investigation to concentration camps despite threats and attempted reprisals. At Oranienburg one of his informers—a prisoner named Rothe—was saved at the last moment from a public execution designed to warn other inmates not to collaborate with Morgen. Even so he won the nickname, "The Bloodhound Judge," bringing some 800 cases of corruption and murder to trial, 200 of which resulted in sentences. Karl Koch of Buchenwald was shot. The commandant of Maidanek was also executed, his chief assistant condemned to death. The commandant of 's Hertogenbosch was posted to a penal unit for maltreatment of prisoners and the head of Flossenburg was fired for drunkenness and debauchery.

These trials caused such reverberations in the hierarchy by the early spring of 1944 that Himmler, undoubtedly at Hitler's order, instructed Morgen to cease further investigations. "The Bloodhound Judge" was going too far, too successfully and was about to launch a full-scale inquiry into Rudolf Höss and the Auschwitz constellation of camps. The shock wave of Morgen's one-man house cleaning had already compromised the Lublin killing complex. Kriminalkommissar Wirth was instructed to destroy three of the four camps he had built—Treblinka, Sobibor and Belzec —without leaving a trace. That task completed, Wirth was dispatched to Italy to defend roads against partisans. Here the man who had escaped

Morgen's justice was soon brought down by a ruder one—a partisan bullet in the back. In the meantime, despite the Himmler-Hitler order, Konrad Morgen was surreptitiously continuing his lonesome attempt to end the Final Solution.* He was particularly interested in a rather low-ranking SD officer named Eichmann.

* Morgen also did his best to convict Ilse Koch, the wife of the Buchenwald commandant. He was convinced that she was guilty of sadistic crimes, but the charges against her could not be proven. After the war Morgen was asked by an American official to testify that Frau Koch made lampshades from the skin of inmates. Morgen replied that, while she undoubtedly was guilty of many crimes, she was truly innocent of this charge. After personally investigating the matter, he had thrown it out of his own case. Even so, the American insisted that Morgen sign an affidavit that Frau Koch had made the lampshades. Anyone undaunted by Nazi threats was not likely to submit to those of a representative of the democracies. His refusal to lie was followed by a threat to turn him over to the Russians, who would surely beat him to death. Morgen's second and third refusals were followed by severe beatings. Though he detested Frau Koch, nothing could induce him to bear false witness. Fortunately, Morgen survived and is presently practicing law in West Germany.

Part 9

INTO THE ABYSS

Chapter Twenty-eight

THE ARMY BOMB PLOT
NOVEMBER 1943–JULY 21, 1944

1

On the eve of the twentieth anniversary of the Beer Hall Putsch Germany's strategic position was frankly revealed to a hundred or so Reichsleiters and Gauleiters by General Jodl. In a top secret lecture at Munich he told of the bitter defeats in Russia, of the failure to draw Spain into the war and thus seize Gibraltar (because of that "Jesuit Foreign Minister Serrano Suñer"), and of the "most monstrous of all betrayals in history"—that of the Italians. Jodl spoke extemporaneously of the future, alarming his listeners with the admission that the Western Allies enjoyed such tremendous air superiority that a mass landing could not possibly be contained by the present defense forces. There was, he concluded, only one solution: to mobilize every German able to bear arms. It would not be possible to drain troops and supplies from the East, he said, since things were indeed "getting warm" there. New ways had to be found to solve the dilemma of manpower shortage in the West. "In my opinion, the time has come to take steps with remorseless vigor and resolution in Denmark, Holland, France and Belgium, to compel thousands of idle ones to carry out the fortification work, which is more important than any other work. The necessary orders for this have already been given."

The glum picture of the present ended with the acknowledgment that the terror air raids by the West "weighed most heavily on the home front" and that U-boat reprisals were declining drastically because of enemy air superiority over the Atlantic. At the same time, he said, there were considerable grounds for confidence in final victory. They were blessed with a leader who was "the soul not only of the political but also of the military conduct of the war," and it was his will power alone that was animating "the whole of the German armed forces, with respect to strategy, organization, and munitions of war. Similarly the unity of political and military command, which is so important, is personified by him in a way such as has never been known since the days of Frederick the Great." He ended with a burst of hyperbole worthy of Hitler. No one could predict what troubles lay hidden in the darkness of the future. One thing alone was certain: Germany would never cease the fight for the culture and freedom of the Continent. "A Europe under the whip of American Jews or Bolshevik commissars is unthinkable."

The politicians cheered. Jodl's talk was a tour-de-force mixture of candor and hope that was followed two days later by a purely inspirational performance on the part of Hitler. In a speech from the Löwenbräu cellar, he spoke with such confidence and fire that many of those listening on the radio were as uplifted as those present.

These attempts to inspire the party and the people were undermined within weeks by deterioration in both the political and the military situation. Hungarians were eying Italy's desertion with envy and Romanians were bitter at the destruction of eighteen divisions on the Don and Volga. The Wehrmacht itself had suffered 1,686,000 casualties in the past twelve months and it was so difficult to find replacements that the conscription law exempting the youngest or only son of a family was suspended, and fifty-year-old men, veterans of the First World War, were deemed eligible for service.

With prospects of another disastrous winter on the eastern front, the atmosphere at Wolfsschanze was glum. The Führer completely ignored the holiday season. There was no Christmas tree, not a single candle to celebrate the festival of love and peace. Early in 1944, on January 26, he summoned several hundred generals and admirals to Rastenburg. After explaining the ideological basis of the war, he made it clear that his officers must take an unequivocal stand in regard to National Socialism. They must support its principles from inner conviction. He said all this in a calm, matter-of-fact manner and so his next words, uttered with an intense sincerity, caught his listeners off balance. "My generals and admirals," he said, "if Providence should actually deny us victory in this battle of life and death, and if it is the will of the Almighty that this should end in catastrophe for the German people, then you, my generals and admirals, must gather around me with upraised swords to fight to the last drop of blood for the honor of Germany—I say, gentlemen, that is the way it actually *must* be!"

There was deathly silence in the room. Everyone, it seemed, was holding his breath. Finally the silence was broken by an officer in the first row who felt insulted. In an ironic voice Field Marshal von Manstein said, "My Führer, it shall be so!" There followed another silence, this one fearful, as Hitler waited for his military leaders to rise as one man and cheer these words—even though they had been uttered sarcastically. But there was not a sound, not a movement. On the rostrum, Hitler paled. He scanned the room, his eyes like searchlights, finally stopping at Manstein in the front row. "Field Marshal," he said harshly, "I have good reason to doubt the faith which your response implies." There was another long, embarrassing pause. Finally he said he knew all about the anti-Hitler movement in the Wehrmacht, the strong negative attitude of numerous officers. He had proof positive that some of these gentlemen were refusing to execute certain Führer orders. Yes, and he knew all about the Free Germany movement among certain officers captured by the Soviets!

These impromptu accusations broke his concentration and he was unable to finish his speech as planned. Instead he brought it to an abrupt close and stalked out of the room. Moments later Manstein was ordered to report at once to the Führer's study. Hitler glared at him. "Field Marshal," he said, "I must forbid you ever to interrupt me again during a speech. How would you like it if someone broke in while *you* were addressing your subordinates?"

One of the few pleasures of Hitler's life in those dreary winter days was the excellent cuisine of his new diet cook. Marlene von Exner was also young, attractive and Viennese. He enjoyed her company and the two would talk at length about Austria and her family, which had supported the National Socialist movement when it was illegal. Her only complaint was Hitler's limited menu. How monotonous, she confided to Traudl Junge, to live on vegetarian soup, carrots, potatoes and soft-boiled eggs! She feared he might get so bored with her meals that he would send her away—and she had fallen in love with a young SS adjutant. She was destined to leave for quite another reason. Bormann, whose advances had been repelled by Frau von Exner, discovered there was Jewish blood on her mother's side and got his revenge by pressing the matter until Hitler, who wished it had never been raised, felt obliged to dismiss her. But he gave her six months' salary and made the entire Exner family honorary Aryans.

Late that February Hitler returned to the Obersalzberg so that the Wolfsschanze buildings could be reinforced against Russian air raids. But life at the Berghof was scarcely more cheerful. "The forced gaiety, the light conversations and the variety of guests," recalled Traudl Junge, "could not hide the disquiet which we all felt in our hearts." Eva had not seen her lover for some time and was shocked by his appearance. "He has become so old and somber," she confided to Traudl. "Do you know what is troubling him?"

The secretary was embarrassed. "You know the Führer much better than I do and you must be able to guess about those things he doesn't speak of." The military situation alone, she said, must be sufficient cause for deep concern. Later in the day, at the tea hous, Eva scolded Hitler for his stoop but he turned it into a joke. "That's because I have heavy keys in my pocket. Besides I tote along a full pack of troubles." He grinned facetiously. "Now you and I will go better together. You are always wearing high heels to be taller so if I bend down a little we will harmonize well."

On the last day of February an unusual guest arrived at the Berghof. Hanna Reitsch, the aviator and glider pilot, had come to tell the Führer how to win the war. The new V-1 rocket, she argued, was too inaccurate. A piloted rocket was the answer and she offered to be the first volunteer. Hitler rejected the project out of hand. This was not the right psychological moment for such a suicidal idea to be accepted by the German people. He changed the subject to the jet plane, one of his secret weapons. Hanna knew that jet propulsion was only in its early stages of development and could not resist interrupting him in mid-sentence. "Mein Führer, you are speaking of the grandchild of an embryo." He was poorly informed about the German jet program, she said, and again brought up the subject of suicide pilots. Surprisingly, he gave peevish permission to begin experimental work on the project so long as he was not pestered during the development stage.

It snowed almost continuously at the Obersalzberg, but the isolation seemed to improve the Führer's spirits. At lunch he began deriding the water colors he had painted in Vienna and which now commanded high prices. It would be crazy, he said, to pay more than two hundred marks for such amateurish efforts. "I did not really want to be a painter," he confessed. "I only painted these things to live and study." He had disposed of them but kept his architectural sketches—"my most treasured possessions, my mental property, which I could never part with. One must not forget that all my present ideas, my architectural plans, go back to those years when I worked all night long."

Life at the Berghof seemed to give him renewed confidence and by the time Goebbels arrived in March, deeply depressed over the first daylight American bombings, Hitler had to instill him with hope for the future. Yet the next day it was the Führer who suffered an attack of nerves. In a conference on March 17 at nearby Klessheim Castle he lost his temper with Admiral Horthy, Regent of Hungary, and accused the Hungarians of planning an Italian-style betrayal. Schmidt, waiting outside, was astounded to see the aged Horthy rush out, red in the face, with Hitler at his heels, looking angry and embarrassed, calling out to come back.

The affronted Horthy sent for his special train but, before it could move, Ribbentrop faked a convincing air raid, including a smoke screen over the castle, which successfully kept the Regent a prisoner. When he had cooled down Ribbentrop informed him that he could leave and read the draft of a joint communiqué stating that the entry of German troops into Hungary had been arranged by mutual consent. "You may as well have added," protested the admiral, "that I begged Hitler to have Hungary occupied by Slovak and Romanian troops, which is another of the threats he made!" This sentence was deleted but by the time Horthy arrived in Budapest he found his country occupied by eleven German divisions.

Hitler's nerves had led to a petty triumph that was a military as well as a political blunder. It took divisions away from the West, where there were increasing indications of an impending invasion, and from the East where, reported intelligence expert Gehlen, the enemy was about to launch a massive offensive in the Ukraine which could have imminent and "far-reaching political, military and economic repercussions on the rest of the war in Europe." The only prospect of regaining the initiative, Gehlen added, was to make bold strategic withdrawals. In line with his policy of hanging tenaciously to every bit of conquered territory, the Führer turned down the recommendation.

This decision may have been influenced by bad health. Others besides Eva noticed how his knees would tremble if he stood too long; and his left hand would shake enough to rattle a cup in its saucer. Early in May he was again plagued by agonizing stomach spasms. While ignoring Dr. Morell's advice to submit to gentle massage and go on long walks, he did agree to take Cardizol and subject himself to intravenous injections of two other drugs (Glucad and Testoviron) to combat increasing fatigue.

Morell also urged Hitler to get to bed earlier, but he said that was impossible. He could not sleep until the last British bomber had left the Reich.

That spring enemy planes ravaged Bavaria. Almost every day the warning sirens screeched and Hitler would climb down the sixty-five steps to the deep bunker under the Berghof. But no bombs dropped on the Obersalzberg; the raiders were bound for Vienna, Hungary or other populated targets. In clear weather one could see the red of the fires in Munich and Eva begged permission to drive there to see if her house on the Wasserburgerstrasse was safe. She persisted until the Führer finally let her go. She returned so shocked by the havoc that Hitler vowed vengeance. "Panic will break out in England!" he promised and told her about the new rocket. "The effect of this weapon will be too much for anyone's nerves. I shall pay back those barbarians who are now massacring women and children and destroying German culture."

The air raid alerts became so common that some of the guests at the Berghof began to ignore them. One early morning Traudl rushed from her bed to safety but found no one in the bunker. When she came up to see why, there was Hitler standing at the entrance like Cerberus, scanning the skies anxiously. He wagged an admonishing finger at her. "Don't be so careless, young lady. Get back to the bunker; the alarm is not yet over." She didn't tell him that the other guests were still in their beds but obediently descended the long flight of steps. During lunch Hitler delivered a lecture on the stupidity of not taking shelter. "My co-workers, some of whom are irreplaceable, simply have an obligation to go to the bunker," he scolded. "It is idiotic to prove your courage by placing yourself in danger of being struck by a bomb."

He was placing his own body in jeopardy by steadfastly refusing to exercise, rest or undergo massage, while depending more and more on medication. In addition to the other pills and injections, he allowed himself to be dosed with a heart and liver extract and four to six multivitamin tablets a day. It was almost as though his health was no longer important and he was only keeping himself alive until he had accomplished his mission in life. He did succeed in lifting himself out of depression and resumed preaching his message of hope. One fine day, he assured the family circle, something would change the entire situation. The Anglo-Saxons would eventually realize their best interests lay with his anti-Bolshevist crusade. *It had to happen.*

The Allies responded with a new strategic bombing campaign of coordinated and concentrated raids. By early May attacks by American daylight bombers on fuel plants in central and eastern Germany seriously endangered Hitler's entire armament program. The daily output of 5850 metric tons abruptly fell to 4820 tons. "The enemy has struck us at one of our weakest points," Albert Speer reported to Hitler. "If they persist this time, we will soon no longer have any fuel production worth mentioning. Our one hope is that the other side has an air force General Staff as scatterbrained as ours!"

Keitel hastily protested that there was still a huge reserve of fuel but Hitler was more realistic and called a meeting, a few days later, to discuss the problem. Four industrialists agreed that the situation was hopeless if the air raids continued systematically.* At first Hitler replied with the usual argument that they had survived worse crises—with Keitel and Göring nodding in unison—but when the industrialists supported their conclusions with data and comparative figures, Hitler made an abrupt about-face. He seemed, thought Speer, eager at last "to hear the unpleasant truth"; the Führer, he hoped, had finally realized that this was the beginning of the collapse of German economy.

2

The war of mobility which the Germans had so successfully employed in the early stages of the war was now turned against them. In the First World War the protracted stalemate had enabled German propaganda to argue plausibly almost to the end that the war could still be won. No such assertions were possible amid the military realities of World War II. There could no longer be any question of another German summer offensive. Last year's defeat at Kursk had ended all hopes for success and it was now only a question of how long the Wehrmacht could hold back the resurgent Red Army. Notwithstanding the staggering losses of manpower in the past three years, Russia still had some 300 divisions of over 5,000,000 men in the field, opposing 20 undermanned German divisions totaling 2,000,000 men. The most painful surprise to the Germans was not the astounding reserve strength of the Red Army but its tenacious fighting spirit. During the siege of Stalingrad Hitler had captiously explained the inability of Paulus to take the city with the fact that the Russians fought like "swamp animals." Whatever the designation, the vigor and valor of these *Untermenschen* of the East had proved more than a match for the Teutonic race. So much for the underlying premise of Hitler's *Ostpolitik*. He had no thought of even a token victory in 1944. His concern, in fact, was invasion from the West. "It will decide the issue not only of the year

* In a similar meeting the previous fall, industrialist Paul Pleiger had asserted that there simply was not sufficient coal and coke to expand steel production. "To my boundless surprise," recalled one witness, "Hitler in the course of the conversation quite dryly said, 'Pleiger, if we cannot produce more coal and steel, the war is lost.'"

but of the whole war," he told his military advisers one day in early June as he gazed absently out the window. "If we succeed in throwing back the invasion, such an attempt cannot and will not be repeated within a short time. It will mean that our reserves will be set free to use in Italy and the East." Then the latter front could at least be stabilized. But if they could not throw back the Western invaders it meant final defeat. "We cannot win a static war in the West for the additional reason that each step backward means a broadening of the front lines across more of France. With no strategic reserves of any importance it will be impossible to build up sufficient strength along such a line. Therefore," he concluded, "the invader *must* be thrown back on his first attempt." He did not add something he told General Heusinger in private: "If the invasion succeeds, then I must try to bring the war to an end by political means."

Hitler had turned over the task of repelling the West to Rommel, who had already presided over one catastrophe, the loss of North Africa, through no fault of his own. Rommel was convinced that the invasion could best be stopped at the beaches where the enemy was at his weakest. "The troops are unsure and possibly even seasick," he argued. "They are unfamiliar with the terrain. Heavy weapons are not yet available in sufficient quantity. That is the moment to strike and defeat them." His elderly superior, Gerd von Rundstedt, Commander-in-Chief West, held the opposite view. The decisive battle should be fought far behind the coast. All armor and tactical reserves, therefore, should be well inside France so they could encircle and destroy the oncoming enemy. Hitler settled the dispute by a compromise that pleased neither. He took all armored units from Rommel but placed them much closer to the coast than Rundstedt wanted.

On the morning of June 4 Rommel set out for Germany by car, ostensibly to visit his wife, whose birthday fell on the sixth, but his main purpose was to drive on to Berchtesgaden and persuade Hitler to transfer two additional armored divisions and one mortar brigade to Normandy. "The most urgent problem," he wrote in his diary, "is to win the Führer over by personal conversation." It was an appropriate time for a brief holiday. The Luftwaffe meteorologist in Paris had just reported that no Allied invasion could be expected for two weeks because of stormy conditions.

Across the Channel General Dwight Eisenhower, the Allied commander-in-chief, was faced with his own dilemma. The invasion, Operation Overlord, was scheduled to start the next day but the unfavorable weather reports induced him to postpone the great venture for at least another twenty-four hours. He spent most of the day alone in his cramped house trailer in a woods near Portsmouth, mulling over the pros and cons of risking an attack under bad conditions or waiting until July. More than 200,000 men had already been briefed on the operation and it seemed inevitable that the secret would leak out by that time. That evening a new weather front was reported: there would be relatively good conditions until the morning of June 6, when the weather would deteriorate. Eisenhower polled his commanders. Air Chief Marshal Sir Arthur Tedder feared the cloud cover would hinder his plans but Montgomery's reply was, "I would say go." Eisenhower made the decision: On June 6 the Allies would hit the beaches of Normandy.

June 6 was barely fifteen minutes old, British Double Summer Time, when an eighteen-year-old paratrooper named Murphy dropped into the garden of a schoolmistress in Ste. Mère Église. It was the beginning of D-Day. Within an hour vague and contradictory reports began flooding German Seventh Army command posts. It was 3 A.M., German time, before Rundstedt informed Supreme Headquarters, presently located on the Obersalzberg, that major paratroop and glider landings had been made in Normandy. Three hours later Rundstedt's chief of staff informed Warlimont that this, in all probability, was the invasion. He urged that the four motorized-armored divisions of OKW reserves be sent nearer the landing area.

But Jodl was positive it was merely a diversionary attack. He had been tricked by a secret Allied operation known as Bodyguard: a fake war plan was cleverly leaked to Führer Headquarters indicating the main landings would be farther north near Calais where the Channel was narrowest. In consequence, Jodl refused to wake up Hitler for consultation.

This caused consternation at Rundstedt's headquarters. The elderly field marshal, according to his chief of operations, "was fuming with rage, red in the face, and his anger made his speech unintelligible." Another commander might have telephoned Hitler directly but the aristocratic Rundstedt, who openly referred to his Führer as "that Bohemian corporal," would not stoop to petition. He left the entreaties to his subordinates, who kept pestering OKW with phone calls in an effort to change Jodl's mind.

It was not until 9 A.M. that the Führer was finally wakened. This, in fact, was earlier than usual but he was scheduled to receive Horthy, Tiso and Antonescu—the dictators of Hungary, Slovakia and Romania—at Klessheim Castle. Emerging from his bedroom in dressing gown, Hitler listened placidly to the latest reports before sending for Keitel and Jodl. He was not so calm by the time they arrived. "Well, is it or isn't it the invasion?" he shouted, then spun on his heel and left. But before long his mood abruptly changed. He clapped people on the back with unaccustomed familiarity as if revitalized by at last coming to grips with the West. "Now, we can give them a nice little packet!" he exclaimed with a slap on his own thigh. He was jubilant throughout the hourlong scenic auto trip to Klessheim. "I can hold the Russians as long as I like," he told his companions and then boasted how he would destroy the Anglo-Saxon powers in front of the Atlantic Wall.

Events in the West dominated the midday situation conference, which was held just before the meeting with the three dictators. As Hitler entered the conference room his military advisers, anxiously clustered around maps and charts, turned with some excitement and apprehension. To their amazement he strode in confidently, face beaming. In exceptionally broad Austrian he said, "So, we're off!" and began chuckling in a carefree manner. What he had wanted all the time had finally come true, he told them. "I am face to face with my real enemies!"

In Berlin DNB, on the authority of a minor official, announced that the invasion had begun but apparently Goebbels himself did not take it too seriously. The most important event of the day, according to Press Officer Wilfred von Oven's diary, was a party at which Goebbels played a piano duet with a countess: "Sounds off on culture at length then disappears with countess behind bar at piano," he recorded. "She sings chansons. Everybody drunk."

At 4 P.M. Hitler was back at the Berghof in time for a late lunch with Eva and a number of party dignitaries and their wives. The highlight of the meal was his comment on vegetarianism: "The elephant is the strongest animal; he also cannot stand meat." The party adjourned as usual to the tea house where the Führer treated himself to lime-blossom tea. This was followed by an hour's nap and another military conference at 11 P.M. He doubted, he said, that this was the real invasion. It was only a feint to trick him into deploying his forces to the wrong place. The main invasion would surely come at Calais since it was the shortest route across the Channel. He could not be shaken from the lie so assiduously planted by Bodyguard—perhaps because that was the route in reverse he had selected when he was planning to invade England.

By midnight the Allies had broken into Hitler's western *Festung* on a front of thirty miles. The Germans had been completely taken by surprise, their air force and navy rendered powerless and their coast defenses shattered. The enemy had achieved a great victory at the cost of fewer than 2500 lives but there was still time to throw them back into the Channel—if the right decisions were made without delay.

3

On June 3 Goebbels had given up smoking. Three days later he got drunk. On the seventh he assured his press officer that it was a genuine invasion and that same noon astonished a select audience of high officials and industrialists by remarking, according to the diary of former Ambassador von Hassell, "that one day the 'Great Powers' would certainly sit down again at the same table and 'shake hands,' and ask one another: 'Now, how did all this come about?' The last word in wisdom!" Goebbels was merely mouthing the views of his master but on the tenth he did his best to persuade Hitler that Germany's only hope was "bloody rejection of the invasion." Then the West would eagerly seek an understanding.

Hitler was still so convinced that the Normandy landing was a trick that he had not yet taken resolute action against this bridgehead, and by refusing to give his field commanders a free hand he had deprived them of their last chance to seize the initiative. The battle was already lost. By now it was obvious that the Allies had won complete air supremacy over France, and Hitler turned to Göring, whom he had praised a few days earlier. He sarcastically asked whether it was true that his vaunted Luftwaffe had taken out a "knock-for-knock" insurance policy with the West.

In desperation the Führer inaugurated the V-1 rocket campaign against London on June 12, two days ahead of schedule. The harassed catapult crews could launch only ten flying bombs. Four crashed immediately, two disappeared, and the others destroyed a single railway bridge. After this fiasco Göring hastily reminded Hitler that this was Milch's program, not his, but when the second launching of 244 rockets two days later set disastrous fires in London the Reichsmarschall was quick to claim the credit.

All this had no effect on the situation in Normandy. Within ten days the Allies had managed to land almost a million men and 500,000 tons of matériel. The situation was so desperate that on June 17 Hitler motored west to a village north of Soissons. Here, for the first time since D-Day, he met Rundstedt and Rommel. "He looked pale and sleepless," recalled General Hans Speidel, "playing nervously with his glasses and an array of colored pencils which he held between his fingers . . . then in a loud voice he spoke bitterly of his displeasure at the success of the Allied landings, for which he tried to hold the field commanders responsible."

It was Rommel, not Rundstedt, who carried the burden of rebuttal. He pointed out, "with merciless frankness," that the struggle was hopeless against the Allies' overwhelming superiority in the air, at sea and on land. There was but one chance: to abandon the suicidal policy of holding onto every meter of ground and abruptly withdraw German forces so that all armored forces could be reorganized for a decisive battle to be fought outside the range of the withering enemy naval fire. Hitler answered by assuring his commanders that his new rocket bombs "would make the British willing to make peace." This was a sore subject to Rundstedt and Rommel, whose request to use these bombs against English south coast ports supplying the invasion had been declined by Hitler on the grounds that all rockets must be concentrated on a political target. The two field marshals confined themselves to criticism of the Luftwaffe: how could one win on the ground without a minimum of help from the air? Hitler's answer was that "masses of jet fighters" would soon sweep the skies clear of American and British planes. He neglected to explain that, against the vigorous opposition of Milch, the jet plane in production was a hybrid fighter-bomber which was efficient at neither task.

The distant drone of approaching enemy planes forced adjournment to an elaborate underground concrete bunker. The change of venue encouraged Rommel to become even more forceful. The West, he said, would inevitably smash through the Normandy front and break into the homeland. Hitler listened with compressed lips as Rommel further predicted that the eastern front would also collapse and the Reich would become politically isolated. He urgently requested, therefore, that the war be brought to an end. "Don't you worry about the future course of the war," Hitler interrupted sharply. "Look to your own invasion front."

During a break for a one-dish lunch, two SS men standing guard behind the Führer's chair tested his plate of rice and vegetables before he would take a bite. It was, concluded Speidel, visible proof of his distrust of the military. Moments after the meeting ended a V-1 bound for London erratically reversed itself and exploded on top of their bunker. Uninjured, Hitler set off at once for his refuge on the Obersalzberg, arriving in a bad temper to announce: "Rommel has lost his nerve; he's become a pessimist. In these times only optimists can achieve anything."

Within two days he received a despairing phone call from another pessimist. Rundstedt explained that the Americans had broken through and were pushing across the Cotentin Peninsula. Unless German forces hastily pulled out of Cherbourg they would be cut off. "The fortress of

Cherbourg is to be held at all cost," replied the Führer, then gave sensible permission for the defenders to withdraw at the last possible moment to avoid capture.

His compromise did not mean that Hitler was weakening in his own resolve, despite disheartening news from his one strong ally. The Japanese had just been dealt a crushing blow in the Battle of the Philippine Sea, losing 3 heavy cruisers and 475 planes. Hitler's nerves remained steady in the face of defeat on all sides, exhibiting composure that amazed his family circle. Nor was it true that he no longer listened to any voice of criticism. During the late evening conference of June 23 General Dietl, incensed at the Führer's derisive comments about the Finns surrendering to Russia, smashed a fist on the table. "Mein Führer, now I must talk to you like a Bavarian!" he exclaimed in dialect and accused Hitler of speaking unjustly. To everyone's amazement, Hitler told Dietl he was absolutely correct, bade him a warm farewell, then turned to the others and said, "Gentlemen, I wish all my generals were like that."

He had shown similar respect for Admiral Dönitz from the first day of his appointment as navy chief when he, with equal frankness, had vigorously opposed a Hitler proposal. From that moment Hitler treated him with marked civility and heard him out with unlimited confidence. During this season of anxiety the Führer would even take criticism from his youngest secretary. One day while watching him examine photographs of air raids Traudl Junge could not help saying that pictures could never portray the true misery of reality. He should go out just once and see the people "warm their hands on the charred rafters as all their possessions go up in smoke." Hitler was not at all angry. "I know how it is," he said with a sigh. "But I'm going to change everything. We have built new planes and soon this whole nightmare will come to an end!"

One group he stubbornly refused to hear out were his field commanders in Normandy and as a result the situation there was beyond repair. On June 26 Cherbourg fell to American troops. Largely because of Hitler's abiding fear of a main invasion at Calais and Ultra intercepts, which were often read in London within minutes of their origin, Germany had no hope of regaining the initiative. With her armies now dedicated to a dreary, enervating period of purely passive resistance, the Third Reich faced catastrophe.

In the coffee room of the Hotel Platterhof, just above the Berghof, a disconcerted, somewhat absent-minded Führer was assuring a hundred representatives of the armaments industry of the inviolability of private property and the retention of free enterprise. Near the close of his uneasy speech, Hitler promised to show his gratitude to businessmen "again and

again" once peace returned but there was so little applause that he concluded with a threat: "There is no doubt that if we were to lose this war,
German private business would not survive." If defeat came, he said
derisively, his listeners would not have to worry about shifting to a peace-
time economy. "Then all anyone will have to think about is how he himself will accomplish his shift from this world to the hereafter. Whether he
wants to take care of it himself, or let himself be hanged, or whether he
prefers to starve or to labor in Siberia—these are some of the questions
which the individual will have to face."

Three days later Hitler summoned Rundstedt and Rommel to the
Berghof. He refused to consider the latter's suggestion that he fight a rearguard action back to the Seine so that the armies in southern France
could be withdrawn and help create a new line along the river all the way
to Switzerland. Instead he spoke optimistically of another offensive. There
would be no general withdrawals, nor even tactical adjustments of the
line.

The war would be won by new miracle weapons, he said, in a monologue that struck Rundstedt's chief of staff as one "lost in fantastic digres-
sions." The two field marshals, committed to a futile policy of aggressive
and obstinate defense, left the meeting disgruntled. Keitel shared their
dejection and admitted resignedly to Rommel, "I, too, know there is nothing to be done."

Within two days Hitler's counterattack failed miserably and inspired
Rundstedt to warn Keitel that this was the writing on the wall. "Then
what shall we do?" asked Keitel. "What shall we do?" "Make peace, you
fools!" exploded Rundstedt. "What else can you do?" Keitel reported this
to Hitler, who chanced to be talking to Field Marshal Günther von Kluge.
On the spur of the moment he put Kluge in charge of the western front
and wrote Rundstedt a polite and proper letter of dismissal.

4

"Nothing works against the success of a conspiracy so much as the
wish to make it wholly secure and certain to succeed. Such an attempt
requires many men, much time and very favorable conditions. And
all these in turn heighten the risk of being discovered. You see, therefore, how dangerous conspiracies are!"

FRANCESCO GUICCIARDINI
Ricordi (1528–30)

The men who had already tried in vain to destroy Hitler's plane with
brandy bottles filled with explosives or to blow him up with bombs con-

cealed in an overcoat were not at all deterred by failure. They made four more attempts between September 1943 and February 11, 1944. First a general, Helmuth Stieff by name, attempted to plant a time bomb to go off during a noon conference at Wolfsschanze but lost his nerve at the last moment. A month later an infantry captain, Bussche, agreed to blow up himself and Hitler while demonstrating a new army coat, but fate in the form of an enemy aerial bomb intervened. The day before the demonstration the model coats were destroyed in a British air raid and Bussche was returned to the front.

The day after Christmas, 1944, another young front-line officer entered the noon conference with a briefcase containing a bomb. For some reason the meeting was canceled at the last moment. A few weeks later another "overcoat" attempt was made. This time the volunteer model was Ewald Heinrich von Kleist, son of one of the original conspirators. Again the RAF saved Hitler, an air raid just before the demonstration forcing its cancellation.

This last failure was followed a fortnight later by a crippling blow to the Resistance. Hitler ordered Himmler to amalgamate the Abwehr and the SD. This meant the virtual destruction of the heart of the conspiracy. General Oster had already been dismissed on suspicion. Although he was at liberty he was too closely watched to be of use. It seemed as though fate indeed was protecting Hitler and a sense of hopelessness permeated the ranks of the conspirators. This might have been the end of their secret war against Hitler but for the inspiration of a new leader, Count Claus Schenk von Stauffenberg, a staff officer with the rank of lieutenant colonel. A great-grandson of Gneisenau, a military hero in the war of liberation against Napoleon, Stauffenberg had abandoned plans to become an architect and entered the Reichswehr in 1926. Like so many other German officers, he applauded Hitler's introduction of conscription, approved the Anschluss with Austria as well as the occupation of Czechoslovakia, and was caught up in the glory of victory in Holland and France. It was Barbarossa that destroyed his illusions. He heartily approved Rosenberg's attempt to free the non-Russian peoples of the Soviet Union and, after this policy was superseded by oppression and murder, he told a fellow officer that the only solution for Germany now was to kill the Führer. By chance he met resistance leaders who had no trouble enlisting him in their cause. His role, however, seemed short-lived; his car ran over a mine and he lost an eye, his right hand and two fingers of the other hand. Almost any other man would have retired, but Stauffenberg was convinced that he alone could assassinate Hitler and was back on duty late in 1943. It was he who had brought the bomb in the briefcase to the Führer conference the day after Christmas. The failure spurred him to a similar but more ambitious plan. This time assassination would be followed by a well-planned military take-over in Berlin, Paris and Vienna.

His new position as chief of staff to the commander of the General Army Office in Berlin made it possible for him to rebuild the weakened ranks of the conspiracy. He seized the reins from the tired, older leaders and, by the dynamism of his personality, got definite commitments from a powerful group in the Wehrmacht: his own chief, the first quartermaster general of the army, the chief of signals at OKW, the general whose troops would take over Berlin after the assassination, and other key officers of middle rank.

As yet, however, not a single field marshal wholeheartedly supported the plot. Kluge was a dubious factor and Manstein refused to commit himself prematurely since he felt "any such coup d'état would collapse the eastern front." The most promising candidate was Rommel but even he had reservations. "I believe it is my duty to come to the rescue of Germany," he said—but opposed assassination. It would only make Hitler a martyr. The Führer should be arrested by the army and brought before a German court to answer for his crimes.

Rommel was brought deeper into the plot during the spring of 1944 by his new chief of staff, Lieutenant General Dr. Hans Speidel, a soldier-philosopher who had received his doctorate in philosophy summa cum laude from the University of Tübingen. Speidel persuaded Rommel to meet secretly with General Karl Stülpnagel, military governor of France, in a country home near Paris. Here the two men, with the help of their energetic chiefs of staff, worked out a plan to end war in the West by an armistice. All German troops would retire into Germany and the Allies would cease bombing the homeland. Hitler would be arrested, with the resistance forces temporarily taking over the country. In the meantime the war in the East would continue, the assumption being that American and British troops would join the crusade against Bolshevism. Rommel was now so enthusiastic, he tried to involve Rundstedt in the plot but, while approving it, he refused to be personally involved. "You are young," Rundstedt said. "You know and love the people. *You* do it."

Stauffenberg and his group were not too pleased with the entrance of Rommel into the conspiracy, for they considered him a Nazi who was only deserting Hitler because the war was lost. They also disapproved of the plan to continue fighting Russia, and felt it was unrealistic to expect the West would make a separate peace. Further, the Stauffenberg circle was dedicated to assassination rather than arrest and by the first of June 1944 they felt it had to be done before the Allied invasion. Once enemy forces overran the homeland there would be no possibility for any decent kind of peace. By now they had a definite scenario for a coup d'état based, ironically, on a measure approved by the Führer himself. The official operation was entitled Walküre and was Hitler's plan to put down any unrest among the millions of war and foreign slave workers employed in Germany. It called for a proclamation of a state of emergency and instant mobilization of adequate forces to quell any uprising. Stauffenberg's scheme was to use the Walküre alert as the signal to start their own coup throughout the Reich and on every battle front. Hitler had specified that the orders to issue the Walküre alert be issued by the commander of the Reserve Army, General Friedrich Fromm—who was flirting halfheartedly with the idea of joining the Resistance.

D-Day caused consternation among the conspirators. The older ones argued that even a successful coup would not save Germany from enemy occupation. It was best to rely on the West to treat Germany decently and prevent Russia from ravaging the homeland. But Stauffenberg was resolved to make one final assassination attempt and chance almost immediately took a hand. He was promoted to full colonel and made Fromm's chief of staff. Now the coup did not depend on such a dubious factor. Stauffenberg himself could issue orders directly to the Reserve Army and thus seize Berlin. The new post also gave him frequent access to the Führer. He made plans to act early in July: he would report to the Führer at the daily conference, plant a time bomb which would blow up Göring and Himmler as well as the Führer, then fly back to Berlin and personally direct the military take-over of the capital.

His confederates at General Staff headquarters were inspired by the assured way he organized the complicated plan. "It was a pleasure," recalled one young lieutenant, Urban Thiersch, a sculptor, "to watch him conduct the telephone conversations—giving brief and definite orders, behaving with natural courtesy toward important people, and always in command of the situation."

Stauffenberg's chance came at last on July 11 when Hitler summoned him to report on replacements. He arrived at the Berghof with a briefcase carrying official papers and an English bomb but, to his dismay, Himmler was not in the conference room. He excused himself to phone the huge General Staff building on the Bendlerstrasse near Berlin's Tiergarten. "Shouldn't we do it anyhow?" he asked the chief of the General Army Office, General Olbricht. The bomb could still kill both Hitler and Göring. Olbricht advised him to wait until he could kill all three at once.

The opportunity came in four days; Stauffenberg was again ordered to see Hitler, who had moved his headquarters to Wolfsschanze. He arrived with bomb in briefcase and this time the conspirators were so sure of success that General Olbricht issued the orders for Operation Walküre at 11 A.M., two hours before the scheduled conference. This would give the troops of the Reserve Army and the tanks from the nearby Panzer school time to move into the capital by early afternoon.

At exactly 1:10 P.M. the conference began. Stauffenberg briefly reported to the Führer, then left the room to telephone the Bendlerstrasse that Hitler was in the room and he was going back to plant the bomb. But on his return he discovered that Hitler had left for some reason and would not be back. It took Stauffenberg another quarter of an hour to excuse himself again and warn Berlin. By this time it was 1:30 P.M. and troops were already converging on Berlin. Olbricht hurriedly canceled the Walküre alarm and the units on march were returned to their barracks as inconspicuously as possible.

Some of the conspirators were discouraged and shaken by this latest fiasco but not Stauffenberg. He met with younger colleagues at his home in Wannsee and they heard an encouraging report from a cousin of Stauffenberg, who was their liaison with the Rommel-Speidel group in France. An imminent Allied breakthrough was expected, he said, and Rommel was determined to support the conspiracy no matter what Rundstedt's replacement, Marshal von Kluge, did. But again fate intervened on behalf of Hitler. The very next day Rommel was badly injured when his car was strafed by Allied planes.

The staff returning to the Wolfsschanze could hardly recognize the area. In place of small, low bunkers were colossal concrete and iron structures, their roofs cleverly camouflaged by transplanted grass and trees. It was so hot that Hitler spent most of his time in the new bunkers, which were much cooler than the wooden barracks. "He was in a bad mood," recalled Traudl Junge, "and complained about sleeplessness and headache." The adjutants did their best to divert him with amusing guests. Hoffmann, who drank more than ever, had become a bore but Professor Giesler, the architect, never failed to bring a smile with his clever imitations. Hitler may have been short-tempered during these sultry days, but he gave the appearance of optimism. He assured Goebbels (who had resumed smoking and was resorting to sleeping pills) that the pendulum of history was about to swing back in favor of Germany.

5

On the afternoon of July 18 Stauffenberg received a summons from Wolfsschanze to report in two days. He was to brief Hitler on replacements that might be thrown into the battle in the East, where the central front was in peril of imminent collapse following recent defeats on both flanks. Stauffenberg spent the nineteenth at the Bendlerstrasse making last-minute preparations and that afternoon presided over a final conference of conspirators. The signals for the following day were hastly arranged; it was agreed that most of the messages would be passed orally in a prearranged sequence. Code words would be used on telephone and teleprinter and would be reserved for important matters since the entire system of communications was tapped by the Gestapo.

The conspirators knew this since their number included several Gestapo officials, including the SS general who had taken over the Gestapo main office in Berlin. There was, in fact, considerable anti-Hitler feeling throughout the SS. General Felix Steiner, for instance, had already evolved a vague plan of his own to kidnap the Führer, then "declare him mentally deranged," and with other Waffen SS commanders had recently assured Rommel of support in any revolt against Hitler. The hierarchy of the SD itself was infected with rebellion. Secretly the head of the Foreign Intelligence Service, Schellenberg, was as eager as the army conspirators to get rid of Hitler in the interest of German survival. In late 1942 he had inveigled Himmler into endorsing a secret plan to bring about a separate peace with the West at the price, if need be, of betraying Hitler. With Himmler's approval Carl Langbehn, a civilian member of the Resistance, met with British and American representatives in Stockholm to explore the chances of peace negotiations; then journeyed to Bern so he could personally confer with the German-born assistant of Allen Dulles, the OSS representative in Switzerland. At this point everything went wrong. The Gestapo chanced to intercept and decode a radio message which revealed that "Himmler's lawyer" had arrived in Switzerland to talk peace, and sent it directly to Hitler. Face to face with the Führer, Himmler swore eternal loyalty—and complete innocence. Hitler chose to believe him, probably because his services were so vital. The Reichsführer, on his part, arrested Langbehn, sent him to a concentration camp and promptly broke off all relations with members of the Resistance lest his master investigate further. Schellenberg, on the other hand, continued to plot, becoming involved with American military men in Spain, in an elaborate operation worthy of a spy novel to kidnap Hitler and turn him over to the Allies.

Incredibly, neither Schellenberg nor Himmler was aware on July 19 that the underground army plot was about to materialize. They knew about the resistance efforts of the conservative officials, retired officers, right-wing Christian intellectuals and socialist politicians but never even suspected Stauffenberg and his circle of younger officers. Several months earlier Schellenberg had consulted Wilhelm Wulff, one of the astrologers on the SS payroll, about a possible removal of Hitler. Wulff said that a mere deposition from office would not change the course of events. "Far too much has happened for that. I have been studying Hitler's horoscope for twenty years now. I have a pretty clear idea of what is ultimately in store for him. He will probably die under the hand of an assassin, certainly in 'Neptunian'—that is enigmatic—circumstances, in which a woman will play a part. The world will probably never know the precise details of his death, for in Hitler's horoscope Neptune has long been in bad aspect to other planets. Moreover, Neptune is extremely strong in his horoscope, and it was always to be expected that his great military projects would have a dubious outcome."

At the Bendlerstrasse late on the afternoon of the nineteenth Stauffenberg completed arrangements for the next day's operation. He instructed his driver, who knew nothing at all about the plot, to collect a briefcase from a certain colonel in Potsdam. It contained, Stauffenberg explained, two very important and confidential packages and was not to be left out of sight. As instructed, the chauffeur kept the case next to his bed that night. It held two bombs.

During evening tea at Wolfsschanze, Hitler was so nervous and uneasy that Fräulein Schröder asked why he was so preoccupied. "I hope nothing is going to happen to me," he replied cryptically. After an awkward silence, he said, "It would be too much if something troublesome happened now. I cannot allow myself to fall ill, since there is no one who can replace me in the difficult situation Germany finds herself in."

July 20, 1944

Shortly after 6 A.M. Stauffenberg was driven from his home to the city. Here he was joined by his adjutant, a lieutenant. At Rangsdorf airfield they met General Stieff and all boarded a plane provided by the quartermaster general. It touched down at the air base near Rastenburg at 10:15 A.M. The pilot was instructed to stand by until noon to take the passengers back to Berlin.

After half an hour's drive through woods, the three conspirators were passed through the first gate of Führer Headquarters. They proceeded through minefields and a ring of fortifications for almost two miles to a second gate. This opened into a large compound surrounded by electrified barbed wire. After another mile they reached the officers' checkpoint. As usual their passes were examined but not their briefcases. In two hundred yards they arrived at a third enclosure. This was Security Ring A, where Hitler and his staff lived and worked. This innermost compound, surrounded by a barbed-wire fence, was constantly patrolled by SS guards and Secret Service personnel. To enter, a field marshal himself needed a special pass issued by Himmler's chief of security, but again the shiny briefcase containing the bombs was not inspected.

While his adjutant took charge of this case, Stauffenberg carried another containing official papers. He proceeded nonchalantly to a mess hall where he had a leisurely breakfast with the camp commander's adjutant. Outwardly unperturbed and casual in bearing, he later sought out General Fellgiebel, OKW chief of signals, the key to success once the bomb exploded. It was his task to inform the Berlin conspirators that it was time to act, then to isolate Wolfsschanze by cutting all telephone, telegraph and radio communications.

Assured that Fellgiebel was ready to do his part, Stauffenberg chatted briefly with another OKW officer and at noon strolled over to the office of Keitel. The field marshal greeted him with slightly disconcerting news: since Mussolini was due to arrive that afternoon, the midday situation conference would start half an hour earlier—in just thirty minutes. Keitel urged Stauffenberg to keep his report brief since the Führer wanted to leave as soon as possible. Keitel kept glancing impatiently at the clock and, just before 12:30 P.M., said it was time to walk over to the conference barracks. In the hallway Stauffenberg approached Keitel's adjutant, Ernst John von Freyend, and asked where he could clean up. He was directed to a nearby lavatory. His own adjutant was waiting here with the brown briefcase. It was not a suitable place to arm the bombs so they returned to the hall and asked Freyend where the colonel could change his shirt. Freyend took them to his own bedroom and left them alone. Stauffenberg grasped a pair of tongs in the three fingers of his only hand and began shoving in the fuse of one bomb. This crushed a glass capsule containing acid which would eat through a thin wire within fifteen minutes and set off the bomb. His adjutant was entrusted with the second "back-up" bomb.

No sooner was the armed bomb carefully packed in the brown briefcase than a sergeant entered to hurry them up and from the hall Freyend shouted, 'Come on, Stauffenberg! The Chief is waiting." As Stauffenberg left the room Freyend suggested he carry the brown briefcase tucked under the colonel's one good arm. Stauffenberg declined the offer and they set out on the short walk along a path to the conference barracks. The two talked casually as they passed through the checkpoint to the Security Ring. Upon nearing their destination, Freyend once more offered to relieve Stauffenberg of his burden and this time he accepted with a request: "Could you place me as closely as possible to the Führer so I can understand everything?" His hearing was impaired.

Keitel was waiting impatiently at the doorway. The conference was already under way. He led the way down the central corridor of the building past the telephone room and into the conference room through a double-winged door. There were ten or so windows and all were open against the sultry midday heat. The conferees gathered around a long, narrow oak map table, notable for its thick top and two massive supports. Only Hitler was sitting, his back to the door, at the middle of the table. A pair of spectacles rested on the map. He toyed with a magnifying glass as General Adolf Heusinger, standing to his immediate right, read out a glum report on the eastern front. Hitler looked at the newcomers, acknowledged their salutes. Stauffenberg moved to the other side of Heusinger, then casually shoved the brown briefcase under the table as close to Hitler as possible. The case leaned against the inside of the heavy oaken support only six feet from the Führer. It was twelve thirty-seven and in five minutes the bomb would explode. The others were so engrossed by Heusinger's tale of doom that Stauffenberg managed to sidle out of the room without being noticed. He hurried down the long corridor and out of the building.

Heusinger was also on the periphery of the anti-Hitler conspiracy but knew none of the details of the plot. When he saw Stauffenberg enter it hadn't occurred to him that anything was awry since the conspirators had promised to warn him when the next assassination attempt would take place. But he happened to glance down just as Stauffenberg shoved the brown briefcase under the table and thought fleetingly: "Something might happen!" But under Hitler's absorbed attention, Heusinger's suspicion evaporated almost as soon as it was aroused. His aide leaned over the conference table to get a better look at the map but was impeded by the brown briefcase. He couldn't budge it with his foot so leaned down and transferred it to the *outside* of the heavy table support. It was a trivial move which would alter the course of history.

Admiral von Puttkamer had moved to a window to get some air and was perched on the sill debating whether he should quietly leave and change to his best trousers for the Mussolini visit. It was twelve forty-one. The Führer was intently leaning far over the table to check the map. Heusinger was saying, "Unless at long last the army group is withdrawn from Peipus, a catastrophe . . ."

At exactly 12:42 P.M. his words were obliterated by a deafening roar. Flames shot up and a hail of glass splinters, timber and plaster rained down. Smoke erupted in the room. Puttkamer had felt a strange jerk a split second before the explosion. Falling down, he saw the heater under the window and thought, "My God, it exploded!" then realized this was nonsense; it was summer. Maybe it was a plot by the foreign laborers who were working on the construction. Dazed as he was, he realized the best thing was to remain on the floor. Then he heard someone shout, "Fire!" and scrambled for the door. It was lying flat on the floor and he leaped over it. Suddenly he wondered where everyone else was and turned to locate the Führer. Just then Hitler, trousers in tatters, face blackened by soot, came toward him with Keitel. Both men were covered with dust and wood fiber. They passed him as if sleepwalking and he realized he could hardly breathe the acid air. He followed Hitler and Keitel down the long corridor. Outside a knee gave way and he collapsed on the ground. He gulped air greedily and saw Hitler and Keitel heading toward the Führer bunker, followed by some third person.

SS Adjutant Günsche didn't even hear the explosion. His eardrums had burst. His forehead bled, his eyebrows were burned off. The room was black with smoke; the floor had buckled up at least three feet. "Where is the Führer?" he wondered. With the instinct of a soldier, he scrambled out a shattered window and hurried to the other side of the building just as Keitel and Hitler were emerging. The Führer's trousers were in tatters, his hair tousled, but there was no blood in sight. "*Was ist los?*" asked Hitler as Günsche helped guide him down the path. A bomb from a Russian plane?

Upon leaving the conference room, Stauffenberg had hurried to the OKW Signals Office in Bunker 88. He and General Fellgiebel stood outside waiting for the bomb to explode. They were talking as unconcernedly as possible when the headquarters signal officer reported that Stauffenberg's car was ready, then reminded him that the headquarters commandant was expecting him for lunch. Stauffenberg confirmed the invitation but said he would first have to return to the conference. Just then came an explosion.

"What's happening?" exclaimed Fellgiebel and the signals officer nonchalantly explained that some animal must have set off another land mine. Stauffenberg now contradicted himself. He said he was *not* going back to the conference but would drive directly to the commandant's for lunch. He bade Fellgiebel a knowing farewell and set off with his adjutant in the car. Moments later their driver, wondering why Stauffenberg wore neither hat nor belt, pulled to a stop at the first checkpoint. The guard there had closed the gates upon hearing the explosion and refused to open them. Without a word, Stauffenberg hurried to the guard room and asked the lieutenant on duty, an acquaintance, for use of the telephone. He dialed, said a few quiet words, replaced the receiver and said calmly, "Lieutenant, I am allowed to pass." The barrier was opened without question and at 12:44 P.M. the Stauffenberg party was through the gate.

Ninety seconds later an alarm was sounded and Stauffenberg could not talk his way through the next barrier. A sergeant major of the guard battalion refused flatly to let any car pass. Once more Stauffenberg used the phone, this time calling the camp commandant's aide. "Colonel Count von Stauffenberg speaking," he said, "from outer Checkpoint South. Captain, you'll remember we had breakfast together this morning. Because of the explosion the guard refused to let me pass. I'm in a hurry." Then he told a lie. "Colonel General Fromm is waiting for me at the airfield." He hastily hung up. "You heard, Sergeant Major, I'm allowed through." But the sergeant major could not be bluffed. He telephoned for confirmation and, to Stauffenberg's relief, got it.

It was almost 1 P.M. by the time Stauffenberg and his adjutant drove up to their Heinkel 111. Moments later they were in the air. Ahead lay a three-hour flight. There was nothing to do but worry since the plane's radio did not have the range to hear any announcements from Berlin. Had Fellgiebel gotten the word through to the conspirators in the Bendlerstrasse? If so, would they have the resolve to seize the capital and send out the prepared messages to the military commanders on the western front?

Hitler would probably have been killed had not the brown briefcase been shifted to the outer side of the table support. It was also fortunate for the Führer that the door behind him led to a long narrow hallway through which the main force of the explosion escaped. Again, luck, incredible luck, had saved Adolf Hitler.

Doctors and rescue workers were in action minutes after the explosion. Ambulances took the seriously wounded to the field hospital at Rastenburg. Dr. Hanskarl von Hasselbach, the Führer's personal physician, was the first to treat him. He bandaged Hitler's wounds, then put his right arm—the elbow was rather badly sprained—in a sling. "Now I have those fellows!" he exclaimed with more glee than anger. "Now I can take steps!"

Dr. Morell arrived, examined Hitler's heart and administered an injection. The patient was in a state of ecstasy, repeating over and over, "Think of it. Nothing has happened to me. Just think of it." To Morell's amazement his pulse was normal. The three secretaries rushed in to see with their own eyes that the Führer still lived. Traudl Junge almost burst into laughter at the sight of his hair, which stood on end like a porcupine's. He greeted them with his left hand. "Well, my ladies," he said with a smile, "once again everything turned out well for me. More proof that Fate has selected me for my mission. Otherwise I wouldn't be alive." He was talkative, blaming the plot on a "coward," undoubtedly one of the construction workers. "I don't believe *in any other possibility*," he emphasized, turning to Bormann for confirmation. As usual Bormann nodded.

The next to arrive with congratulations was Himmler. He too thought laborers had built the bomb into the barracks. It took an amateur to set the trail straight. Valet Linge went to the conference barracks and learned from the sergeant in charge of the telephone room that Stauffenberg had been expecting an urgent call from Berlin. Then someone recalled that the colonel had left a briefcase under the table. A telephone call to the airstrip revealed that Stauffenberg had left hastily for Berlin a little after 1 P.M. Hitler now had no doubts that Stauffenberg alone was responsible. He ordered his arrest.

This order never was transmitted to Berlin because of a curious set of circumstances. Moments after the explosion one of Hitler's adjutants ordered the headquarters signals officer Colonel Sander, to cut all telephone and teleprinter communications. He did so, then told Chief Signals Officer Fellgiebel what he had done. Fellgiebel, whose assignment as a conspirator was to isolate Führer Headquarters, solemnly agreed that proper action had been taken by Sander but upon discovering, moments later, that Hitler was not dead, the general called his own office. "Something frightful has happened," he told his chief of staff. "The Führer is *alive*. Block *everything!*" The chief of staff understood the odd message, for he too was a conspirator. Within minutes the major switch centers at *both* Führer and army headquarters went dead.

This communication blackout gave the conspirators in Berlin time to seize the capital, but they failed to act since confusion was the order of the day at the Bendlerstrasse. The plotters, uncertain whether Hitler had been killed or not, were reluctant to activate Operation Walküre. The information from Wolfsschanze was too vague to risk a repetition of the false alarm of July 15.

And so everyone stood about nervously at the general staff building, waiting for Stauffenberg, who was still half an hour's flight away. The two titular leaders of the conspiracy, General Beck and Field Marshal von Witzleben, should have been issuing the prepared proclamation and commands. They should have been broadcasting to the nation that the end of Hitler's tyranny had come at last. But neither man had yet arrived at the Bendlerstrasse.

Perhaps it was the weather. The sky was murky, the air heavy. One conspirator noted glumly that it was no weather for a revolution but someone pointed out that the French had stormed the Bastille on an equally oppressive day in July. Precious time passed as the conspirators waited for further word from Fellgiebel at Wolfsschanze. None came.

Hitler refused to rest before the midday meal. He insisted on taking a walk all by himself and made a point of chatting with the construction workers he had first suspected. Watching from a distance, his SS adjutant guessed he wanted to show that he was still alive and let everyone know he no longer thought the workers were involved. At lunch Fräulein Schröder was surprised to find his countenance youthful and calm even under the dazzling light of bare electric bulbs in the spartan dining room. Without prompting he told in detail what had happened. "I had incredible luck," he said and explained how he had been protected by the heavy table support. He proudly exhibited his shredded trousers. If the explosion had occurred in the large conference room of the bunker and not in a wooden barracks, he was sure all would have been killed. "A curious thing. For some time I had a presentiment that something extraordinary was going to happen."

After the meal he was driven to the small railroad platform adjoining the Wolfsschanze. The sky was overcast and the few scattered raindrops failed to bring any relief to the sultry afternoon. He paced the platform, cap pulled down over face, black cape swirling behind him, until Mussolini's train pulled in. His guest seemed a ghost of himself; he had managed to form a new Fascist regime, but in so doing he had been forced by Hitler to execute a number of "traitors," including his own son-in-law, Ciano. The Führer was thinking only of the events of the day. "Duce," he said excitedly, extending his left hand, "a few hours ago I experienced the greatest piece of good fortune I have ever known!" He insisted on taking his guest immediately to the scene of the crime. On the three-minute drive Hitler told him what had happened "almost in a monotone as though he had no part in it."

The two men silently surveyed the wrecked conference room. As Mussolini took a chair Hitler seated himself on a box and, with the expertise of a guide at the ruins of Rome, explained exactly what had happened. Mussolini's eyes rolled in wonderment. Then Hitler displayed his tattered trousers and rather lightheartedly remarked he was saddened by the damage to a new pair of pants. Mussolini forced a laugh. Hitler then showed the back of his head where the hair was singed.

Mussolini was horrified. How could such a thing happen at Führer Headquarters? Hitler was exhilarated. He told again how other conferees were badly injured and one was blown out of the window. "Look at my uniform! Look at my burns!" He told of his other narrow escapes from assassination attempts. "What happened here today is the climax!" he exclaimed. This last miraculous escape from death was surely a sign that the great cause he served would survive its present peril. Infected by such enthusiasm, Mussolini brightened. "Our position is bad," he said, "one might almost say desperate, but what has happened here today gives me new courage."

They walked out of the wreckage down the path to resume discussion at tea. On the way Hitler walked over to a wire fence and once more began talking with the workers. He told them his first suspicions were unfounded and his investigators had found the real culprit. At the tea house his mood abruptly changed. He was restless, distracted, and—communications having been partially reopened—his conversation with Il Duce was frequently interrupted by telephone calls from generals who wanted to know if the report of his death was true. Hitler lapsed into moody suspicious silence. He sat staring ahead, sucking brightly colored pills, ignoring an angry argument among Göring, Keitel and Ribbentrop, each claiming the other's mistakes had led to Germany's desperate situation. The wrangle took a new twist once Admiral Dönitz, just arrived from his command post north of Berlin, accused the army of treason. When Göring chorused agreement, Dönitz turned his wrath on the miserable performance of the Luftwaffe. Ribbentrop chimed in but the Reichsmarschall raised his baton as if to thrash him. "Shut up, Ribbentrop, you champagne salesman!" "I'm still Foreign Minister," he retorted, "and my name is *von* Ribbentrop!"

Light rain pattered unceasingly on the windowpanes. Only mention of the Röhm Putsch brought Hitler to life. He leaned forward and began to repeat that he was the child of Fate. He got to his feet in a burst of anger. "Traitors in the bosom of their own people deserve the most ignominious of deaths—and they shall have it!" His voice rasped menacingly. "Exterminate them, yes, exterminate them!" His rage disappeared as rapidly as it had come. He was suddenly empty as the vision of vengeance faded. His eyes were drained, his face ashen.

Mussolini must have felt with his Italian flair that it was up to him to save the situation. He laid a hand on Hitler's and looked at him with a gentle smile. This brought the Führer out of his reverie. Someone had opened the outside door. Hitler sent for Il Duce's coat, explaining that a fresh east wind usually sprang up in the afternoon. He did not want his guest to catch cold. Mussolini replied in Italian, "At a time like this, a Duce does not catch cold!" But he put on his heavy army overcoat.

At 3:42 P.M. Stauffenberg finally landed at an airport outside Berlin. To his surprise, no one was waiting, friend or foe. His aide telephoned the

Bendlerstrasse, got General Olbricht and gave the code word signifying that the assassination attempt had succeeded. Olbricht's vague reply made it clear that Walküre had not even been activated. Stauffenberg seized the phone, demanded they do so without waiting for his arrival. He commandeered a Luftwaffe car to take him to Berlin.

Only at 3:50 P.M. did Olbricht act. The Wehrmacht commandant of Berlin, General Kortzfleisch, was ordered to alert all units of the guard battalion, the Spandau garrison and two army weapons training schools. Kortzfleisch, who was not in the plot, did so.

To speed matters, General Olbricht personally alerted General von Hase, the Berlin garrison commander, another conspirator. By 4:10 P.M. his troops were ready to march. So were those outside Berlin. At the Bendlerstrasse itself the guards were alerted and their commander orally instructed by Olbricht to use force if any SS units tried to enter. Within minutes transit traffic was stopped, all exits blocked.

Olbricht was now doing what he should have been doing three hours earlier. He burst in on General Fromm, who was neither all the way in nor all the way out of the conspiracy, and explained that Hitler was really dead. He urged Fromm, as commander of the Replacement Army, to issue the Walküre alert to the military district commanders. Fromm, an ambitious man with a grand manner, hesitated as he had been doing for months. He insisted on telephoning Keitel for assurance that Hitler was dead.

"Everything is as usual here," said Keitel from the tea house, and when Fromm said that he had just received a report that the Führer had been assassinated, he exploded. "That's all nonsense." The Führer was alive and only slightly injured. "Where, by the way, is your chief of staff, Colonel von Stauffenberg?" The agitated Fromm replied that the colonel had not yet reported to him—and silently resigned from the conspiracy.

A few minutes later most of the conspirators were congregated in Olbricht's large office waiting anxiously for Stauffenberg. Someone announced excitedly that he had just driven into the courtyard! In moments the colonel bounded energetically into the room, bringing with him a spirit of enthusiasm and confidence. Stauffenberg told what he had seen —a great explosion, flames and smoke. "As far as one can judge," he said, "Hitler is dead." They must act decisively without wasting another moment! Even if Hitler was alive they should do their utmost to overthrow the regime. Beck agreed.

Stauffenberg put through a call to his cousin at General von Stülpnagel's headquarters in Paris. He told about the explosion. "The way to action is open!" he said. The good news sent Stülpnagel into motion. He ordered senior signals officers in France to cut all radio and telephone communications between France and Germany except those lines needed for their own traffic with Berlin.

Back at the Bendlerstrasse, Stauffenberg was doing his utmost to bring General Fromm back into the conspiracy. He assured him that Hitler was truly dead, but Fromm repeated what Keitel had said. "Field Marshal Keitel is lying as usual," said Stauffenberg and proceeded to lie. "I myself saw Hitler being carried out dead."

"In view of this," cut in Olbricht, "we have sent out the code signal for internal unrest to the military district commanders." Fromm leaped from his chair, a startling act for such a huge, ponderous man. He banged the table and shouted in his best parade ground manner. "This is rank insubordination. What do you mean by 'we'?" He ordered the Walküre alert canceled.

Stauffenberg made another attempt to convince Fromm that Hitler was dead. "No one in that room can still be alive," he argued but Fromm was not impressed. "Count von Stauffenberg," he said, "the attempt has failed. You must shoot yourself at once." Stauffenberg refused and Olbricht added his plea to strike now. Otherwise the Fatherland would be ruined forever. Fromm turned on him. "Olbricht, does this mean that you, too, are taking part in the coup d'état?" "Yes, sir. But I am only on the fringe of the circle."

Fromm glared down from his height at Olbricht. "Then I formally put all three of you under arrest." Olbricht was not cowed. He returned the glare. "You can't arrest us. You don't realize who's in power. It's we who are arresting you." The two generals went from words to blows. Stauffenberg intervened and in the scuffle was struck in the face. Big Fromm was subdued only under threat of a drawn pistol. He was placed under arrest and locked in the next room. By 5 P.M. guards were posted at all entrances to the huge building, as well as the bombed area in the rear. Everyone entering now needed an orange pass signed by Stauffenberg; no one could leave without a similar pass or signed orders.

6

Although the Bendlerstrasse was at last under the complete control of the conspirators, their comrade, General von Hase, was in deep trouble at his office on Unter den Linden. An hour earlier, as commandant of the Berlin Garrison, he had ordered the guard battalion to seal off the government quarter; not a general or minister was to cross the barrier. Major Otto Remer, commander of the battalion, was a former Hitler Youth

Leader and he first wanted assurance that his Führer was really dead. Hase gave it, adding that he had been murdered by the SS. Who was his successor? asked Remer, who felt "something was fishy." Hase told him to stop asking stupid questions and get his battalion on the move.

Remer's companion, Lieutenant Hans Hagen (in Berlin to lecture the guard battalion on National Socialism), was equally suspicious and once they were alone he convinced Remer that this looked like a military Putsch. He asked for permission to clarify the matter with Goebbels, his prewar employer. Remer put a motorcycle at his disposal with instructions to report back immediately. As the major set out to supervise the blockade of the inner city, Hagen (an author in civilian life) was bouncing in the sidecar of a motorcycle bound for the official residence of the Minister of Propaganda. He was heard to shout out periodically, like a Teutonic Paul Revere: "Military Putsch!"

The Goebbels establishment was already a center of confusion. The burgomeister of Berlin was there, along with a city councilor, and both were bewildered by the conflicting rumors. So was Speer, who had just noticed a group of Remer's men trotting toward Brandenburg Gate with machine guns; others stood guard outside the ministry. Sweating profusely, Goebbels was on the telephone querying party officials and regional military commanders. Troops from Potsdam and provincial garrisons, it seemed, were already marching toward the city. The situation was desperate but Goebbels saw a ray of hope in the fact that the rebels hadn't yet broadcast their success over the radio. He now busied himself making arrangements for his own broadcast, a tricky matter since a simple account of the facts might cause panic.

Just then Hagen, rumpled from his motorcycle ride, pushed his way into Goebbels' presence. After listening impatiently to the soldier-author's breathless account, Goebbels demanded to know if Remer could be trusted. Absolutely! Hadn't he been wounded eight times in action? Still somewhat suspicious, Goebbels instructed Hagen to fetch Remer. If the two were not back within half an hour, Goebbels would assume the major was either a traitor or held by force—and he would order SS troops to seize the headquarters of the Berlin Garrison at Unter den Linden.

Moments later, at 5:30 P.M., Goebbels was again called to the telephone. It was Hitler, who urged an immediate broadcast to let the people know that his life had been spared. Goebbels promptly phoned the text of a broadcast to the Rundfunkhaus. It was already occupied by rebellious troops of the infantry school but their commanding officer was so confused—or terrified—by Goebbels' voice that he readily agreed not to interfere with transmission of the announcement.

Eva Braun, right, and sister Ilse. FR. SCHNEIDER

Eva at nineteen. Hitler's favorite photograph. FR. SCHNEIDER

The wedding of Eva's friend Marion Schönemann to Herr Theissen, at the Berghof, August 1937. Kneeling near groom, Gretl Braun, Eva's sister. Standing, l. to r., Heinrich Hoffmann, Frau Honni Morell, Erma Hoffmann, Eva Braun, Frau Dreesen (her husband owned the Hotel Dreesen), Dr. Morell, Herta Schneider (Eva's best friend), two unidentified men and Hitler. U. S. ARMY

Eva poses for photographer Hoffmann. N. GUN

Eva in the war years. FR. SCHNEIDER

Eva's bedroom at the Berghof. N. GUN

The passageway leading to Eva's bedroom. N. GUN

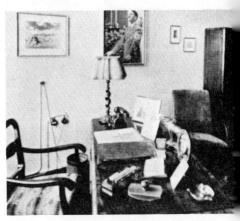

Hitler's study in the Reich Chancellery. N. GUN

His favorite tea house, just below the Berghof. FRENTZ

Adolf dozes after dinner with Eva at the tea house. N. GUN

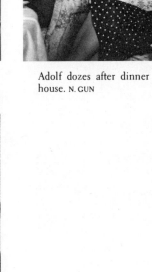

Hitler reading at the tea house. (Note glasses) N. GUN

Above, omnipresent Bormann in the
Führer's car. FRENTZ

Left, Frau Gerda Bormann with one of
their nine children. FATH

Above, Frau Gertraud "Traudl" Junge (Hitler's youngest secretary) and her husband, Hans Junge (Hitler's valet), dine on the Führer's train with the oldest secretary, Fräulein Wolf. (Note reflection) FRENTZ

Left, the two other Hitler secretaries waiting for the train. Gerda Daranowsky Christian, left, and Christa Schröder. FRENTZ

Hitler leaves the eastern front for relaxation on the Obersalzberg. FRENTZ

Left, Hitler and SS adjutant
Günsche on the Obersalzberg.
GÜNSCHE

Below, Hitler and ordnance
officer Wünsche visit a
girls' school in Berchtesgaden.
WÜNSCHE

In the meantime Hitler, swayed by agitated advisers, had come to suspect his Propaganda Minister was a traitor. He again phoned Goebbels, this time bitterly reproaching him for delaying the newscast so long. Goebbels gave vehement assurance that he was not to blame; it was someone in the Radio Division. Hitler believed him—at least he said he did—and hung up.

The early rumor of Hitler's death brought hysteria and tears to scores of girl telephonists. The story spread and caused consternation until the reassuring newscast brought new tears, these of joy. Messages of congratulation descended on the Wolfsschanze. Field Marshal Milch for one telegraphed his "HEARTFELT JOY THAT A MERCIFUL PROVIDENCE HAS SHIELDED YOU FROM THIS BASE MURDER ATTEMPT AND PRESERVED YOU FOR THE GERMAN PEOPLE AND ITS WEHRMACHT." These expressions of relief were not completely self-serving. The great majority of Germans felt that the nation's future depended on the Führer.

In Berlin, Major Remer had just finished sealing off the government area. He was glum, for he had not yet heard that the Führer was alive. Remer had carried out his mission with misgivings, reinforced when he reported back to Hase only to be given vague answers to every question. Dissatisfied, Remer was in a rebellious mood by the time Hagen accosted him outside with the news that Minister Goebbels demanded his immediate presence! This was civil war, Remer thought, and brought Hagen upstairs to repeat Goebbels' message to Hase. The general pretended to be alarmed and, when Remer said he must report at once to the Propaganda Minister, ordered him to remain in the anteroom. But another conspirator, also a major, intervened, with a knowing wink at Hase; he suggested that it *was* Remer's duty to see Goebbels—and place him under arrest. Remer left the building in a state of confusion. "Well, I've got to gamble for my life," he finally told his adjutant and set off for the Propaganda Ministry with twenty men.

Goebbels was checking the time. He had been unsuccessful in attempts to reach Remer by phone and it was only two minutes before the deadline—7 P.M. Then Remer marched in. He did not tell Goebbels he had orders to arrest him nor did he believe the Minister's claim that he had just spoken to the Führer. He would believe Hitler was alive only, he said, if he heard it from his own mouth.

"As you wish, Major," said Goebbels and put in a call to Rastenburg. In less than a minute he was telling Hitler, "Here is Major Remer, commander of the guard battalion." Remer took the receiver warily. It could be a recording or someone imitating the Führer. "Are you on the line, Major Remer?" he heard. "What are you doing now?" The voice certainly sounded like the Führer's and Remer told what he had done to date. But he must have sounded doubtful. "Do you believe that I am alive?" The answer was Jawohl even though Remer was not entirely convinced.

Hitler said that he was giving Remer complete authorization to insure the security of the government. "Do whatever you think necessary. Every officer, regardless of rank, is now under your command." He ordered Remer to restore full order immediately. "If necessary by *brachial* (brutal) armed force." The *"brachial"* completely convinced Remer this really was Hitler. He snapped to attention. "You are responsible only to me," repeated Hitler and promoted him to the rank of colonel.

Remer turned the ministry into a command post. First he telephoned General von Hase and said he had just spoken to the Führer, who had put him in complete command. He ordered Hase to reported to him at once. Hase refused indignantly. "Since when does a general come trotting to a little major?"

"General, if you don't want to come, I will have you arrested," said Remer and sent troops to occupy Hase's headquarters. He then informed all military units in the Berlin area that they were now under his personal command, and was not surprised that their commanders, regardless of rank, accepted his authority without protest. As a finishing touch, Colonel Remer assembled his own battalion in the ministry garden so they could hear about the *Attentat* (assassination attempt) from the lips of Goebbels himself.

By this time a subdued General von Hase had arrived. He was no longer angry and, in fact, seemed at the point of embracing Remer. He was so full of compliments and questions that Remer had to politely put him off so he could get on with the job of restoring order. Goebbels was somewhat condescending to Hase, who began to stammer slightly under his curt questioning. Would the Minister mind if he telephoned his wife and had something to eat? "There go our revolutionaries," jibed Goebbels after the general left to enjoy his snack. "All they think about is eating, drinking and calling up Mamma."

The switchboard at the Bendlerstrasse was jammed with calls from officers seeking fuller details on the newscast. The recipients of the Walküre alert were also asking for direct confirmation from Fromm of the earlier report of Hitler's death. They were answered by Stauffenberg, who insisted that Hitler *was* dead and, if they were conspirators, he gave assurance that the plot was still operative. He told them the newscast was a trick. The army was in control and all was well.

At last one of the titular leaders of the revolt, Field Marshal von Witzleben, appeared in full uniform to take charge. He had held himself aloof all day but made up for his tardiness, just before 7:30 P.M., by sending out a strong directive, as new head of the Wehrmacht:

> The Führer, Adolf Hitler, is dead. An unscrupulous clique of non-combatant party leaders utilizing this situation, has attempted to stab our fighting forces in the back and seize power for their own purpose.
>
> In this hour of extreme danger the Government of the Reich, to maintain law and order, has decreed a military state of emergency and placed me in supreme command of the German Armed Forces. . . .

This message put new life into another field marshal. Kluge, on the point of abandoning the Paris conspirators, exclaimed: "An historical hour has struck!" He proposed they seek an immediate armistice in the West. The new German regime would agree to cease the rocket attacks on London if, in return, the Allies stopped their bombing. Kluge's enthusiasm was interrupted by a telegram from Keitel: the Führer was alive and orders from the traitorous Witzleben-Beck group in the Bendlerstrasse were to be ignored.

Kluge's resolve crumbled. He asked his chief of staff to find out what was really going on at Führer Headquarters. But Warlimont could not be reached by telephone, nor could Jodl or Keitel. Their absence was so curious that Kluge's hope revived. Perhaps Beck had told the truth after all and Hitler *was* dead! A call was put in to a fellow conspirator at Wolfsschanze. But he could only confirm the worst possible news: the Führer *was* alive! Kluge put down the telephone despondently. "Well," he said, "the attempt on his life has failed." That ended the matter for the marshal. "Gentlemen," he said, "leave me out of the question!"

In Berlin the man who had signed the order to seize power had also just abandoned the conspiracy. Field Marshal von Witzleben, expressing disgust at the confusion in the Bendlerstrasse, marched out of the building and drove to army headquarters in Zossen. Here he told Quartermaster General Wagner that all was lost and proceeded toward his country estate.

At Wolfsschanze Keitel had just succeeded in dispatching an order putting Himmler in command of the Replacement Army. Keitel added that "only orders from him and myself are to be obeyed." This teleprint went out at 8:20 P.M. Ten minutes later Party Chancellor Bormann dispatched an urgent message informing all his Gauleiters of the "murderous attempt on the Führer's life by certain generals." He ordered his people to honor only orders from the Führer himself.

At 9 P.M. the people were informed by radio that the Führer would soon speak to them in person. There would be a long delay, however, since there were no facilities at Wolfsschanze to broadcast directly. The nearest recording van was in Königsberg, the capital of East Prussia, and it would take several hours to fetch it.

By chance Hitler's favorite commando, Otto Skorzeny, was in Berlin, but once he heard that the Führer was alive he saw no reason to delay a trip to Vienna to inspect his school of frogmen saboteurs. As he was boarding the train at Anhalt Station at dusk an officer raced down the platform shouting that there was a military revolt in the city and Skorzeny had been commanded to establish order.

He hurried to SD headquarters where he was told that some traitorous military leaders were seizing control of the capital. "The situation is obscure and dangerous," said Schellenberg. His face was pale; a revolver lay in front of him on the table. He made a dramatic gesture. "I'll defend myself here if they come this way!" It was a ridiculous picture and Skorzeny could not resist laughing. He advised Schellenberg to put his weapon away before he shot himself.

Skorzeny alerted a company from another of his sabotage schools located in the Berlin suburbs before setting out on a personal reconnaissance of the city. Everything was quiet in the government compound. Checking a report that the Waffen SS was in the conspiracy, he hastily inspected their barracks at Lichterfeld. All was serene. He drove to the headquarters of the SS Leibstandarte Division for information but learned very little and continued at top speed to paratroop headquarters near the Wannsee. He found General Student on the terrace of his villa poring over a mass of papers. The general was wearing a long dressing gown; his wife sat beside him, sewing. It was comic, in a way, to see one of Germany's most important commanders presiding over such a placid scene during a revolt. Student refused to take the matter seriously until a phone call from Göring confirmed Skorzeny's alarm: all orders except those issued from Wehrmacht headquarters were to be ignored. While Student began relaying these orders, Skorzeny raced back to Schellenberg's office. No sooner had he arrived than he was called to the phone. "How many men have you?" asked Jodl. Only one company. "Good. Take them to the Bendlerstrasse and support Major Remer and his guard battalion who have just been ordered to surround the building."

There was a feeling of growing desperation at the Bendlerstrasse. The guard battalion units which had been protecting the high command head-quarters were withdrawing, on orders from their commander to assemble in the garden behind Goebbels' official residence. This left only about thirty-five soldiers at the main gate. Inside, General Olbricht collected his officers at 10:30 P.M. for the third time that evening and said they would now have to take over the protection of the building since the guards had left. Each of the six exits, he said, would have to be manned by a General Staff officer.

No one objected but one armed group of loyalists was secretly deter-mined to stand by their oath to the Führer. At about 10:50 P.M. these men, eight in all, burst into Olbricht's office, grenades fastened to their belts and armed with submachine guns and pistols. As Olbricht was trying to calm them, Stauffenberg entered. He spun around and escaped in a fu-sillade through the anteroom. He staggered as if hit, then darted into an adjoining office. But in short order he was captured along with Beck, Olbricht and other conspirators. Soon they were faced by Fromm, who had been released from captivity. "Well, gentlemen," said the big general, brandishing a pistol, "I am now going to treat you as you treated me." He told them to lay down their weapons.

"You wouldn't demand that of me, your former commanding officer," said Beck quietly. "I will draw the consequences from this unhappy situa-tion myself." He reached for a revolver on a suitcase.

Fromm warned him to keep the gun pointed at himself. The elderly Beck began to reminisce. "At a time like this I think of the old days . . ." "We don't want to hear about that now," interrupted Fromm. "I ask you to stop talking and do something." Beck mumbled something and fired. The bullet grazed his head; he reeled back, slumped in a chair. "Help the old gentleman," Fromm told two junior officers. They approached Beck and tried to take his gun. He resisted so he could try again but dropped back in a daze. Fromm turned to the other conspirators. "Now, you gentlemen, if you have any letters to write you may have a few minutes to do so." He returned in five minutes and informed them that a court-mar-tial "in the name of the Führer" had just pronounced death sentences on Olbricht, Stauffenberg and their two adjutants. Stauffenberg, his left sleeve soaked in blood, stood stiffly as he and his three colleagues were led into the courtyard.

Beck's face was splotched with blood. He asked for and was given a pistol. He was left in the anteroom but those outside heard him say: "If it doesn't work this time, please help me." There was a shot. Fromm looked in and saw that the former chief of the General Staff had failed again.

"Help the old gentleman," he told an officer, who refused. A sergeant dragged the unconscious Beck from the room and shot him in the neck.

Outside, the courtyard was dimly lit by the hooded lights of an army vehicle. It was midnight. The four condemned men were lined up in front of a sand pile for use in air raids. Olbricht was calm. At the order to fire, Stauffenberg shouted, "Long live our sacred Germany!" and died.*

The huge form of Fromm appeared at the doorway of the building. He marched across the yard to review the firing squad. He talked briefly, ending with a resounding "Heil Hitler!" then somewhat pompously made for the gate. He called for his car and disappeared in the darkness. At the message center in the Bendlerstrasse a teleprint message was being transmitted: "Attempted Putsch by irresponsible generals bloodily crushed. All ringleaders shot. . . ."

Just as Fromm was walking through the gate a white sports car arrived with a screech of brakes. The driver was Speer, his passenger Colonel Remer. "Finally an honest German!" said Fromm as if he himself were innocent. "I've just had some criminals executed." And when Remer said he wouldn't have done that, Fromm blustered. "Do you intend to give me orders?"

"No, but you'll have to be responsible for your actions." Remer suggested the general report at once to Goebbels. As Fromm drove off with Speer, Otto Skorzeny arrived with his men. He wondered why such an important general was leaving at such a time, then asked Remer, "What's going on?" Remer had no idea either, he only had orders to surround the building.

Skorzeny said that he was going inside and, after posting his company in the courtyard, bounded up the stairs toward the chief of staff's office. In the corridor he passed several officers, all armed with machine pistols. They glared at him with hostility. In Olbricht's anteroom he found several staff officers of his acquaintance who gave a brief account of what had happened. It all sounded very wild but confirmed what he had guessed. After trying in vain to telephone Führer Headquarters, he realized he must act on his own to restore peace and order "to this disturbed hive." Resumption of work was the best cure and, after gathering those officers he knew personally, he suggested they get on with their jobs; the battle fronts were still in dire need of reinforcements and supplies.

The staff officers agreed, but who would sign orders? Those in command were either dead or vanished. Skorzeny said he would sign and take all responsibility. As the machinery of the high command began to move

---

* Bendlerstrasse presently is named the Stauffenbergstrasse.

again, Skorzeny finally was connected to Jodl, who told him to stay in charge. "Send some general," suggested Skorzeny, but Jodl insisted he take over in the name of the Führer. Skorzeny began by sending out orders countermanding the Walküre alert and ordering all commanders to stand by for new instructions.

Speer chauffeured Fromm back to the Propaganda Ministry where Goebbels disregarded the latter's demand to speak privately with Hitler. Instead he put him in another room, asked Speer to leave, and telephoned the Führer in private. After some time Goebbels came to the door of his office and ordered a guard posted in front of Fromm's room.

Himmler was among those present at the ministry. He had recently arrived from Rastenburg with express orders and full powers from the Führer to crush the rebellion. "Shoot anyone who resists, no matter who it is," Hitler had told him. Despite such credentials—including a temporary assignment as commander-in-chief of the Reserve Army—he let Goebbels take over the visual command, remaining his usual quiet, contained self. To Goebbels' assistant, Naumann, he even seemed to be indifferent, whereas Goebbels was exhilarated. His version of the day gave the impression that he had crushed the rebellion in Berlin practically singlehanded. "If they hadn't been so clumsy!" he boasted to Himmler. "They had an enormous chance. What dolts! What childishness! When I think how I would have handled such a thing. Why didn't they seize the radio station and spread the wildest lies?"

The placid Himmler nodded politely without revealing that before coming to Goebbels' he had already unleashed the terror of a counter-Putsch and set up the machinery for a special investigation of the uprising.

At Wolfsschanze General Fellgiebel knew his fate was decided but he did not attempt to kill himself since he wanted to testify to his motives at an official trial. "If you believe in a Beyond," he told his youthful aide in farewell, "we could say *auf Wiedersehen!*"

Hitler was in his tea house impatiently waiting for the recording van from Königsberg so that he could make his speech to the nation. In anticipation of its imminent arrival, he summoned his family circle to hear him read a hastily drafted message. The secretaries and adjutants arrived along with Keitel and the bandaged Jodl, but there was still no van and Hitler used the time to enlarge on the Attentat. "These cowards!" he shouted. "That's exactly what they are! If they had had the courage at least to shoot me I'd have some respect! But they didn't want to risk their lives!"

At last the van arrived and just before 1 A.M., July 21, there was a fanfare of military music over every German radio station. After a brief pause Hitler began telling of the plot, and of the death and injury to colleagues very dear to him. He repeated his mistaken conviction that the circle of conspirators was extremely small and had nothing in common with the spirit of the Wehrmacht or the German people. It was a tiny band of criminal elements which would be promptly and ruthlessly exterminated. "I was spared a fate which held no horror for me, but would have had terrible consequences for the German people. I see in it a sign from Providence that I must, and therefore shall, continue my work."

He was followed briefly by Göring, who pledged the loyalty and deep affection of the Luftwaffe, and Dönitz, who declared that the navy was "consumed with holy wrath and boundless fury at the criminal attempt on our Führer's life." Then came the official announcement that the ringleaders of the criminal officer plot had either committed suicide or been shot by the army. "There have been no incidents, anywhere. Others who are implicated in the crime will be brought to account."

These words chilled the chief conspirators in Paris, who were gathered around a radio at the staff club in the Hotel Raphael. They had just succeeded in occupying every SS barracks in the area and arresting the two senior SS men in France, Karl Oberg and Helmut Knochen. As he listened, General von Stülpnagel was almost sure this was their own death sentence. But there was one last desperate hope. Perhaps Oberg and Knochen would have the decency to shield them. These two were released and brought to the Hotel Raphael. When Stülpnagel rose in greeting Oberg lunged at him. Ambassador Otto Abetz intervened. "What happens in Berlin is one thing," he said. "Here what matters is that the Normandy battle is raging and so here we Germans must show a united front." Oberg calmed down and agreed that he and Knochen would secretly join forces with the Wehrmacht against Himmler's RSHA. They would pretend that the SS and SD arrests had simply been staged by Oberg and Stülpnagel as a trick to deceive the Putschists.

Once his speech was finished, Hitler retired to his bunker where he was again examined by Dr. Morell. The Führer wanted confirmation that he had sustained no serious injuries. His inner circle waited in the tea house until Morell returned to announce that Hitler's pulse was normal. All was well. The Führer himself, shaken by the events of the day, had not yet realized the extent of the plot against him and still felt some exhilaration at his miraculous escape. He decided to send his tattered uniform to Eva Braun in Berchtesgaden for safekeeping. It would be a historical relic, proof that Providence really did intend him to complete his mission.

7

Soon after midnight, July 21, Otto Skorzeny was in complete command of the Bendlerstrasse, and the affairs of the high command were again on course. He also found details of the Putsch in Stauffenberg's safe and placed a number of officers under arrest.

At the Propaganda Ministry, Goebbels and Himmler were interrogating a number of generals including Fromm. They were treated courteously, given wine and cigars, and some, like Kortzfleisch, were allowed to go home when their innocence was established. At 4 A.M. the investigations ended. Goebbels emerged from his office with a radiant smile. "Gentlemen," he announced, "the Putsch is over." He escorted Himmler to his car, taking leave of his old rival with a long handshake, then returned upstairs to regale his closest associates with his own exploits. Utterly pleased, he spryly perched himself on a table next to a bronze bust of the Führer. "This was a purifying thunderstorm," he said. "Who would have dared to hope when the horrible news arrived early this afternoon that all this would end so quickly and so well." It was nothing short of a miracle. If Hitler had died the people would have believed it was God's judgment. "The consequences would have been incalculable. For in history only facts speak as evidence. And they are this time on our side." The press consequently should be instructed to belittle the conspiracy.

At Wolfsschanze Bormann was still sending out instructions to his Gauleiters. At 3:40 A.M. he informed them that the Putsch "may now be considered closed," and at 11:35 A.M. he passed on an urgent request from Himmler "that you should stop any further independent action against officers whose attitude was ambiguous or even against those who have to be classified as open adversaries." In other words, the Reichsführer himself was in full charge of restoring order and implementing a thorough investigation. In his methodical way he had already set up machinery staffed by four hundred officials in eleven sections.

In Paris Kluge's chief of staff—with the continued co-operation of the two most powerful SS officials in France, Oberg and Knochen—was doing his utmost to cover up the tracks of Kluge and Stülpnagel. But the latter, so recently the most powerful man in the City of Light, assumed all hope was gone upon receiving an order to report to Berlin. Instead of going by plane Stülpnagel set off later that morning in the rain by car. He ordered his chauffeur to drive past the battlefields of the First World War, Château-Thierry and the Argonne Forest, then to Sedan where so many old comrades of the Darmstadt Grenadiers had fallen in 1916. He continued the sentimental journey throughout the afternoon, finally disembarking for "a little walk." Soon after he disappeared over a rise near the Meuse Canal the driver heard a shot, perhaps two. He found the general floating in the canal, face upturned. Stülpnagel was barely alive but by wounding himself he had established his guilt beyond doubt. He was destined to be hanged.

At the Wolfsschanze it was apparent that Hitler's head injury was not superficial. He could hear nothing with his right ear and his eyes constantly flickered to the right. That evening while strolling outside he twice wandered off the path. Dr. Karl Brandt urged him to rest in bed for several days, but the Führer would not listen. "That's impossible." He had too much work to do. Besides it would certainly look ridiculous to foreign guests to see such a healthy man lying in bed.

The next day, despite a persistent earache, he insisted on visiting his wounded officers at the nearby field hospital. Two were at the point of death. General Schmundt was in critical condition. Deeply disturbed, Hitler unburdened himself to the two injured navy men, Puttkamer and Assmann, who shared a room. Sitting on the latter's bed, he expressed sorrow that they were victims of the plot. "These gentlemen had me, and only me, in mind." Yet miraculously he had escaped assassination once more. "Don't you agree that I should consider it a sign of Fate that it intends to preserve me for my assigned task?" The twentieth of July, he said, "only confirmed the conviction that Almighty God has called me to lead the German people—not to final defeat but to victory."

As the day progressed the pain in his ear became so intense that Morell sent for Professor van Eicken, the eminent Berlin eye-ear-nose-throat specialist who had operated on the Führer's throat in 1935. He was unavailable and the EENT specialist at a nearby field hospital was summoned. Dr. Erwin Giesing was well qualified, having worked two years in Professor van Eicken's clinic before opening his own office. Giesing found that the eardrum was badly ruptured and the inner ear was damaged. But, he said, it was not serious provided no infection of the middle ear set in.

At this point Dr. Morell appeared, breathing heavily. He sharply reprimanded Giesing for not reporting to him first and was told stiffly that "an officer was required to report only to his superior and not to any civilian." Although Hitler could hear little of this exchange, he noticed Morell's look of indignation. "Come now, end this quarrel, my dear Professor," he placated. "Dr. Giesing was van Eicken's assistant and he has told me that tomorrow he will have to do a small drum cauterization if the bleeding does not stop." Morell wanted to inject a hemostat but grudgingly agreed to send to Berlin for the medication prescribed by his rival.

Although Hitler was convinced he would never hear with his right ear, he remained in relatively good spirits. He took the time to peck out a letter on a typewriter to "My dear Tschapperl," the Viennese diminutive which he often used affectionately for Eva Braun. Illustrated by a sketch of the bombed barracks, it assured her that he was fine, just somewhat tired. "I hope to come back soon and so be able to rest, putting myself in your hands. I greatly need tranquillity."

She replied at once on her blue monogrammed stationery that she was deeply unhappy. "I am half dead now that I know that you are in danger." She asserted she could not go on living if anything happened to him. "From the time of our first meetings, I promised myself to follow you everywhere even in death. You know that my whole life is in loving you."

On July 23 Gestapo investigators by accident found incriminating diaries in the ruins of a bombed house which implicated Canaris and other important officials in the coup. The admiral was arrested, as was former Minister of Economics Schacht. At first Hitler could not believe that such high-ranking people—and so many of them!—were involved. It was a blow to his convictions that only a small clique of traitors existed and he was hurt. "My life is so full of sorrow, so heavily leaden," he told Traudl Junge, "that death itself would be salvation." And another secretary heard him chide his dog for disobeying him: "Look me in the eyes, Blondi. Are you also a traitor like the generals of my staff?"

At the situation meeting the next morning he declared that the English had backed Stauffenberg, then tried to convince his listeners that the plot was *not* really so widespread. "The important thing is to explain to the whole world that the overwhelming multitude of the officers' corps had nothing to do with those swine." It should be emphasized in the press that the commanders in the Bendlerstrasse had refused to go along with the handful of traitors and, in fact, executed four of them out of hand. "I am too much of a psychologist," he concluded, "not to see that a divine hand led this man with the bomb here at precisely the most favorable time for us. If I and the entire staff had been killed, it would have been a real catastrophe."

Goebbels followed Hitler's instructions in an address broadcast over all German radio stations. It was a clever speech replete with dramatic moralizing and appeal to the emotions. He pictured Stauffenberg as the satanic leader of a relatively small officers' clique that did not represent the Wehrmacht as a whole. He charged that Stauffenberg had been conspiring with the Western Allies and listed four evidences of proof: constant reference in their press to a group of German generals opposed to Hitler; use of an English bomb; relationship of Stauffenberg to the English aristocracy; and the hope expressed in London papers, after first news of the bombing, that the collapse of Germany was at hand.

Reports to the Gauleiters indicated that Goebbels' propaganda effectively aroused the people. At a hospital in Braunschweig, for example, the patients spontaneously decorated every picture of the Führer with flowers. Loyalty demonstrations were organized in numerous cities. High school teachers told their pupils that the conspiracy now explained the military defeats in Africa and Russia; traitors had prevented the Führer's orders from filtering down to the divisions.

On July 25 Dr. van Eicken arrived from Berlin to be greeted warmly by the Führer, who predicted that with all his worries he would "only last another two or three years." There was one consolation: by then he would have accomplished his task and others could continue the work. He eased himself painfully into a chair and described his symptoms in detail.

Dr. Giesing, who prided himself on his memory, was unobtrusively jotting down everything Hitler said in a yellow pocket almanac. So that no one else could decipher his notes he wrote in code, using Latin and a combination of personal symbols. Professor van Eicken confirmed Giesing's diagnosis and treatment but the Führer refused his advice to rest in bed for at least a week. "You have all conspired among you to make a sick man out of me!"

The following day Hitler complained to Giesing that his left ear still bled internally and he wanted it cauterized again, no matter how painful. "I don't feel any more pain," he said, adding as an afterthought, "Pain is meant to make a man *hard*." He proved it a minute later when an adjutant brought in reports on the assassination attempt. "Ja," he said, ruffling through the pages, "I would not have thought this Helldorf was such a scoundrel." He vowed "to tear out those traitors by the roots," then reviled Stauffenberg for his cowardice. "He at least should have had the courage to stand next to me with his briefcase. The bullet that killed him was too good for him."

Two days later Hitler complained of insomnia and when Giesing recommended cancellation of the nightly tea session Hitler said he had already tried that but it only made sleep more difficult. "I have to relax beforehand and talk about other things. If not, I see before me in the dark the General Staff maps and my brain keeps working. It takes hours before

I can get rid of such visions. If I put on the light I can draw an exact map of each army group position. I know where every single division stands— and so it goes on and on for hours until I fall asleep around five or six. I know this is not good for my health but I can't change my habits."

8

The day after the bombing Hitler replaced his ailing chief of staff, Zeitzler, with a man he had previously banished from a front-line command for differing with him. By the time Heinz Guderian, perhaps the most respected Panzer expert in the Wehrmacht, arrived in Rastenburg to take charge, he found the offices of OKH practically deserted. Zeitzler had already departed in semi-disgrace. Heusinger was gone and many department heads had been removed by the Gestapo.

One of Guderian's first tasks was to issue a loyalty order of the day, pledging to Hitler "the unity of the generals, of the officer corps and of the men of the army." By the end of the week Guderian went further; he ordered every General Staff officer to be a National Socialist officer-leader "by actively co-operating in the political indoctrination of younger commanders in accordance with the tenets of the Führer." Any officer who could not conform was ordered to apply at once for transfer. None did and the subjugation of this elite band, begun in 1933, came to a degrading finale.

By now the western front was collapsing in the face of a savage American attack on the western flank of the Normandy beachhead. At dusk of July 30 a fierce tank battle raged for the Avranches defile, the last barrier to an American breakthrough into the open spaces of France. Warlimont and others pressed for an immediate withdrawal from France while there was still time but Jodl contented himself with presenting to the Führer a draft of an order "for possible withdrawal from the coastal sector."

By the next evening American tanks were storming into Avranches. Hitler wanted to rush west and take personal charge, but both Giesing and Eicken forbade him to fly. Restricted to Wolfsschanze, he was forced to do nothing while six of George Patton's divisions poured through the gap at Avranches and sealed the fate of France. This was but one of many concerns. On August 1, 35,000 ill-armed Poles of all ages assaulted the German garrison in Warsaw and the next day Turkey broke off diplomatic relations with the Reich.

Somehow he managed to put all these cares behind him and on that second of August play the role of budding medical student. He inundated Giesing with questions on the inner ear, then donned a surgeon's white coat and, with mirror strapped to head, began peering intently into Linge's right ear. He could see nothing. When he tried again in vain, Giesing suggested he use an electric mirror. "Ja!" he exclaimed in wonder. "Now I can see something. . . . I see clearly a small light yellow line; that will probably be the well-known eardrum." He told Linge to turn around and inserted the orthoscope into his left ear, and became so enthralled that he had to test Linge's hearing with tuning fork and stop watch. "You know, Doctor," he said somewhat shyly, "when I was young I always wanted to be a doctor. But my other career came along and I realized what my true mission was." No sooner had Giesing left than Dr. Hitler resumed his research. He summoned Linge and two SS orderlies, examining them all until he had mastered the electric mirror; then he requested a copy of Professor Knick's book on the treatment of eye, ear and throat.

If Hitler's spirits had improved, he was still so dizzy he had to walk with legs astride like a sailor on a pitching ship. Even so he insisted on talking to his Gauleiters on August 4. He went from man to man shaking hands. Many, like Friedrich Karl Florian of Düsseldorf, could not restrain their tears at the sight of his condition. "You won't misunderstand me," said Hitler, "when I assure you that for the past eighteen months I was firmly convinced I would one day be shot by someone in my own close circle." He asked them to try and imagine how terrible it was to realize that certain violent death could come at any moment. "How much inner energy I had to summon to do all that was necessary for the maintenance and protection of our people! To contemplate, cogitate, and work out these problems. And I had to do all this by myself, without the support of others and with a feeling of depression hanging over me." After the lugubrious speech, a one-pot meal was served. Finally Hitler slowly got to his feet. "Now I will retire," he said, "and you gentlemen . . ." He put two fingers to his mouth and they took out cigarettes as he walked off trying to hide his stagger.

Himmler had recently assured this same group that he would ruthlessly bring to justice not only the criminals in the conspiracy but their families. "The Stauffenberg family," he said, "will be exterminated root and branch!" Enthusiastic applause. "That will be a warning example, once and for all." He pressed the investigation in this spirit. Next of kin and other relatives of the chief conspirators were arrested, including at least a dozen women over seventy. Scores of detectives covered every angle of the conspiracy—with such dispatch and thoroughness that the first trial got under way on August 7. Eight officers were brought before a People's Court presided over by Roland Friesler, an expert on Soviet law and methods of punishment. Characterized by Hitler as "our Vishinsky," he had been instructed by the Führer to proceed harshly and "with lightning speed."

The defendants entered the great courtroom of the Kammergericht in Berlin wearing old clothes. They looked haggard and unkempt, as movie cameras recorded the event so the German people could see what happened to traitors. Field Marshal von Witzleben, deprived of his false teeth, looked like a tramp in a comedy as he kept hitching up his oversized beltless pants. Friesler, dramatically clothed in red, began shouting like one of the Soviet judges he so admired: "You dirty old man, why do you keep fiddling with your trousers?"

This was the tone and level of the show trial. "Never before in the history of German justice," recalled one shorthand secretary, "have defendants been treated with such brutality, such fanatic ruthlessness as at these proceedings." The judgment was foreordained and, in a trumpet voice, Friesler pronounced all eight men guilty of treason against the Führer (which, in fact, they were) and against German history (which they were not). In line with Hitler's specific instructions, the eight men were trucked to Plötenzee prison, then into a small room where eight meathooks dangled from the ceiling. Here the condemned were stripped to the waist and hung by nooses of piano wire. Their agonized jerking was recorded by a movie camera, and that same evening was reproduced on a screen at the Wolfsschanze. According to Speer, "Hitler loved the film and had it shown over and over again," but Adjutant von Below and others in the family circle still assert he never saw it.

There were further investigations and other trials but only the execution of the first eight victims was publicized. Almost 5000 other men and women, most of them not even directly involved in the uprising of July 20, were also executed.

9

On August 15 the Allies landed in southern France and Guderian's comment that the bravery of the Panzer forces was not enough to make up for the failure of the air force and navy infuriated Hitler. In an effort to contain himself, he adjourned to another room for a tête-à-tête with Guderian, but their voices became so loud that an adjutant had to caution the Führer that every word was clearly audible outside. Could he please close the window?

This exhibition was mild compared to one later in the evening when Hitler learned that Field Marshal von Kluge had mysteriously disappeared. It seemed that the Commander-in-Chief West had driven up to the front that morning to confer with his armored commander but never arrived at the rendezvous. Hitler shouted that Kluge must have been involved in the bombing plot and had now sneaked off for secret surrender talks with the enemy!

Kluge, in fact, had been delayed up front by an enemy fighter-bomber attack, his car destroyed along with two transmitters. He was not only trapped, incommunicado, on congested roads but caught in a personal dilemma. While doing his best to stem the Allied breakthrough, he was convinced his was a hopeless task. Depressed ever since a serious auto accident in Russia, he would pace his office like a caged beast, torn between the oath he had sworn to Hitler and "his responsibility before God, before his nation, before his conscience."

Kluge finally reached his destination late that night but by then Hitler had already decided to replace him with Field Marshal Model. On August 17 Model arrived in France with a handwritten note from the Führer and took over command of the western front. Kluge sat at his desk dazed by the dismissal. "Here at Avranches all my reputation went," he told his chief of staff, pointing to a map. "It's all up with me." The following day he headed east, like Stülpnagel, on a leisurely motor trip across the old battlefields of France. Like Stülpnagel, he intended to take his own life. But Kluge was successful. Near Clermont-en-Argonne, after lunching under the shade of a tree, he gave his aide a letter for his brother —then swallowed cyanide.

Another letter was already on its way to the Führer. After outlining the reasons for his failure to stem the Allies, he implored Hitler to end the war and put an end to the people's unspeakable sufferings. At Wolfsschanze Hitler read the letter, then, without comment, handed it to Jodl, who was surprised by the last lines wherein Kluge praised Hitler for his iron will and genius and the "great and honorable fight" he had fought. "Prove yourself now to be so great as to put an end, if need be, to the hopeless struggle." It seemed to epitomize the final humiliation of the Wehrmacht but was not at all self-serving. Kluge stood to gain nothing. He had only made a last effort to serve his country by sounding a warning.

It was a futile one; Hitler was still bound by his ultimate mission: to rid the world of Jews, a task, so Eichmann reported in August, that was nearing its end. He told Himmler that six million Jews had already been eliminated—four million in the killing camps and the rest in mobile operations. Spurred by the rapid advance of the Red Army and the continuing investigations of the inexorable Konrad Morgen, who also calculated a figure of at least six million dead Jews, Hitler instructed Himmler to prepare the dismantling of all the killing camps except Auschwitz.* There were still Jews from Hungary, Lodz, Slovakia and Theresienstadt to be gassed but Commandant Höss had the facilities to wind up the entire job, provided the troops in the East did not allow a Soviet breakthrough.

10

The military situation was so desperate that only a man with such motivation would have banished all thoughts of surrender. From the Baltic to the Ukraine, Red Army offensives had routed or surrounded the Wehrmacht along the entire eastern front. In the south Soviet troops were seizing the oilfields of Romania; in the north they had just surrounded fifty German divisions; and in the center they were closing in on Warsaw. On Hitler's personal orders, preparations were made to remove the coffin of President von Hindenburg from the tomb at Tannenberg, scene of his great victory in the First World War.

In the emergency, Goebbels proclaimed a new Draconian policy on August 24: all theaters, music halls, drama schools and cabarets were to be closed within a week. Soon, he warned, all orchestras, music schools and conservatories (except a few leading ones) would be shut down and the artists put either in uniform or in armaments factories. There would be an end to publication of fiction or belles-lettres and of all but two illustrated papers.

On the following day Paris was liberated after four years of occupation; both Romania and Finland sued for an armistice. Twenty-four hours later the Romanians, who had thrown out Marshal Antonescu by a coup, declared war on Germany. With defeat imminent on all fronts, Hitler did not waver. His answer to signs of disintegration within the Wehrmacht was a threat to arrest the kin of any deserter.

He told Keitel and two other generals on the last day of August that the time was not yet ripe for a political decision. "Such moments come only when you are victorious." There was still hope of success, he said. The tension between the Allies would soon become so great that a major break would occur. "The only thing is to wait, no matter how hard it is, for the right moment." He mused glumly on the problems facing him in both East and West, then began feeling sorry for himself. "I think it's pretty obvious that this war is no fun for me. I've been cut off from the world for five years. I haven't been to the theater, I haven't heard a concert, and I haven't seen a film." His voice rose in wrath. "I accuse the General Staff of failing to give the impression of iron determination and

---

* The order to close the killing centers was issued by Himmler on November 24, 1944.

so of affecting the morale of combat officers—and when General Staff officers go up front I accuse them of spreading pessimism!" He would fight until Germany got a peace which secured the life of the nation for the next hundred years "and which, above all, does not besmirch our honor a second time, as happened in 1918." His thoughts reverted momentarily to the bomb plot. Death, he said, "would only have been a release from sorry, sleepless nights and great nervous suffering. It is only a fraction of a second and then a man is freed from everything and has quiet and eternal peace."

This mood of fatalism might have been the result of deteriorating health. Although he joked with his secretaries about his right hand, which trembled so much he could no longer shave himself, he was seriously affected by a head cold which was aggravated in turn by an incessant earache. His condition was complicated a few days later by a slight feeling of pressure in his head, particularly in the brow area. His voice grew hoarse. He began complaining of stomach pains but disregarded Dr. Giesing's warning that this might be the result of the numerous pills prescribed by Dr. Morell. By the beginning of September, however, Hitler had come to accept Dr. Giesing's prescription of a ten per cent cocaine solution to relieve the sinus pain and would faithfully crouch for hours each morning and evening over an inhalator.

Giesing's visits indeed became so pleasurable that Hitler began to show the same gratitude he had bestowed on Morell. Gratitude ripened into trust and before long the new doctor enjoyed a rare personal relationship with the Führer. The treatments were invariably followed by long discussions on a variety of subjects, ranging from the future of the Reich to the evils of smoking. During all these conversations Giesing continued to take detailed notes. He also undertook something even more dangerous: secret psychological tests. This was done so subtly and over such a long period that Hitler never guessed he had been the object of, in Giesing's terms, "rather primitive psychological tests," and had been diagnosed as "a neurotic with Caesar-mania."

Touchy as he was in these days of pain and depression, Hitler never lost his temper with his youngest secretary, Traudl Junge, or failed to show keen interest in her personal welfare. But at one noonday meal she noticed he acted strangely. He said not a word to her and when their eyes met his were serious and probing. She wondered if anyone had spread gossip about her. Later in the day SS General Otto Hermann Fegelein phoned and asked if she could come to his barracks. Putting an arm around her in a fatherly manner, he revealed that her husband had been killed in action. The Chief, he explained, had known about it since yesterday but was unable to tell her the bad news. Later she was summoned to the Führer's study. He took both her hands and said softly, "Oh, child, I am so sorry. Your husband was such a fine fellow." He asked her to remain on the job and promised to "always help" her.

In early September Professor van Eicken returned for another examination and, upon learning of Morell's injections and pills, became as concerned as Giesing and Hitler's two surgeons, Brandt and Hasselbach. The four doctors met secretly but Eicken doubted that their patient would heed his warnings any more than those of his three colleagues since Morell enjoyed Hitler's complete confidence.

A week later Hitler reported that he was getting almost no sleep. He would lie awake all night long from the agony of stomach spasms. Nor was there any relief from the sinus inflammation; the left side of his head continued to ache constantly. This was aggravated by the rattle and grind of pneumatic drills used around the clock by construction workers in an effort to strengthen his bunker from expected Soviet air attacks. A side effect of his bad health was deterioration of his remarkable memory. He had always been able to glance at a long document and repeat it word for word; now he had difficulty remembering names. It was fortunate, he wryly observed, that he only had to deal with a few people these days.

On September 12 Hitler suddenly became dizzy immediately after Giesing had administered the cocaine treatment. He complained that everything was going black and grabbed a table to keep from falling. His pulse was rapid and weak but in ninety seconds the attack—it might have been a mild coronary—passed and the pulse returned to normal. Hitler suffered a similar attack on the fourteenth. This time he broke out into a cold sweat. He summoned Morell, who gave him three injections which gave him temporary relief, but on September 16 there was a third mild attack. This time he agreed to do what Giesing had been urging for a month: undergo head X rays.

Chapter Twenty-nine

THE BATTLE OF THE BULGE
JULY 21, 1944–JANUARY 17, 1945

1

That same day Hitler issued an order demanding "fanatical determination" from every able-bodied combat man in the West. The Americans had just reached the German frontier and at one point, south of Aachen, pierced it. "There can be no large-scale operations on our part. All we can do is to hold our position or die." Hitler seemed to be calling only for a last-ditch defense of the Fatherland but it was a ruse to fool the enemy who, he feared, had a spy at Führer Headquarters privy to all directives. (The spy, of course, was Ultra.) No sooner had the regular Führer conference ended than Hitler invited four men to an inner chamber. Keitel and Jodl were followed into the new conference room by Chief of Staff Guderian and General Kreipe, representing Göring. As they were conjecturing in undertones on what surprise the Führer had in store for them, he entered, stooped, still wan and wary from the third attack. His blue eyes were watery and distant, his mouth slack.

He nodded to Jodl, who succinctly summed up their position: their allies were either finished, switching sides or attempting to do so. While the Wehrmacht listed more than 9,000,000 men under arms, there had been 1,200,000 casualties in the last three months—almost half of them on the western front. There was a respite in the East where the Soviet summer offensive seemed to have run its course. "But in the West we are getting a real test in the Ardennes." This was the last hilly area in Belgium and Luxembourg that had been the highway to German victory in the Great War and again in 1940.

At the word "Ardennes" Hitler abruptly came to life. Raising his hand, he exclaimed: "Stop!" There was a dead pause. Finally Hitler spoke: "I have made a momentous decision. I am taking the offensive. Here—out of the Ardennes!" He smashed his left fist on the unrolled map before him. "Across the Meuse and on to Antwerp!" The others stared in wonder. His shoulders were squared, his eyes luminous, the signs of care and sickness gone. This was the dynamic Hitler of 1940. In the next few days he was a model of his former vigor as he pressed preparations for the ambitious counteroffensive: he issued orders for the establishment of a new Panzer army and envisaged ways of bringing 250,000 men and thousands of machines up to the Ardennes in absolute secrecy.

Only then did he keep his promise to get X rays taken of his head. Late in the afternoon of September 19 he was driven to the field hospital at Rastenburg and escorted to the X-ray room, which had been searched carefully for hidden explosives. Afterward he again visited his wounded officers but this time the sight of the dying Schmundt brought tears.* Outside Hitler was greeted by loud shouts of "Sieg heil!" from a crowd of civilians from the town and recuperating soldiers. Their excitement at the sight of their Führer—probably for the first time—was understandable but what impressed Giesing most was the ardent enthusiasm in the eyes of the amputees and other badly wounded men.

The following morning Giesing checked the three X rays with Morell and was amazed that his colleague identified the cheekbones as the sinuses. There followed the daily examination of the patient in his bunker and Giesing noticed Hitler's face had an odd reddish tinge in the artificial light. Afterward Hitler was stricken with stomach pains and insisted on taking more than half a dozen of the "little black pills" prescribed by Morell. Concerned by the continuing dosage, Giesing began to make cautious inquiries. Linge showed him the pill container. Its label read: Antigas Pills, Dr. Koster, Berlin, Extract nux vomica 0.04; Extract belladonna 0.04.

Giesing was appalled. Hitler had been heavily dosing himself with two poisons—strychnine and atropine. Perhaps that explained his attacks, his growing debility; his irritability and aversion to light; his hoarse throat and

---

* After Schmundt's death, Hitler again wept. "Don't expect me to console you," he told Frau Schmundt. "You must console me for my great loss."

the strange reddish tinge of his skin. Two cardiograms revealed clearly ab-
normal T waves. It could be hardening of the arteries or high blood pressure, but in any case it was an alarming development in the light of his
other disabilities. At their regular session Hitler again complained to Giesing of intestinal discomfort. "The cramps are so severe that sometimes I
could scream out loud."

After their next meeting on September 25 Dr. Giesing chanced to see
his patient outside the bunker. To his surprise the tinge of Hitler's skin
was not red in sunlight but yellow. His eyes were starting to turn yellow.
He obviously had jaundice. After a night of agonizing pain, Hitler could
not get out of bed the following morning. His secretaries, adjutants and
servants were in a state of alarm; no one could remember the Führer staying in bed no matter how sick. He would see no one, wanted no food. In
great excitement, Günsche told Traudl Junge that he had never seen the
Chief so listless, so indifferent. Even the critical situation on the eastern
front failed to interest him.

Morell advised Hitler to remain in bed all day but he insisted on getting up for his regular examination by Giesing. He, in turn, advised dis-
continuance of the cocaine treatment but Hitler wearily shook his head.
"No, dear Doctor," he said. "I think that my physical weakness the past
few days is due to the poor functioning of my intestines and cramps."
Giesing hesitated, then warned his patient to take care lest he suffer another collapse. On his way out he confiscated a box of Morell's black pills
and showed them to Dr. von Hasselbach. He too was horrified to learn
they contained strychnine and atropine but warned Giesing to say nothing
until they could confer with Dr. Brandt.

In the meantime Morell gave orders that no other doctor was to see
the Führer and when Giesing reported on the twenty-seventh he was
turned away by Linge. Even Dr. van Eicken, who came from Berlin to irri-
gate the patient's swollen sinuses, was refused admittance. For the rest of
the month Morell did his utmost to isolate the patient from the other
doctors. He insisted that the Führer was *not* suffering from jaundice. It
was more likely a temporary gall bladder inflammation. During this time
Hitler lost six pounds and lay in bed, racked with pain. He ate nothing
and showed little interest in the battle fronts. Occasionally he would see
his secretaries but then he would almost immediately dismiss them. "It
gave me a feeling of despair," recalled Traudl Junge, "to see the one man
who could have stopped this tragedy with a single stroke of a pen lying
disinterested in his bed, looking around with tired eyes—while around him
all hell had broken out. It seemed to me that his body had suddenly real-

ized how senseless had been all the efforts of brain and will and gone on strike. He had just laid down and said, 'I will not do anything any more.' "

Physical pain was not the only cause of Hitler's deep depression. Another cache of incriminating documents was unexpectedly discovered in a safe at army headquarters in Zossen. They implicated a considerable segment of the army leadership in the assassination plot. The Führer was shattered and some of those in the family circle felt that this, more than the jaundice or the stomach pains, which he had endured for years, had broken his spirit.

Dr. Brandt returned to the Wolfsschanze on the twenty-ninth. Enthusiastic at the chance to finally unmask Morell as a charlatan, he managed to get into Hitler's room that afternoon. At first the patient took Brandt's denunciation seriously; but Morell convinced the Führer that he was absolutely innocent of any wrongdoing. If Hitler suffered aftereffects from the anti-gas pills it was because he himself increased the daily dosage. Disconsolate, Brandt now left it up to his colleagues to discredit Morell. Hasselbach went to Bormann. He was the last one the doctors should have sought as an ally since he had been doing his best for months to get Brandt dismissed. Bormann's ulterior motive was Byzantine; he looked on Brandt as the accomplice of Speer, whose "dangerous" influence on the Führer had to be diminished at all costs. After listening politely to Hasselbach and expressing shock at the pill stories, Bormann promptly went to Hitler and warned him that Brandt had been joined by Hasselbach and Giesing in an effort to ruin poor Dr. Morell for their own personal gains.

No doctor but Morell was allowed to see Hitler and it appeared that Bormann had won. Then, late in the afternoon on October 1, Linge telephoned Giesing. The Führer was suffering from a bad headache and insisted on seeing Giesing at once. He was lying on his spartan bed in a nightgown. He lifted his head slightly to greet Giesing but immediately dropped back to the pillow. His eyes were empty, expressionless. He complained of pressure in his head. He also could not breathe through his left nostril. As Giesing seated himself next to the bed, Hitler abruptly changed the subject. "Doctor," he asked, "how did you come upon the story of the anti-gas pills?"

Giesing explained. Hitler frowned. "Why didn't you come directly to me? Didn't you know that I have great confidence in you?" The doctor felt chills—not from the excessive air conditioning in the little cell. He explained that he had been prevented from coming. Hitler shrugged this off as well as Giesing's conviction that his intestinal problems were due to strychnine. He had suffered similar attacks frequently, if not as severely.

"It is the constant worry and irritation that give me no rest; and I must work and think only of the German people day and night." He was already feeling much better and should be out of bed in a few days. "You gave Morell a great fright," he said. "He looked quite pale and disturbed and reproaches himself. But I have assured him. I myself always have believed they were simple pills to absorb my intestinal gases and I always felt very well after taking them." Giesing explained that the feeling of well-being was an illusion. "What you say is probably right," interrupted Hitler, "but the stuff did me no harm. I'd have had intestinal cramps anyway because of the continuous nervous strain of the last month and, after all, at some time the twentieth of July would have reacted on me. Up to now I'd had the will power to keep all this inside me—but now it has broken out."

Giesing diagnosed his problems as jaundice but Hitler protested. "No, you want to make a gall bladder patient out of me! Go ahead, examine my gall bladder." He folded back the bedclothes so Giesing could make his own examination. It was Giesing's first chance to give his patient a complete physical. He examined Hitler's neurological reflexes, his glands, every part of his body. Giesing satisfied himself, for instance, that the malicious rumor about the Führer's deficient sex organs was a canard; in this respect he was intact and normal.*

Hitler was once more the medical student, absorbed by each detail of the process. "You see, Doctor," he said as Linge and Giesing helped him into the nightgown, "aside from this nervous hyperactivity, I have a very healthy nervous system and I hope that soon all will be well again." He was talking himself into a state of euphoria. He thanked Giesing for everything he had done to relieve his discomfort. "And now Fate has sent you again to ferret out this anti-gas story and you have saved me further damage because I would have kept on taking these pills after I recovered." This paradoxical conclusion was followed by a perplexing outburst of gratitude and praise. "My dear Doctor, it was Providence that led you to make this examination and discover what no other doctor would ever have noticed. I am in any event very grateful to you for everything and will remain loyal to you—even if you did attack Morell—and I thank you again for everything." He took both of Giesing's hands, pressed them tightly, then requested another dose of "that cocaine stuff." The Führer instantly luxuriated under the treatment. His head was clearing up, he said, and he would soon be well enough to get up. But his words began to fade and his

---

* At least two other doctors gave Hitler a complete physical. Dr. Morell found his sexual organs "completely normal." So did a physician at Berlin's Westend Hospital soon after the Führer's accession to power; this man, having heard of Hitler's "alleged homosexual tendencies," paid special attention to his penis and testicles."

eyes fluttered. His face turned a deathly white. Giesing grasped Hitler's pulse. It was rapid and weak. "My Führer, are you all right?" he asked but got no answer. Hitler had passed out.

The doctor looked around but Linge had left to answer a knock on the door. It suddenly occurred to Giesing that Hitler was entirely at his mercy. He saw before him a tyrant whose knowledge of people seemed very inadequate. "At that moment," so he claimed in his diary, "I did not want such a man to exist and exercise the power of life and death in his purely subjective manner." Some inner command drove him to plunge a swab stick into the cocaine bottle—a second dose could be lethal—and he rapidly began brushing the interior of Hitler's nose with the substance that had just knocked him out. As Giesing finished the left nostril he was startled by a voice: "How much longer will the treatment take?" It was Linge.

Giesing forced himself to say he was about finished. Just then Hitler's face, paler than before, twitched and he drew up his legs as if in pain. "The Führer is having another one of his intestinal cramps," observed Linge. "Let him rest." Outwardly composed, Giesing bade farewell to Linge and quickly bicycled back to the field hospital, still wondering if he had killed Hitler. In a state of terror, he telephoned Hasselbach, telling what had happened and that he was taking a day off, ostensibly to check on his Berlin office, which had been bombed.

The next day Giesing phoned from the capital to learn that Hitler was alive and no one suspected the double cocaine treatment. It was safe to return to Wolfsschanze. He arrived in an atmosphere of suspicion but not from the Führer, who was as friendly as ever. Still he made it clear that he wanted the whole anti-gas pill episode relegated to the past since he had "total faith" in Morell. He was personally going to clear up the matter and had asked Brandt to see him that afternoon.

Hitler settled the question by dismissing both Brandt and Hasselbach. Early that evening Giesing was summoned to Bormann's quarters. "But, my dear Doctor," Bormann said, upon observing that the doctor had come in full uniform, "why do you come in such official style? I only wanted to discuss something with you." He seemed amused at Giesing's apprehension. "There's no need to take the whole matter so tragically. We have nothing against you. On the contrary, the Führer is full of praise and asked me to give you this letter." It thanked him for his excellent treatment. Enclosed was a check for 10,000 marks. The doctor laid the check on the table. But Bormann forced it upon him with the warning that a refusal would be an insult to Hitler.

After packing, Giesing reported to the Führer bunker. Hitler extended his hand. "You will understand," he said, "that this anti-gas pill business has to be cleared up once and for all. I know that you yourself acted only out of idealism and purely professional motives." He again thanked Giesing for his excellent treatment and promoted him on the spot.

So ended the affair of the little black pills—with the dismissal of three doctors of good reputation. Few in the family circle gave any credence to the growing rumor that Dr. Morell had willfully attempted to poison the Führer. Most of them shared Gerda Christian's opinion that Morell was a good doctor despite his slovenly appearance. Even the trio who denounced Morell for incompetence did not believe he was trying to poison Hitler. They remembered the truly shocked look on his face when Brandt pointed out that these pills—though harmless if taken in moderation—contained some strychnine. Morell, it seemed, had never checked the analysis on the label, only the name, nux vomica. And it came as a blow to discover that this was a strychnine-containing seed.

By the time Hitler left his sickbed there was considerable evidence of Rommel's implication in the bomb plot and the Führer assigned two generals the unpleasant task of offering him a deadly proposition. On October 14 they visited Rommel, who was recuperating at his castle near Ulm from the auto accident. When they left an hour later an ashen Rommel told his wife, "In a quarter of an hour I shall be dead." He explained that he had been accused of complicity in the plot and Hitler offered him the choice of taking poison or facing the People's Court.

After bidding his wife and son farewell, he took his aide aside. "Aldinger," he said, "this is it." He repeated Hitler's proposition and plan: he was supposed to drive to Ulm with the two generals and, en route, take poison. Half an hour later his death by accident would be reported. He would be given a state funeral and his family would not be persecuted. Aldinger begged him to resist but Rommel said that was impossible. The village was surrounded by SS men and the lines of communication to his own troops had been cut. "I have therefore decided to do what, obviously, I must do."

At 1:05 P.M., wearing his Afrika Korps leather jacket and carrying his field marshal's baton, Rommel was driven off. In transit to the Ulm Hospital he committed suicide. His death, according to the medical report, was caused by an embolism due to previous skull fractures. The field marshal's face, recalled his relatives, was marked by an "expression of colossal contempt."

2

By the end of September 1944 Hitler had lost three allies: Finland, Romania and Bulgaria. October brought a further defection. Horthy, the Hungarian admiral without a navy, who was nominally ruler of a kingdom without a king, sent envoys to Moscow to beg for an armistice. After all, the fiction of his independence had ended with the Nazi occupation of Hungary earlier that year—and Soviet troops were less than a hundred miles from the capital. Since a secret in Budapest was usually discussed loudly in cafés, Hitler knew all about the negotiations. While the Hungarian deputies were arguing fruitlessly in Moscow for better conditions, Hitler sent his favorite commando, Otto Skorzeny, to Hungary to bring her leaders back in line. He did so with a minimum of bloodshed in probably the most imaginative operation of the war, aptly titled Mickey Mouse. He simply kidnaped Horthy's son Miki, wrapped him in a carpet (Skorzeny got the idea from Shaw's play, *Caesar and Cleopatra*) and delivered him to the airport. He then proceeded to capture the citadel where Admiral Horthy lived and ruled with a single parachute battalion. It took half an hour and cost seven lives.

Six days later he was greeted at Wolfsschanze by Hitler with a warm "Well done!" His description of the kidnaping of young Horthy greatly amused Hitler. As Skorzeny rose to go, Hitler stayed him. "I am now going to give you the most important job of your life." He told of the surprise attack in the Ardennes. Skorzeny, he said, would play a leading role by training men to masquerade as Americans. They would work behind American lines—in American uniforms, with American vehicles. They would seize bridges over the Meuse, spread rumors, issue false orders, breed confusion and panic.

By this time Jodl had presented Hitler with the draft of his plan for the offensive. First it was given the symbolic name of Christrose but that morning the Führer himself changed it to Watch on the Rhine to deceive any spy. It called for the use of three armies with a combined strength of twelve Panzer and eighteen infantry divisions. Watch on the Rhine was based on two premises: complete surprise, and weather that would ground Allied planes. It was designed to break through on a wide front, cross the Meuse on the second day and reach Antwerp on the seventh day. It would not only destroy more than thirty American and British divisions but drive a great wedge—psychological as well as physical—between the Americans and British. The defeat would be so smashing that the West would sue for a separate peace. Then all German troops would be thrown against the Red Army.

To insure absolute secrecy only a select few were told of the offensive; a different code name for the offensive was to be used at every command level and changed every two weeks; nothing of the offensive was to be trusted to telephone or teletype; officers, sworn to silence, would be used as couriers. Only with such precautions, reasoned Hitler, could the spy at his headquarters be foiled.

Field Marshal Model, the Führer's personal choice to command the offensive, read the plan with dismay. "This damned thing hasn't got a leg to stand on!" he complained. Rundstedt shared his concern and offered a counterplan, a more modest attack of twenty divisions on a forty-mile front. "Apparently you don't remember Frederick the Great," Hitler remarked sarcastically. "At Rossbach and Leuten he defeated enemies twice his strength. How? By a bold attack." It was the same old story. His generals lacked imagination for the Big Solution. "Why don't you people study history?"

He patiently explained how Frederick had taken his great risk and then, as if in reward for daring, a bolt from the blue had come—*an unpredictable historical accident*: the alliance against Prussia suddenly split apart. And Frederick, doomed to defeat by every expert in Europe, went on to win the Fatherland's greatest victory.

"History will repeat itself," he said. His eyes shone. This was the Hitler of old, full of confidence and visions. "The Ardennes will by *my* Rossbach and Leuten. And as a result another unpredictable historical accident will take place: the alliance against the Reich will suddenly split apart!"

His own alliance with Japan, incidentally, was of little value. The Nipponese had just suffered another catastrophic loss. MacArthur had not only successfully landed in force on the Philippine island of Leyte but in the ensuing naval battle of Leyte Gulf the imperial navy had lost 300,000 tons of combat shipping: four carriers, three battleships, six heavy cruisers, three light cruisers and ten destroyers. Never again would the Japanese navy play more than a minor role in the hopeless defense of the homeland. And Japanese troops in Manchuria were no longer any threat to Hitler's nemesis, the Red Army, for they were being shipped out in force to stem the Americans.

On November 10 Hitler signed an order to prepare for the Ardennes offensive. He made it clear that this was a do-or-die proposition, a last gamble. The tone of his directiveness incurred the protests of the senior commanders in the West and Hitler decided to leave Wolfsschanze so he could explain his purpose in person despite a sudden relapse in spirit and body. His hoarseness had increased and the examination of Professor van Eicken revealed a small polyp on his right vocal cord. He was cranky and depressed; visitors were shaken to see him propped up on his spare cot, pale and drawn. Ignoring Morell's orders, he would drag himself out of bed to the map room, feeling his way like an old man. Breathing heavily, he would finally flop into a chair and wipe his brow. To keep him going during the ensuing briefings Dr. Morell had to administer numerous injections.

Hitler was advised to take a brief vacation before undertaking a trip to the western front that would be arduous, if not dangerous, in his present condition. But he was obsessed by the need to inspire those who must lead the offensive. On November 20 he entrained with his entourage. He must have known it was the last time he would ever see the Wolfsschanze, but he kept up the fiction of returning by allowing the reconstruction work to continue. His train did not leave until dawn since Hitler wanted to arrive in Berlin after dark. He sat in his compartment with all the shades drawn until lunch, then joined the others in the dining car. Traudl had never seen him so downcast and absent-minded. "His voice was only a soft whisper; his eyes were either glued to his plate or staring at a spot on the white tablecloth. It was such a depressing atmosphere that all of us had a strange ominous feeling."

Without preamble Hitler announced that Professor van Eicken would perform another operation on his throat. It was not dangerous, he said, as if assuring himself. "But it is quite possible that I am losing my voice and . . ." He never finished the sentence. He remained in seclusion for the next few days and the family circle knew only that Eicken had removed a polyp the size of a millet seed. Finally he appeared unexpectedly for breakfast; he was obviously looking for company. Everyone extinguished cigarettes; windows were opened to clear the air. He could only whisper. Doctor's orders, he said, and before long everyone was unconsciously imitating him. "My ears are fine and there is no need to spare them," he murmured softly, and everyone laughed, more in relief that he was again in good spirits than at the joke.

He returned to work with a resilience that astonished his entourage, vigorously applying himself to the Ardennes offensive that would turn around the course of the war. On December 7 he approved the final draft. It was almost exactly the same plan he had first proposed. To guarantee security radio operators dispatched coded messages to fictitious headquarters, fictitious messages to genuine headquarters, genuine messages to headquarters a hundred miles from their advertised location. False rumors were spread in lower echelons, in beer halls, in restaurants for the ears of Allied agents.

By now Otto Skorzeny, wielding more power as lieutenant colonel than some colonel generals, had reached mid-term of his "School for Americans." Though he had never been to the United States, his volunteers were doing well. The course: American slang, habits, folkways, and how to spread panic as pseudo GIs behind enemy lines. On December 11 the build-up was nearly complete. The Reichsbahn, achieving a miracle in railroading, had delivered the first wave to the Zone of the Offensive— without being observed by the enemy. Early that morning Hitler moved into his new headquarters near the medieval castle of Ziegenberg. This was Eagle's Eyrie, his headquarters for the 1940 invasion of the West, but now he and his entourage were housed in deep underground shelters.

Later in the day he met with half of his division commanders; the rest would come tomorrow. Upon arrival the first group of generals and their staffs were stripped of revolvers and briefcases by the Gestapo. Each man was forced to swear on his life that he would reveal nothing of what he was about to hear. Not one knew why he had been summoned; only that every division had been going in circles for weeks.

The meeting took place in a large underground room. The Führer sat at a narrow table flanked by Keitel and Jodl. Across were Rundstedt, Model and Lieutenant General Hasso von Manteuffel, who would command the most powerful of the three armies in the offensive. A descendant of a famous family of Prussian generals, Baron von Manteuffel was an ex-gentleman jockey and German pentathlon champion. Standing little more than five feet tall, he was tough-minded, possessed formidable energy and was one of the few who dared to disagree openly with Hitler.

For over an hour Hitler lectured to the sixty or so officers on Frederick the Great, the history of Germany and National Socialism. His voice was strong, his eyes flashed excitedly as he explained the political motives for deciding upon an all-out offensive. Then Autumn Fog—its final code name—was explained in detail. It would start at 5:30 A.M. on December 15. The divisional commanders listened in awe, impressed not only by the grandiosity of the plan but by the Führer's vigor and good health. But Manteuffel was almost close enough to touch him and saw he was actually "a broken man, with an unhealthy color, a caved-in appearance in his manner, with trembling hands; sitting as if the burden of responsibility seemed to oppress him, and compared to his looks at the last conference in the beginning of December, his body seemed still more decrepit; he was a man grown old." Manteuffel also caught the Führer surreptitiously maneuvering his hands under the table so one could move the other which was almost completely limp.

Those out front could see none of this and remained impressed to the end, which came with a ringing pronouncement: "The battle must be fought with brutality and all resistance must be broken. In this most serious hour of the Fatherland, I expect every one of my soldiers to be courageous and again courageous. The enemy must be beaten—now or never! Thus lives Germany!"

The next day, December 12, the second group heard the same exhortations. There was one difference: the offensive was once more postponed (as in 1940). *Null*-Day was now set for December 16. This, said Hitler, was a definite date. Definite, that is, if the weather was bad enough to ground Allied aircraft.

3

The night of December 15 was cold and quiet along the Ardennes front. Twisting eighty-five miles through terrain similar to New England's Berkshires, it was held by six American divisions. Of these, three were new, the other three exhausted and bled white in battle. This was known as the Ghost Front—a cold quiet place where for over two months both sides had rested and watched and avoided irritating each other.

That night no Allied commander seriously feared a German attack. Hours earlier Montgomery had stated flatly that the Germans "cannot stage major offensive operations." In fact things were so dull he asked Eisenhower if there was any objection to his going off to England the next week.

Three German armies—250,000 men and thousands of machines—had been moved secretly to the line of departure, the noise of half-tracks drowned out by low-flying planes. By midnight of the fifteenth the troops were assembled at their assault posts. They stood shivering but listened with genuine enthusiasm as officers read a message from Field Marshal von Rundstedt:

> *We gamble everything!* You carry with you the holy obligation to give all to achieve superhuman objectives for our Fatherland and our Führer!

The excitement of old victories rose in the men. Once more they were on the attack. Deutschland über Alles!

At 5:30 A.M. an eruption of flame and smoke burst all along the Ghost Front. For eighty-five miles mortars coughed, rockets hissed up their launching platforms, 88s roared. The ground shook. Hundreds of tanks rumbled and clanked, and from the rear came the hollow boom of railroad guns hurling their fourteen-inch shells at targets miles behind the American lines.

After an hour the barrage stopped. There was a stunned, momentary silence. Ghostly white-sheeted forms, almost invisible against the new-fallen snow, came out of the haze toward GIs advancing in a slow ominous walk twelve and fourteen abreast. As Hitler's infantrymen filtered into the American forward position, planes of a new design came out of the east with a strange crackling roar, streaking by at unbelievable speed. The Germans looked up at their new jets and many cheered, wild with excitement. Hitler's "miracle weapons" were not talk but fact.

The power, fervor and surprise of their attack were met with a stubborn, if makeshift, defense by the green or worn-out American troops. Cooks and bakers, clerks and musicians, loggers and truck drivers were thrown pell-mell into the line to stem the tide. Some turned in terror and ran; many stood and fought. In some places the Americans held; in others the Germans burst through almost unopposed. In the north a narrow valley called the Losheim Gap was lightly defended even though this had been the classic gateway from east to west. Through this seven-mile corridor invading German armies had poured in 1870, in 1914 and in 1940. Once more German troops—this time accompanied by tanks, armored cars and assault guns—advanced unimpeded into the Gap.

By dusk the northern part of the United States lines was in a shambles but General Omar Bradley, leader of more combat troops than any American field commander in history, had received such fragmentary reports that he assured Eisenhower it was merely a "spoiling attack." Eisenhower disagreed. "This is no local attack, Brad," he said. "It isn't logical for the Germans to launch a local attack at our weakest point." He didn't think they could afford "to sit on their hands" until they found out, and told Bradley to send two armored divisions to the rescue.

Hitler was elated at the reports of breakthrough in the north. Late that night he telephoned the commander of Army Group B far south of the Ardennes. "From this day on, Balck," Hitler said, "not a foot of ground is to be given up. Today we march!" He told how his tanks were already poised on the heights above the road to Bastogne. And the weather was still "Hitler weather." Fog, drizzle and haze, it was forecast, would continue to ground Allied planes. "Balck, Balck," he exclaimed, "everything has changed in the West! Success—complete success—is now in our grasp!"

Success continued and at noon, December 18, German broadcasters raised the hopes of the people. "Our troops are again on the march," said one announcer. "We shall present the Führer with Antwerp by Christmas." At Eagle's Eyrie Hitler was learning that a Manteuffel column had opened up the road to Bastogne. Major penetrations had been achieved just as predicted and he talked confidently of a victory that would turn the tide. He felt so good he took a short walk in the countryside and was so refreshed he decided to do it every day.

In Paris there was near panic in many French government offices. The Blitzkrieg of 1940 was still a fresh, bitter memory. At SHAEF headquarters in Versailles an excited delegation of high-ranking French officers headed by General Juin had arrived to find out what was happening in the Ardennes. The Frenchmen were amazed at the succession of calm orderly offices. "I don't understand," exclaimed one agitated general. "You're not packing!"

By midnight the Ardennes battlefield was in turmoil, a scene of indescribable confusion to those involved in the hundreds of struggles. No one —German or American, private or general—knew what was really happening. In the next two days a series of disasters struck the defenders. On the snowy heights of the Schnee Eiffel at least 8000 Americans—perhaps 9000 for the battle was too confused for accuracy—were bagged by Hitler's troops. Next to Bataan, it was the greatest mass surrender of Americans in history.

Only seven jeeploads of Skorzeny men in American uniforms managed to break through the lines but these were raising havoc beyond his initial hopes. The leader of one team was directing an American regiment down the wrong road while his men were changing signposts and snipping telephone wires. Another jeepload, stopped by a United States column for information, feigned fear so convincingly that the Americans caught their panic and turned tail. A third group severed the main telephone cables connecting the headquarters of Bradley and his commander in the north, General Courtney Hodges.

But the greatest damage was done by a team that had been captured. When the four confessed their mission to an American intelligence officer the news was immediately broadcast that thousands of Germans in American uniforms were operating as saboteurs behind the lines. At once this information was associated with a verified report of widely dispersed parachutists north of Malmédy—an abortive paradrop which had failed even more dismally than Skorzeny's operation. Out of two fiascos was developing a formidable success.

By December 20 half a million Americans throughout the Ardennes were quizzing each other on lonely roads, in dense pine forests and in deserted villages. Passwords and dog tags no longer proved identity. You were an American only if you knew the capital of Pennsylvania, the identity of "Pruneface" or how many homers Babe Ruth had hit.

In Paris terror of Skorzeny and his men had reached panic peak. According to one hysterical report, Skorzeny men dressed as nuns and priests had just floated to earth. Their destination, according to the confession of a captured Skorzenyite, was the Café de la Paix. There they would join forces and kidnap Eisenhower. American security officers firmly believed this fabrication. SHAEF headquarters was surrounded with barbed wire and the guard quadrupled. Tanks stood at the gates, passes were examined and re-examined. If a door slammed, Eisenhower's office was pestered with calls asking if he was still alive. Skorzeny's twenty-eight men had done their work well.

By the following morning, the twenty-first, the battle had assumed a recognizable shape. It was a giant bulge. In the middle, at Bastogne, completely surrounded, was a collection of Americans under an acting commander of the 101st Airborne Division, Brigadier General Anthony McAuliffe, the division artillery officer. Called upon to surrender by a German *parlementaire*, he offhandedly replied, "Nuts." The one-word message spread throughout the Ardennes and helped raise the flagging spirits of the defenders. The time for running had stopped. The spirit of resistance was followed by an abrupt end of "Hitler weather." A bright sun shone next morning on the Ardennes for the first time and before noon sixteen big C-47s were dropping supplies to the encircled men at Bastogne.

The tide of battle was threatening to turn but Hitler did not yet know it. Manteuffel's tanks were already far beyond the American enclave of Bastogne and approaching the Meuse. But Manteuffel himself was deeply concerned; the German infantry army on his left was far behind. On December 24 he phoned Führer Headquarters from a château near La Roche. "Time is running short," he told Jodl. His left flank was exposed and the time had come for a complete new plan. He could not keep driving toward the Meuse and still take Bastogne. When Jodl protested that the Führer would never abandon the drive to Antwerp, Manteuffel argued that there was still a chance for a great victory *if* they followed his plan. "I'll wheel north on this side of the Meuse. We'll trap the Allies east of the river." The proposal shocked Jodl but he promised to pass it on to the Führer.

But Hitler would not believe that full success could not be achieved. His confidence carried over to Christmas, which he celebrated, to the amazement of his circle, with a glass of wine. It was the first time Fräulein

Schröder had ever seen him take wine with any pleasure. Later in the day he refused another request by Manteuffel to abandon the attack on Bastogne even though his most advanced Panzer division had just been cut off by an American armored division and was being smashed to pieces. December 26 was a day of Allied might. The snows that now blanketed the entire Ardennes were red with blood but nowhere was the carnage greater than in the pocket a few miles from the Meuse River where General Ernest "Gravel Voice" Harmon's 2nd Armored Division was savaging Manteuffel's 2nd Panzer Division in a hundred small engagements.

At Eagle's Eyrie an argument over Autumn Fog had continued since morning. Jodl was now saying, "Mein Führer, we must face the facts squarely. We cannot force the Meuse." The 2nd Panzer was close to disaster and Patton had just opened up a narrow corridor from the south to besieged Bastogne. Throughout the Ardennes it was the same story. For the moment it was a static struggle; the great offensive had been temporarily stalled.

Everyone had a plan and Hitler listened to them all. Finally he spoke. "We have had unexpected setbacks—because my plan was not followed to the letter." He frowned. Then his face lightened with a new hope. "But all is not yet lost." He issued new orders: Manteuffel was to turn to the northeast, thus outflanking most of the Americans in the top half of the bulge. "I want three new divisions and at least 25,000 fresh replacements rushed to the Ardennes," he announced to a semicircle of somber faces. Granted the Allies could not be wiped out in a single dramatic blow as planned, Autumn Fog could still be turned into a successful battle of attrition. And this would surely bring Germany a substantial political victory.

These orders were intercepted by the Ultra team and passed on to Eisenhower—and he was assured that Hitler's attack had shot its bolt. What Ultra did not learn was that the Führer and his chosen successor had just engaged in a violent quarrel. At least the violence was on Hitler's side when Göring proposed they seek a truce. "The war is lost," he said. "Now we must get in touch with Count Bernadotte." Folke Bernadotte, whose father was Swedish King Gustavus V's brother, would surely act as mediator for any armistice negotiations.

Hitler, so a pale-faced Göring reported shortly to his wife, had raged and screamed about betrayal and cowardice but he himself had replied in an earnest and composed manner: "Mein Führer, I could never do anything behind your back." He assured Hitler that he would remain faithful in bad times as well as good, then repeated his conviction that an immediate armistice was essential. Hitler, he said, calmed down a bit but then sharply replied: "I forbid you to take any step in this matter. If you go against my orders I will have you shot." Never had Frau Göring seen her husband so shaken as he told her all this. "This is the final break," he said glumly. "There is no sense my attending any more daily briefings. He does not believe me any more. He does not listen to me."

4

To the Germans the classic struggle was known as the Ardennes Offensive but to the Americans it was the Battle of the Bulge. By December 28 its third and final phase was fast approaching. At a special meeting of his top military leaders that day Hitler admitted the situation was desperate, but he had never learned the word "capitulation" and would pursue his aim with fanaticism. "As much as I may be tormented by worries and even physically shaken by them, nothing will make the slightest change in my decision to fight on till at last the scales tip to our side." He was, therefore, launching a new offensive, North Wind, on New Year's Day south of the Ardennes. Chances of victory were bright. The final assembly of troops had been completely camouflaged from the Allies, who had failed even to send up any air reconnaissance in the area. "These people did not think it necessary to look around. They did not believe it at all likely that we could take the initiative. Perhaps they were even influenced by the conviction that I am already dead or that, at any rate, I suffer from cancer . . ." The irrelevant allusion to cancer near the anniversary of his mother's death from that disease was revealing.

He went on to say that their first aim was to clear up the situation in the West by offensive action. "We must be fanatical in this aim," he said and resorted to sarcasm. "Perhaps there are still some who will secretly object, saying: 'All right, but will it succeed?' Gentlemen, the same objection was raised in the year 1939. I was told in writing and vocally that the thing could not be done; that it was impossible. Even in the winter of 1940 I was told: 'You cannot do that. Why don't we stay behind the Westwall?'" His voice hardened. "What would have happened to us if we had not attacked them? You have exactly the same situation today."

During the military conference that same day Rundstedt made the mistake of urging Hitler to abandon Autumn Fog and retreat before an Allied counteroffensive started. Hitler flared up. They would renew the drive to the Meuse, he said, just as soon as North Wind got under way. He jabbed a finger at a point on the large wall map a hundred miles south of the Bulge. Throughout German history New Year's Eve had always been a night of good omen for German arms and this year's would be an unpleasant surprise for an enemy who always celebrated New Year rather than Christmas. The certain success of North Wind, he said, would "automatically bring about the collapse of the threat to the left of the main offensive in the Ardennes"—he stressed the next few words—"*which will then be resumed* with a fresh promise of success." His listeners were impressed by his ardor, belied as it was by a trembling left hand and wan appearance. "In the meantime," he continued, "Model will consolidate his holdings and reorganize for a new attempt on the Meuse. And he will also make another powerful assault on Bastogne. Above all, we must have Bastogne!" By midnight nine Panzer and Volksgrenadier divisions began to converge on the town Hitler wanted at all costs.

"Military qualities don't show themselves in an exercise on a sand model," he told General Thomale, inspector general of the armored forces, the following night. "In the last analysis they show themselves in the capacity to hold on, in perseverance and determination. That's the decisive factor in any victory. Genius is a will-o'-the-wisp unless it is founded on perseverance and fanatical determination. That's the most important thing in human existence." World history, he said, could only be made by a man with fanatical determination who had the courage of his convictions. "No one can last forever. We can't, the other side can't. It's merely a question of who can stand it longer. The one who must hold out longer is the one who's got everything at stake." If America gave up nothing would happen to her; New York would still be New York. "But if we were to say today, 'We've had enough,' Germany would cease to exist." That was why Hitler doggedly continued a war that seemed lost. To a gambler like him a thousand-to-one chance was worth taking. What would be sheer madness to another was only logical for one with his obsession.

His chief propagandist was not as sanguine—at least in private. At an intimate New Year's Eve supper, which included Hans Ulrich Rudel, the famous Stuka pilot, Josef Goebbels remarked sardonically that his title as Reich Plenipotentiary for the Total War Effort was quite hollow. "Now there is nothing left to put into effect," he said. "Everything, including all the flower shops, have been closed by British bombers."

At this point Frau Goebbels interrupted with a remark that the guests found hard to believe. "Why don't you tell these old soldiers that for the past three and a half years you have seldom managed to see the Führer alone." Goebbels was embarrassed and tried to stop her, but she would not be quieted: "These people have the right to know about this." Goebbels turned to Hein Ruck, who had warned him in the first days of Hitler's chancellorship that many SA men like himself were not at all happy with Hitler's compromise with the German nationalists. Such a compromise, according to Ruck, would lead eventually to the death of National Socialism. At that time Goebbels had angrily accused Ruck of being an opportunist but now the Propaganda Minister said ruefully, "I should have taken your words more seriously back in 1933." The talk switched to the political and military blunders made in the past few years and there was almost general agreement that the end was at hand. All except Rudel, who exclaimed that the Führer's new secret weapons would bring a surprise victory.

Just before midnight Operation North Wind, designed to take Allied pressure from the Bulge, was launched and eight German divisions rushed from their Westwall position with great élan to assault the Seventh U. S. Army near the boundary of northern Alsace. To the north in the Ardennes, a tremendous artillery barrage erupted at the stroke of midnight. The irrepressible George Patton had ordered every available gun in his command to fire a New Year's salute.

Five minutes later Adolf Hitler's voice, somewhat raspy but confident, was broadcast throughout the Reich. Germany, he said, would rise like a phoenix from its ruined cities and go to ultimate victory. Afterward he entertained the family circle in his private bunker. Everyone was relaxed by champagne but there was a subdued atmosphere. The most enthusiastic was Hitler, who needed no alcohol. The others listened in silence to his prophecies of great success for Germany in 1945. At first Bormann alone seconded them but as Hitler went on for more than an hour the others became infected by his enthusiasm in spite of themselves.

At 4:35 A.M. the Führer left the gathering so he could hear the first reports of North Wind. It started auspiciously but the Ultra team had succeeded in passing on his battle directives to Eisenhower, who quickly reduced the U. S. Seventh Army front and prevented the Germans from cutting off a salient. Thanks to the warning, the Americans were able to hold off the German attack, which came to a standstill after a fifteen-mile advance.

In the Ardennes the Allies went over to the offensive on January 3, 1945, with massive attacks on the center of the Bulge from north and south designed to cut the huge salient in two. The Germans fought tenaciously, yielding every yard of snow at heavy cost to both sides. They were dug in with their usual efficient use of terrain. American troops moved slowly since the dense fog eliminated air support and cut down the use of artillery. Tanks and self-propelled guns slipped and skidded on the iced trails and roads, often crashing into each other.

Churchill flew over from England to observe the counteroffensive, which was being supported by a considerable British assault on the western tip of the Bulge. On January 6 he met with Eisenhower, who was vexed by the slow, arduous progress of the British and American troops. Was it possible, he asked, to get help from the Russians to take pressure from the Ardennes? Churchill knew that Stalin was mounting a new offensive but not when it would start. "You may find many delays on the staff level," he told Eisenhower. "But I expect Stalin would tell me if I asked him. Shall I try?" The answer was a relieved yes, and that same day Churchill cabled a request for a major Russian offensive during January. The response from Moscow was immediate. A large-scale attack, said Stalin, would be launched not later than the second half of January.

Simultaneously Allied drives from north and south, designed to pinch the Bulge in its midriff, began to gain ground on the morning of January 7 and by the following day had drawn so close together that Hitler was forced to authorize a withdrawal of those units in the western half of the salient. Within an hour those Panzers which had almost crossed the Meuse did an about-face and hastened to get east of the Bastogne–Liège highway.

It was the end of Hitler's great dream. Now the question was: would the hundreds of thousands of German tanks and self-propelled guns lumbering eastward cross the highway in time or be caught in a sack? Would the attempted retreat be another Stalingrad?

On the ninth of January Guderian once more journeyed to Eagle's Eyrie and warned Hitler for the third time that the Red Army was about to launch a massive offensive. Today he brought maps and charts made up by Gehlen, his chief of intelligence, showing the relative distributions of strength—and Gehlen's recommendation that East Prussia be evacuated immediately if Berlin itself were to be held.

When Guderian displayed the maps and charts, Hitler angrily labeled them "completely idiotic" and ordered his chief of staff to have the man who had made them shut up in a lunatic asylum. Guderian lost his temper. "The man who made these," he said, "is General Gehlen, one of my best General Staff officers. I should not have shown them to you were I in disagreement with them. If you want Gehlen sent to a lunatic asylum, then you had better have me certified as well!" Hitler's flare-up subsided and he mixed reassurances with praise. "The eastern front," he said, "has never before possessed such a strong reserve as now. That is your doing. I thank you for it."

Guderian was not placated. "The eastern front," he said, "is like a house of cards. If the front is broken through at one point all the rest will collapse, since twelve and a half divisions are far too small a reserve for so extended a front." Hitler, as usual, had the last word. He refused to deprive the Ardennes of any of its reserves on the ground that there was still hope of limited success there. "The eastern front," he concluded, "must help itself and make do with what it's got." As Guderian drove back to his headquarters at Zossen he was glum. He knew that both Hitler and Jodl were as aware as he that any major Soviet offensive could easily break through the unreinforced lines. Had they blinded themselves to the catastrophe that was imminent in the East because neither had been born in that region? To Prussians like himself, it was a homeland won at great cost—to be defended at all cost.

Three days later Stalin kept his word to Churchill. Almost 3,000,000 Red Army troops—more than a dozen times those landed by the Allies on D-Day—attacked some 750,000 poorly armed Germans on a four-hundred-mile front extending from the Baltic Sea right down the middle of Poland. Supported by massed artillery and led by seemingly inexhaustible streams of "Stalin" and T-34 tanks, hordes of Red infantrymen began storming the pitifully inadequate defense system devised by Guderian. Although weather grounded most of the Red Air Force tactical support, by dusk the first echelon of attackers had pushed forward as much as twelve miles.

Germany was now caught between powerful forces on east and west, for that day also saw substantial victory in the Ardennes. American infantry divisions—including Vice-President Truman's old outfit, the 35th—joined with the 6th Armored Division to trap thousands of first-rate German troops east of Bastogne.

At Eagle's Eyrie Hitler appeared serene to Traudl Junge, who was just returning from Christmas holidays in Munich. At dinner he answered her grim stories of the heavy air raids on Munich with a promise. "This nightmare will abruptly stop in a few weeks," he said. "Our new jets are coming out in quantity now, and then the Allies will be leery of flying over Germany." In mid-January Hitler and his entourage left Eagle's Eyrie for new headquarters in Berlin. Outwardly Hitler did not appear at all depressed, and in fact laughed with the others when someone joked that Berlin was now the only practical place for headquarters since one could travel between the west and east fronts by subway.

A fresh pincer attack had just been launched on the evaporating Bulge from north and south. On January 16 the two forces met a few miles north of Bastogne. In one great bite, half of the Bulge had been eliminated and about 20,000 Germans cut off. The feat was marred by bitterness between Americans and Britons. It had started a few days earlier when Montgomery, in charge of the northern half of the Battle of the Bulge, gave correspondents the impression that he had personally saved the day and that British troops in large numbers were helping extricate the Americans from their hole. Most American correspondents were irritated at what they considered a patronizing tone in the announcement since it was well known that relatively few British troops were involved and that American generals, for the most part, felt impeded by Montgomery's deliberate tactics. For a few days it appeared as if Hitler's dream of driving a wedge between the two Allies had, thanks to human nature, succeeded. But Eisenhower, as much diplomat as soldier, effectively smoothed out ruffled feathers in both camps.

By January 17 there was no consolation at all for Hitler. Manteuffel's army had joined the full retreat. A few picked infantrymen were left behind—the very young, old and useless. These men fought a gallant rearguard battle in lonely hopelessness. Boys of fourteen and fifteen died, rifles frozen to their hands; men in their fifties were found in cellars, feet black with putrefaction. The retreating columns were harassed by planes and big guns. None who survived would ever forget the overpowering American artillery. Winding lines of trucks, tanks and self-propelled guns rumbled toward the Fatherland over icy roads and trails clogged with snowdrifts. Long columns of infantrymen tramped in the snow, tormented as much by the bitter weather as by the retreating enemy.

The Battle of the Bulge was over. Left behind were two tiny ravaged countries, destroyed homes and farms, dead cattle, dead souls, dead minds —and more than 75,000 bodies.

Autumn Fog was creeping back to the Führer like some huge wounded beast. It reminded many of Napoleon's retreat from Moscow. Men shuffled painfully through the snow, feet encased in burlap bags, with shawls wound around their heads like careless turbans. They plodded on frozen feet, bedeviled by biting winds, bombs and shells. The wounded and sick crept back to the homeland with rotting insides, ulcers oozing, pus running from destroyed ears. They staggered east on numb feet with despair in their hearts, stricken by dysentery, which left its bloody trail of filth in the snow.

Their will was broken. Few who survived the retreat believed there was now any chance of German victory. Almost every man brought back a story of doom, of Allied might and of the terrifying weapon forged in the Ardennes: the American fighter. The GI who came out of the battle was the quintessential American, the man Hitler did not believe existed.

Chapter Thirty

"THIS TIME WE MUST NOT SURRENDER FIVE MINUTES BEFORE MIDNIGHT" JANUARY 17–APRIL 20, 1945

1

By January 17, 1945, the Red Army had overrun or by-passed German troops in the Baltic and crossed the Vistula River from Warsaw to Lower Silesia. The Soviets were so close to Auschwitz that inmates could hear the rumble of their artillery. For the past weeks SS guards had been burning storehousefuls of shoes, clothing and hair to hide traces of mass exterminations. Within two days most German officials in the area were in flight and the over-age *Volkssturm* (People's Militia) had disintegrated. That afternoon guards lined up 58,000 ill-clothed, hungry inmates in a freezing wind and marched them to the west for possible use as hostages. Some 6000 others, too ill to struggle to their feet, were left behind, it was hoped, to be disposed of by bombs and shells in the Soviet advance, but when the Red Army troops finally, on January 27, streamed through the front gate with its slogan Work Brings Freedom, there were still almost

5000 emaciated survivors, so weak they could barely cheer. Efforts to obliterate all traces of the murders at the vast complex had continued until that morning with the final blasting of the gas chambers and five crematoria, but even this could not wipe out the grisly proof of what had gone on in Hitler's death factory. Despite fires and detonations, Red Cross officials found 368,820 men's suits, 836,255 women's coats, 13,964 carpets and seven tons of hair. They came upon mountains of toothbrushes, eyeglasses, shoes, artificial limbs—and the mass graves of hundreds of thousands of human beings.

In Berlin that afternoon General Guderian and his aide climbed the dozen steps up to the main door of the chancellery to attend the Führer military conference. Once inside they took a long detour to Hitler's office; direct passage was closed off by damage from Allied bombs. They passed windows covered by cardboard, through corridors and rooms barren of pictures, carpets and tapestries, finally reaching an anteroom where guards stood poised with machine pistols. An SS officer politely requested them to hand over their side arms and carefully examined their briefcases. This, a regulation since July 20, applied even to the army chief of staff.

By four o'clock the room was filled with military leaders, including Göring, Keitel and Jodl. Moments later the doors to the Führer's office were opened, revealing a spacious room sparingly decorated. In the middle of one wall was a massive desk, behind it a black-upholstered chair facing the garden. The high-ranking conferees seated themselves in heavy leather chairs while their aides and the lesser members either stood or found straight chairs.

At 4:20 P.M. Adolf Hitler shuffled in, shoulders stooped, left arm hanging loose. He greeted a few with a limp shake from his incapacitated right hand, then heavily sank into a chair pushed forward by an aide. The conference opened with Guderian reporting realistically on the growing disaster in the East. Hitler made remarkably few suggestions, almost as if it were beyond his scope, but once the western front came up for discussion he showed lively interest, interspersing criticism with nostalgic reminiscences from his war ("Usually, in the First World War, in 1915 and 1916—we really had an ammunition allowance that would make your hair stand on end"), then engaging in a lengthy argument with Göring about the reduced rank given officers called out of retirement to active duty. The conference ended at 6:50 P.M. and Guderian started back to Zossen. He was disgusted. They had talked for two and a half hours without reaching a single important decision on the problems of the critical eastern front.

One of those problems was Himmler, who had just been placed in command of an emergency army group designed to stop the main thrust of Marshal G. K. Zhukov. To Guderian his selection was plain idiocy but Hitler had argued that the Reichsführer was the only man capable of forming a major force overnight; his name alone would inspire a fight to the end. Bormann had encouraged this appointment but those close to Himmler were convinced it was a plot to ruin their chief. Sending him to the East would not only keep him away from Führer Headquarters and allow Bormann to strengthen his growing hold on Hitler, but would inevitably give convincing proof of Himmler's military incompetence.

Himmler, an ex-army cadet who secretly longed to lead troops into battle, took the bait, if a bit reluctantly. While he feared Bormann, it never occurred to him that his rival was preparing his downfall. He started east in his special train determined to halt the Russians at the Vistula River. To do so he had a few staff officers, one outdated map and a name for his unit, Army Group Vistula. Except for several scattered units, his command existed only on paper. As new divisions arrived, Himmler foolishly began forming an east-west defense line running from the Vistula to the Oder, which merely served as protection for Pomerania to the north. In other words, he barricaded the side door while leaving the front gate wide open.

Zhukov, consequently, simply by-passed this lateral line and kept moving due west, impeded only by isolated groups, and, as the Führer conference ended on January 27, his troops were a hundred miles from Berlin. Ahead lay the Oder, the last major geographical obstacle they would have to hurdle before reaching the Reich chancellery.

Three days later Hitler spoke to the people. He raised the specter of international Jewry and Asiatic Bolshevism before calling on every German to do his duty to the last. "However grave the crisis may be at the moment," he concluded, "it will, despite everything, finally be mastered by our unalterable will, by our readiness for sacrifice and by our abilities. We shall overcome this calamity, too, and this fight, too, will not be won by central Asia but by Europe; and at its head will be the nation that has represented Europe against the East for 1500 years and shall represent it for all times: our Greater German Reich, the German nation."

During the afternoon Bormann found time to advise his "beloved Mummy-Girl" to lay in a supply of dried vegetables and, "say, fifty pounds of honey"; he also wrote her of the atrocities in the East where the Bolsheviks were ravaging every village. "You and the children must never fall into the hands of these wild beasts!"

Despite such news, the Führer was in good spirits. After the evening's briefing, some of the conferees stayed while he talked informally of the political situation. Relaxed, he spoke like a professor to a group of favorite students, first explaining that he had launched Autumn Fog to split the Allies. Although the battle had been lost, he said, the Americans and British were publicly wrangling over its conduct, a split between these Allies was imminent.

Guderian kept looking impatiently at his watch but the younger officers seemed mesmerized as the Führer predicted that the West was bound to realize before long that Bolshevism was their real enemy and then would join Germany in the common crusade. Churchill knew as well as he that if the Red Army conquered Berlin half of Europe would immediately become Communist and in a few years the other half would be digested. "I never did want to fight the West," he said bitterly. "They forced it on me." But Russia's program was becoming more and more obvious and Roosevelt himself must have had his eyes opened when Stalin recognized the Communist-backed Lublin Government in Poland. "Time is our ally," he said. That was why he demanded last-ditch defenses in the East. Wasn't it obvious that every Festung they hung onto would eventually be a springboard in the German-American-British crusade to wipe out Jewish Bolshevism? His voice rose as he reminded his listeners that in 1918 the Fatherland had been stabbed in the back by the General Staff. But for its premature surrender, Germany would have gained an honorable peace and there would have been no postwar chaos, no Communist attempts to seize the country, no inflation, no depression. "This time," he said, repeating an earlier vow, "we must not surrender five minutes before midnight!"

On the last day of January Hitler was wakened with alarming news: enemy tanks had just crossed the Oder River! No natural barrier of any consequence lay between them and Berlin. The panic in the capital was heightened three days later when the city was subjected to the heaviest bombing of the war. Almost a thousand American bombers leveled much of the center of the city and among the victims was Roland Friesler, president of the People's Court, who was trying Fabian von Schlabrendorff for the July 20 plot. Now Friesler lay pinned in death by a huge beam, still clutching the folder containing Schlabrendorff's evidence of guilt. "The way of God is miraculous," thought Schlabrendorff. "I was the accused; he was the judge. Now he is dead and I am alive."

He and two other defendants were hurriedly transferred by small car to the Gestapo prison. It was still early afternoon but the sky was dark from the smoke and falling ashes. Flames were everywhere. The Gestapo building at 9 Prinz Albrechtstrasse was burning yet its bomb shelter was only slightly damaged and as Schlabrendorff passed another prisoner, Admiral Canaris, he called out, "Friesler is dead!" The good news was passed along to other prisoners. With luck, the Allies would free them before the next trials.

Hitler's headquarters was also badly damaged in the raid and the next day Bormann described its woeful state to his wife. There was no communication with the outside, not even any light, power or water. "We have a water cart standing before the Reich chancellery, and that is our only supply for cooking and washing up! And the worst thing of all, so Müller tells me, is the toilets. These Kommando pigs use them constantly, and not one of them ever thinks of taking a bucket of water with him to flush the place." By this time Bormann, who now attended the daily military discussions, had insinuated himself into an impregnable position with the Führer. No longer were Göring, Speer and Himmler rivals for his trust and affection, and Goebbels had come to realize his own influence depended on a continuation of the uneasy alliance with the Reichsleiter.

A final mark of honor came to Bormann early in February. The Führer began dictating to him a political testament. If the Reich *did* fall— and Hitler still entertained the faint hope of some miracle—he wanted to record for history how closely he had come to achieving his magnificent dream. It was typical that he wanted the last word. And so on February 4, with the Bolsheviks at the gates of Berlin, the indefatigable Bormann began jotting down the Führer's final explanation to history of what went wrong. The British, he said, could have put an end to the war at the beginning of 1941. "But the Jews would have none of it. And their lackeys, Churchill and Roosevelt, were there to prevent it." Such a peace would have kept America from meddling in European affairs and, under German guidance, Europe would have speedily become unified. With the Jewish poison eliminated, unification would have been simple. And Germany, her rear secure, could have achieved "the ambition of my life and the raison d'étre of National Socialism—the destruction of Bolshevism." How simple it all would have been if only the English had been logical and reasonable! But they were neither and so he had been forced, as custodian of the fundamental interests of Germany, to wage total war.

Two days later there was another session. "Our enemies," dictated Hitler, "are gathering all their forces for the final assault." It was the final quarter of an hour. The situation was desperate. "We have facing us an incongruous coalition, drawn together by hatred and jealousy and cemented by the panic with which the National Socialist doctrine fills this Jew-ridden motley." This will to exterminate the Third Reich left but one alternative: a fight to the end. "No game is lost until the final whistle." If

Churchill were suddenly to disappear, everything could change in a flash! He began to daydream out loud of the possibility of an about-face by the British aristocracy. "We can still snatch victory in the final sprint!"

Next to Bormann, the man he saw most in these days was his favorite architect, Paul Giesler. They would spend many hours poring over an illuminated wooden model of the new Linz, which would outrank Vienna as the jewel of Austria, or talk until early morning of architecture and Bolshevism, of art and the Western Allies, of his dream of saving Europe and uniting it into one grand unity. It was the large model city that was an unfailing inspiration to him and sometimes Goebbels would be dragged out of bed so Hitler could demonstrate with lights how Linz would look in morning, noon and night. He could have been the young Hitler lecturing to Kubizek on the wonders of their rebuilt city.

2

On February 12 the Big Three announced that a meeting at Yalta had just concluded with unanimity on the defeat of the Axis and the world of the future. The communiqué was widely acclaimed in the United States, England and the Soviet Union. It also delighted Goebbels, for it gave him an opportunity to resurrect the bogey of unconditional surrender. The decision of Roosevelt, Churchill and Stalin at Yalta to dismember Germany and force her to pay crushing reparations, he argued, proved that Germany must fight with renewed vigor—or be obliterated.

Hitler's satisfaction at the propaganda windfall was tempered by an irritating conflict with Guderian at the next day's noon conference. The general bluntly declared that Himmler had neither the experience nor the proper staff to lead the proposed counterattack against the Zhukov spearhead at the Oder. "How dare you criticize the Reichsführer!" exclaimed Hitler. Guderian had gone too far to back down and insisted that his own deputy, Walter Wenck, take command of the operation. Hitler was incensed and the two men began to argue so strenuously that one by one the conferees unobtrusively left the room until only Himmler, Wenck and a few blank-faced adjutants remained. For about two hours their argument continued. Each time Hitler shouted, "How dare you!" and took a deep breath, Guderian would stolidly reiterate his demand that Wenck be made Himmler's assistant. And each time the demand was made, Himmler seemed to get a shade paler.

At last Hitler broke off his awkward pacing, stopped in front of the Reichsfuhrer's chair and said, with a sigh of resignation, "Well, Himmler, General Wenck is going to Army Group Vistula tonight to take over as chief of staff." He sat down, exhausted. "Let us please resume the conference," he murmured and smiled wryly. "Herr Generaloberst, today the army General Staff won a battle."

Hitler found the time for more dictation the following day. The National Socialists, he told Bormann, had purged the German world of the Jewish poison by *action*, not words. "For us, this has been an essential process of disinfection, which we have prosecuted *to its ultimate limit* and without which we should have ourselves been asphyxiated and destroyed." He revealed that his elimination of Jews had become the most important aim of the war. On the eve of the attack on Poland he had warned them that "they would not be spared if they precipitated another war, and that I would exterminate the vermin throughout Europe, and this time once and for all." This was not a threat, he said, but his chief historical mission. "Well, we have lanced the Jewish abscess; and the world of the future will be eternally grateful to us."

The following evening Dr. Giesing chanced to meet Hitler in the chancellery air raid shelter. The Führer was pale, his right arm trembled; he could not walk any distance without grasping something for support. Hitler seemed quite absent-minded and several times asked the same question almost as if a needle was stuck on a record. "Where are you from, Doctor? Oh yes, Krefeld, Krefeld, yes, Krefeld . . ." He rambled on, first assuring Giesing that the Americans would never break through the Westwall, then declaring that if Germany *should* lose the war he would die with his troops, and finally boasting about a new weapon called an atom bomb, which he would use "even if the white cliffs of England disappear into the water." So saying, he walked off without a word of farewell.

Others noted this occasional absent-mindedness; and his growing shortness of temper was aggravated by the Allied bombing of Dresden on February 13. The old town was almost completely destroyed in a terrifying fire storm which lay waste 1600 acres—almost three times the damage done to London during the entire war. The preliminary report stated that at least 100,000 people, probably more, had been killed in two successive raids. The final report by the area police chief listed a probable death toll, "primarily women and children," of 25,000 with 35,000 listed as missing.

At first Goebbels refused to believe that Dresden had been destroyed, then wept. When at last he found voice it was to castigate Göring. "What a burden of guilt this parasite has brought on his head for his slackness and interest in his own comfort. Why didn't the Führer listen to my earlier warnings?" Hitler reserved his ire for the British and American fliers who had dropped the bombs, yet rejected Goebbels' suggestion that the Allied air force prisoners be executed in retaliation. He agreed in principle, he said, but wanted to wait before making the final decision. Ribbentrop and others were able to dissuade him.

That February rumors of peace negotiations appeared in newspapers of neutral European countries. They had been inspired largely by the latest efforts of Peter Kleist, who had been ordered explicitly by Hitler to cease all dealings with the Russians. He did so but then, on his own initiative, embarked on a new adventure in Sweden which led eventually to another attempt for peace, this time with the West. He had begun by agreeing to talk with Gilel Storch, an important representative of the World Jewish Congress. At their first conference in a Stockholm hotel Storch proposed that they negotiate for the release of some 4300 Jews from various concentration camps.

Kleist said it was impossible to solve the Jewish problem by such individual operations. It could only be done politically. "If the preservation of Jewry can be traded for the preservation of Europe," said Kleist, "then we will have a genuine 'deal' that's worth risking my life."

Storch was enthusiastic. He suggested Kleist speak with an American diplomat in the Stockholm Embassy, Ivor Olson, the personal adviser to Roosevelt for the War Refugee Committee of Northern and Western Europe. Storch made the contact, reporting back excitedly that President Roosevelt was willing to redeem the lives of the 1,500,000 Jews in concentration camps "with politics." This was exactly what Kleist wanted and he repeated Storch's words to Werner Best, the Nazi commissioner of Denmark, whose advice was to approach Himmler's assistant, Kaltenbrunner.

Upon return to Berlin Kleist did so and was placed under house arrest, just as he had been for dealing with Clauss. But after a few days Kaltenbrunner informed him that Himmler was "willing to take up this Swedish possibility." Kleist was to go to Stockholm to start negotiations and, as a token of good faith, bring a gift of 2000 Jews with him. Interest in trading with Jews was not new to Himmler. He had been tentatively negotiating on this line in other quarters, using them as blackmail for a negotiated peace. He was being encouraged by two men of dubious character. One was his masseur, a doctor without a medical degree, Felix Kersten, a Balt, born in Estonia. The second self-seeker was Himmler's chief of espionage, Schellenberg. He too was attempting to convince Himmler that a show of humanity to political and war prisoners would prove to the world that he was no monster. Convinced that Hitler was leading Germany and himself to destruction, Schellenberg had been tirelessly urging Himmler to explore every possible avenue to peace.

This was no easy task since these negotiations had to be conducted without Hitler's knowledge; nor did it help that Kaltenbrunner was faithful to his Führer and, moreover, disliked and distrusted Schellenberg. Kaltenbrunner had continuously urged Himmler not to get into schemes that might result in Hitler's displeasure—or worse. That is, until he heard Kleist's latest proposition. He did trust Kleist, and that was undoubtedly one reason Himmler had been persuaded to send him back to Sweden.

But the machinations within the SS were such that no sooner did Kleist begin preparing for his trip than he was recalled to Kaltenbrunner's office and told that the case no longer concerned him. Kaltenbrunner could not explain that Schellenberg, his enemy, had just persuaded Himmler not to share any credit with the Foreign Office—and so was sending Dr. Kersten instead of Kleist to handle the transaction. Kersten promptly began negotiations with the Swedish Minister of Foreign Affairs for the freedom of Scandinavian prisoners in concentration camps, and these went so smoothly it was agreed that Count Folke Bernadotte should come to Berlin to make final arrangements with Himmler personally.

Since Kleist had been warned to keep quiet, his own chief, Ribbentrop knew nothing of all this until the Swedish ambassador in Berlin innocently sent an official message to Himmler requesting that Bernadotte be granted an interview with the Reichsführer—and being official, of course, it had to go through the Foreign Office. For the first time Ribbentrop realized that negotiations were being carried on by his rival behind his back. He sent for Fritz Hesse, who had so tirelessly worked for peace with England before the war. Did Hesse think that Count Bernadotte would be a suitable person to transmit "peace feelers"? Hesse responded with a question of his own: had the Führer given his consent for such negotiations? No, Ribbentrop admitted, but perhaps he could be persuaded. Together they prepared a memorandum on the subject which was presented to Hitler. While it did not contain the key word "capitulation," Hesse was not deceived. It was, he observed, little better than an offer to capitulate. He doubted that the West would consider such proposals but said, "Very well, you can try but I don't think anything will come of it."

Ribbentrop began by negotiating with a personal enemy, Himmler. To his surprise, the Reichsführer was more than willing to co-operate; he was terrified that the Führer might find out that Bernadotte was coming to Berlin to discuss other than humanitarian matters. First he gave assurance that the Foreign Office would have his full personal support in the future, then promised to issue an order canceling Hitler's instructions to destroy prisoners of war and inmates of concentration camps rather than abandon them alive to the enemy. Ribbentrop struggled to hold back tears of joy as he revealed all this to Hesse. "Yes, now we can at least try to save the German people," he said, and so dispatched Hesse to Stockholm on February 17.

Himmler must have regretted his rash promises to Ribbentrop almost immediately. He became terrified that the Führer might discover—and misinterpret—his actions and, once informed of Bernadotte's arrival in Berlin, he refused to see him unless two of his own antagonists—Kaltenbrunner and Ribbentrop—first met with the count. That, he figured, would prevent them from carrying tales to Hitler. Both were happy to oblige. Kaltenbrunner was first in line but Bernadotte wanted to deal directly with Himmler and decided to tell as little as possible to his assistant. Bernadotte merely proposed that the Swedish Red Cross be allowed to work in the concentration camps and was surprised that Kaltenbrunner not only nodded but said he "quite agreed" that Bernadotte should see Himmler personally.

Within the hour the count was talking to Ribbentrop at the Foreign Office, or rather, was listening. Curious as to how long this would go on, Bernadotte surreptitiously set his stop watch. Ribbentrop went from one subject to another, parroting Nazi platitudes without pause, and finally declared that the living man who contributed most to humanity was "Adolf Hitler, unquestionably Adolf Hitler!" He fell silent and Bernadotte snapped the stop watch at sixty-seven minutes.

The next day Bernadotte was driven to Dr. Gebhardt's sanatorium at Hohenlychen, seventy-five miles north of Berlin, Himmler's unofficial headquarters. Bernadotte found him disconcertingly affable. There was nothing at all diabolic in his appearance; he was quiet and polite, his small hands were meticulously manicured. Bernadotte told him that what had aroused indignation in Sweden was the seizure of hostages and the murder of innocent people. The count, Himmler replied earnestly, obviously was misinformed, and he asked if his guest had any concrete proposals.

Bernadotte proposed that Himmler release Norwegians and Danes from concentration camps for custody in Sweden. This modest request touched off a stream of vehement accusations against the Swedes that made no sense at all to Bernadotte but had probably been inspired by one of Himmler's sudden flashes of fear. "If I were to agree to your proposal," he said, his eyes blinking spasmodically, "the Swedish papers would announce with big headlines that the war criminal Himmler, in terror of punishment for his crimes, is trying to buy his freedom." Then he tacked and said he might just do what Bernadotte asked—if Sweden and the Allies assured him that sabotage would stop in Norway.

"That's unthinkable," replied the count and asked for several other small concessions, which were granted. Encouraged, Bernadotte wondered if Swedish women married to Germans could return to their homeland. This brought a blunt refusal. Himmler had been pushed to the limit, and his mood changed. "You may think it sentimental, even absurd, but I have sworn loyalty to Adolf Hitler, and as a soldier and as a German I cannot go back on my oath. For that reason I cannot do anything in opposition to the Führer's plans and wishes." Only a moment before he had granted concessions that would have infuriated Hitler, but now he began to echo him on the "Bolshevik menace" by prophesying the end of Europe if the eastern front collapsed. This was succeeded by sentimental reminiscences of the "glorious" early days of the Nazi movement—"the most wonderful years of my life."

Bernadotte managed to break in with a polite question on German treatment of the Jews. "Won't you admit there are decent people among the Jews, just as there are among all races? I have many Jewish friends." "You're right," was the reply, "but you in Sweden have no Jewish problem and therefore can't understand the German point of view." At the end of the two-and-a-half-hour conference Himmler promised to give definite answers to all of Bernadotte's requests before he returned to Sweden, and Bernadotte presented his host, who was extremely interested in Scandinavian folklore, with a seventeenth-century work on troll-drums.

Bernadotte returned to Ribbentrop's office. The Foreign Minister seemed more eager to help than before, but his overbearing good humor only irritated Bernadotte, who excused himself as soon as he could do so politely. Ribbentrop immediately called Kleist and asked who was backing Bernadotte. What did he *really* want besides saving the Scandinavians? Kleist noticed a large leather billfold bulging with papers in a chair. It was Bernadotte's. Kleist handed it over, assuming that Ribbentrop would examine the papers inside, but he put the billfold in a large plain envelope and asked that it be returned to the owner. Kleist was impressed. It seemed a unique "gesture of chivalry amidst the dissolution of a total war."

Ribbentrop's agent in Stockholm, Hesse, was receiving little encouragement from the Swedish banker, Wallenberg, who maintained that both Roosevelt and Churchill were determined to destroy Germany. He suggested that the Germans try the East. A clearly defined proposal to Stalin might succeed. "Stalin," he said, "is not committed to the West."

A few days later Hesse saw a photograph in the Swedish papers which raised his hopes. It showed Wallenberg's brother on the steps of the Russian Embassy, arm in arm with Madame Kollontai, the Russian ambassador. This could be a signal that the Kremlin was dissatisfied with the West and ready to talk with Hitler. Encouraged, Hesse returned to Berlin but found his chief completely disinterested in any tidings from Sweden. Ribbentrop lay in bed, ill and depressed. It was all in vain, he said wanly. There was no chance whatever of starting any conversations with the West. "Our enemies want to destroy Germany altogether. That is why they reject every chance of negotiation that might save German lives."

When Hesse insisted that there still were two genuine possibilities of opening conversations, one with the West (he had been assured by Olson, Roosevelt's personal adviser, that the President was willing to negotiate) and another with the East, Ribbentrop came to life. He kept Hesse at his bedside until late that night and sent for him again in the morning. March 16 was a clear sunny day and this time Ribbentrop was out of bed, pacing impatiently. "I have given your reports and comments the most careful thought," he said and confounded Hesse by ordering him to return to Stockholm and start conversations with Madame Kollontai. His instructions would be ready in a few hours. "I am sending them to the Führer for final approval. Your airplane is ready. You can leave for Stockholm tonight."

All that afternoon and late into the night Ribbentrop and his staff gave Hesse advice on how to deal with the Russians. Just after midnight they were interrupted by the telephone. It was Hewel of the Foreign Office, still one of the Führer's most trusted advisers. As Ribbentrop listened, his face turned chalk white. "Please repeat," he said tersely, then, moments later, put down the receiver. He seemed composed but his voice was not. "Gentlemen," he said, "the Führer has prohibited any further conversation with any foreign power! I thank you. You can go now!"

Later Hewel told Hesse what had happened at the chancellery. Hitler had first agreed to a contact with the Russians but, upon reading over the instructions, hesitated. He paced around his room while a phonograph ground out music from *Götterdämmerung*, then tore up the instructions, page by page. "I forbid any further contact with the enemy," he told Hewel. "It is all senseless. Whoever talks to the enemy is a traitor to the Idea. We may fall in the fight against Bolshevism but we shall not negotiate with it. Good night!"

3

A month earlier Hitler had complained to Fräulein Schröder, "I am lied to on all sides." He could rely on no one, and if anything happened to him Germany would be without a Führer. His successor, Göring, had lost the sympathy of the people, and Reichsführer Himmler would be rejected by the party. He apologized for talking politics during lunch, then said:

"Rack your brains again and tell me who my successor is to be. This is a question that I keep on asking myself, without ever getting an answer."

His spirits were raised a week later by Eva Braun's return to Berlin. She had been ordered out of the capital earlier in the month for the relative safety of Munich but after two weeks announced to her friends that she had to return to her man's side no matter what happened. She told them that death no longer mattered and she had to share the fate of the one she loved. Hitler pretended to be angry at her sudden reappearance and made a show of scolding her, but all that evening he repeated how proud he was of Fräulein Braun's devotion.

Several days later, near the end of February, Hitler convened his Gauleiters for a final meeting. They were alarmed by his appearance. He had to be supported by Schaub. His voice was low, his left hand shook badly. Everyone expected a sensational announcement, but instead he delivered a paradoxical sermon that was both inspiring and depressing. First he assured the Gauleiters that, although no wonder weapon was going to rescue the Reich at the last moment, the war could still be won so long as they inspired a "Teutonic fury" in the German people. If the nation failed to respond it had no moral worth and deserved destruction.

He thanked the Gauleiters for their co-operation and loyalty before doing something totally unexpected: he told them frankly of his failing health. He confessed that the trembling in his leg had traveled to his left arm, and made a joke: hopefully it would not move to his head. His last words were vague but ominous: in the future he would be forced to take harsh measures. He hoped they would not feel betrayed should he take steps they did not understand.

Faced as he was by almost certain disaster, Hitler's dominant mood in the days to follow became one of defiance and ire. He railed at Allied airmen who had already killed half a million civilians, and reviled those Germans who were greeting the advancing Americans almost as though they were liberators. His fury knew no bounds on March 7. The railroad bridge over the Rhine at Remagen was seized intact by Hodges' First Army before the defenders could blow it up. To Hitler this was another betrayal and he was determined to punish those responsible. It also gave him an excuse to get rid of the aging Rundstedt, who seemed only bent on retreat. In the emergency he ordered his most trusted trouble-shooter, Otto Skorzeny, to destroy the bridge. One group of Skorzeny frogmen managed to approach it with packages of "Plastit," a plastic explosive, but were discovered in time by an Allied secret weapon, Canal Defense Lights, a powerful beam whose source was undetectable.

By this time the entire German defense system in the West was in jeopardy. Model's Army Group B had been smashed, its remnants shoved back across the Rhine. To the south Hausser's Army Group G had been backed up against the river's west bank and was about to be surrounded. The situation in the East was no better and during these desperate days of mid-March Hitler decided to visit this front. His generals warned him that the situation was so fluid he might be captured or killed but he would not listen. As a concession he had Kempka drive him forward in a Völkswagen rather than the famous Mercedes. Their destination was a castle near the Oder where he pleaded with the commanders of the Ninth Army to contain the Russian drive on Berlin. Every day, every hour was precious, he said, since new secret weapons would be ready momentarily. On the trip back to Berlin, Hitler sat silently beside Kempka, deep in thought. He knew that his talk of secret weapons was visionary and had recently confessed so to his Gauleiters. His atom bomb was many months from completion and his other secret weapons were unrealistic political ones, such as the hope that the West would join in the crusade against Bolshevism. By the time he returned to the city he had seen enough out front. Never again would he venture beyond the chancellery grounds. His only hope was a last-minute political miracle.

Hitler was aware that plots were being woven around him. He knew, for example, of Ribbentrop's negotiations in Sweden and that Himmler was dickering with the Jews but he continued to allow these men to negotiate as if in his own name, even while declaring that all negotiations were futile. If a negotiation failed, he would deny any knowledge of it; if it succeeded, he could take the credit.

It is doubtful, however, that Hitler knew his trusted Speer was urging commanders such as Manteuffel to disobey orders to destroy bridges, dams and factories rather than leave them to the enemy. On March 18 Speer brought his protest against this "scorched earth" policy directly to the Führer. "At this stage of the war," he wrote in a memorandum, "it makes no sense for us to undertake demolitions which may strike at the very life of the nation." If Hitler had ever wavered in determination to scorch German earth, Speer's words spurred him to action. He summoned his quondam architect moments after reading his memorandum and said icily, "If the war is lost, the people will be lost also. It is not necessary to worry about what the German people will need for elemental survival. On the contrary, it is best for us to destroy even these things. For the nation has proved to be the weaker, and the future belongs to the stronger Eastern nation [the Soviet Union]. In any case only those who are inferior will remain after this struggle, for the good have already been killed."

4

In the year 900 Germany's borders were the Oder and the Rhine. By the beginning of March 1945 Hitler's Grossdeutschland was compressed between the same rivers. And his thousand-year Reich was coming to an end. From both east and west his enemies were poised for massive attacks which they were certain would bring quick final victory. On the morning of the third, Montgomery launched his assault across the Rhine. Two airborne divisions—one British and one American—dropped across the river to support the infantrymen, and by nightfall the Germans were in full retreat. A hundred and fifty miles upriver, the unpredictable George Patton had also crossed the Rhine, surprising Montgomery as much as the Germans. It was a brilliant, improvised maneuver done in secret, without a round of artillery preparation and at a cost of only twenty-eight men killed or wounded. A pontoon bridge was thrown across the Rhine and as Patton crossed it he stopped in the middle. "I've been looking forward to this for a long time," he said and urinated into the river.

The rapid advance east of both Montgomery and Patton in the next few weeks caused consternation at Führer Headquarters. Hitler was particularly aroused by the action of Cardinal Galen, who drove out from Münster to surrender the city to an American unit. "If I ever lay hands on that swine," exclaimed Hitler, "I'll have him hanged!" He had also reached the limit of tolerance for his outspoken and feisty army chief of staff. Guderian knew it and, on the morning of March 28, drove up to Berlin determined to have a showdown. He was particularly upset by the fate of 200,000 German soldiers needlessly trapped hundreds of miles behind Russian lines in Kurland. Once inside the partially destroyed chancellery, Guderian and his aide were escorted by a guard down a flight of stairs to a steel-reinforced door guarded by two SS men. This was the entrance to Hitler's new home: a huge bunker buried far below the chancellery garden.

They descended more stairs to a narrow corridor, which was covered with a foot of water. They balanced their way across duckboards to a door, then went down another short flight of stairs to the upper level of the bunker. Twelve small rooms opened on a central vestibule which also served as the general mess hall. Guderian and his aide traversed this passageway, then proceeded down a curving stairway and a final dozen steps to the lower level. Here, in the Führer bunker, were eighteen cubicles, separated by an entrance hall which was divided into a waiting room and the conference room. Beyond these, in a small vestibule, was the emergency exit to four steep flights of concrete steps leading up to the chancellery garden. On the left of the conference room was a small map room, a rest room for the Führer's bodyguard and the six-room suite of Hitler and Eva Braun. The air was stuffy despite a ventilating system whose shrill, monotonous whine penetrated every room of the bunker. The whole structure was protected by a twelve-foot-thick reinforced ceiling, topped by thirty feet of concrete. This would be Hitler's tomb or his bastion of miraculous victory. Perhaps it reminded him of the terrible but heroic trench life of the Great War.

Hitler shuffled in from his adjoining apartment and the noon conference opened with a report by General Theodor Busse on his unsuccessful attempts to relieve a town on the east bank of the Oder. Hitler's criticism of Busse was interrupted by a spirited defense from Guderian. Stung, Hitler suddenly got to his feet with an agility which amazed the conferees. But Guderian was not intimidated. He boldly brought up the subject he and Hitler had fought over for weeks. "Is the Führer going to evacuate the Kurland army?" he asked. "Never!" exclaimed Hitler with a wave of an arm. Large red blotches appeared on his deathly white face. Guderian stood rooted to the spot, then started toward Hitler. Jodl and his deputy shepherded Guderian away, but he kept talking in a loud voice. Finally his aide inveigled him into the anteroom "to answer a phone call" and by the time Guderian returned to the conference room he had control of himself.

Hitler was back in his chair, face pinched, and though his hands trembled, he too had regained his poise. He quietly asked all to leave the room except Guderian and Keitel, then said, "General Guderian, the state of your health requires that you immediately take six weeks' sick leave." As Guderian started to leave Hitler told him to remain until the end of the conference. It continued as if nothing had happened. After several hours, which seemed interminable to Guderian, the session was over. But he was not yet free to go. "Please take good care of yourself," the Führer said solicitously. "In six weeks the situation will be very critical. Then I shall need you urgently." Guderian said he would pick a place to rest that wouldn't be overrun before the weekend, raised his arm in salute and walked away.

On Easter Sunday all resistance in the Ruhr collapsed and Hitler was forced to face the reality of total defeat—a Reich hacked to pieces by the victors, his people exposed to the savage excesses of the Soviets and Americans. But he prophesied, in dictation to Bormann, "The laws of both history and geography will compel these two powers to a trial of strength, either military or in the field of economics and ideology. These same laws make it inevitable that both powers should become enemies of Europe. And it is equally certain that both powers will sooner or later find it desirable to seek the support of the sole surviving nation in Europe, the German people. I say with all the emphasis at my command that the Germans must at all costs avoid playing the role of pawn in either camp."

Bormann wrote his wife that same day, April 2, describing the latest raid on Berlin and the pall of desperation that hung over the city. He warned her to expect the worst at Vienna; if the Russians overpowered that citadel she should flee the Obersalzberg. A few days later Red Army troops were streaming into Vienna almost at will while resistance men carrying stolen passes and wearing Volkstürm armbands moved openly through the streets, sniping at anyone in German uniform. By evening the already frantic exodus from the city grew as fire brigades, air raid wardens and even police joined the disorderly mob fleeing the city.

5

Even as fronts everywhere were collapsing, Hitler did his utmost to instill hope of a last-minute miracle. He pointed out that the foundation for the Brave New Europe set up by his enemies at Yalta was already beginning to crack. This was not wishful thinking. The Big Three had drawn up the plan in relative harmony but were indeed already deeply embroiled in its implementation. Their representatives, meeting in Moscow to form a new Polish government, had reached an impasse, with Molotov proclaiming that the Lublin Government truly represented the people of Poland, whereas Averell Harriman and the British ambassador contended that a more representative government must be set up to include émigré Poles.

This conflict was but a preamble to a more disruptive one. For several months General Karl Wolff—formerly Himmler's personal adjutant and presently SS chief in Italy—had been negotiating with the Americans through an agent of Allen Dulles, the OSS representative in Switzerland. Wolff had the Führer's vague approval to explore the matter but on his own initiative proposed surrendering all German troops in Italy, then secretly met with two Allied generals in Ascona, Switzerland, to discuss how this could be done without Hitler's knowledge.

From the beginning the Allies had kept Stalin informed about Operation Sunrise, as this venture was named, and from the beginning he had adamantly demanded that a Soviet officer take active part in the negotiations. The Allies explained, with reason, that Wolff would never come to a meeting under such circumstances but this merely raised Stalin's suspicions. When he learned of the rendezvous at Ascona his reaction was violent. He accused the Allies of conniving with Germany, "behind the backs of the Soviet Union, which is bearing the brunt of the war against Germany," and labeled the whole affair "not a misunderstanding but something worse."

By the end of March Stalin was charging that, because of the talks at Ascona, the Germans had felt free to send three divisions from Italy to the eastern front. He further complained that the agreement at Yalta to attack Hitler simultaneously from the east, west and south was not being observed in Italy by the Allies. An explanation by Roosevelt resulted in an irate cable from Stalin openly accusing the Allies of playing a deceitful game. This so irritated the President that on April 5 he sent off the most aggressive and indignant message he had ever addressed to an ally: "Frankly I cannot avoid the feeling of bitter resentment toward your informers, whoever they are, for such vile misrepresentations of my actions or those of my trusted subordinates." Stalin hastily replied that he had never doubted Roosevelt's integrity or trustworthiness. But it was an aggressive apology; he added that a Russian should have been invited to the Ascona meeting and described his own point of view as "the only correct one."

Hitler did not know the details of the discord in the enemy camp, only that there was one and he had predicted it. It fanned the faint hope of a miracle and he was in a receptive mood when Goebbels read to him Carlyle's description of the desperate days of the Seven Years' War: Frederick the Great, dejected by apparent defeat in Prussia, declared that if there was no change before February 15 he would take poison. "Brave King," wrote Carlyle, "wait yet a little while, and the days of your suffering will be over. Already the sun of your good fortune stands behind the clouds, and soon will rise upon you." On February 12 the Czarina died and brought about the incredible change in Frederick's fortunes.

"At this touching tale," Goebbels later told Schwerin von Krosigk, "tears stood in the Führer's eyes." It also whetted Hitler's interest in his own horoscope and he sent for two that were kept in Himmler's research departments. Both predicted victories until 1941, and then a series of reversals culminating in disaster during the first half of April 1945. But there would be a temporary success in the second half of that month, followed by a lull until peace in August. Germany would endure hard times until 1948 when she would rise once more to greatness.

A skeptic by nature, Goebbels was not averse to grabbing at a straw. He was so impressed by the historical parallel that he repeated the story during a visit to General Busse's headquarters near the Oder on April 12. One officer asked caustically, "Well, what Czarina is going to die this time?" "I don't know, but Fate holds all kinds of possibilities," replied Goebbels and headed back for Berlin in the gathering dusk.

Across the Atlantic, in Warm Springs, Georgia, Franklin Roosevelt was murmuring, "I have a terrific headache," before losing consciousness. He died two hours and twenty minutes later. Goebbels received the news upon arrival at his office. "This is the turning point!" he exclaimed and then asked incredulously, "Is it really true?" Some ten people hung over him as he telephoned Hitler. "My Führer," he said, "I congratulate you! Roosevelt is dead. It is written in the stars that the second half of April will be the turning point for us." It was a miracle! He listened to Hitler a moment before mentioning the possibility that Truman would be more moderate than Roosevelt. Anything could happen now. Goebbels hung up, eyes shining, and launched into an impassioned speech. It was as if the war was nearly over.

Ribbentrop did not share his enthusiasm. Next morning, April 13, he returned from a short visit with Hitler in a black mood. "The Führer," he told his staff, "is in seventh heaven!" That scoundrel Goebbels had convinced him that Roosevelt's death was the turn of the tide. "How nonsensical, and how criminal! How could Roosevelt's death change anything to our advantage?"

Goebbels counseled the press to write objectively and non-committally about Truman; to say nothing to irritate the new President; and to hide any rejoicing at Roosevelt's death. But by afternoon the Propaganda Minister's elation had begun to wane. When General Busse called to ask if Roosevelt's death was the situation he had alluded to the day before, Goebbels replied halfheartedly, "Oh, we don't know. We'll have to see." The reports from the fronts indicated that the change of Presidents had not at all affected the enemy's military operations, and late in the day Goebbels confessed to his staff, "Perhaps Fate has again been cruel and made fools of us. Perhaps we counted our chickens before they were hatched."

If Hitler suffered a similar letdown, he gave the opposite impression. He called a special meeting and revealed a bizarre strategy to save Berlin: German troops falling back toward the capital would create a hard nucleus of defense which would irresistibly draw Russian troops toward it. This would relieve other German forces from pressure and enable them to attack the Bolsheviks from the outside. The decisive battle would be won in Berlin, he assured a dubious audience; and he himself would remain in the city to inspire the defenders. Several urged him to go to Berchtesgaden but he would not consider it. As commander-in-chief of the Wehrmacht and as leader of the people, it was his obligation to stay in the capital. He drafted an eight-page proclamation—the last he would write to the troops —and sent it to Goebbels. Even the Propaganda Minister thought its bombast too ridiculous. He began revisions with a green pencil but had to give up and threw the statement in the wastebasket. Then he pulled it out and changed a few sentences. Without bothering to clear the final version, Goebbels had copies distributed along the front on the fifteenth. If every soldier on the eastern front did his duty, it said, Asia's last assault would fail. For Fate had removed Roosevelt, the greatest war criminal of all times, from the world, and the war would take a decisive turn.

Incredibly, many of the soldiers were heartened by Hitler's words. Even the majority of citizens still kept faith with him, despite the relentless bombings from the West and the rapidly shrinking borders of the Reich. To the average German the Führer was more than a man, he was a supernatural phenomenon. They held positive belief in his invulnerability, many clinging to the popular myth that a house wall bearing his picture could withstand any bomb. His miraculous escape on the twentieth of July bore witness to his indestructibility, making it that much easier to raise their spirits and hopes with such slogans as "Hitler Is Victory Itself."

In private, the creator of this slogan had lost his own faith. Goebbels disconsolately began preparing for the end, and started by burning his papers and personal mementos. He hesitated before destroying a large autographed photograph of his great love, Lida Baarova. "Now, there's a beautiful woman!" he remarked. After staring at the picture a long moment, he ripped it into pieces then threw them into the fire.

The following day Germany received two great blows: one from the West where all German troops within the Ruhr pocket surrendered; another from the East where Zhukov's all-out attack on Berlin breached the ridge defense lines west of the Oder, thus opening the road to the Führer bunker forty-five miles away. Though he still talked of victory, Hitler prepared for the worst. He entrusted a visiting party official with two assignments: he was to remove the German gold reserves to a salt mine in Thuringia and convey to safety a sealed package that Bormann would give him. The package contained Hitler's dictations to Bormann, his testament to Germany and the world.*

It was a time for supermen and later in the day Hitler gave orders to

---

* The document was deposited in the vault of a bank in Bad Gastein by the party official, who was later arrested for war crimes and imprisoned. Fearing the testament would incriminate him further, the official asked a legal friend to destroy it. The lawyer did so, but not before making a photostatic copy. In 1959 these revealing statements, each page authenticated by Bormann's signature, were finally published under the title *The Political Testament of Adolf Hitler, the Hitler-Bormann Documents.*

place one in command of all jet fighter planes. Hans Ulrich Rudel was already a legend. With his Stuka dive bomber he had sunk a Soviet battleship and knocked out 500 Red tanks. Several months earlier he had lost a leg in a crash but was already ambulatory and ready for more action. Göring's chief of staff was appalled at the choice, since Rudel knew nothing about jets, but Hitler would not listen. "Rudel is a fine fellow," he said. All the others in the Luftwaffe were actors and clowns.

Rudel himself violently opposed the assignment since he preferred to fly. He refused point-blank to take the job and began making excuses. It was only a question of time before the Russians and Allies met, he told Hitler. This would split Germany into two pockets and make jet operations impossible. Why didn't Hitler seek an armistice in the West, so a victory could be achieved in the East? "It is easy for you to talk," said Hitler with a tired smile. He had tried ever since 1943 to conclude a peace, but the Allies persisted in demanding unconditional surrender. "Therefore we must do everything to surmount this crisis so that decisive weapons may yet bring us victory."

It was late—after midnight—by the time Rudel was dismissed. As he limped into the waiting room, he noticed it was already filled with those eager to be the first to congratulate the Führer on his fifty-sixth birthday.

At Dr. Gebhardt's sanatorium Himmler was preparing to celebrate the birthday. But it was far from a happy occasion. The Reichsführer's face was lined with worry and he kept nervously twisting his snake ring around and around. Like Hitler, he too seemed on the brink of physical collapse. There was good reason. His office was an incredible nest of plots. Some of his people were secretly negotiating in Sweden with his reluctant approval, while SS General Wolff was still dealing with the Allies in Switzerland despite Himmler's flat order to desist.

Himmler was not sure just how much Hitler knew and consequently lived in terror. For the past months he had been endlessly urged to make momentous decisions. Everyone, it seemed, wanted him to do something. Kersten and Schellenberg wanted him to overthrow Hitler by a coup d'état, and earlier that day Count Schwerin von Krosigk had entreated him to persuade Hitler to seek a negotiated peace through the Pope. Himmler would only say that the Führer had a different notion. "But he won't reveal what the notion is."

The count was exasperated. "Then you must do away with the Führer whichever way you can."

"Everything is lost! And as long as the Führer lives there is no possibility of bringing the war to a proper end!" Himmler looked around in such terror that Schwerin von Krosigk wondered if he had "gone mad all at once." Himmler became hysterical, repeating several times that he couldn't promise to do a thing. Instead he fled to the sanatorium where more problems awaited him. Kersten had just landed at Tempelhof with a representative of the World Jewish Congress, Norbert Masur, a last-minute substitute for Storch. That was not all. Count Bernadotte was expected shortly in Berlin and wanted another meeting with the Reichsführer. All of Himmler's problems seemed to have come to a head.

Completely unnerved, he began to make feeble excuses. How could he meet two people at once? Couldn't both meetings be postponed? Finally, in desperation, he asked Schellenberg to "have a preliminary talk" with Masur. Schellenberg agreed and, since it was just past midnight, they toasted the Führer's birthday with champagne.

FIVE MINUTES
PAST MIDNIGHT, OR,
"THE CAPTAIN ALSO GOES
DOWN WITH THIS SHIP"
APRIL 20–30, 1945

1

The Allies celebrated the occasion with another thousand-bomber raid on the capital. But nothing seemed to dampen Hitler's confidence. Throughout the twentieth of April he told birthday visitors that he still believed the Russians would suffer defeat in Berlin. In the afternoon he met a group of Hitler Youth in the chancellery garden and thanked them for their gallantry in the battle for the capital. Then he climbed down into the bunker and received Grossadmiral Karl Dönitz, who thought he looked like a man carrying an intolerable burden. Afterward he greeted Keitel with warmth. "I will never forget that you saved me at the time of the Attentat and that you got me out of Rastenburg—you made the right decisions and took the right actions."

Keitel blurted out that negotiations for peace should be initiated at once before Berlin became a battlefield. Hitler interrupted. "Keitel, I know

what I want. I am going to go down fighting, either in or outside Berlin."
After a tête-à-tête with Jodl, he slowly passed down a line of military and
civilian leaders—including Bormann, Ribbentrop and Speer—shaking
hands and saying a few words to each man. Almost everyone urged Hitler
to flee to Berchtesgaden while there was still an open road but he was
adamant. From now on, he said, the Reich would be divided into two
separate commands, with Dönitz in charge of the northern sector. Field
Marshal Albrecht Kesselring, commander of the western front, was the
logical choice for the south, but Hitler was also considering Göring—perhaps for political expediency—and said he would leave it to Providence to
decide. He recommended that the various command staffs split in two, and
those selected for the south should leave that evening for Berchtesgaden.
Göring asked if he should go south or send his chief of staff, Koller. "You
go," said the Führer. The two old comrades, once so close, parted with
polite coolness. Göring headed for Karinhall where his butler was waiting
with fourteen carloads of clothing and art treasures.

Hitler dined alone with Eva and his secretaries. Again he was urged
to go south but he said that would be like a Tibetan lama turning an
empty prayer wheel. "I must force a decision here in Berlin—or perish!"
After midnight he summoned the two older secretaries to his private room
and revealed that they were to leave in half an hour or so by car for the
Obersalzberg along with Admiral von Puttkamer and eighty others.* The
two women were wide-eyed with astonishment. His explanation was that
they had been with him the longest. Besides, Fräulein Wolf supported her
mother. "I will join you as soon as possible." He spoke in a whisper, vainly
trying to hide the trembling of his left hand. A sigh escaped him; one,
thought Fräulein Schröder, which seemed to come from a man without
hope. A little later he phoned her to say that Berlin was surrounded. She
could not leave until first light. A second call followed in minutes. The
plane would take off as soon as the air raid all-clear was sounded. She
didn't quite understand, since his voice gurgled imperceptibly, and asked
him to repeat himself. He said nothing. His last words to her colleague
Fräulein Wolf were: "It is all over."

Earlier that evening Himmler, after paying respects to the Führer on
his birthday, left the bunker and drove through the beating rain for several hours to meet Masur, the representative of the World Jewish

* Among those sent south was Dr. Morell. He was banished in anger for suggesting that
Hitler take an injection of caffeine for his fatigue. "You will probably give me morphine!" shouted Hitler and ordered him to remove his uniform as the Führer's private
physician. "And act as if you've never seen me." Morell collapsed at Hitler's feet and
had to be led away. He died, a broken man, soon after the war.

Congress. Himmler explained that he had been empowered to solve the Jewish problem and had first planned a humane solution through emigration. But even those countries which boasted of their friendliness toward the Jews refused to take them. "Through the war," Himmler said, "we came into contact with the masses of the Eastern Jewish proletariat, and this created new problems. We could not have such an enemy in our back." These Jews not only helped the partisans but were infected by typhus and other diseases. "In order to curtail the epidemics," he explained, "we had to build crematoria where we could burn the corpses of the large number of people who died because of these diseases. And now they'll get us just for doing that!"

"Much has happened which cannot be undone," Masur said. "But if we are ever to build a bridge between our peoples for the future, then all Jews who are today alive in the areas dominated by Germany must remain alive." Himmler protested that he had always intended turning over the camps to the Allies without resistance. Hadn't he done so with Bergen-Belsen and Buchenwald? And look what he got in return: faked atrocity pictures were being circulated by the Americans! And when he let 2700 Jews go to Switzerland, the foreign press claimed that he had done so only to get himself an alibi. "I don't need an alibi. I have always done what I felt would fill the needs of my people, and I take full responsibility. It certainly didn't make me a rich man."

While Masur was out of the room Himmler suddenly asked his masseur, Kersten, if he would fly to Eisenhower's headquarters and discuss immediate cessation of hostilities. "Make every effort to convince Eisenhower that the real enemy of mankind is Soviet Russia and that only we Germans are in a position to fight against her. I will concede victory to the Western Allies. They have only to give me time to throw back Russia. If they let me have the equipment, I can still do it."

On Masur's return Himmler said he would show his good faith by releasing 1000 Jewish women from Ravensbrück at once. He stipulated that their arrival in Sweden be kept secret, suggesting that they be designated "Polish" instead of "Jewish." Just before dawn Himmler bade Masur farewell and drove to the Gebhardt sanatorium where Count Bernadotte was waiting. The two sat down to breakfast. Himmler's exhaustion did not seem to affect his appetite, though he compulsively kept tapping his front teeth with his fingernails. Unaccountably, he objected to Bernadotte's modest request that the Scandinavian prisoners be allowed to continue from Denmark to Sweden, then spontaneously offered to let the Swedish Red Cross have *all* the women at Ravensbrück and retired to get some sleep. Early that afternoon Himmler summoned Schellenberg to his bedroom and said he felt ill; and as their car crept along the jammed highway toward their nearby headquarters the Reichsführer said, "Schellenberg, I dread what is to come."

"That should give you courage to take action."

Himmler was silent, and once Schellenberg began criticizing the unrealistic policy of evacuating all the concentration camps, he pouted like a scolded child. "Schellenberg, don't you start too," he said. "Hitler has been raging for days because Buchenwald and Bergen-Belsen were not completely evacuated."

At the moment Himmler assured Masur that all evacuations had ceased, the inmates of Sachsenhausen, which lay directly athwart the path of Zhukov's advance on Berlin, were being herded out of the barracks into the rain and lined up for departure; ten miles to the east Zhukov's guns roared ominously. The Red Cross delegate requested the camp commandant to turn over Sachsenhausen to his organization, but he refused, on the grounds that he had standing orders from Himmler to evacuate everything except the hospital at the approach of the Russians. And so almost 40,000 prisoners—starved, sick, poorly clothed—were shoved into two surging columns. The guards harried them through the pummeling rain in a northwesterly direction, and those who couldn't keep up the pace were shot and left in the ditches.

"What can you do with a people whose men don't even fight when their women are raped!" It was Goebbels, bitterly admitting to his aides later in the day that the war was irrevocably lost—not because of Hitler but because the people had failed him. "All the plans, all the ideas of National Socialism are too high, too noble for such a people. . . . They deserve the fate that will now descend upon them." He even turned on his own aides. "And you—why have you worked with me? Now you'll have your little throats cut! But when we step down, let the whole earth tremble!" Throughout the day Goebbels went from despair to resentment. Upon learning that two secretaries had fled to the country on bicycles, he complained, "Now I ask you, how could that ever have happened? How can there be any guarantee now of keeping regular office hours?"

On the eastern front there were rumors that the leaders in Berlin had given up all hope and that OKW was fleeing to Berchtesgaden. The Russians had broken through the lines of Army Group Vistula at half a dozen points and one Red Army task force was but twenty miles from Berlin and the Führer's bunker. By noon of April 21 it had closed to artillery range, and the explosions of its shells could be heard faintly in the bunker as Jodl reported that a Zhukov column was threatening to encircle Manteuffel's army. To counter this, the last small reserve under SS General Felix Steiner had just been positioned twenty-five miles north of Berlin.

Hitler jerked upright from a slump. Like Skorzeny and Rudel, Steiner was a magic name; it was his desperate attack from Pomerania that had slowed Zhukov's advance in February. Hitler began poring over a map. Finally he looked up. His eyes glistened. Counterattack! he said with rising excitement. Steiner was to drive to the southeast and cut straight through the Zhukov spearhead: this would, with one bold blow, save Berlin and prevent Manteuffel from being encircled. He dispatched a personal order to Steiner expressly forbidding any retreat to the west. "Officers who do not comply unconditionally with this order are to be arrested and shot immediately. You, Steiner, are answerable with your head for execution of this order." Of all the impossible orders Steiner had received from the Führer, this was the most fantastic. His Panzer corps was one in name only. He had no intention of sacrificing his troops in such a hopeless cause and would only make a show of compliance—an easy decision for a man who had once considered kidnaping the Führer.

Bormann also knew there was no hope. He telephoned his wife at Berchtesgaden and told her he'd found a "wonderful hiding place" for their children in the Tyrol. She was to pose as a director of bombed-out children seeking refuge. He had kidnaped six youngsters from the party kindergarten in Garmisch to make the group look more plausible.

2

In the bunker, on the morning of April 22, Steiner was the main topic of conversation. Had his attack from the north been launched to relieve Berlin? If so, how far had it gone? With each passing hour Hitler became increasingly upset every time General Hans Krebs, Guderian's replacement as OKH chief of staff, told him there was nothing definite to report. At the afternoon Führer conference, after learning that Berlin was three fourths surrounded, Hitler demanded to know once and for all how far Steiner had progressed in his attack. At last Krebs was forced to admit that the Steiner corps was still being organized and there just wasn't anything to report.

Hitler's head jerked and he began breathing heavily. Harshly he ordered everyone out of the room except his generals and Bormann. The rest stumbled over one another in their eagerness to escape. In the waiting room they stood in silent apprehension. Once the door closed Hitler lunged to his feet. As he lurched back and forth, swinging his right arm wildly, he shouted that he was surrounded by traitors and liars. All were too low, too mean to understand his great purpose, he shouted. He was the victim of corruption and cowardice and now everyone had deserted him. His listeners had never before seen him lose control so completely. He flung an accusing finger at the generals and blamed their ilk for the disasters of the war. The only protest came from Bormann. The officers were surprised, but Bormann's words were undoubtedly meant not so much as a defense of the military as to calm the Führer.

Hitler shouted something about Steiner and abruptly flopped into his chair. In anguish he said, "The war is lost!" Then with a trembling voice he added that the Third Reich had ended in failure and all he could do now was die. His face turned white and his body shook spasmodically, as if torn by a violent stroke. Suddenly he was still. His jaw slackened and he sat staring ahead with blank eyes. This alarmed the onlookers more than his fury. Minute after minute passed—afterward no one could remember how many. Finally a patch of color came to the Führer's cheeks and he twitched—perhaps he had suffered a coronary attack or fibrillation. Bormann, Keitel and Burgdorf, chief of army personnel, begged him to have faith. If *he* lost it, then all indeed was lost. They urged him to leave for Berchtesgaden immediately, but he slowly shook his head and in a dead, tired voice said that if they wanted to go they were free to do so, but he was meeting his end in the capital. He asked for Goebbels.

Those in the outer room had heard almost everything. Fegelein grabbed a phone and told Himmler what had happened. The shaken Reichsführer phoned Hitler and begged him not to lose hope. He promised to send SS troops at once. In the meantime Hitler sent for Traudl Junge, Gerda Christian and his new cook, Konstanze Manzialy. They came to his anteroom where he was waiting with Eva Braun. His face was expressionless, his eyes dead. In an impersonal yet imperious manner he told the four women to prepare to leave for the south by plane within the hour. "All is lost, hopelessly lost," he said.

The women stood rigid with shock. Eva was the first to move. She went up to Hitler, took both his hands in hers. She smiled softly as if to a sad child. "But you surely know that I shall stay with you. I won't let you send me away." This brought life back to his eyes and he did something no one in the family circle had ever before seen: he kissed Eva on the lips.

In spite of herself, Traudl found herself saying, "I also am staying." Gerda and the cook joined the chorus. Hitler again ordered them to leave but they stood firm. He seized their hands in turn and said with emotion, "If only my generals were as brave as you are!" As if totally exhausted, he dragged himself to the next room where a group of officers was waiting. "Gentlemen," he said, "this is the end. I shall remain here in Berlin and shoot myself when the time comes. Each of you must make his own decision on when to leave."

Goebbels was still at home when he learned that the Führer wanted him immediately. As he was preparing to leave the ministry word came that Hitler also wanted to see Magda and the children. At five o'clock Frau Goebbels calmly told the nurse to get the children ready for a visit to the Führer. They were delighted. Would Uncle Adi give them chocolate and cake as usual? The mother, guessing they might all be going to their death, put on a smile and said, "Each of you may take one toy, but no more than that."

Keitel finally cleared the conference room so that he could talk alone with Hitler. He wanted to convince him to go to Berchtesgaden directly and initiate surrender negotiations from there. But Hitler interrupted. "I already know exactly what you're going to say: 'The decision must be made at once!'" His voice was rasping. "I have already made a decision. I will never leave Berlin; I'll defend the city to my last breath!" Jodl appeared and Hitler repeated his decision to die. "I should already have made this decision, the most important in my life, in November 1944, and should never have left the headquarters in East Prussia."

Hitler summoned Bormann and ordered him to fly to Berchtesgaden with Jodl and Keitel. The latter would take command, with Göring as the Führer's personal representative. When Keitel protested, Hitler said, "Everything is falling to pieces anyway and I can do no more." The rest, he added, should be left to Göring. "There's mighty little fighting to be done, and if it comes to negotiating, the Reichsmarschall can do it better than I can. I will either fight and win the Battle of Berlin, or die in Berlin." He could not run the risk of falling into enemy hands, he said, and would shoot himself at the very last moment. "That is my final, irrevocable decision!"

The generals swore that the situation was not completely lost. Wenck's Twelfth Army could be turned around and brought to the relief of Berlin. All at once Hitler's eyes brightened. Incredibly, hope returned and with it determination. He began by asking questions, then outlining in detail exactly how Berlin could be saved. No sooner had Keitel left to give orders to Wenck in person than the Führer sank into another depression. He told his family circle that there was no hope. When someone pointed to the painting of Frederick the Great and asked if he no longer believed in a similar miracle of history, the Führer tiredly shook his head.

"The army has betrayed me, my generals are good for nothing," he said. "My orders were not carried out. It is all finished. National Socialism is dead and will never rise again!" Perhaps in a hundred years a similar idea would arise with the power of a religion and spread throughout the world. "But Germany is lost. It actually was not quite ready or quite strong enough for the mission I set for the nation."

3

That evening General Eckard Christian, the Luftwaffe chief of operations, burst into Koller's headquarters just outside Berlin. "The Führer is in a state of collapse!" He gave a frightening account of what had happened. Koller drove to the new OKW headquarters and asked Jodl for confirmation of Christian's incredible story. Jodl calmly replied that it was true. Koller asked if the Führer would carry out his threat to commit suicide. Yes, he was stubborn on that point. Koller was indignant. He said he must leave at once to tell Göring in person that the Führer had said: "If it comes to negotiating, the Reichsmarschall can do it better than I can."

Just before dawn on April 23 Koller and his staff left for Munich in fifteen JU-52s. At Berchtesgaden Göring had already learned much of what had happened from an unlikely source. That morning he had told his caretaker—and no one else—of a secret radio message from Bormann informing him that the Führer had suffered a nervous breakdown and that Göring was to take over command. Göring was torn between suspicion and credulity. What should he do? Act at once or wait?

Koller did not reach Göring's comfortable, unostentatious house on the Obersalzberg until noon. Excitedly he told about Hitler's collapse. Göring, of course, knew most of this and to Koller's surprise showed little reaction. He asked if Hitler was still alive. Had he appointed Bormann as his successor? Koller replied that the Führer was alive when he left Berlin and that there were still one or two escape routes. The city would probably hold out for a week. "Anyway," he concluded, "it is now up to you to act, Herr Reichsmarschall!"

Göring was hesitant. Might not Hitler have appointed Bormann as his successor? he asked again. Bormann, an old enemy, could have sent the telegram to make him usurp power prematurely. "If I act, he will call me a traitor; if I don't, he will accuse me of having failed at a most critical time!" He sent for Hans Lammers, the legal expert and custodian of the two official documents establishing a successor, drafted by Hitler himself in 1941. In these directives Göring was appointed Hitler's deputy upon his death. He would also be Hitler's successor in case the Führer was prevented—permanently or temporarily—from performing his office.

Göring wanted to know if the military situation in Berlin warranted his taking over, but Lammers could make no decision. Well aware that his influence with the Führer had waned as Bormann's waxed, Göring asked if Hitler had issued any orders since 1941 which might have invalidated his own succession. No, said Lammers, he had made sure from time to time that the documents had not been rescinded. The decree, he declared, had the force of law and didn't even need to be promulgated again.

Someone suggested that a radio message be sent asking the Führer if he still wanted Göring to be his deputy. One was drafted: "My Führer, is it your wish, in view of your decision to stay in Berlin, that I take over complete control of the Reich, in accordance with the decree of June 29, 1941?" Göring read it and added: ". . . with full powers in domestic and foreign affairs," so that he might negotiate a peace with the Allies. Still concerned, he said, "Suppose I don't get any answer? We must give a time limit, a time by which I must receive an answer."

Koller suggested that they make it eight hours and Göring scribbled down a deadline, then added hastily, "You must realize that I feel for you in this most difficult hour of my life and I can find no words to express myself. God bless you and speed you here as soon as possible. Your most loyal, Hermann Göring." Leaning back heavily, he said, "It's frightful." If no answer came by 10 P.M. he had to do something drastic. "I'll stop the war at once."

At the bunker his telegram—the last from Göring to be intercepted in England by Ultra—seemed to outrage Bormann more than anyone else. He demanded Göring's execution. Hitler refused to go that far and sent his Reichsmarschall three conflicting messages. The first offered to disregard the death penalty for high treason if Göring resigned all his offices; the second rescinded the decree establishing Göring as his successor; and the third, perhaps more accurately reflecting Hitler's confused feelings, was couched in such vague terms ("Your assumption that I am prevented from carrying out my own wishes is an absolutely erroneous idea whose ridiculous origin I do not know") that Bormann must have feared it was a prelude to forgiveness. On his own he radioed the SS commandant at the Obersalzberg to arrest Göring for treason.

Krebs phoned Keitel from the bunker and told him in detail about Göring's dismissal. Horrified, Keitel kept insisting there must be some misunderstanding. Suddenly Bormann's voice broke into the conversation. He shouted that Göring had been fired "even from his job as Reich Chief Hunter." Keitel did not deign to reply. The situation, he thought, was "too serious for such sarcastic remarks." After a brief, frustrating meeting with Hitler that afternoon, Keitel drove back to his headquarters with Jodl. "On the way we frankly agreed that we could not leave things as they were—we discussed the possibility of abducting the Führer from his bunker, possibly even by *force*." But they gave up the idea; it would be impossible to get the collaboration of the Führer's SS guards and Security Service bodyguard.

4

With the Russians closing in on the capital, Eva Braun's normal cheerful nature had changed to one of controlled terror. Once she seized Traudl Junge's hands and in a trembling voice confessed how frightened she was. "If only everything would finally be over!" She penned a farewell letter to her best friend, Herta: "These are my last lines, and therefore the last sign of life from me," she began and explained that she was sending her jewelry to be distributed according to her will. She apologized for the letter's incoherence; the Goebbelses' six children were in the next room making an infernal racket. "I can't understand how all this can have happened, it's enough to make one lose one's faith in God!" In a postscript she added that Hitler himself had lost hope. But the next day, Monday, April 23, Eva wrote her sister that there was still a chance. "It goes without saying, however, that we will not let ourselves be captured alive." She asked Gretl to destroy all her business papers but to pack the Führer's letters and her replies in a watertight package and bury them. The message ended with a pitifully hopeful postscript: "I just spoke to the Führer. I think he is also more optimistic about the future than he was yesterday."

Himmler was making last-minute preparations. Just before midnight he again met Folke Bernadotte, this time in the Swedish Consulate at Lübeck, the German port on the Baltic. "The war must end," he unexpectedly said with a resigned sigh. "I admit that Germany is defeated." The Führer might be dead and so he was no longer bound by his personal oath. He was willing to capitulate on the western front, he said, but not in the East. "I have always been, and I shall always remain, a sworn enemy of Bolshevism." He asked if the count was willing to forward this proposal to the Swedish Minister of Foreign Affairs for transmittal to the West.

Bernadotte did not like the idea but agreed to pass it on to his government. What would Himmler do if his offer was turned down? "In that event," was the answer, "I shall take over command on the eastern front and be killed in battle." Himmler added that he hoped to meet Eisenhower and was willing to surrender unconditionally to him without delay. "Between men of the world, should I offer my hand to Eisenhower?" he asked.

After remarking that it was the bitterest day of his life, Himmler strode purposefully into the darkness and got behind the wheel of his car. He stepped on the accelerator and the vehicle lunged through a hedge into a barbed-wire fence. The Swedes and the Germans managed to push the car clear and Himmler lurched off. There was, commented the count, something symbolic about it all.

At the military conference next morning, April 24, Hitler learned that Manteuffel's army had been completely cut off by a deep Soviet tank thrust. "In view of the broad natural barrier formed by the Oder," he said after a tense silence, "the Russian success against the Third Tank Army can only be attributed to the incompetence of the German military leaders there!" Krebs tried to defend the front-line commander but this only reminded Hitler of Steiner's abortive attack. He pointed shakily at a map and said that another drive from north of Berlin must be started within twenty-four hours. "The Third Army will make use of all available forces for this assault, ruthlessly depleting those sections of our front line which are not under attack. It is imperative that the link to Berlin from the north be restored by tomorrow evening. Have that passed on at once." A suggestion that Steiner lead the attack incensed him. "Those arrogant, tedious, indecisive SS leaders are no good to me any more!"

Goebbels left the meeting to issue his last proclamation to the citizens of Berlin. He hoped that by telling the truth he could frighten them into continuing the holy crusade against the Reds to the end. "Our hearts must not waver and not tremble. It must be our pride and our ambition to break the Bolshevist mass onslaught which is surging from the East against the heartland of Europe at the walls of the Reich capital." Even as these last words were disseminated, Julius Schaub was burning the last of the Führer's private correspondence. This done, Hitler's personal adjutant enplaned for the south with orders to destroy other private documents in the Munich apartment and at the Berghof.

5

The SS commandant at Berchtesgaden had acted immediately upon receipt of Bormann's telegram by placing Göring and his family under house arrest. The past two days had been the most tempestuous in the Reichsmarschall's dramatic career: his Führer had collapsed; he thought

he himself had been called upon to inherit the Third Reich; then came
Hitler's three telegrams; and now he feared he was going to be executed.
That morning—April 25—several SS officers tried to persuade Göring, in
the presence of his wife and his butler, to sign a document stating that he
was resigning all positions because of poor health. Göring refused; in spite
of the telegrams he could not bring himself to believe Hitler really meant
what he said. But once the SS men drew their guns Göring quickly signed.
The ceremony was interrupted by the drone of approaching aircraft.

Allied planes had often passed over Berchtesgaden on their way to
Salzburg, Linz and other targets, but as yet Hitler's retreat was un-
damaged. Today, however, 318 Lancaster bombers were bent on wiping it
out. At 10 A.M., the first wave swept over the mountain, dumping high
explosives on the edge of the Führer area. Half an hour later came a larger
wave. For almost an hour plane after plane unloaded blockbusters directly
onto the Obersalzberg. After the last bomber had disappeared Air Force
General Robert Ritter von Greim, commander of Luftflotte 6 in Munich,
drove up to the Berghof. It was a mass of twisted wreckage. Greim looked
around in dismay. The Führer's home had been hit directly; one side was
demolished and the blasted tin roof hung in mid-air.

A dedicated Nazi (he gave Hitler his first plane ride in 1920), Greim
had received a telegram from Berlin to report to the bunker, and he now
sought out Koller, who, he had been told, had a similar order. Greim
began berating Göring for leaving the capital and performing "treasona-
ble" acts. Koller apologized for his chief. But Greim was not at all
impressed. Göring's actions should not be defended, he declared, and
headed for Berlin.

By midmorning the Red Army pincers around Berlin were about to
close and the conferees at the 10:30 A.M. meeting waited in an atmosphere of gloom for Hitler's arrival. He too was despondent until Heinz
Lorenz of the official German news agency reported that he had just
monitored an announcement from a neutral country that an argument
had broken out between Russians and Americans at the first meeting of
their troops on the Mulde River. There were disagreements regarding the
sectors to be occupied, with the Russians accusing the Americans of in-
fringing on area agreements made at Yalta.

Hitler sat upright, eyes gleaming. "Gentlemen," he said, "here again
is striking evidence of the disunity of our enemies. The German people
and history would surely brand me as a criminal if I made peace today
while there is still the possibility that tomorrow our enemies might have a

falling out!" He seemed to gather strength as he spoke. "Isn't it possible that at any day—yes, at any hour—war could break out between the Bolsheviks and the Anglo-Saxons over their prize, Germany?" He turned to Krebs, signaling him with a slight nod to begin the conference. The army chief of staff launched into his report only to be interrupted twice by Hitler: where was Wenck? The answer was a sheepish "No report."

The intercepted news report preoccupied Hitler, and he spent the next hour daydreaming out loud of another last-minute miracle. The time had come, he said, when the Anglo-Saxons must oppose the Reds out of a sense of self-preservation. "If it is really true that differences among the Allies are arising in San Francisco [delegates were gathering there for the first United Nations conference]—and they will occur—a turning point can be achieved if I can administer a beating to the Bolshevik colossus at some point. This might convince the others that only one person is able to contain the Bolshevik colossus, and that person is represented by me, the party and the present German state." The DNB report was incorrect. There was no disagreement between Russian and American advance troops. They did not meet, in fact, until the next day, the twenty-sixth, when two separate American patrols made contact with the Red Army at Strehla and Torgau on the Elbe. This junction cut Hitler's diminishing Reich in two.

By late morning it appeared that General Wenck's army was driving to the rescue of Hitler. Radio reports of his steady progress heartened Berliners. No one waited more eagerly than Hitler. He was counting on Wenck to prolong the battle at least until May 5 so he could die on the same day as Napoleon. It was a vain hope. Only a single corps of Wenck's army, the XX, was attacking toward the capital, and its limited mission was to reach Potsdam and provide a corridor of retreat for the Berlin garrison. The bulk of Wenck's army was driving east—against the Führer's orders—to save comrades of the entrapped Ninth Army.

Early that evening another general, the epitome of loyalty, was risking death to report to his Führer. Ritter von Greim was at the controls of a small observation plane flying at treetop level toward embattled Berlin. Overhead the sky raged with dogfights. Suddenly a gaping hole appeared in the flooring of the cockpit and Greim slumped over. As the plane plunged down out of control his passenger, Hanna Reitsch, reached over and seized the stick. Somehow she managed to right the Storch and make a safe landing on the broad avenue running through the Brandenburg Gate. She commandeered a car and helped Greim aboard.

After his injured right foot was treated, Greim was carried on a stretcher down to the Führer bunker. The little party encountered Magda Goebbels, who stared wide-eyed, marveling that any living soul could have found his way there. She had never met Hanna Reitsch but embraced her and began sobbing. In a moment they came upon Hitler in the narrow passageway. His head drooped heavily, his arms twitched continually, his eyes were glassy. But Greim's report gave Hitler new life. He seized both Greim's hands, then turned to Reitsch. "Brave woman! So there is still some loyalty and courage left in the world!"

Hitler told them about the treacherous telegram Göring had sent. "An ultimatum, a blatant ultimatum! Now there's nothing left. Look what I have to go through: no allegiances were kept, no honor lived up to; there are no disappointments or betrayals I have not experienced—and now this above all." He stopped as if unable to go on. Then, looking at Greim with half-closed eyes, said in little more than a whisper, "I hereby declare you Göring's successor as Oberbefehlshaber der Luftwaffe. In the name of the German people I give you my hand." Deeply moved, both newcomers asked to be allowed to remain in the bunker to atone for Göring's deceit. Equally moved, Hitler assented. Their decision, he said, would long be remembered in the history of the Luftwaffe.

By dawn April 27 Berlin was completely encircled and the last two airports overrun by the Red Army. Still a flurry of optimism swept through the bunker with arrival of a radiogram from Wenck, announcing that XX Corps had come to within a few miles of Potsdam. Goebbels' office immediately proclaimed over the radio that Wenck had reached Potsdam itself and predicted that he would soon be in the capital. And if Wenck made it, why not others? "The situation has changed decisively in our favor," Berliners were told. "The Americans are marching toward Berlin. The great change of the war is at hand. Berlin must be held till Army Wenck arrives, no matter at what costs!"

The daily army communiqué, also broadcast in the clear, divulged Wenck's exact position. He was appalled. "We won't be able to move a single step farther tomorrow!" Wenck exclaimed to his chief of staff. The Russians surely had heard the same broadcast and would concentrate everything available at his position. It was, he said, almost a betrayal.

At the noon military conference Hitler expressed his utmost faith in Wenck, whom he called "a real man," but a moment later, as if realizing how empty hopes of rescue were, he said, "I shall lie down today somewhat calmer and do not wish to be awakened unless a Russian tank is just outside my bedroom, so that I can make my preparations." In the next breath he expressed the hope that the Russians would bleed themselves to death in Berlin; then immediately closed the meeting with a philosophic quotation from Richelieu: "What have I lost! The dearest remembrances! What does all this mean? Sooner or later the entire beastly mess must be left behind."

After the conference Hitler pinned an Iron Cross on a small, bleary-eyed boy who had just blown up a Russian tank. The youngster silently turned and walked to the corridor, where he crumpled to the floor, fast asleep. Krebs's two aides were so affected that they began to complain loudly of the unbearable situation. Bormann came up behind them, draping his arms familiarly around their shoulders. There was still hope. Wenck was on the way and would soon relieve Berlin. "You, who stayed here and kept faith with our Führer through his darkest hours," he said unctuously, would be rewarded with great estates. The two aides gaped incredulously. As professional soldiers they had always been treated with the greatest suspicion by Bormann and his people.

Hanna Reitsch spent much of the day in Goebbels' suite. He seemed unable to forget Göring's treachery. The Reichsmarschall, he said, with extravagant gesticulation, was an incompetent; he had destroyed the Fatherland with his stupidity and now he wanted to lead the entire nation. This itself proved that "at heart he was always weak and a traitor." Goebbels gripped the back of a chair as a lectern and proclaimed that those in the bunker were making history and dying for the glory of the Reich so that the name of Germany could live forever.

Reitsch thought Goebbels was too theatrical, but she had only admiration for his wife. In the presence of her six children Magda was always cheerful; and when she felt self-control slipping she left the room. "My dear Hanna," she said, "you must help me to help the children out of this life. They belong to the Third Reich and the Führer, and if those two things cease to exist, there will be no place for them." Her greatest fear was that at the last moment she would weaken. Reitsch told the children stories of her flying experiences and taught them songs which they later sang to Uncle Adi. She also visited Eva Braun, and thought she was a shallow woman who spent most of her time polishing her fingernails, changing her clothes and combing her hair. It must have been a shock to Reitsch, who adored the Führer, to find him living openly with a woman.

In the second conference of the day, Hitler reverted to reminiscences. He talked of compromises he had been forced to make upon assuming power in 1933 and how this situation had lasted until Hindenburg's death.

This led to another pledge to remain in Berlin. He did so, he said, so he could proceed harshly against weakness. "I would otherwise not have this moral right. I cannot constantly threaten others if I run away from the German capital in a critical hour. I must now obey the dictates of Fate. Even if I could save myself, I would not do so. The captain also goes down with this ship."

At the evening briefing the military commandant of Berlin, General Helmuth Weidling, tried to get Hitler to realize that the city was completely surrounded and that the circle of defense was fast shrinking. It was no longer possible, he said, to get supplies by air. He enlarged on the misery of the civilians and the wounded, but Hitler was more interested in complaining about those who had betrayed him. "Many cannot understand my bitterness. I cannot imagine that a party leader, to whom I have given an order, could possibly conceive of not carrying it out. This damages the total result, and the individual suffers. The greater the area of responsibility of the individual, the greater the necessity for obedience." He recalled how Field Marshal von Blomberg had told him that obedience only went up to the rank of general. "It was a mechanism," he commented sarcastically, "which allowed situations to be avoided by false reports, etc., when difficulties arose."

He began to worry about his own fate. He had no intention of allowing Stalin to exhibit him in a cage. "I must have absolute certainty," he said, "that I will not be captured by a Russian tank due to some clever trick by the enemy." At the same time he could not possibly leave Berlin. How could he ask anybody to die for the Fatherland when he himself refused to direct the battle from the heart of the nation?

During one of these reveries Goebbels' assistant, Werner Naumann, was called to a phone outside the room and informed of reports in American newspapers that "a group of highly placed Nazis acting without authority of Hitler but with the backing of the high command" had just offered to surrender to the West. Himmler's offer, submitted through the Swedish government, had somehow leaked out but his name was not mentioned nor was the source of the story revealed.

Naumann returned to the conference and whispered the news to Hitler, who then exchanged a few urgent but subdued words with Goebbels. The Berlin commandant, Weidling, was dismissed and he went to the anteroom where he found Bormann, the Führer's adjutants and the two women secretaries chatting. Frustrated in the conference room, Weidling ("Bony Karl" to his troops) poured out all the things that Hitler had refused to hear. Their only hope, he said, was to leave Berlin before it was too late. Everyone agreed, even Bormann. This encouraged Weidling to repeat the suggestion to Krebs as soon as he emerged from the conference room. Krebs too was receptive and promised to present the breakout plan in detail at the next conference.

Fifty-five miles away at Wenck's Twelfth Army headquarters a radio operator was tapping out a message to Weidling:

COUNTERATTACK OF THE TWELFTH ARMY IS STALLED SOUTH OF POTSDAM. TROOPS ARE ENGAGED IN VERY HEAVY DEFENSIVE FIGHTING. SUGGEST BREAKTHROUGH TO US. WENCK.

The operator waited for acknowledgment. None came.

6

Hitler's closest ally was also facing his last days. Ever since his rescue by Skorzeny, Mussolini had hoped to bring about some sort of "Italian political solution" to the disastrous war. He sent his son Vittorio to the Archbishop of Milan with a verbal proposition to open negotiations with the West. The proposal was duly forwarded to the Allies by the Vatican— but was summarily rejected.

Il Duce never reported this to Hitler, with whom he'd had little communication lately, nor did he withhold from journalists his disapproval of the Führer's "megalomaniacal" attack on Russia. He confessed that he was little more than a prisoner of the Germans and that his own star had set. On April 25 Mussolini left Milan in a ten-car caravan for a last stand in the north with his most faithful Blackshirts. In one of the cars, an Alfa-Romeo with Spanish license plates, was Clara Petacci, his mistress. "I am following my destiny," she wrote a friend. "I don't know what will become of me, but I cannot question my fate." Mussolini left his wife behind, giving her documents, including letters from Churchill, which he hoped would get her safely across the frontier with their children. "If they try and stop you or harm you," he said, "ask to be handed over to the English."

Before dawn of the twenty-sixth, the Mussolini party started up the winding west shore of Lake Como, beautiful even in the heavy drizzle. Twenty-five miles later the party stopped at a hotel to wait for the 3000 Blackshirts who were supposed to join them. But none appeared and the next day the caravan continued north. Near Dongo they were captured by partisans; an argument broke out between those who wanted to kill the Fascists immediately and those who wanted to turn Mussolini over to the Allies. The issue was resolved on April 28 by a three-man execution squad from Milan which gunned down Mussolini and Clara Petacci with their machine pistols.

By that morning the German forces in the East were almost completely disjointed, their leadership on the verge of open rebellion. Manteuffel's Third Panzer Army, for instance, was making a fighting withdrawal to the west in defiance of Hitler's order to stand fast. Its goal was surrender to the Anglo-Americans.

The disintegration of the military hierarchy was evident in the bunker itself. Just before dawn Bormann, Krebs and Burgdorf had been embroiled in a drunken argument. "Nine months ago I approached my present task with all my strength and idealism!" railed Burgdorf. "I tried again and again to co-ordinate the party and the Wehrmacht." And because of this, he said, his fellow officers came to despise him and even called him a traitor to the officers' caste. "Today it is clear that these accusations were justified, and my labors were for nothing. My idealism was misplaced, and not only that, I was naïve and stupid!"

Krebs tried to quiet him but the noise had already wakened his two aides in the next room. They could hear Burgdorf shout down the conciliatory Krebs: "Let me alone, Hans—all this has to be said! Perhaps it will be too late to do so in another forty-eight hours. . . . Young officers with faith and idealism have gone to their death by the thousands. For what? The Fatherland? No! They have died for you!" Burgdorf turned his attack on Bormann. Millions, he shouted, had been sacrificed so that party members could further themselves. "For your life of luxury, for your thirst for power. You've annihilated our centuries-old culture, annihilated the German nation. That is your terrible guilt!"

"My dear fellow," soothed Bormann, "you shouldn't be so personal about it. Even if all the others have enriched themselves, I at least am blameless. That much I swear on everything I hold sacred. Your health, my friend!" In the next room the two eavesdroppers heard a clink of glasses, then there was silence.

All that morning General Weidling worked on his plan to break out of Berlin in three echelons. It was obvious that the Russians would soon reach the chancellery and "Bony Karl" was so sure that he could get approval from the Führer at the evening conference that he ordered all his commanders to report at the bunker by midnight.

In her quarters Frau Goebbels was writing her son by a previous marriage, now an Allied prisoner of war. She told him that the "glorious ideas" of Nazism were coming to an end "and with them everything beautiful and noble and good I have known in my life." A world without Hitler and National Socialism was not worth living in. That was why she had brought the six children to the bunker. They were too good for the life that was coming after defeat "and a merciful God will understand my reason for sparing them that sort of life. . . . May God give me strength for my last and most difficult duty." Bormann was sending his wife a radiogram that "all was lost" and there was no hope for him. She was to leave Berchtesgaden at once for the Tyrol with their children and the half dozen kidnaped youngsters.

7

In San Francisco, where the conference to set up a United Nations Organization was in session, a Reuters reporter was told that Himmler had just offered to surrender Germany unconditionally. His telegram got through to Reuters without censorship and a bulletin was dispatched throughout the world. A DNB man on the upper level of the bunker heard a BBC version of this story just before 9 P.M. on the twenty-eighth and brought it to Hitler. He read the message without emotion, as if resigned that the end had come, then summoned Goebbels and Bormann. The three conferred behind locked doors.

All day long Bormann had been making wholesale charges of treason and only an hour earlier had radioed Dönitz: TREACHERY SEEMS TO HAVE REPLACED LOYALTY. The brother-in-law of Eva Braun was one of those under grave suspicion. Otto Hermann Fegelein, Himmler's liaison officer at the bunker, had been arrested by the Gestapo at his city apartment. Since he was wearing civilian clothes and carried jewelry and considerable money, including Swiss francs, the Gestapo agents concluded he was planning to escape to a neutral country. Brought back to the bunker in disgrace, he was saved by Eva's intercession; she pleaded for mercy on the grounds that his wife, her sister, was having a baby. Hitler had merely dressed him down for cowardice, ripped off his epaulets and Knight's Cross, and locked him in a nearby room for punishment. But the BBC news report convinced the Führer that Fegelein's flight was connected with the betrayal of his chief, Himmler. Fegelein must be bound for Switzerland to start peace talks. In the space of an hour he was court-martialed, found guilty of treason and condemned to death. This time Eva, though her eyes were red from crying, did not defend him. She had since learned that some of the jewelry in his suitcase was hers—and that he was betraying her sister. Fegelein, it seemed, was leaving Berlin with the attractive wife of a Hungarian diplomat.

The bunker was in a turmoil by the time Weidling arrived for the evening conference. He informed Hitler of the latest Russian advances.

All ammunition, food and supply dumps were either in enemy hands or under heavy artillery fire. In two days his troops would be out of ammunition and no longer able to resist. "As a soldier, I suggest therefore that we risk the breakout at once." He immediately launched into the details of his plan before Hitler could comment. Pure hysteria! Goebbels exclaimed. But Krebs said it was feasible from a military viewpoint. "Naturally," he added quickly, "I must leave the decision to the Führer." Hitler was silent. What if the breakout did succeed? he finally asked. "We would merely flee from one frying pan to another. Am I, the Führer, supposed to sleep in an open field or in a farmhouse, and just wait for the end?"

He left the conference to visit the wounded Greim; Hanna Reitsch was already there. He slumped down on the edge of Greim's bed, his face ashen, and told them of Himmler's betrayal. "Our only hope is Wenck," he said, "and to make his entry possible we must call up every available aircraft to cover his approach." He ordered Reitsch to fly Greim to the Rechlin airport so he could muster his aircraft from there. Only with Luftwaffe support could Wenck get through. "That's the first reason you must leave the shelter. The second is that Himmler must be stopped." His lips and hands trembled, his voice quavered. "A traitor must never succeed me as Führer. You must get out to make sure he will not." Painfully Greim began to dress. In tears, Reitsch asked Hitler for permission to stay. Hitler refused. "God protect you."

Frau Goebbels gave Reitsch two letters to her son. She took off a diamond ring and asked her to wear it in her memory. Eva Braun also gave Hanna a letter for her sister, Frau Fegelein. Later Reitsch couldn't resist reading it; she thought it was "so vulgar, so theatrical and in such poor, adolescent taste" that she tore it up.

The dark night was lit up by flaming buildings, and Greim and Reitsch could hear intense small-arms fire as an armored car brought them to an Arado 96 trainer, hidden near the Brandenburg Gate. She taxied the little plane down the east-west axis, taking off in a hail of fire. At rooftop level Russian searchlights picked up the Arado and flak explosions began tossing it about like a feather. With full power she climbed out of the maelstrom—below lay Berlin, a sea of flames. She headed north.

8

"Better to reign in hell than serve in heaven."
Lucifer in MILTON's *Paradise Lost*

Himmler's betrayal brought an end to Hitler's last hesitation and flickering hope. Despite his show of confidence to Greim, he admitted to himself that Wenck too was a lost cause and that the time had come to prepare for the end. He sent for Traudl Junge. She wondered what he had to dictate, then noticed a table elaborately decorated for some festivity: a tablecloth with the initials A.H., the silver service, champagne glasses. Was he intending to celebrate his final farewell?

He winked. "Perhaps we can begin now," he said and led the way to the conference room. He stood at his usual place before the map table— today it was barren—and stared at the polished surface. "My last political will," he said. As she took down his words her hand trembled. This was history in the making! She was sure it was going to be a confession, a justification. Who would lie at the brink of death? But the words she jotted down were only recriminations, accusations. Usually he made numerous corrections, rephrasing every sentence. Tonight he spoke almost without pause, his eyes glued on the table. He charged that neither he nor anyone else in Germany wanted war and that it had been "provoked exclusively by those international statesmen who either were of Jewish origin or worked for Jewish interests."

He declared that he would die "with a joyful heart" but had ordered his military commanders "to continue to take part in the nation's continuing struggle." To Traudl's wonder he began to name a new government. As his successor—both as President of the Reich and Supreme Commander of the Armed Forces—Hitler appointed Admiral Dönitz. Goebbels was made Chancellor and Bormann Party Minister. Traudl could not understand, if everything was lost, if Germany was destroyed, and National Socialism dead forever, what would these new officials do?

He was still staring at the table when he finished. For a moment he said nothing; then he began to dictate his personal will. "Since I did not feel that I could accept the responsibility of marriage during the years of struggle, I have decided now, before the end of my earthly career, to take as my wife . . ." Traudl looked up, startled, at last realizing why the table had been set for a celebration. She recalled Eva's cryptic words an hour earlier to Gerda Christian and herself: "This evening I bet you I shall cry!" But Traudl could find no tears. ". . . as my wife," continued Hitler, "the girl who, after many years of loyal friendship, came of her own free will to this city, already almost besieged, in order to share my fate. At her own request she goes to her death with me as my wife. Death will compensate us for what we were both deprived of by my labors in the service of my people." He left his possessions to the party, "or if this no longer exists, to the state," and appointed his most faithful party comrade, Martin Bormann, executor of his will. He ended with words that might have been inspired by Wagner and the opera libretto he himself composed as a young man in

Vienna: "My wife and I choose to die in order to escape the shame of overthrow or capitulation. It is our wish that our bodies be burned immediately, here where I have performed the greater part of my daily work during the twelve years I served my people."

While Traudl retreated to a small room to type out the two documents, Hitler joined the wedding party in the map room. He had often told his friends he could not undertake "the responsibility of marriage." Perhaps he had also feared that it might diminish his uniqueness as Führer; to most Germans he was almost a Christlike figure. But now all that was over and the bourgeois side of his nature impelled him to reward his faithful mistress with the sanctity of matrimony.

There were eight guests: Bormann, the Goebbelses, Gerda Christian, Chief Adjutant Burgdorf, Krebs, Arthur Axmann, head of the Hitler Youth, and Fräulein Manzialy, the cook. A minor official was found in a nearby Volkssturm unit and brought into the bunker to officiate—appropriately, his name was Wagner. Eva wore a long gown of black silk taffeta; Hitler was in uniform. The ceremony was brief and notable only for two slight mishaps and a minor embarrassment. The rings were too big; they had been hastily located in the Gestapo treasury. Then Eva signed the marriage certificate and, like many nervous brides, made a mistake. She started to sign it "Eva B . . . ," then hastily crossed out the "B" and wrote, Eva Hitler, née Braun. Wagner also was so nervous he signed his name wrong—with a double "a"—then Goebbels and Bormann added their signatures as witnesses. It was just before midnight, April 28.*

Arm in arm with his bride, Hitler led the way into the study for the wedding feast. He joked and drank a little Tokay. Eva was radiant. She sent for the phonograph with its single record, "Red Roses," and went out into the corridor to receive congratulations from the staff. The word spread and smaller parties began celebrating the event throughout the bunker. Hitler was jovial but distracted and kept leaving the festivities to find out how Traudl was progressing with the two testaments. Just as she was finishing, Goebbels rushed in, pale and excited. He exclaimed that the Führer had ordered him to quit Berlin so as to take over a leading position in the new government. But how could he leave his side? He stopped abruptly, oblivious of the tears rolling down his cheeks. "The Führer has

---

* It is generally believed the marriage took place in the early hours of April 29 since this is the date that appears on the document. In his nervousness Wagner had placed one paper on top of the other when the ink was wet. Half an hour or so later he noticed the original date was obliterated by a blot and began to retrace the figures. Before doing so, he checked his watch; it was thirty-five minutes past midnight and so, thoughtlessly, he wrote down April 29. This revision is evident in the original document at the Eisenhower Library, if not in photostatic copies.

made so many decisions too late! Why this one, the last one, too early?" He made her leave the typewriter so she could take down *his* last will, one to be attached to Hitler's. "For the first time in my life," he dictated, "I must categorically refuse to obey an order of the Führer. My wife and children join me in this refusal." In the nightmare of treachery surrounding Hitler, he continued, there must be at least one willing to stay unconditionally with him until death.

It was almost 4 A.M. by the time Traudl finished all three documents. By then Bormann, Goebbels and Hitler were hovering over her and one of them ripped the last page from her typewriter. The three returned to the conference room where Hitler scratched his signature at the bottom of his official political testament. Goebbels, Bormann, Burgdorf and Krebs signed as witnesses. It reaffirmed the obsession of his life and career by taking credit for the annihilation of the Jews. They had started the war, he said, and he had made them pay, "even if by more humane means, for their guilt." He had no remorse for what he had done. He was proud that he had never weakened. "Above all," he concluded, "I enjoin the leaders of the nation and those under them to uphold the racial laws to their full extent and to oppose mercilessly the universal poisoner of all peoples, International Jewry." He was proud for having accomplished his mission of extermination and his words reaffirmed that, though he had many accomplices, without him there would have been no Final Solution.

9

By mid-morning of April 29 Russian ground forces were driving toward the bunker in three main attacks: from the east, south and north. The circle around the dying city tightened as advance Soviet units infiltrated the zoo. A mile away in the bunker Martin Bormann was making preparations to send Hitler's testament as well as his personal will to his successor, Admiral Dönitz. To help guarantee their delivery, Bormann decided to dispatch two separate emissaries: his own personal adviser and Heinz Lorenz. Goebbels also wanted his testament to reach the outside world and gave a copy to Lorenz.

A third copy of Hitler's political testament was entrusted to the Führer's army adjutant by General Burgdorf, who ordered it delivered to the newly appointed commander-in-chief of the army, Field Marshal Schörner. The messenger was also given a handwritten covering note, explaining that the will had been written "'under the shattering news of Himmler's treason," and was the Führer's "unalterable decision." It was to be published "as soon as the Führer orders it, or as soon as his death is confirmed."

Eva did not get up until midday. She was greeted by an orderly with an embarrassed "Gnädiges Fräulein." With a smile she told him it was all right to call her Frau Hitler. She asked her maid, Liesel, to take her wedding ring and nightgown to her best friend, Herta Schneider, then gave Liesel a ring as a keepsake. A little later she turned over to Traudl Junge another cherished possession, her silver fox coat. "I always like to have well-dressed people around me," she said. "Take it, and I hope it will give you much pleasure." Traudl was too overwhelmed by the gift to foresee how absurd it would be to escape Berlin in such style.

The day dragged on for those in the bunker. There was little to do but gossip and smoke. By now everyone—even Eva—was smoking openly. The fumes did not seem to bother the Führer. Finally, at 6 P.M., he assembled the family circle in his study, which was screened from the anteroom by a red velvet curtain with gold fringes. After announcing that Wenck was not coming, he said that he and his wife were going to die unless some miracle intervened. He passed out phials containing cyanamide. It was a poor parting gift, he told the two secretaries, and again praised their courage. Goebbels wondered if the phials had lost their deadly effect with time. Hitler was seized with doubts of a different nature: they had been supplied by that traitor Himmler. He sent for his new surgeon, Dr. Ludwig Stumpfegger—who proposed one phial be tested on Blondi. Hitler agreed, then, recalling that Stumpfegger himself belonged to the SS, sent for a doctor in the hospital bunker. This man dutifully forced the liquid down the throat of the dog Hitler adored. It killed her.

Early that evening word arrived that Mussolini and his mistress had been assassinated by Italian partisans, their bodies strung up by the feet in a Milan gas station. "I will not fall into the hands of the enemy dead or alive!" said Hitler. "After I die, my body shall be burned and so remain undiscovered forever!" The news from Italy depressed Hitler and he would have suffered additional anguish had he known that SS General Wolff had just succeeded in secretly surrendering to the Allies all German forces in Italy.

At the final briefing of the day General Weidling told of the bitter, hopeless battles in the streets. His divisions, he said with heavy heart, were little more than battalions. Morale was poor, ammunition almost exhausted. He brandished an army field newspaper filled with optimistic stories of the imminent relief of Berlin by Wenck. The troops knew better, he charged, and such deceptions only embittered them. Goebbels sharply accused Weidling of defeatism; and another argument erupted. It took Bormann to calm them down so that Weidling could continue. He concluded his report with the devastating prediction that the battle would be over within twenty-four hours.

There was a shocked silence. In a tired voice Hitler asked the commandant of the chancellery area, an SS general, if he had observed the same conditions. He had. Weidling again pleaded for a breakout. Hitler pointed to a map and, in a resigned but sarcastic tone, said he had marked down the positions of the troops according to information from foreign radio announcements, since his own troop staffs were not even bothering to report to him any longer; his orders were not executed any more and so it was useless to expect anything.

As he rose painfully from his chair to say good-by, Weidling once more begged him to change his mind before ammunition ran out. Hitler murmured something to Krebs, then turned to Weidling: "I will permit a breakout of small groups," he said, but added that capitulation was out of the question. Weidling walked down the passageway wondering what Hitler meant. Wasn't the breakout of small groups a capitulation? He radioed all his commanders to congregate at his headquarters in the Bendlerstrasse the next morning.

After midnight Hitler bade farewell to a group of twenty officers and women secretaries in the main dining room. His eyes were covered with a film of moisture and, to Frau Junge, he seemed to be looking far away. He passed down the line shaking hands, then descended the curving staircase to his suite.

Throughout the bunker barriers dropped and high-ranking officers chatted familiarly with their juniors. In the canteen where soldiers and orderlies ate, a dance began spontaneously. It became so boisterous that a messenger from Bormann brought a warning to hold the noise down. He was trying to concentrate on a telegram he was writing to Dönitz. In it Bormann complained that all incoming reports were "controlled, suppressed or distorted" by Keitel, and ordered Dönitz "to proceed at once, and mercilessly, against all traitors."

10

By late morning of April 30 the Tiergarten was overrun by the Soviets and one advance unit was reported in the street next to the bunker. It was difficult to see that this news had any effect on Hitler. During lunch with the two secretaries and the cook, he chatted as if it were merely another family circle gathering. He was self-possessed and, if anything, quieter than usual. To Traudl it seemed to be "a banquet of death under the cheerful mask of resignation and composure."

But it was no ordinary day and no sooner had the three ladies left than Hitler summoned them back, along with Bormann, the Goebbelses and several others. More stooped than ever, he slowly came out of his room with Eva, who was wearing the black dress that was his favorite; her hair was neatly combed. Hitler began shaking hands with everyone. He was pale and there were tears in his eyes. He looked directly at Traudl as he held her hand but did not seem to see her, and mumbled something she could not understand. She stood motionless in a trance, oblivious of everything in the room. The spell was broken somewhat when Eva Hitler, with a sad smile, put an arm around her. "Please, at least try to get out of here," she said. Her voice broke into a sob. "Then please greet Munich for me."

Hitler took Günsche aside and said that he and his wife were going to commit suicide. He wanted their bodies burned. "After my death," he explained, "I don't want to be put on exhibition in a Russian wax museum." Günsche phoned Kempka's quarters at the bunker, asked for something to drink and said he was coming over. Kempka knew something was wrong. In the last days no one had thought of alcohol. He found a bottle of cognac and waited. The phone rang. It was Günsche again. "I need two hundred liters of gasoline immediately," he said huskily. Kempka thought it was some kind of joke and wanted to know why he needed so much fuel.

Günsche could not tell him on the phone. "I want it at the entrance of the Führer bunker without fail." Kempka said the only gasoline left—about 40,000 liters—was buried in the Tiergarten, which was under deadly fire. They would have to wait until five o'clock when the barrage let up.

"I can't wait a single hour. See what you can siphon out of the wrecked cars."

Hitler was bidding his personal pilot for so many years an emotional farewell. As they clasped hands, Baur begged him to escape by plane to Argentina, to Japan, or to one of the Arab countries where his anti-Semitism had made him such staunch friends. But the Führer would not listen. "One must have the courage to face the consequences—I am ending it all here! I know that by tomorrow millions of people will curse me —Fate wanted it that way." He thanked Baur for his long service and offered his cherished portrait of Frederick the Great as a present. "I don't want this picture to get lost. I want it to remain for the future. It has great historical value."

Baur said he would take it only if he were allowed to turn it over, later, to a museum or gallery. Hitler insisted it was for him personally, then with a small smile recalled how often Baur had grumbled about transporting the large portrait from headquarters to headquarters. He grasped the pilot's hands. "Baur," he said bitterly, "I want them to write on my tombstone: 'He was the victim of his generals!' "

The Hitlers sat together on a couch in their suite. Behind them was the bare space where the portrait of Frederick had hung. Eva was the first to die—by poison. At about 3:30 P.M. Hitler picked up his 7.65-caliber Walther pistol (Geli killed herself with a Walther and Eva had tried to but failed). It had been his companion for years: a defense against the Reds in the early days of the party; the means of gaining attention at the Bürgerbräukeller in 1923. He had threatened to kill himself with it during several fits of depression. This time his intention was genuine. On a console was a picture of his mother as a young woman. He put the pistol barrel to his right temple and pulled the trigger.

On the upper floor, Traudl Junge was telling the Goebbels children a fairy story to keep them from going downstairs, when a shot echoed along the damp concrete. Young Helmut thought it was an enemy bomb and said, "Bull's-eye!" In the conference room Goebbels, Bormann, Axmann and Günsche hesitated momentarily after hearing the shot, then broke into Hitler's anteroom with Goebbels in the lead. Günsche saw the Führer on the couch sprawled face down across a low table. To his left lay Eva, slumped over the armrest, her lips tightly closed in death, her nostrils discolored by cyanamide. Her dress was wet, but not with blood. A jug lying on the table must have been knocked over as the Führer pitched forward. Unnerved, Günsche stumbled back into the conference room where he was accosted by Kempka.

"For God's sake, Otto," the chauffeur said, "what's going on? You must be crazy to have me send men to almost certain death just for two hundred liters of gasoline." Günsche brushed past him, slamming the door to the cloakroom so that no one else could wander in. Then he closed the door to the Führer's suite and turned, eyes wide. "The Chief is dead!"

The only thing Kempka could think of was that Hitler had had a heart attack. Günsche lost his voice. Though he had seen the bullet hole in Hitler's right temple, he pointed a finger like a pistol and put it in his mouth, his shocked gesture inspiring the widely believed story that Hitler had shot himself in the mouth.

"Where is Eva?"

Günsche indicated Hitler's anteroom and was finally able to say,

"She's with him." It took Günsche several minutes to stammer out the whole story.

Linge peered out of Hitler's anteroom and asked for the gasoline. Kempka said he had about a hundred and seventy liters in jerricans at the garden entrance. Linge and Dr. Stumpfegger carried out Hitler's body in a dark brown army blanket. The Führer's face was half covered, his left arm dangled down. Bormann followed, carrying Eva. Her hair was hanging loose. The sight of her in Bormann's arms was too much for Kempka. She had always hated Bormann and the chauffeur thought, "Not one more step." He called to Günsche, "I'll carry Eva," then took her away from Bormann. Halfway up the four flights of stairs to the garden, her body almost slipped from his grasp. Kempka stopped, unable to continue until Günsche moved to his aid, and together they carried Eva into the garden.

Another Russian barrage had begun, with shells smashing into the rubble. Only the jagged walls of the chancellery remained and these trembled with every shattering explosion. Through a cloud of dust Kempka saw Hitler's body not ten feet from the bunker entrance. His trousers were pulled up; his right foot was turned in—the characteristic position he always assumed on a long auto trip.

Kempka and Günsche stretched Eva's body out on Hitler's right. All at once the artillery barrage increased in tempo, forcing them to take cover in the bunker entrance. Kempka waited a few minutes, then seized a jerrican of gasoline and ran back to the bodies. He placed Hitler's left arm closer to his side. It was done only to delay a repellent duty; he could not bring himself to drench the body with gasoline. A gust of wind moved Hitler's hair. Kempka opened the jerrican. A shell exploded, showering him with debris; shrapnel whizzed past his head. Again he scrambled back for refuge.

Günsche, Kempka and Linge waited in the entrance for a lull in the shelling. When it came they returned to the bodies. Shivering with revulsion, Kempka sprinkled them with gasoline. He thought, "I can't do it but I'm doing it." He saw the same reaction in the faces of Linge and Günsche, who were also pouring gasoline. From the entrance Goebbels, Bormann and Dr. Stumpfegger peered out with morbid concern.

The clothing of the corpses became so soaked that even the strongest gust of wind brought no stirring. The bombardment resumed, but the three men emptied can after can until the shallow depression in which the Hitlers lay was filled with gasoline. Günsche suggested igniting it with a hand grenade but Kempka said no. The idea of blowing up the bodies was too repugnant. He saw a large rag lying near a fire hose at the entrance He pointed it out to Günsche, who doused it with gasoline.

Goebbels handed Kempka a pack of matches. He set fire to the rag and tossed it onto the bodies. A boiling ball of fire mushroomed, followed by dark clouds of smoke. It was a small blaze in a burning city, but horrifying. The men watched, hypnotized, as the fire slowly began to consume Adolf and Eva Hitler. Shaken, Günsche and Kempka stumbled back to the entrance. More jerricans of gasoline were delivered, and for the next three hours they kept pouring the liquid on the smoldering corpses.

In a daze, Günsche finally climbed back into the bunker. On the upper level he noticed Traudl sitting on a small bench, a bottle of Steinhäger beside her. He took a drink, his big hands trembling. "I executed the Führer's last order," he said very softly. "His body is burned." She said nothing but when he left to make another inspection of the bodies she was impelled to see Hitler's apartment. The door was open. On the floor next to the couch was the brass hull of a poison capsule. It looked like an empty lipstick. On the right cushion of the couch she saw blood—Hitler's blood. On an iron clothes rack hung the dog leash and his plain gray overcoat; above it his cap with the golden party emblem and his light deerskin gloves. She decided to take the gloves as a souvenir—at least one of them, but something stayed her hand. She noticed a silver fox coat in the wardrobe. It was the one Eva had bequeathed her but Traudl could not take it. What use would it be? All she needed was a poison capsule.

That evening the charred remains of Hitler and Eva were swept into a canvas and, so Günsche recalled, "let down into a shell hole outside the exit from the bunker, covered over with earth, and the earth pounded firm with a wooden rammer."

He was buried in the rubble of defeat; not, as he had instructed architect Giesler, in Munich ("Here I was born, here I started this movement, and here is my heart"). There should have been someone present to recite the poem Baldur von Schirach had made from the Führer's own words:

> *Could be that the columns which halt here,*
> *That these endless brown rows of men,*
> *Are scattered in the wind, split up and dispersed*
> *And will desert me. Could be, could be . . .*
> *I shall remain faithful, even though deserted by all—*
> *I shall carry the flag, staggering and alone.*
> *My smiling lips may stammer mad words,*
> *But the flag will only fall when I fall*
> *And will be a proud shroud covering my corpse.*

The flag fell where he fell and when he died so did National Socialism and the Thousand-Year Third Reich. Because of him, his beloved Germany lay in ruins.

The greatest irony of all was that the driving force of his life—his hatred and fear of Jews—was thwarted. He had intended the elimination of six million Jews to be his great gift to the world. It would lead, instead, to the formation of a Jewish state.

Epilogue

1

To the surprise of the world, Hitler's death brought an abrupt, absolute end to National Socialism. Without its only true leader, it burst like a bubble. There were no enclaves of fanatic followers bent on continuing Hitler's crusade; the feared Alpine Redoubt proved to be a chimera. What had appeared to be the most powerful and fearsome political force of the twentieth century vanished overnight. No other leader's death since Napoleon had so completely obliterated a regime.

In death the Führer remained controversial and mysterious. Even as his body smoldered, a rumor spread in the bunker that Axmann, the Youth leader, had put some of Hitler's ashes in a box with instructions to secrete it outside of Berlin. News of his suicide was received with disbelief by some Germans. The parents of Fegelein, for instance, assured an American counterintelligence agent that a courier had brought a message from their son that he and Hitler were "safe and well in Argentina." Stalin also professed doubt. He told Harry Hopkins that Hitler's end struck him as "dubious." Hitler had surely escaped and was in hiding along with Bormann. This version became U.S.S.R. history until 1968 when a Soviet journalist, Lev Bezymenski, published a book revealing that the Russians *had* found the bodies of Adolf and Eva Hitler outside the bunker on May 4, 1945. As evidence, Bezymenski included an autopsy report of the Forensic Medical Commission of the Red Army, which stated that splinters of a poison ampule had been found in the Führer's mouth—and there was no bullet hole in the skull. In other words, the Soviets implied that Hitler had taken a cowardly route to death. Moreover, added the report, he had but one testicle—a conclusion made much of by some psychohistorians despite reports from three doctors who had examined Hitler indicating he was normal. The long-delayed Soviet revelation was received with some suspicion. Although the detailed report was authenticated by five pathologists and experts in forensic medicine, it was supported only by photographic evidence of Hitler's corpse. The remains themselves, Bezymenski admitted, had been "completely burned and their ashes strewn to the wind."

Skeptics wondered why Stalin had spread the story in 1945 that Hitler had escaped when he knew the body had been found. They were not at all convinced by Bezymenski's explanation: "First, it was resolved not to publish the results of the forensic medical report but to 'hold it in reserve' in case someone might try to slip into the role of 'the Führer saved by a miracle.' Secondly, it was resolved to continue the investigations in order to exclude any possibility of error or deliberate deception." Neither reason accounts for the wait of twenty-three years, nor was any explanation given for the destruction of the remains. Pictures of the corpse's dentures had been kept on file and in 1972 Dr. Reidar Soggnaes, a dental forensic expert from U.C.L.A., discovered that these teeth exactly matched those in the X-ray head plates of Hitler taken in 1943. This hard evidence, Dr. Soggnaes told the 6th International Meeting of Forensic Sciences at Edinburgh, proved beyond doubt that Hitler was dead and that the Soviets had autopsied the right body. But where was the proof that Hitler had not shot himself? The skull "proving" that there was no bullet hole had been conveniently destroyed. Moreover, none of the eyewitnesses in the bunker had noticed the telltale discolorations of cyanamide on Hitler's lips; and only one empty poison capsule had been found.

No mystery clouded Goebbels' death. On the first of May, after a futile attempt to negotiate with the Soviets, he told his adjutant, Günther Schwägermann, "Everything is lost." He handed Schwägermann a silver-framed photograph of Hitler and bade him farewell. Frau Goebbels roused their six children from bed. "Children, don't be afraid," she said, "the doctor is going to give you an injection, a kind that is now given to all children and soldiers." After a dentist named Kunz injected morphine to make the children sleepy, Frau Goebbels herself placed a crushed ampule containing potassium cyanide in the mouth of each child.

Others in the bunker were getting last-minute instructions for escape. They were divided into six separate groups. At 9 P.M. the first section would make a run for the nearest subway entrance and walk along the tracks to the Friedrichstrasse station. Here they would emerge, cross the

Recently rescued by the famous commando Otto Skorzeny (September 1943), Mussolini is about to face Hitler. From rare movie film. TIEFENTHALER

Hitler's trousers after the blast. BUND-ESARCHIV

Shortly after the explosion, Hitler has changed his uniform and had a bandage put on his left hand, which is supporting his injured right arm. L. to r., Keitel, Göring (Günsche and Jodl in background), Hitler, Below. To the right, Himmler jabs finger at General Lörzer. BIBLIO. FÜR ZEIT.

Hitler marveling at his miraculous escape from death earlier that day. L. to r., Mussolini (who had just arrived for a visit), Bormann, Admiral Dönitz, Hitler, Göring, SS General Fegelein (husband of Eva's sister Gretl), General Lörzer. BIBLIO. FÜR ZEIT.

Major Otto Remer, promoted to major general by Hitler for his part in squashing the army bomb plot, is congratulated by Goebbels. On left, Hans Hagen, an author in uniform, who helped Remer. REMER

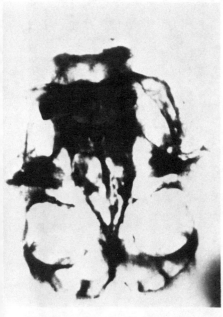

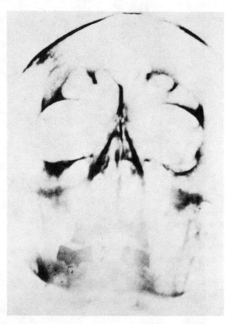

After the bombing, Dr. Erwin Giesing persuaded Hitler to allow X rays of his skull taken. NATIONAL ARCHIVES

Field Marshal Rommel was forced to take poison for participating in the plot. Here, two years earlier, he is being honored for his victories in the desert. Behind, l. to r., Engel, Keitel and Schulze. U. S. ARMY

Right, Field Marshal Walther Model, Hitler's personal choice to command his last gamble, the Battle of the Bulge, December 1944. Left, Bodenschatz; center, Luftwaffe General von Richthofen. U. S. ARMY

General Hasso von Manteuffel, German pentathlon champion, whose tanks almost reached the Meuse River. MANTEUFFEL

Left, the Reich Chancellery, March 1945. FRENTZ. Right, Hitler driven underground by Allied bombs. The waiting room of the Führer bunker. Extreme left, Dr. Morell. Center, Hitler's former valet Krause and Admiral von Puttkamer. PUTTKAMER

Cologne. AMERICAN COMMISSION FOR THE PROTECTION AND SALVAGE OF HISTORICAL MONUMENTS

Nuremberg, home of the Nazi Party Day. AMERICAN COMMISSION FOR THE PROTECTION AND SALVAGE OF HISTORICAL MONUMENTS

In the midst of destruction, Hitler dreams of a new Munich, above, and a new Linz, below. Both cities were designed by Professor Hermann Giesler with Hitler's help. Behind, as usual, is Bormann. FRENTZ

One of the last pictures of Hitler. He visits Oder front, March 1945. BIBLIO. FÜR ZEIT.

On October 10, 1943, Hitler congratulates Himmler, who has just revealed that six million Jews have been exterminated. U. S. ARMY

Millions more Jews and non-Jews died in concentration camps in the spring of 1945. Belsen. U. S. OFFICE OF WAR INFORMATION

. Nachdem nunmehr beide Verlobte die Erklärung abgegeben
haben die Ehe einzugehen, erkläre ich die Ehe vor dem Gesetz
rechtmäßig für geschlossen.

Berlin, am ✠ April 1945

        Vorgelesen und unterschrieben:

1.) Ehemann:

2.) Ehefrau:

3.) Zeuge zu 1:

4.) Zeuge zu 2:

5.)

    als Standesbeamter

The wedding certificate of Eva and Adolf Hitler, dated May 29, 1945. Note blurred date—it was
originally May 28 and then mistakenly altered—and Eva's writing mistake. EISENHOWER LIBRARY

The End. After twelve years of imprisonment in the East, SS adjutant Günsche views the ruins of
the Berghof. Left, personal adjutant Schulze. MONIKA SCHULZE-KOSSENS

Spree River and head west or northwest until they reached the Western Allies or Dönitz. The other five groups would follow the same course, at intervals. Some were captured but, miraculously, few died.

At 8:45 P.M. Kempka went to the Goebbels suite to say good-by. The children were already dead. Frau Goebbels asked Kempka in a calm voice to send greetings to her son Harald and tell him how she had died. The Goebbelses left their room arm in arm. Utterly calm, he thanked Naumann for his loyalty and understanding; Magda could only hold out her hand. Naumann kissed it. Goebbels wryly remarked that they were going to walk up the steps to the garden so that their friends wouldn't have to carry them. After shaking hands with Naumann, he escorted his silent, pale wife toward the exit. They disappeared up the steep concrete stairway. Then came a shot, followed by a second. Schwägermann and the Goebbelses' chauffeur hurried up the stairs to find the Goebbelses sprawled on the ground. An SS orderly was staring at them—he had shot them. He and the two newcomers poured four jerricans of gasoline on the bodies and set them afire. Without waiting to see the effect of the blaze, they returned to the bunker, which they had been ordered to destroy. They dumped the last can of gas in the conference room and ignited it.

The fate of Martin Bormann was more controversial than his master's. It was generally assumed that he had died while attempting to escape from Berlin but declassified United States and British intelligence documents indicated that he might have escaped to Bolzano, Italy, where his wife had already fled from Berchtesgaden with their nine children. For the next twenty-seven years there were recurring reports of Bormann's reappearance, particularly in Argentina. Then, late in 1972, an American author, Ladislas Farago, claimed he had positive proof Bormann was alive in South America. This sensational announcement was followed a few days later by another. The German authorities declared that they had just found Bormann's body near the Führer bunker. Dr. Soggnaes, who had authenticated the Hitler corpse, asked permission to examine the skull so he could corroborate the dental identification. At first permission was withheld, adding suspicion that the corpse might be a hoax. Finally in the summer of 1973 Dr. Soggnaes was allowed to examine the skeletal remains as well as the maxillary incisor bridge which had been found three months after the skull was unearthed. Dr. Soggnaes returned to U.C.L.A. to prepare a forensic analysis of the data. In September 1974 he presented his material to the World Congress of the Federation of Dentaire Internationale in London. The skull, he concluded, was indeed that of Bormann. And the mystery of Hitler's most faithful servant was finally solved.

2

To the very end, Heinrich Himmler hoped for some arrangement with the Allies while fearing that something would go wrong. After Hitler's death he fled to the north and requested the Führer's successor to appoint him the second man in his new German state. But Admiral Dönitz said, "That is impossible. I have no job for you." In desperation Himmler turned to Schwerin von Krosigk for advice. "Please tell me what is going to become of me?" he asked the new Foreign Minister. "I am not interested in the least what will happen to you or any other man," was the exasperated answer. "Only our mission interests me, not our personal destinies." Krosigk gave Himmler two choices: either commit suicide or disappear with a false beard. "But if I were you I would drive up to Montgomery and say, 'Here I am, Himmler the SS general, and ready to take responsibility for my men.'"

That evening Himmler cryptically told his closest friends that an important new task remained. A few could accompany him. He shaved off his mustache, put a patch over one eye, changed his name and—with some nine followers, including his chief Waffen SS adjutant, Werner Grothmann—went into hiding. When Grothmann discovered his chief had a cyanide capsule and intended to use it if necessary, he accused Himmler of taking an easy way out that was not open to his followers. It was the Reichsführer's duty, he said, not only to assume responsibility for his men's actions but to make clear that the Waffen SS, the SD and the concentration camp guards were from distinctly different organizations. Himmler demurred. "After I take the poison," he said, "then you young officers must tell the world what happened here in Germany—what I did and what I did not do." Within two weeks Himmler was captured by the British. A doctor conducting a routine examination noticed something in his mouth, but when he reached in to pull out the object Himmler bit down on the cyanide capsule and died instantly. There were other suicides but their number were fewer than expected, particularly among the hierarchy, one of whom—Robert Ley—did commit suicide while awaiting trial at Nuremberg.

Göring was by far the most defiant prisoner at Nuremberg. He arrived at the prison with an incredibly large cache of Paradocin pills and was taking forty daily. By the time he testified, however, he was completely free of the drug habit and had cut his weight down more than forty per cent to 153 pounds. In the courtroom he, almost alone, defended his Führer. Unlike so many of the other defendants, he never put blame on others or hid behind the figure of Hitler. He took charge of the prisoners' dock, aggressively dictating a concerted strategy of defense. Back in the cell block, he would rub his hands enthusiastically and call himself the captain of the first-string team, boasting that he would give the prosecutors and the audience a run for their money. If any fellow defendant protested or weakened, the revivified Göring would bully and insult him into silence. "It makes me sick to see Germans selling their souls to the enemy!" he said during one lunch, then banged a fist on the table. "Damn it," he added, "I just wish we could all have the courage to confine our defense to three simple words: *Lick my ass!*"

Of the twenty-two major defendants only three (Schacht, Papen and Fritzsche) were acquitted. Eight received long terms of imprisonment; the rest were sentenced to death. At 10:45 P.M. October 15, 1946, Göring cheated the hangman with a cyanide capsule. Two hours later the executions began. The first to climb the thirteen steps of the gallows was Ribbentrop. "God protect Germany," he said loudly. "My last wish is that Germany's unity shall be preserved and that an understanding be reached between East and West." It had taken the incontrovertible evidence at Nuremberg to convince him that masses of Jews had been killed, for Hitler had assured him time and again that the Jewish problem would be solved by deportation. "I never dreamed," he told G. M. Gilbert, an American psychologist, "it would end like this!"

Next came Keitel. Minutes earlier he had sobbed while the chaplain gave him a last benediction. Now his chin was thrust out. "I call on the Almighty God to have mercy on the German people. For Germany—everything. Thank you!" He turned to the chaplain, an American. "I thank you and those who sent you with all my heart." The hangman, Master Sergeant John Woods, had looked forward with relish to these executions. He adjusted the rope around Keitel's neck, then placed a black hood over his head. At the very last moment the field marshal shouted, "Deutschland über Alles!" During the trial Keitel had confided to Gilbert that Hitler had betrayed him. "If he did not deceive us by deliberate lies, then he did it by deliberately keeping us in the dark and letting us fight under a false impression!"

3

A surprising number of Hitler's family circle survived the last cataclysmic days: the four secretaries; his two favorite architects, Speer and Giesler; his pilot, Baur; his chauffeur, Kempka; his valet, Linge; Heim and Koeppen, who copied down his table conversations; the best friend of his wife, Frau Schneider; his two favorite fighters, Skorzeny and Rudel; the three women he particularly admired: Leni Riefenstahl, Gerdy Troost and Helene Hanfstaengl.

A number of his adjutants and ordnance officers not only survived but were willing to talk freely of their experiences: Puttkamer, Engel, Below, Wünsche, Schulze and Günsche. When the last returned to West Germany after twelve years of imprisonment in the Soviet Union and East Germany, he was bewildered by the sight of young men with beards and long hair. "Dear friend," Schulze told him, "we have lost the war and all is now changed. The young people don't live as we did." To shock Günsche back to reality, Schulze took him to the Berghof. The building had been set afire by the SS on May 4, 1945, and its remains had been gradually destroyed by the Americans. Everything looked different and it was very difficult even to figure out where the long flight of steps leading up to the house had been. As the two men surveyed the scene, Schulze's wife took their picture, capturing in their stunned faces, as no words could, the definitive end of the man they had worshiped. The most extraordinary figure in the history of the twentieth century had vanished—unlamented except by a faithful few.

Acknowledgments

Without the co-operation of numerous people in Germany, Austria, England and the United States this book could not have been written. Archives and libraries contributed immeasurably: the National Archives (John E. Taylor, John Mendelsohn, Robert Wolfe, George Wagner); the Library of Congress; the main branch of the New York Public Library; the Danbury, Ct., Public Library; the Yale University Library; the Franklin D. Roosevelt Library (Bettie Sprigg, Robert Parks); the Wiener Library, London; the Imperial War Museum, London (Rose Coombs); the Institut für Zeitgeschichte, Munich (Frl. Danyl); the Bayerisches Hauptstaatarchiv, Munich; the Forschungstelle für die Geschichte des Nationalsozialismus, Hamburg (Werner Jochmann); the Bibliothek für Zeitgeschichte, Stuttgart (Werner Haupt, Gerhard Buck, Dr. Jurgen Röhwer); the Bundesarchiv, Koblenz; the Institut für Zeitgeschichte, Vienna (Dr. Ludwig Jedlicka); and the Landesarchiv, Linz (Dr. Hans Sturmberger).

Numerous agencies, organizations and individuals made substantial contributions to this book:

United States: Charles MacDonald and Hannah Zeidlik of the Office of the Chief of Military History, Department of the Army; U. S. Army Intelligence Command, Fort Holabird, Md. (Elaine M. Pospishil); fellow authors and historians: Richard Hanser, Telford Taylor, Richard Walton, Dr. John Lukacs, Dr. Harold J. Gordon, Jr., Dr. Eberhard Jäckel, Dr. Ernst Deuerlein, Dr. Dietrich Orlow, Dr. Reginald Phelps, Dr. Oron Hale, Dr. Bradley F. Smith; contributors of documents: Edward Whalen, Dave Stanton, Peter Thayer and Ben E. Swearingen; psychiatrists and physicians: Drs. Wolzar, Richmond Hubbard, Jason Weiner and Warren Sherman; Edward Weiss; Raymond Garthoff; Michael Erlanger; Arthur Shilstone; Sig Muller; Otto Zundricht; Peter Repetti; John Stillman and Stewart Richardson of Doubleday & Company.

Austria: Alfred Janicek, Heimleiter, Männerheim, Vienna; Josef Adler, Asylum, Vienna; Dr. Wilfried Daim; and Dr. Eleonore (Kandl) Weber.

England: Ellic Howe, Walter Henry Nelson and Hugh Trevor-Roper.
Spain: Otto Skorzeny.
Germany: Bavaria Atelier Fernsik-Productions (Dr. Helmut Pigge);
Bayerischer Rundfunk and Fernseher (Thilo Schneider and Dietmar Ebert);
Prof. Gerdy Troost; Nerin Gun; Egon Hanfstaengl; Harry Schulze-Wilde
(H. S. Hegner); Günter Syrup; Klaus Wiedemann; Major General Gustav
Lombard; Erich Kempka; Dr. Werner Koeppen; Heinrich Heim; Erich Kern-
mayer; Helmut Sündermann; Admiral Karl Jesko von Puttkamer; General
Hasso von Manteuffel; Frau Luise Jodl; Dr. H. D. Röhrs; Hein Ruck; Richard
Schulze-Kossens; Max Wünsche; Hans Ulrich Rudel; Frau Ilse (Braun) Fucke-
Michels; and two research assistants and interpreters: Inge Gehrich and Wolf-
gang Glaser.

Finally I would like to thank eleven people who contributed outstandingly
to the book: Roger Bell, The Society for the Studies of the E.T.O. 1944–45,
London, for supplying numerous books; Dr. Rudolph Binion, John Jamieson,
Dr. George Breitbart and Dr. Eric Roman, all of whom read the entire manuscript and made valuable suggestions; my chief research assistant and interpreter in Germany, Karola Gillich, an indefatigible aide since 1957; my secre-
tary-translator-typist, Ann Thomas, whose suggestions and corrections have
been of inestimable value; my two editors at Doubleday, Carolyn Blakemore
and Ken McCormick, who somehow managed to make the revisions a pleasure;
and my wife, Toshiko, for putting up with Adolf Hitler more than five years.

Glossary

ABWEHR Espionage, counterespionage and sabotage service of the German high command.

ANSCHLUSS Union. Especially the political union of Austria and Germany in 1938.

BLITZKRIEG Lightning warfare.

BLUE POLICE Municipal police, so called for color of their uniform.

EINSATZGRUPPE An operational task force of the SD and Sipo for special missions in occupied Eastern territory. Its task was to maintain law and order but its primary occupation was liquidation of partisans, Jews and other "dangerous elements." There were four Einsatzgruppen and, although they were administratively subordinated to the military command, the RSHA retained functional control over them.

ENDLÖSUNG The Final Solution, extermination of Jews.

FESTUNG Fortress.

GAU Territorial division of the NSDAP.

GAULEITER High-ranking, Nazi Party official in a Gau. Responsible for political and economic activity as well as mobilization of labor and civil defense.

GENERALGOUVERNEMENT German-occupied Poland. Administered by a German civilian, Hans Frank.

GESTAPO Abbreviation for Geheime Staatspolizei. Secret state police. (See SS.)

GLEICHSCHALTUNG Unification. Nazi program begun in 1933.

GREEN POLICE State police, so called for the color of their uniforms.

HEER German army.

HITLERJUGEND (HJ) Hitler Youth.

KREIS Administrative district in a Gau.

KREISLEITER Head of Kreis.

KRIPO Kriminalpolizei. Criminal police which, with the Gestapo, formed the Sipo, secret police.

LEBENSBORN Spring of Life. SS maternity organization to promote Himmler's racial policy.

LEBENSRAUM Living room. Living space. Additional territory desired by a nation for expansion.

LEIBSTANDARTE SS ADOLF HITLER Adolf Hitler Bodyguard Regiment.

LUFTWAFFE German air force.

NSDAP Nationalsozialistische Deutsche Arbeiter Partei, National Socialist German Worker's Party. Nazi Party.

OBERKOMMANDO DES HEERES (OKH) High command of the German army.

OBERKOMMANDO DER WEHRMACHT (OKW) High command of the German armed forces.

OSTMINISTERIUM Ministry of the East.

REICHSFÜHRER Highest rank in SS.

REICHSLEITER Highest-ranking Nazi official.

REICHSSICHERHEITSHAUPTAMT (RSHA) Reich Central Security Department. Under Heydrich, then Kaltenbrunner. (*See* SS.)

REICHSWEHR The 100,000-man army Germany was restricted to under the Treaty of Versailles.

SCHUTZSTAFFEL (SS) Guard Detachment. It contained the following sections:

1. *Allgemeine* (General) SS. Strictly civilian. Most diplomats, top-level state employees, industrialists, lawyers, doctors, etc., held high ranks in the *Allgemeine* SS.
2. RSHA (*Reichssicherheitshauptampt*, National Central Security Office). Civilian and paramilitary. Of its seven departments, the most important were: Bureau III, the SD (*Sicherheitsdienst*, Security Service inside the Reich); Bureau IV, the Gestapo (State Security Police); Bureau V, Criminal Police; and Bureau VI, Foreign Intelligence.
3. *Waffen* (Armed) SS. Strictly elitist military organization with recruitment open not only to Germans but to qualified Aryans of other nations. Its divisions included volunteers from Belgium, France, Holland, Norway, Lithuania, Denmark, Sweden, Hungary, Romania, etc., who had joined primarily to fight Bolshevism.
4. *Totenkopfverbände* (Death's Head units). Paramilitary. Concentration and death camp guards. By 1943 the majority were elderly or wounded soldiers unfit for front-line duty. In 1940 the youngest and healthiest were formed into an elite battle unit, the *Totenkopf* Division, and thus became a genuine part of the Waffen SS. Those who remained as concentration and death camp guards also ranked as members of the Waffen SS, carrying the same pay-books and wearing the same uniforms. It was an insult to those Waffen SS troops who had fought gallantly at the front and were not at all involved in the terrorism of the camps. But

their commanders did not protest and, besides providing the bulk of the troops for the annihilation of the Warsaw ghetto, contributed some 1500 men to the notorious Einsatzgruppen squads.

SICHERHEITSDIENST RFSS (SD) SS Security Service. (*See* RSHA and SS.)

SICHERHEITSPOLIZEI (Sipo) Security police consisting of Gestapo and Kripo.

STAHLHELM Steel Helmet. Nationalist ex-servicemen's organization founded in 1918. Absorbed into SA in 1933.

STURMABTEILUNG (SA) Storm Detachment. The Brownshirts, storm troopers.

TOTENKOPFVERBÄNDE Death's Head Detachments. (*See* SS.)

VERTRAUENSMANN (V-mann) An intelligence agent or informer. Hitler was a V-mann in 1919.

VOLKSSTURM Home Guard.

WAFFEN SS Armed SS. Militarized SS units. Almost 40 divisions were fielded in World War II. (*See* SS.)

WEHRMACHT The German armed forces—army, navy and air force.

Table of Ranks

SS	GERMAN ARMY	BRITISH ARMY	U.S. ARMY	RED ARMY (Soviet ranks compiled by Raymond Garthoff)	NSDAP (The first entry in each section represents a function, the second denotes the appropriate rank)
Reichsführer	Generalfeldmarschall	Field Marshal	General of the Army	Marshal of the Soviet Union [Marshal Sovetskogo Soiuza] Chief Marshal of (an Arm: i.e., Artillery, Armor, Aviation, Signals, Engineers) [Glavnyi Marshal—(Artillerii)]	Reichsleiter Hauptbefehlsleiter
Obergruppenführer (from 1942 only)	Generaloberst	General	General	Marshal of an Arm (as above) [Marshal (Artillerii)] General of the Army [General armii]	Gauleiter Oberbefehlsleiter
Obergruppenführer	General (der Infanterie etc.)	Lieutenant-General	Lieutenant General	Colonel General (also, Col. Gen. of an Arm) [General polkovnik]	Gauleiter (or deputy) Befehlsleiter
Gruppenführer	Generalleutnant	Major-General	Major General	Lieutenant General (also, Lt. Gen. of an Arm) [General leytenant]	Gauleiter (or deputy) Hauptdienstleiter
Brigadeführer	Generalmajor	Brigadier	Brigadier General	Major General (also, Maj. Gen. of an Arm) [General Mayor]	Gauleiter (or deputy) Oberdienstleiter
Oberführer	....	....	no such rank	....	Gauleiter (or deputy) Oberdienstleiter
Standartenführer	Oberst	Colonel	Colonel	Colonel [Polkovnik]	Kreisleiter Dienstleiter or Hauptbereichsleiter
Obersturmbannführer	Oberstleutnant	Lieutenant-Colonel	Lieutenant Colonel	Lieutenant Colonel [Podpolkovnik]	(a) Kreisleiter Oberbereichsleiter or Bereichsleiter Hauptabschnittsleiter (b) Ortsgruppenleiter Oberabschnittsleiter
Sturmbannführer	Major	Major	Major	Major [Mayor]	

SS	GERMAN ARMY	BRITISH ARMY	U.S. ARMY	RED ARMY	NSDAP
Hauptsturmführer	Hauptmann or Rittmeister (Cav.)	Captain	Captain	Captain [Kapitan]	(a) Ortsgruppenleiter Abschnittsleiter (b) Zellenleiter Hauptgemeinschaftsleiter or Obergemeinschaftsleiter
Obersturmführer	Oberleutnant	Lieutenant	First Lieutenant	Senior Lieutenant [Starshiy leytenant] Lieutenant [Leytenant]	(a) Zellenleiter Gemeinschaftsleiter (b) Blockleiter Haupteinsatzleiter
Untersturmführer	Leutnant	Second Lieutenant	Second Lieutenant	Junior Lieutenant [Mladshiy leytenant]	Blockleiter Obereinsatzleiter Einsatzleiter
Sturmscharführer	Stabsfeldwebel Stabswachtmeister	Regimental Sergeant-Major	Sergeant Major	Sergeant Major [Starshina]	Hauptbereitschaftsleiter
Stabsscharführer	Hauptfeldwebel	....		no such rank	
Hauptscharführer	Oberfeldwebel Oberwachtmeister	Sergeant-Major	Master Sergeant	Sergeant Major [Starshina]	Oberbereitschaftsleiter
Oberscharführer	Feldwebel Wachtmeister	Quartermaster-Sergeant	Technical Sergeant	...no such rank...	
Scharführer	Unterfeldwebel	Staff Sergeant	Staff Sergeant	Senior Sergeant [Starshiy serzhant]	Bereitschaftsleiter
Unterscharführer	Unteroffizier	Sergeant	Sergeant	Sergeant [Serzhant]	Hauptarbeitsleiter
Rottenführer	Stabsgefreiter Obergefreiter Gefreiter	Corporal	Corporal	Junior Sergeant [Mladshiy serzhant]	Oberarbeitsleiter
Sturmmann	Oberschütze Obergrenadier etc.	Lance-Corporal	Private 1st Class	Private First Class [Yefreitor]	Arbeitsleiter Oberhelfer
SS-Mann	Schütze Grenadier etc.	Private	Private	Private [Ryadovoi]	Helfer

Sources

A. INTERVIEWS (partial list)

Dieter Allers (SA), 1971, taped
Countess Haiga von Arco auf Valley, 1971
Stephen Bauchner (Leonding), 1971, taped
Flugkapitan Hans Baur, 1970, taped
Oberst Nicolaus von Below, 1971, taped
Werner Benecke (SA), 1971, taped
Countess Estelle Manville Bernadotte, 1963
Generalleutnant Günther Blumentritt (2 interviews), 1957 **
Wolfgang Boigs (DNB), 1963
Otto Bräutigam (Rosenberg office), 1971, taped
Carl J. Burckhardt, 1963
General Theodor Busse, 1963
Gerda Daranowsky Christian (2), 1971, taped
Wilfried Daim (3) (author), 1971, taped
Léon Degrelle (2), 1963, 1971, taped
General Erich Dethleffson, 1971, taped
Wallace Deuel (Chicago Daily News), 1972
Prof. Ernst Deuerlein, 1971, taped **
SS Oberstgruppenführer Josef (Sepp) Dietrich, 1963 **
Eugen Dollmann (3), 1971, taped
Grossadmiral Karl Dönitz (2), 1963; 1971, taped
Allen Dulles, 1963
Hans Ehard, 1971, taped
General Gerhard Engel (2), 1971, taped
Hermann Esser (2), 1971, taped
Hildegard Fath (3), 1971, taped
Werner Fink, 1971, taped **

** Deceased

F. K. Florian (Gauleiter), 1971, taped
André François-Poncet, 1971, taped
Albert Frauenfeld (2), 1971, taped
Walter Frentz, 1971, taped
Helmuth Fuchs (SS), 1971, taped
Gero von Gaevernitz (4), 1963–64
General Adolf Galland, 1971, taped
General R. Chr. von Gerstdorff, 1971, taped
Dr. Erwin Giesing (3), 1971, taped
Paul Giesler (2), 1971, taped
G. M. Gilbert, 1972, taped
Walter Görlitz (historian), 1971
SS Lieutenant Colonel Werner Grothmann (2), 1971, taped
Nerin Gun (4), 1970–71, taped
SS Major Otto Günsche (2), 1963, 1971
Dolly Haas, 1971, taped
Otto von Habsburg, 1971, taped
General Franz Halder, 1963 **
Egon Hanfstaengl (4), 1971, taped
Ernst Hanfstaengl (15), 1970–71, taped **
Helene Hanfstaengl, 1971, taped **
Heinrich Härtle (2) (Rosenberg office), 1970–71, taped
Dr. Hanskarl von Hasselbach, 1971, taped
Heinz Haushofer, 1971, taped
SS General Paul Hausser, 1963
Heinrich Heim (6), 1971, 1974–75, taped
Richard Helms (2), 1971–72, taped
Ilse Hess, 1971, taped
Fritz Hesse (2), 1971, taped
General Adolf Heusinger, 1971, taped
Hans Hitler, 1971, taped
Wilhelm Hoegner, 1971, taped
Ellic Howe (author), 1971
Werner Huppenkothen (SS), 1971
Werner Jochman, 1971
Frau Luise Jodl (5), 1970–71, taped
Rudolf Jordan (Gauleiter), 1970, taped
Traudl Junge (2), 1971
Erich Kempka (3), 1963, 1971, taped **
Robert M. W. Kempner, 1970
Josef Keplinger (Linz), 1971, taped
Erich Kernmayr (historian), 1970
General H. Kissel, 1971, taped
August Klapprott (German-American Bund) (2), 1971–72, taped
Ewalt Heinrich von Kleist (2), 1971, taped
Peter Kleist (4), 1963, 1970–71, taped **
Werner Koeppen (4), 1971, taped
Admiral Theodor Krancke, 1971, taped

**   Deceased

Carl-Vincent Krogmann (Bürgermeister of Hamburg), 1971, taped
Robert Kropp (Göring's butler), 1963
G. Wilhelm Kunze (German-American Bund), 1972, taped
Helmut Kurth (Göring's photographer), 1971, taped **
Hermann Lauterbacher (Gauleiter) (2), 1971, taped
Georg Leibbrandt (2) (Rosenberg office), 1971, taped
General Gustav Lombard (2), 1970–71, taped
Major Bernd Freytag von Loringhoven (Krebs adjutant), 1963
SS Major Heinz Macher (Himmler adjutant), 1971, taped
Field Marshal Erich von Manstein, 1971, taped **
General Hasso von Manteuffel (5) 1956, 1963, 1970, 1971, taped
Fräulein Johanna Mayrhofer (Leonding), 1971, taped
Dennis McEvoy, 1971
Hubert Meyer (SS), 1971, taped
General W. Meyer-Detring, 1971, taped
Field Marshal Erhard Milch (4), 1971, taped **
Konrad Morgen, 1971, taped
Lady Diana Mosley, 1972
Sir Oswald Mosley (3) 1971–72, taped
Josef (Oxensepp) Müller (2), 1963
Johannes von Müllern-Schönhausen, 1971
Werner Naumann (2), 1971, taped
Theodor Oberlaender (2), 1971, taped
Piotr Olender (Auschwitz), 1971, taped
Dr. Raimund von Ondarza (Göring's doctor), 1971, taped
Ambassador Hiroshi Oshima (4), 1966–67, 1971
General Eugen Ott (German ambassador to Japan), 1963
General Albert Praun, 1971, taped
Admiral Karl Jesko von Puttkamer (7), 1970–71, taped
Ambassador Count Edward Raczynski, 1963
General Otto Remer (3), 1971, taped
Annelies von Ribbentrop, 1971, taped **
Leni Riefenstahl (6), 1971, taped
Ambassador Emil von Rinteln, 1971, taped
Frau Annalies Röhm (Ernst Röhm's sister-in-law), 1971, taped
Robert Röhm (Ernst Röhm's brother), 1971, taped
Dr. H. D. Röhrs, 1971, taped
Hein Ruck (3), 1971, taped
Colonel Hans Ulrich Rudel (2), 1963, 1971
Admiral Friedrich Ruge, 1971, taped
Hjalmar Schacht (2), 1963 **
Prince Schaumberg-Lippe, 1971, taped
Gustav Scheel (Gauleiter), 1971, taped
Dr. Ernst Schenck (doctor in Führer bunker), 1971, taped
Fabian von Schlabrendorff, 1963
Dr. Gustav Schlotterer (2) (Funk office), 1971, taped

**   Deceased

General Arthur Schmidt (2), 1971, taped
Frau Anneliese Schmundt (wife of Hitler's chief adjutant), 1971, taped
Frau Herta Schneider (4), 1971, taped
Field Marshal Ferdinand Schörner (2), 1963 **
Professor Percy Ernst Schramm (OKW diarist) (2), 1963 **
General Wilhelm Ritter von Schramm, 1971, taped
Frau Ada Schultze (3), 1974, taped
Dr. Walter Schultze (4), 1974, taped
Sigrid Schulz (3), 1971–72, taped
Harry Schulz-Wilde (2) (author), 1971, taped
Richard Schulze (Schulze-Kossens) (6), 1971, 1973–74, taped
Kurt von Schuschnigg, 1971, taped
Martin Schwaebe, 1971, taped
Count Lutz Schwerin von Krosigk (2), 1963; 1971, taped
Vera Semper (Lambach), 1971, taped
Ramon Serrano Suñer, 1963
SS Colonel Otto Skorzeny (7), 1956, 1963; 1971, taped **
Albert Speer (2), 1970–71, taped
SS General Felix Steiner, 1963 **
Otto Strasser (2), 1971, taped **
Johann Stütz (Spital), 1970–71, taped
Helmut Sündermann (3), 1970–71, taped **
Günter Syrup (5), 1971, taped
General Wolfgang Thomale, 1963
Professor Gerdy Troost (4), 1971, taped
Olga Tschechowa, 1971, taped
Ignacio, Marquis de Valdeglesias, 1971, taped
Admiral Gerhard Wagner, 1971, taped
General Walter Warlimont, 1971, taped
Rolf Wehser, 1971, taped
General Walter Wenck, 1963
Klaus Wiedemann (son of Fritz Wiedemann), 1971
Colonel Otto Wien (2) (Luftwaffe), 1971, taped
Johann Wiesinger (Leonding), 1971, taped
SS General Karl Wolff, 1963
Lieutenant Max Wünsche (2), 1971, taped
Dr. Werner Zabel, 1971, taped
Hans Severus Ziegler (author), 1971, taped

B. DOCUMENTS, RECORDS AND REPORTS

British Government Archives:
    The Cabinet Minutes and Memoranda, 1937–39
    Foreign Office, 1937–39
    Minutes of the Foreign Policy Committee of the Cabinet and Memoranda, 1937–39

** Deceased

Papers of the Prime Minister's Office, 1937–39
Records of the Committee of Imperial Defense. London: Her Majesty's Stationery Office.

Correspondence Between the Chairman of the Council of Ministers of the U.S.S.R. and the Presidents of the U.S.A. and the Prime Ministers of Great Britain during the Great Patriotic War of 1941–1945, 2 vols. Moscow: Foreign Language Publishing House, 1957.

Correspondence between Göring and Negrelli 1924–25. Ben E. Swearingen collection.

Der Hitler-Prozess. Munich: Deutscher Volksverlag, 1924.

Documents and Materials relating to the Eve of the Second World War, 1937–39, 2 vols. Moscow: Foreign Language Publishing House, 1948.

Documents at the Bibliothek für Zeitgeschichte, Stuttgart; Institut für Zeitgeschichte, Munich; Institut für Zeitgeschichte, Vienna; Imperial War Museum, London; the National Archives, Washington; the Library of Congress, Washington; U. S. Army Military History Research Collection, Carlisle Barracks, Pa. (including dossiers of U. S. Army Intelligence); Bayerisches Hauptstaatarchiv, Munich; Bundesarchiv, Koblenz.

Documents on British Foreign Policy 1919–1939, 7 vols. London: Her Majesty's Stationery Office

Documents on German Foreign Policy, Series C, The Third Reich: Vols. I–IV. Washington: U. S. Dept. of State.

Documents on German Foreign Policy, Series D, Vols. V–XII. Washington: U. S. Dept. of State.

The French Yellow Book, diplomatic documents, 1938–39, London: Hutchinson, 1940.

Halder, General Franz. *Kriegstagebuch*. Stuttgart: Jacobsen, 1962.

Hitler Diary (January 1, 1934–June 12, 1943). *Sekretar des Führers. Führers Tagebuch*. Washington, Library of Congress, Appendix 5, Safe 5,5.

Hitler e Mussolini–Lettere e documenti. Milan: Rissoli, 1946.

Hitler's speeches:
Baynes, Norman H. ed. *The Speeches of Adolf Hitler*, April 1922–August 1939, 2 vols. New York, 1942. Prange, Gordon W., ed. *Hitler's Words*, Washington, 1944.

Hitler War Directives 1939–1945. London: Sidgwick and Jackson, 1964.

International Military Tribunal, *Trial of the Major War Criminals before the International Military Tribunal*, 14 November 1945 to 1 October 1946, 42 vols.

Koeppen, Werner. Hitler's Tabletalk. 28 surviving reports. National Archives.

Linge, Heinz. *Diaries*, March 1943 to February 1945, National Archives.

Lochner, Louis. Letters and Papers. State Historical Society of Wisconsin, Madison, Wisc.

Milch, Field Marshal Erhard. Papers and Memoirs. Unpublished.

Nazi Conspiracy and Aggression, 10 vols. Washington: U. S. Government Printing Office, 1946.

Nazi-Soviet Relations, 1939–1941. Documents from the Archives of the German Foreign Office. Washington: U. S. Dept. of State, 1948.

OSS *Hitler Source Book.* 1943. For the Langer Report.

Smith, Captain Truman. *Notebook and Report* (on trip to Munich, November 15–22, 1922). Yale University Library.

Trials of War Criminals before the Nuremberg Military Tribunals, 15 vols. Washington: U. S. Government Printing Office, 1951–52.

U. S. Embassy, Berlin Reports 1930–1939. National Archives.

Wehrmacht, Oberkommando des. *Kriegstagebuch des Oberkommandos der Wehrmacht 1940–1945.* Frankfurt am Main, 1961–65.

C. NEWSPAPERS AND MAGAZINES

Assmann, Heinz. "Adolf Hitler." *U. S. Naval Institute Proceedings,* Vol. 79, No. 12.

Bach-Zelewski, Erich von dem. "Life of an SS-General," New York *Aufbau,* August 23, 1946.

Binion, Rudolph. "Hitler's Concept of *Lebensraum:* The Psychological Basis," *History of Childhood Quarterly,* Fall 1973.

Bloch, Dr. Edward. "My Patient Hitler," *Collier's,* March 15 and 22, 1941.

Deuerlein, Ernst. "Hitlers Eintritt in die Politik und die Reichswehr." *Vierteljahreshefte für Zeitgeschichte,* April 1959.

Earle, George H. "F.D.R.'s Tragic Mistake," *Confidential,* 1958.

Eastman, Lloyd E. "Fascism in Kuomintang China: The Blue Shirts," *China Quarterly,* January/March 1972.

Elstein, David. "Operation Sea Lion," *History of the Second World War,* Part 8.

Glaser, Kurt. "World War II and the War Guilt Question," *Modern Age,* Winter 1971.

Goldhagen, Erich. "Albert Speer, Himmler, and the Secrecy of the Final Solution," *Midstream,* October 1971.

Hale, Oron James. "Gottfried Feder Calls Hitler to Order," *Journal of Modern History,* December 1958.

Hanisch, Reinhold. "I Was Hitler's Buddy," *New Republic,* April 5, 12 and 19, 1939.

Hoffmann, Peter C. "The Attempt to Assassinate Hitler on March 21, 1943." *Canadian Journal of History,* No. 1, 1967.

Kempner, Robert M. W. "Blueprint of the Nazi Underground," *Research Studies of the State College of Washington,* June 1945.

Linge, Heinz. "The Hitler I Knew," Chicago *Daily News,* October–December 1955.

Loewenberg, Peter. "The Unsuccessful Adolescence of Heinrich Himmler," *Journal of Modern History*, September 1959.

Mayr, Captain Karl. "I Was Hitler's Boss," *Current History*, November 1941.

Morell, Dr. Theodor. Interview, New York *Times*, May 22, 1945, p. 5.

Nyomarkay, Joseph L. "Factionalism in the National Socialist German Workers' Party, 1925–26," *Political Science Quarterly*, March 1965.

Orlow, Dietrich. "The Conversion of Myths into Political Power," *American Historical Review*, April 1967.

Phelps, Reginald H. "Hitler als Parteiredner im Jahre 1920," *Vierteljahreshefte für Zeitgeschichte*, 1963: 3.

———. "Hitlers Grundlegende—Rede über den Antisemitismus," op. cit., 1968: 4.

———. "Hitler und die Deutsche Arbeiter Partei," *American Historical Review*, July 1963.

Sauer, Wolfgang. "National Socialism: Totalitarianism or Fascism?" *American Historical Review*, December 1967.

Speer, Albert. Interview, *Playboy*, by Eric Norden, June 1971.

Thompson, Larry V. "*Lebensborn* and the Eugenics Policy of the Reichsführer-SS," *Central European History*, March 1971.

D. BIOGRAPHIES, DIARIES, MEMOIRS,
STUDIES OF HISTORY

Absagen, K. H. *Canaris*. London: Hutchinson, 1956.

Alfieri, Dino. *Dictators Face to Face*. New York: New York University Press, 1955.

Allen, William Sheridan. *The Nazi Seizure of Power*. Chicago: Quadrangle Books, 1965.

Andrus, Burton. *I Was the Nuremberg Jailer*. New York: Coward, McCann & Geoghegan, 1969.

Ansel, Walter. *Hitler Confronts England*. Durham, N.C.: Duke University Press, 1960.

———. *Hitler and the Middle Sea*. Durham, N.C.: Duke University Press, 1972.

Ausubel, Nathan. *Voices of History*. New York: Gramercy, 1946.

Barnett, Corelli. *The Collapse of British Power*. London: Eyre Methuen, 1972.

Baur, Hans. *Ich flog die Mächtige der Erde*. Kempten: Pröpster, 1960.

Berndt, A. I. *Der Marsch ins Grossdeutsche Reich*. Munich: Eher, 1939.

Best, S. Payne. *The Venlo Incident*. London: Hutchinson, 1950.

Bewley, Charles. *Hermann Göring and the Third Reich*. Devin-Adair 1962.

Bezymenski, Lev. *The Death of Adolf Hitler.* New York: Harcourt, Brace & World, 1968.

Blackstock, Paul W. *The Secret Road to World War II.* Chicago: Quadrangle Books, 1969.

Boelcke, Willi A., ed. *The Secret Conferences of Dr. Goebbels.* New York: E. P. Dutton, 1970.

Boldt, Gerhard. *Hitler: The Last Ten Days.* New York: Coward, McCann & Geoghegan, 1973.

Bormann, Martin and Gerda. H. R. Trevor-Roper, ed. *The Bormann Letters.* London: Weidenfeld and Nicolson, 1954.

Bracher, Karl. *The German Dictatorship.* New York and Washington: Praeger, 1970.

Bramsted, Ernest K. *Goebbels and National Socialist Propaganda, 1925–1945.* East Lansing: Michigan State University Press, The Cresset Press, 1965.

Bräutigam, Otto. *So Hat Es Sich Zugetragen* . . . Würzburg: Holzner Verlag, 1968.

Breker, Arno. *Im Strahlungsfeld der Ereignisse.* Preussisch Oldendorf: K. W. Schutz, 1972.

Brook-Shepherd, Gordon. *The Anschluss.* Philadelphia and New York: J. B. Lippincott, 1963.

Broszat, Martin. *German National Socialism 1919–1945.* Santa Barbara, Calif.: Clio Press, 1966.

Brown, Anthony Cave. *Bodyguard of Lies.* New York: Harper & Row, 1975.

Bullitt, Orville, ed. *For the President, Personal and Secret.* Correspondence between Franklin D. Roosevelt and William C. Bullitt. Boston: Houghton Mifflin, 1972.

Bullock, Alan. *Hitler, A Study in Tyranny.* New York: Bantam, 1961.

Burckhardt, Carl. *Ma mission à Dantzig.* Paris: Arthème Fayard, 1961.

Burdick, Charles B., and Lutz, Ralph H., eds. *The Political Institutions of the German Revolution 1918–1919.* New York and Washington: Praeger, 1966.

Cadogan, Sir Alexander. *The Diaries of Sir Alexander Cadogan 1938–1945.* New York: Putnam, 1972.

Carell, Paul. *Invasion—They're Coming!* New York: E. P. Dutton, 1963.

———. *Hitler Moves East: 1941–1942.* New York: Bantam Books, 1966.

———. *Scorched Earth.* Boston: Little, Brown, 1970.

Carr, William. *A History of Germany 1815–1945.* New York: St. Martin's, 1969.

———. *Arms, Autarky and Aggression.* London: Arnold, 1972.

Cecil, Robert. *The Myth of the Master Race.* New York: Dodd, Mead, 1972.

Cervi, Mario. *The Hollow Legions.* Garden City: Doubleday, 1971.

Chambers, Frank. *This Age of Conflict*. New York: Harcourt, Brace & World, 1962 (1943).

Ciano, Galeazzo. *The Ciano Diaries 1939–1943*. Garden City: Doubleday, 1946.

Colvin, Ian. *The Chamberlain Cabinet*. London: Gollancz, 1971.

———. *Hitler's Secret Enemy*. London: Pan Books, 1957.

Compton, James V. *The Swastika and the Eagle*. Boston: Houghton Mifflin, 1967.

Craig, Gordon. *The Politics of the Prussian Army: 1650–1945*. London, Oxford, New York: Oxford University Press, 1968.

Creveld, Martin van. *Hitler's Strategy 1940–1941*. Cambridge: Cambridge University Press, 1973.

Dahlerus, Birger. *The Last Attempt*. London: Hutchinson, 1948.

Dahrendorf, Ralf. *Society and Democracy in Germany*. New York: Doubleday-Anchor, 1969.

Daim, Dr. Wilfried. *Der Mann, der Hitler die Ideen gab*. Munich: Isar, 1958.

Dallin, Alexander. *German Rule in Russia, 1941–1944*. London: 1957.

Dallin, David. *Soviet Russia's Foreign Policy, 1939–1942*. New Haven: Yale University Press, 1942.

Davidson Eugene. *The Trial of the Germans*. New York: Macmillan, 1966.

Dawson, Raymond. *The Decision to Aid Russia 1941*. Chapel Hill: University of North Carolina Press, 1959.

Deakin, F. W. *The Brutal Friendship*. New York: Harper & Row, 1962.

Delarue, Jacques. *The Gestapo*. New York: William Morrow, 1964.

Delmer, Sefton. *Trail Sinister*. London: Secker & Warburg, 1961.

———. *Black Boomerang*. New York: Viking, 1962.

Dennis, Peter. *Decision by Default*. London: Routledge and Kegan Paul, 1972.

Deuerlein, Ernst. *Der Aufsteig der NSDAP 1919–1933 in Augenzeugen Berichtet*. Düsseldorf: Rauch, 1968.

———. *Der Hitler Putsch*. Stuttgart: Deutsches Verlags-Anstalt, 1962.

———. *Hitler*. Munich: List, 1969.

Dickinson, John K. *German and Jew*. Chicago: Quadrangle Books, 1967.

Dietrich, Otto. *Hitler*. Chicago: Henry Regnery, 1955.

———. *Mit Hitler in die Macht*. Munich: Franz Eher Verlag, 1934.

Dirksen, Herbert von. *Moscow, Tokyo, London*. Norman: University of Oklahoma Press, 1952.

Dodd, Martha. *My Years in Germany*. London: Gollancz, 1939.

Dodd, William. *Ambassador Dodd's Diary, 1933–1938*. London: Gollancz, 1941.

Dollmann, Eugen. *The Interpreter*. London: Hutchinson, 1967.

Dönitz, Admiral Karl. *Memoirs*. London: Weidenfeld and Nicolson, 1958.

Dorpalen, Andreas. *Hindenburg and the Weimar Republic*. Princeton: Princeton University Press, 1964.

Douglas-Hamilton, James. *Motive for a Mission*. London: Macmillan, 1971.

Eden, Anthony. *Facing the Dictators*. London: Cassell, 1962.

———. *The Reckoning*. Boston: Houghton Mifflin, 1965.

Eich, Hermann. *The Unloved Germans*. New York: Stein & Day, 1965.

Engel, Gerhard. *Heeresadjutant bei Hitler 1938–1943*. Stuttgart: Deutsche Verlags-Anstalt, 1974.

Falls, Cyril. *The Great War*. New York: Putnam, 1959.

Feiling, Keith, *The Life of Neville Chamberlain*. London: Macmillan, 1946.

Fest, Joachim. *The Face of the Third Reich*. New York: Pantheon Books, 1970.

———. *Hitler*. New York: Harcourt Brace Jovanovich, 1974.

Fischer, Fritz. *Germany's Aims in the First World War*. New York: W. W. Norton, 1967.

Fischer, Louis. *Russia's Road from Peace to War*. New York: Harper & Row, 1969.

Flannery, Harry. *Assignment to Berlin*. London: The Right Book Club, 1943.

François-Poncet, André. *The Fateful Years*. London: Gollancz, 1949.

Frank, Hans. *Im Angesicht des Galgens: Deutung Hitlers und seiner Zeit auf Grund eigener Erlebnisse und Erkenntnisse*. Munich: Beck, 1953.

Franz-Willing, Georg. *Die Hitlerbewegung: Der Ursprung, 1919–22*. Hamburg: Decker, 1962.

Fredborg, Arvid. *Behind the Steel Wall*. New York: Viking, 1944.

Freund, Gerald. *Unholy Alliance*. New York: Harcourt, Brace, 1957.

Friedländer, Saul. *Prelude to Downfall: Hitler and the United States, 1939–1941*. New York: Alfred A. Knopf, 1967.

———. *Pius XII and the Third Reich*. New York: Alfred A. Knopf, 1966.

———. *Kurt Gerstein: The Ambiguity of Good*. New York: Alfred A. Knopf, 1969.

Frischauer, Willi. *Hermann Goering*. New York: Ballantine Books, 1951.

———. *Himmler*. New York: Belmont Tower Books. 1962.

Fromm, Bella. *Blood and Banquets*. London: Bles, 1943.

Gallagher, Matthew. *Soviet History of World War II*. New York: Praeger, 1963.

Galland, Adolf. *The First and the Last*. New York: Ballantine Books, 1957.

Gallo, Max. *The Night of Long Knives*. New York: Harper & Row, 1972.

Gasman, Daniel. *Scientific Origins of National Socialism*. New York: American Elsevier, 1971.

Gatzke, Hans, ed. *European Diplomacy Between Two Wars, 1919–1939.* Chicago: Quadrangle Books, 1972.

Gedye, G. E. R. *Betrayal in Central Europe.* New York: Harper, 1939.

Gehlen, Reinhard. *The Service.* New York: World, 1972.

Giesing, Dr. Erwin. *Diary.* Unpublished.

Gilbert, Felix. *Hitler Directs His War.* New York: Oxford, 1950.

Gilbert, G. M. *Nuremberg Diary.* New York: Signet, 1961.

———. *The Psychology of Dictatorship.* New York: Ronald Press, 1950.

Gisevius, Hans B. *To the Bitter End.* Boston: Houghton Mifflin, 1947.

Goebbels, Josef. *The Early Goebbels Diaries.* London: Weidenfeld and Nicolson, 1962.

———. Louis P. Lochner, ed. *The Goebbels Diaries.* Garden City: Doubleday, 1948.

Goerlitz, Walter. *The German General Staff.* New York: Praeger, 1959.

———. *Paulus and Stalingrad.* New York: Citadel Press, 1963.

Goodspeed, D. J. *Ludendorff.* London: Hart-Davis, 1966.

Gordon, Harold J., Jr. *Hitler and the Beer Hall Putsch.* Princeton: Princeton University Press, 1972.

Greiner, Joseph. *Das Ende des Hitler-Mythos.* Vienna: Amalthea, 1947.

Griffiths, Richard. *Marshal Pétain.* London: Constable, 1970.

Grunberger, Richard. *The 12-Year Reich.* New York: Holt, Rinehart and Winston, 1971.

Guderian, Heinz. *Panzer Leader.* New York: Ballantine Books.

Gun, Nerin. *Eva Braun,* New York: Bantam Books, 1969.

———. *The Day of the Americans.* New York: Fleet, 1966.

Halder, General Franz. *Hitler as Warlord.* London: Putnam, 1950.

Hale, Oron J. *The Captive Press in the Third Reich.* Princeton: Princeton University Press, 1964.

Hamilton, Alistair. *The Appeal of Fascism.* London: Blond, 1971.

Hanfstaengl, Egon. *Memoirs.* Unpublished.

Hanfstaengl, Ernst. *Biographical Sketch of Hitler and Himmler.* OSS report, Dec. 3, 1943.

———. *The Missing Years.* London: Eyre and Spottiswoode, 1957.

———. *Zwischen Weissem und Braunen Haus.* Munich: R. Piper & Co. Verlag, 1970.

———. *Out of the Strong.* 1974. Unpublished.

Hanfstaengl, Helene. *Notes.* Unpublished.

Hanser, Richard. *Putsch!* New York: Peter H. Wyden, 1970.

Hassell, Ulrich von. *The Von Hassell Diaries, 1938–1944.* Garden City: Doubleday, 1947.

Hegner, H. S. (Harry Schulz-Wilde). *Die Reichskanzlei.* Frankfurter Societats, 1959.

Heiber, Helmut. *Goebbels.* New York: Hawthorn Books, 1972

Heiden, Konrad. *Der Führer.* Boston: Houghton Mifflin, 1944.

Hedin, Sven. *Germany and World Peace.* London: Hutchinson, 1937.

Heinz, Heinz A. *Germany's Hitler.* London: Hurst and Blackett, 1934.

Henderson, Archibald. *GBS: Man of the Century.* New York: Appleton-Century-Crofts, 1956.

Henderson, Nevile. *Failure of a Mission.* New York: Putnam, 1940.

Herzstein, Robert. *Adolf Hitler and the Third Reich.* Boston: Houghton Mifflin, 1971.

Hess, Rudolf and Ilse. *Prisoner of Peace.* London: Britons, 1954.

Hesse, Fritz. *Hitler and the English.* London: Wingate, 1954.

———. *Das Spiel um Deutschland.* Munich: List, 1953.

Higgins, Trumbull. *Hitler and Russia.* New York: Macmillan, 1966.

Hilberg, Raul. *The Destruction of the European Jews.* Chicago: Quadrangle Books, 1967.

Hildebrand, Klaus. *The Foreign Policy of the Third Reich.* Berkeley: University of California Press, 1973.

Hillgruber, Andreas. *Staatsmänner und Diplomaten bei Hitler.* 2 vols. Frankfurt am Main: Bernard und Graefe, 1967–70.

———. *Hitlers Strategie.* Frankfurt am Main: Bernard und Graefe, 1965.

———. *Die Weltpolitische Lage: 1936–1938: Deutschland in Weltpolitik 1933–1939.* Oswald Hauser, ed. 1965.

Hills, George. *Franco.* New York: Macmillan, 1967.

Hirszowicz, Lukasz. *The Third Reich and the Arab East.* London: Routledge and Kegan Paul, 1966.

Hitler, Adolf. *Hitler's Secret Conversations.* New York: Signet, 1961.

———. *Hitler's Secret Book.* New York: Grove Press, 1961.

———. *Mein Kampf.* Boston: Houghton Mifflin Company, 1943.

———. *Mein Kampf.* Munich: Eher, 1925–26.

———. *The Testament of Adolf Hitler.* The Hitler-Bormann Documents. London: Cassell, 1961.

Hitler, Brigid. *My Brother-in-law Adolf.* Unpublished. Main Branch NYPL Manuscript and Archives Room.

Hoare, Samuel. *Complacent Dictator.* New York: Alfred A. Knopf, 1947.

Hoffmann, Hans Hubert. *Der Hitlerputsch*; Munich: Nymphenburger Verlag, 1961.

Hoffmann, Heinrich. *Hitler Was My Friend.* London: Burke, 1955.

Höhne, Heinz. *The Order of the Death's Head.* New York: Coward, McCann & Geoghegan, 1970.

———. *Codeword Direktor*. New York: Coward, McCann & Geoghegan, 1971.

Holborn, Hajo, ed. *Republic to Reich*. New York: Pantheon Books, 1972.

———. *Germany and Europe*. Garden City: Doubleday, 1970.

Horthy, Admiral Nicholas. *Memoirs*. London: Hutchinson, 1956.

Howe, Ellic. *Rudolph von Sebottendorf*. Unpublished.

———. *Urania's Children*. London, Kimber, 1967.

Howe, Quincy. *Ashes of Victory*. New York: Simon & Schuster, 1972.

Hull, David. *Film in the Third Reich*. Berkeley: University of California Press, 1969.

Huss, Pierre. *Heil and Farewell*. London: Jenkins, 1943.

Irving, David. *Breach of Security*. London: Kimber, 1968.

———. *Hitler und seine Feldherren*. Berlin: Ullstein, 1975.

———. *The Rise and Fall of the Luftwaffe*. Boston: Little, Brown, 1973.

Isherwood, Christopher. *The Berlin Stories*. New York: New Directions, 1963.

Jäckel, Eberhard. *Hitler's Weltanschauung, A Blueprint for Power*. Middletown: Wesleyan University Press, 1972.

Jenks, William A. *Vienna and the Young Hitler*. New York: Columbia University Press, 1972.

Jetzinger, Franz. *Hitler's Youth*. London: Hutchinson, 1958

John, Otto. *Twice Through the Lines*. London: Macmillan, 1972.

Jones, Ernest. *The Life and Work of Sigmund Freud*. Vols. I and II. New York: Basic Books, 1953.

Jones, Thomas. *A Diary with Letters, 1931–1950*. London: Oxford University Press, 1954.

Junge, Gertraud. *Memoirs*. Unpublished.

Kallenbach, Hans. *Mit Adolf Hitler auf Festung Landsberg*. Munich: Kress and Horning, 1943.

Keitel, Wilhelm, *Memoirs*. London: Kimber, 1965.

Kele, Max H. *Nazis and Workers*. Chapel Hill: University of North Carolina Press, 1972.

Kelem, Emery. *Peace in Their Time*. New York: Alfred A. Knopf, 1963.

Kelley, Douglas M. *22 Cells in Nuremberg*. New York: Greenberg, 1947.

Kempka, Erich. *Ich habe Adolf Hitler Verbrannt*. Munich: Kyburg, 1952.

Kennan, George. *From Prague After Munich*. Princeton: Princeton University Press, 1968.

———. *Memoirs 1925–1950*. Boston: Little, Brown, 1967.

Kirkpatrick, Clifford. *Nazi Germany, Its Women and Family Life*. Indianapolis and New York: Bobbs-Merrill, 1938.

Kirkpatrick, Ivone. *Mussolini*. New York: Hawthorn, 1964.

Klein, Burton. *Germany's Economic Preparations for War*. Cambridge: Harvard University Press, 1959.

Kleist, Peter. *European Tragedy*. London: Antony Gibbs & Phillips, 1965.

Knickerbocker, H. R. *Is Tomorrow Hitler's?* New York: Reynal & Hitchcock, 1941.

Koehl, Robert L. *RKFDV, German Resettlement and Population Policy 1939–1945*. Cambridge: Harvard University Press, 1957.

Koehler, Hans Jürgen. *Inside Information*. London: Pallas, 1940.

Koller, General Karl. *Der letzte Monat*. Mannheim: Wohlgemuth, 1949.

Kramary, Joachim. *Stauffenberg*. New York: Macmillan, 1967.

Krause, Karl. *Zehn Jahre Kammerdiener bei Hitler*. Hamburg: Laatzen, 1949.

Krausnick, Helmut etc. *Anatomy of the SS State*. New York: Walker, 1968.

Kubizek, August. *The Young Hitler I Knew*. Boston: Houghton Mifflin, 1955.

Kuby, Erich. *The Russians and Berlin 1945*. New York: Hill & Wang, 1968.

Kühnl, Reinhard. *Die Nationalsozialistische Linke, 1925–1930*. Meisenheim am Glan: Hain, 1966.

Lammers, Donald. *Explaining Munich*. Stanford: Hoover Institution Press, Stanford University, 1966.

Lane, Barbara Miller. *Architecture and Politics in Germany 1918–1945*. Cambridge: Harvard University Press, 1968.

Langer, Walter C. *The Mind of Adolf Hitler*. New York: Basic Books, 1972.

Laqueur, Walter. *Russia and Germany*. Boston: Little, Brown, 1965.

Levin, Nora. *The Holocaust*. New York: Schocken Books, 1973.

Lewy, Guenter. *The Catholic Church and Nazi Germany*. New York: McGraw-Hill, 1964.

Lochner, Louis. *Always the Unexpected*. New York: Macmillan, 1946.

———. *What About Germany?* New York: Dodd, Mead, 1942.

Lüdecke, Kurt G. W. *I Knew Hitler*. London: Jarrolds, 1938.

Ludendorff, Erich. *Auf dem Weg zur Feldherrnhalle*. Munich: Ludendorffs, 1938.

Lukacs, John. *The Last European War*. Garden City: Anchor Press/Doubleday, 1976.

———. *The Passing of the Modern Age*. New York: Harper & Row, 1970.

Maass, Walter. *Assassination in Vienna*. New York: Scribner's, 1972.

MacLeod, Iain. *Neville Chamberlain*. New York: Atheneum, 1962.

Macmillan, Harold. *Winds of Change*. New York: Harper & Row, 1966.

———. *The Blast of War*. New York: Harper & Row, 1968.

Maisky, Ivan. *Memoirs of a Soviet Ambassador*. New York: Scribner's, 1968.

Manchester, William. *The Arms of Krupp*. New York: Bantam Books, 1970.

Mandell, Richard D. *The Nazi Olympics*. New York: Macmillan, 1971.

Manvell, Roger, and Fraenkel, Heinrich. *Dr. Goebbels*. New York: Simon & Schuster, 1960.

————. *Hess*. London: MacGibbon and Kee, 1971.

————. *Himmler*. New York: Putnam, 1965.

Maschmann, Melita. *Account Rendered*. London: Abelard-Schuman, 1964.

Maser, Werner. *Die Frühgeschichte der NSDAP*. Frankfurt am Main: Athenäum, 1965.

————. *Adolf Hitler*. Munich: Bechtle, 1971.

————. *Hitler*. New York: Harper & Row, 1975.

————. *Hitlers Briefe und Notizen*. Düsseldorf: Econ, 1973.

McRandle, James. *The Track of the Wolf*. Evanston: Northwestern University Press, 1965.

McSherry, James. *Stalin, Hitler and Europe, 1933–1939*. Cleveland: World, 1968.

————. *Stalin, Hitler and Europe, 1939–1941*. Cleveland: World, 1970.

Mellow, James R. *Charmed Circle*. Washington: Praeger, 1974.

Mend, Hans. *Adolf Hitler im Felde*. Munich: Eher, 1931.

Meskill, Johanna. *Hitler and Japan*. New York: Atherton, 1966.

Milward, Alan S. *The German Economy at War*. London: Athlone Press of University of London, 1965.

Mitchell, Allan. *Revolution in Bavaria*. Princeton: Princeton University Press, 1965.

Mitchell, David. *1919 Red Mirage*. New York: Macmillan, 1970.

Mosley, Philip. *The Kremlin and World Politics*. New York: Vintage, 1960.

Mosley, Sir Oswald. *My Life*. London: Nelson, 1970.

Mosse, George. *Nazi Culture*. New York: Grosset & Dunlap, 1966.

Müllern-Schönhausen, Dr. Johannes von. *Die Lösung des Rätsels Adolf Hitler*. Vienna: Verlag zur Förderung wissenschaftlicher Forschung.

Murphy, Robert. *Diplomat Among Warriors*. Garden City: Doubleday, 1964.

Mussolini, Benito. *Memoirs 1942–1943*. London: Weidenfeld & Jacobson, 1949.

Nelson, Walter. *The Soldier Kings*. New York, Putnam, 1970.

Nicolson, Harold. *The War Years 1939–1945*. New York: Atheneum, 1967.

Nogueres, Henri. *Munich*. New York: McGraw-Hill, 1965.

Nolte, Ernst. *Three Faces of Fascism*. New York: Holt, Rinehart and Winston, 1966.

Nyomarkay, Joseph. *Charisma and Factionalism in the Nazi Party.* Minneapolis: University of Minnesota Press, 1967.

Oechsner, Frederick. *This Is the Enemy.* Boston: Little, Brown, 1942.

Offner, Arnold A. *America and the Origins of World War II.* Boston: Houghton Mifflin, 1971.

O'Neill, Robert. *The German Army and the Nazi Party.* New York: Heineman, 1966.

Orlow, Dietrich. *The History of the Nazi Party, 1919–1933.* Newton Abbot: David and Charles, 1971.

——. *The History of the Nazi Party, 1933–1945.* Pittsburgh: University of Pittsburgh Press, 1973.

Oven, Wilfred von. *Mit Goebbels bis zum Ende.* 2 vols. Buenos Aires: Dürer-Verlag, 1949–50.

Papen, Franz von. *Memoirs.* London: Deutsch, 1952.

Parkinson, Roger. *Peace for Our Time.* New York: McKay, 1971.

Peterson Edward. *Limits of Hitler's Power.* Princeton: Princeton University Press, 1966.

Phillips, Peter. *The Tragedy of Nazi Germany.* New York: Praeger, 1969.

Piotrowski, Stanislaw. *Hans Frank's Diary.* Warsaw: Panstwowe Wydawnictwo Naukowe, 1961.

Pope, Ernest. *Munich Playground.* New York: Putnam, 1941.

Price, G. Ward. *I Know These Dictators.* London: Harrap, 1937.

Pridham, Geoffrey. *Hitler's Rise to Power.* New York: Harper & Row, 1973.

Raczynski, Count Edward. *In Allied London.* London: Weidenfeld and Nicolson, 1962.

Reitsch, Hanna. *Flying Is My Life.* New York: Putnam, 1954.

Remak, Joachim. *Nazi Years.* Englewood Cliffs, N.J.: Prentice-Hall, 1969.

Ribbentrop, Annelies von. *Die Kriegsschuld des Widerstandes.* Leoni: am Starnberger See Druffel, 1974.

Ribbentrop, Joachim von. *Ribbentrop Memoirs.* London: Weidenfeld and Nicolson, 1962.

Rich, Norman. *Hitler's War Aims.* 2 vols. New York: Norton, 1973, 1974.

Riess, Curt. *Joseph Goebbels.* New York: Ballantine Books, 1948.

Ringelblum, Emmanuel. *Notes from the Warsaw Ghetto.* New York: McGraw-Hill, 1958.

Roberts, Stephen. *The House That Hitler Built.* London: Methuen, 1937.

Röhl, J. C. G. *From Bismarck to Hitler.* New York: Barnes & Noble, 1970.

Rosenberg, Alfred. With commentary by Serge Land and Ernst von Schenck. *Memoirs.* Chicago: Ziff-Davis, 1949.

————. *Das politische Tagebuch Alfred Rosenbergs.* Fragmentary diaries. Göttingen: Hans-Günther Seraphim, 1956.

————. *Alfred Rosenberg, Selected Writings.* London: Cape, 1970.

Rothenbücher, Karl. *Der Fall Kahr.* Tübingen: Mohr, 1924.

Rudel, Hans Ulrich. *Stuka Pilot.* New York: Ballantine Books, 1958.

Rumpf, Hans. *The Bombing of Germany.* New York: Holt, Rinehart and Winston, 1963.

Ryder, A. J. *The German Revolution of 1918.* Cambridge: Cambridge University Press, 1967.

Santoro, Cesare. *Hitler Germany.* Berlin: Internationaler Verlag, 1938.

Sayers, Michael, and Kahn, Albert. *The Plot Against the Peace.* New York: Dial, 1945.

Schacht, Hjalmar. *Account Settled.* London: Weidenfeld and Nicolson, 1948.

————. *Confessions of the "Old Wizard."* Cambridge: Houghton Mifflin, 1956.

Schellenberg, Walter. *Hitler's Secret Service.* New York: Pyramid, 1958.

Schirach, Henriette von. *The Price of Glory.* London: Muller, 1960.

————. *Der Preis der Herrlichkeit.* Wiesbaden: Limes, 1956.

Schlabrendorff, Fabian von. *The Secret War against Hitler.* New York, Putnam, 1965.

Schmidt, Paul. *Hitler's Interpreter.* London: Heinemann, 1951.

Schramm, Percy. *Hitler: The Man and the Military Leader.* Chicago: Quadrangle Books, 1971.

Schramm, Wilhelm Ritter von. *Conspiracy Among Generals.* New York: Scribner, 1957.

Schuschnigg, Kurt von. *Brutal Takeover.* New York: Atheneum, 1971.

————. *Austrian Requiem.* London: Gollancz, 1947.

Schweitzer, Arthur. *Big Business in the Third Reich.* Bloomington: Indiana University Press, 1964.

Seaburg, Paul. *The Wilhelmstrasse.* Berkeley: University of California Press, 1954.

Seaton, Albert. *The Russo-German War, 1941–45.* London: Barker, 1971.

Sender, Toni. *Autobiography of a German Rebel.* New York: Vanguard, 1939.

Serrano Suñer, Ramon. *Entre les Pyrénées et Gibraltar.* Geneva: Cheval Ailé, 1947.

Shirer, William L. *Berlin Diary.* New York: Alfred A. Knopf, 1941.

————. *End of a Berlin Diary.* New York: Alfred A. Knopf, 1947.

————. *The Rise and Fall of the Third Reich.* New York: Simon & Schuster, 1960.

Siemsen, Hans. *Hitler Youth.* London: Lindsay Drummond, 1940.

Simpson, Amos. *Why Hitler?* Boston: Houghton Mifflin, 1971.

Skorzeny, Otto. *Skorzeny's Special Missions.* London: Hale, 1957.

———. *Lebe gefährlich.* Siegburg-Niederpleis: Ring, 1962.

———. *Wir kämpften—wir verloren.* Siegburg-Niederpleis: Ring, 1962.

Smith, Bradley. *Adolf Hitler.* Stanford: Hoover Institution Press, Stanford University, 1967.

———. *Heinrich Himmler,* Stanford: Stanford University Press, 1971.

——— and Peterson, Agnes F. *Heinrich Himmler Geheimreden 1933 bis 1945.* Frankfurt am Main: Propyläen, 1974.

Smith, Howard K. *Last Train from Berlin.* New York: Alfred A. Knopf, 1942.

Sontag, Raymond James, and Beddie, James Stuart, eds. *Nazi-Soviet Relations 1939–1941.* New York: Didier, 1948. (Selections from U. S. Department of State publications.)

Speer, Albert. *Inside the Third Reich.* New York: Macmillan, 1970.

Spengler, Oswald. *Spengler Letters.* London: Allen & Unwin, 1966.

Starhemberg, E. R. von. *Between Hitler and Mussolini.* London: Hodder and Stoughton, 1942.

Stein, George. *Hitler.* Englewood Cliffs, N.J.: Prentice-Hall International, 1968.

Stern, Fritz. *The Failure of Illiberalism.* New York: Alfred A. Knopf, 1972.

Strasser, Otto. *Hitler and I.* London: Cape, 1940.

———. *Mein Kampf.* Frankfurt am Main: Heinrich Heine, 1969.

———. *Ministersessel oder Revolution?* Berlin: Kampf Verlag, 1930.

Tobias, Fritz. *The Reichstag Fire.* New York: Putnam, 1964.

Toland, John. *Battle: The Story of the Bulge.* New York: Random House, 1959.

———. *The Last 100 Days.* New York: Random House, 1966.

———. *The Rising Sun.* New York: Random House, 1970.

Trevor-Roper, H. R. *The Last Days of Hitler.* New York: Macmillan, 1947.

Trunk, Isaiah. *Judenrat.* New York: Macmillan, 1972.

Wagner, Dieter. *Anschluss.* New York: St. Martin's, 1971.

Wagner, Friedelind. *The Royal Family of Bayreuth.* London: Eyre and Spottiswoode, 1948.

Waite, Robert G. L. *Vanguard of Nazism.* New York: W. W. Norton, 1952.

Warlimont, Walter. *Inside Hitler's Headquarters.* Washington: Praeger, 1964.

Watt, Richard. *The Kings Depart.* London: Weidenfeld and Nicolson, 1968.

Weinberg, Gerhard L. *The Foreign Policy of Hitler's Germany.* Chicago: University of Chicago Press, 1970.

Weiner, Jan. *The Assassination of Heydrich.* New York: Grossman Publishers, 1969.

Weiss, John. *Nazis and Fascists in Europe, 1918–1945*. New York: Harper & Row, 1967.

Weizsäcker, Ernst von. *Memoirs*. London: Gollancz, 1951.

Werth, Alexander. *France—1940–1955*. New York: Holt, Rinehart and Winston, 1956.

———. *Russia at War 1941–1945*. New York: E. P. Dutton, 1964.

Wheeler-Bennett, John. *Munich, Prologue to Tragedy*. London: Macmillan, 1966.

———. *The Nemesis of Power*. New York: Viking, 1967.

Wiedemann, Fritz. *Der Mann, der Feldherr werden wollte*. Velbert, 1964.

Williams, Robert C. *Culture in Exile*. Ithaca: Cornell University Press, 1972.

Windsor, Duke of. *A King's Story*. London: Cassell, 1951.

Winterbotham, F. A. *The Ultra Secret*. London: Weidenfeld and Nicolson, 1974.

Wiskemann, Elizabeth. *The Rome-Berlin Axis*. London: Collins, 1966.

Wulff, Wilhelm. *Zodiac and Swastika*. New York: Coward, McCann & Geoghegan, 1973.

Zeller, Eberhard. *The Flame of Freedom*. Coral Gables: The University of Miami Press, 1969.

Ziegler, Hans Severus. *Wer war Hitler?* Tübingen: Grabert, 1970.

Zoller, Albert. *Douze ans auprès d'Hitler*. (Memoirs of Christa Schröder.) Paris: Julliard, 1949.

Chapter Eighteen. CRYSTAL NIGHT

pages 587–88
Schacht conference, Aug. 20, 1935: ND, NG-4067.

page 588
Streicher quote: speech before German Labor Front mass meeting, Oct. 4, 1935; ND, M-35.

page 588
Fromm quote: Fromm 235–36.

page 588–89
Grynszpan quote: Arthur Morse, *While Six Million Died* (New York, 1967), 222.

page 589
Himmler memorandum: Affidavit by Schallermeier, July 5, 1946, ND, SS(A) 5.

page 589
Himmler speech: Bradley Smith and Agnes Peterson 24–49.

page 589
Heydrich teletyped orders: ND, PS-3051.

page 590
"must have been exceeded considerably." Levin 80.

page 590
Tolischus story: New York *Times*, Nov. 11, 1938.

page 590
Frau Funk account: Affidavit by Louise Funk, Nov. 5, 1945, Funk-3.

page 590
Göring testimony: IMT, IX, 277.

pages 590–91
Hitler to Frau Troost: Interview with Gerdy Troost, 1971.

page 591
Hesse account: HH 59–61.

page 591
Footnote: Hassell 123.

page 591
Footnote: Gutterer affidavit, signed in Neuengamme, Oct. 19, 1947; notarized by Moritz Augustus von Schirrmeister.

page 592
Göring quote: Levin 87.

page 592
Hauptmann quote: *Die Welt*, Nov. 10, 1962.

pages 592–93
Dieckhoff report: GFP, D, IV, #501.

page 593
Roosevelt news conference: Morse, op. cit., 231.

page 594
Hitler at the Bruckmanns': Hassell 28.

page 594
Ilse Braun account: Gun, *Eva Braun*, 104–5.

pages 594–95
Schacht account: *Account*, 134–37.

page 595
Hitler-Wiedemann; Wiedemann 146–47 (tr.).

pages 596–97
Piechler story: Interview with Gerdy Troost, 1971.

page 597
Hitler to Chvalkovsky: *French Yellow Book*, 210; Krausnick 44.

page 597
Foreign Ministry circular: GFP, IV, 932–33.

pages 597–98
Hitler speech: Baynes 740–41.

page 598
"During this month he plans . . ." Ciano 3.

page 599
Cadogan comment: Cadogan 151–52.

page 599
Henderson report: BFP, 3rd, IV, 165.

page 599
Henderson on Hitler: N. Henderson 209.

page 599
Newton report: BFP, IV, 183–84.

pages 599–600
Henderson letter: Ibid. 210–11.

page 600
Henderson telephone call: Ibid. 223.

page 601
"When I get worked up . . ." Schmidt 236.

page 601
Tiso-Hitler: BFP, IV, 439; GFP, D, IV, 243–45.

page 601
Chamberlain quote: BFP, IV, 250.

pages 602–4
Hacha-Hitler: Schmidt 122; GFP, IV, 263–69; HSC 211; *French Yellow Book*, 96.

page 604
Footnote: IMT, IX, 303–4.

page 604
Hitler to secretaries: Zoller 91–92.

page 604
Hitler to Hoffmann: Hoffmann 95.

page 605
Kennan account: *Memoirs*, 98.

page 605
Henderson phone calls: BFP, IV, 255, 257.
page 605
Henderson letter: Ibid. 595.
page 605
Hitler to Linge: Linge ⚡14.
page 606
Kempka account: Interview, 1971.
page 606
"The Italians will laugh at me," Ciano 44: Bullock 433.
page 606
"I knew it. In fourteen days . . ." Erich Kordt, *Nicht aus den Akten* (Stuttgart, 1950), 298.
page 607
Halifax quote: BFP, IV, 271.
page 607
"has so lost its fibre . . ." *British Blue Book*, 5.

Chapter Nineteen. THE FOX AND THE BEAR

page 609
Phipps note: BFP, IV, 596.
page 611
"You want to negotiate . . ." *Polish White Book*, No. 64.
page 611
Chamberlain statement: Bullock 444.
pages 611–12
Hitler speech: Prange 303–4.
page 612
Canaris-Hitler: Gisevius 363
page 612
Hitler to Keitel: Keitel 84.
page 613
Footnote: Höhne, *Order*, 232.
pages 614–15
Kleist account: Kleist 15.
page 615
Merekalov-Weizsäcker: NSR 2.
page 615
Hitler to Gafencu: Grégoire Gafencu, *Derniers jours de l'Europe* (Paris, 1946), 89.
page 616
Song: Gregor Ziemer, *Education for Death* (London and New York, 1941), 120

page 616
Talking dog: *Schwarzes Korps,* July 31, 1935; Grunberger 86.
page 617
Bishop of Mainz quote: *Amtsblatt Mainz,* No. 7, Apr. 17, 1939.
page 617
Footnote: New York *Post,* 1974; correspondence with Senator Cranston, 1975.
pages 617–18
Hitler speech: Prange 306; Shirer, *Rise,* 471–75.
page 619
"like a cannon ball." A. Rossi, *Deux ans d'alliance germano-soviétique* (Paris, 1949), 27.
page 619
Hitler-Hilger: Kleist 21–22; Gustav Hilger and Alfred Meyer, *The Incompatible Allies* (New York, 1953), 293–97; McSherry I, 149–50.
page 620
Hitler conference: GFP, D, VI, 574–80; Shirer, *End,* 233.
page 621
"sell more dearly its own goods." McSherry I, 153.
page 621
Ribbentrop instructions, May 26, 1939: Louis Fischer 337–38. This watershed message, not published in any collection of official documents, was discovered in 1966 by Fischer in the German Foreign Office archives in Bonn.
page 621
Message to Schulenburg: NSR 5.
page 622
Halifax to Maisky: CAB 23/100, Cabinet 33 (39).
page 622
Mussolini letter to Hitler, May 30, 1939: Deakin 8.
page 623
Hitler-Kubizek meeting: Kubizek 287–89.
page 624
Molotov-Schulenburg meeting, Aug. 3, 1939; NSR 41.
page 625
Schnurre to Astakhov: NSR 45.
page 625
Hitler to Speer: Speer, *Inside,* 161.
pages 625–26
Hitler-Burckhardt meeting: Burckhardt 378–88.
pages 626–27
Hesse account: HH 71–74; interview with Hesse, 1971.
page 627
Ribbentrop-Ciano meeting: Wiskemann 191–92.
page 628
Ciano-Hitler meetings: Dollmann 168; Schmidt 132–33; Wiskemann 194–98; Ciano 119–20.
pages 628–29
Hesse-Ribbentrop meeting: HH 75.
page 629
Ribbentrop to Schulenburg: NSR 63.

pages 629–30
Trade agreement: NSR 83
page 631
"I have them!" Speer, *Playboy*, 88.
page 631
Hoffmann account: Hoffmann 102–3.
pages 631–32
"one of the extraordinary figures . . ." HSC 38.
page 632
"If Stalin did commit a bank robbery . . ." Hitler to Baur: Baur section in Ziegler; interview with Baur, 1970.
page 632
"In actual fact, he identifies himself . . ." HSC 190–91.
pages 632–33
This is not a verbatim account of the August 22 conference but based on notes taken by several officers present. GFP, D, VII, 200–6, 557–59; Shirer, *End*, 252–55.
page 633
Göring leads applause: IMT, IX, 492.
page 634
Kleist quote: Kleist 35.
pages 634–35
Chamberlain letter to Hitler: BFP, 3rd, VII, 171.
page 635
Hitler-Henderson meeting: GFP, VII, 210–13; Weizsäcker 203.
page 636
Second Hitler-Henderson meeting: BFP, VII, 201–2; GFP, VII, 214.
page 636
"Odd Moscow customs." J. von Ribbentrop, *Memoirs*, 111.
pages 636–37
Ribbentrop-Stalin meeting: Ibid. 111–13; J. von Ribbentrop, *De Londres à Moscou* (Paris, 1954), 147; NSR 72; Schmidt 137; interview with Richard Schulze, 1971; GFP, VII, 228.
page 638
Hitler to Bormann: TAH 99–100.
page 638
"We've won!" Dietrich 64.
page 639
Speer comment; Hitler quote: Speer, *Inside*, 161

Chapter Twenty. "A CALAMITY WITHOUT PARALLEL IN HISTORY"

page 640
Henderson report: BFP, VII, 212–13.
page 641
Hiranuma announcement: Toland, *Rising*, 59.
page 641
"ingrown and Jewish . . ." Delmer, *Trail*, 386.

page 641
"The signing of the pact . . ." Hoffmann 113.
page 642
"*My* servants and *my* house . . ." Zoller 141.
page 642
Schmidt account: Schmidt 142.
page 642
"to make a move toward England . . ." GFP, VII, 279.
page 642
Henderson-Hitler meeting: Ibid. 280–81; Schmidt 143.
page 643
Mackensen report: GFP, VII, 293.
page 643
"military supplies and raw materials . . ." Ibid. 285–86.
pages 643–44
Schmidt account: Schmidt 145–46.
page 644
Hitler-Attolico: GFP, VII, 286.
page 644
Hitler to Keitel: IMT, X, 514.
page 644
Engel comments: Engel 59–61.
page 644
Schmundt to Warlimont: Warlimont 3.
page 645
Dahlerus phone call to Göring: Dahlerus 53.
page 646
"Why, at once, before hostilities begin." Wiskemann 206.
page 646
Hitler to Mussolini: GFP, VII, 314.
page 646
Hitler to Mussolini, Ibid. 232.
pages 647–48
Dahlerus-Hitler: Dahlerus 60–62.
page 649
Hitler to Daladier: GFP, VII, 357–59.
pages 649–50
Dahlerus-Chamberlain: Dahlerus 72–73.
pages 651–52
Henderson-Hitler: GFP, VII, 332; N. Henderson 276; BFP, VII, 351, 381–82, 388.
page 652
Engel comments: Engel 61.
pages 652–53
Henderson-Hitler: N. Henderson 280; Schmidt 149; BFP, VII, 393.
page 653
Dahlerus-Göring: Dahlerus 90–94.

pages 653–54
"They would sooner fight . . ." BFP, VII, 395.
page 654
Dahlerus-Chamberlain: Dahlerus 98–99.
page 654
Schmidt comment: Schmidt 150.
page 655
Kleist-Schmenzin story: BFP, VII, 415–17.
pages 655–56
Henderson-Ribbentrop: Schmidt 151–53; J. von Ribbentrop, *Memoirs*, 124.
page 657
Wiretap: Irving, *Breach*, 113, 32.
page 657
"get ahead of the clock . . ." BFP, VII, 442.
page 658
Berndt story: HH 82–83.
page 658
Directive ⚡1: HWD 3–4.
page 658
Operation Himmler: Naujocks affidavit, ND 2751-PS; Höhne, *Order*, 264–65.
pages 658–59
Lipski-Ribbentrop: Schmidt 154; GFP, VII, 463.
page 659
Hitler-Attolico: Ibid. 465.
page 659
Polish broadcast: *German White Book* (German Library of Information, New
     York, 1939), 35–36.
page 659
"a pact with Satan . . ." Fest, *Hitler*, 585.
page 660
"The English will leave the Poles in the lurch . . ." Interviews with Engel,
     Below, Puttkamer, 1970–71.
page 660
"it disturbed the formation of his intuition." Irving, *Breach*, 39.
page 660
"England is bluffing . . ." Hoffmann 115.
page 660
"Now you've got your damned war!" Albert Kesselring, *A Soldier's Record*
     (New York, 1954), 37.
pages 660–61
Hitler to Mussolini: GFP, VII, 483.
page 661
Eva Braun quote: Gun, *Eva Braun*, 151–52.
page 662
Lawrence quote: D. H. Lawrence, *Movements in European History* (London,
     1922), 306.

page 662
"his policy has broken down . . ." BFP, VII, 517.
page 662
Dahlerus-Göring: Dahlerus 119.
pages 662–63
Ribbentrop-Hitler-Abetz: Kleist 70.
page 663
Raczynski account: Raczynski 25–26.
pages 663–64
"We only pity you people . . ." GFP, VII, 521.
page 664
Chamberlain speech: Feiling 415.
pages 664–65
Hesse-Hewel: HH 84–85; Hesse, *Das Spiel*, Chap. 4; interview with Hesse,
1970.
    On Hitler offer: Annelies von Ribbentrop 380; interview with Frau von
    Ribbentrop, 1971.
page 665
Nicolson account: Nicolson, *Diaries and Letters*, 1930–1939 (London, 1969),
412.
page 665
Chamberlain speech: BFP, VII, 521.
page 665
Greenwood quote: Parkinson 215.
page 666
Hesse-Wilson: HH 85–88; interview with Hesse, 1971.
page 666
"I therefore suggest that Sir Nevile Henderson . . ." CAB 23/100, Cabinet 49
    (39); Parkinson 216.
page 667
Henderson-Schmidt meeting: Schmidt 157.
pages 667–68
Schmidt at Chancellery: Schmidt 158.
page 668
Dahlerus-Göring: Dahlerus 129–30.
page 668
Henderson-Ribbentrop meeting: N. Henderson 300.
page 669
Chamberlain broadcast: Feiling 415–16; Colvin, *Chamberlain Cabinet*, 253–
    54.
page 669
Ribbentrop to Schulenburg: GFP, VII, 541.
page 669
Hitler to Mussolini: Ibid. 538–39.
page 670
"Now, all my work crumbles . . ." Zoller 175.
page 670
Hitler to Linge: Linge ⁂15.

Chapter Twenty-one. VICTORY IN THE WEST

page 673
Hitler motto: Zoller 156–57.
pages 674–75
Hesse-Hewel: Hesse, *Das Spiel*, Chap. 5; interview with Hesse, 1971.
page 675
Ribbentrop to Schmidt: Schmidt 162.
page 676
"the Polish national problem . . ." GFP, D, VIII, 161.
page 676
Ribbentrop-Stalin meeting: J. von Ribbentrop, *Memoirs*, 129–31; GFP, VIII, 943.
page 677
"his intention of settling questions . . ." J. von Ribbentrop, *Memoirs*, 129.
page 677
Heydrich to SS commanders, Sept. 21, 1939: ND, EC-307, PS-3362.
page 677
Hitler speech at Danzig: Irving, *Hitler*, 28.
pages 677–78
Footnote: Interviews with Richard Schulze, Helmuth Fuchs, and Herbert Meyer, 1971.
page 678
Hewel to Hesse: Hesse, *Das Spiel*, Chap. 5.
page 678
"The British can have peace . . ." GFP, VIII, 140–45.
page 678
"clearly taken aback." Warlimont 37.
page 679
Cadogan on Dahlerus: Cadogan 220.
page 679
Hitler speech: Prange 173; Shirer, *Rise*, 641–42.
pages 679–80
Hitler memorandum: *Nazi Conspiracy and Aggression*, VII, 800–14.
page 680
Footnote: Remak 113–14.
page 681
"My attempts to make peace . . ." IMT, IX, 50; interview with Milch, 1971.
page 682
Müller account: Interview with Müller, 1963.
pages 682–83
Brauchitsch-Hitler meeting: Halder Diary, Nov. 4–5, 1939; Brauchitsch testimony, IMT, XX, 575; Wheeler-Bennett, *Nemesis*, 471.

page 683
Krafft warning: E. Howe, *Urania's*, 169.
pages 683–84
Hitler-Frau Troost meeting: Interview with Gerdy Troost, 1971.
page 684
Footnote: Interviews with Sir Oswald Mosley and Lady Diana Mosley, 1971–72.
page 684
Elser account: Record of interrogation, *Der Stern*, May 10, 1966.
page 685
Hitler at Bürgerbräukeller: interviews with Kempka and Wünsche, 1971.
pages 684–85
Footnote: Interview with Hein Ruck, 1971.
page 686
"Now I am completely content!" Zoller 204. There is conflicting evidence on when Hitler learned of the bombing. Höhne wrote it was at the Munich railroad station (*Order*, 286). Herta Schneider and Kempka agreed it was near Augsburg (Interviews, 1971).
page 686
"What idiot conducted this interrogation?" *Schellenberg Memoirs* (London, 1961), 110.
page 687
Official version: Wheeler-Bennett, *Nemesis*, 481.
page 687
Cardinal Faulhaber story: Lewy 311.
page 687
Hitler comment on Pope: Frank 408.
page 687
Hitler to Hoffmann: Hoffmann 119.
page 688
Nov. 23 conference: Shirer, *End*, 256–62; GFP, VIII, 439–46; IMT, IX, 311; Warlimont 58–59; interview with Warlimont, 1971.
page 689
"for the first time he desired German defeat." Ciano 183.
page 689
Footnote: GFP, VIII, 683.
pages 689–90
Mussolini letter to Hitler: Ibid. 607–9.
page 690
Shirer comment: *Berlin*, 234.
page 690
Sir Kingsley Wood quote: John Lukacs, *The Last European War* (Garden City, 1975).
pages 690–91
Goebbels' propaganda methods: Interview with Naumann, 1971.
page 691
Goebbels' instructions: Boelcke 8.

page 691
Diesing story: Irving, *Rise*, 83.
page 692
"I doubt very much . . ." CAB 65/5, War Cabinet 30 (40).
page 693
War Directive: HWD 23–24.
page 693
"most daring and most important . . ." Rich I, 142.
page 693
Soviet mission to Berlin: Interview with Schlotterer, 1971; GFP, VIII, 722.
page 693
Trotsky quote: Higgins 34.
page 693
"The agreement means a wide-open door . . ." GFP, VIII, 817.
page 693
Hitler on Stalin: Zoller 178.
page 694
Hitler-Mussolini meeting: Schmidt 173; Ciano 223–24; Dollmann 183.
pages 694–95
Hitler-Schirach: Schirach 171–72.
page 696
"You Germans have done the incredible again!" ND, 3596-PS; Shirer, *Rise*, 700.
page 696
Hitler-Brauchitsch: Assmann; Warlimont 77–78.
page 697
"beside himself with joy." Warlimont 79; interview with Warlimont, 1971.
page 697
Hitler on Milch: Irving, *Breach*, 88.
pages 697–98
Hitler's plan: Interviews with Wünsche, Below, Puttkamer, Manstein, 1970–71; Dietrich, *Hitler*, 81; Keitel 102–3.
page 698   *b*
"The swine has gone . . ." Allen Dulles, *Germany's Underground* (New York, 1947), 58–61; interview with Dulles, 1963.
page 699
"I was filled with rage." HSC 93.
page 699
"When the news came that the enemy . . ." Ibid. 94.
page 701
"I have always said . . ." London *Times*, Nov. 7, 1938.
page 701
Goebbels conference: Boelcke 40.
pages 701–2
"This raid on the night of the 11th May . . ." F. J. P. Veale, *Advance Towards Barbarism* (Appleton, Wisc., 1953), 120.
page 702
Goebbels conference: Boelcke 42.

page 702
"This one here is yours . . ." Gerd von Klaus, *Krupps, the Story of an Industrial Empire* (London, 1954), 415.

page 703
"Talks in words of appreciation . . ." Jodl diary, May 20, 1940.

page 703
Göring incident: Engel 80; Irving, *Rise*, 89–90.

page 704
"Our left wing, consisting of armor . . ." Halder diary, May 24, 1940.

page 704
"Only fish bait will reach . . ." Engel 81.

page 705
"It is always good to let . . ." Ansel, *Hitler Confronts*, 87.

page 705
"Churchill was quite unable to appreciate . . ." TAH 96.

page 706
Puttkamer on Hitler: Interview, 1971.

page 706
Hitler to Frau Troost: Interview with Gerdy Troost, 1971; correspondence, 1975.

page 706
François-Poncet on Hitler: Interview, 1971.

page 706
"She lost her nerve . . ." Engel 85.

page 706
On Unity Mitford: Interviews with Sir Oswald Mosley and Lady Diana Mosley, 1971–72; Oswald Mosley 411–12.

page 707
"I have decided to stay . . ." *Belgian Rapport*, Annexes, 69–75.

page 707
"I have quite often in the past . . ." Engel 82.

page 708
Warlimont account: Warlimont 102; interview, 1971.

page 708
Hitler's "jig": Interview with Walter Frentz, 1971; correspondence, 1975; Ansel, *Hitler Confronts*, 92; Hoffmann 121; Zoller 92; *Esquire*, Oct. 1958.

page 709
Mussolini-Hitler meeting: Ciano 265–66.

page 709
Mussolini-Hitler autographs on postcard: Müllern-Schönhausen 159.

page 709
"In truth the Duce fears that . . ." Ciano 266.

page 710
Shirer account: *Berlin*, 422.

page 710
"We will destroy everything . . ." Linge #17.

pages 710–11
French surrender: Schmidt 181–83.

page 711
Breker account: Breker 151–67; correspondence, 1975.
page 712
"Now your work begins . . ." Interview with Giesler, 1971; correspondence, 1975.
page 712
Footnote: Interview with Giesler, 1971.
page 712
Hitler to Speer: Speer, *Inside*, 172.
page 713
"It was a great responsibility," Breker 167; Speer, *Inside*, 170–71.

Chapter Twenty-two. "EV'N VICTORS BY VICTORY ARE UNDONE"

page 714
Hitler to Hoffmann: Hoffmann 122.
page 715
Hitler to Hewel: HH 114.
page 716
Halder diary: July 13, 1940.
pages 716–17
Ribbentrop to Schmidt: Schmidt 185.
page 717
Delmer account: *Black Boomerang*, 10–11.
page 717
Shirer account: *Berlin Diary*, 453
page 717
Dieckhoff report: GFP, D, X, 260.
page 717
Footnote: Ibid. 298.
pages 717–18
Conference, July 21: Ansel, *Hitler Confronts*, 163–65. Halder diary, July 22, 1940.
pages 718–19
Orwell review: *New English Weekly*, Mar. 21, 1940.
page 719
Kubizek account: Kubizek 292.
page 720
Jodl-Warlimont: Warlimont 111–12; interview, 1971; Ansel, op. cit., 181.
pages 720–21
Conference, July 31: GFP, X, 370–74; Ansel, op. cit., 184–89; Shirer, *Rise*, 764–66.
page 722
Directives: HWD 37–38; *Führer Conferences on Naval Affairs*, 82–83.
page 723
"Neither type of fighter . . ." Irving, *Rise*, 101.
page 723
Shirer comment: *Berlin Diary*, 486.

pages 723–24
Hitler speech: Ibid. 496; Ansel, op. cit., 283.

page 724
Raeder-Hitler conference: Report of CIC Navy to Führer, dated Sept. 7, 1940; Ansel, op. cit., 284–86.

page 724
Göring broadcast: Ibid. 250.

page 725
Churchill speech: Churchill, *Their Finest Hour* (New York, Bantam), 1962, 282.

page 726
Hitler to Puttkamer: Interview with Puttkamer, 1971.

pages 726–27
Churchill conference: Brown 41.

page 726
Hitler-Serrano Suñer meeting: GFP, D, XI, 93–98.

page 727
Hitler letter to Franco: Ibid. 106–8.

page 730
Ribbentrop letter to Stalin: Ibid. 296–97; Toland, *Rising*, 64.

page 730
Hitler-Mussolini meeting: Ansel, *Hitler and Middle Sea*, 33; GFP, XI, 250–51.

pages 730–34
Hitler-Franco meeting: HSC 532; Schmidt 193–97; Hills 345, 342; GFP, XI, 371–79; interviews with Puttkamer, Schulze (1971) and Serrano Suñer (1963); Linge ₦19; Keitel 126.

page 735
Franco to Pétain: Francisco Franco, *Discursos y mensajes del Jefe del Estado, 1951–54* (Madrid, 1955), 41.

pages 735–36
Hitler-Pétain meeting: Hamilton 231–32; Griffiths 271.

page 737
Ciano comment: Ciano 305; Martin van Creveld, *Hitler's Strategy 1940–1941: The Balkan Clue* (London, 1973), 43–47.

page 737
Ribbentrop quote: Schmidt 199.

page 737
"Ribbentrop approved this . . ." Weizsäcker 244.

page 737
Engel account: Engel 88.

pages 737–38
Mussolini meeting: Keitel 126–27; Linge ₦19; Ciano 300; Ciano Minute, Oct. 28, 1940; Wiskemann 283; GFP, XI, 411–22.

Chapter Twenty-three. "THE WORLD WILL HOLD ITS BREATH"

pages 740–41
Ribbentrop-Molotov meeting: Schmidt 210–13; GFP, XI, 537–38.

pages 741–42
Hitler-Molotov meeting: Ibid. 542–61; Schmidt 213–19.
pages 742–43
Molotov-Ribbentrop meeting: GFP, XI, 562–70; Louis Fischer 431–32.
page 743
Hitler to Bormann: TAH 65–66.
page 744
"more godlike than human." Public Record Office, London, FO 800/316, H/XV/212.
page 744
Hitler-Serrano Suñer meeting: GFP, XI, 598–606; Hills 348; HSC 567.
page 745
Footnote: Interview with Marquis de Valdeglesias, 1971.
page 745
Franco part Jewish: Interview with Otto Skorzeny, 1971; Hoare 31.
page 746
"Only completely ossified . . ." Halder 41.
page 746
"Hegemony over Europe . . ." McSherry II, 191.
page 746
Hitler speech: Prange 32–33.
page 746
Goebbels conference: Boelcke 110, 112.
pages 746–47
Directive: HWD 49–50.
page 747
Hitler to Bormann: TAH 17.
page 748
Hitler speech: Flannery 107–9; Hitler, *My New Order* (New York, 1941), 901–24.
page 748
"When Barbarossa commences . . ." ND, 872-PS; Shirer, *Rise*, 822.
page 749
"struck a blow at the belief . . ." TAH 97–98.
pages 749–50
Lochner account: *What About Germany?*, 122.
pages 750–51
Hitler and Yugoslavia: GFP, D, XII, 364, 369–75; Weizsäcker 25; Keitel 138–39; Jodl testimony at Nuremberg, June 5, 1946, 422.
page 751
Matsuoka to Hitler: Schmidt 227.
page 752
Matsuoka to Göring and Ribbentrop: Toland, *Rising*, 65–66, GFP, XII, 376–83, 386–94.
page 752
Hitler letter to Mussolini: Ibid. 397–98.
page 753
"I was haunted . . ." TAH 97.

page 753
Hitler lecture: Keitel 134–36. Halder affidavit at Nuremberg, Nov. 22, 1945;
   Warlimont 160–61; Halder diary, Mar. 30, 1941.

pages 754–55
"Thus, the (Jewish) wife . . ." GFP, XII, 446.

page 755
Stalin notation: David Dallin, *Die Sowjetspionage* (Cologne, 1956); Carell,
   Hitler Moves, 59.

page 755
Matsuoka-Stalin: Toland, *Rising*, 66–67.

page 755
Stalin to Schulenburg: GFP, XII, 537.

page 756
"wanted to try one more . . ." J. von Ribbentrop, *Memoirs*, 152.

page 756
"I do not intend a war . . ." GFP, XII, 66–69.

page 756
Footnote: Letters from Trevor-Roper and Lee, 1975.

page 757
Jodl to Warlimont: Warlimont 140.

page 757
"had succeeded in infecting . . ." Guderian, 125.

page 757
Hitler to Hanfstaengl: *Out of the Strong*, 34.

page 758
"I was confronted by a very hard . . ." Hess 14.

pages 758–59
Background information on Hess: Interview with Hildegard Fath, 1971.

page 759
Hess letter to wife: Hess 138.

pages 759–60
Events of May 10: Hess 19–21, 31–37; correspondence with Frau Hess, 1975.

pages 760–61
Engel account: Engel 103–4.

page 760
"Oh, my God, my God!" Speer interrogation, June–July 1945, Field Intelligence Agency; Bodenschatz interrogation, May 30, 1945.

pages 760–61
Hess letter: Hess 27; Dietrich, *Hitler*, 62–63.

page 761
"I hope he falls into the sea!" Schmidt 233.

page 761
Fath account: Interview, 1971.

page 761
Frau Hess account: Hess 21–22; correspondence with Frau Hess, 1975.

page 762
"well, Hess or no Hess . . ." Douglas-Hamilton 163.

page 762
"As is well known in party . . ." Ibid. 197–98.
page 762
Goebbels conference: Boelcke 162.
page 762
Frank account: Frank 411.
page 763
Hess interrogation: Douglas-Hamilton 167.
page 763
Haushofer story: Interview with Heinz Haushofer, 1971; correspondence, 1975.
page 763
"The Jewish tainted professor . . ." Engel 105.
page 764
Engel quote: Idem.
page 764
Herbert poem: "Let Us Be Glum."
page 764
Ciano comment: Ciano 451.
page 764
Hitler did not think Hess mad: Interview with Schwaebe and Florian, 1971.
pages 764–65
Hitler to Frau Bruckmann: Hess 26–27.
page 765
"True, I achieved nothing . . ." Ibid. 138.
page 766
Molotov-Schulenburg meeting: GFP, XII, 870.
page 766
"This stroke would be more deadly . . ." Shirer, *Rise*, 829.
page 767
Hitler-Oshima meeting: Interview with Oshima, 1966.
page 767
"I cannot demand that my generals . . ." Jodl testimony at Nuremberg, June 3, 1946, 308.
page 767
"These commissars are the originators . . ." Krausnick 519–20.
page 768
Tass communiqué: Werth, *Russia*, 125–26.
page 768
"No use beating an alarm." A. M. Nekrich, *June 22, 1941* (Moscow, 1965), 144–45.
pages 768–69
Hitler-Frank meeting: Frank 408, 414.
page 769
Cripps to Maisky: Maisky 156.
page 769
Hitler letter to Mussolini: GFP, XII, 1066–69.
page 769
Molotov to Schulenburg: GFP, XII, 1072.

page 770
Hitler to troops: Carell, *Hitler Moves*, 4–5.
page 770
"that some tremendous action . . ." Dietrich, *Hitler*, 66.
page 770
"In three months at the latest." Interview with Puttkamer, 1971.
page 771
Mussolini to Ciano: Ciano 372.
page 771
Molotov-Schulenburg meeting: Winston Churchill, *The Grand Alliance*
      (Boston, 1950), 366–67.
page 771
Ribbentrop-Dekanozov meeting: Schmidt 234.
page 771
Hitler's message: Ansel, *Hitler and Middle Sea*, 441.

Chapter Twenty-four. "A DOOR INTO A DARK, UNSEEN ROOM"

page 772
Goebbels conference: Boelcke 176.
pages 772–73
Olga Tschechowa account: Interview, 1971.
page 773
Churchill quotes: *Grand Alliance*, 370–72.
page 773
Kennan note: *Memoirs*, 133.
page 774
Roosevelt quotes: James M. Burns, *Roosevelt: the Soldier of Freedom* (New
      York, 1970), 103.
page 774
"high-handed gallantry . . ." Friedländer, *Pius*, 78.
page 774
"We have only to kick . . ." Bullock 587.
page 774
"At the beginning of each campaign . . ." Zoller 160.
page 774
Hitler to Dietrich: Dietrich, *Hitler*, 89.
pages 774–75
"to all intents and purposes . . ." Warlimont 180.
page 775
"Contrary to the opinions . . ." Leo Alexander, *Journal of Criminal Law and
      Criminology*, Sept.–Oct. 1948, 315.
page 775
"Stange is the calmness . . ." ND, RSHA IV-A-1, Operational Report, Sept.
      12, 1941, No. 3154.
page 776
Himmler in Minsk: Bach-Zelewski, *Aufbau*, Aug. 23, 1946.

pages 776–77
Conference, July 16: GFP, D, XIII, 149–56; 606–8. Interviews with Koeppen, Bräutigam and Leibbrandt, 1971.
pages 777–78
Hitler-Ribbentrop meeting: U. S. State Dept. interrogation of Steengracht, Sept. 4, 1945.
page 779
"A black day for the army!" Engel 110.
pages 779–80
Hitler-Mussolini meetings: Dollmann 191–92; Alfieri 159.
page 780
"In several weeks we will . . ." Zoller 160.
page 780
Table conversations: Interviews with Koeppen and Heim, 1971, 1974–75.
page 782
Sept. 17 conversation: HSC 58–60.
page 783
"They are brutes . . ." HSC 66.
page 783
"In a few days a youth . . . preservation of the species," Ibid. 69–70.
page 784
"Before I became Chancellor . . ." Fabian von Schlabrendorff, *Offiziere gegen Hitler* (Zurich, 1946), 47–48; Halder diary, Aug. 4, 1941.
page 784
Hitler speech: VB, Oct. 5, 1941; Stein 78–82.
page 785
"The city will be destroyed . . ." Koeppen notes, Oct. 9, 1941.
page 785
Smith account: Smith 86–88.
page 786
Goebbels conference: Boelcke 186.
page 786
Ribbentrop to Hesse: HH 145–46.
pages 786–87
Supper conversation, Oct. 17: Koeppen notes; interview with Koeppen, 1975; HSC 91–93.
pages 787–88
Stalin speeches: Werth, *Russia*, 246, 248–49.
pages 788–89
Oshima-Hitler meeting: Interview with Oshima, 1966.
page 789
Guderian account: Guderian 191–92.
page 789
Rundstedt-Hitler telegrams: U.S. interrogation of Rundstedt, 1945; Shirer, *Rise*, 861.
page 790
"I myself, for instance, am not . . ." Testimony of General August Winter at Nuremberg, June 8, 1946, 604.

page 790
"victory could no longer be achieved . . ." Percy Schramm 26–27.
page 791
"The United States and England will always . . ." Hillgruber, *Staatsmänner,*
   300ff.
page 792
Hassell comment: Hassell 208.
page 792
Hitler to Raeder: *Brassey's Naval Annual,* 232–33.
page 793
Hitler speech: Prange 366.
pages 793–94
Hitler to Huss: Huss 208–22.
page 794
Ribbentrop-Oshima meeting: Interview with Oshima, 1966; intercepted message, Oshima to Tokyo, Nov. 29, 1941, ND, D-656.
pages 794–95
Message to Oshima, Nov. 30, 1941: ND, 3598-PS.
page 795
Dietrich account: Dietrich, *Hitler,* 70–71.
page 795
Keitel account: Keitel 162.
page 795
Hitler to Hewel: Irving, *Hitler,* 354.
page 795
Directive: HWD 107.
page 795
Hitler to Bormann: TAH 87–88.
pages 795–96
Hitler-Ribbentrop meeting: TMWC 297–98; Shirer, *Rise,* 894.
page 796
Hitler to Reichstag: Prange 97, 367–77.
pages 796–97
Warlimont-Jodl: Warlimont 208.
page 797
"Stand fast, not one step back!" Keitel 166.
page 797
Brauchitsch-Keitel: Keitel 164.
pages 797–98
Hitler-Halder: Halder 49.

Chapter Twenty-five. "AND HELL FOLLOWED WITH HIM"

page 801
"to make all necessary . . ." Göring to Heydrich, July 31, 1941, ND, PS 710.
page 802
Höss account: IMT, XI, 398.

page 803
"but the first thing, above all . . ." HSC 91.
page 803
"From the rostrum . . ." Ibid. 108–9, 111.
page 803
"I am now as before a Catholic . . ." Engel 31.
page 804
Frank account: ND, PS-2233; IMT, XXIX, 498ff.
pages 804–5
Wannsee conference: Eichmann minutes, ND, NG 2586; Hilberg 264–65;
 ND, PS-709; Krausnick 82–87; Röhl 163; interviews with Leibbrandt and
 Hesse.
page 805
After conference: *Life*, Nov. 28, 1960, pp. 24, 101.
pages 805–6
"One must act radically . . ." HSC 238.
page 806
Hitler speech: Prange 83.
page 806
Fredborg comment: Fredborg 69.
page 807
Guderian-Hitler: Guderian 205–6.
page 807
Hitler to Speer and Milch: Irving, *Hitler*, 357; interview with Milch, 1971.
page 807
"As long as there . . ." HSC 257; Percy Schramm 28.
pages 807–8
Hewel quote: HH 148.
page 808
Hitler to Speer: Speer, *Inside*, 195.
page 808
Hitler to lieutenants: Interview with Richard Schulze, 1973; correspondence,
 1975.
page 808
"I've always detested snow." HSC 309.
page 808
"Boys, you can't imagine . . ." Ibid. 327.
page 809
Koeppen account: Interviews with Koeppen, 1971, 1975.
page 809
"My prophecy shall be fulfilled . . ." *Keesings Archiv der Gegenwart*, 1940,
 5409.
page 810
Fritzsche account: IMT, XVII, 172–73.
page 810
Goebbels comment: *Goebbels Diaries*, 138.

pages 810–11
Hitler speech: BBC Monitoring Report; ND, 1961-PS.
page 811
Mussolini-Hitler meeting: Ciano 478–79.
page 812
Heydrich to Syrup: Interview with Syrup, 1971.
page 812
"He plays cat and mouse . . ." *Goebbels Diaries*, 88.
pages 812–13
Heydrich assassination: Jan Wiener, *The Assassination of Heydrich* (New York, 1969), 82–90; Höhne, *Order*, 494–95.
page 813
Schellenberg account: Schellenberg 294.
page 813
Merin quote: *Commentary*, Dec. 1958, 481–83.
page 813
Footnote: Charles Wighton, *Heydrich* (London, 1962), 270; Höhne, *Order*, 496.
page 814
Eichmann-Wisliceny: Wisliceny affidavit, Nov. 18, 1946; Levin 300.
page 814
"The occupied Eastern territories . . ." Himmler to Berger, July 28, 1942; ND, NO-626.
pages 814–15
Gerstein account: Friedländer, *Kurt Gerstein*, 104–13.
page 816
Tojo-Emperor: Toland, *Rising*, 476.
page 817
"If I listen to Halder . . ." Interview with Richard Schulze, 1972.
page 818
Hitler-Halder: Halder diary, Aug. 24, 1942; A. Heusinger, *Befehl im Widerstreit* (Tübingen, 1950), 200–1.
page 819
Hitler-Jodl: Jodl testimony at Nuremberg, June 3, 1946, 300–1; Warlimont 256–57; interviews with Warlimont, Heusinger and Wien, 1971.
page 820
Keitel-Warlimont: Interview with Warlimont, 1971.
page 820
Hitler-Paulus: Goerlitz, *Paulus*, 159–60.
page 821
Hitler-Warlimont: Warlimont 258.
page 821
"He trusts none of his generals . . ." Engel 127–28.
page 821
Hitler-Halder: Halder diary, Sept. 24, 1942; Keitel 184; correspondence with Halder, 1971; Shirer, *Rise*, 917–18.
pages 821–22
Hitler-Zeitzler: Interview with Heusinger, 1971.

page 822
Zeitzler to officers: Warlimont 260.
pages 822–23
Sportpalast speech: *Keesings Archiv*, op. cit., 5657.
page 823
Song: Fredborg 129.
page 823
Bräutigam memorandum: TMWC, XXV, 331–42, ND 294-PS; interview with Bräutigam, 1971.
page 824
Warlimont-Keitel: Interview with Warlimont, 1971; correspondence, 1975.
page 824
Jodl comment: "Answers to Questions Put to General Jodl," OCHM, MS ※A-914.
pages 824–25
Hitler speech: BBC Monitoring Report.
page 825
"the God of war had now turned . . ." Percy Schramm 27.
page 825
"All I want to discuss . . ." J. von Ribbentrop, *Memoirs*, 169.
page 825
Hitler-Oshima: Interview with Oshima, 1966.
pages 825–26
Gehlen report: Gehlen 59.
page 826
"repeatedly overestimated the enemy . . ." Percy Schramm 109.
page 826
"Führer himself completely unsure . . ." Ibid. 113.
page 826
"Absolute dismay . . ." G. K. Zhukov, *Memoirs of Marshal Zhukov* (New York, 1971), 409.
page 827
Paulus to Schmidt: Goerlitz, *Paulus*, 210.
page 827
Hitler to Paulus: Carell, *Hitler Moves*, 635.
page 828
Manstein to Paulus: Goerlitz, op. cit., 234; interview with Schmidt, 1971.
page 828
Paulus to Manstein: Goerlitz, op. cit., 236.
page 829
Conference, Dec. 12: Warlimont 292.
page 829
On breakout: Interview with Schmidt, 1971; correspondence, 1975.
page 829
Manstein-Paulus: Interview with Manstein, 1971; Goerlitz, op. cit., 277.
page 829
Manstein-Führer HQ: Ibid. 280.
page 830
Goebbels message and conference: Boelcke 312, 314–15.

page 830
Hube story: Carell, op. cit., 664; Goerlitz, op. cit., 260–61: interview with
    Schmidt, 1971.
page 831
"this fellow Göring, this fat . . ." HH 152.
pages 831–32
Hitler-Zitzewitz: Carell, op. cit., 669; Goerlitz, op. cit., 264.
page 832
Paulus to Hitler: Jan. 29, 1943.
page 833
Paulus letter: Goerlitz, op. cit., 250.
page 833
Footnote: Interview with Hans Hitler, 1971; Maser, *Adolf Hitler*, 479;
    Svetlana Alliluyeva, *Twenty Letters to a Friend* (New York, 1967),
    161–63.
page 833
Zeitzler to Paulus: Carell, op. cit., 670.
page 833
Schmidt account: Interviews with Schmidt, 1971.
pages 833–34
Conference Feb. 1, 1943: Warlimont 300–6; Felix Gilbert 17–22.
page 834
De Gaulle quote: William Craig, *Enemy at the Gates* (New York, 1973)
    XV.

Chapter Twenty-six. THE FAMILY CIRCLE

page 836
"You don't have to get excited . . ." Unpublished memoirs of Gertraud
    (Humps) Junge; interview, 1971.
page 836
"After Stalingrad Hitler would not . . ." A. Zoller, *Hitler Privat* (Düsseldorf,
    1949), 44–45.
page 837
Goebbels speech: *Josef Goebbels Reden*, II, 1939–45 (Düsseldorf, 1971),
    177–83.
page 837
Bormann letter: Bormann 6–7.
page 837
Goebbels speech: Holborn, *Republic*, 316.
pages 837–38
Göring-Goebbels: *Goebbels Diaries*, 266–69.
pages 838–39
Milch-Hitler: Interviews with Milch, 1971; Irving, *Rise*, 202.
page 839
Lochner account: *Always the Unexpected*, 294–95.
pages 839–40
Schlabrendorff account: Interview with Schlabrendorff, 1963.

page 840
Gerstdorff account: Interview with Gerstdorff, 1971; Gerstdorff correspondence, 1975; Peter Hoffmann, *Canadian Journal of History*, 1967.
page 841
Gertraud Humps (Junge) account: Junge, *Memoirs*.
page 842
Footnote: Bormann 42–43.
page 844
"Either give up smoking or me." Interview with Herta Schneider, 1971.
page 845
"They seem like two invalids." A. Pozzi, *Come li ho visto Io* (Mondadori, 1947), 147–48.
page 845
"As a general rule . . ." Dostoevski, *The Brothers Karamazov* (Modern Library, New York), 5.
page 845
"But after the war . . ." HSC 306.
page 845
Traudl-Hitler: Junge, *Memoirs*; correspondence, 1975.
pages 845–46
Hitler-Henriette von Schirach: Schirach 187–88.
page 846
Traudl account: Junge, *Memoirs*.
page 847
"If it be true today . . ." *Goebbels Diaries* 354–59.
pages 847–48
Hitler diet: Interview with Zabel, 1971.
page 848
Traudl account: Junge, *Memoirs*; correspondence, 1975.
page 849
On Citadel: Interviews with Manstein and Puttkamer, 1971; Guderian 246–47; Seaton 356; Gehlen 64–65.
pages 849–50
Hitler-Mussolini: *Hitler e Mussolini* 165–90; Alfieri 237–48.
pages 850–51
Two conferences: Warlimont 342–586; Felix Gilbert 39ff.
page 851
"Mussolini is much weaker . . ." Junge, *Memoirs*.
pages 851–52
"At such a time one can't have a better adviser . . ." Felix Gilbert 44.
page 852
Goebbels in "blue funk": Diary of Wilfred von Oven, Aug. 4, 1943.
page 852
Galland account: Galland 163.
pages 852–53
Hitler to Ribbentrop: HH 154–55; interview with Hesse, 1971.
page 853
Hesse-Ribbentrop: HH 155–56.

pages 853–56
Kleist-Clauss negotiations: Kleist 145–52, 162–68; interviews, 1963, 1970–71; Vojtech Mastny, "Stalin and the Prospects of a Separate Peace," Dec. 1942, 1371, 1387.
pages 856–57
Hitler-Goebbels: *Goebbels Diaries* 435–37.
page 857
Hitler speech: Prange 384.
page 857
"I must admit that for a while . . ." Oven diary, Sept. 10, 1943.
pages 857–59
Skorzeny-Mussolini: Skorzeny, *Special Missions*, 70–90; interviews with Skorzeny, 1956, 1963, 1971; correspondence, 1975.
pages 859–60
Hitler-Mussolini: F. Anfuso, *Da Palazzo Venezie al Lago di Garda* (Cappelli, 1957), 326–27; Zoller 180; J. von Ribbentrop, *Memoirs*, 170–71.
page 860
Goebbels-Hitler: *Goebbels Diaries*, 477.
page 860
Kleist to Sweden: Kleist 169–70.
page 860
Japanese peace bid: Mastny, op. cit., 1384, 1388.

Chapter Twenty-seven. "AND WITH THE BEASTS OF THE EARTH"

pages 861–62
Lammers account: IMT, XI, 52–53.
page 862
Frank comment: Interview with G. M. Gilbert, 1972; Gilbert, *Nuremberg.*
page 862
"was necessary in the interests of Europe." Piotrowski 281–82.
page 862
"People are now clinging." Krausnick 371.
page 863
Hitler to Himmler: Ibid. 123.
page 863
Hitler to Bormann: TAH 57.
pages 863–64
Warsaw ghetto: Hilberg 320–26; Ringelblum 310, 326; Stroop Report, ND 1061-PS.
page 864
Pius XII quote: Alexis Curvers, *Pie XII, Le Pape outragé* (Paris, 1964), 139.
pages 865–67
Morgen story: Interview, 1971.
pages 867–68
Comments on Himmler: Höhne, *Order*, 30; interviews, Gudrun Himmler (1974), Wehser (1971).

page 868
Poem: Werner Angress and Bradley Smith, "Diaries of Heinrich Himmler's
Early Years," *Journal of Modern History*, Sept. 1949, 223–24.

page 868
Footnote: Larry V. Thompson 54ff.

pages 868–70
On Himmler: Toland, *Last*, 132–33; interviews with Hausser, 1963, Sündermann (1970), Richard Schulze, Milch, Wehser, Grothmann (1971).

page 870
Höss quotes: Gilbert, *Nuremberg*, 230; Gilbert, *Psychology*, 255.

page 871
"The SS commander must be hard . . ." *Die Zeit*, June 25, 1965.

page 871
"If the motive is selfish . . ." Krausnick 315.

page 871
"I do not want to see . . . put an end to it," Smith and Peterson, 38, 89.

page 872
Himmler speech, Oct. 4, 1943: ND, 1919-PS.

pages 872–73
Himmler speech, Oct. 6, 1943: Smith and Peterson 162ff.; Goldhagen 44–48.

pages 873–74
Kleist account: Kleist 126–28; interview, 1971.

page 875
"All that rubbish . . ." *Goebbels Diaries*, 279.

page 876
Hitler's handwritten notes: Müllern-Schönhausen 220–24.

pages 876–77
Himmler speech, Jan. 26, 1944: Interview with Gerstdorff, 1971; Kunrat von
Hammerstein, *Spaehtrupp* (Stuttgart, 1963), 192–93; Smith and Peterson
201.

page 877
Himmler speech to Navy at Weimar, Dec. 16, 1943: Ibid. 201.

page 877
Himmler speech to generals at Sonthofen, May 24, 1944: Ibid. 202.

pages 877–80
Morgen story: Interview, 1971; Morgen testimony at Nuremberg, Aug. 7–8,
1946, 488–515.

Chapter Twenty-eight. THE ARMY BOMB PLOT

pages 883–84
Jodl speech: Shirer, *End*, 279–86.

pages 884–85
Hitler to military leaders: Assmann, op. cit.; interview with Manstein, 1971.

pages 885–86
Junge account: Junge, *Memoirs*.

page 886
Reitsch account: Reitsch 212.
pages 886–87
Hitler on painting: Hoffmann transcript for Mar. 3, 1944, from Heinrich
    Heim.
page 887
Horthy story: Horthy 213–16; Warlimont 412–13.
page 887
Gehlen report: Gehlen 96.
page 888
On air raids: Junge, *Memoirs*.
page 888
It *had to happen:* Interview with Günsche, 1971.
pages 888–89
Speer account: Speer, *Inside*, 346–47.
page 889
Footnote: Percy Schramm 27.
pages 889–90
"It will decide the issue . . . an end by political means." Interview of
    Warlimont by Major Kenneth Hechler, July 19, 1945, 5.
page 890
"If the invasion succeeds . . ." Interview with Heusinger, 1971.
page 890
Rommel account: Carell, *Invasion*, 14–16.
page 892
"Now we can give them . . ." Linge ⚡34; interview with Günsche, 1971.
page 892
Hitler conference: Interview with Warlimont, 1971; Warlimont 427.
page 892
"Sounds off on culture . . ." Oven diary, June 6, 1944.
page 893
Hassell comment: Hassell 349–50.
page 893
Hitler to Göring: Irving, *Rise*, 285.
pages 893–94
Hitler near Soissons: Hans Speidel, *Invasion* (Chicago, 1950), 93; Shirer, *Rise*,
    1039–41: Speer, *Inside*, 356; OCMH, Speidel monograph.
page 895
Dietl story: Assmann, op. cit.
page 895
Junge-Hitler: Junge, *Memoirs*.
pages 895–96
Hitler at Platterhof: Speer, *Inside*, 359–61.
page 896
"I, too, know . . ." Speidel monograph, op. cit.
page 896
Keitel-Rundstedt: Chester Wilmot, *The Struggle for Europe* (London, 1952),
    347.

page 898
"any such coup d'état . . ." Interview with Manstein, 1971.

page 898
"I believe it is my duty . . ." Desmond Young, *Rommel—The Desert Fox* (New York, 1950), 223–24.

page 898
"You are young . . ." Speidel, *Invasion*, op. cit., 71.

page 899
Thiersch account: Zeller 286.

page 901
Steiner account: Interview with Steiner, 1963; Höhne, *Order*, 513.

page 901
Langbehn story: Rainer Hildebrandt, *Wir sind die Letzten* (Berlin, 1950), 135–37; Allen Dulles, *Germany's Underground*, 153–63; Douglas-Hamilton 219–23.

page 902
Wulff account: Wulff 97.

page 902
Hitler to Schröder: Zoller 207–8.

pages 903–4
Freyend account: *Walküre*, a TV special produced by Bavaria Atelier, Munich, and based on interviews with survivors; Zeller 302–3.

page 904
Heusinger account: Interview, 1971.

pages 904–5
Puttkamer account: Interview, 1973. Günsche account: Interview, 1971.

page 905
Fellgiebel account: Zeller 345–48; *Walküre*, op. cit.

pages 905–6
Stauffenberg escape: Ibid.; Zeller 304, 344.

page 906
Hitler-Hasselbach: Interview with Hasselbach, 1971.

pages 906–7
Hitler-secretaries: Junge, *Memoirs*.

page 907
Fellgiebel account: Zeller 346–48; Peter Hoffmann article on July 20 plot.

page 908
Hitler-Schröder: Zoller 206–7.

pages 908–9
Hitler-Mussolini: Dollmann 324; interview with Dollmann, 1971; Schmidt 275–77; *Walküre*, op. cit.; Zeller 337–38.

page 910
Keitel-Fromm: Zeller 306; Fabian von Schlabrendorff, *They Almost Killed Hitler* (New York, 1947).

pages 910–11
Stauffenberg at the Bendlerstrasse: Zeller 307–9; *Walküre*, op. cit.

pages 911–12
Remer account: Interview, 1971.

page 912
Hagen story: *Walküre*, op. cit.; Zeller 355; Bramsted 338–39.
pages 913–14
Remer story: Interviews with Remer, 1971; Zeller 339–41, 355–56; Bramsted 339–40; *Walküre*, op. cit.; Speer, *Playboy*, 193; Oven diary, July 20, 1944.
page 915
Witzleben message: *Brassey* 408
page 915
Kluge story: OCMH, MS⚡B-272, monograph by Günther Blumentritt, "20 July 1944,"; interview with Blumentritt, 1957.
pages 915–16
Bormann message: Bormann 61–62.
page 916
Skorzeny account: Interview, 1971.
pages 917–18
Fromm-Beck: Zeller 315–18; Höpner testimony, TMWC XXXIII, 299–530.
page 918
Teleprint message: Zeller 319.
page 918
Fromm-Remer: Interview with Remer, 1971.
pages 918–19
Skorzeny account: *Special Missions*, 117–18; interview, 1971.
page 919
Himmler at Goebbels': Zeller 339; interviews with Remer, 1971.
page 919
Fellgiebel to aide: Zeller 349.
page 919
Hitler quotes: Junge, *Memoirs*; interview with Christian, 1971.
pages 919–20
Hitler and Göring speeches: Zeller 342–43.
page 920
Stülpnagel-Abetz: Wilhelm von Schramm, *Der 20 July in Paris* (Bad Wörishofen, 1953), 105; interview with Schramm, 1971.
page 921
Goebbels quotes: Oven diary, July 21, 1944.
page 921
Bormann instructions: Bormann 64–65.
page 922
Hitler-Assmann-Puttkamer: Interview with Puttkamer; Assmann, op. cit.
page 922
Giesing account: Interview, 1971; Giesing unpublished *Diary*.
page 923
Hitler-Eva Braun correspondence: Gun, *Eva Braun*, 179–80.
page 923
Hitler quotes: Junge, *Memoirs*; Zoller 193; *Walküre*, op. cit.
page 924
Hitler-Eicken: NA Film, ML/125, 131; U.S. interrogation of Eicken, Sept. 30, 1945.

page 925
Guderian order of the day: Shirer, *Rise*, 1080–81.

pages 925–26
Hitler-Giesing: Giesing *Diary*; interview with Giesing, 1971.

page 926
Hitler to Gauleiters: Interview with Florian, 1971.

page 926
"The Stauffenberg family will be exterminated . . ." *Vierteljahreshefte für Zeitgeschichte*, Vol. 4, 1953, 363–94.

page 927
Trial and executions: Zeller 371–75; IMT, XXXIII, 2999, for testimony of Peter Vossen, shorthand secretary at trial; Shirer, *Rise*, 1070.

page 927
On film of executions: Speer, *Playboy*, 193; interview with Below, 1971; correspondence with Hasselbach, 1975.

page 927
Guderian-Hitler argument: Guderian 296.

pages 927–28
Kluge story: Wilhelm Schramm 189–90, 207–8; Carell, *Invasion*, 260; Percy Schramm 167–68.

pages 928–29
Morgen account: Interview with Morgen, 1971.

pages 929–30
Hitler to Keitel: Felix Gilbert 105–6; Warlimont 450–55.

pages 930–31
Junge account: *Memoirs*.

page 931
Giesing account: *Diary*.

Chapter Twenty-nine. THE BATTLE OF THE BULGE

page 932
Directive: HWD 197.

pages 932–33
Hitler special conference: OCMH, A-862, "The Preparations for the German Offensive in the Ardennes" by Percy Schramm; interview with Schramm, 1957.

page 933
Footnote: Interview with Frau Schmundt, 1971.

pages 933–34
Giesing account: *Diary*; cardiograms in "Hitler as Seen by His Doctors," NA USFET, OI/CIR/4.

pages 934–35
Junge comment: *Memoirs*.

page 935
Bormann-Brandt rivalry: Bormann 79–80; Giesing *Diary*.

pages 935–36
Giesing-Hitler: Giesing *Diary*; interview, 1971.

page 937
Dr. von Hasselbach does not believe that Giesing gave Hitler the double cocaine dose (correspondence, 1975).

pages 937–38
Giesing account: *Diary*; interview, 1971.

page 938
Rommel story: Speidel, op. cit., 152; Desmond Young, op. cit., 251–52; Milton Schulman, *Defeat in the West* (New York, 1948), 138–39; Zeller 378–79; Shirer, *Rise*, 1077–79.

pages 939–40
Skorzeny account: Interviews with Skorzeny, 1957, 1963, 1971.

page 940
Model quote: Interview with Percy Schramm, 1957. Hitler-Rundstedt: Schramm, "Preparations," op. cit.

page 941
Hitler-Junge: Junge, *Memoirs*.

pages 942–43
Dec. 11 conference: Interviews with Manteuffel, Blumentritt and Percy Schramm, 1957; OCMH, MS⫻B-151, Manteuffel; Percy Schramm, op. cit.

page 944
Bradley-Eisenhower: Dwight Eisenhower, *Crusade in Europe* (Garden City, 1948), 350; interview with Bradley, 1957.

page 944
Balck-Hitler: Toland, *Battle*, 51; interview with Balck, 1963.

page 946
Manteuffel-Jodl: Interview with Manteuffel, 1957.

page 947
Jodl-Hitler: OCMH, A858, "The Course of Events of the German Offensive in the Ardennes" by Percy Schramm.

pages 947–48
Hitler-Göring: Frau Göring account in Ziegler.

page 948
Special meeting: Felix Gilbert 158–74.

pages 948–49
Military conference: Percy Schramm, op. cit.; interview with Blumentritt, 1957.

page 949
Hitler-Thomale: Warlimont 495–96.

pages 949–50
At the Goebbels': Interview with Ruck, 1971.

pages 950–51
Churchill-Eisenhower: Churchill, *Triumph and Tragedy* (Bantam, New York, 1962), 240–41.

pages 951–52
Hitler-Guderian; Guderian 315; interview with Praun, 1971.

page 952
Hitler-Junge: Junge, *Memoirs*.

Chapter Thirty. "THIS TIME WE MUST NOT SURRENDER FIVE MINUTES BEFORE MIDNIGHT"

page 956
Hitler speech: Ausubel 46.
page 956
Bormann letter: Bormann 164.
page 957
Hitler lecture: Guderian 337; interviews in 1963 with two SS officers who were present but wish to remain anonymous.
pages 957–58
Schlabrendorff account: Interview, 1963.
page 958
Bormann letter: Bormann 168–69.
pages 958–59
Hitler to Bormann: TAH 33–34; 38–41.
page 959
Hitler-Giesler: Interview with Giesler, 1971.
pages 959–60
Feb. 13 conference: Interviews with Generals Wenck and Thomale, and Major Bernd Freytag von Loringhoven, 1963; Guderian 342–44.
page 960
Hitler to Bormann: TAH 50–57.
page 960
Giesing-Hitler: Giesing *Diary*; interview with Giesing, 1971.
page 960
Goebbels comment: Rudolf Semmler, *Goebbels: The Man Next to Hitler* (London, 1947).
page 961
Kleist account: Kleist, 184–90; interviews with Kleist, 1963, 1970.
page 961
The account of Kersten's achievements in his own book is unreliable. For instance, his claim to have persuaded Himmler to rescind Hitler's orders to deport masses of Dutch civilians was disproved in 1972 by the eminent Dutch historian, Professor Lou de Jong. He discovered that Kersten had forged four documents purporting to authenticate the act that won him Holland's highest award and a place in Dutch schoolbooks as a national hero.
page 962
Hesse-Ribbentrop: HH 194–303; interview with Hesse, 1971.
pages 963–64
Bernadotte account: Folke Bernadotte, *The Curtain Falls* (New York, 1945), 25–61; interview with Estelle Bernadotte, 1963.
page 964
Kleist-Ribbentrop: Kleist 191–92; interview with Kleist, 1970.
pages 964–65
Hesse account: HH 202–15; interview with Hesse, 1971. After checking this

section of his story, Dr. Hesse wrote in March 1975: "I was forced to give up my 'Stockholm Mission' in consequence of an indiscretion in the Swedish press. . . . It pretended that I had sought out the British Embassy in Stockholm but that the British envoy had refused to even speak to me. This was entirely untrue. I spoke to no British person in Stockholm. The indiscretion, in fact, was initiated by no other person than Schellenberg. But I found this out only years after the publication of my book through Dr. Kleist. Schellenberg told Kleist that he and Himmler could not allow Ribbentrop to conduct negotiations in behalf of the Jews, nor peace feelers; he felt it therefore necessary to torpedo my negotiations in Stockholm by a calculated indiscretion. But they never intended to harm me personally. This explains why Schellenberg tried to take up the negotiations at the very end of the war—unsuccessfully, of course—and, what is more important—why Himmler *did not rescind* the order to stop the killing of the Jews. Thus it came that approximately 3 million Jews fell *alive* (*still alive*) into the hands of the victorious Russians and why later on approximately 2 millions of Jews managed to emigrate to Israel."

pages 965–66
Hitler to Schröder: Zoller 230–31.

page 966
Hitler to Gauleiters: Interviews with Florian, Jordan and Scheel, 1971.

page 967
Kempka-Hitler: Interview with Kempka, 1971.

page 967
Speer account: Speer, *Inside*, 436–37, 440.

page 968
"If I ever lay hands . . ." Boldt 84.

pages 968–69
March 28 conference: Guderian 356–57; interviews with Puttkamer (1971), Freytag von Loringhoven, and Generals Thomale and Busse (1963).

page 969
Hitler to Bormann: TAH 104–8.

pages 970–71
Operation Sunrise: Interviews with Generals Wolff, Airey and Lemnitzer, Allen Dulles, Gero von Gaevernitz, 1963–64.

page 971
Stalin and Roosevelt messages: *Correspondence Between the Chairman of the Council of Ministers of the U.S.S.R. and the Presidents of the U.S.A. and the Prime Ministers of Great Britain during the Great Patriotic War of 1941–45*, II, 206–10.

page 971
Hitler-Carlyle story: Schwerin von Krosigk's diary (Shirer, *End*, 193). Carlyle is misquoted; the Czarina died on Jan. 5, 1762.

page 971
Hanussen's horoscope of Jan. 1, 1933, it will be recalled, predicted that Hitler would rise to power in thirty days and enjoy tremendous successes until the "union of the three" was broken. At this point his work would disappear during the spring of 1945 "in smoke and flames." Although Hitler

often ridiculed astrology to his family circle, he had shown a genuine interest not only in Hanussen's horoscope but in that of Frau Ebertin in 1923.

pages 971–72
Goebbels-Busse: Interview with Busse, 1963.

page 972
Goebbels quotes: Semmler, op. cit., 192ff.

page 972
Ribbentrop quote: HH 218–19.

page 972
Goebbels to Busse: Busse interview, 1963.

pages 972–73
Hitler proclamation: Max Domarus, *Hitler: Reden und Proklamationen* (Würzberg, 1962–63), 2223–24.

page 973
"Now, there's a beautiful woman!" Oven diary, Apr. 18, 1945.

pages 973–74
Rudel-Hitler: Rudel 217–20; interview, 1963.

pages 974–75
Himmler-Schwerin von Krosigk: Interview with Schwerin von Krosigk, 1963.

page 975
Masur as substitute: "I was prevented from leaving Sweden for several reasons," Storch wrote the author in 1965. "Firstly I did not receive in the last minute the Swedish passport, but this was not the main reason. Secondly, Kleist had learnt that I was to go and, therefore, I did not want to leave Stockholm. Thirdly, we had, in fact, already carried through our aims of delivering concentration camps and transferring 10,000 Jews to Sweden. The only motive was to prevent Kaltenbrunner from counteracting, as he had done in Buchenwald. . . . As I was prevented from going, I chose Masur in the last minute. I preferred him to the others because he had a moustache and looked older than the others. But, unfortunately, Masur was not familiar with our negotiations and, in view of the short notice (2 hours), I could not tell him about them."

Chapter Thirty-one. FIVE MINUTES PAST MIDNIGHT

pages 976–77
Hitler-Keitel: Keitel 197.

page 977
"I must force a decision . . ." Junge, *Memoirs.*

page 977
Hitler to secretaries: Zoller 247–48.

page 977
Footnote: New York *Times,* Apr. 21, 1945.

pages 977–78
Himmler-Masur: Norbert Masur, *En Jood talar med Himmler* (Stockholm, 1946); *The Memoirs of Doctor Felix Kersten* (Garden City, 1947), 284–86; Schellenberg 385–86.

pages 978–79
Himmler-Schellenberg: Schellenberg 387.

page 979
Goebbels to aides: Oven diary, Apr. 21, 1945; Semmler, op. cit.

page 980
Hitler to Steiner: Interview with Steiner, 1963; Cornelius Ryan, *The Last Battle* (New York, 1966), 426.

page 980
Bormann story: CIC Document 03649, 12 Oct. 1945, Carlisle Barracks.

pages 980–82
Hitler collapse: Trevor-Roper 117–19; interview with Freytag von Loringhoven, 1963; Junge, *Memoirs*.

page 982
Goebbels family: Semmler, op. cit.; Trevor-Roper 120.

page 982
Hitler to Keitel: Keitel 201.

page 982
"I should already . . ." Memorandum dictated by Jodl to his defense counsel's wife in 1946; quoted in Percy Schramm 204.

page 982
Hitler to Keitel: Keitel 202; *Generalfeldmarschall Keitel, Verbrecher oder Offizier?* edited by Walter Görlitz (Göttingen, 1961).

page 983
"The Army has betrayed me . . ." Junge, *Memoirs*.

pages 983–84
Koller story: Koller diary, *Die Letze Monate* (Mannheim, 1949); Trevor-Roper 128–31.

page 984
Hitler's dismissal of Göring: Trevor-Roper 138–39; Toland, *Last*, 431–32.

pages 984–85
Keitel account: Keitel 206; *Generalfeldmarschall Keitel*, op. cit.; Toland, *Last*, 432.

page 985
Eva to Traudl: Junge, *Memoirs*.

page 985
Eva letter to Herta: Gun, *Eva Braun*, 209–10; interview with Herta Schneider, 1971.

page 985
Eva letter to sister: CIC, Fegelein File, inclosure 18, Carlisle Barracks.

pages 985–86
Himmler-Bernadotte: Bernadotte 106–14.

page 986
Apr. 24 conference: Interview with Freytag von Loringhoven, 1963; Boldt 166–67.

page 986
Goebbels proclamation: *Drahtloser Dienst* (Nord), Apr. 24, 1945, BBC monitoring.

pages 987–88
Hitler quotes: *Der Spiegel*, Jan. 1966.

pages 988–89
Reitsch-Greim story: Reitsch 229; U.S. interrogation of Reitsch, Oct. 8, 1945,
"The Last Days in Hitler's Air Raid Shelter," Ref. AIU/IS/1.

page 989
Wenck account: Interview with Wenck, 1963.

pages 989–90
Noon conference: *Der Spiegel,* op. cit.

page 990
"You, who stayed here . . ." Interview with Freytag von Loringhoven, 1963;
Boldt 183–84.

page 990
Reitsch account: Reitsch 229; Reitsch interrogation, op. cit.

page 991
Hitler quotes: *Der Spiegel,* op. cit.

pages 991–92
Naumann account: Interview, 1971.

page 992
Wenck message: Interview, 1963.

pages 992–93
Mussolini story: F. Bandini, *Le Ultime Ore di Mussolini* 95 (Suger ed.,
1959); Deakin 814–17; Toland, *Last,* 475–513.

page 993
"Nine months ago . . . Your health, my friend!" Interview with Freytag von
Loringhoven, 1963.

pages 993–94
Frau Goebbels letter: Manvell, *Dr. Goebbels,* 272–73.

page 994
Bormann radiogram: CIC Bormann file ₰03649, Carlisle Barracks.

pages 994–95
Evening conference: Weidling Diary.

page 995
Reitsch account: Reitsch interrogation, op. cit.

pages 996–97
Hitler-Junge: Junge, *Memoirs.* Text of Hitler's two wills: ND 3569-PS; English translation, Stein 83–87.

pages 997–98
Junge-Goebbels: Junge, *Memoirs.*

page 999
Frau Hitler-Junge: Junge, *Memoirs.*

page 999
"I will not fall into the hands . . ." Ibid.

pages 999–1000
Weidling-Hitler: Weidling diary.

pages 1000–1
Junge account: Junge, *Memoirs.*

page 1001
Hitler-Günsche: Interview with Günsche, 1963.

page 1001
Günsche-Kempka: Interviews with Günsche and Kempka, 1963.

pages 1001–2
Baur-Hitler: Baur chapter in Ziegler; interview with Baur, 1970.
pages 1002–4
Death of Hitler and Eva: Junge, *Memoirs*; interviews with Kempka and Günsche, 1963, 1971.
page 1004
Poem: Schirach 192.

Epilogue

page 1007
"safe and well in Argentina," CIC, Fegelein File, interrogation, Carlisle Barracks.
page 1008
Bezymenski quotes: Bezymenski 66.
page 1008
Dr. Soggnaes account: Correspondence, 1973.
page 1008
"Children, don't be afraid . . ." Bezymenski 63.
page 1009
Kempka account: Interview, 1971.
page 1009
Naumann account: Interview, 1971.
page 1009
Dr. Soggnaes account: Correspondence, 1975.
page 1010
Dönitz to Himmler: Interview with Dönitz, 1963.
page 1010
Schwerin von Krosigk to Himmler: Interview with Schwerin von Krosigk, 1963.
page 1010
Grothmann account: Interview with Grothmann, 1971.
page 1011
Göring quote: Gilbert, *Psychology*, 109–10.
page 1011
Ribbentrop quote: Gilbert, *Nuremberg*, 260.
page 1011
Keitel quotes: Andrus 195–96; Gilbert, *Nuremberg*, 300.
page 1012
Günsche-Schulze: Interviews with Richard and Monika Schulze-Kossens, 1973.

Index